Third Edition

Marketing Research Principles:

Putting Theory into Practice

Kenneth E. Clow
University of Louisiana-Monroe

Karen E. James
Louisiana State University at Shreveport

TEXTBOOK\MEDIA

The Quality Instructors Expect.
At Prices Students Can Afford.

Replacing Oligarch Textbooks since 2004

Marketing Research Principles: Putting Theory into Practice/3e,
Kenneth E. Clow and Karen E. James

For more information, contact
Textbook Media Press
795 Dodd Road
Suite 100
West Saint Paul, MN 55118

Or you can visit our Internet site at
http://www.textbookmedia.com
or write
info@textbookmedia.com

For permission to use material from this text or product, submit a request online at
info@textbookmedia.com

Print (4-color paperback)	978-1-891002-55-7
Print (black & white paperback)	978-0-9969962-1-1
Print (black & white loose-leaf)	978-1-891002-54-0
E-book access card	978-1-891002-56-4

Textbook Media Press is a Minnesota-based educational publisher.

We deliver textbooks and supplements with the quality instructors expect, while providing students with media options at uniquely affordable prices.

Brief Contents

Contents

Preface

"The only thing constant in life is change." This famous quote, largely attributed to French philosopher François de la Rochefoucauld, seems custom-made for marketing research. Clearly the field is changing. New technologies and emerging social trends make marketing research one of the most interesting and possibly volatile career choices possible.

We developed *Marketing Research Principles 3e* because we concluded that the methods used to teach marketing research do not reflect practices occurring in the marketing research industry. Further, we believe that the currently available texts do not meet the needs of the majority of students enrolled in the Marketing Research course required for marketing majors. Toward that end, this book features four themes that make it distinct from other books and more useful to marketing students. These include:

- strong emphasis on how to use marketing research to make better management decisions
- focus on understanding and interpreting marketing research studies
- application of marketing research to marketing and business situations
- integration of data analysis, interpretation, application, data presentation, and decision making throughout the entire text.

First, we *put research into practice* in every chapter. The goal is to show students how research is used by marketing professionals to make more informed decisions. While uncertainty cannot be eliminated, marketing research can reduce the uncertainty faced by managers in the decision-making process.

Second, the book has a *focus on understanding, interpreting, and reporting marketing research studies*. While statistics and analytical techniques are presented in the text and are important, the focus of this text is on how to understand those findings and, more important, how to interpret the findings in a practical manner. Data analysis may show something to be significantly different, but what does that mean? How can it be interpreted and is it of managerial significance? How can data be visually reported to decision makers? These types of questions are answered in every chapter of the text so that students can see how marketing research is used by businesses in the twenty-first century.

Third, this text focuses on the *application of marketing research to marketing and business situations*. The marketing situations faced by businesses today are different from those businesses faced even ten years ago. Social media especially has revolutionized the way consumers communicate and how businesses market their brands. These changes have also affected marketing research, especially in terms of data collection. However, they have also affected reporting of results and the role marketing researchers have in the development of marketing strategies.

Key Features

This textbook is designed to help students learn, understand, and apply the concepts and theories of marketing research. A variety of methods are used to reach this goal. Each has a special purpose that addresses a component of learning.

Chapter Openings

Each chapter begins by describing the results of a research study that apply to the topics presented in that chapter. The research results are taken from a variety of industries, with an emphasis on social media and digital marketing. This approach allows students to better understand how marketing research is used by firms to make decisions. It also exposes students to research findings of practical value. Thus, students not only benefit from a better understanding of how research results guide decision making, but also their understanding of marketing tactics and decision making is enhanced.

Statistics Review

Chapters 1 through 12 each have a "Statistics Review" section that revisits basic principles of statistics. Rather than focusing on theory and formulas (as is common in statistical textbooks), the Statistics Review sections emphasize the practical interpretation and application of the statistical principle being reviewed. Because many students take statistics two to four semesters prior to the Marketing Research class, this content provides a necessary and helpful refresher of statistical topics. Furthermore, the section addresses a common problem among undergraduate students in that many suffer from a disconnect between statistical theory, as explained in statistics courses, and practical application and usage of statistics, as is required in marketing research courses.

Statistics Reporting and Statistics Reporting Exercises

As the name implies, the Statistics Reporting section focuses on the various methods by which data can be visualized and presented to decision makers. A variety of graphing and charting techniques are explored with special emphasis paid to the type of data appropriate for each chart as well as proper labelling of information. The importance of data visualization and infographics are also discussed in the final chapter. The Statistics Reporting Exercise provides students with the opportunity to practice the creation of graphs, charts, and infographics.

Dealing with Data

As with the Statistics Reporting section, each chapter has a feature called "Dealing with Data." Most marketing research textbooks wait until the final few chapters to present data analysis and interpretation. Starting with Chapter 1, this text provides students with multiple opportunities to practice interpretation and application of results to marketing decisions throughout the entire semester. When the section is used on a regular basis, repetition helps students to internalize the information, allowing for true learning to occur. Because students begin "Dealing with Data" in the first chapter and continue through the rest of the book, they develop a superior understanding for how to interpret and apply research results. Multiple SPSS data sets are provided at the textbook's accompanying website (www.clowjames.net/students.html) for instructor and student use. These data sets can be used for the purposes outlined in each chapter's Dealing with Data section or can be adapted by the instructor for use with additional assignments. For instructors who do not want to spend time teaching SPSS during class, step-by-step instructions for running analyses in SPSS are available at the textbook website. These instructions can also be used by students for review of the analytical process.

Lakeside Grill (Comprehensive Case)

The "Lakeside Grill" is a comprehensive case and is positioned at the end of each chapter. The unique feature of this case is that students conducted it. As such, it can be a valuable teaching tool in a number of ways. While the team of students makes some very good decisions in the research process, they also make some decisions that are not optimal. Questions follow each of the cases. These can be used for class discussion, in-class group work, or individual assignments. Because it is a continued case, Lakeside Grill shows potential trade-offs, difficulties, and flaws that often occur during the implementation of a research project. Students can critically evaluate the decisions made, how they were implemented, and suggest improvement. When assigned on a regular basis, this section is useful for reinforcing the chapter material and is very helpful in terms of developing students' critical thinking and analytical reasoning skills.

Chapter Terms

Key terms are presented in **bold face** and are listed and defined in the page margins throughout the chapter, and every key term is listed in alphabetical order in the end-of-chapter Key Term list. This helps students to both review the chapter and re-examine the terms to make sure they understand them.

Critical Thinking Exercises

These are not review questions. These critical thinking exercises are application-oriented and emphasize key chapter concepts as well as understanding marketing research results and how they can be applied to decision making. The exercises require students to utilize critical thinking and analytical skills. Critical thinking exercises can easily be incorporated into class discussion or assigned as homework. They might also be used as exam questions for those who prefer short-answer or problem-oriented testing.

Resources for Students

Several resources are available to students via the textbook website found at www.clowjames.net/students.html. Data sets and files related to the Dealing with Data and Lakeside Grill exercises can be downloaded from the student website, along with step-by-step SPSS instructions. Links to a variety of videos related to marketing research are also available. These can provide an excellent review of marketing research topics.

Resources for Professors

One of our goals in creating this textbook is to make sure professors can augment each chapter's content with additional teaching resources available at the authors' website (www.clowjames.net/students.html. For the resources mentioned below, please click Contact Us at the publisher's website (www.textbookmediapress.com). The total package for this book includes the following.

Instructor's Manual

The instructor's manual provides an outline of each chapter that can be used as a guide for lectures. Answers to the Critical Thinking Exercises and Dealing with Data feature are provided. Notes related to the Lakeside Grill continuing case are also included. Suggestions for class discussion and the use of the other teaching resources are also provided.

Test Bank

The test bank consists of true-false, multiple-choice, and short-answer questions. Answers to each are given along with the chapter section from which the question was taken. The questions range from simple memory exercises to those requiring more sophisticated thought processes and answers. The test bank is available in formats compatible with all major LMS platforms.

SPSS Data Sets

A number of data sets are provided at the accompanying website, (www.clowjames.net/students.html). While these data sets are designed to accompany specific sections of the text, such as Dealing with Data, they can be used for additional exercises or analysis. In addition to the data sets, detailed instructions are provided for using SPSS on the website. These instructions can be used to supplement classroom instruction or be assigned to students, allowing the instructor to focus class time on other topics. For individuals teaching an online course, these instructions are especially valuable.

PowerPoint® Lecture Slides

A full set of PowerPoint® lecture slides is provided for each chapter. These slides highlight the key points of the chapter. Especially useful are all of the graphs, tables, and charts that are featured in the text. In addition, SPSS results are shown for the Statistics Review and Dealing with Data sections.

Videos

The authors have identified some excellent YouTube videos that can be used with the textbook. These are available at http://www.clowjames.net/videos.html. These videos can be used as a review of major topics presented in the chapters. Since they are not created by the authors, the videos present the information from a different angle. Hearing the same thing from different sources can enhance recall and learning of materials. The videos can be especially useful for online marketing research classes. The video list is continually updated to ensure research topics are adequately covered.

Acknowledgments

Kenneth Clow would like to thank many of the individuals at the University of Louisiana at Monroe. He would also like to thank his sons Dallas, Wes, Tim, and Roy, who offer continuing encouragement and support. Karen James would like to thank Dr. Nancy Albers, Caitlyn Miller, and the Management and Marketing faculty at Louisiana State University in Shreveport for their support. Finally, she wishes to thank and acknowledge many former students who served as guinea pigs for the Critical Thinking and Dealing with Data exercises.

We would like to especially thank our spouses, Susan Clow and Marc James, for being patient and understanding during those times when the work seemed monumental. They have been enthusiastic and supportive for many, many years.

PART I

Introduction to Marketing Research

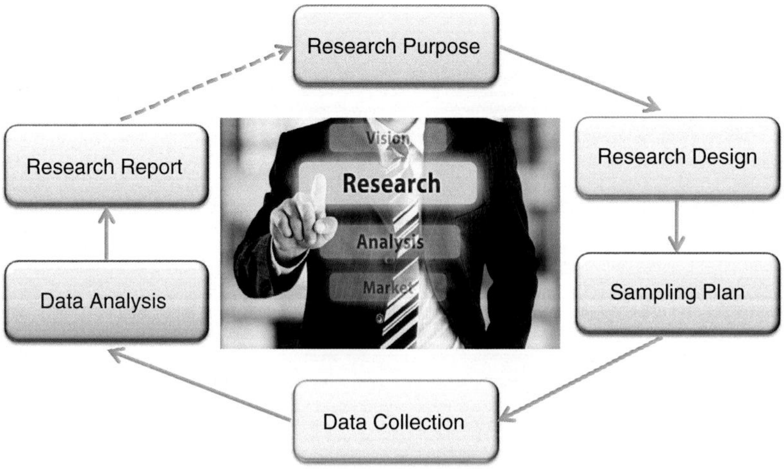

Source: Milos Vucicevic/Shutterstock.

The Role of Marketing Research

CHAPTER 1

Source: one photo/Shutterstock.

Chapter Outline

Learning Objectives

After studying this chapter, you should be able to:

- Discuss the basic types and functions of marketing research.
- Identify marketing research studies that can be used in making marketing decisions.
- Discuss how marketing research has evolved since 1879.
- Describe the marketing research industry as it exists today.
- Discuss the emerging trends in marketing research.

1.1 Chapter Overview

LEARNING OBJECTIVE 1.1
Discuss the basic types and functions of marketing research.

Internet of Things (IoT) growing network of home appliances, vehicles, security systems, heart monitors, and items other than computers and smartphones that connect to the Internet.

Marketing research systematic gathering and analysis of marketing-related data to produce information that can be used in decision-making.

The **Internet of Things (IoT)** refers to the growing network of home appliances, vehicles, security systems, health monitors and items other than computers or smartphones that connect to the Internet.[1] These stand-alone Internet-connected devices are becoming more popular as they allow consumers to remotely control the lights in their home or monitor who is at the front door via an IoT security system. Often, smartphone applications help control IoT devices and contribute to their functionality. Cameras built-in to a smart refrigerator allow users to check the appliance's contents from a smartphone application while they are shopping in a grocery store.

With more than 30 billion IoT devices forecasted to be in service by 2020, marketers are anxious to tap into the multi-trillion dollar market.[2] Understanding current adoption trends of existing smart devices, and barriers to consumer purchase is of the utmost importance.

A recent survey by Fluent LLC found that 55% of US Internet users owned a smart device. Figure 1.1 shows the percentage of people who own various smart devices, including TVs, lighting, thermostats, security systems and kitchen appliances. When examining the data, one might wonder why ownership is so low for smart kitchen appliances. Marketing research can help to provide answers.

Marketing research is defined as the systematic gathering and analysis of marketing-related data to produce information that can be used in decision-making. Marketing research involves following a systematic sequence of steps that will produce reliable and valid data. Through analysis and interpretation the data are transformed into information suitable for decision-making purposes by managers. Typically, data alone is simply not useable. It is the analysis and interpretation of the data that makes it useful to managers.

Figure 1.2 provides an example of marketing researchers turning data into information that can be used by smart appliance marketers. Recall that Figure 1.1 indicated that only 7% of Internet users owned a smart kitchen appliance. In June of 2018, a poll conducted by YouGov found that many consumers (62%) simply don't know much about either smart kitchen appliances or smart thermostats, even though they are aware that they exist. While 26% of consumers aged 18–34 claimed to know a lot about these devices, 52% of the

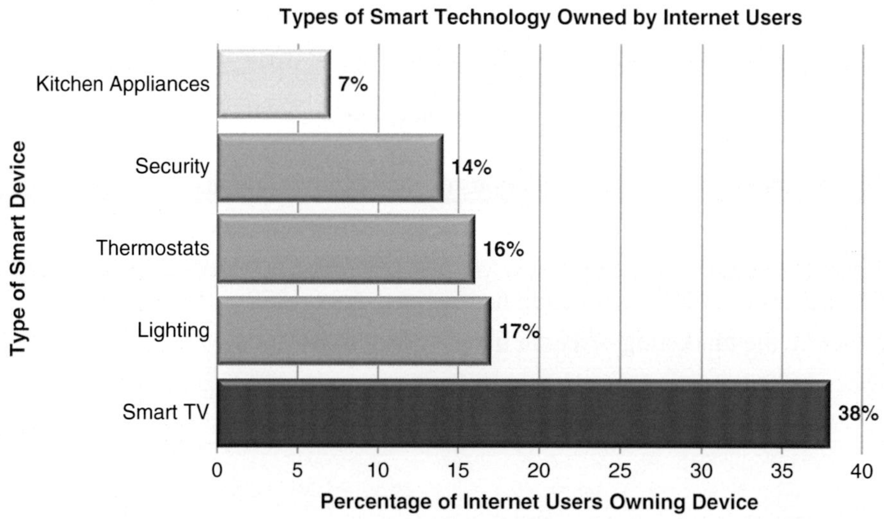

FIGURE 1.1 A Bar Chart of the Types of Smart Technology Owned by Internet Users
Source: Author created with data from Krista Garcia, "Smart Appliances Haven't Found a Home But That Could Change if Prices Come Down and Understanding Grows," July 5, 2018, eMarketer.com, accessed July 5, 2018.

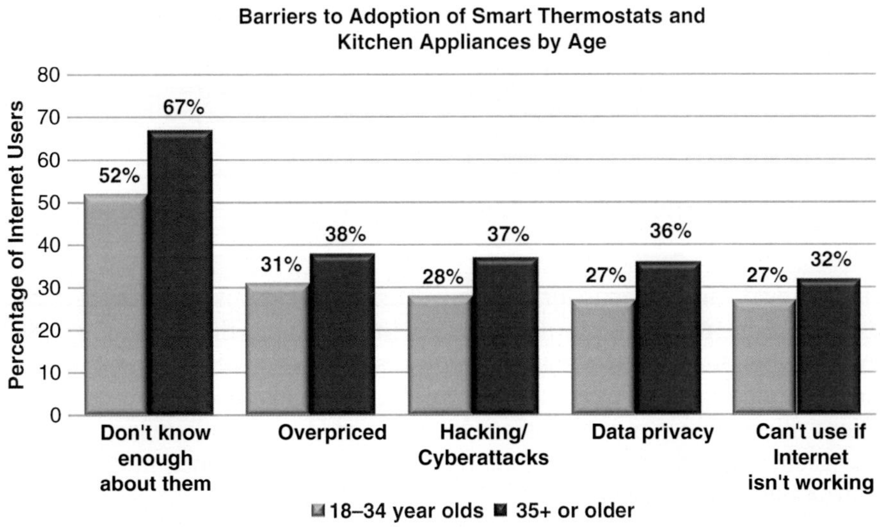

FIGURE 1.2 A Bar Chart Comparison of Potential Barriers to Purchase of Smart Thermostats and Kitchen Appliances by Age
Source: Adapted from Krista Garcia, "Smart Appliances Haven't Found a Home Yet But That Could Change if Prices Come Down and Understanding Grows," July 5, 2018, https://www.emarketer.com/content/smart-appliances-haven-t-found-a-home-yet?ecid=NL1009 accessed July 5, 2018.

same age group were aware, but didn't fully understand smart appliances or thermostats. The poll also identified four additional potential barriers to the purchase of smart kitchen appliances and thermostats. A significant proportion of the population believe that these devices are overpriced, while others feared hacking or cyberattacks. Data privacy is also a concern, while a smaller percentage of respondents worry about not being able to use their smart devices if their Internet is not working. In all cases, these concerns are more prevalent among consumers 35 years of age and older.[3]

The data presented in Figure 1.2 are important as they underscore the fact that marketers must do more than simply create awareness for new products. Clearly, consumers do not understand the smart technology and the benefits it provides, and without a clear understanding of these benefits, they cannot see the value of a smart thermostat or refrigerator. As a result, consumers compare the cost of smart appliances to that of regular appliances, and this comparison influences their perceptions that smart devices are overpriced. Smart thermostat and kitchen appliance marketers need to develop marketing campaigns to better educate consumers as to the nature of smart technology and its benefits, and why this warrants a higher price than traditional appliances. Additional message points can address fears related to data privacy and hacking or cyber attacks. Manufacturers can assist retailers in selling smart kitchen appliances or thermostats by offering cooperative advertising and special in-store display materials, especially around holidays or other times when smart appliances might be featured or placed on sale.

1.2 Marketing Research

Marketing research may be conducted internally by a firm's marketing department or may be performed externally by a marketing research firm. The information gathered is then used to make decisions related to the marketing mix or other marketing functions. The **marketing mix** is the specific combination of product, pricing, promotional and distribution decisions made for the purpose of targeting a particular group of consumers. Some of the more common marketing uses of research information include market segmentation, identifying specific target markets and their media habits, analyzing consumer behavior and needs, tracking customer satisfaction and the user or customer experience, journey mapping the various media and touchpoints used by consumers, developing new

Marketing mix specific combination of product, pricing, promotional and distribution decisions made for the purpose of targeting a particular group of consumers.

- Exploratory
- Descriptive
- Diagnostic
- Predictive

FIGURE 1.3 Functions of Marketing Research

products, and evaluating various forms of advertising executions and pricing tactics. But, the use of marketing research information is not limited to just the marketing department. It can be used by all levels of management to make decisions that impact other aspects of a firm's operation. It can guide top management in making strategic decisions about acquisitions, divestitures, and expansion. It can be used by middle managers to develop production schedules, purchase raw materials, develop departmental budgets, and determine appropriate staffing levels.

1.2a Functions of Marketing Research

Exploratory function occurs when researchers have a limited understanding or no knowledge at all about a marketing situation or a particular outcome.

As shown in **Figure 1.3**, marketing research serves four primary functions within an organization. The **exploratory function** of marketing research occurs when researchers have a limited understanding or no knowledge at all about a marketing situation or a particular outcome. For example, a company may be losing customers or sales may be declining, but managers are not sure why. Marketing research can be used to explore some of the possible causes of lost sales or customers. Alternately, a firm may be considering offering a new product in a category with which they have little experience. In this case, marketing research could be used to delve deep into a consumer's mind to uncover some of the hidden reasons or thought processes that go into making a purchase decision for the type of product being considered.

Descriptive function gathering and presentation of information about a marketing phenomenon or situation.

Marketing research often serves a **descriptive function**, which refers to the gathering and presentation of information about a marketing phenomenon or situation. For example, marketing research can be used to describe the primary customer of a product, such as a Panasonic HDTV or a John Deere tractor. It can be used to describe the process a customer uses in deciding on a restaurant for dinner, such as the Macaroni Grill or Outback Steakhouse. **Figure 1.4** illustrates the descriptive function of marketing research since it shows the primary way that NFL fans watch football on TV. While the majority, 52%, watch games live, 19% record games using their DVR for later viewing, 17% stream games and 8% use some other process. Only 4% buy games on demand.[4]

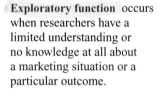

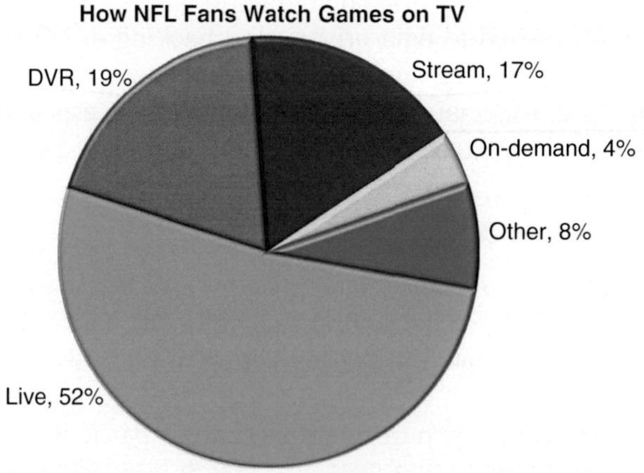

FIGURE 1.4 Methods Used by NFL Fans to View Games on TV
Source: Adapted from Jenna Enright, "Study Looks at Common Traits of NFL Fans," Quirk's Media, October 4th, 2017, accessed on July 18, 2018.

The **diagnostic function** of marketing research is particularly helpful in many situations. Here, data analysis techniques are used to investigate relationships and phenomena within data that has been gathered through marketing research. The analysis may show that females eat at Olive Garden more frequently than males. It may show how potential barriers to adoption of smart appliances vary by age, as was shown in Figure 1.2. The diagnostic function is important to marketers because it allows marketers to discover inter-relationships within data.

Diagnostic function data analysis techniques used to investigate relationships and phenomena within data that has been gathered through marketing research.

The **predictive function** of marketing research allows data to be used to predict or forecast the results of a marketing decision or consumer action. Retailers use predictive research to determine what items a consumer is likely to purchase together so suggestive selling can be used. Amazon utilizes this technique when website customers select a particular book and the software then suggests other books they might also want to purchase. Marketing research can be used to estimate the impact of a coupon or other sales promotional offer. It is often used to estimate the market share of a brand extension or new product introduction.

Predictive function marketing research used to predict or forecast the results of a marketing decision or consumer action.

1.2b Applied versus Basic Research

Marketing research can be either applied or basic. **Applied marketing research** is designed to solve a specific marketing problem, to investigate a particular marketing phenomenon, or to understand the results of previous decisions. The previous research investigating potential factors that act as barriers to the purchase of smart thermostats and kitchen appliances is an example of applied studies, as is the study on NFL game viewing habits. Most commercial marketing research and studies conducted internally by research departments within businesses is applied research since companies are seeking solutions to problems or information that can help them exploit potential opportunities. Marketing research should provide information that will allow managers to make better marketing decisions.

Applied marketing research research designed to solve a specific marketing problem, to investigate a particular marketing phenomenon, or to understand the results of previous decisions.

Basic marketing research is more theoretical in nature and is conducted to advance marketing knowledge in general or to verify a proposed marketing theory or concept. Findings from basic research studies cannot be implemented by managers in the short run. This is because basic research is typically not conducted in the context of a particular brand or firm, or for the purpose of solving a specific marketing problem or exploiting an opportunity facing a given brand or firm. Most basic marketing research is conducted by academicians in an effort to advance our knowledge of the marketing discipline. For instance, many research studies use questions to assess how consumers claim they will act when confronted with a given situation. One basic research study evaluated four different methods by which consumers' willingness to pay for an item are commonly measured in consumer research studies, and compared the results with actual purchase data in an effort to ferret out the relative strengths and weaknesses of each measurement technique.[5] The results of this study cannot be immediately applied to any particular problem facing a firm, but rather serve to advance our knowledge of marketing research practices. However, in the future, the results of the study may influence the types of questions asked as part of an applied research study commissioned by a firm that needs to investigate consumers' willingness to pay for their products.

Basic marketing research research conducted to advance marketing knowledge in general or to verify a proposed marketing theory or concept.

1.2c The Philosophy of Science

The philosophy of science underlies researchers' efforts to make sense of the world and its various activities and events in a wide variety of disciplines. The philosophy of science assumes that for a given event or activity, causes or "antecedents" can be identified, meaning that things just don't happen, they happen for a reason. Thus, scientific research seeks rational and logical explanations for activities or events that are true the vast majority of the time. Most marketing researchers desire to be 95% confident that the results of their research efforts are accurate and unlikely to have occurred by chance. The philosophy of science also tends to value a more general understanding of events or phenomena. This is because such knowledge is useful in forming theories and because it allows a scientific law to be generalized, meaning it can be applied to a larger group of activities or events. By contrast, the marketing tactics that can be used on Facebook to spur in-store sales for small businesses is helpful to local retailers, but from a broad scientific standpoint, the information would be not at all useful in the formulation of theory or scientific law.

Another characteristic inherent in the philosophy of science is that science, by its very nature, is empirically verifiable, meaning that the theories and laws created can be tested through the collection and analysis of data. The nature of science and empirical testing is such that we can never totally prove a theory to be true; however, the more a theory is subjected to testing under different conditions, and the more empirical testing fails to disprove the theory, the more confident researchers can be in the validity, or truthfulness of the results. So part of the research process is to also investigate the specific conditions under which a law or theory could be disproved.

Finally, the philosophy of science requires that researchers remain open to the possibility of change and modification. It is common for a scientific theory to be tested over time and if eventually disproven in too many circumstances, the theory must be revisited. This ultimately leads to better theories with greater explanatory value[6] assuming that the scientific method is followed when researchers perform their studies.

Source: Panos Karas/Shutterstock.

The philosophy of science dates back to the time of Aristotle, and underlies researchers' efforts to make sense of the world and its various activities and events in a wide variety of disciplines.

1.2d The Scientific Method

In conducting marketing research, it is important that researchers follow the scientific method shown in **Figure 1.5**. The research process begins with a thorough investigation of current knowledge. Whether applied or basic research, marketing researchers should examine current knowledge on the topic and review prior research. This is often called a literature review and typically involves examining past research studies, academic articles, news articles, and facts, figures, and statistics from a variety of sources. From this state of current knowledge, researchers can develop a theory which explains the nature of what is being studied, followed by a research question and one or more hypotheses, which are discussed in Chapter 2. The next step is to design a study and then collect the data to test the hypothesis. It is important to state the hypothesis prior to collecting data to prevent the data from biasing the hypothesis in any way. From the results of the data analysis, the researcher can draw conclusions, advance theories, and create new knowledge that can then be used for future research. The cycle then begins again.

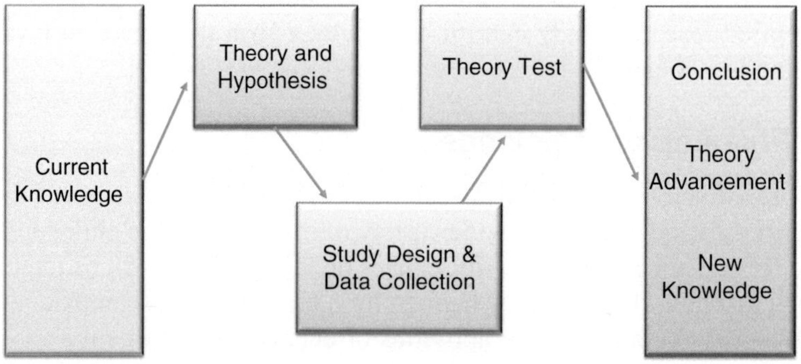

FIGURE 1.5 The Scientific Method

1.3 Marketing Research and Decision Making

The primary objective of conducting marketing research is to support marketing decisions. Managers will never have perfect knowledge and as a result there will always be some uncertainty in choosing a course of action. But, through marketing research, the amount of uncertainty can be reduced allowing the manager to be more confident that the correct or best decision is being made. Marketing research plays a role in a number of marketing decision areas, as shown in **Figure 1.6.**

LEARNING OBJECTIVE 1.2
Identify marketing research studies that can be used in making marketing decisions.

1.3a Segmentation and Targeting

Marketing research provides essential information for decisions on segmentation and targeting. **Benefit and lifestyle studies** examine the similarities and differences consumers seek in products and how these benefits fit into particular lifestyles. This information is then coupled with **target market analysis**, which provides basic demographic, geographic, psychographic, and behavioral information about specific target markets. From these research studies, marketers can decide which segments best match the features of their brands. Details such as usage patterns, attitudes, preferences, and lifestyles will allow a company to make better segmentation and targeting decisions.

Benefit and lifestyle studies research that examines the similarities and differences consumers seek in products and how these benefits fit into particular lifestyles.

Target market analysis research that provides basic demographic, psychographic, and behavioral information about specific target markets.

1.3b Customer Experience and Satisfaction

Customer experience studies (CX) provide information on how customers interact with a firm and the type of experiences they have with the company. This information helps firms to better understand customer needs and how to build consumer loyalty. **User experience studies** (UX) specifically seek to understand how consumers use a product to achieve their goals. Understanding user behaviors, needs, and motivations—often through observation research—allows researchers to design better websites, better marketing content, or better products. **Customer satisfaction** studies track satisfaction levels of current customers with a firm's product's services, facilities, or experiences on an ongoing basis. Satisfaction studies may serve as an early warning system of problems when satisfaction is tracked monthly or more frequently.

Customer experience studies provide information on how customers interact with a firm and the type of experiences they have with the company.

User experience studies seek to understand how consumers use a product to achieve their goals.

Customer satisfaction studies track satisfaction levels of current customers with a firm's product's services, facilities, or experiences of current customers on an ongoing basis.

1.3c Product Development

Marketing research is used in all stages of product development. Research can be used in the concept stage to gather customer input on ideas for a new product, or modifications of a current product. **Product testing studies** identify how a product fits the needs of consumers and what changes need to be made to the product to make it more attractive. **Test markets** can be conducted to provide information on how well a new product or product modification will sell before the product is launched. Modifications and decisions that will increase the probability that the new product will be successful can be made based on the results of the test market.

Product testing studies research that identifies how a product fits the needs of consumers and what changes need to be made to the product to make it more attractive.

Test markets research that provides information on how well a new product or product modification will do in a limited market before a national or international launch.

- Segmentation and targeting
- Customer experience and satisfaction
- Product development
- Marketing communications and media selection
- Market and competitive analysis
- Pricing and sales potential/forecast studies
- Site selection and distribution studies

FIGURE 1.6 Marketing Research and Marketing Decisions

1.3d MARCOM and Media Selection

Advertising effectiveness research research that examines the effectiveness of advertising and marketing communications.

Media studies research that identifies the most appropriate media to reach a specific target market.

Marketing research can provide valuable information concerning marketing communications (MARCOM) and media selection. **Advertising effectiveness research** examines the effectiveness of advertising and marketing communications. These studies can be conducted on a continuous basis and compared to a benchmark, previous ad campaigns, or competitive advertising. Input from these research studies allows marketers to develop more effective advertising and marketing communications. It also can identify when consumers are not paying attention any longer and allows for detection of when an ad is wearing out. **Media studies** are used to identify the most appropriate media to reach a specific target market, such as television, radio, magazines, etc. In addition to the best media, media studies will also identify the best vehicles, such as the specific magazine titles or the best television shows in which to place an ad.

1.3e Market and Competitive Analyses

Market analysis study research that examines the current marketing situation faced by a company or brand and then identifies potential markets.

Competitive analysis studies research that examines competitors within a market industry.

A **market analysis study** will examine the current marketing situation faced by a company or brand. Factors to be assessed include the product's ability to meet consumers' needs, the perceived image of the product, the current channels of distribution and other internal factors in addition to external factors such as trends in the socio-cultural, technological, economic, or legal-political environments that may impact the marketing of the brand. The ultimate goal of the market analysis is to identify potential markets for the firm. While market analysis studies are especially important for new products or entry into new markets, the studies are also important for current products, as market dynamics change. Companies can lose market share quickly if they do not stay in touch with current consumer behavior trends. Just like market analysis studies, **competitive analysis studies** should be conducted regularly to ensure market share is not lost to competitors. Understanding the competition's pricing, distribution, and marketing communications strategy provides useful information as will a competitive analysis of actual brands and the features/benefits they provide. Many organizations will use a marketing information system to gather market and competitive information on a continuous basis.

1.3f Pricing and Forecasting

Pricing studies research that evaluates the elasticity of a brand's price and the impact pricing changes will have on demand.

Sales forecasts research that estimates future sales for a company or brand.

Sales potential studies research that estimates potential sales for a product industry.

Pricing is an important determinant in buying decisions, so **pricing studies** can be used to evaluate the elasticity of a brand's price and the impact pricing changes will have on demand. Part of a pricing study is to examine competitors' prices and determine how consumers (or businesses) evaluate price relative to product features. Additional studies, such as **sales forecasts** and **sales potential studies** are used to estimate future sales. These studies are often used for budgeting, production, and staffing decisions. The *Statistics Review*, *Statistical Reporting*, and *Dealing with Data* sections at the end of this chapter will examine sales forecasting further.

Source: Gestur Gislason/Shutterstock.

Site selection research studies help retailers such as Starbucks determine the best locations for their stores.

1.3g Site Selection and Distribution

Site selection studies help retailers determine the best locations for their stores. Other research studies can help determine whether a single or multi-channel distribution system will be most effective, which channels a manufacturer should use, how logistics can be improved and so forth.

Marketing research is an essential input into marketing management decisions. The studies cited are just a few examples of the types of information marketing research can provide. Because of the impact marketing decisions make on a firm's income and profit generation, obtaining good information through marketing research has become more critical.

Site selection research study to help retailers determine the best locations for retail outlets.

1.4 Brief History of Marketing Research

LEARNING OBJECTIVE 1.3
Discuss how marketing research has evolved since 1879.

The first documented instance of marketing research occurred in 1879 and was conducted by the advertising agency N.W. Ayer. The company surveyed state and local officials about expected levels of grain production. This information was used by a manufacturer of farm equipment in the preparation of an advertising schedule. From that first beginning marketing research slowly evolved. The basic foundation of marketing research was developed during the first 30 years of the twentieth century. The first textbook on marketing research was published in 1921 and the first marketing research courses taught on college campuses occurred in the 1930s.[7]

The early years of marketing research focused on methods of sampling, collecting data, and analytical techniques. Researchers also focused on ways to measure concepts such as opinions, perceptions, preferences, attitudes, personality, and lifestyles. The primary goal of marketing research at that time was to measure marketing phenomena and consumer characteristics. Raw data were converted to information which was then passed on to managers to make decisions.

The period of the 1970s and 1980s is often referred to as the "golden age of consumer research." During this time marketing research techniques became more scientific. Computing power made collecting and analyzing data faster, easier, cheaper, and more accurate. Companies invested substantial dollars into marketing research to better understand the market, the consumer, and the decision process. Few decisions were made that were not supported by marketing research. Research study results became the support or rationale for choosing particular marketing strategies and marketing tactics.[8]

During the late 1990s and early 2000s a cultural shift in marketing research began to occur. Decision makers wanted more than support for marketing decisions. They wanted marketing researchers to offer insights into what the data meant. Simply describing potential markets, characteristics of consumers, and the decision process was no longer sufficient. Decision makers wanted insights into why particular choices were made by consumers and how the results of a marketing research study could provide a better understanding of the best strategies and tactics. Marketing researchers were no longer just data providers. They were to assist in providing discernments into marketing situations.

Some marketing researchers believe we are now beginning to enter another, newer phase of marketing research—the consultative stage. Just providing insights may no longer be sufficient. Managers want marketing researchers to be part of the solution, to provide input and direction into marketing decisions. As part of the 2018 *Greenbook Research Industry Trends Report* study, professional marketing researchers were asked to self-categorize their company type. Only 6% of respondents selected "Full Service Research Firm" while 42% of respondents indicated that "Strategic Insights Consultancy" best categorized their firm, and this figure grew to over 60% when response options for consultancies of any kind were combined.[9]

Source: Elnur/Shutterstock.

Many firms are looking to hire graduates with skills in data analytics, data science, big data, data modeling, story-telling, data visualization, sales and general business knowledge.

Job titles have also evolved, with "research analyst" giving way to titles containing phrases such as "market (or business) intelligence," "brand (or

- Big Data
- Business Intelligence
- Data Analysis
- Data Visualization
- Market Intelligence
- Market Research
- Questionnaire/ Survey Research
- R Statistics
- Strategic Marketing
- User Experience (UX)
- Behavioral Science/ Behavioral Economics
- Customer Experience (CX)
- Customer/Consumer Insights
- Focus Groups
- Marketing Research
- Predictive Analytics
- Quantitative Research
- SPSS
- Strategic Insights
- Voice of Consumer (VOC)

FIGURE 1.7 Top 20 Job Requirements for Marketing Research and Consumer Insights Positions in May of 2017
Source: Kathyrn Korostoff, "Today's MR jobs are Expanding Traditional Roles," *Quirk's Media*, (www.quirks.com), Article ID 20170806, August 2017.

consumer, category, shopper, strategic) insights," and "consumer (or user) experience." Job titles reflect the link between research, insights, and strategy, and also suggest a wider range of career paths for those entering the research field. Unfortunately, job hunting can be a little confusing because while titles may differ between firms, the duties are often the same. The industry hasn't yet developed standardized expectations for many of these positions.[10]

However, the skills set needed by those filling research positions have changed from the traditional skills expected a decade or more ago. **Figure 1.7** lists the top 20 job requirements (in alphabetical order) found in an analysis of May 2017 job postings for marketing research and insights professionals. The list contains skills that go beyond the nearly *universal* requirements for data analysis, analytical thinking, written and verbal communication, project management, and presentation skills, which were not included in the list.[11] The importance of the skills shown in Figure 1.7 is underscored by the 2018 Quarter 3-4 *Greenbook Research Industry Trends* report, which asked researchers, "If you could add one individual with a needed skill in your organization, what skill would it be?" Thirty-four percent of respondents selected data analytics and data science, which also includes big data, data modeling and other analytical skills. Twenty-one percent chose story-telling and visualization, while 19 percent selected sales and business knowledge.[12]

For traditional marketing researchers, the new skill sets shown in Figure 1.7 and described in the GRIT report represent a challenge. They were trained and educated in traditional research methods and data analysis. Now, they must familiarize themselves with new research-related data tools, or hire individuals who specialize in areas such data visualization, big data, and customer experience. Previously isolated corporate data functions are evaporating, and the teams responsible for marketing research, customer or web analytics, business intelligence and competitive analysis are being reorganized and integrated. Furthermore, they are being asked to assist in developing marketing strategy and strategic insights. It means not only does the researcher need a thorough understanding of marketing research and the ability to synthesize data; they must also have a thorough understanding of marketing and especially marketing planning and strategy. Clients expect research partners to understand their business, and create research that links to business objectives. Clients need practical recommendations for marketing strategies and tactics that will help to grow their sales, so the results of research must be actionable.[13] **Figure 1.8** highlights the various historical stages or marketing research.

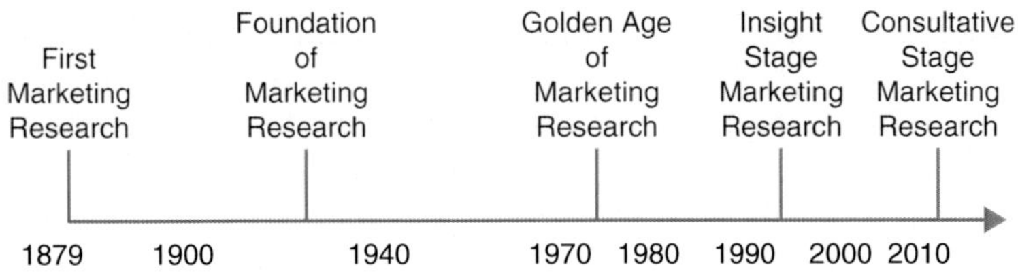

FIGURE 1.8 Historical Stages of Marketing Research

1.5 The Marketing Research Industry Today

LEARNING OBJECTIVE 1.4
Describe the marketing research industry as it exists today.

Major catalysts of the significant changes in marketing research in the last two decades are 1) the rise of international competition and 2) the explosion of communications and computer technology. **Figure 1.9** provides a pictorial illustration of the marketing research industry as it exists today.[14] While it looks complicated, it is not. But, it does illustrate how inter-related marketing research has become and how a research project often involves multiple entities.

The client companies illustrated in the figure are the numerous firms such as Nike, Kraft Foods, The Home Depot, Toyota, and Sony. These companies are called "client companies" because they are the ones that are seeking information for making decisions through marketing research. Chapter 2 will provide an overview of the research process and the request for proposal (RFP) that is issued by client companies.

1.5a Conducting Research In-House vs. Outsourcing

When the decision has been made to conduct marketing research, client companies have three alternatives: 1) they can conduct the research study themselves, 2) they can hire a marketing research firm, or 3) they can do most of the study themselves but outsource some duties, such as data collection, or sample recruitment. If the company is large and has a research division, then the marketing research study may be conducted internally within the firm. Even though a company has a research division, it may not conduct all of the studies that are needed. The department may be overloaded and need to commission a research firm to conduct particular studies. Or, it may want an independent research firm to conduct a particular study to prevent internal bias from impacting the outcome. Also, when commercially available research studies are available that could provide the information needed to solve a research problem; the research division may simply purchase

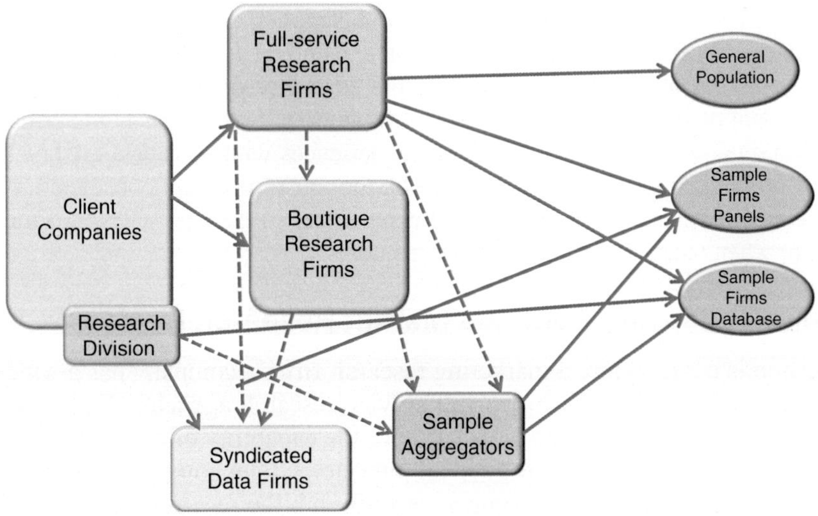

FIGURE 1.9 The Marketing Research Industry Today

this information from a commercial syndicated data firm. Many full-service marketing research firms also subscribe to a wide variety of syndicated data sources.

The decision to conduct research in-house versus hiring a marketing research firm rests on many factors. Generally, it is less expensive and faster to conduct research in-house, so the budget and time available for a given study are two key factors. The proliferation of Do-It-Yourself (DIY) research tools has helped internal research departments to minimize costs and time. The level of specialization required for the study is also a critical factor. It would make sense to hire a firm that specializes in Hispanic Marketing research, such as ThinkNow Research, than it would to attempt such research in-house. In fact, when asked why they outsource, 31 percent of corporate researchers who indicated their firm fully or partially outsourced marketing research did so to obtain expertise that wasn't available from the internal staff.[15] But in other cases, in-house corporate research departments are chosen over external suppliers when a full-service firm lacks the business or technical knowledge necessary to truly understand the industry or problems facing the firm. However, lack of experience with a product category can also be beneficial, particularly when a firm is seeking exploratory research that needs "an open-mind with no preconceived notions."

The current workload of those employed by the firm's internal research division might also be important. The *Q-Report* work life study of corporate researchers provides valuable insight into why firms outsource market research, and what type of tasks are outsourced. The *Q-Report* gathers data from an invite-only set of pre-qualified market research clients/users who subscribe to *Quirk's Media*, a market research trade magazine, and to members of ESOMAR, a global professional organization known for advancing market research worldwide. In total, 1,075 usable responses were obtained for the June 2018 online survey, with results demonstrating a 2.9 percent margin of error at the 95 percent confidence interval. While 49 percent of survey respondents conducted research in-house—an increase from previous years—51 percent either fully outsourced (33 percent) or partially outsourced (18 percent) marketing research. Among those who partially outsourced research duties, the most common task was data collection (28 percent) followed by respondent recruitment (26 percent) and data analysis and tabulation (22 percent). One-third of respondents who outsourced did so due to a lack of internal staff, indicating that research departments are often chronically understaffed. In addition to the 31 percent who outsourced to gain expertise not available internally, perceptions that outsourcing was faster and cheaper influenced 16 percent and 7 percent, respectively. Finally, 6 percent outsourced simply due to management preferences, which may indicate a lack of trust or respect for the internal research department.[16]

When it comes to selecting a particular research supplier, data quality is the number one consideration for research clients, followed by an existing relationship with the firm, thought leadership, and general pricing. According to the 2018 *Greenbook Industry Trends Report*, the fact that data quality is the top consideration indicates two things, 1) the critical importance of data quality and, 2) client's previous experiences with poor data quality. Logically, if all firms provided quality data, it wouldn't be the most important consideration. Since it is, it suggests that clients have had negative experiences in the past when outsourcing data collection or when outsourcing entire research studies.[17]

1.5b Full-Service and Boutique Market Research Firms

If the decision is made to hire a marketing research firm, a company has a wide array of choices from small boutique firms to full-service research agencies. Full-service agencies, called "full-servs" within the industry, have the capability of conducting all types of research, including focus groups, individual interviews, telephone surveys, mail surveys, internet surveys and more. These companies start with the research objectives the client firms want to accomplish. The full-serv will then design the study, collect data, analyze the data, and make a report.

While full-service research firms offer a full array of services, boutique firms specialize in either a particular type of research or a particular type of audience. For instance, ThinkNow Research focuses only on Hispanic respondents and firms that want to research the Hispanic market. EC Insights is a boutique research agency that specializes in providing meaningful insights and strategic guidance for a brand throughout its life cycle. The Realise Group is a boutique marketing research agency that focuses on mystery shopping in the retail sector providing retailers with a full measurement and evaluation of customer experiences. Axion is a boutique agency that specializes in creative research methods that utilize focus groups, in-depth interviews and other one-on-one approaches. Customer Care Measurement & Consulting is a firm that helps measure and manage the customer experience, "moments of truth" and customer contacts throughout the firm and with various media. Thirdeye Data is a Big Data service company that works with Big Data, cloud consulting, and artificial intelligence. Big Data boutique firms have become much more common in the industry, as have data analytic boutique firms.

Source: Vgstockstudio/Shutterstock.

Axion is a boutique agency that specializes in research methods that utilize focus groups, in-depth interviews and other one-on-one approaches.

1.5c Sample Aggregators

Both full-service research firms and boutique research firms design the research study, interpret the data, and make a report to the client. When it comes to collecting the data, the research firm has three basic choices. First, it can use the general population and one of the sampling techniques that will be discussed in Chapter 8 of this text. The second option is to use one of the many companies that specialize in providing samples and collecting data. Third, the research agency can go to a **sample aggregator**, which is a firm that collects data through utilizing multiple sampling companies. While some full-serve and boutique agencies will collect their own data using the general population, most are moving away from doing their own data collection to using companies that specialize in sampling.

Sample aggregator firm that collects data through utilizing multiple sample companies.

Research firms are shifting the sample selection and data collection to independent companies for two primary reasons: cost and time. It is more cost effective to use sampling firms that already have sample panels (groups of individuals who have agreed in advance to participate in research studies) or databases. It is also more time efficient as many firms use programmatic sampling that relies on automation to find samples that match certain characteristics. Both are important as client companies push for fast results, but lower costs.

A new player in the research industry is the sample aggregator. This is a company that knows the sample and data collection industry and can work with either a client company or a marketing research firm to expedite the data collection process and at the same time provide a better quality, more valid sample. For instance, if a company wants to survey decision makers related to the purchase of computer software in medium to large companies internationally, a sample aggregator such as ReRez can identify various sample firms that have these types of respondents. It is unlikely any one sample provider will have enough people within their panel or database to fill the quota desired by the client. Thus, ReRez can contract with a number of different sampling firms throughout the countries specified by the client. Furthermore, extensive experience with various sample firms allows the sample aggregator to limit their selection to only those firms that practice strong quality control practices. As you will learn later, the quality of the sample—particularly when it is Internet-based—is extremely important in assuring that the information provided to the client is accurate and meaningful. Thus, an aggregator such as ReRez can better ensure that the responses are valid and truly represent software decision makers. Finally, through the firm's expertise, the data can be collected accurately, and in a timely and cost-effective manner.

1.6 Emerging Trends in Marketing Research

LEARNING OBJECTIVE 1.5
Discuss the emerging trends in marketing research.

For many years marketing research relied on land line telephones and mail surveys to conduct research. While other methods were used, mail and phone surveys were the mainstay; then came the dawn of the 21st century. A number of significant changes occurred that have and will continue to have a profound effect on marketing research. Some of these changes are still occurring and marketing research firms have to adapt quickly or be left behind by smaller, more nimble start-up research agencies that can see what is occurring. The major factors influencing the changes are listed in **Figure 1.10**. While these factors are listed separately and discussed separately, they are all inter-related, which has created a synergistic impact that is having a profound effect on the way research is being conducted now and how it will be conducted in the future.[18]

1.6a Data Privacy and Security

The General Data Protection Regulation (GDPR) policy, implemented by the European Union (EU) in late May of 2018, fundamentally altered how digital information is protected, stored, and used. The primary policy goal is to give individuals control over their data. For example, personal data must be stored using pseudonyms or in a fully anonymous format. What constitutes personal data is more stringently defined, and includes any piece of information that can be used to personally identify an individual. The GDRP stipulates that buyers, processers and users of personal data must follow a set of standards designed to obtain participants consent, provide notification of data breaches, allow consumers to remove their consent or have their data erased, and receive full disclosure of how their data will be used and how long it will be retained.[19]

At first glance, it may appear that firms that do not do business in the EU are not affected, but this is a common misperception. Data shared, used or purchased from a third party in the EU makes a firm subject to the terms of the GDPR, regardless of their geographic location. Data transfers must be encrypted, secure FTP servers with properly managed credentials and limited access rights must be used to store the data, and a data retention policy must be in place to remove the data after it has served its purpose. Another common misperception surrounds what constitutes personal identifiable information or personal data. Phone numbers and email addresses would both fall into this category, as would cookies and ISP addresses associated with mobile addresses.[20]

U.S. firms that wish to be compliant with the GDPR will need to embrace the concept that they no longer *own* data—the customer does! Embracing this viewpoint also requires acceptance of a broader view of personal data, respecting consumers right to revoke usage of their data, and keeping data only as long as necessary. The GDPR guidelines[21] are explained in **Figure 1.11**.

- Data Privacy and Security
- Technology
- Economics and DIY
- Automation and Artificial Intelligence
- Research Panels and Crowdsourcing
- Competition

FIGURE 1.10 Factors Impacting the Marketing Research Industry

- **Consent:** Consumers cannot be tricked or confused into giving their consent; personal data collection activities must be clearly disclosed and consumers must be allowed easy withdrawal of their consent.
- **Breach notification:** Firms must report data breaches and corresponding risks to consumers within 72 hours.
- **Right to access information:** Inform customers how their personal data is being processed and provide an electronic copy for free if consumers desire access to their data.
- **Right to be forgotten:** Requests from consumers to delete their data should be honored.
- **Data protection officers:** Should be hired by firms whose core business tasks include processing or using personal data.
- **Privacy by design:** Data protection measures should be present throughout the design of use of software, websites, etc.
- **Full disclosure:** Any data collection must be clearly disclosed, including the purpose of data collection, length of data retention, and whether data will be shared outside of the EU.

FIGURE 1.11 General Data Protection Guidelines
Source: Adapted from Douglas Pruden and Terry Vavra, "Complying with GDPR—a U.S. Perspective," *Quirks Media*, (www.quirks.com), May 30, 2018.

1.6b Technology

Advances in telecommunications, smartphones, social media, the Internet, and IoT have impacted consumers all over the world and have created a significant change in the way individuals communicate with each other, with brands, media, and with companies. Social media, the Internet and smartphones have not just changed the way people communicate, but have also created cultural changes as well. Individuals regularly communicate with one another through social media, such as Facebook, or through Twitter, instead of talking in person or even calling on the phone. An individual in Maine can communicate with someone in California or even in Spain or Japan at a fraction of the cost that talking via phones would incur. Smartphones allow these individuals to take the Internet with them which means they don't even have to telephone someone to talk. They can use text messages, or access the Internet and correspond through email, Skype, or some type of social media platform.

Media consumption habits have been impacted as well, with ever-growing numbers of consumers "cutting the cord" of their cable/satellite provider, and choosing instead to stream TV shows via smartphones, tablets, laptops or TVs. Online news organizations and online magazines have seriously undermined subscription rates for traditional print media, while local radio stations have attempted to broaden their reach via the Internet, and to better compete with satellite radio and other online radio stations. These changes present greater challenges for marketers, who correspondingly have shifted their media strategies to embrace more online and social media, that more effectively reach their target markets, especially younger consumers.[22]

Technology has also changed the way brands and firms are influenced by word-of-mouth communication. If consumers have a bad experience with a brand, they are not limited to telling just a few of their friends and family members verbally. They can now use social media and instantly be "heard" by thousands of consumers all over the world within hours and many times within minutes. The potential for negative word-of-mouth can be devastating to a brand. On a positive note, this same technology can be used to engage consumers and stimulate positive endorsements.

The cultural shift in communications is also impacting the marketing research industry. Marketing researchers have for decades relied on surveys to gather information.

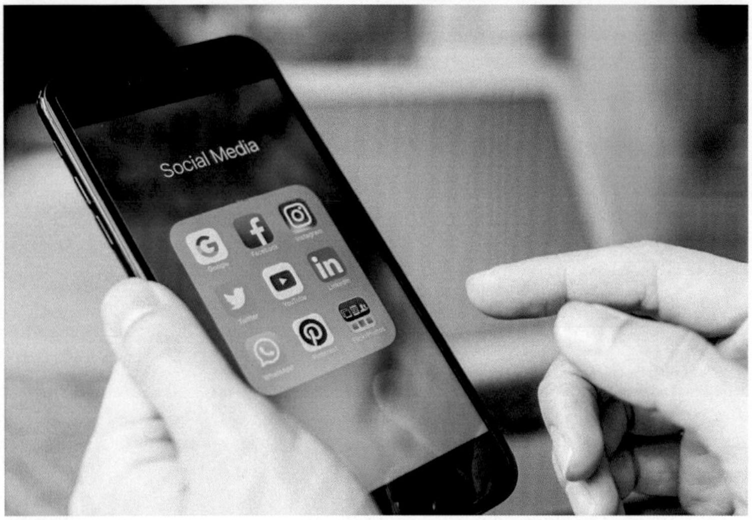

Source: Vasin Lee/Shutterstock.

Advances in telecommunications, smartphones, social media, the Internet, and IoT have created significant change in the way individuals communicate with each other, with brands, media, and with companies.

Virtual voice interviewing respondents dial into a telephone line and leave voice mail responses to a set of automated questions.

While online and mobile surveys remain the most frequently used techniques for quantitative survey data collection, there are signs that change may be forthcoming. For example, as people become more comfortable with voice-activated technology such as Alexa, it is predicted that data collection may in the future move away from computers, tablets and cell phones, in favor of voice-response devices.[23] The medical industry has already experimented with **virtual voice interviewing** (VVI), in which respondents dial into a telephone line and leave voice mail responses to a set of automated questions. While VVI's are in their infancy and certainly not appropriate for most situations[24], marketing researchers will be considering the potential of this tool as technology improves. Furthermore, the industry as a whole is embracing a more agile approach to marketing research that favors mixed methodologies of quantitative and qualitative primary research, with big data, third party data, and unstructured data, as required by the study objectives.[25] In short, the days of relying on surveys alone are gone.

Emphasizing this fact is a clear trend that market researchers are expanding their data collection efforts to include information gathered from market research online communities (MROCs), social media and other sources of "unstructured" or free-form information, such as consumer review sites. The growing interest and usage of MROCs and social media listening demonstrates that researchers have embraced the attitude espoused by Joan Lewis, global consumer and marketing knowledge officer of Procter & Gamble. Lewis stated that the marketing research industry should get away from "believing a method, particularly survey research, will be the solution to everything. We need to be methodology agnostic. Social-media listening isn't only replacing some survey research but also making it harder to do by changing consumer behavior and expectations."[26]

Business firms continue to monitor social media and listen to what consumers are saying so that they can respond appropriately. They see social media as a means of engaging consumers in two-way communication. For marketing research firms, it is another avenue for collecting data and monitoring consumers' conversations about brands.

Many companies have embraced marketing research online communities (MROC) as a method of engaging potential research participants. Research communities allow participants to offer feedback organically through blog discussions or forum posts. Research firms often find value in monitoring the peer-to-peer interactions that take place on a research community website.[27]

Although it remains mostly untapped for now, the IoT has made an enormous amount of data available. Any digitally connected and enabled device—from cars, to Fitbits, to smart refrigerators and business devices—can be used to gather information, *assuming* the proper privacy protocols are followed. What makes IoT devices so attractive to researchers is that they report actual behavior in real-time. Researchers could answer questions such as, "What is the average temperature of New Orleans homes with smart thermostats in July?" "How often do people with smart refrigerators snack at night and what do they eat?" As the vast majority of people are grossly inaccurate in reporting their behavior, the potential of IoT devices is of interest to researchers, particularly as the number of connected devices is forecast to grow to over 64 billion by 2025.[28]

In today's research environment, mobile market research and online research go hand-in-hand. Surveys must be created with a "mobile first" mindset to maximize response rates, as mobile participants are more likely to drop-off from a mobile survey if they have a poor experience. With smartphone penetration in the U.S. estimated by eMarketer to top 73.2 percent and 73.8 percent in 2022 and 2023, respectively,[29] making certain that quantitative surveys are easy to read and answer on mobile devices is a must. The vast majority of emails are read on smartphones, and since online survey invitations typically are sent via email, the likelihood of survey participants answering via a mobile device by clicking on an email link from within their phone is quite high. In fact, millennials are so attached to their mobile devices that some fear they will quit participating in research studies altogether unless they are presented in a mobile-friendly format that can be used on any device.

A new type of mobile survey is the chat survey, which is hosted through a messaging app such as Facebook Messenger. Mobile chat surveys are not simply online surveys optimized for a smartphone apps, but instead are delivered in a unique fashion. The surveys are shorter, featuring fewer questions. The tone is informal, friendly even, and questions are presented in a conversational manner. Early results appear to indicate that respondents enjoy chat surveys more than traditional online surveys, which could lead to enhanced usage in the future if respondents continue to be more engaged in the survey-taking process.[30]

Industry experts cite several benefits offered by mobile research beyond its ability to reach millennials. For example, respondents' answers may be more valid than answers gained via social media research, as studies have shown that respondents "self-censor" in social networking situations. A critical advantage of mobile research is that it can facilitate immediate "in-the-moment" feedback when consumers are shopping in-store, eating at a restaurant, or when experiencing some type of activity or event. Typically this information is captured using **micro surveys**, which generally contain no more than 5 questions which can be answered in a short amount of time, often a minute or less.

Micro surveys mobile surveys that contain no more than 5 questions which can be answered in a short amount of time, often a minute or less.

Furthermore, mobile research adds the benefit of being able to observe consumers' travel patterns via geolocation and mobile analytics.[31] When research is conducted via a mobile app, a smartphone's features—such as the microphone and camera—can be used to gather data. For instance, it allows users to easily view videos, take and submit photos, "and provide in-the-moment quick, multimedia-rich feedback."[32]

1.6c Economics and DIY Research

The financial crisis that hit the world in the beginning of the 21st century produced significant changes in the marketing research industry. It was stressful for traditional marketing research firms, but an opportunity for startup companies and traditional full-service agencies that recognized changes were about to occur. Business as usual had vaporized. Tighter corporate budgets meant finding firms that could produce more results for less money and do it more quickly than research had been completed in the past. Faced with these demands from clients, marketing research firms had two choices: 1) earn less revenue and less profit or 2) find a cheaper and faster way of conducting marketing research. The solution: both!

Marketing research firms had to do what the rest of the business, private and governmental sector experienced—lower their costs and learn to operate on lower revenues and lower profits, yet produce the same or higher levels of results. Unfortunately, as a result of this experience, client companies realized they could get the same research done at lower costs and that huge sums of money were not necessary to fund research studies, an attitude that prevails today, despite the fact that the economy has recovered.

Research firms were forced to look for cheaper ways to conduct research. The solution was to utilize online marketing research, mobile research, and online panels and databases. The cost of conducting a survey online versus in-person or by telephone is considerably cheaper and typically faster. Another advantage, with smartphones, consumers can be reached anywhere, anytime. Of course the survey methodology needs to be changed, but research firms knew that could be done!

Research firms also began migrating qualitative and observation research efforts online in a similar effort to save money. As you will see in chapter five, ethnographic research has changed substantially, with the Internet and technology playing a large role in reducing costs and providing more timely results. As virtual reality technology becomes more cost-effective, it may offer another channel by which researchers can understand consumer's decision-making process. Virtual store simulations are already used by some firms to help in packaging, pricing, and product shelf placement decisions.

Today, market research firms face an additional challenge. Client firms are now engaging in DIY research, or "Do It Yourself" research. DIY research may mean that the former client now conducts all phases of a research project, or that they outsource a portion of the project to one or more research partners, and do the rest themselves. For example, the client might contract with a sampling firm to recruit participants, but undertake their own observation study, focus group or field their own online survey. The DIY trend stems from several factors. First, programmers and engineers from outside of the research industry have brought new perspectives that have enhanced DIY software, making it much easier to use. Competition has increased, making DIY tools for text analytics, online surveying, data analysis, and data visualization readily available. Clients understand the market research process to an extent far beyond their knowledge a decade ago, and are hiring skilled talent who can complete research projects for the firm. Perhaps most telling, client budgets remain restricted, providing the key motivation to save money with DIY solutions.[33]

1.6d Automation and Artificial Intelligence

In the continuing effort to make marketing research faster, cheaper and better, automation has changed the face of the research industry. More than 20% of the 3,930 global market research client and research suppliers surveyed for the 2018 quarter 1–2 *Greenbook Research Industry Trends Report* indicated that they had adopted automation platforms for charting and infographics, survey data analysis, text analysis, and social media analysis. Another 24–30% or more were in the process of pilot testing software platforms for these purposes. **Figure 1.12** shows the top five uses of automation in marketing research, and the percentage of firms who have adopted these platforms, or who were piloting platforms at the time of the survey.[34]

Automation simplifies processes and automates time-consuming tasks. For example, automation allows firms to access high quality, diverse samples from multiple sources

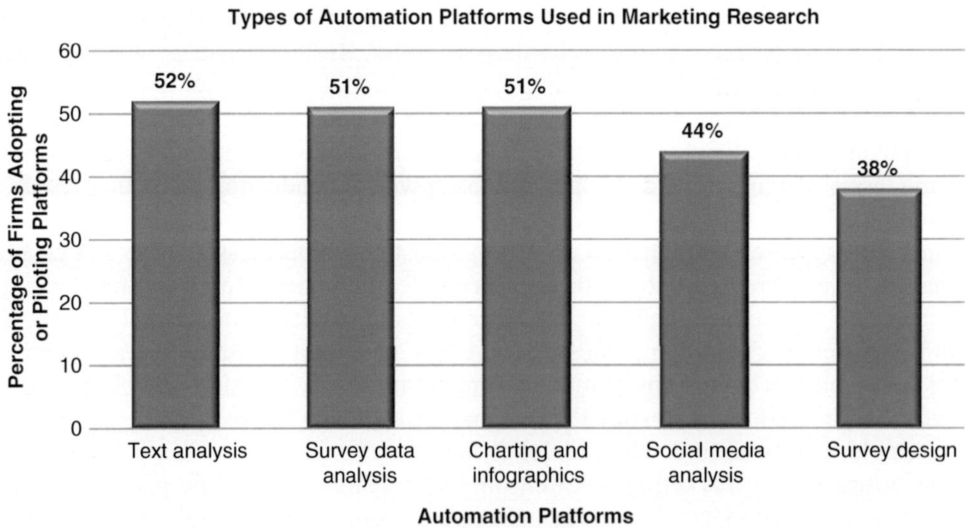

FIGURE 1.12 Bar Chart of Automation Platforms Used in Marketing Research

Source: Adapted from "Adoption and Consideration of Automation Platforms," GRIT Report. *Greenbook Research Industry Trends Report,* Quarters 1–2, 2018, (www.greenbook.org/grit) retrieved on June 26, 2018.

and blend them together via programmatic sampling.[35] Automation has also improved the speed of product concept and advertising copy testing, allowing for quicker rejection of poor ideas in favor of those that deserve more attention.[36] Researchers benefit from automation by having more time to focus on creating insights, recommendations, or strategies that require human thought, innovation, and creativity.[37] Some research, such as customer satisfaction studies, can be more easily automated as identical research objectives can often be fulfilled by the same research tool or questions. Defining a standardized customer satisfaction survey template that would be auto-administered is helpful to both research suppliers and clients. Standardization of data allows for easy comparison across studies. It also reduces error, and when applied within an industry, offers benchmarks that individual firms can compare their results against.[38] Now there are solutions that automate a particular methodology from start to finish. These and other automated tools are affordable, which helps those DIY in-house researchers who are struggling with the need to complete more research without a corresponding increase in budget.[39]

Artificial intelligence (AI) relates to computers that are programmed to learn in a way that mimics how humans think and act. One day, AI computers will be able to work autonomously without human interaction, but currently AI systems such as IBM Watson interface with humans, providing (mostly) accurate answers to a set of domain-specific questions, and "learning" from each new interaction or exposure to structured or unstructured data. AI has garnered a great deal of attention throughout the research industry and its impact is already making waves. Advancements in text analytics featuring artificial intelligence have increased the practicality of social media listening and unstructured data analysis, offering richer and deeper insights that go beyond simple sentiment coding, while making the process more cost-effective and less time-consuming. Other artificial intelligence programs feature predictive functions that analyze market segment or target market data, then deliver customized predictions related to churn (loss of customers) or lead-scoring. AI systems can also analyze the results of a marketing, advertising, or sales promotion campaign, and even generate marketing recommendations for a given target market. Of course, the usefulness of any AI system is highly dependent on its programming as algorithms categorize information based on filters or instructions input by the user.[40]

Artificial intelligence (AI) relates to computers that are programmed to learn in a way that mimics how humans think and act.

In layman's terms, Big Data describes the large volume of structured and unstructured data that businesses are exposed to a daily basis. Depending on the computing infrastructure, data storage, and data acquisition processes, the amount of data can be truly massive. Big Data includes all information internal to the organization that is stored in a digital format, including sales records, customer call center transcripts or voice recordings, past research studies, and existing customer databases, primary research data, and web analytics specific to the firm's websites. It also includes information gathered externally by the firm, such as social media text data, images gathered from Instagram or other sources, customer review data, MROC data, IoT data, third party research studies found or purchased by the firm, and any other structured or unstructured data that is available and relevant. These massive datasets truly benefit from artificial intelligence that is able to categorize and analyze disparate pieces of information and look for patterns, and insights that can be used by businesses to improve their operations and marketing decisions.

1.6e Research Panels and Crowdsourcing

Online research panels and research databases have become the "go-to" source for data collection. **Research panels** are individuals who have agreed to provide input on research topics and are asked to participate in research studies on a regular basis. Details of how the panels are formed are discussed in Chapter 8. **Research databases** consist of individuals who are part of a firm's database and are asked to participate in research studies sporadically. The primary function of the database is some other purpose than to conduct marketing research.

Research panels group of individuals who have agreed to provide input on research studies and are asked to participate in research studies on a regular basis.

Research databases group of individuals who are part of a firm's database and are asked to participate in research studies sporadically.

While the panels and databases can exist apart from the Internet, the trend is to utilize online research panels and databases. Data can be collected via a laptop at an individual's home or office. Data can also be collected via a smartphone or tablet either via social media, web surveys, or specially created mobile research applications. The smartphones and tablets means that collecting data can occur anytime, 24/7, and regardless of where the consumer is located. This makes data collection faster and easier as it is no longer necessary to reach consumers at their home or place of business.

MindSumo.com is a crowdsourcing website that has been used by more than 100 Fortune 500 companies interested in gathering ideas from Millennial and Generation Z consumers. A cost-effective alternative to panel research, companies that use MindSumo present research problems as "challenges" to college students, who offer their solutions for a chance to win a portion of a financial reward. The company receives multiple "entries" and is exposed to numerous ideas proposed by the targeted group. One challenge asked, "Can you come up with the next great sustainable product idea of 2019?" Participants were asked to either redesign an existing product into a sustainable version, OR to suggest a new sustainable product that satisfied an existing need only met by a less sustainable competitor. The top twelve entries shared $400, a small price to pay for accessing new ideas from generations that are notoriously difficult to engage in research.[41]

1.6f Competition

Competition sparked two additional changes in marketing research—accelerated timelines and an increased focus on international research. Because of global competition, firms are increasingly seeking to conduct research internationally. If a brand is distributed in 14 countries, then in most cases, research should be conducted in all 14 countries. If a company is planning to expand into a new region of the world, then research should be conducted in that region and within each country or province of that region.

Coupled with the need to do research in multiple countries, research firms continue to face a compression of the timeline. Instead of having months to complete a marketing research study, many companies now expect the entire project to be completed within 6 to 8 weeks.[42] Time-compressed deadlines are challenging, especially as studies today tend to mix multiple research techniques more often than not. The time compression for research studies contributed to an increased reliance on automation and artificial intelligence, as well as contracting with firms specializing in sample provision, primarily online or mobile samples. In almost all cases, online and mobile data collection can occur considerably faster than other methods.

1.7 Global Concerns

Because of the increase in global competition and due to the elimination of geographic barriers and lower costs provided by the Internet, marketing research is now being conducted on a broader scale that involves multiple countries. Compared to the past, few studies by major firms are limited to the United States or just one country. Expanding research into additional countries involves some unique challenges that will be highlighted in each of the following chapters.

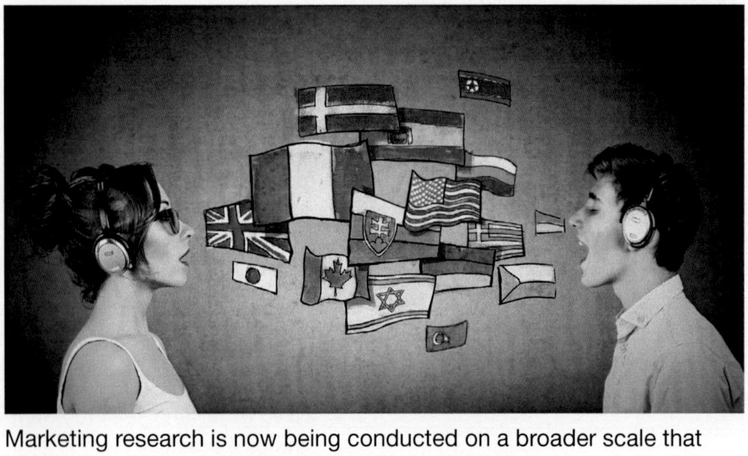

Source: pathdoc/Shutterstock.

Marketing research is now being conducted on a broader scale that involves multiple countries. A primary challenge is the translation of surveys into various languages.

A primary challenge of course is the translation of surveys into various languages. English is a very rich language, and sometimes there is not an equivalent word available in a foreign language, forcing the question to be reworded to ensure a similar meaning. But, more problematic is the difference in cultures. What is appropriate to ask in one country may be deemed to be inappropriate in another. For instance, interviewing females in western countries is perfectly acceptable. But for many Middle Eastern countries, it is not acceptable unless a male is present. Furthermore, in most cases it needs to be a female–female surveyor and respondent relationship.

In some countries like the United States, getting individuals to participate in studies is difficult. That is one reason for the increased usage of online panels and databases as well as the growth of mobile marketing research. But, in some of the developing countries individuals are eager to participate in studies. It is novel and new to them. Of course, this raises questions of how representative the samples are in both situations, in the United States where participation is difficult to obtain and in other countries where individuals are eager to participate.

1.8 Marketing Research Statistics

1.8a Statistical Review

To obtain sales forecasts, companies will typically turn to the marketing department. Common techniques used include moving averages, trend analysis, and salesforce estimates. Of these three the moving averages method is the simplest to calculate because it is just the average of X number of periods. Moving averages works well for an existing product with sales that are relatively stable such as products like milk, eggs or other items bought regardless of the time of year, price, or changes in the economy. It does not work well for sales with significant upward or downward trends or sales with high volatility, such as products that are new to the market. Figure 1.13 illustrates sales forecasting using moving averages. The second column is the actual sales figures. The third, fourth, and fifth columns calculates a sales forecast averaging the last 5 years, 4 years, and 3 years respectively. The number of years (or periods) used in the moving average depends on the stability of the sales data and knowledge the marketing manager has of the company and its operating environment.

Year	Actual Sales	5-year	4-year	3-year
2009	$187,527			
2010	$194,049			
2011	$190,113			
2012	$209,696			$190,563
2013	$210,009		$195,346	$197,953
2014	$229,946	$198,279	$200,967	$203,273
2015	$248,346	$206,763	$209,941	$216,550
2016	$259,253	$217,622	$224,499	$229,434
2017	$271,951	$231,450	$236,889	$245,848
2018	$284,822	$243,901	$252,374	$259,850
2019	$278,766	$258,864	$266,093	$272,009
2020	$270,537	$268,628	$273,698	$278,513
	Forecast	$273,066	$276,519	$278,042

FIGURE 1.13 Creating a Sales Forecast Using the Moving Average Technique

SUMMARY OUTPUT					
Regression Statistics					
Multiple R	0.961043117				
R Square	0.923603872				
Adjusted R Square	0.915964259				
Standard Error	10708.21553				
Observations	12				
ANOVA	df	SS	MS	F	Significance F
Regression	1	13862724931	1.39E+10	120.8967	6.61855E-07
Residual	10	1146658797	1.15E+08		
Total	11	15009383728			
	Coefficients	Standard Error	t Stat	P-value	
Intercept	-19549124.1	1799441.517	-10.864	7.4E-07	
Year	9845.91958	895.4659674	10.9953	6.62E-07	

FIGURE 1.14 SPSS Regression Output that Identifies the Trend Based on Past Sales

Trend analysis is a common method of sales forecasting especially if the data displays an upward or downward trend in sales. Sales in 2009 was $187,527 and by 2020 had grown to $270,537. Examining the sales figures between 2009 and 2020 shows a tendency for sales to increase over time. The trend, which is the average yearly increase or decrease in sales, can be calculated by using regression analysis in Excel. The y-values would be the actual sales figures and the x-values would be the year. **Figure 1.14** shows the output from the regression analysis. The number of primary interest is the coefficient for the year. It is 9845.91958. This figure indicates that, on the average, sales increase $9,846 per year. To forecast sales for 2021, the trend amount of $9,846 is added to the 2020 sales figure ($270,537) producing a forecast of $280,383, as shown in **Figure 1.15.**

With the salesforce estimate, salespeople are asked to estimate or forecast their sales for the next year or period. These estimates are then aggregated into a corporate forecast. **Figure 1.16** shows the sales forecast for a company with seven salespeople. Each was asked to estimate his/her sales for the next year. The total estimates were then added to produce a company forecast of $1.285 million.

Because salespeople tend to be optimistic in terms of future sales, a sales manager will often discount the total forecast based on historical data. **Figure 1.17** shows the actual sales figures since 2007. The third column is the salesforce estimate of sales for each of those years. Notice in all cases, the sales force tended to overestimate sales. The last column compares the actual sales to the salesforce estimate. Thus, for 2007 actual sales was 85.47 percent of the salesforce estimate. If the sales/estimate percentage is averaged for all of the years, the actual sales tends to be 85.84 percent of the salesforce estimate.

Year	Actual Sales
2009	$187,527
2010	$194,049
2011	$190,113
2012	$209,696
2013	$210,009
2014	$229,946
2015	$248,346
2016	$259,253
2017	$271,951
2018	$284,822
2019	$278,766
2020	$270,537
Trend	$9,846
Forecast	$280,383

FIGURE 1.15 Final Sales Forecast Using Trend Analysis

Salesperson	Sales Estimate
Michael	$165,000
Ashley	$200,000
Jessica	$215,000
Matt	$200,000
Josh	$200,000
Andy	$155,000
Brittany	$150,000
Total	$1,285,000

FIGURE 1.16 Sales Estimates Submitted by Each Salesperson

Using this information, a sales manager would take 85.84 percent of the $1,285,000 sales estimate obtained from the seven salespeople. This would produce a final sales forecast of $ 1,103,044 ($1,285,000 * 85.84 percent).

1.8b Statistical Reporting

Sales figures as well as profits are commonly reported using line charts. The data can also be reported through area graphs. Both line charts and area graphs require continuous data. **Continuous data** can take on any value within a specified range. Sales, profits, and contribution margins are examples of numbers that can take on any value within a range,

Continuous data can take on any value within a specified range including decimals.

Year	Actual Sales	Salesforce Estimate	Sales/Estimate Percent
2007	$595,865	$697,162	85.47%
2008	$627,350	$721,453	86.96%
2009	$642,500	$803,125	80.00%
2010	$657,750	$762,990	86.21%
2011	$686,487	$775,730	88.50%
2012	$735,115	$904,191	81.30%
2013	$795,621	$899,052	88.50%
2014	$805,102	$958,071	84.03%
2015	$862,919	$1,009,615	85.47%
2016	$875,025	$1,067,531	81.97%
2017	$925,000	$1,017,500	90.91%
2018	$940,250	$1,081,288	86.96%
2019	$956,923	$1,090,892	87.72%
2020	$1,034,897	$1,179,783	87.72%
		Average	**85.84%**

FIGURE 1.17 Calculation of the Ratio of Actual Sales to Salesforce Estimates

Discrete data have specific integer values with no decimals.

including decimals. **Discrete data**, on the other hand, have specific integer values without decimals. Examples would be the number of products a company sells, the number of ads placed on television, and the number of salespeople within a salesforce. Integer values are also called whole numbers.

Figure 1.18 displays the sales figures for KEC Equipment using a line chart in which sales for each year is plotted on the graph and connected via a line. The same data are presented in **Figure 1.19** using an area chart. Since sales are continuous data it is appropriate to use a line or area chart to display the information.

In creating graphs it is critical that both the x-axis and the y-axis are labelled. A title should also be given that explains what is being graphed, or lists the specific survey question respondents answered. The idea behind these titles is to make the graph stand alone. Someone looking at the graph should be able to understand the information being presented and interpret the data without reading any written explanation.

1.8c Statistical Reporting Student Exercise

Access the authors' website at www.clowjames.net/students.html and open the Excel file for this chapter entitled "Chapter01Thunderhead." Graph the sales figures provided for Thunderhead Biotics Company using a line chart. Be sure to provide a chart title, an x-axis title, and a y-axis title. Graph the same data using an area chart. Again, make sure the x-axis, y-axis, and chart are titled correctly.

1.8d Dealing with Data

Access the authors' website at www.clowjames.net/students.html and open the Excel file entitled "Chapter01Thunderhead." Tyler began Thunderhead Biotics in 1993. The first

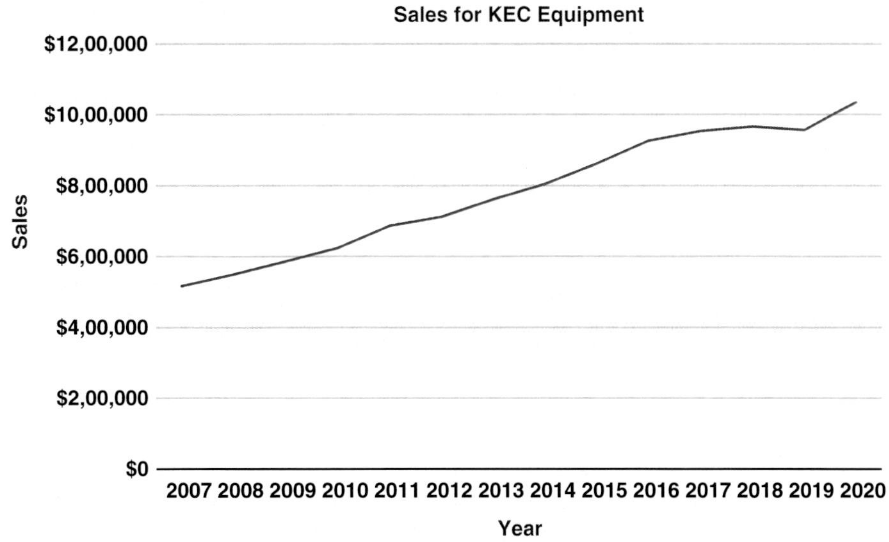

FIGURE 1.18 A Line Graph Showing the Sales for KEC Equipment Company

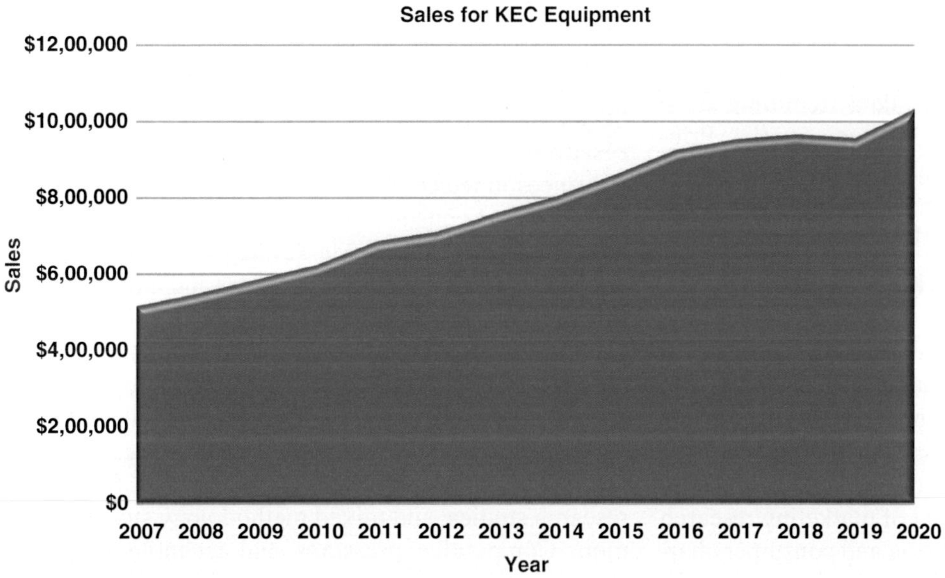

FIGURE 1.19 An Area Chart Displaying Sales Figures for KEC Equipment Company

year, he was the sales staff, CEO, accountant, janitor and all other jobs that needed to be done. In 1994, he hired his first salesperson. He now has 4 individuals in sales. In 2007 he began using the salesforce estimate approach to forecasting future sales. Use the data provided in the Excel spreadsheet under the heading "Chapter 1 Dealing with Data" for the following exercises.

1. Use regression analysis and the sales figures from 1998 through 2020 to estimate a trend and forecast for 2021.
2. Calculate the 2021 sales estimate based on the input of the four salespeople.
3. Using the data provided, calculate the average ratio of sales to sales force estimate.
4. Using the information from Question 2 and Question 3, forecast the sales for Thunderhead for 2021.
5. Calculate 2021 forecasts for Thunderhead using a 5-year, 4-year, and 3-year moving average.
6. Based on all of the forecasts you obtained, which should Tyler use? Why?

Summary

Objective 1: Discuss the basic types and functions of marketing research.

Marketing research studies can perform one or more of the following functions: exploratory, descriptive, diagnostic, and predictive. Most commercial marketing research studies are applied research, while basic marketing research is typically conducted in University settings. The philosophy of science and scientific method guides the marketing research process.

Objective 2: Identify marketing research studies that can be used in making marketing decisions.

Segmentation and targeting decisions often rest on data obtained via benefit and lifestyle studies and target market analysis. Product testing studies and test markets provide essential information as part of the new product development process. Existing brands benefit from market analysis and competitive analysis studies, which allow decision makers to understand changes in the dynamic marketplace and how their brands will be affected. Marketing communication decisions are enhanced by data stemming from advertising effectiveness research and media studies. Pricing studies evaluate the impact that pricing changes have on demand, and studies of sales potential and sales forecasting efforts are used many departments within the firm.

Objective 3: Discuss how marketing research has evolved since 1879.

The first documented instance of marketing research occurred in 1879 with the basic foundation of marketing research being developed during the first 30 years of the twentieth century. The early years of marketing research focused on methods of sampling, collecting data, and analytical techniques. The primary goal of marketing research was to measure marketing phenomena and consumer characteristics. During the "golden age of consumer research" (1970s and 1980s) marketing research techniques become more scientific, computing power made collecting and analyzing data faster, easier, cheaper, and more accurate. Marketing research became the support, the rationale for choosing particular marketing strategies and marketing tactics. During the late 1990s and early 2000s a cultural shift resulted in researchers being asked to provide insights into what the data meant and to assist in providing insights into marketing situations. The current stage of marketing research is "the consultative stage." Now, marketing researchers are being asked to assist in developing marketing strategy.

Objective 4: Describe the marketing research industry as it exists today.

Client firms conduct research in-house or hire full-service or boutique marketing research firms to provide information needed for decision-making. Data collection can be undertaken with the general population, or a firm may be hired to provide a sample from its panel or database. Research agencies are increasingly relying upon sample aggregators to obtain more representative, reliable samples.

Objective 5: Discuss the emerging trends in marketing research.

Advances in telecommunication technology have changed the ways that consumers interact with each other, companies, media and brands. Marketing researchers monitor social media, MROCs, review websites and mobile marketing research as a result. Economic constraints have tightened client budgets, and led many researchers to embrace DIY research options, automation and artificial intelligence in order to complete research cheaper, quicker and better.

Research panels, research databases, MROCs and crowdsourcing are increasingly being used for marketing research studies, and mixed methodology studies are common. Competitive pressures and technological changes continue to compress research deadlines. Furthermore, the globalization of business has resulted in a greater need for multi-country marketing research efforts.

Key Terms

advertising effectiveness research, p. 10
applied marketing research, p. 7
artificial intelligence (AI), p. 21
basic marketing research, p. 7
benefit and lifestyle studies, p. 9
competitive analysis studies, p. 10
continuous data, p. 25
customer experience studies (CX), p. 9
customer satisfaction studies, p. 9
descriptive function, p. 6
diagnostic function, p. 7
discrete data, p. 26
exploratory function, p. 6
Internet of Things (IoT), p. 4
market analysis study, p. 10
marketing mix, p. 5
marketing research, p. 4
media studies, p. 10
micro surveys, p. 19
predictive function, p. 7
pricing studies, p. 10
product testing studies, p. 9
research databases, p. 21
research panels, p. 21
sales forecasts, p. 10
sales potential studies, p. 10

Critical Thinking Exercises

1. Have you ever participated in a marketing research study? If so, describe how the research was conducted. Was the study exploratory, descriptive, diagnostic, or predictive in nature? Justify your answer.
2. What impact do you think IoT, virtual reality and other forms of emerging technologies will have on the way companies conduct marketing research in the future?
3. Think about the place where you currently work, or a place you have worked in the past. Describe how marketing research could be used to gather information that would be beneficial to the business or organization.
4. Interview a professor at your school other than your instructor. Ask the professor about the types of research he/she conducts. Would it be applied or basic research? Show the individual the diagram in Figure 1.5. Ask if that process applies to his or her research process.
5. A research study investigated the factors that influence and determine a firm's reputation. The study included 150 firms from a variety of industries, and several factors which influence or determine firm reputation under various conditions were identified. Is this an example of applied research or basic research?
6. Find an article in each of the following journals: *Services Marketing Quarterly, Journal of Services Marketing, Business Communication Quarterly, Journal of Healthcare Marketing,* and *Journal of Advertising.* Identify whether the research is applied or basic in each article. For applied research studies, briefly describe how the data were collected. If you classified an article as basic research, explain the theory or concept that was proposed or tested.
7. A student bookstore conducted a series of group interviews with several groups of students in order to try to understand why textbook sales were declining, despite the fact that enrollment had increased during the same semester. Which function of research does this illustrate?
8. Give an example of how a health club, fashion retailer, or manufacturer of fishing boats might conduct four separate studies that exemplify each of the types of research: exploratory, descriptive, diagnostic, and predictive.
9. Have social media and smartphones changed our culture? Explain. Have they changed the way humans communicate with each other? Explain.
10. Do you use Twitter? Why do you use it? If so, how has it impacted your life? Have you ever used Twitter to communicate with a company or brand? What happened as a result? If you have not used Twitter, why not?
11. Are you a Facebook fan of one or more brands? If so, which ones? Why did you join?
12. Interview five individuals of different ages ranging from young teenagers to a senior. Ask them about their use of social media, cell phones, and smartphones. Write a short report contrasting the differences and how age impacts the use of modern technology.
13. A researcher investigated whether an individual's technological ability varied according to their age. A total of 20 respondents participated in the study. Respondents indicated their age in years, and rated themselves according to the scale shown in **Figure 1.20.** Critique the graph shown in **Figure 1.21.** What elements are missing? What needs to be changed? Are the data collected appropriate for a line chart? Why or why not? Do you think this study provides valid information? Why or why not?

Rating	Technical Ability Scale	Examples
0	Very little technical ability	i.e., cannot turn a computer on, would need step by step instructions 99% of the time
1	Below average technical ability	i.e., can turn it on a navigate a few things, needs help from others often
2	Average technical ability	i.e., knows a few programs, uses them often, sometimes help from others
3	Above average technical ability	i.e., has computer/smartphone, knows it well without much help from others
4	Ultimate technical ability	i.e., expert ability, helps other with technical issues, uses technology for almost everything daily

FIGURE 1.20 Scale for Rating Technical Ability (Q. 13)

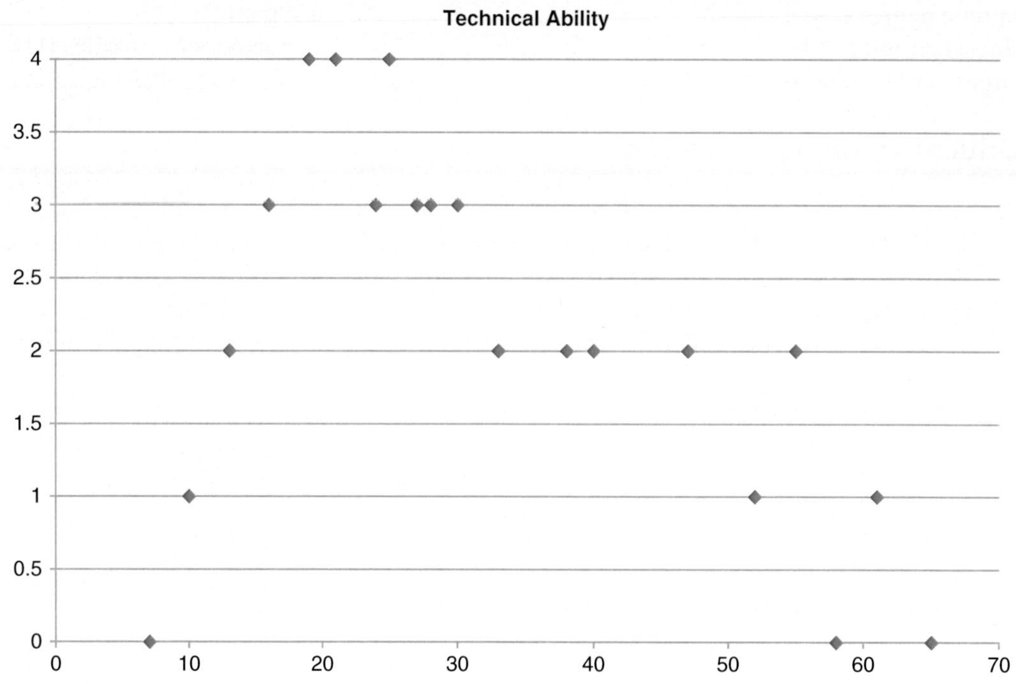

FIGURE 1.21 Graph of Age and Rating Technical Ability (Question 13)

Lakeside Grill

(Comprehensive Student Case)

As part of their annual service project, five students of the American Marketing Association student chapter have agreed to conduct marketing research for a local business—the Lakeside Grill.

This "Lakeside Grill (Comprehensive Student Case)" section provides a summary of how these students used the information in each chapter for their research project. Because it is a continuous project that flows throughout the entire text, it will be possible to see a research project from beginning to end. However, being students, the team does not always make the most optimal decisions. Following a description of their actions, questions will encourage a critique of the decisions made by the student team. This section allows a glimpse of a marketing research project conducted by a team of students from inception to completion.

Critique Questions:

1. How important is it for students to conduct a real-world project while taking a course in marketing research? What are the pros and cons of doing this?
2. What could a local business realistically expect from a student team conducting a research project?
3. How much guidance or direction should a faculty member or instructor of the course provide for the student team? Explain.
4. If you were part of a student team conducting research for a local business or non-profit, what type of business or non-profit organization would provide the best learning experience? Why?
5. Is it fair to the local marketing research firms for a business to use a student team to conduct research rather than hiring the marketing research firm? Justify your answer.

Notes

1. Andrew Meola, "What Is the Internet of Things (IoT)? Meaning & Definition," *Business Insider* (May 10, 2018), http://www.businessinsider.com/internet-of-things-definition.
2. Ibid.
3. Garcia Krista Garcia, "Smart Appliances Haven't Found a Home Yet, but That Could Change if Prices Come Down and Understanding Grows," emarketer, July 5, 2018, https://www.emarketer.com/content/smart-appliances-haven-t-found-a-home-yet.
4. Adapted from Jenna Enright, "Study Looks at Common Traits of NFL Fans," *Quirk's Media* (October 4, 2017), https://www.quirks.com/articles/study-looks-at-common-traits-of-nfl-fans.

5. Klaus M. Miller, Reto Hofstetter, Harley Krohmer, and Zhand Z. John, "How Should Consumers' Willingness to Pay Be Measured? An Empirical Comparison of State-of-the-Art Approaches," *Journal of Marketing Research* 48, no. 1 (2011): 172–184.
6. This section is based on Earl R. Babble, *Survey Research Methods* (Belmont, CA: Wadsworth Publishing Company, 1973), 10–19.
7. David W. Stewart, "From Methods and Projects to Systems and Processes: The Evolution of Marketing Research Techniques," *Marketing Research* 3, no. 3 (September 1991): 25–36.
8. Scott Christofferson and Beverly Chu, "The Client-Side Researcher 2.0," Research World, http://rwconnect.esomar.org/2011/05/10/the-client-side-researcher-2.0.
9. "Market Research Industry Lumascape," in *GRIT Report: GreenBook Research Industry Trends Report, Quarters 1–2, 2018* (New York: GreenBook, 2018), http://www.greenbook.org/grit.
10. Kathyrn Korostoff, "Marketing Research Job Titles in 2018," *Quirk's Media* (February 21, 2018), https://www.quirks.com/articles/marketing-research-job-titles-in-2018.
11. Kathyrn Korostoff, "Today's MR Jobs Are Expanding Traditional Roles," *Quirk's Media* (August 2017), https://www.quirks.com/articles/today-s-mr-jobs-are-expanding-traditional-roles.
12. "The Evolving Researcher Role & Skills," in *GRIT Report: Greenbook Research Industry Trends Report, Quarters 3–4, 2018* (New York: GreenBook, 2018), http://www.greenbook.org/grit.
13. This section is based on Kathyrn Korostoff, "Today's MR Jobs Are Expanding Traditional Roles," *Quirk's Media* (August 2017), https://www.quirks.com/articles/today-s-mr-jobs-are-expanding-traditional-roles; and Uwana Evers, "The Changing Face of Value: Clients Want New Technology, Data Analytics, and Strategic Consultancy," in *GRIT Report: Greenbook Research Industry Trends Report*, Business & Innovation Edition (New York: GreenBook, 2019).
14. Interview with Debbie Peternana and Carrie Bellerive, ReRez, February 25, 2011.
15. "One More Squeeze Left," *The Q Report. Corporate Researcher Report 2018*, August 2019, https://www.quirks.com/tools/corporate-researcher-report.
16. Ibid.
17. "Drivers of Supplier Selection," in *GRIT Report: Greenbook Research Industry Trends Report, Quarters 3–4, 2018* (New York: GreenBook, 2018).
18. This section is based on an interview with Leonard Murphy, Brandscan 360, April 14, 2011; and "Will Social Media Replace Surveys as a Research Tool?" *Ad Age* (March 21, 2011), http://adage.com/print/149509.
19. Douglas Pruden and Terry Vavra, "Complying with GDPR—a U.S. Perspective," *Quirks Media* (May 30, 2018), https://www.quirks.com/articles/complying-with-gdpr-a-u-s-perspective.
20. Zoltan Szuhai, "Does Your Business Rely on CATI? Prepare for GDPR," *Quirks Media* (May 10, 2018), https://www.quirks.com/articles/does-your-business-rely-on-cati-prepare-for-gdpr.
21. Douglas Pruden and Terry Vavra, "Complying with GDPR—a U.S. Perspective," *Quirks Media* (May 30, 2018), https://www.quirks.com/articles/complying-with-gdpr-a-u-s-perspective.
22. Alicia Hamilton, "The Future of Connected Devices and MR Methodologies," *Quirk's Media* (May 2016), https://www.quirks.com/articles/the-future-of-connected-devices-and-mr-methodologies.
23. Melanie Courtright, "Introducing the Dynata Global Trends Report," *Quirk's Media* (April 29, 2019), https://www.quirks.com/articles/introducing-the-dynata-global-trends-report.
24. Corinne Shanahan and Jessica Spilman, "Leverage Virtual Voice Response Interviews," *Quirk's Media* (March 25, 2019), https://www.quirks.com/articles/leveraging-virtual-voice-response-interviews.
25. Matt Warta, "Industry Challenge: Making the Strategic A&U More Agile," in *GRIT Report: Greenbook Research Industry Trends Report*, Business & Innovation Edition (New York: GreenBook, 2019).
26. "Will Social Media Replace Surveys as a Research Tool?" *Ad Age* (March 21, 2011), http://adage.com/print/14950.
27. Alex Osbaldeston, "Are You Embracing the Increase in Consumers Willing to Participate in MROCs?" *Quirk's Marketing Research Review* (July 2016), https://www.quirks.com/articles/are-you-embracing-the-increase-in-consumers-willing-to-participate-in-mrocs.
28. This section is based on Ed Crowley, "Will IoT and Advanced Analytics Be the Death of Traditional MR?" *Quirk's Media* (June 12, 2017), https://www.quirks.com/articles/will-iot-and-advanced-analytics-be-the-death-of-traditional-mr.
29. "Smartphone Penetration Rate as Share of the Population in the United States from 2010 to 2021," Statista, May 29, 2018, https://www.statista.com/statistics/201183/forecast-of-smartphone-penetration-in-the-us.
30. Jennifer Reid, "Chat Surveys. How They Compare to Traditional Online Surveys and Their Impact to Research Experience and Data Quality," Rival Tech, 2018, https://www.rivaltech.com/chat-effectiveness-thank-you?submissionGuid=f76c73e9-1f2f-40a6-9b6f-3588ada45959.
31. Bob Yazbeck and Susan Scarlet, "10 Reasons Why You Should Go Mobile Right Now," *Quirk's Marketing Research Review* (July 2013): 52.

32. Patricia Graham and Sean Conry, "Making the Move to Mobile Research: A Primer for Client and Supplier-Side Professionals," *Quirk's Marketing Research Review* (February 2014): Article ID 20140210.
33. Eric Whipkey, "Why Researchers Are Embracing DIY," *Quirk's Media* (April/May 2019), https://www.quirks.com/articles/why-researchers-are-embracing-diy.
34. "Adoption and Consideration of Automation Platforms," in *GRIT Report: Greenbook Research Industry Trends Report, Quarters 1–2, 2018* (New York: GreenBook, 2018).
35. Bob Fawson, "Something Old, Something New. The Evolution of Automation in Research and Why It's a Net Gain," in *GRIT Report: Greenbook Research Industry Trends Report, Quarters 1–2, 2018* (New York: GreenBook, 2018).
36. Matt Warta, "The Missing Ingredient to Product Innovation Success: Agile Audience Intelligence," in *GRIT Report: Greenbook Research Industry Trends Report, Quarters 3–4, 2018* (New York: GreenBook, 2018).
37. Melanie Courtright, "The Benefits of Automation and AI: Moving from Concept to Reality," in *GRIT Report: Greenbook Research Industry Trends Report*, Business & Innovation Edition (New York: GreenBook, 2019).
38. Roddy Knowles, "Using MR Automation to Keep Up with the Speed of Business," *Quirk's Media* (June 26, 2017), https://www.quirks.com/articles/using-mr-automation-to-keep-up-with-the-speed-of-business.
39. Cassandra McNeill, "Marketing Research and Automation Can Co-Exist," *Quirk's Media* (May 6, 2019), https://www.quirks.com/articles/marketing-research-and-automation-can-co-exist.
40. Brian Heikes, "A Look at Artificial Intelligence vs. Intelligence Amplification," *Quirk's Media* (May 8, 2017), https://www.quirks.com/articles/a-look-at-artificial-intelligence-vs-intelligence-amplification.
41. This section adapted from "Discover the Power of the Crowd," MindSumo, 2019, https://www.mindsumo.com/business; and "Can You Come Up with the Next Great Sustainable Product Idea of 2019?" MindSumo, 2019, https://www.mindsumo.com/contests/sustainability-product-brainstorm.
42. Interview with Michael Patterson, Probit Research, April 14, 201

The Marketing Research Process

CHAPTER 2

Source: Konstantin Chagin/Shutterstock.

Chapter Outline

Learning Objectives

After studying this chapter, you should be able to:

- Compare and contrast the three types of research designs.
- Explain the marketing research process.
- Describe the components of a request for research (RFP) and a research proposal.
- Provide an overview of qualitative and quantitative research.
- Recite the ethical considerations in designing research studies.

2.1 Chapter Overview

Marketers are interested in several generational cohorts that exist within America. Members of a generation share history, values, and experiences that often influence their lifestyles, expectations, media habits and purchasing behaviors. Generations are classified according to a range of birth dates though not all sources agree on the defining dates for some generations. The "Greatest Generation" was also the smallest in size in 2017, as shown in **Figure 2.1**, and is composed of individuals born prior to 1928. Members of the "Silent Generation" were born between 1928 and 1945, while "Baby Boomers" are those born following World II through 1964. The "Generation X" label is generally assigned to those born between 1965 and 1980, while "Millennials" (also called "Generation Y") identify the group born between 1981 and 1996. The final generation is composed of individuals born from 1997 to 2015, and is called "Generation Z".[1]

Interest in Generation Z has grown as its members enter into their teens and young adult years. Gen Z will become the largest generation by 2020, and members currently directly or indirectly influence over $600 billion in spending by their families. Gen Z differs from previous generations in meaningful ways. They are the first truly digital native generation to grow up with technology, such as tablets, from an early age. The vast majority use social media regularly, particularly Snapchat, Instagram, and to a lesser extent, Facebook. In fact, Gen Z is more likely to use social media to communicate with friends and family than any other Generation as 20 percent prefer this mode of communication over phone calls, texting, mobile message apps and email. As demonstrated in **Figure 2.2**, brands are important to Gen Z, as 16 percent indicated that brands were more important than price. By comparison, only 11 percent of Millennials indicated that brands were more important than price, with percentages declining further for Generation X (9 percent) and Baby Boomers (7 percent). In looking at the percentage of those who selected price as being more important (either by a little or a lot), a pattern becomes clear. With the exception of Baby Boomers 41 percent of whom indicated that price was more important than brands Gen Z (42 percent) is less price conscious when compared to Millennials (50 percent) and Generation X (45 percent). Having witnessed the impact of the last recession, Gen Z is financially savvy, risk adverse and trusts banks less compared to the other Generations. This makes them a challenging target for financial institutions, and early research on Gen Z shows that marketers must develop trust and authenticity when marketing to Gen Z.[2]

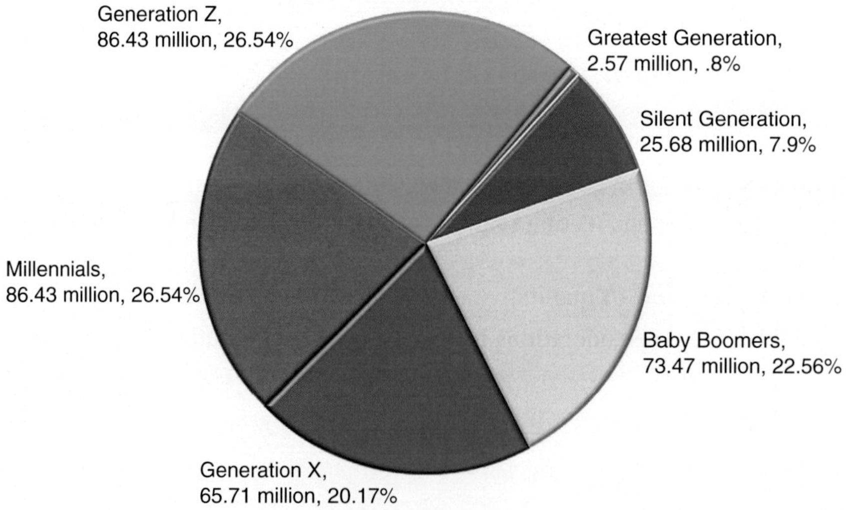

FIGURE 2.1 U.S. Population by Generation

Source: Author-created with data from US Census Bureau. "Resident population in the United States in 2017, by generation (in millions)," https://www-statista-com.ezproxy.lsus.edu/statistics/797321/us-population-by-generation/, accessed July 9, 2018.

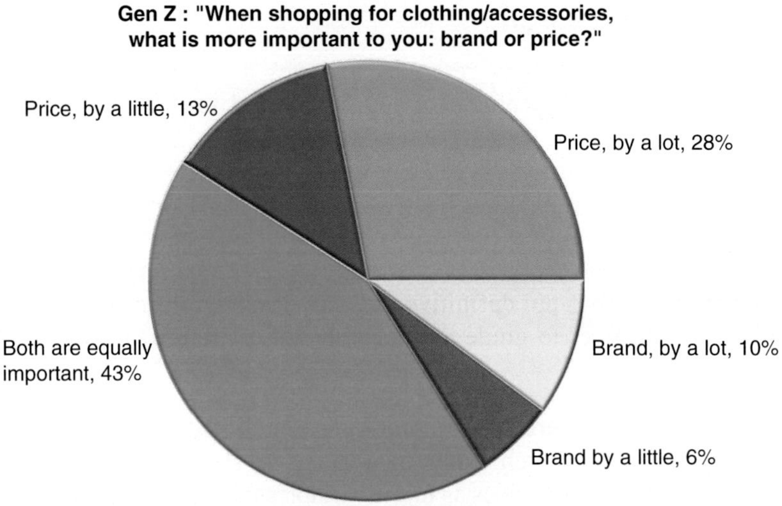

FIGURE 2.2 Pie Chart Showing Gen Z Responses to a Survey Question

Source: Author-created with data from "Guide to Gen Z: Debunking the Myths of our Youngest Generation," NPD Group, 2017, https://www.npd.com/lps/pdf/guide-to -gen-z.pdf, accessed July 17, 2018.

This chapter explores the different types of research and the research process that can be used to obtain information similar to what has just been discussed. Following a detailed research process allowed the researchers to go beyond collecting data, to providing insights that can be utilized by individuals marketing to Generation Z consumers. The chapter discusses the two primary types of research: qualitative and quantitative. Finally, the chapter concludes with a discussion of ethics and identifies where unethical conduct may creep into marketing research studies.

2.2 Types of Research Designs

LEARNING OBJECTIVE 2.1 Compare and contrast the three types of research designs.

As previously stated, the purpose of marketing research is to help managers make better decisions. While it is impossible to remove all uncertainty, information can help managers understand the problem being faced and the possible ramifications of decision options. For example, many companies are struggling with what to do about providing online reviews of products. Recent research found that trustworthy reviews influenced 68 percent of online U.S. shoppers in 2017. Furthermore, 71 percent of online shoppers indicated it was important to read online reviews before making major purchases. Finally, product ratings and reviews have influenced 42 percent of U.S. Internet users choice of shopping venue.[3] Based on these findings, it would appear that companies should offer some type of online reviews on their websites. But, what type of reviews? And, if reviews are provided, how and where should they be posted? An even more pertinent question is revealed by examining who responded to this particular survey. The study stated online shoppers were interviewed, which begs the question, "Who were the online shoppers and are they different from consumers who shop primarily in retail stores?"

> **Aspen Pet Self Warming Beds**
> by Petmate
> ★★★★☆ ⌄ 2,434 customer reviews | 126 answered questions
> **#1 Best Seller** in Cat Beds
>
> Trustworthy reviews influenced 68 percent of online U.S. shoppers in 2017.

While research can provide information, managers must be able to interpret that information and relate it to the problem or opportunity they are facing and the decisions that need to be made. This process requires an understanding of the basic types of research design, shown in **Figure 2.3**.

Exploratory Research	Descriptive Research	Causal Research

FIGURE 2.3 Types of Research Design

2.2a Exploratory Research

Exploratory research preliminary examination of a problem or situation to identify parameters to be studied further or to define the research problem itself.

As the name implies, **exploratory research** involves a preliminary examination of a problem or situation to identify parameters to be studied further and in some cases to even define the problem itself. Researchers will often launch exploratory research when the problem they are facing is not clear. They have symptoms, such as declining sales or a decrease in market share, but do not fully understand what is causing the sales or market share to decline. The goal of exploratory research in such cases is to help researchers understand the situation, the problem being faced, and perhaps even some possible solutions. Exploratory research is not definitive. It is not designed to be used by managers for making decisions, but rather to guide the development of future research projects or to better understand a situation.

Uses of Exploratory Research Exploratory research is often used in the first stage of a more comprehensive research study. In addition to shedding light on the problem, exploratory research can provide clues as to the variables that should be studied. Additional types of research can then be used to determine the relationships among variables and any cause-and-effect relationships that may exist.

Research hypothesis expected research outcome which seems reasonable in light of existing information.

Exploratory research can provide information that can be used to develop hypotheses for future studies. A **research hypothesis** states an expected research outcome relevant to one or more variables that seems reasonable in light of existing information. In simpler terms, research hypotheses represent educated guesses with respect to what the researcher expects to find after analyzing the research data. For example, if a marketing researcher wished to explore the impact of consumers' online shopping behavior in greater detail, he or she might develop the following hypothesis after reading an article about how consumers use online reviews, ratings, and search.

Hypothesis: *When researching branded products online prior to purchasing, 75 percent of consumers will start with a search engine.*

Types of Exploratory Research Methods of exploratory research include secondary research, focus groups, in-depth interviews, case studies, and even pilot studies. With the widespread availability of the Internet and easy access to large article databases, conducting secondary research can be done rather quickly and inexpensively. After all, someone else may have faced a similar problem. Articles relating to the situation may provide useful information and understanding, and possibly help lead to hypothesis development. Internally, the firm can review previous research studies that might shed some light on the issue at hand.

Focus groups and in-depth interviews will be discussed in more detail in a later chapter, but both methods allow researchers to gather information from individuals. With the focus group, researchers talk with a small group of individuals about a specific topic, exploring their thoughts and ideas in detail. With in-depth interviews, the researcher is talking to individuals one-on-one to explore a particular topic in greater depth or to better understand the thought process behind an individual's actions or behaviors. Both forms of research can provide rich, detailed information and consumer insights that can help researchers to better understand important aspects of a current situation.

Pilot study an abbreviated study with a limited number of respondents designed to provide information to the researcher useful in developing a larger, more definitive study.

Occasionally, a researcher will launch a **pilot study**, which is an abbreviated study with a limited number of respondents designed to provide information to the researcher in developing a larger, more definitive study. A researcher may not know exactly what questions to ask. A pilot study can be helpful, especially by asking open-ended questions. Suppose a researcher wants to study the impact of various factors on the consumer decision process that is used in determining whether online reviews will be consulted before purchasing a product. A pilot study might be used and respondents asked to identify what factors influence whether they conduct an online search for information prior to making a purchase decision. Pilot studies are also useful in testing aspects of research methodology, such as sampling and data collection procedures.

2.2b Descriptive Research

As the name implies, **descriptive research** answers the questions who, what, when, where, and how in describing the characteristics of consumers, brands, and other marketing factors. In contrast to exploratory research, marketers who use descriptive research already have a good understanding of the marketing problem or situation. They are just seeking additional information in order to make more informed decisions.

Descriptive research answers the questions who, what, when, where, and how in describing the characteristics of consumers, brands, and other marketing phenomena.

Descriptive research often relies on surveys to obtain data. Consider the example of descriptive research findings presented in Figure 2.4.

In cooperation with the National Retail Foundation, IBM surveyed 15,600 Generation Z consumers between the ages of 13 and 21 in sixteen countries. One question asked how they typically made purchases. Notice that over two-thirds of those surveyed will shop in a retail store most of the time. Despite having grown up with technology, only 22 percent shop the Internet using web browsers most of the time, while only 13 percent use a smart phone app to make purchases. Yet 52 percent of respondents use their smartphone most of the time to shop other stores for price comparisons, while 51 percent look for coupons, discounts, or promotions on their phone most of the time. This type of information can be valuable to marketing managers in developing in-store and digital marketing tactics.[4]

Descriptive research is appropriate for a large number of research situations and is the most frequently used type of research. In most cases, descriptive studies provide discrete and continuous data. Counts, percentages and averages are commonly computed, which allows for statistical and mathematical relationships to be examined. Caution should be used when interpreting these relationships because descriptive research findings cannot be used to prove causality. For instance, descriptive research may show that there is a relationship between online product reviews and purchase behaviors, but this fact alone does not prove that one causes the other. It is merely a description of the relationship.

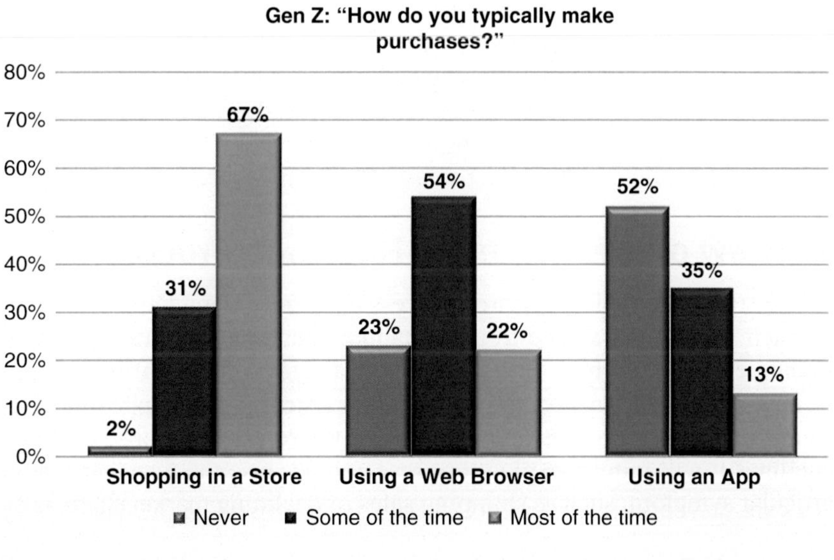

FIGURE 2.4 Bar Chart Showing Results from a Descriptive Research Study

Source: Adapted from Jane Cheung, Simon Glass, Karl Haller and Christopher K. Wong, "What do Gen Z shoppers really want?," IBM Corporation, Armonk: NY, 2018, p. 3.

An ad campaign that appears to triple the sale of snow shovels over a weekend may be a spurious association, rather than a causal factor if 14 inches of snow falls the same weekend as the sale.

2.2c Causal Research

To determine if one variable causes another, researchers utilize **causal research**. Most causal research designs involve experimentation, which is the topic of Chapter 7. Care has to be taken to ensure that the relationship is truly cause-and-effect and not just a coincidence, or spurious association. **Spurious associations** occur when two variables appear to be related and one appears to be causing something else to happen, when in fact it may be due to other factors. For instance, a hardware store might run a special advertising campaign on snow shovels. Over the weekend, sales triple. It would appear that the increase in the sale of the snow shovels was caused by the advertising campaign. However, the more likely cause is the 14 inches of snow that fell at the beginning of the weekend. The goal of causal research is to control or eliminate all other possible causes of an effect except the one being studied.

Causal research research used to determine cause-and-effect relationships between variables.

Spurious association apparent cause-and-effect relationship between two variables that is actually caused by other factors.

Temporal sequence condition for causality in which the cause precedes the effect.

Concomitant variation condition for causality in which the two items thought to be linked in a causal relationship vary or change together and in the direction hypothesized.

In determining cause-and-effect, two conditions must be met. The first, called **temporal sequence**, is related to timing issues and simply means that the cause must precede or occur at the same time of the effect. In the case of the hardware store, the ad campaign must precede or occur simultaneously with the increase in the sales of snow shovels. In the case of understanding the impact of online customer reviews on purchase decisions, the viewing of the review by the shopper must occur prior to or at the time of the purchase and not after the purchase. Assuming that such behavior is the norm would be dangerous since many individuals will in fact read product reviews after making a purchase, as one method of alleviating buyer's remorse (also called cognitive dissonance or buyer's regret).

The second condition for establishing causality is **concomitant variation**, which means the two items thought to be part of a causal relationship vary or change together and in the direction hypothesized. In the case of the hardware store, if the researcher wants to show a cause-and-effect between the ad campaign and the sale of snow shovels, then an increase in ad spending should result in an increase in the sales of snow shovels, rather than no sales increase, or even worse, a decrease in sales. Correspondingly, a decrease in ad expenditures would be expected to create a decline in the sale of snow shovels, though perhaps not immediately, due to advertising's carry-over or lag effect. From this example, it can be seen that to show a cause-and-effect between advertising and sales is difficult. While marketers believe there is a strong relationship, they also understand there are a large number of other factors that affect sales beyond an advertising campaign.

2.3 Overview of the Marketing Research Process

LEARNING OBJECTIVE 2.2
Explain the marketing research process.

Figure 2.5 illustrates the typical research process. It starts with understanding the research purpose, which stems from a need to understand a situation, opportunity, or a particular problem being experienced by a firm or brand. Managers often confuse symptoms with problems, so it is up to the market researcher to persistently investigate or question management until the true problem is understood, and the research purpose is clearly identified. Sometimes it will require exploratory research because the manager may not know why a particular symptom, such as slumping sales or declining market share, is occurring.

2.3a Research Purpose

Research purpose statement that broadly specifies the situation, phenomenon, opportunity, or problem to be investigated, and guides the creation of research questions and hypotheses.

Market research is conducted with a specific purpose in mind. The **research purpose** might be to gain a better understanding of a situation or phenomenon, to investigate an opportunity, or to understand or address one or more problems which may be negatively affecting the firm. As **Figure 2.6** illustrates, defining the research purpose is a multi-tiered

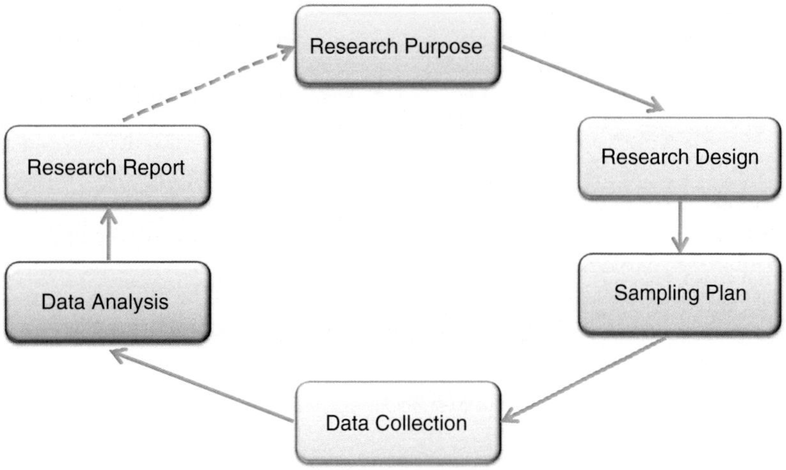

FIGURE 2.5 The Marketing Research Process

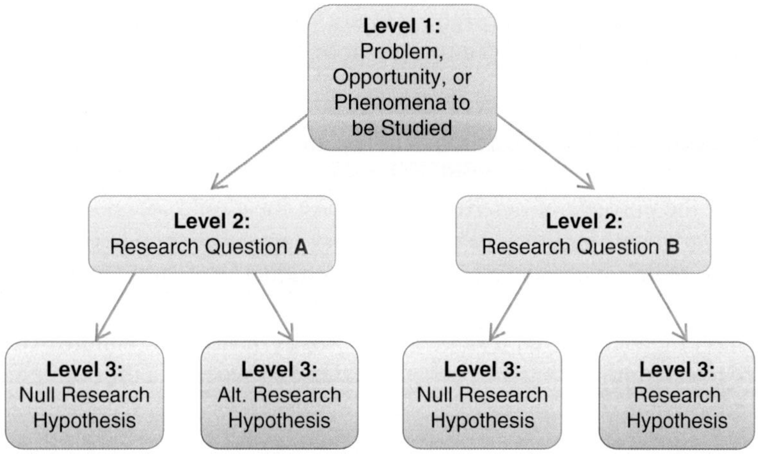

FIGURE 2.6 Defining the Research Process

process in which the research purpose statement serves as a springboard for developing research questions and research hypotheses. Although not an easy task, its importance cannot be overstated because the research purpose affects every aspect of the research design.

Symptoms or Problems This task is particularly challenging when the purpose of the research relates to a problem being experienced by the firm or brand. Too often management's preconceived notions of the problem are incorrect, which may result in research that isn't helpful because it doesn't collect the proper data. This can occur when symptoms are confused with the problems, or the true underlying cause of the problem is not properly identified. The difference between symptoms and problems can be illustrated by the *iceberg principle*. With an iceberg, typically less than 20 percent of the iceberg is visible above the water. The portion below the water is much larger, and poses a much greater risk to ships. Most managers see the part above the water, such as declining sales. It is the task of the marketing researcher to discover the part under the water, the problem or cause of the symptoms.

Sales may be lost due to declining levels of customer satisfaction. But the decline in customer satisfaction may in turn have been caused by something else—perceptions of inferior product quality, poor product performance, unsatisfactory customer service, a price that is too high for the benefits received, entrant of a new competitor, and so forth. Determining the true problem is akin to peeling an onion—researchers must continually ask, "what caused that" as they strip away each layer in an attempt to uncover the root cause or causes.

Investigating Problems which May Cause Symptoms	Investigating Opportunities
• Poor brand image • Lower quality products • High pricing • Poor distribution • Poor customer service • New competition	• New product or service development • Site selection for store • Shifts in consumer wants **Investigating Phenomena** • Top 100 advertisers • Impact of social media

FIGURE 2.7 Typical Research Purposes

Some typical research problems which may trigger research studies are shown as part of Figure 2.7. The symptom for each of the research problems identified in the figure may have been declines in key marketing metrics related to the problem, slumping sales or declining market share. But, the problems causing the symptom are vastly different. In terms of research design, a study examining poor brand image will be conducted differently from one examining a poor distribution system or poor customer service.

Exploiting Opportunities Research studies are also conducted for the purpose of exploiting an opportunity. A few examples also appear in Figure 2.7. Site selection research is conducted for the purpose of determining the best location to open a new retail store or restaurant. Similarly, with millions of dollars at risk, consumer goods firms often invest in a great deal of research when developing a new product. Research conducted during the new product development process typically includes concept testing in the early stages to ascertain whether the idea is even feasible. Later stages of research will involve a variety of studies geared toward optimizing the package design and aspects of the marketing mix, such as price and marketing communications. In some instances, research culminates in a test market, where the product is introduced on a limited basis in an actual store and promoted via the initial marketing communications campaign. As an example, a recent syndicated research study by MRI-Simmons explored the cannabis market in the US. For many firms, marketing cannabis could be an opportunity as more states seek to legalize its status. The national study provided profiles of user and non-user segments, descriptive data of how cannabis is being using medicinally and recreationally, key benefits, barriers, and attitudes towards cannabis use, and consumer purchasing behavior and marketplace information. Insights from the study can be used by marketers as they develop product offerings, create advertising messages, and select advertising media to reach both those who support and oppose widespread legalization, as well as current users or nonusers of cannabis.[5]

Investigating Phenomena Not all research studies involve a marketing or business problem. Researchers or managers may be seeking a better understanding of a situation or phenomenon. For instance, in the study referred to earlier in this chapter, researchers wanted a better understanding of Generation Z consumers. In another example, Global Reputation Pulse conducts a survey every year to determine the top 100 global brands in terms of each company's reputation. Nielsen Online conducted a survey to investigate consumer attitudes towards purchasing products that contain organic or all-natural ingredients. In all three situations, marketers were seeking a better understanding of the marketplace and consumers in order to develop more effective marketing strategies.

Research Questions Once the research purpose and the related problem, opportunity, or situation to be studied has been clearly identified, research questions and hypotheses are formed. Typically, multiple research questions are formed for a

Research Question	Research Objective
• What is the demographic, geographic, and psychographic profile of the credit union's depositors, investors, and mortgage holders? • Which of three test package designs has the greatest impact on consumer attitudes and purchase intentions?	• To determine the demographic, geographic, and psychographic profile of the credit union's depositors, investors, and mortgage holders. • To identify which of three test package designs has the greatest impact on consumer attitudes and purchase intentions.

FIGURE 2.8 Research Questions vs. Research Objectives

particular research purpose. Research questions should not be confused with survey questions. **Research questions** specify the *type of information* needed in order to successfully fulfill the research purpose and make important managerial decisions. As such, they should be clearly written and stated as specifically as possible in order to help guide the research process down the line. A research question which asks, "What is the profile of the credit union's target market?" would not be as helpful in guiding survey development as would one which asks, "What is the demographic, geographic, and psychographic profile of the credit union's depositors, investors, and mortgage holders? Some researchers prefer forming research objectives. The only difference between these two concepts is that one is phrased as a question, while the other is phrased as a statement. **Figure 2.8** illustrates how the same information can be phrased as a research question or a research objective.

Research question specifies the type of information needed to fulfill the research purpose and to make managerial decisions.

Research Hypotheses Research hypotheses are included only when the researcher has reason to suspect, or "conjecture" an answer to a particular research question. Sources of potential hypotheses include secondary research, focus group results, other exploratory research findings, or theory.

Consider a study conducted by Socratic Technologies and JP Morgan Chase. The research purpose was to better understand how visual gamification affects respondents' behavior towards surveys. **Visual gamification** occurs when "fun" game elements are mixed into an online survey. The research questions for this study were three-fold:

Visual gamification occurs when "fun" game elements are mixed into a survey.

1. Does visual gamification increase the engagement level of respondents?
2. Do the gaming aspects enhance the respondent's survey-taking experience (according to self-reported satisfaction scores)?
3. How does visual gamification affect data quality?

Secondary data was consulted to see if reasonable research hypotheses could be developed. Efforts included both a review of the academic literature and a review of previous research findings conducted by Socratic Technologies. The secondary data suggested that engaging individuals through interactive surveys results in greater satisfaction with the survey process and higher response rates. On the basis of this information, the following research hypotheses was formed:

a. The engaged version of the survey will result in higher levels of self-reported satisfaction.
b. The engaged version of the survey will result in better data quality.[6]

To test hypotheses empirically once data has been collected, the research hypotheses are rephrased as null hypotheses. Null hypotheses are stated in terms of equality or "no difference," also called "status quo." For example, the first null hypothesis shown in **Figure 2.9** is an example of a "no-difference" hypothesis. Alternatively, it could have

Research Purpose
To understand how visual gamification impacts respondents' behavior towards surveys.
Research Questions and Hypotheses
1. Does visual gamification increase the engagement level of respondents?
2. Do the gaming aspects enhance the respondent's survey-taking experience according to self-reported satisfaction scores?
Research hypothesis: The engaged version of the survey will result in higher levels of self-reported satisfaction.
H_0: There will be no difference in the satisfaction scores reported by those who took the engaged and non-engaged survey versions.
3. How does visual gamification impact data quality?
Research hypothesis: The engaged survey version will result in better data quality.
H_0: The response rates for the engaged version of the survey will not differ from response rates of the non-engaged survey.

FIGURE 2.9 Research Purpose, Questions, Hypotheses

Source: Adapted from Trish Doran and Shellie Yule, "How Game-enhanced Design Can Improve Respondent Data Satisfaction and Quality," *Quirk's Marketing Research Review*, January 2015.

been written as, "The satisfaction scores for respondents who took the engaged version of the survey will be equal to the satisfaction scores of those who took the non-engaged survey version." The hope is that data analysis will provide sufficient evidence to reject the null hypothesis or, in this case, show that satisfaction scores between the engaged and non-engaged survey takers are not equal.

The null hypothesis is often confusing because it appears to state the opposite of what researchers believe to be true. Yet this custom is the norm for researchers because it provides a more rigorous test of the data. Information gathered from samples may not be representative of the population. Testing the null hypotheses reduces the likelihood that the researcher will make a mistake in claiming that the research hypothesis is true based on the data from the sample, when in fact it is not true in the larger population. The Statistics Review section for this chapter describes research hypotheses, null hypotheses, and alternative hypotheses in more detail.

2.3b Research Design

Research design plan to address the research problem, question, and/or hypothesis.

The **research design** is the plan that will be used to address the research problem, question, or hypothesis. It guides the research process and outlines how data will be collected. The specific design chosen will vary depending on the problem being studied and the constraints imposed by management. Typical constraint issues that affect the design include time, costs, and quality of information. If time to conduct the study is short, then the researcher must look for quicker methods of collecting data, which often drives up costs and may affect the quality of the information obtained in a negative manner. If management wants a high level of information quality, it will lengthen the time for the study and, again, increase the budget to accommodate the correspondingly higher costs. If management is concerned about costs then it limits the researcher's options, which then usually has an inverse impact on the quality of data. Therefore, management and the researcher must come to an agreement on the desired level of precision of the information needed in light of costs and time constraints.

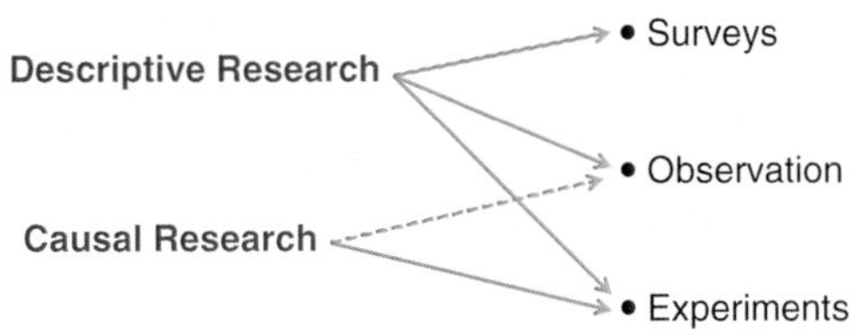

FIGURE 2.10 Methods of Collecting Data

Descriptive or Causal Approach The first research design decision involves whether to use a descriptive or causal approach. As described earlier, both designs assume the researcher has a good grasp on the problem or question to be studied. If not, then further exploratory research needs to be conducted. If the researcher is looking for an understanding of specific variables or relationships among variables, then a descriptive approach is appropriate. For example, suppose a credit union was interested in profiling the characteristics of its current mortgage holders. In this instance, the credit union is looking to describe the relationship between those who hold home mortgages with the credit union and factors such as gender, marital status, type and number of other accounts held within the credit union, income, and so forth. If the purpose of the study is to prove a cause-and-effect relationship, then a causal design works better. So if the credit union was interested in learning whether a $50 savings bond, $25 gift card, or free dinner for two at Red Lobster was the most effective incentive for enticing new customers to open an account, causal research could be used. In making the decision, time, costs, and quality of information must be considered. While causal research will normally provide a higher level of information, it tends to take longer and costs are higher. For most marketing decisions, descriptive research provides ample information for managers to make decisions.

The second component of research design is how the data will be collected. As shown in Figure 2.10, researchers have three basic methods of collecting data. For descriptive research, the most common approaches are surveys and observation. For causal research, the typical approach would be to use an experiment.

Survey research research in which individuals are asked a series of questions about the topic under study.

Survey Research **Survey research** can be conducted in a number of ways, but the overall methodology involves a researcher asking individuals a series of questions about the topic under study. It can be done one-on-one with an interviewer asking individuals questions. It can be done through distributing a questionnaire to individuals. Today, the majority of surveys are distributed via the Internet and mobile technology. Survey research can also include interaction with a group of individuals who meet to discuss a particular topic. Surveys are a primary method of conducting descriptive research since the typical who, when, where, what, and how questions can be asked of participants.

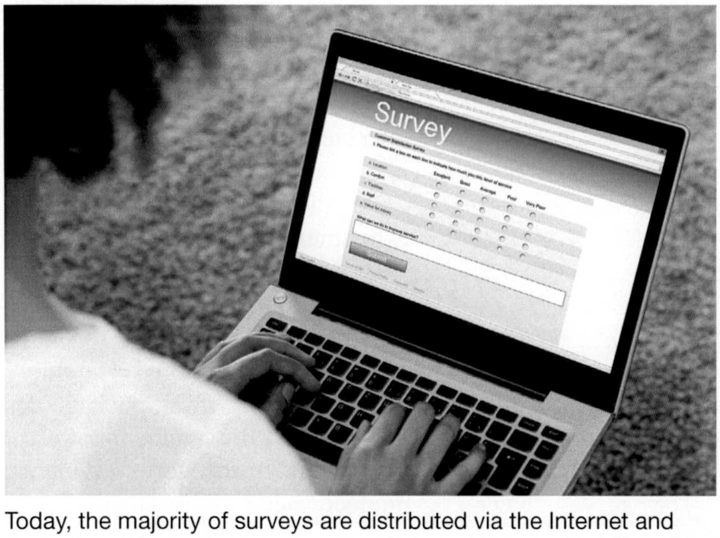

Source: Andrey Popov/Shutterstock.

Today, the majority of surveys are distributed via the Internet and through mobile technology.

Observation Research Instead of asking individuals a series of questions, researchers can observe their behaviors or observe the result of their behaviors in the **observation approach**. Researchers can watch individuals interact with a point-of-purchase display at a retail store or watch children playing with a new toy. Research can even involve giving children money to spend at a toy store and then watching how they go about deciding

Observation research research in which the behaviors of those being studied or the results of their behaviors are observed by researchers.

which toy to purchase. It may be watching how an adult buys groceries. In all of these examples, the researcher observes, but does not interact with the subject being studied. If the researcher believes his presence may influence the subject's behaviors, then the observation is normally done through a two-way mirror or recorded with a digital camera and watched later.

Mystery shopping is a key form of observation research commonly used by restaurants and retail stores to help assess the customer service provided by employees, or other factors such as the condition of the facility. When customer service is assessed, the mystery shopper pretends to be a customer and does interact with employees to some degree.

Instead of watching the behavior, a common approach is to observe the results of behavior. Technology, especially, retail scanners, has increased the desirability of this approach. Instead of actually watching shoppers at a point-of-purchase display, scanner data from the store's cash register system can identify how many individuals purchased the items on display. If the store has loyalty cards, even the person who made the purchases can be identified. This information can then be tied into an individual's demographic information and past purchase history for richer information.

The Internet offers a wealth of observation data. Through cookies, a company can track individuals that visit a website. Data such as how long they stay on a page, what links they click on, and where they go on the particular website can all be tracked. This type of data is very useful in studying the impact of mobile marketing, search engine marketing, and Internet advertising.

Observation can be used in descriptive research since the actions of individuals can be described and measured. It can also be used in causal research, but requires more controls to ensure there is truly a cause-and-effect situation. When used for causal research, most marketers would use the results of behavior rather than observing the behavior itself. Scanner data and Internet tracking data can be used in more tightly controlled situations and can possibly show a cause-and-effect.

Experiments a research study where all variables are held constant except the one under study consideration.

Experimental Research The last method of collecting data is **experiments**, which involves a research study where all variables are held constant except the one under study. Most experiments are conducted in tightly controlled environments, such as laboratories. In advertising, it might take place in a movie theater where individuals are shown a documentary or new television show with ads that would normally be in a television show. Embedded among the ads is one the researchers are studying. Questions asked before and after can provide information on any impact the target ad may have had on the participants in the study.

Field experiments conducting an experiment in a real-world setting.

Another approach is what is called a **field experiment**, which involves conducting an experiment in a real-world setting. Controlling all of the variables except the one under study becomes much more difficult because a number of extraneous factors could have an impact on the results. A company such as Tyson could create a study examining three different package designs for its fajita chicken. Price and location of the product is the same in all of the stores. The only difference is the package design. Sales could then be examined to see if the package design affected the purchase decision. The challenge is ensuring that any change in sales was due to the package design and not some other factor, such as one of the stores having a special sale on a competing brand or complementary product, such as fajita steak.

2.3c Sample Selection

Population the group that is being studied, from which samples are drawn.

Because of time and cost constraints, researchers in most studies will select a sample, or subset of individuals to study rather than the entire population being considered. The sample selection process begins by defining the **population**, which is the group that a researcher wants to study. It can be as small as the students at a university or as large as the entire population of the United States. It can be broadly defined, such as online shoppers, or narrowly defined, such as women living in Louisiana who have given birth to a child within the last six months. Once the population of study has been defined, then the researcher designs a method for selecting a sample from the population. Chapter 8 describes the process of sample selection in greater detail. Most critical to the selection process is the assurance that the sample is representative of the population. If it is, then conclusions and findings of the research obtained from the sample can be applied to the population being studied. If it is not, then regardless of how large the sample and how detailed the information, inference cannot be made to the population.

Suppose J.P. Morgan Chase conducted a survey of 500 randomly selected individuals who accessed their financial account information (mortgage, credit card, checking, savings) online during the month of April. If the purpose of the study is to assess customer satisfaction of checking account holders, then the population for this study should include all Chase customers who have a checking account with the financial institution. Unfortunately, in the situation described above, the survey administration and resulting sample is flawed because it is restricted to online users only, as those individuals who do not use online banking (or who did not access their account information online in April) have no opportunity to participate in the study. Because certain demographics might be associated with those unlikely to use online services (older, financially disadvantaged), the study results would clearly not be representative of the population, and satisfaction levels could realistically differ between users and nonusers of online services. An additional problem stems from the fact that many of Chase's online account information users may not have checking accounts with the bank, but instead use the online service to track or pay credit card bills or a home mortgage. If such an individual were randomly selected to participate in the study, his or her ratings of checking account services would "confound" the data, meaning that the information provided would not be relevant because the checking services being rated were not those offered by Chase.

2.3d Data Collection

For a marketing researcher, now the fun begins! It is time to collect the data. How the data are collected depends on the research design process. If survey research is used, then data can be collected online, via a mobile platform, or through personal interviews, telephone interviews, mail surveys or email. It can be distributed at a mall, in a class at a university, or stuffed in a credit card bill. The method that is chosen goes back to the three criteria already identified—time, costs, and quality of information. Chapter 6 provides a discussion of these topics as well as relative advantages of various methods of survey research.

Source: Mangostar/Shutterstock.

While every study will have some random error, the goal of the researcher is to minimize error as much as possible.

For observation research, multiple methods are available. It can be done in person or with a digital camera or smart phone camera. Scanner data from cash registers can be used. Internet metrics can be utilized through cookie information. Again, time, costs, and quality of information will affect the decision. Methods involving human observation are almost always more expensive and take longer.

Data collection can vary widely for experimental research. It can take the form of questionnaires given at the end of an experiment which assess attitudes, thoughts, feelings, or intentions. It can be observation of human behavior, such as electronic tracking of eye movement when viewing a print ad, or results of human actions. With experiments, the type of experiment that is conducted will have the most impact on how the data is collected.

Regardless of the method used to collect data, the goal should be to produce data that are free of errors. This requires identifying ways errors can possibly occur and then designing methods of reducing the probability. For instance, an interviewer's facial expression or tone of voice in asking someone questions may influence the respondent's answers, creating error. This type of error can be reduced by proper training of interviewers or by switching to a self-administered questionnaire. Errors can occur in recording of data or in selecting the sample. While every study will have some random error, the goal of the researcher is to minimize error as much as possible. The various types of errors and more specific methods of reducing them will be discussed in future chapters, especially Chapter 6. For now, it is important to understand that in collecting data, errors should be minimized and steps should be taken in the design of the research to reduce errors.

2.3e Data Analysis

Once the data have been collected, it is time for the analysis. The purpose of the analysis is to make sense of the data and turn raw numbers into meaningful information that management can use to make informed decisions. In some studies, simple procedures such as frequency counts and averages are sufficient. In other studies, more complex analyses are needed to understand the relationships among variables. This is especially true for causal research.

Listed in **Figure 2.11** are the results of an analysis of the dollars spent buying clothing on sale in the U.S. for four generations. Analyses do not always need to be complex to be of value. The results presented in Figure 2.11 provide valuable and useful information to marketers. However, a deeper analysis may provide additional information that will allow a marketer to make better decisions. For instance, statistical tests can be run that will show if there is a difference between males and females in terms of purchasing apparel on sale. Further analysis could involve examining categories of apparel purchased, or online vs. in-store sales.

2.3f Research Report

Once the analysis is complete, it is time to write the research report. The purpose of the report is to present the research findings. In preparing the report, the intended audience of the report should guide how it is prepared. Executives tend to be extremely busy and

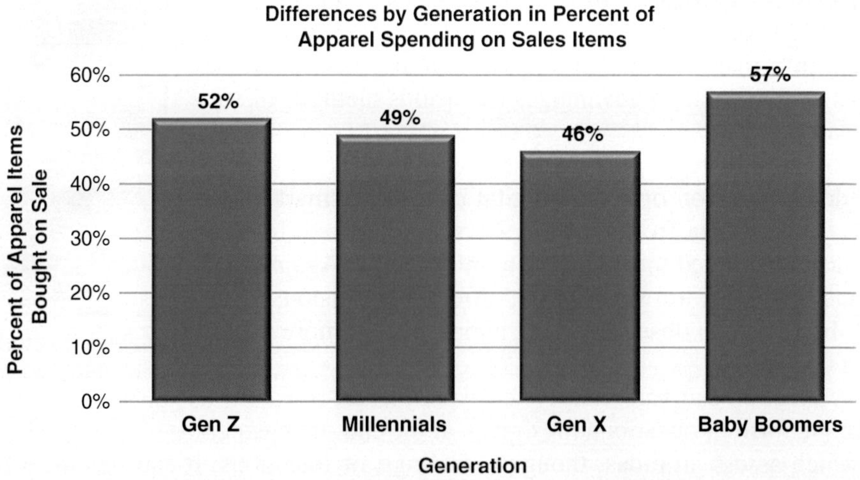

FIGURE 2.11 Percent of U.S. Apparel Dollars Spent on Sale Items
Source: Adapted from "Guide to Gen Z: Debunking the Myths of our Youngest Generation," NPD Group, 2017, https://www.npd.com/lps/pdf/guide-to-gen-z.pdf, accessed July 17, 2018, p. 9.

do not have time to read long, lengthy reports. They prefer reports that summarize the findings of the research and have clear, succinct conclusions and recommendations.

The report should begin by stating the research purpose, problems, questions or hypotheses. This should be followed by a description of the methodology that includes how the sample was chosen and then how the data were collected. Seldom will executives or managers care about how the data were analyzed. They just want to see results. Using graphs and charts provides pictures that are easier and quicker to read than having results listed in a table or in the written part of the report. For oral presentations, graphs are especially effective. Infographics are commonly used.

In reporting the results, it is easy to overwhelm executives with a large number of graphs, charts, and tables and jargon. Not everything has to be reported. The report should focus on the research purpose and identify the portion of the analysis that answers the research questions and supports the findings of the research. Additional information can be put in an appendix for reference.

While researchers love to talk about results, executives want to know the conclusions and the corresponding recommendations. As discussed in Chapter 1, executives now are looking to researchers to supply insights and to be consultants in the decision process. Just supplying the results is insufficient. They must be put into context. How do those results affect the company and how do they affect the decision that management needs to make? More information about the content of the report and how it is written is provided in Chapter 14.

2.4 Preparing the Research Proposal

LEARNING OBJECTIVE 2.3
Describe the components of a request for research (RFP) and a research proposal.

The research process typically starts with some type of **request for proposal (RFP)**, which is a request soliciting proposals from research companies. This document is especially important for firms seeking to hire an external research firm. But, it can also be part of the research process for companies that house an internal research department. In such situations, companies will often have more requests than can be funded by the company, so the RFP can be an internal approval process in which research projects move forward.

Request for proposal (RFP) written document containing an official request for a research proposal (also referred to as an "invitation to bid").

Typically, a RFP will provide a background for the research request to justify why the study is needed. The research objective or question will be stated as well as the population of the study. While the RFP typically does not specify the exact methods of sample selection and data collection, it may contain information on what is expected and an approximate sample size since these two criteria are primary determinants of costs. It makes a difference whether a company wants to use an online data collection methodology with a desired sample size of 500 compared to face-to-face personal interviews of 300 people. Most RFPs will close with a time frame when the study needs to be completed. Other factors, such as nondisclosure agreements, payment terms and deliverables, are important. For instance, an on-site presentation of the research findings might be specified as a key deliverable. Other deliverables may include data models, written reports, written management summaries, on-site workshops, and interactive reporting tools.[7]

Research proposal written document prepared in response to a RFP that provides basic information about the research process that will be used.

The **research proposal** is prepared by a marketing research firm in response to a RFP. It can also be developed by internal marketing research staff for executives within the company. In either situation, the research proposal provides basic information about the research process that will be used. **Figure 2.12** identifies the primary components of a research proposal. The depth of information within each section will depend primarily on the cost and complexity of the study.

The research proposal begins by providing a background of the study and any issues that may have prompted the research or that are pertinent to the research situation. Understanding the background may require additional conversations with an in-house client on a one-on-one basis. While this is typically not possible when bidding on external research contracts, research suppliers can use email to solicit additional information, and use any available secondary data to learn as much as they can about the client.[8] Next, the research

- Introduction and background information
- Research objectives or questions
- Research design
- Target population
- Sample size and method
- Data collection methodology
- Cost and time schedule for study

FIGURE 2.12 Components of a Research Proposal

objectives or questions are stated. While this may have been stated in the RFP, it is important to re-state it in the proposal because the proposal then becomes a contract or an agreement between management and whoever is conducting the research.

The focus of the research proposal should be on how the firm can best meet the client's needs. The research design identifies if the research will be exploratory, descriptive, or causal. The target population is defined, because it is from the target population that the sample will be drawn. Sample size and method of selection should be stated with the goal of ensuring the sample will be representative of the target population. As stated earlier, the size of the sample has a significant impact on the cost and time frame of the study as does the method of collecting the data.

The last part of the proposal is the cost of the study and the time frame. When hiring an external firm this information is critical to the decision process. However, it is just as important for firms using an internal research department. In addition to using the research proposal to make decisions about which studies to approve, it provides information for budgeting.

LEARNING OBJECTIVE 2.4
Provide an overview of qualitative and quantitative research.

Qualitative research unstructured data collection methods that provide results that are subjectively interpreted.

Quantitative research structured data collection methods that provide results that can be converted to numbers and analyzed through statistical procedures.

2.5 Qualitative and Quantitative Research

Another facet of marketing research is examining the difference between qualitative and quantitative research. These differences are highlighted in Figure 2.13. **Qualitative research** involves unstructured data collection methods that provide results that are subjectively interpreted. **Quantitative research** involves structured data collection methods that provide results that can be converted to numbers and analyzed through statistical procedures.

2.5a Qualitative Research

Qualitative research is typically used for exploratory research. It can also be used after a descriptive study to explore more deeply into the minds of consumers or whoever the research participants may be, or as part of a planned mixed methods research project. A major advantage of qualitative research is that it is unstructured. The researcher will normally follow a guide sheet to ensure all of the study topics are covered, but the researcher is free to depart from it in order to ask probing questions to better understand the respondent's thoughts, feelings, behaviors, or ideas.

Most qualitative research is conducted with a small sample. Interviews can be with individuals or they can be with a small group ranging from just three or four to as many as 10 or 12 people. When groups become too large it is difficult to probe individual thoughts, and the advantages of group dynamics begin to disappear.

Since qualitative research involves probing via open-ended questions, the results become subjective. That makes generalizing the findings to a larger population or other consumers more difficult. Also, business executives are reluctant to make major decisions on the thoughts of just a few individuals, and most data obtained by qualitative methods is subjected to verification using larger samples that allow for quantitative analysis.

Feature	Qualitative	Quantitative
Type of research	Exploratory	Descriptive/Causal
Sample size	Small	Large
Types of questions	Unstructured	Structured
Type of analysis	Subjective	Objective, statistical
Generalizability	Limited	High
Costs (Typically)	Lower	More expensive
Timeframe (Typically)	Shorter	Longer

FIGURE 2.13 Comparison of Qualitative and Quantitative Research

That said, Dave Snell of The Richards Group states, "that you should never underestimate the power of qualitative data." The Richards Group is an advertising firm in Dallas, Texas and has clients such as Motel 6, Bridgestone, Home Depot, and Chick Fil-A. The agency regularly tests print and broadcast ads through Millward Brown, a marketing research firm. In addition to quantitative measures such as awareness, level of interest, and liking, Millward Brown solicits open-ended thoughts from test participants about the ads they are viewing. Dave Snell says, "These verbatim remarks are extremely valuable. It provides clues into what people are thinking, and how they see the ad, and how they feel about it." Typically, Millward Brown will use a sample of about 150 people. According to Snell, "When you read all of the comments and see some patterns or a number [of people] that speak about a certain aspect of the commercial, then you know you've got to go back and look at that ad again or you've hit the sweet spot that really speaks to people." While the qualitative data will not tell The Richards Group what to do or exactly what worked, it does provide valuable insight into ads the agency produces.[9]

The approach used by Millward Brown in evaluating ads for The Richards Group is growing in popularity with researchers. This type of qualitative research is less costly and normally can be conducted in a shorter time frame since it is part of a quantitative study. More important, it can add richness and depth to quantitative studies.

2.5b Quantitative Research

Because of the issue of accountability that managers and business executives now face, they prefer research that can provide numbers. Quantitative research is a structured approach that is used for descriptive and causal research. It is objective and, because of its numerical data format, it is subject to statistical tests and procedures.

The Nielsen Company conducted a global survey about connectivity to the Internet and commerce. One component of the study was examining offers that might entice global shoppers to buy online. Results are shown in **Figure 2.14**. The highest percentage of individuals, 49 percent, would be more likely to buy if a money back guarantee was provided in case the delivered product did not match what was offered. Same day replacement service for products that were unavailable, and free delivery were also important incentives. The findings indicate that free delivery above a purchase minimum is a greater incentive to purchase than are free deliveries 7 days a week if purchasing an annual pass is required. It also suggests that marketing managers should place information on the brand and retail store website about the guarantee, in order to establish trust with the consumer.

A Nielsen study illustrates some of the other aspects of quantitative research. The survey was conducted in 64 countries with a sample of over 30,000 people. While this number is larger than typical quantitative studies, it does illustrate that the sample size for

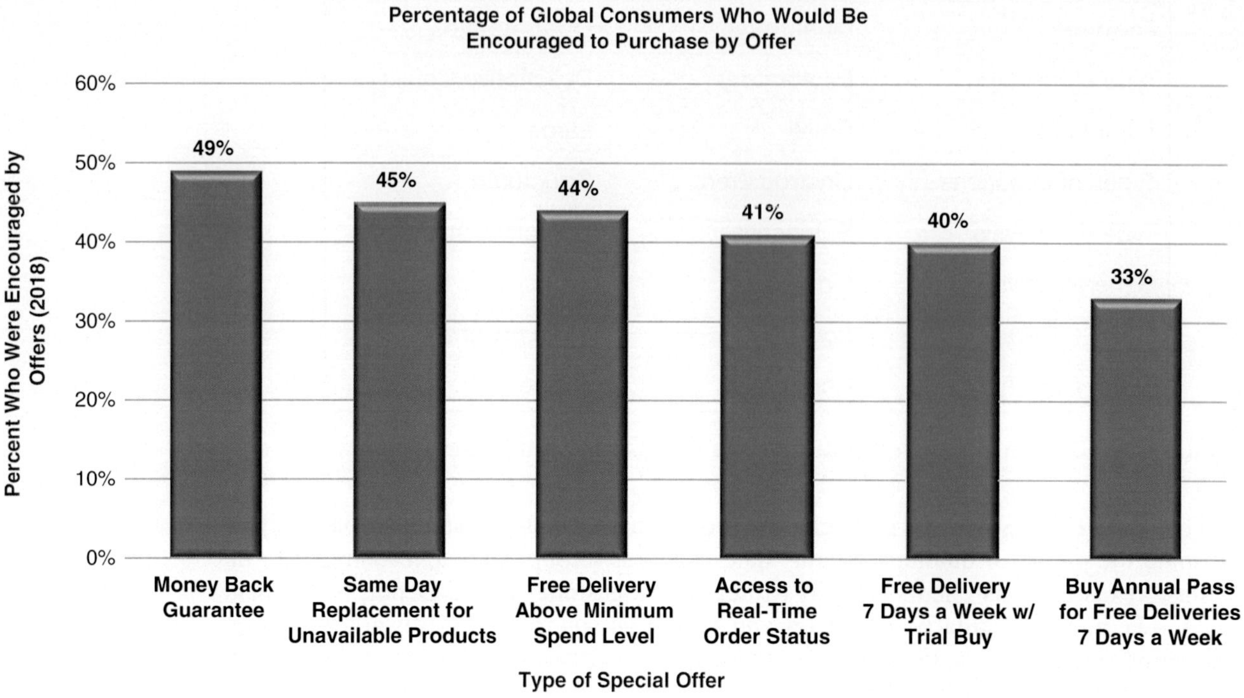

FIGURE 2.14 Impact of Special Offers on Online Buying Behavior
Source: "Connected Commerce," *The Nielsen Company*, November, 2018.

quantitative research is significantly higher than for qualitative studies. The larger sample size means most quantitative studies are more expensive and require a longer time to execute. The benefit from the higher cost and longer time frame is that results are more objective and can normally be generalized to a larger population. Because 30,000 individuals were surveyed by Nielsen, it is rather safe to say that money back guarantees are the number one incentive that might influence global consumers to buy online. Even findings within the various countries can be generalized to those particular countries because of the large sample size, though it is possible that some study results may vary on a country-by-country basis.

In their study, Nielsen highlights the survey was based on respondents with online access in the 60 countries. They further state that the study reflects only the habits of existing Internet users. Individuals who do not have active online access may be different. Thus, a company introducing a new product both online and in physical retail stores and using the results of this study must take this limitation into consideration.

2.5c An Illustration of the Marketing Research Process

To illustrate the marketing research process, consider a study examining the role of Super Bowl marketing and social media today in the United States. The research process began with a RFP by *Adweek* magazine, a trade publication targeting advertising professionals. The research had one main objective, to determine the digital consumption of social media by 18–54 year olds who planned to watch the big game.[10]

Survata was contracted to do the research and served as a study co-sponsor. The research design involved a descriptive study using an online survey. A total of 1,000 consumers between the ages of 18 and 54 were surveyed. The sample was carefully weighted to be representative of the U.S. population in terms of demographic characteristics.

Survata found that 49 percent of the sample was likely to visit Facebook during the Super Bowl. To be able to see how this compares to other social media, Survata's survey also asked about Instagram, Snapchat, Twitter and YouTube. The percentage of the sample planning to visit other social media platforms are displayed in **Figure 2.15**. In addition, 36 percent of the sample indicated they would not visit any of the five listed social media platforms during the game. Because it was a quantitative study, the results can be extrapolated to the general online audience.

Source: Artur Szczybylo/Shutterstock.

Survey results found that only 16% of online users who watched the Super Bowl tweeted a specific hashtag seen in an ad during the big game.

When investigating which digital platform was likely to be used to consume the most content during the Super Bowl, Nielsen found that 51 percent of the sample chose Facebook. Figure 2.15 shows that Facebook was clearly preferred to Snapchat, Twitter and YouTube. In interpreting the results, however, it is critically important to go back to the sample. The Super Bowl is a global event, and it might be tempting for marketers to extrapolate these findings to other countries. To do so would be incorrect. The sample was U.S. online users only. It might be expected, therefore, that their viewing of Facebook would be higher than the global population in general. But we don't know for certain as online users from other countries were not part of the sample. Would these sample percentages hold true for the global population of online users in general? It is unlikely, which means these results can be generalized to U.S. online users, but not to global online population as a whole.

Additional survey findings indicated that only 16 percent of respondents had tweeted a specific hashtag, and that 20 percent has text messaged a code in order to get a special offer or more information after being asked to do so by a Super Bowl advertiser. Only 12 percent were very likely and 26 percent were somewhat likely to search for a brand online after seeing a Super Bowl ad during the game[11]. The Survata research study illustrates the power of marketing research and how companies can obtain valuable information to make important marketing decisions. While the results of this particular study are public, many research studies are owned by companies who commission the research, or by commercial firms that collect data on a regular basis to sell reports to

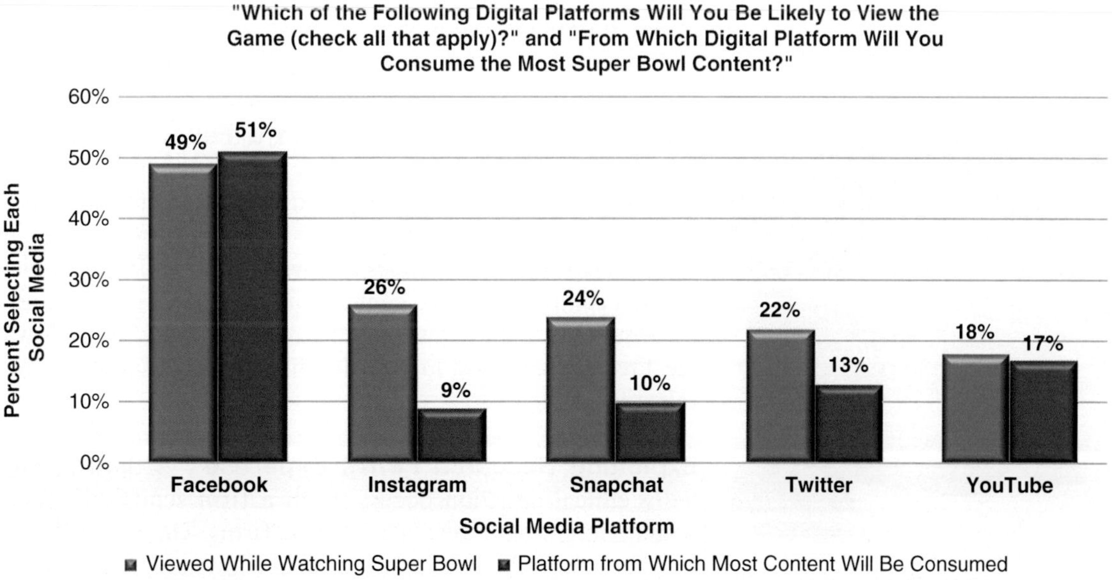

FIGURE 2.15 Results of a Survata Survey

Source: Author created with data from Christopher Heine, "Social Media's Screen Game," *Adweek*, January 30, 2017, Vol. 58, Issue 3, p. 7.

other firms. Syndicated research firms, such as Nielsen, are discussed in more detail in Chapter 3.

2.6 Ethical Considerations in Designing Research Studies

LEARNING OBJECTIVE 2.5
Recite the ethical considerations in designing research studies.

A number of potential ethical situations could occur when requesting, designing, and conducting research studies. Honesty and integrity should be the guiding principles of marketing research firms, individuals conducting the research, and client companies. Unethical situations can arise easily due to competitive pressures among firms and the desire for companies to succeed in the marketplace, whether it is a research firm or a client. Within companies, individuals have a desire to succeed to obtain promotions and bonuses, and they can be tempted to engage in unethical behaviors.

2.6a Ethics and the RFP

Most research firms will spend time, effort, and money on preparing a research proposal in response to a RFP. These companies expect the RFP to be accurate, honest, and truthful. In the vast majority of situations, this is true. However, there are opportunities for unethical behavior.

Source: garagestock/Shutterstock.

Research firms spend time, effort, and money in preparing a response to a RFP and expect the RFP to be accurate, honest, and truthful.

Securing Multiple Bids to Satisfy Policy The first ethical situation is when a company sends out a RFP to various companies, but the decision has already been made about who will do the research. Some companies have policies requiring that multiple bids be acquired, especially when the research project is projected to cost over a certain dollar value. The RFPs are sent to various companies in order to satisfy this policy. A second instance in which RFPs may be sent despite the fact that a firm has already been selected occurs when a vice-president or other business executive requests additional bids, to cover their decision in case anyone questions why a particular research firm was selected. Regardless of the reason, it is not fair to request companies to spend time, effort, and money in preparing a research proposal when they have no chance of winning the contract.

Source: kan_chana/Shutterstock.

Sending out RFPs to various companies to secure multiple bids that satisfy policy is unethical when a vendor has already been selected, and the firms have no chance of winning the contract.

Sharing Competitive Bids with a Favored Firm A closely related ethical situation may occur when the company sending out the RFP has a favored research firm they want to hire, for whatever reason. It may be due to a personal friendship or past experiences that were positive. To ensure the favored company gets the contract, information from the other proposal bids is shared with the favored company. This allows the favored company to then modify its proposal to ensure selection.

Exploiting Research Firm's Expertise A third potentially ethical situation occurs when a firm sends out RFPs with no intention of hiring any of the firms. They are seeking information on how to do the study. They may even ask for additional details on questionnaire design or sample selection under the guise of wanting to make sure the objectives will be met. The company then hires freelancers to conduct the study, completes the study using their own employees, or goes to a data collection firm to just collect the data rather than design the entire study.

Making False Promises A fourth ethical consideration is when a firm makes false promises to a marketing research firm with the goal of enticing them to conduct a study at a lower price in exchange for future studies. The future studies never come, or if they do, they have been modified drastically. A firm may say "we have a number of large studies we want to conduct that will involve extensive research designs and large samples of several thousand." The marketing research firm is told that if they will do this first study at a substantially lower price, then they will be given the larger studies, without further bidding.

2.6b Ethics and the Research Proposal

Similarly, firms that prepare the research proposals may engage in unethical behavior. The two most common ethical situations that can occur with the research proposal are low-ball pricing and bait-and-switch. **Low-ball pricing** is submitting a bid with an extremely low price in order to get the contract, when in fact the firm has no intention of doing the work at the quoted price. Once the contract is obtained, then the research company identifies some means of increasing the price. For instance, the client company may be told that the fee for the sample respondents was not included in the bid price, or that interviewer expenses were not included. The research company identifies some fee that was not included in the bid price and of course must be added to the bill.

Low-ball pricing submitting an extremely low-priced bid in response to a RFP simply for the purpose of getting the contract, with no intention of doing the work at the quoted price.

The second unethical situation is bait-and-switch. With this approach the marketing research firm submits a price that is legitimate. But, once the contract is signed and they start working on the study, the research firm identifies some means of upgrading the study. Instead of 250 respondents, the research firm convinces the client that to obtain reliable results they need to interview 400 respondents. Instead of the basic questions that are on the current survey, the research firm convinces the client they need to add more questions or a supplemental research study of an additional topic to better validate the results the client is seeking. With the bait-and-switch tactic, the original bid is legitimate, but often only addresses a stripped-down version of what should be done. While the research company could perform the original bid contract, their goal was to get the contract and then convince the client to switch to a more expensive research design.

2.6c Ethics and the Research Process

When it comes to the research process itself, a number of potential ethical situations can occur. Some are easy to identify, others are more difficult. As shown in **Figure 2.16**, ethical issues that may occur include advocacy research, biased or unrepresentative sample selection, distorted data collection procedures, data falsification, improper statistical manipulations, and confidentiality issues with proprietary studies.

Advocacy Research Advocacy research occurs more often with internal marketing research projects than it does with outside research agencies. **Advocacy research** is designed to advocate or support a company's position. Perhaps a company wants to justify a mobile marketing campaign or a direct response campaign. The company is looking specifically to find statistical evidence that the decision already made or the decision they want to make is the best course of action. Thus, the research is clearly to prove a particular point of view or decision. The research is then designed and carried out to increase the probability the results the company wants are obtained. The manager can then submit the research report to superiors as support for the decision.

Advocacy research research which is purposively designed to advocate or support a particular position.

- Advocacy research
- Biased or unrepresentative sample selection
- Distorted data collection procedures
- Data falsification
- Improper statistical manipulations
- Confidentiality issues with proprietary studies

FIGURE 2.16 Ethics and the Research Process

Sample Representativeness Obtaining a sample that is representative of the target population can be a challenge for a marketing research firm. Once the company has the contract, the firm may look for alternative or more convenient methods of identifying the sample participants to cut costs. For instance, the sampling plan may call for a mall intercept survey in which every 12th person who walks into the mall is supposed to be interviewed. Instead, researchers just pick individuals that they think will complete the survey, or they may go to the bookstore in the mall and ask individuals who are reading a book or having coffee to complete the survey. Either process violates the procedure for selecting the sample outlined in the sampling plan, detracting from the quality of data gathered.

Similarly, rather than randomly selecting and soliciting respondents in the population, a research firm may use professional research respondents who have agreed to participate in research studies as part of a panel or use respondents from a previous study. In both cases, the respondents are easy to identify and have experience in participating in research studies. In such situations, it is very likely the respondents do not match the target sample of the study; or, if they do, because they have participated in other studies, they may not be representative of consumers in general. It is very tempting for a research firm to look at alternative ways of selecting a sample in an effort to control costs while disguising the fact that these individuals may not match the target sample. Ethical research firms must make full disclosure of how the sample is recruited, and be certain the client understands the risks associated with using panel members or other easily obtainable samples. Increasingly, firms are outsourcing sampling to firms that specialize in this area. However, that doesn't absolve them of the responsibility to make certain that the final sample matches the target population.

Distorted Data Collection Procedures To reduce data collection errors, it is important for the research firm and researchers not to intervene or influence the respondents in any way. Data collection distortion can occur in a number of ways. For instance, when conducting personal interviews, the interviewer's tone of voice can influence the option selected by the respondents or inhibit the degree to which they respond to open-ended questions. In a telephone survey, the interviewer may skip some of the answer options under a question to save time, or tell the respondent to tell them when they come to a response that matches their feelings, thus not reading the entire list of options. Data collection distortion is very difficult to detect unless the client company actually observes the data collection process.

Data Falsification A more serious data collection problem is falsification of data. Companies rely on accurate data to make decisions. Any type of falsification is a very serious ethical, and potentially legal, problem. In order to produce the sample size a client wants, a research company might be tempted to manufacture data or duplicate data to reach the required number of responses. This can be particularly true in telephone surveying if data recorders are contract employees who are paid on a per completed-survey basis rather than an hourly wage. It may also be tempting for data recorders to fill in answers to partially completed surveys which the respondent terminates midway through, or even particular questions which the respondent left blank.

For example, many individuals resist answering questions about their race, age, or income. In recording survey responses, the data recorder may be unclear about which answer a respondent selected, and arbitrarily choose one rather than clarify the answer with the respondent, or leave the answer to a particular question blank.

Improper Statistical Manipulations Improper statistical manipulations occur most often in advocacy studies. When researchers are requested to provide a particular type of support, then the temptation is to use statistical procedures or manipulate the data to ensure the pre-determined results are obtained. Suppose a significance level of .05 was stipulated prior to data collection, but results indicate a significance level of .0598. While technically it is not significant, the researcher could just leave off the last two decimal points and not round up, indicating it was significant at the .05 level.

A more serious type of data manipulation might occur when researchers leave out part of the sample in the analysis in order to obtain significant results. Suppose that in analyzing the differences between business travelers and leisure travelers, researchers find no significant difference in how much money they spend on merchandise in a common airport store. But, when business travelers who make fewer than 10 trips per year are left out of the analysis, there is a significant difference, and this result is ultimately reported in the study. Such an action would be highly unethical if in the report nothing is said about the data manipulation, and the fact that the difference is actually only between business travelers who make more than 10 trips per year, versus leisure travelers, rather than business travelers in general.

Confidentiality of Propriety Studies The last ethical issue in terms of the research process is the confidentiality of propriety studies. When companies hire marketing research firms to conduct studies, in most cases the results are confidential and are the property of the client. Without the client's approval, nothing from the research studies may be made public or used in other studies. But, it is very easy for a company conducting research for another company to go back and pull data or results from a prior study to include in the current study.

In every aspect of marketing research, there is the potential for unethical conduct. Some behaviors are clearly wrong and unethical. Others are more difficult to judge. Each person working in marketing research must keep an eye open to potential ethical situations and strive to always perform work that is of the highest integrity.

2.6d Ethics and Respondents

Marketing research firms also have ethical responsibilities toward research participants. ESOMAR (www.esomar.org) is a global organization serving the marketing research industry. Among their many contributions, ESOMAR developed a guide to ethical research practices that is currently in use in more than 130 countries worldwide. The guide was revised in 2016 to address issues stemming from technology and its influence on data collection and storage.[12] Many of ESOMAR's ethical guidelines became part of the European Union General Data Protection Regulations that govern data collection, sharing, and processing practices discussed in chapter 1. While the GDPR are regulatory standards that impact firms collecting, processing, or sharing data from consumers within the European union, the ESOMAR guidelines do not have regulatory authority, but rather serve as a set of industry standards that ethical research firms should strive to maintain. Researchers' ethical responsibilities to data subjects are categorized into six broad categories, as illustrated in Figure 2.17.

A key duty of researchers is to "ensure that data subjects are not harmed as a direct result of the personal data being used for research."[13] Additionally, researchers must be cognizant of data collection circumstances that may cause respondents mental distress. The expectation of safety and freedom from mental or physical harm is one of the basic respondent rights that many researchers respect. Several of the additional provisions outlined in ESOMAR's code of standards address respondent issues, and are shown in Figure 2.18 as basic rights of respondents.

- Respecting respondent's rights and providing a duty of care when conducting research
- Taking extra precautions with children, young people, and other vulnerable individuals
- Minimizing data collection to items relevant to the research study
- Explaining the primary data collection process
- Vetting the original collection process of secondary data that includes personal data
- Protecting data and subjects privacy by maintaining confidentiality

FIGURE 2.17 Researchers Responsibilities to Data Subjects

Source: Adapted from "ICC/ESOMAR International Code on Social Science and Market Research," https://ana.esomar.org/document/10513?query=ESOMAR%20Codes%20And%20Guidelines&offset=60, accessed July 17, 2017.

- Respondents have the right to the expectation of safety and freedom from harm
- Respondents have the right to refuse to participate
- Respondents have the right to stop participating in a research study at anytime
- Respondents have the right to require that their information remain confidential and secure
- Respondents have the right to require that personal information be deleted after use
- Respondents have the right to verify the identity and bonifides of the researcher without difficulty

FIGURE 2.18 Ethical Responsibilities to Research Respondents

Source: Adapted from, "ICC/ESOMAR International Code on Social Science and Market Research." http://www.esomar.org/uploads/pdf/professional-standards/ICCESOMAR_Code_English_.pdf, accessed July 17, 2017.

Treating respondents ethically means respecting their rights. According to ESOMAR, respondents have the right to refuse to participate in a market research project; to withdraw from the market research interview at any time; to require that their personal data are not made available to others; to delete or to rectify incorrect personal data obtained by the researcher and to verify the identity of the researcher without difficulty.

It is important to be honest and not abuse the trust of respondents in the process of conducting the research. Respondents should not be misled as to the purpose of the research. It is also imperative to ensure respondents will not be harmed in any way, or experience any negative reactions to the research.

Children and vulnerable populations require special consideration. Researchers must obtain parental consent or that of a legal guardian when collecting data from children. When vulnerable populations are studied, such as the elderly, immigrants or the mentally disadvantaged, special care must be taken to ensure that are not unduly pressured to participate, and that they are capable of making an informed decision.

Cognitive neuroscience research process involving brain-image measurements through the tracking of brain activity.

Ethical researchers should limit data collection to information relevant to their study. Researchers should also explain how the data will be collected and fully inform respondents of the recording and observation techniques being used. If there is any activity that will require contact at a later time, participants must be informed upfront and researchers must gain agreement for a future contact. For instance, participants of a focus group should understand that the session is being digitally recorded and will be analyzed later, and permission to recontact participants must be obtained before administering a follow-up survey or an invitation to a second focus group held at a later date. In **cognitive neuroscience**, which is a brain-image measurement process that tracks brain activity, researchers need to explain to participants how the process works and how data are used.

This principle does not apply, however, to observation techniques in public places if the respondent's identity or information about the respondent is not in any way tied to the results. For instance, in studying respondent behavior at a point-of-purchase display in a retail store, individuals do not need to be informed they are part of the study. If some of the individuals are recognized as the leave the store and the researcher wants to append the research entry to include any personal information about the person, then consent from the respondent would have to be obtained.

ESOMAR's guidelines indicate that researchers who use secondary data that contains personal information must first make certain the intended use is compatible with the purpose for which the data were originally collected. Additionally, the burden is on the researcher to determine that the data collection process did not violate any laws. Finally, the researcher must examine the privacy notice provided to respondents during the original data collection to determine that the intended use of the secondary data was not specifically excluded by the privacy notice.

Data protection and confidentiality are absolutely critical, especially if there is any way the respondent can be identified through personal information. Easily understood privacy notices that outline the usage terms for the data must be provided at the time of data collection. Researchers have the responsibility to carefully guard research results against unauthorized use, disclosure, loss, misuse and manipulation, and to ensure that no one can tie data to specific respondents. Finally, researchers should not share a subject's personal data with a client unless the subject has expressly agreed to do so.

Related to confidentiality is the protection of a respondent's identity. It is common for demographic and even psychographic and behavioral information to be part of the data collection process or appended to the research results at a later time. If this is done, researchers have the obligation to protect respondents' privacy and ensure information about respondents remains confidential.

2.7 Global Concerns

Conducting global marketing research involves a number of concerns and potential ethical situations, which makes planning the research process even more critical. Differences in language and cultures across countries can easily lead to poor market research results and embarrassing situations. To prevent costly errors, companies may have to invest in more exploratory research that not only aids in identifying the problem to be studied, but provides relevant information about the target population to be studied.

For instance, quantitative analysis tends to be dominant in Central and Eastern Europe. Between 70 and 85 percent of all research in Europe involved quantitative data collection methods, with face-to-face interviews the most frequently used.[14] Though not broken down by country, more recent research by Greenbook, an organization that surveys marketing research clients and suppliers worldwide, indicates that qualitative research remains an important tool. In fact, qualitative accounted for 33 percent, 35 percent, and 34 percent of global research efforts according to the 2016, 2017 and 2018 GRIT reports, respectively. Sixty-two percent, 60 percent, and 62 percent of research was quantitative, with the remaining percentages classified as "other" over the same time period. Online research has also grown in recent years.[15] The challenge in many countries with online research, however, is the dependability of Internet connections and bandwidth to handle visuals that may accompany a research study.[16]

Another area of concern in global marketing research is ethical standards and conduct. Ethical beliefs vary widely across the world and even within countries with different cultures and subcultures. In the United States, bribes are considered unethical as well as illegal. In other countries it is a standard business practice and even permitted as a tax write off. Obtaining a marketing research contract may require paying a bribe to government officials or to the RFP issuing company. Gift giving can also be an accepted practice during the business negotiations, and even how negotiations are conducted will vary widely from eastern cultures to western cultures.

To avoid potential pitfalls, companies will often engage local marketing research firms or international firms with experience in various countries. Alternatively, nationals from the country where the research is to be conducted can be contracted to provide valuable insights into the do's and don'ts of that country or culture.

2.8 Marketing Research Statistics

Good marketing research should include the development of hypotheses, which is the topic of the statistical review for this chapter. Outlining a hypothesis or multiple hypotheses will provide guidance in developing a research study that is beneficial to management for making marketing decisions.

Proper statistical reporting ensures that managers understand information and can use it to make decisions. The statistical reporting section of this chapter addresses bar graphs. The key is to make these graphs stand alone with proper labeling and titling.

Most market researchers use SPSS for data analysis. The section on dealing with data will expose you to this program. While Microsoft Excel can be used for statistical analysis, SPSS is more robust and allows for quicker and easier data analysis.

2.8a Statistical Review

The research hypothesis, null hypothesis, and alternative hypothesis are related concepts, which often causes confusion. As discussed earlier, a research hypothesis states an expected research outcome relevant to one or more variables that seems reasonable in light of existing information. Research hypotheses are linked to specific research questions or research objectives, and typically describe the anticipated nature of a variable or the expected relationship between two variables.

Suppose the purpose of a research study was to introduce a new type of snowmobile. Several research questions must be answered in order to fulfill the research purpose, including, "How does demand for snowmobiles vary by region of the country?" The research hypothesis, "Demand for snowmobiles will be lower in the southeast area of the country than in the northwest area of the country," seems reasonable in light of average temperature and average annual snowfall data for various regions of the U.S. Research hypotheses aren't always developed in response to research questions, but they are useful in guiding the data analysis process when sufficient information exists to create logical hypotheses.

Taking the time to create well-written research hypotheses is time well spent. Well-designed research hypotheses should be as specific as possible, yet restricted to a single sentence. Hypotheses should also be concise; words that add little to the meaning of the sentence should be deleted. Since data analysis is only accurate within a determined margin of error, the word "prove" should never be included as part of a research hypothesis, because error exists in all market research studies. A research hypothesis should clearly indicate the phenomenon or variable to be studied, without referencing possible implications of the research or making other improper statements. A research hypothesis which states, "Tobacco advertising is bad for society" is judgmental and does not specify the variable to be investigated. Conversely, one which proposes that, "Greater exposure to tobacco advertising increases the likelihood of smoking" indicates the variables to be investigated (level of tobacco advertising exposure; likelihood of smoking) and their expected relationship, without passing judgment or jumping ahead to implications. Research hypotheses that compare groups (users vs. nonusers, males vs. females, etc.) should be stated in the plural form, and the subgroups to be compared specifically identified. Furthermore, when the hypothesis features a stated comparison (lower, higher, more, less, etc.), the variables being compared should be explicitly referenced, using consistent terminology. Finally, the word "significant" should not be incorporated in the research hypothesis, since it is understood that tests of significance will be used during hypothesis testing.[17]

The concept of null and alternative hypotheses is a basic statistics principle, although often confusing. Represented by the symbol "H_0", the null hypothesis is a statement or claim that can be statistically tested. When the subject of a research hypothesis is a single variable, the null hypothesis is stated in terms of equality. For instance, a research hypothesis might propose that, "Individuals most likely to purchase a yacht for personal use have an average annual income of $5 million or more." This research hypothesis would be rephrased into the following null hypothesis: "Individuals most likely to purchase a yacht for personal use have an average annual income equal to $5 million."

The alternative hypothesis, designated as H_A, states that which must be true when the null hypothesis is false. In the example above, H_A would be designated as, "Individuals most likely to purchase a yacht for personal use have an average annual income not equal to $5 million." Or, two separate alternative hypotheses specifying income levels of less than $5 million and greater than $5 million, respectively, could be created (so long as both were included).

In the case of group comparisons, the null hypothesis is sometimes called the status quo or "no-difference" hypothesis, because it essentially states that no differences exist between the groups. The snowmobile research hypothesis conjectured that, "Demand for snowmobiles will be lower in the southeast area of the country than in the northwest area of the country." Prior to data analysis, the null hypothesis would be phrased as, "Demand for snowmobiles does not vary by region of the country," and the research hypothesis can be listed as one of several potential alternative hypotheses. The process of hypothesis testing would then be used to determine whether or not sufficient evidence exists, based on the results of the study, to reject the null hypothesis. Recall that the null hypothesis is only rejected when the study results are unlikely to have occurred by chance, as determined by the appropriate significance test. A more in-depth discussion of hypothesis testing is provided in Chapter 13.

2.8b Statistical Reporting

Bar or column graphs are a major method of reporting discrete data. As discussed in chapter 1, discrete data have specific integer values with no decimals. The graphs are based on counts, or percentages derived from counts of different categories, such as age groups or gender. The graphs are easy to construct and relatively easy for managers to interpret. As with all graphs, the title needs to state clearly the data being presented. Both the x-axis and y-axis should be appropriately labeled. This is especially true for the values being graphed so anyone looking at the chart will know what the values mean.

Figure 2.19 is a bar or vertical column chart showing the U.S. market share of major credit cards according to purchase volume. The percentages do not total 100 as many smaller suppliers of credit cards are not listed in the chart. The title of the graph is clearly labeled. The x-axis title indicates the labels are credit cards. The y-axis is in percent of total market share. Value labels are presented above the bars so someone looking at the graph can immediately see what the market share is for each of the credit cards. Thus, it is easy to see American Express has the highest market share, at 20.6 percent, and Chase is a close second, at 20.0 percent. To provide further useful data, the purchase volume in billions of dollars might also be added to the data labels, or provided separately in another chart.

Another way to use bar graphs is to make the bars horizontal rather than vertical. **Figure 2.20** shows the measured media spending by the same U.S. credit card brands. In this instance, the title of the graph is not directly shown on the chart, but instead is listed below the illustration as the name of Figure 2.20. Measured media is tracked by WPP

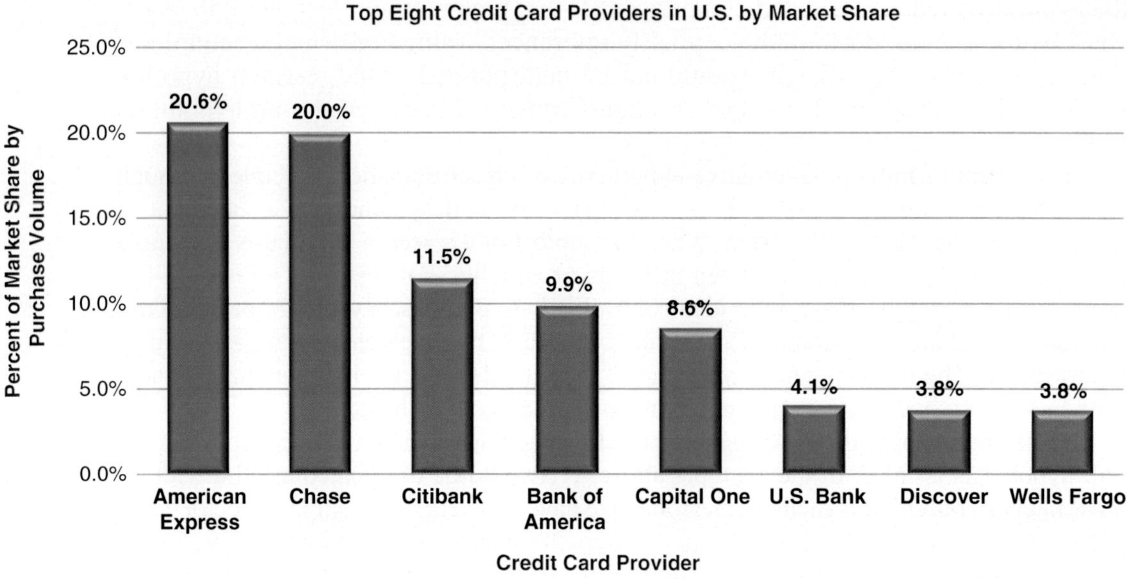

FIGURE 2.19 A Bar Graph Showing Market Share for Major U.S. Credit Cards
Source: Author adapted from *Advertising Age 2019 Marketing Fact Pack*, p. 13.

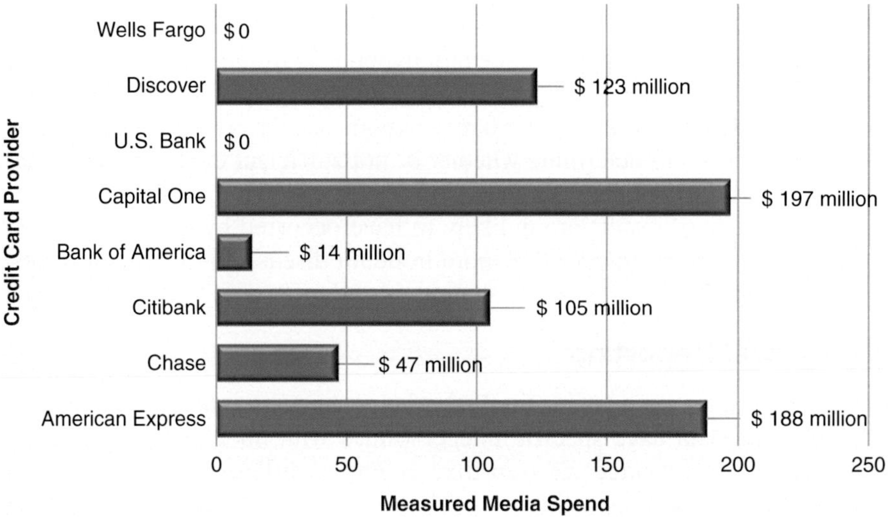

FIGURE 2.20 A Horizontal Bar Graph Showing Measured Media Spending for Major U.S. Credit Cards
Source: Author adapted from *Advertising Age 2019 Marketing Fact Pack*, p. 13.

Kantar Media and includes multiple forms of TV, digital, magazine, newspaper, radio, and outdoor and cinema advertising. **Figure 2.21** lists the forms of measured media tracked.

Labelling a graph is extremely important. In Figure 2.20, the data labels indicate that the values are in millions of dollars. Often the label on the bottom of the graph includes the measurement level (millions) and the data are numeric (123). The important point is that the level of measurement must be included in either the label or data values. Otherwise it would be unclear what the values mean. Comparing the two graphs, it is interesting to note that American Express has the highest market share, but Capital One spends the most money in measured media advertising. American Express ranks second in terms of measured media spending. Even more interesting is the lack of measured media spending by Wells Fargo and U.S. Bank. Does this mean they don't advertise at all? The answer is likely "no", as measured media does not include direct response advertising, digital advertising other than that shown on Figure 2.21, social media advertising, mobile advertising,

- **TV advertising**
  - Broadcast network TV
  - Cable TV networks
  - Spanish-language TV
  - Spot TV
  - Syndicated TV
- **Radio advertising**
  - Local
  - National spot radio
  - Network radio
- **Digital advertising**
  - Internet display
  - Paid search advertising
- **Magazine advertising**
  - Consumer magazines
  - B2B magazines
  - Local magazines
  - Sunday magazines
  - Spanish language magazines
- **Newspaper advertising**
  - Free-standing inserts
  - Local newspaper
  - National newspaper
  - Spanish language newspaper
- **Outdoor advertising**
- **Cinema advertising**

FIGURE 2.21 Measured Media Tracked by WPP Kantar Media
Source: "About 200 Leading National Advertisers 2018," *AdAge*, https://adage.com/article/datacenter/ad-age-ranked-200-leading-national-advertisers/313786, June 24, 2018, accessed June 13, 2019.

email marketing, or special events or promotions. So while Wells Fargo and Discover have identical market shares, Discover spent $123 million in measured media advertising in 2018 compared to the zero dollars invested by Wells Fargo, Wells Fargo may be investing in other forms of advertising or retention marketing that are currently not being tracked.

2.8c Dealing with Data

SPSS is a software application used by many research professionals and university professors to analyze data. SPSS allows users to perform a variety of analyses, ranging from simple procedures such as basic descriptive statistics and non-parametric tests such as chi-square analyses, to more involved and complex processes such as regression, ANOVA, time series analysis, classification analysis, correlation analysis, and more. SPSS also provides extensive charting capabilities and export options to facilitate the creation of research reports.

The purpose of this exercise is for you to become acquainted with SPSS. You will need to download the following two files that are on the student website for this textbook at www.clowjames.net/students.html

- Chapter 02 Dealing with Data (SPSS file)
- Chapter 02 Dealing with Data Survey (Word file)

The first file is the actual data file that contains the results obtained from a student research project. The second file is the questionnaire composed by the student. If you are not familiar with SPSS, detailed step-by-step instructions are provided for each chapter's exercise on the student website for the textbook at www.clowjames.net/students.hml.

Open the questionnaire. It may be helpful to print the one-page questionnaire so you can refer to it as you complete this exercise. Open the SPSS data file and save it to your hard drive or a flash drive. Go through the following steps to become acquainted with SPSS.

1. Notice SPSS has two views or sheets. The data view contains the raw data numbers; the second is the variable view that provides information about each variable.
2. Change to the variable view so you can understand what the raw data means. The survey question is listed under the "Label" column. Click on the "Label" cell for the variable named, "Q1Often" and read the information, and compare it to the questionnaire. If you cannot see the entire question, widen the cell as you would in Excel.

3. Next, click on the cell under the "Value" column for the "Q1Often" variable. These are called "value labels." Value labels show what the data mean by providing the actual answer the respondent indicated. For example, switching back to the data view, you'll see that the first respondent is coded as "3" under the "Q1Often" column. Returning to the variable view, the "Values" column shows that "3" represents "two or three times a month" on question 1 of the survey. Go to the variable view and examine each column. Compare it to the questionnaire.
4. Write a short description of each column. For instance, the first column is the name of the variable. It is a short abbreviated name with no spaces and identifies the question number in the survey. It is also beneficial to click on a cell in each column to examine the different options available. You can see other options by clicking the grey box with three dots that appears when you select a cell for certain variables, such as "Type."
5. Two columns that are especially important for you to examine closely are the columns entitled "Label" and "Values." Why do you think these are important?

Summary

Objective 1: Compare and contrast the three types of research designs.
Exploratory, descriptive, and causal research designs are each appropriate under certain conditions. Exploratory research uses focus groups, one-on-one interviews, secondary research, and/or pilot studies to develop a better understanding of a particular problem or situation that may otherwise be ambiguous. An exploratory study might seek to define the marketing research problem, identify parameters or variables to be studied further, or to generate potential research hypotheses for testing. Descriptive research studies are the most common form of marketing research and typically seek to describe existing characteristics, attributes, or behaviors of people, brands, organizations, or other objects. Survey and observation research form the bulk of descriptive research studies. Causal research is appropriate when we attempt to investigate whether a change in one item causes a change to occur in another. Establishing causality requires both a temporal sequence and concomitant variation. Carefully controlled laboratory experiments and field experiments are used in the determination of causality.

Objective 2: Explain the marketing research process.
The marketing research process is organized into six key steps: 1) defining the research problem, 2) developing the research design, 3) determining the sampling plan, 4) implementing data collection procedures, 5) analyzing the data, and 6) preparing and sharing the research report. Defining the research problem starts by establishing the research purpose. Next is the development of research questions or objectives that outline the scope of the research project and guide the development of the research design, followed by the creation of hypotheses. Research design decisions include determining the nature of the approach (descriptive or casual), and selecting the method of data collection (survey, observation, or experimentation). The sampling plan begins with a determination of the population to be studied, then describes the process by which the sample group of study participants will be selected. During data analysis, researchers apply mathematical and statistical processes to raw numbers for the purpose of providing meaningful information that can assist managers in making decisions. The final stage of the research process involves writing and presenting the research report to include a set of actionable recommendations.

Objective 3: Describe the components of a request for research (RFP) and a research proposal.
Requests for research proposals, commonly referred to as RFPs, are created by firms commissioning a research study. RFPs typically include background information, an overview of the research purpose, problem or question, and a description of the target audience for the study. Important expectations that influence the cost of the study should be provided, such as desired sample size, data collection methodology, and the time frame for the study. A research proposal is prepared by firms who wish to bid on RFPs and contain the following information: 1) introduction and background to the RFP, 2) research questions, 3) research design, 4) target population, 5) sample size and method, 6) data collection methodology, and 7) study cost and time schedule.

Objective 4: Provide an overview of qualitative and quantitative research.
Qualitative research involves the use of small samples and unstructured data collection methods, such as focus groups, personal interviews, case studies, and other techniques. It is subjective and exploratory in nature, and results should not be interpreted as providing definitive answers. In contrast, quantitative research is a more structured process in which data is collected objectively using larger, more representative samples. Research designs allow for data to be represented numerically, permitting statistical tests and analyses. Results are more definitive and can be generalized to the population. Quantitative research is most commonly associated with descriptive and causal studies.

Objective 5: Recite the ethical considerations in designing research studies.
Ethical considerations affect research decisions as well as various entities involved in the research industry. Firms seeking to commission research studies may behave unethically if RFPs are issued that are not sincere requests for bids. Marketing research suppliers who submit research proposals in response to RFPs behave unethically when engaging in lowball pricing or bait-and-switch tactics. Numerous opportunities for unethical behavior exist throughout the research process, and include, but are not limited to, purposively engaging in advocacy research, biasing the sample selection, distorting the data collected, falsifying data, improperly analyzing data or manipulating statistics, and violating the confidentiality of proprietary studies. Respondent's rights to confidentiality and safety should be protected, and to withdraw their participation from the study, and to correct inaccurate information. Special care should be taken when studying children and vulnerable populations. Researchers must limit data collected to that relevant to the research at hand, and ensure that secondary data containing personal information meets certain criteria prior to use. Finally, researchers must make every effort to protect data from misuse, disclosure, loss, and unauthorized manipulation.

Key Terms

advocacy research, p. 53
causal research, p. 38
cognitive neuroscience, p. 56
concomitant variation, p. 38
descriptive research, p. 37
experiments, p. 44
exploratory research, p. 36
field experiments, p. 44
low-ball pricing, p. 53
observation research, p. 43
pilot study, p. 36
population, p. 44
qualitative research, p. 48
quantitative research, p. 48
request for proposal (RFP), p. 47
research design, p. 42
research hypothesis, p. 36
research proposal, p. 47
research purpose, p. 38
research question, p. 41
spurious association, p. 38
survey research, p. 43
temporal sequence, p. 38
visual gamification, p. 41

Critical Thinking Exercises

1. Visit **https://theharrispoll.com** and select or search for the "News" link (which may be at the bottom of the home page). Review the titles of the various articles available. Select a study that has implications for marketers and is of interest to you. Summarize the results of the study. Is this an example of exploratory, descriptive, or causal research? Was it gathered via observation, survey, or experimental methods? What type of businesses could make use of this information and how could it be useful?
2. Is it ethical for churches, charities, governmental organizations, or other not-for-profit organizations to request pro-bono or discounted rates in their RFP? Why or why not?
3. Critique the following research hypotheses. Describe what is wrong with each one. Rewrite each research hypothesis to address the problems noted, following the principles outlined in the *Statistics Review* section. Next, write both a null and an alternative hypothesis for each revised research hypothesis.
   a. Demand for new technology products will be higher among students.
   b. All drivers should purchase automobile insurance.
   c. Coupon redemption rates vary significantly by income.
   d. Among brand-loyal consumers, those who have higher levels of brand loyalty will be more willing to pay higher prices, while brand-loyal consumers who have moderate levels of brand loyalty will be less willing to pay higher prices.
   e. Search engine advertising will be proven to be more effective than banner advertising.
4. A veterinarian has commissioned a research study to investigate whether or not selling specialty dog food, cat food, and other pet products at her clinic would be profitable for business. You have been working as a receptionist at the clinic for the past six months and she has asked for your help in creating research questions that will provide the information necessary to make the correct business decision. Develop a minimum of three research questions or objectives that can help to achieve the purpose of the study.
5. Search for the American Marketing Association's "Statement of Ethics" found at **https://www.ama.org.** Do any of the items discussed in this document apply specifically to marketing research? Can the existing ethical standards be generalized to marketing research? If so, explain. Contrast the AMA's statement

of ethics to that of the Insights Association which can be found when searching the term "code of ethics" at **https://www.insightsassociation.org**. Which ethical code is more useful for the marketing research profession? Does the Insights Association code apply to all forms of marketing research? If not, what forms are missing?

6. Requests for proposals (also called invitations to bid) are commonly listed on the website of the client firm, and sent directly to research entities that the client hopes will submit a bid. Using the search engine of your choice, search either or both of the following terms: "request for proposal market research" or "invitations to bid market research." Review the search results until you find an actual RFP document. Read through the document, and prepare a one- to two-page report which answers the following questions:
   a. Based on your understanding of the RFP, will the research project be primarily qualitative or quantitative in nature, or will both forms of research be required? Explain.
   b. Would you classify the research likely to result from the RFP as exploratory, descriptive, or casual? Why?
   c. Are surveys, observation, experiments, or some other form of data collection likely to be involved? Explain.
   d. Does the RFP contain all of the components of a RFP discussed in this chapter? Is it clearly written, or are some portions of the RFP ambiguous? Would you feel comfortable responding to the RFP based on the information provided?
   e. What ethical concerns might be raised by the RFP?

   Your report should be accompanied by a link to the RFP, hard copy of the RFP or electronic copy of the RFP.
7. A mystery shopper visits a Chick-Fil-A restaurant and places an order for a sandwich at the counter. After leaving the restaurant, the mystery shopper submits a report that lists:
   - the amount of time he stood in line waiting to place his order
   - whether or not the order-taker smiled when taking the order, suggested the purchase of a drink or fries with the sandwich, and thanked the shopper for placing an order
   - the amount of time that it took to receive the food after placing the order
   - whether the order was filled correctly
   - whether or not the windows, floor, counter tops, restrooms and empty tables in the restaurant were clean.

Is this research study an example of qualitative or quantitative research?

Would you describe the research as exploratory, descriptive, or casual? Does the research method described in this scenario reflect survey, observation, or experimental research? Are there any other factors that might be added to those evaluated by the mystery shopper? Justify each of your answers.

Lakeside Grill

(Comprehensive Student Case)

Students Brooke, Alexa, Juan, Destiny, and Zach began their research proposal by outlining the background for the study and specifying the research problem and research objectives. According to the group, "The purpose of this research study is to determine why sales at the Lakeside Grill are declining, and what changes to the marketing mix are needed in order to improve sales and profitability." Based on the research purpose, the group wrote the following research questions:

1. What is the current level of customer satisfaction with various operational aspects of the Riverside Grill, such as the menu, hours of operation, atmosphere, quality of service, and quality of food?
2. Why have customers reduced their level of patronage at Lakeside Grill?
3. How has the addition of a new competitor down the street affected the Lakeside Grill's customer base?
4. Would changing the Lakeside Grill's menu, prices, advertising and/or promotional practices increase sales and profitability?

In terms of type of research, Juan explained, "We will conduct descriptive research and collect primarily quantitative data. We really don't need to conduct any exploratory research because Mr. Zito (owner of Lakeside Grill) has provided us with information about the restaurant's background and the situation that he is facing now."

Critique Questions:

1. Evaluate the research purpose. Is it clear? Should "determine why sales are declining" be part of the research purpose, or is it a symptom? What about "changes in the marketing mix?" Is this a strategy or can this be a legitimate purpose for the study?
2. Based on information provided in this chapter, improve and re-write the research purpose statement for the student group.
3. Are the research questions appropriate for the research purpose you wrote in response to Question 2, or do they need to be re-written also? If so, please re-write the research questions to match your new research purpose.

4. Would you agree with Juan's statement that the best approach is descriptive research and quantitative data? Why or why not?
5. Would you agree with Juan's statement that "We really don't need to conduct any exploratory research because Mr. Zito (owner of Lakeside Grill) has provided us with information?" Why or why not?
6. What ethical issues could arise with the AMA student team conducting this research project? What steps should the students and faculty advisor take to ensure no unethical behaviors occur?

Notes

1. Erin Duffin, "Resident Population in the United States in 2017, by Generation (in Millions)," U.S. Census Bureau, last updated July 1, 2019, https://www.statista.com/statistics/797321/us-population-by-generation/.
2. This section based on Joe Sciara, "The Power of Gen Z Influence," Millennial Marketing, January 2018, http://www.millennialmarketing.com/wp-content/uploads/2018/01/Barkley_WP_GenZMarketSpend_Final.pdf; "Generation Z Will Account for 40 Percent of Shoppers by 2020," RYMNTS, August 18, 2018, https://www.pymnts.com/news/retail/2018/generation-z-consumer-spending-teens/; "Guide to Gen Z: Debunking the Myths of our Youngest Generation," NPD Group, 2017, https://www.npd.com/lps/pdf/guide-to-gen-z.pdf.
3. This section is based on "Leading Purchase Influences of U.S. Online Shoppers 2017" (Study ID 50566) Statista, 2017, https://www.statista.com/statistics/788185/us-online-shoppers-purchase-influences/, p. 9; "U.S. Online Review Importance during Selected Circumstances, 2017" (Study ID 50566), Statista, 2017, https://www.statista.com/statistics/713258/online-review-importance-circumstances-usa/, p. 13; "U.S. Internet Users Factors Influencing Where to Shop Online in 2017" (Study ID 50566), Statista, 2017, https://www.statista.com/statistics/311421/us-internet-users-online-shopping-factors-decision/, p. 21.
4. Jane Cheung, Simon Glass, Karl Haller, and Christopher K. Wong, *What Do Gen Z Shoppers Really Want?* (Armonk, NY: IBM Corporation, 2018), 3.
5. "Seven Surprising Cannabis Insights for Marketers," MRI-Simmons, 2019, https://www.simmonsresearch.com/reports/seven-surprising-cannabis-insights-marketers/, p. 8.
6. Trish Doran and Shellie Yule, "How Game-Enhanced Design Can Improve Respondent Data Satisfaction and Quality," *Quirk's Marketing Research Review* (January 2015).
7. Kathryn Korostoff, "A Few Helpful Reminders on RFPs," GreenBook, September 20, 2010, http://www.greenbook.org/marketing-research/creating-rfps-helpful-reminders-hm20.
8. John C. Frederic, "10 Heresies in Marketing Research. Wrong Symptoms, Wrong Cures." *Quirks Media* (November 2017), https://www.quirks.com/storage/attachments/59f20e41d82f1c22e654278e/59f20e41d82f1c22e6542798/original/201711_quirks.pdf, pp. 24–27.
9. Interview with Dave Snell, The Richards Group, May 11, 2010.
10. This section is based on Christopher Hiene, "Social Media's Screen Game," *Adweek* 58, no. 3 (January 30, 2017): 7.
11. Ibid.
12. Information from this section is adapted from "ICC/ESOMAR International Code on Social Science and Market Research," ESOMAR, 2016, https://www.esomar.org/uploads/pdf/professional-standards/ICCESOMAR_Code_English_.pdf.
13. Ibid.
14. Danuta Babinska and Aleksandra Nizielska, "International Marketing Research on the Markets of Central and Eastern Europe," *Journal of Economics & Management* 6 (2009): 5–19.
15. This section is based on "Use of Traditional Methodologies," in *GRIT Report: GreenBook Research Industry Trends Report, Quarters 3–4, 2016* (New York: GreenBook, 2016), 20; "Use of Traditional Methodologies," in *GRIT Report: GreenBook Research Industry Trends Report, Quarters 3–4, 2017* (New York: GreenBook, 2017), 28.
16. Anuta Babinska and Aleksandra Nizielska, "International Marketing Research on the Markets of Central and Eastern Europe," *Journal of Economics & Management* 6 (2009): 5–19.
17. Adapted from Fred Pyrczak and Randall R. Bruce, *Writing Empirical Research Reports: A Basic Guide for Students of the Social and Behavioral Sciences*, 6th ed. (Glendale, CA: Pyrczak Publishing, 2007).

PART II

Types of Marketing Research

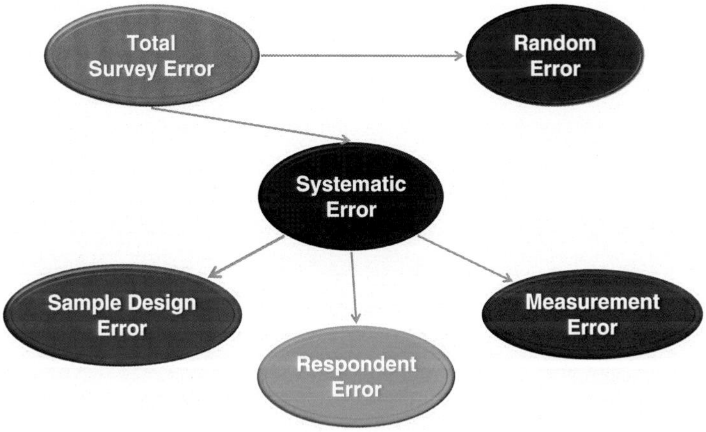

Secondary Data and Research

CHAPTER 3

Source: alexskopje/Shutterstock.

Chapter Outline

Learning Objectives

After studying this chapter, you should be able to:

- Discuss the advantages and disadvantages of secondary data.
- Identify key uses of secondary data.
- Explain how internal sources of data and big data can be used for secondary research.
- Describe the open access sources of secondary data.
- Summarize the primary differences among the bibliographic digital databases.
- Identify and explain the types of data available from syndicated sources.

3.1 Chapter Overview

A number of marketing research firms, such as the NPD Group (https://www.npd.com), collect data about retail sales on a regular basis. The data are organized, analyzed, and then sold to clients and other interested businesses. It is cheaper for firms to purchase data from a firm such as the NPD Group than for each company to collect its own data. An example of this type of data is shown in **Figure 3.1**. The graph shows the percentage of private label dollar sales, also known as the share of sales, for various product categories, as tracked by point-of-sale (POS) data.[1] **Private labels** are products manufactured by a third party and sold under a retailer's brand name. Equate is one of Walmart's private label brands just as Archer Farms brand is a private label sold at Target.

Private labels products manufactured by a third party and sold under a retailer's brand name.

Private label apparel not only represents nearly one-third of all apparel sales, it is a growth market, with a year-to-year growth rate of 2.1 share points. Private label sales of housewares is growing at an annual rate of 1 share point, while technology and accessories are growing at 0.4 and .03 share points, respectively. However, when compared to the selling prices of manufacturer branded merchandise, private label prices are declining for apparel, housewares, and technology, while accessories experienced a 30 cent increase on average compared to the $3.70 average increase for branded accessories. Still, a deeper dive into the data revealed that in premium product categories, private labels are growing at twice the rate of name brands. The lines between national brands and private labels are blurring, offering retailers the ability to introduce more private labels, and increase profit by eliminating wholesalers and distributors. Retailers are also in a position to capitalize on trends that could warrant higher prices. For example, private label sales in the grocery industry have increased when marketing organic and non-GMO goods. This type of information is very useful to both brick-and-mortar and online retailers, as well as manufacturers who sell through retail outlets. It can be used to make pricing decisions, merchandise mix decisions, and branding decisions designed to better meet the needs of consumers. It is clear that branded manufacturers must consider the competitive impact of private labels in today's market. Companies do not always have to collect their own data to make good marketing decisions. Often, data can be purchased from another source, such as the NPD Group, MRI-Simmons, IRI, Nielsen, or Retail Metrics.

Secondary data data collected previously for purposes other than for the current study at hand.

Primary research research studies specifically developed to help fulfill the research purpose currently being investigated.

3.2 It All Begins with Secondary Data

LEARNING OBJECTIVE 3.1
Discuss the advantages and disadvantages of secondary data.

Data previously collected for purposes other than the current study at hand is **secondary data**. By contrast, **primary research** involves focus groups, questionnaires, experiments, or observation studies specifically developed to help answer the research questions

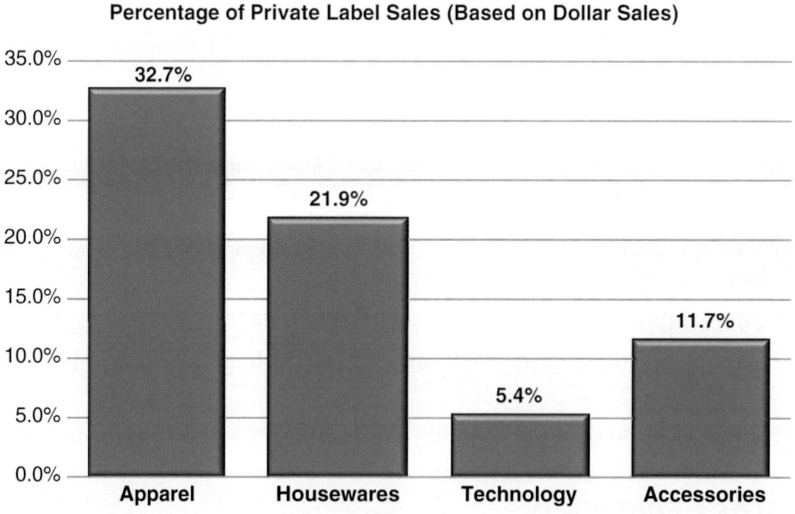

FIGURE 3.1 A Bar Chart Showing the Share of Private Label Sales in Key Product Categories
Source: Adapted from, Marshal Cohen, *How Private Label Goes Premium*. NPD Group, June 2019. https://www.npd.com/wps/portal/npd/us/news/thought-leadership/2019/is-private-label-peaking/, retrieved June 10, 2019.

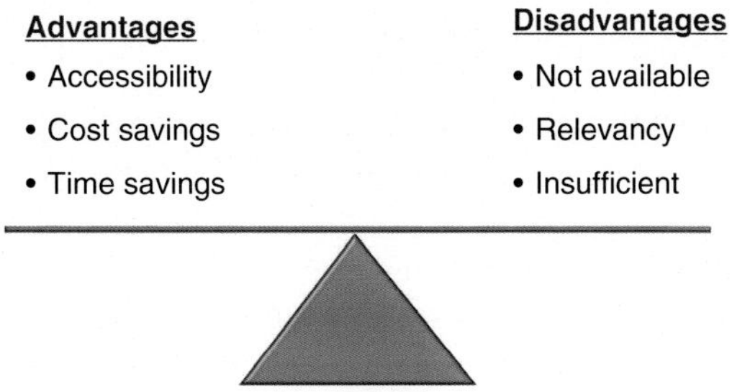

FIGURE 3.2 Advantages and Disadvantages of Secondary Data

currently being investigated. While both types of research may be necessary to fulfill the research purpose, research studies should always begin with secondary data research. Secondary data is an important method for gathering competitive intelligence, understanding public opinion, and adding context and background information to a study.[2] While this type of research may not answer all of the questions being posed by the researcher, gathering secondary data is almost always a useful exercise that can produce a number of benefits. It is well worth the time and effort and, in some cases, secondary data can provide adequate information that can be used by management for making better-informed decisions. The primary advantages and disadvantages of using secondary data are listed in **Figure 3.2.**

3.2a Advantages of Secondary Data

The major advantage of secondary data is its accessibility, which in turn produces cost and time savings. A marketing researcher may be able to locate useful information from the Internet, online publications, reputable websites, expert blogs, libraries, databases, syndicated data sources, governmental sources or internal company sources. If so, the amount of time it takes to acquire the information will be considerably less than if primary research was undertaken. It also would be much less costly to acquire for several reasons. First, internal data and many forms of high-quality secondary data are available free of charge (such as census data from the government). Secondly, compared to collecting primary data, even data purchased from syndicated sources costs less, because the overall study expense is shared among multiple subscribers, making each individual purchaser's cost a fraction of the whole. A **syndicated research service (or data source)** is a marketing research firm, such as the NPD Group or Nielsen, that supplies standardized information to a number of clients for a fee. Clients often include advertising agencies and consumer goods producers, as well as business-to-business marketers. Finally, secondary data will cost less and take less time than collecting primary data because each of the steps outlined in Chapter 2 for the primary research process would not have to be followed.

Syndicated research service a marketing research firm that supplies standardized information to a number of clients for a fee.

Consider a company with multiple retail locations in many cities needs to make a decision on how much, if any, of its advertising budget should go toward location-based mobile advertising. The proposed media change might be based on the belief that, since so many individuals have mobile phones, the probability of the ad being seen on a cell phone is greater than the probability of it being seen via television or one of the other traditional media. In addition, if location-based mobile advertising is used, then only individuals within a specified distance from the firm's retail outlets would receive the ad. Faced with this decision, management may request a research study to determine if some of the advertising budget should be allocated for location-based mobile phone advertising. Competitive intelligence and insight into the marketing strategies of other retail businesses or franchisees might be particularly helpful.

In conducting secondary research, the researcher might locate an analysis of 1,500 franchisees located in MSAs across the USA. According to research partners Vya

Targeted social ads use behavioral data, demographic data, geo-targeting and other profile data gathered by social platforms to target only those consumers whose profiles interest marketers.

Geo-aware ads mobile ads triggered by a consumer's location around a retail outlet.

and BIA Advisory Services, the study sample closely matches the distribution of local businesses according to size of market. Interestingly, this study found that 84 percent of franchisees used **targeted social ads** as a form of local advertising, while 71 percent used **geo-aware ads**. Targeted social ads use behavioral data, demographic data, geo-targeting and other profile data gathered by social platforms to target only those consumers whose profiles interest franchisees. Geo-aware ads are mobile ads triggered by a consumer's location around a retail outlet. The study also found that while 74.8 percent of those surveyed rated the return on investment (ROI) of targeted social ads excellent (9 or 10 on a ten point scale), the Internet Yellow Pages outperformed all media in ROI excellence, as 83.9 percent of the sample rated it a 9 or 10 using the same scale.[3] Thus, if the company wants to spend money on mobile phone advertising, then using targeted social ads may be a wise strategy, supplemented with Internet Yellow Pages for those who are actively searching for businesses. While primary research might provide more specific information related to the firm's current and potential customers, the secondary research may be sufficient for management to make a decision on whether or not to allocate money for geo-aware ads, targeted social ads, and Internet Yellow Pages advertising. If so, the company has saved considerable time and money since the information could have been obtained within a few hours compared to the several weeks or months required when conducting a primary research study.

3.2b Disadvantages of Secondary Research

A number of disadvantages are associated with secondary data. First, the exact information needed may not be available. This occurs when the information that management is seeking has not been studied by someone else. For example, a company such as John Deere may want information about how consumers and commercial customers feel about its line of lawn mowers with a hydrostatic transmission. They may also wish to know if there is a difference in attitudes between consumers who purchase the lawn mower and commercial customers such as golf courses, school districts, hospitals, and parks. A study identified via secondary research may rank the various brands of lawn mowers. Another study may have examined consumer preferences in terms of the desirability of lawn mower features. However, neither secondary study tells John Deere what consumers and commercial customers think of their lawn mower featuring the hydrostatic transmission. Such is often the case with new products that have just been introduced to the market. Some primary research would be needed to answer such questions.

Unfortunately, a great deal of secondary data will be irrelevant to the research purpose. Carefully crafted search phrases can limit the degree to which superfluous information is found when searching electronic databases or the Internet. A major source of frustration for many marketers occurs when secondary data is found which is "close" to what is being searched for, but which uses irrelevant units of measure in defining the target market or other variables of interest.

A researcher might be seeking information on the number of unique (separate) individuals who use mass transportation in an average month. Suppose a secondary research study was found which listed the number of fares (cash/debit and electronic bus pass) collected each month by type of public transportation. Unfortunately, this information would be irrelevant; the number of fares collected cannot be used as a proxy for the number of unique riders. Fares are collected each time a rider—any rider—uses the bus or city train system. Thus, a commuter who takes the bus to work each day would log ten fares in a single week. Using fares as a proxy for riders would overstate the number of individual people using the transportation system. While it may be possible to separate out those with electronic passes as unique individuals, other riders might still be double-counted.

Secondary data might be available and it might be relevant to the current research topic, but still be insufficient to answer the research question. Suppose that three years ago John Deere conducted a study that examined how customers felt about its line of lawn mowers and the various features that it offered. The study may have compared the John

- Data source
- Purpose of study
- Sample selection
- Data collection process
- Data analysis
- Data interpretation

FIGURE 3.3 Issues in Examining Accuracy of Secondary Data

Deere brand to other brands. But, the study did not survey commercial customers. Thus, the secondary data is not sufficient to answer the current research question of whether the feature was desired by its commercial customers.

3.3 Evaluating the Accuracy of Secondary Data

In using secondary data, it is important to assess its accuracy. As shown in Figure 3.3, a number of issues need to be examined. Data may be easily accessible and save a company money and time, but if it is inaccurate and of poor quality, then flawed decisions will be made that could cost the firm more than if it had conducted primary research initially.

3.3a Data Source

Evaluating the accuracy of secondary data begins with determining the source of the data. With the Internet, secondary data is readily available. It is not, however, always easy to determine who produced the data. Websites do not always clearly identify the company or organization behind the site or the data. This is especially true with blogs and microsites that companies have developed for specific purposes. It is also true of sites hosted by individuals. The researcher must be very careful not to mistake statements of opinion for statements of fact. Anyone can say anything on a website, but without insight into the source of the data, the sample studied, and the methodology used to collect and analyze data, taking results on blind faith can be dangerous and result in poor decision-making.

Sources of data that tend to be accurate include government organizations, major syndicated data providers, custom research firms, trade organizations, and educational institutions. The federal, state, and even local governments produce a large number of data sets that are publicly available free of charge to individuals and companies. Syndicated data providers exist for the sole purpose of gathering, analyzing, and packaging standardized data to multiple subscribers. Thus, the data they provide must be of high quality in order to keep their subscriber base strong. Custom research firms are also actively involved in collecting data. Similar to syndicated data, some data collected by these research firms may be available for businesses to purchase at a price that is typically much cheaper than collecting the same data through primary research. However, much of the data collected by custom research firms is propriety and belongs to the client who paid for the study.

Custom research firms will sometimes publish the results of studies or an executive summary of the study for free. The rationale for publishing this information is usually to show the research firm's expertise and to encourage additional business from companies interested in the topic. Care should be taken, though, because published studies of this nature—though accurate at the time of data collection—can be out of date. It would be erroneous to assume that the quality and accuracy of data gathered by custom research firms is always inherently strong. Unlike syndicated firms, which rely on repeat business in the form of subscriptions, custom research firms are more dependent upon new business. Bidding low to secure a research project may result in cutting corners during study implementation, or simply failing to pay attention to detail, either of which can damage the accuracy of the information collected. The marketing research profession does not currently require that those who call themselves professionals be licensed or certified. Thus, the quality and accuracy of data provided by custom research firms can vary. The expertise and training of the staff assigned to a project can be a major contributing factor. Reputable firms will disclose the methodology of their studies in detail when asked, maintain strict quality-control measures, and adhere to proper sampling practices.

Trade organizations will collect data unique to the industry and make that information available to firms within the industry. Some of the data will be used as the basis for articles posted in the trade journal and on the trade organization's website. Other data can be purchased by firms within the industry.

The last source of secondary information is educational institutions. Most of this data is free and collected as a public service. Many universities have centers for economic research that study issues affecting the local workforce and economy. Many other types of studies are published in academic journals that can be accessed through a library database subscription.

3.3b Purpose of Study

Accuracy of secondary data is affected by the purpose of a study. Studies are sometimes conducted to justify a particular position (advocacy research). In such cases the results may be biased, or at least the methodology will be suspect, since the goal was to arrive at a pre-determined result. An advertisement for a particular type of toothpaste or toothbrush that states 7 out of 10 dentists recommend the brand is likely an advocacy study.

Often it is difficult to determine the purpose of a study. In such cases it is important to look at the source of the study, why it was conducted, and the sample used. Consider the results shown in Figure 3.4 for a study conducted by BlogHer. Respondents indicated they spent more time reading blogs than they do watching TV, listening to radio, or reading print media. The sample was primarily individuals from the BlogHer Network, which provides a valuable clue as to the results found.[4] Since the respondents were members of the BlogHer Network, they would be more inclined to reading, commenting, and writing

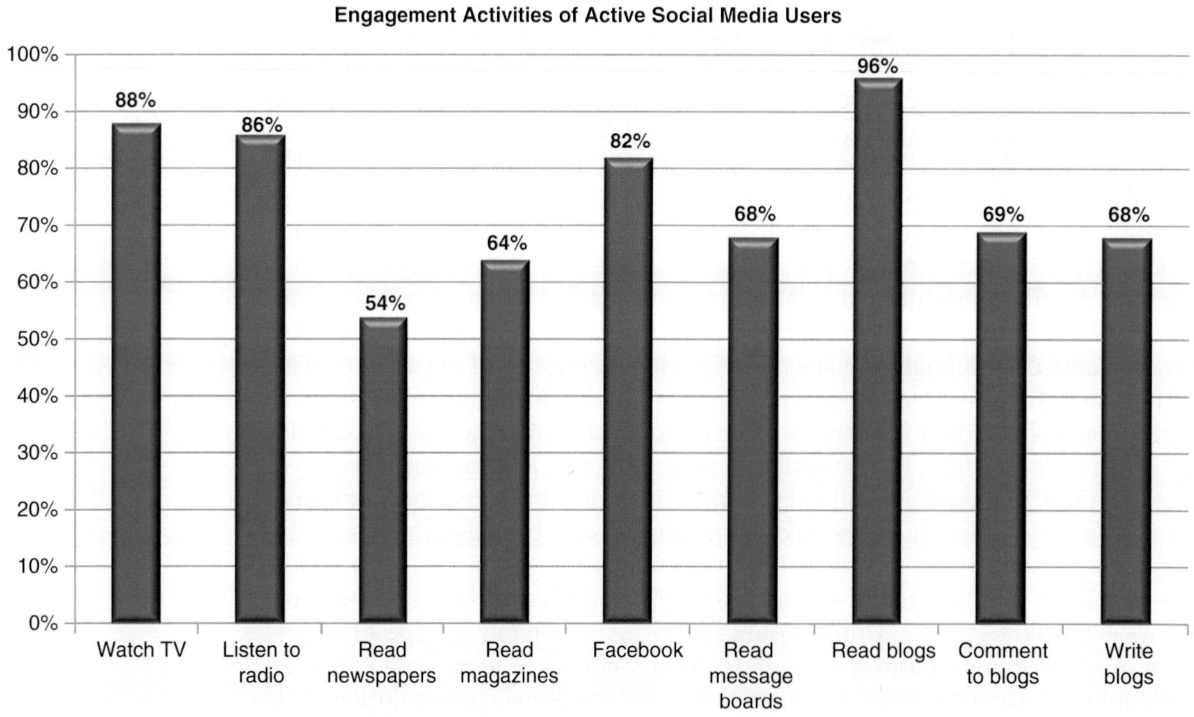

FIGURE 3.4 Results of a Survey by BlogHer
Source: Adapted from *Social Media Matters 2010*, BlogHer Inc., BlogHer Network, sample, N=1,550.

blogs, which helps to explain the results. While the purpose of this study is not fully known, the sample and the source of the study show a bias toward individuals, very likely females, who like blogging. It would be difficult for any company other than BlogHer to use this data to make management decisions. Certainly, it would be inappropriate for another firm to conclude that *all women* like blogging; doing so would lead to added and unnecessary expense should the firm then decide to create blogs on product websites which primarily cater to women.

3.3c Sample Selection

Who constitutes the sample and how they are selected is critically important in determining the accuracy of secondary data. Referring back to Figure 3.4, note that the sample not only is part of the BlogHer Network but they are *active* social media users. By sampling active social media users it is not surprising to see that 96 percent read blogs "weekly or more." If occasional social media users were surveyed or even nonsocial media users, the results would be quite different. Similarly, if Ford surveyed only individuals with incomes of $75,000 or more concerning their attitudes towards the Ford F-150 series pickup trucks, the results would be different than if all consumers, regardless of income, were surveyed.

Source: lev radin/Shutterstock.

The accuracy of secondary data is impacted by the study purpose and the sample. A study conducted by the BlogHer Network used BlogHer members who were active social media users, primarily women, as the sample. The limitations of the sample mean that the results cannot be generalized to bloggers in general, or even female bloggers in general, and thus cannot be used for decision-making purposes in other organizations.

With secondary research the means of selecting the sample may not be stated or otherwise be evident. But it is important because the sample needs to represent the population being studied. If a company wants to use the results of a secondary research study to support a management decision, then the sample needs to represent the company's population or target market for which the decision will be made. For instance, the sample used by BlogHer was predominantly female. It would not be representative of the population as a whole. As mentioned earlier, it isn't even representative of all females, but rather just those who are actively engaged with social media and who are members of BlogHer network.

3.3d Data Collection Process

Even harder to determine when evaluating the quality of secondary data is when the study was undertaken, how the data were collected, what type of analysis was conducted, and how the analysis was interpreted. All of these facets of the research process are important in determining the accuracy of data. A study examining what people do on the Internet would be of little value today if conducted five years ago, or even three years ago. Too much has changed; many people have cut the cord and now stream video from Hulu, Netflix, or other services over the Internet; social networking opportunities have grown exponentially, while new alternatives—such as closing your garage door remotely or viewing who is ringing your doorbell—have been made possible by enhancements in technology and the Internet of Things. In the case of the BlogHer study, what was true in 2010 is very likely different from what is true today, which cast further doubt on the accuracy of the information.

Seldom would the research methodology details be provided within a published report. The information can be obtained, however, if the secondary data is purchased from a marketing research firm. If the source is government data, such information might be contained in footnotes or available upon request.

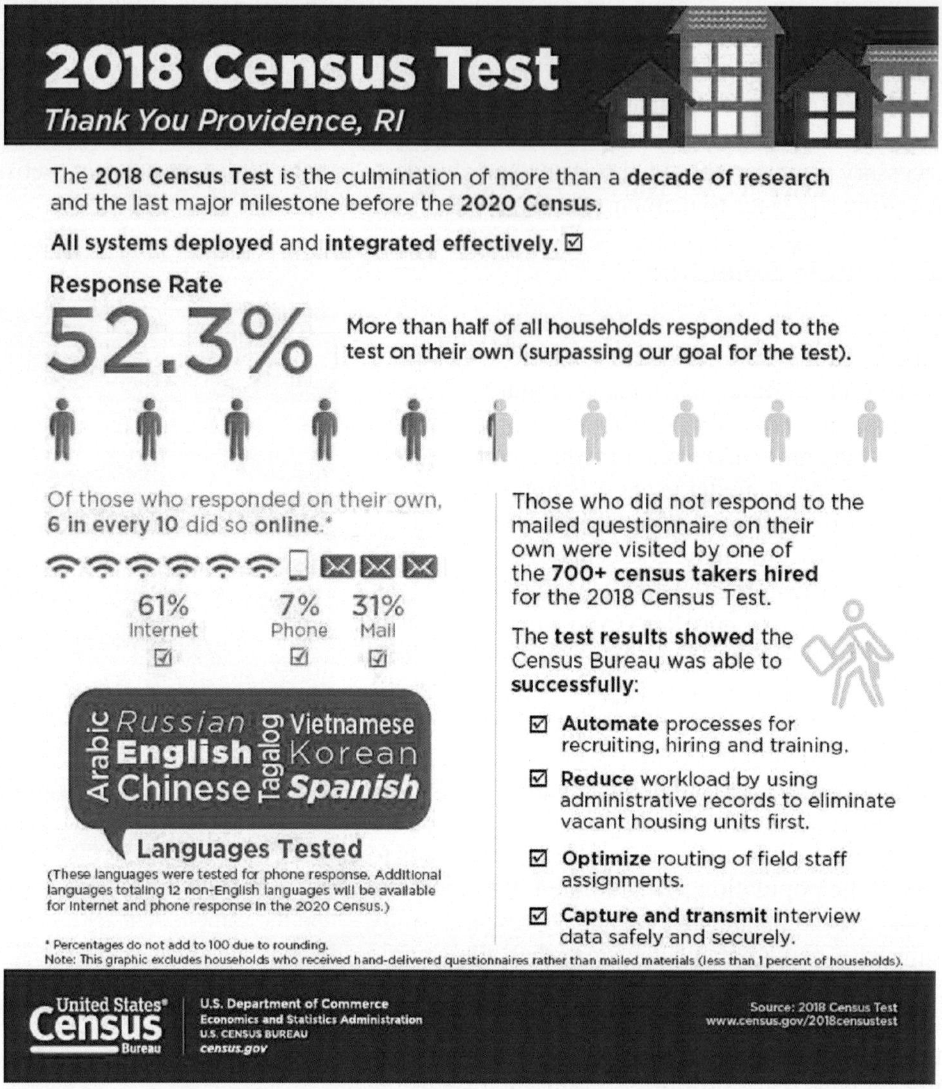

FIGURE 3.5 New Census Methodology Test Results
Source: 2018 Census Test, www.census.gov/2018censustest

The U.S. Census "serves as the backbone for all consumer marketing research."[5] Its accuracy has long been taken for granted, but as the 2020 census grows near, changes are coming which may draw the validity of the census results into question. The first is a change in data collection methodology. As a cost-cutting measure, the U.S. Census Bureau is adding online and phone data collection methods to the existing face-to-face interviewing and mail survey process. However, far fewer dollars will be allocated to the face-to-face interviewing process that has been critical in reaching non-respondents in the past, so the overall response rate may suffer. Only one end-to-end field test of the new methodology occurred, in Rhode Island. The test results are displayed in Figure 3.5. While encouraging, a single test of the new methodology may be insufficient to deem the results acceptable, as people in Rhode Island may behave differently from those in Mississippi. There is a legitimate concern that the new methodology may undercount residents who are more difficult to reach, such as transient populations, or lower income groups who are less likely to have Internet access.[6]

3.3e Data Analysis

The accuracy of the data can be greatly influenced by the type of analysis performed and the degree of error that the researcher finds acceptable. Determining whether the data were properly analyzed can be quite difficult since access to the questionnaire or data collection instrument, results of the full data analyses, and the data set used in analyses is rarely, if ever, available. Furthermore, a strong working knowledge of statistics and the properties of different types of data yielded by the types of questions or data collection methods are essential to understanding whether the analyses undertaken were appropriate. These topics are discussed in greater detail in later chapters, but the following illustration will help make the point. Suppose a survey question asked respondents to indicate their age by checking a category from among the following choices: less than 18, 18–24, 25–34, 35–44, 45–54, 55 and older. An analysis that reported an "average" age of 35, based on this data, would be inaccurate because means cannot be computed on the basis of categorical data. Only counts and percentages would be appropriate to report.

The degree of error allowed by the researcher is also critically important in judging the accuracy of the research. A survey that is purported to be accurate to within "plus or minus 10 percent" indicates a high tolerance of error. Suppose the survey found that 54 percent of the population was in favor of stricter political advertising regulations. In reality, the "true" attitude of the population could be anywhere between 44 percent and 64 percent in favor of stricter control, which is quite different!

3.3f Data Interpretation

Interpretation of some forms of data is highly subjective, such as the various forms of qualitative data that will be discussed in Chapter 4. When subjectivity is introduced into the data interpretation process, the accuracy of the results can vary considerably, depending on who interprets the results. For example, one form of qualitative data asks consumers to tell stories about products or consumption situations. Two psychologists trained in different schools of thought could realistically interpret the same story as having different meanings.

3.4 Key Uses of Secondary Data

LEARNING OBJECTIVE 3.2
Identify key uses of secondary data.

Despite the disadvantages just cited, secondary data is important and useful to companies. It provides information that sometimes is impossible for a company to collect itself. It can also save thousands of dollars and provide quality information sooner than conducting primary research. At times, secondary research may even be superior to data a company can collect through primary research. Figure 3.6 identifies the key uses for secondary data.

3.4a Exploratory Research and Preparing Primary Research

As presented in Chapter 2, secondary data is often used for exploratory research and as preparation for primary research. When a company doesn't really know the problem it is facing, or needs additional information to determine the problem, exploratory research and secondary data can be helpful. In preparing a primary research study, secondary data

- Exploratory research
- Preparation for primary research
- Identifying consumer trends
- Industry information
- Estimating demand
- Selecting target markets, trade areas and sites
- Measuring advertising exposure
- Database marketing
- Data mining
- Behavioral targeting of online advertising

FIGURE 3.6 Key Uses for Secondary Data

can provide excellent background information and guide the primary research process. It can help the researcher decide the best research design, how to word questions, or suggest potential sampling sources (such as databases, panels, and lists). Rather than create an entirely new research design or questionnaire, researchers would do well to review secondary data for information on how previous research was conducted and to understand where improvements need to be made.

3.4b Identifying Consumer Trends

Secondary data is excellent for identifying consumer trends. *Food Service Director* is one of many trade magazines serving the restaurant and food service industry. Staff writers keep pace with trends based on industry news sources or studies and summarize results and implications for their readers. For example, a recent article recounted how plant-based foods were becoming more popular among consumers in general, and presented five recipes for "plant-forward" foods. Another article discussed menu trends for the upcoming year, citing needs for high-protein, portable foods, eating on-the-go, adding ancient grains in food bowls, and more authentic ethnic food.[7]

A Gallup telephone poll conducted in August of 2019, surveyed 1,525 consumers 18 years or age or older to learn more about their restaurant habits.[8] The results are displayed in Figure 3.7. More than 50 percent of U.S. adults 18 or older eat out at a restaurant at least once a week, while 37 percent order restaurant food for takeout or delivery at least one a week.

A more comprehensive study of restaurant trends was compiled by the National Restaurant Association, a key trade association serving the industry. Among other topics, the report identified food and menu trends. This information can be used by restaurant managers to guide their operations as well as marketing programs. The following trends were identified in the report:

- Consumers' desire for sustainable business practices, such as hyper-local sourcing and zero-waste cooking, are likely to impact menu offerings and operational practices.

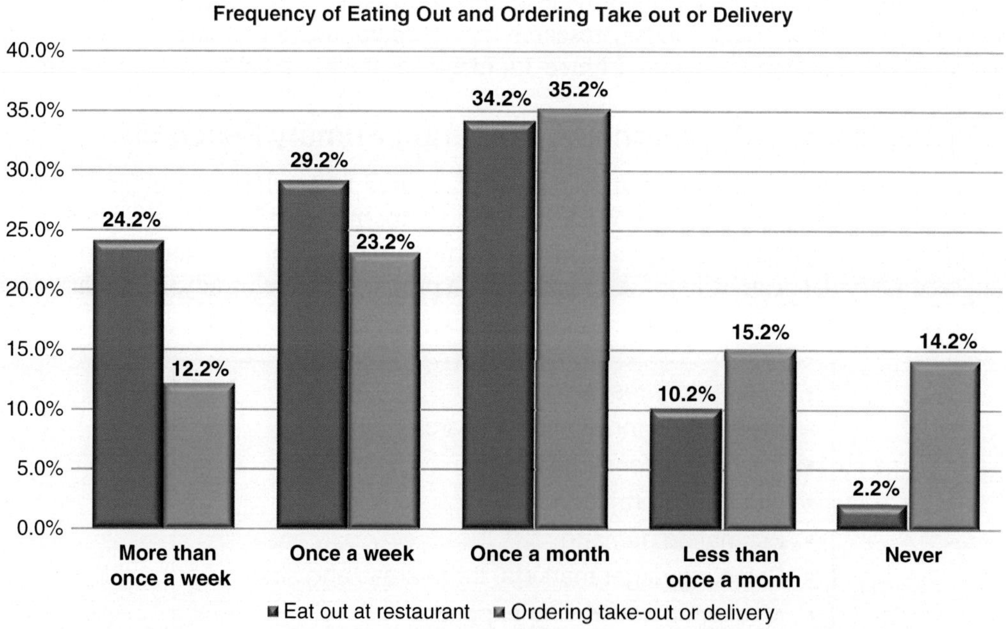

FIGURE 3.7 Bar Chart Showing the Frequency of Eating Out at Restaurants and Ordering Take-out or Delivery from Restaurants
Source: Adapted from "How Do US Consumers Get Their Food?" *eMarketer*, https://chart-na2.emarketer.com/230576/how-do-us-consumers-their-food-of-respondents-by-frequency-of-method-july-2019, accessed on October 28, 2019.

- Natural ingredients and healthy food will continue to be important, and a greater demand is expected for "veggie-forward" cuisines.
- The desire for locally sourced, eco-friendly, healthy food influences the choice of restaurant for many consumers.
- The meal kit trend is presenting new opportunities for restaurants. Consumers are now interested in purchasing food and ingredients from their favorite restaurant, with instructions on how to replicate their favorite dishes at home.[9]
- In a related study, chefs who were surveyed felt that cannabis/CBD oil-infused drinks and food would be a top trend for 2019, along with globally inspired breakfast dishes and kid meals.[10]

Marketing to the majority of adults has become more challenging, as they continue to turn away from network and cable-TV shows in favor of on-demand TV and videos. Young consumers are predicted to the key to building future business, and restaurants plan on using social media and online marketing to reach these coveted consumers.[11]

3.4c Obtain Industry Information

Another use of secondary information is to obtain industry information such as sales, market share, and competitive position. One source for the restaurant industry is *QSR Magazine*. Recently, data for the top 50 quick-service restaurants (QSR) was published. The data includes U.S. system-wide sales, average sales per unit, number of franchised units, number of company units, total units, and total change in units over the previous year. Figure 3.8 is a graph of the system-wide sales for the top 10 QSRs. McDonald's has sales almost three times its closest competitor, Starbuck's.

Other industry information that was reported by *QSR Magazine* included the news that Burger King became the second best-selling burger chain, overtaking Wendy's and topping a billion dollars in sales for the first time. Chick-Fil-A averaged the highest per store sales at $4,090,900, with Whataburger ($2,775,430) and Panera Bread ($2,693,90) a

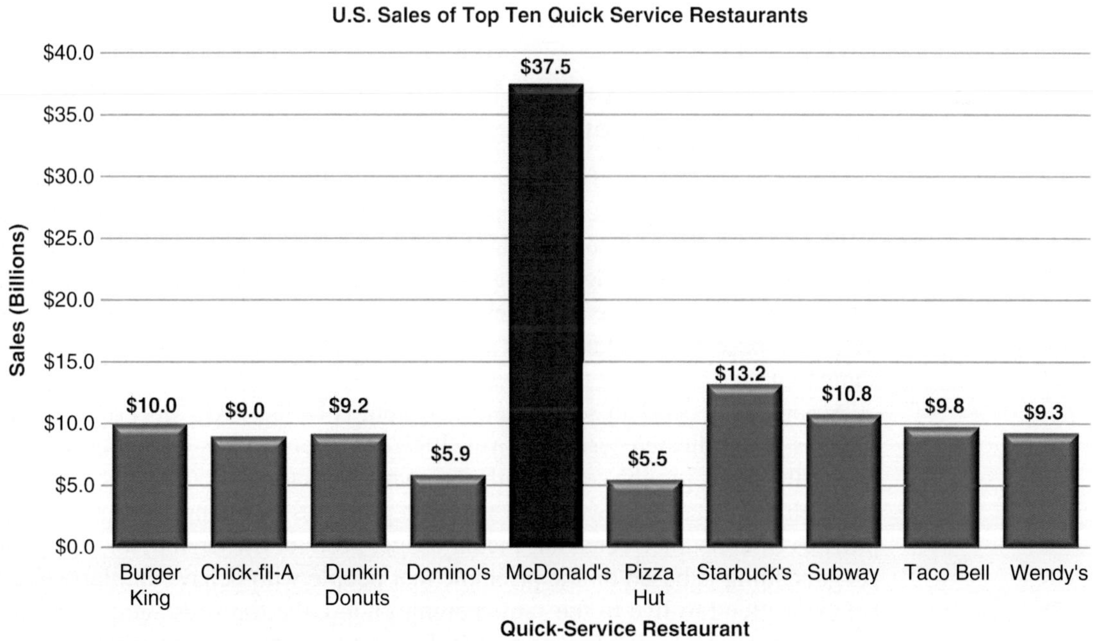

FIGURE 3.8 Sales Data (in billions) for the Top Ten Quick-Service Restaurants
Source: Adapted from "The QSR 50," *QSR Magazine*, http://pdf.qsrmagazine.com/QSR+50+Charts+2008-2018.pdf?AWSAccessKeyId=0VD405H56VDT0B0JCY82&Expires=1561560940&Signature=uhW2laXwFb3%2BkOxcx6VlfXcEwQ8%3D, accessed April 29, 2019.

distant second and third. The fastest growing chains are Moe's Southwest Grill and Jersey Mike's, with respect to growth rate, though Starbucks added the most new stores (758) compared to the previous year. Finally, though number three in terms of overall sales on the top 50 list, Subway closed 866 stores, a 3.34 percent decline over the previous year. Noodles & Co unit growth decline was the most severe of the top 50, as they closed 11.3 percent of their units, while Steak 'n Shake wasn't far behind, closing 11.15 percent of the restaurants that had been open the previous year. This type of information can be used by quick service restaurants to determine their position in the market and to develop marketing strategies.[12]

3.4d Estimating Demand

Secondary data are often used to estimate demand. Demographic information from government sources such as the U.S. Census Bureau can provide raw numbers in terms of population. Industry reports from providers such as MarketLine, and aggregate data from trade associations, government reports, company annual reports and other sources provide valuable information. Often industry reports provide growth estimates or forecasts for business segments as well as competitive information about revenues and profits of particular businesses.[13] Coupled with sales data from a company's own database, estimates of future demand can be forecasted. This information is then used to set production schedules, determine staffing, and set operating budgets. Many trade associations also provide data on sales, market share, and even market potential. For instance, *The Restaurant, Food & Beverage Market Research Handbook* provides sales data for various types of restaurants and the changes in sales during the last year, and over the last 10 years. This information can be used by a company to estimate their demand for the upcoming year. *Sales & Marketing Management's Survey of Buying Power* provides subscribers with statistics, such as effective buying income (EBI) and the buying power index (BPI), for counties and media markets located throughout the U.S. Purchasing data, rankings, and demographics are also provided. The Bureau of Labor Statistics Consumer Expenditure Survey reports consumer spending in food, housing, apparel and services, transportation, healthcare, and entertainment product categories. As demographic data is also collected, marketers can estimate aggregate expenditures for key product categories by age, income, race, or other key variables.

3.4e Selection of Target Markets, Trade Areas, and Facility Locations

Secondary data are beneficial in the selection of target markets, trade areas, and facility location sites. Not only can companies obtain population figures, they can also obtain maps with population densities shown. A number of companies specialize in **geocoding**, which involves combining geographic information with demographic and psychographic information. This can be extremely valuable for companies wanting to locate the right customer base for a retail outlet or even for developing an advertising or direct mail campaign.

Geocoding a secondary data compilation process which involves combining geographic information with demographic and psychographic information.

A popular geocoding segmentation system is called PRIZM® Premier. Developed by Claritas, a syndicated research firm, PRIZM® Premier has currently identified 68 different lifestage groups, each with its own characteristics. Claritas uses both original research and data from over forty research partners, including Nielsen, to create detailed profiles of consumer behavior, media usage, product ownership, and technology habits. As geocoding is based on the principle that people who behave similarly and share characteristics tend to live in the same neighborhood, the top lifestage groups are identified for each zip code in the United States. For instance, in Dallas, Texas the zip code 80205 consists of lifestage groups named the Cosmopolitans, the Connected Bohemians, Young Digerati, Aspiring A-Listers, and American Dreams. The Cosmopolitans are described as highly educated upscale urbanites, working in management and professional careers. They own their own homes, have a median household income of $80,518, and are more likely to own an Audi, attend College sporting events, and eat at Starbucks when compared to the U.S. population. Individuals between the ages of 25–44 make up the largest age segment, and tend to be concentrated in areas where social activities are prevalent.[14]

For local geographic data, traffic counts can be obtained from most state's Departments of Transportation for major streets or highways. Traffic counts may be helpful in selecting the location for a restaurant or retail store. These data will tell a business how many vehicles and what types of vehicles pass certain points on a road. For downtown locations, pedestrian traffic counts may be important. Companies rely heavily on secondary data from transportation departments at the state and local level in choosing site locations.

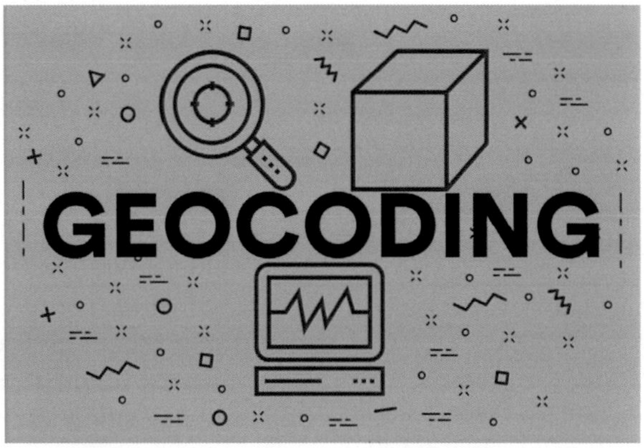

Source: OpturaDesign/Shutterstock.

Geocoding can be extremely valuable for companies wanting to locate the right customer base for a retail outlet or even for developing an advertising or direct mail campaign.

3.4f Measuring Advertising Exposure and Effectiveness

Advertising agencies and companies use syndicated secondary data to measure ad exposure and effectiveness. According to Media Dynamics, the average consumer is exposed to 362 branded messages daily, though only 12 are worthy of attention.[15] The most well-known source of advertising exposure data is Nielsen Media Research, which produces weekly Nielsen ratings for television and radio. The ratings tell companies how many people were tuned into a specific TV program or radio station at a particular time and thus how many potentially saw or heard the advertisement. Nielsen ratings are one of the sources television programs use to determine advertising rates. The higher the Nielsen rating, the more it will cost to advertise on the program, since more individuals are exposed to the ad. Nielsen also produces ratings and measures of effectiveness for digital ads. Similar figures can be obtained from other agencies for magazines (Starch Research, www.starchresearch.com). GfK Mediamark Research & Intelligence provides comprehensive information on consumer use of magazine, cable, and internet websites for specific brands, activities, and usage situations.

3.4g Database Marketing and Data Mining

Database marketing programs utilize secondary data. It can be internal data from a company's own database or it might be data purchased through one of the database marketing firms. For example, to receive a player card, casino patrons must first complete a questionnaire in which they provide contact information, demographic characteristics, and answer questions related to lifestyle interests. Patrons present this card whenever they play at the casino, and the player card system tracks and stores records of individual player behaviors related to the type of gaming activity, amount wagered, amount of time spent playing, and related activities (such as dining on premises and use of casino hotel). Using various computer programs, the data can be parsed to include only individuals that fit a specific target profile or meet some other criteria. A casino may want to target "high rollers" who like country and western music with an offer of a free hotel room and complimentary tickets to a Garth Brooks concert to entice them to "stay and play."

Source: Andy Shell/Shutterstock.

Greater privacy restrictions are under consideration in the U.S. at the state level which will impact programmatic advertising and online behavioral advertising, including the California Consumer Privacy Act which many have likened to a "mini-GDPR."

Secondary data is used for **data mining**, which is the process of scanning and analyzing data to uncover patterns or trends. Many companies now have large databases of customers with millions of records. These can be mined in various ways. They can provide a profile of a firm's best customers. They can indicate which products people tend to purchase together. For retail stores, they can provide information on what merchandise to stock and when it is usually sold.

Data mining the process of scanning and analyzing data to uncover patterns or trends.

3.4h Behavioral Targeting of Online Advertising

Behavioral targeting uses consumers' online behavioral data and some offline secondary data to display relevant advertising and marketing messages, and personalized content such as product recommendations.

Onsite behavioral targeting occurs within a particular website as part of the website's personalization strategy.

Network behavioral targeting collects and shares non-personally identifiable data across multiple Internet sites, and categorizes the consumers based on interests, purchase intent, and other factors.

Programmatic advertising automated software-based advertising auction system.

Behavioral targeting uses consumers' online behavioral data and some offline secondary data to display relevant advertising and marketing messages, and personalized content such as product recommendations. Which websites are visited, what videos are watched, what brands or product categories are viewed, the time spent viewing websites or pages, and whether individuals search, shop, or simply surf from website to website are among the behavioral forms of online data that make behavioral targeting possible. Offline data may include secondary data such as information purchased from data warehouses, store loyalty programs or credit card companies, as well as data found in public records.[16]

Onsite behavioral targeting occurs within a particular website as part of the website's personalization strategy. Amazon uses onsite behavioral targeting to track the webpages visited by consumers within Amazon's site, to suggest products purchased by other users who also purchased items being considered by those who search its website, or to make personalized recommendations based on the visitor's past sales history. The suggestions and personalized content result from data mining of internal information. Data mining is limited to the context of the visitor's current onsite searching or browsing behavior, in this case, Amazon's past sales data for both the visitor and for other customers who have purchased the same and similar items. Given the data used for onsite behavioral targeting, websites often know personally identifiable information for past customers, such as names and addresses, which may raise privacy concerns among some users. However, websites that use onsite behavioral targeting typically adhere to strict privacy policies that prevent the sharing of customer information with advertising networks or other partners, at least without express permission on the part of the consumer.[17]

Unlike onsite behavioral targeting, **network behavioral targeting** collects and shares non-personally identifiable data across multiple Internet sites, and categorizes the consumers based on interests, purchase intent, and other factors. Examples of online advertising networks include Advertising.com, AdKnowledge, SmartyAds, Clicksor, AdBlade and AdMaven, to name just a few. Some networks add offline public record information from the DMV or voter registration bureau, while others add secondary data purchased from credit card companies, so while not all networks may share personally identifiable information, many still collect it and use it as the basis for serving ads. Consumers might also be tracked via IP addresses, device specific IDs, or cookies that are installed on their computer (often without their knowledge). Network behavioral targeting makes assumptions about consumers' characteristics and interests based on their searching and surfing behavior, and then delivers ads that match the interests identified. For example, if a user was tracked visiting a woman's clothing site, a candle website, and visited several webpages related to make-up and hair care products, the software would profile that user as a woman. If a user visited the American Kennel Club, a Pug animal rescue website, and the local animal shelter, it is likely that ads related to dog products would begin to appear on future websites in order to provide relevant marketing messages.[18]

Recently, online behavioral advertising has exploded, in part due to programmatic advertising. **Programmatic advertising** is an automated software-based advertising auction system. The process outlined in **Figure 3.9** takes only microseconds to achieve, so that visitors to a web page see the "winning" ad as the page loads. Unfortunately, programmatic advertising raises privacy concerns, as businesses involved at any step of the process may place tracers or cookies on the consumer's computer to collect data. The number of entities involved in a single page load can be astounding. *Bloomberg Businessweek* reported that a visit to a U.S. news-based website resulted in 20 auction requests being sent to 10 different advertising networks, with each network likely offering the ad impression to hundreds of different advertisers. The single visit also resulted in 47 cookies with unique tracking characteristics that attempted to identify the consumer's likes and dislikes, and demographics based on future browsing behavior.[19]

Consumers take threats to their privacy seriously, and are increasingly blocking online ads. In the U.S., more than 70 million people will block ads in 2019, an increase of more

- Consumer clicks on a web page
- Website publisher (or network) places ad impression up for auction
- Auction is held among advertisers interested in ad impression based on consumer profile
- Advertiser who bids the most for that ad impression wins right to display their ad
- Ad is delivered to page viewed by consumer
- Customer (hopefully) clicks on ad, and ad links to advertiser's website jump page

FIGURE 3.9 Programmatic Advertising Process
Source: Adapted from Robert Allen, "How Programmatic Advertising Works", July 31, 2018, https://www.smartinsights.com/internet-advertising/internet-advertising-targeting/what-is-programmatic-marketing/, accessed April November 4, 2019.

than 5 percent when compared to 2018. eMarketer predicts that by 2021, twenty-seven percent of the population (78.6 million people) will be using software on their computer and mobile devices to delete advertising content from apps and web pages.[20]

While ad-blocking is bad news for marketers in general, researchers are more concerned about consumer's increased frustration with behavioral advertising, and how this may impact the industry's ability to collect data. The Internet Innovation Alliance (IAA) and Civic Science surveyed consumers in April of 2019 regarding their thoughts on data privacy, online data collection, and online advertising. The results were far from reassuring for researchers:[21]

- Fifty-four percent of respondents strongly agreed that they were concerned with how technology and social media firms used their online and location data for commercial purposes. Twenty-two percent somewhat agreed with the same statement.
- Forty-eight percent strongly agreed that there should be a national policy for data privacy in the U.S., while an additional 24 percent somewhat agreed.
- Only 3 percent strongly agreed that they were okay with the collection and use of personal data for making online advertising content and searches more relevant to them, while 56 percent strongly disagreed with this same statement.

The latter finding is particularly important, as marketers have long defended behavioral advertising on the premise that it makes advertising more relevant for the consumer and is thus beneficial. That argument seems to have little merit. When privacy concerns are combined with consistent complaints that ads slow devices and web page load times while consuming limited mobile data, and sometimes delivering malware, it's easy to see why consumers aren't happy with the online advertising industry.

Greater privacy restrictions are on the horizon. Browsers such as Chrome and Safari have added features to limit the worst and most intrusive ads. After being heavily criticized for allowing Cambridge Analytica to collect well over 50 million Facebook profiles without alerting its social media users, Facebook has since ended many partnerships with firms that previously combined Facebook data, data with credit card transactions, and other sources of online and offline customer data. More firms will likely follow suit, as they attempt to comply with the European Union's General Data Protection Regulation.[22] While there is no single national privacy policy in place for the U.S. as of spring 2020, a number of states have privacy bills in the works. The most restrictive is the California Consumer Privacy Act that goes into effect in January of 2020. The bill has been characterized as a "mini-GDPR" in that California residents will enjoy access and control over their personal information to a broad extent, while businesses that violate privacy or

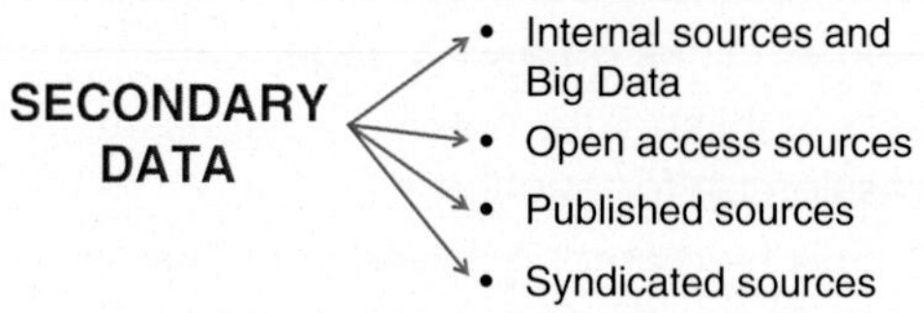

FIGURE 3.10 Primary Source Categories of Secondary Data

suffer data breaches will be subject to punitive financial penalties, and notification obligations.[23] These changes will impact the collection, sharing, and usage of secondary data.

In conducting marketing research, secondary data should never be overlooked. It is an excellent place to start a research project. It is cheaper and quicker. It may provide the information that is needed. If not, secondary data can provide clues or information on how best to conduct additional research.

3.5 Sources of Secondary Data

Secondary data can be obtained from a number of different sources and, with the Internet, is often readily accessible. The primary source categories of secondary data are shown in **Figure 3.10**. The best source depends on the type of information needed, how quickly the information is needed, and if the firm has a budget to purchase secondary data.

3.5a Internal Sources and Big Data

LEARNING OBJECTIVE 3.3
Describe how internal sources of data and big data can be used for secondary research.

Keep in mind that any internal data that has been collected for a purpose other than the current study is secondary data. Even a primary research project that involved data collection just a month ago is secondary data if it was not specifically collected for the current research agenda. Past marketing decisions, sales data, cost data, customer data from the company's database, and internal accounting system data are all secondary data.

Many research studies are undertaken for the purpose of deciding how best to market a good or service. An important form of internal secondary data to be examined in such cases relates to past marketing decisions. Budget allocations by media type, advertising campaign themes, sales force quotas, allocation of sales forces across geographic territories and the like are just some of the factors which might be examined, particularly when considered in conjunction with the outcomes resulting from these decisions.

Rather than conduct primary research or hire a marketing research firm, a number of marketing and management questions can be answered with a company's sales data. If collected and stored correctly, sales data can be used to:

- Build a profile of a firm's customer base or its best customers.
- Determine the profile of customers who purchase a particular product.
- Geographically locate particular types of customers for a variety of marketing programs, such as billboard locations, radio advertising campaigns, or a couponing campaign.
- Identify the best prospects for cross-selling of other products.
- Determine the best channel of communication with customers, or the best channel of distribution.
- Determine the most profitable segments of customers to pursue.
- Determine the best social media venues to use to engage consumers with the brand.
- Identify the most effective digital marketing strategies.

For retail stores, sales data obtained through their own checkout scanners can provide considerable information that can be used for marketing and merchandising decisions. If the store has loyalty cards where the data can be tied to specific customers, it becomes even more valuable. Retailers can use the information to determine what products are often purchased together, then use cross-promotions to encourage purchases. The store can also place items close together that tend to be purchased within the same shopping trip. Special promotions, coupons and point-of-purchase displays can be tested for effectiveness. For retail chains, a number of marketing programs can be tested in various stores and then compared to stores that use a different marketing program or none at all.

Companies that maintain a customer marketing database have an advantage when it comes to secondary internal data. A marketing database is different from an accounting database. An **accounting database** contains a record of customer transactions, follows the rules of accounting, and is used for accounting purposes. A **marketing database** contains records of customers that involve communication interactions, demographic profiles, and any other information that a company has collected or purchased from an independent marketing data research firm.

Accounting database database containing a record of customer transactions which follows the rules of accounting and is used for accounting purposes.

Marketing databases allow researchers to investigate a number of additional questions not possible with accounting data only. A company can examine the various methods customers use to interact with the firm. These can be analyzed further to determine the best channels of communication for various target segments. Demographic profiles and, if it is in the database, even psychographic, behavioral, and attitudinal information can be tied together to create a much richer description of a firm's market segments. How much can be done with a firm's marketing database is determined, of course, by the amount of data it contains and the flexibility of the software used to access the data.

Marketing database database containing records of customers that involve communication interactions, demographic profiles, and any other information that company has collected or purchased from an independent marketing data research firm.

Tying the accounting and marketing databases together allows a researcher to identify various characteristics of market segments based on actual purchases. Rather than arbitrarily selecting the "best" marketing segment for a product, a firm can use the marketing database to systematically determine who is purchasing the product and the characteristics of those buyers. This profile can be valuable for advertising purposes because it will allow advertising agencies and individuals designing ads to better understand the type of consumer who is purchasing the product.

A primary advantage of using internal data first is that it is readily and easily accessible. More important, it provides information about a firm's own customers. If the research agenda involves comparisons with non-customers, then it will be necessary to go beyond a firm's own internal sources. It may, however, be possible to use the firm's internal data for its customers and then purchase data on non-customers to match and compare.

The advancement of machine learning and artificial intelligence, combined with increased computer processing speed and cost effective data warehousing options has allowed many companies to build massive internal databases containing terabytes of information. **Big data** refers to extremely large data sets holding structured and unstructured data that are analyzed to reveal patterns, trends, and associations, especially those related to human behavior and interactions. These data sets are composed of internal information and observation data gathered from social media and Web analytics, though other forms of secondary information may be added over time. Unstructured data may come from integrating written comments, reviews, photos or video transcripts found on social media sites run by the firm or pertaining to the company or its brands. Customer behavioral data, including purchase histories are also added to many internal databases and linked to customer profiles. Past research studies, Web site analytics, internal marketing performance metrics, customer service records, loyalty card data and other forms of secondary data discussed later in the chapter could be part of the big data held by a firm as well. Thus, big data generally begins with internal data, but encompasses any and all data the firm eventually collects.

Big data extremely large data sets holding structured and unstructured data that are analyzed to reveal patterns, trends, and associations, especially those related to human behavior and interactions.

Proponents argue that big data analytics allow for deeper insights into data at the consumer, brand, store, and transaction level, though this requires a strong software product to manage, organize and mine the data. For example, Walmart was able to drill down through billions of data points to the store and product level to determine why avocado sales were below the norm for a given day in a particular town in Texas. The answer—a major store was out of inventory! Problem-solving at the granular level is a key benefit of big data analytics. Broader insights are also possible because of the richness of detail provided by unstructured data via social media comments, open-ended survey question responses, customer reviews, customer service transcripts, video transcripts and more, in addition to the structured data found in quantitative surveys. Insights become more accurate as the additional data provides a better understanding of the complex conditions surrounding the topic of study.[24] When the proper software tools are in place, big data analytics can also reduce costs and increase the speed of insight delivery.

Despite the potential benefits of big data, there are challenges. Many firms are becoming overwhelmed as they gather too much data from too many sources too quickly using automated processes and social media listening tools. In fact, IBM predicted that "knowledge will double every 11 to 12 hours" by 2020.[25] It is easy to see how decision-making may ground to a halt when efforts to verify the accuracy and relevancy of the data cannot keep pace with the constant influx of new information.[26] One recourse is to outsource the collection and analysis of data to a big data analytics firm that has the computing power and advanced software analytical tools capable of real-time processing. Others in the industry argue that the time of collecting and hoarding any and all forms" of information may be waning, and that a more minimalistic approach to data collection and storage may be warranted in the future. **Data minimalism** is a philosophy that examines data collection from the user perspective, and strives to assure that every piece of data collected and stored is not only in the consumer's best interest, but is helpful in driving business outcomes. When evaluating whether to collect or hold data, businesses should consider their liability in case of a data breach, as well as the degree to which the firm is capable of complying with consumer's right to access and other regulatory requirements.[27]

Data minimalism a philosophy that examines data collection from the user perspective and strives to assure that the data collected and stored is in the consumer's best interest and is helpful in driving business outcomes.

The greatest challenge on the horizon revolves around data ownership and changing privacy regulations. Consumers want ownership and control over their own data be it past, present, or future. Firms that maintain big data on internal servers may find themselves rethinking their data collection policies and storage practices. Under many of the new and proposed privacy laws, each additional piece of information linked to a profile or some form of personally identifiable information increases the firm's risk of violating current or future privacy regulations. Many within the industry are looking to cryptographic techniques and blockchain technologies as a potential solution. These technologies will allow consumers to take back ownership of their personal information and allow consumers to store data on their own their own devices. Consumers would have the power to keep sensitive data away from commercial databases, businesses, and research entities, absolving firms of the responsibilities entailed with owning personally identifiable or sensitive information. Of course, that creates its own challenges, as researchers would be tasked with finding new ways of engaging qualified research participants, and encouraging them to share the very information they want to hold private.[28]

3.5b Open Access Sources of Secondary Data

LEARNING OBJECTIVE 3.4
Describe the open access sources of secondary data.

As shown in **Figure 3.11**, open access sources of secondary data include government sources, online blogs, social media networks, website analytics, and independent websites. Most of this information is free and available to the public. A few organizations, however, charge a subscription fee to access the data, or at least for some of the more detailed data.

Government Sources The federal, state, county, and local governments produce volumes of data and secondary information. The most well-known and used data are the

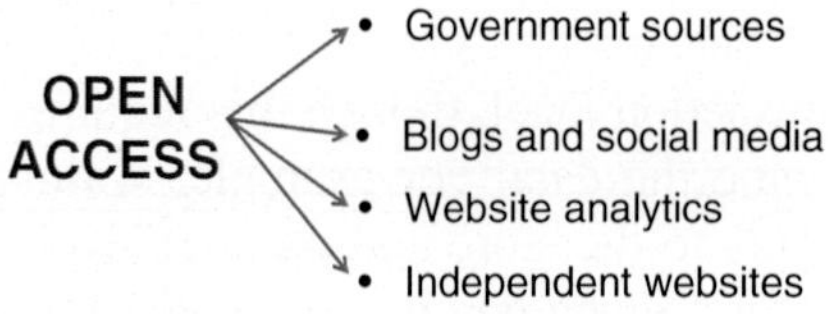

FIGURE 3.11 Open Access Sources of Secondary Data

various census and economic data. Every ten years the United States takes a census of the population and aggregates the data at www.census.gov. The data can be examined and sorted on the website in various ways and also downloaded into Excel spreadsheet files. This demographic information is valuable in developing sales potential forecasts and looking at market size. In addition to population demographics, the Census Bureau also contains business information. This type of information is useful for business-to-business operations.

An excellent starting point for secondary research into government data, reports, and information is USASearch.gov at www.fedworld .gov. It is operated by the United States Department of Commerce and is the gateway to government publications and data. Researchers can search over 30 million government web pages through www.fedworld .gov, which eliminates the need to search individual federal government agency pages. If desired, individuals can gain access to key agencies and federal topic sites through the USASearch.gov website. Any data, report, or information that is made publicly available at a federal agency can be accessed in some way through this site.

Source: Jer123/Shutterstock.

The Department of Commerce is an example of an open-access government source that provides business, trade and economic data and forecasts through the Stat-USA.gov website.

Another site operated by the Department of Commerce that deals specially with data is Stat-USA (www.stat-usa.gov). The site is a single point of access to business, trade, and economic data that is produced by the federal government. It contains over 50,000 current and historical statistical releases, state and regional statistical reports, forecasts, and financial data.

Blogs and Social Media Blogs and social media are a second major source of open access secondary data and information. The Internet provides a wealth of information. The challenge is sifting through it to locate data that are accurate, relevant, and useful.

Blogs are regularly updated webpages containing online discussions or musings. Blogs are typically run by organizations, small groups, or an individual. But, researchers should not be too quick to dismiss them as personal opinions and, therefore, unreliable sources of information. The usefulness of blogs is partly determined by who posted it and how the blog is run. A blog may be the thoughts of a single individual on a particular topic, or it might be maintained by a company. Some blogs allow browsers to post comments, and add files and links. For others, only the administrator can post.

Blogs regularly updated webpages containing online discussions or musings.

The first task in determining the viability of a blog is to determine who posted it and why. Blogs sponsored by companies tend to be more viable than blogs written by individuals. The Nielsen Insights blog provides snippets of information from more comprehensive Nielsen research studies. Blogs provided by trade associations or industry experts that allow browsers to post responses usually are there to seek input and, as such, often can provide more useful information than a blog written by an individual who is simply musing about their everyday life and opinions. The second task is to determine if the information in the blog is that of a single individual (or company) or if it is information that can be supported in some scientific or statistical manner.

Suppose a marketing researcher wants to collect secondary information on the effectiveness of e-mail for a financial service firm. In conducting research on the Internet, a blog is found about e-mail marketing written by Steven MacDonald. In his blog, he states that in 2018, on average, 24.88 percent of emails were opened, meaning that the reader either clicks on the email or displays the email in full with images, in the preview pane.[29]

Can the researcher use this data to support a decision to use an e-mail marketing campaign? Further investigation of the site determines Mr. MacDonald is an employee of the firm that markets SuperOffice, which is a customer relationship management software solution. The statistics he states certainly support a decision to use an e-mail marketing campaign. That is one of the services his CRM solution offers. No citation or information is given in the blog about the origin of the statistics. Was it collected internally by the firm, or was it collected by an independent third party? Without further information, it would be difficult to rely on this information since the writer of the blog has a personal incentive in showing e-mail is an effective online marketing tool. It may very well be valid, but there is no way to know without additional research.

Further investigation reveals that by following various links, users can download the *2019 Email Marketing Benchmark Report* which contains more current information than that found in the blog. Here the reader learns that a firm called Sign-up. To the parent firm marketing the SuperOffice CRM product conducted a study in which they analyzed over 1 billion emails sent through their software between January 1st and December 31st of 2018. More importantly, one learns that the firm is based in the United Kingdom, not the United States, and that emails were delivered primarily to throughout the United Kingdom. If marketing to the United Kingdom, this would be good news, as the data would be highly relevant. But, if the researcher was interested in marketing in the United States, the data would be of less value, as people in the United States may not respond to email in a similar fashion as those do in the United Kingdom. It would be risky to generalize the results of the study to the U.S., as culture and other factors may influence email usage to a different degree in the United Kingdom when compared to the United States.[30]

In contrast, consider the information found on the Campaign Monitor blog website. The blog reports email benchmarks for open rates, unsubscribe rates, click-to-open rate, and bounce rates, organized by industry and day of the week. It offers recommendations on how to use benchmarks to improve email marketing efforts, and provides insights into the best and worst days for email marketing.[31] More importantly, one is able to download the full *2019 Marketing Benchmark Report*, which describes the study methodology and contains a glossary of key terms. The report reveals that data collection occurred in 40 countries during the 2018 calendar year. In the United States, the average open-rate was 24.7 percent, while the click-thru rate increased from 3 percent in 2017 to 3.6 percent in 2018.The average open-rate for emails sent by banks and financial service firms was 25.3 percent, though transactional emails such as password resets and order confirmations had a higher open rate (43.8 percent) than did marketing messages (23.8 percent). Industry data was reported for the entire sample, and not by country. While the banking and financial services industry data is not entirely specific to the U.S., at least some of the data is from the United States, and it may be possible to learn more by contacting a sales representative at Campaign Monitor directly.[32]

The moral of the story is that when using blogs, it is important to evaluate them carefully. Using multiple blogs and tracing a study back to its origins, as in this example, is one way to ensure that the information is valid and not just the opinion of an individual. The date of the posting must also be taken into consideration. To increase confidence in the effectiveness of an e-mail campaign, further research could be conducted using other types of sources, such as articles from journals in the library, or a search for relevant statistics at eMarketer.com or through the Statista database.

Social media and Twitter can be used to gather secondary information, although it will typically be qualitative in nature. Some quantitative data may be available. For instance, one of the fast food restaurants, such as KFC or Burger King, could look at the volume of mentions on social media sites following the launch of a new sandwich or menu item. However, the extent to which useful information can be obtained for research purposes via social media is debatable, and may vary by brand or industry as well as the capabilities of the analytic software. To discover true marketing insights, more advanced analytical capabilities are necessary that go beyond mere counts. Fortunately, technological advances provide that possibility. A study conducted over the five-day period encompassing Thanksgiving demonstrated the power of "listening" when an advanced enterprise software solution was used. The purpose of the study was to understand consumer sentiment and purchase behavior as it related to the Thanksgiving holiday. Using the keyword "Thanksgiving," over four million tweets were analyzed by a software solution which built topics around tweets that were conceptually related. While food was of course a popular topic, 13 percent of the conversations revolved around what type of clothing to wear. Comfort, rather than fashion, was overwhelmingly desired, as leggings and sweatpants were mentioned most often. The study also identified that stress, family, and Thanksgiving were highly related concepts. This type of insight can be valuable to marketers of pain relievers in developing a real-time campaign showing how the pain reliever can help people "get through" the stress of the holidays. Execution of real-time marketing efforts would require at least one person to constantly track the trends, topics, and related concepts found by the software and then immediately initiate an ad or social media campaign.[33]

Most companies now hire individuals to monitor the Internet, especially social media pages, to see what consumers are saying about their brand. Web-scanning software allows researchers to follow conversations on the Internet and to be alerted every time a company's name or particular brand name is mentioned in any social media platform. Mentions can be tabulated if a company just wants to know the volume of online chatter. As previously discussed, identifying relationships between topics provides more detailed information on what individuals are saying and how they feel about a particular company or brand. These insights can then lead to opportunities for real-time marketing campaigns as well as traditional or digital campaigns.

Website Analytics Another important open access source of secondary data is **web analytics**, or information resulting from the analysis of various data, or metrics, collected from a website. A **metric** is a standard of measurement such as a count, percentage, or average. By combining and analyzing various metrics, website analytics can provide valuable information about web traffic, trends and visitor characteristics or behavior at company and brand websites. Figure 3.12 provides examples of various metrics that companies can use.

Web analytics information resulting from the logical analysis of various data, or metrics, collected from a website.

Metric a standard of measurement such as counts, percentages, or averages.

Summary metrics examine website traffic and are good measures when a firm's objective is to drive consumers to its website. Action metrics, on the other hand, examine actions a web visitor takes. The top provider of these types of analytics is Google. With the insertion of HTML code on each page of the website, Google Analytics provides rich insight into who's visiting the website and the effectiveness of various marketing initiatives. The easy-to-use interface makes Google Analytics practical for even small business owners with little website expertise.

Independent Websites The last open access source of secondary data is independent websites. Researchers can access literally thousands of independent websites. Most will not be of value. Some, however, can provide useful information. As with blogs, it is important to determine whose website it is and what purpose it fulfills, and if the information on the site is viable. An advertising agency that specializes in guerilla marketing will probably have information about the effectiveness of guerilla marketing and how it

Summary Metrics	Action Metrics
• Click-thrus	• Search/information requests
• Visit duration	• Subscriptions (RSS, newsletter)
• Visit frequency & recency	• Downloads/free trials
• Page views	• Contest submissions
• Interactions per visit (pages/session)	• Customer reviews/ratings
• Repeat visit %	• Comments/posts/shares
• New visitor %	• Bookmarking/tagging
• Bounce rate	• Viewing key content
• Engagement	• Placing items in shopping cart
• New/unique conversions	
• Incoming traffic sources	
• Sales	
• Lifetime value	

FIGURE 3.12 Key Metrics Used in Web Analytics

is superior to using traditional marketing channels. How that information is conveyed is important to its usefulness and viability. If the site quotes statistics based on their own research and their own guerilla marketing campaigns, then it is highly likely the data will be biased. If, however, the site has information from independent sources and associations, then the viability increases sharply. A company using third party support for their brand, product, or service is seen as more credible than one that touts itself.

Search engines, such as Google, Bing, and Yahoo, allow researchers to search the Internet. Each search engine uses a slightly different algorithm to locate sites. Since about 93 percent of online experiences begins with a search engine, companies strive to have their name on the first page or at least near the beginning of the results.[34] The process of increasing the probability of a particular company's website emerging from a search is called **search engine optimization (SEO)**. Search engine optimization occurs in one of three ways. First, a *paid search insertion* comes up when certain products or information are sought. Companies can speed this process by registering with various search engines in order to have their site indexed and also by paying a higher placement fee for top positions. The placement of the ad on a search page depends on the price the company pays and the algorithm a search engine uses to determine the advertisement's relevance to a particular search word or phrase.

Search engine optimization (SEO) the process of increasing the probability of a particular company's website emerging from an Internet search.

Display/text search ads are similar to paid search insertions, but appear as text messages or small display ads when phrases searched by the consumer match keywords on which the marketer has bid. Other factors, such as the degree to which the web page content at the destination URL or the ad content itself matches the search phrase, influence how likely it is the ad will display toward the top of the list. The amount that a marketer is willing to pay per click also affects the position in which the ad appears.

The third method of optimization is a *natural* or *organic emergence* of the site. This method involves developing efficient and effective organic results that arise from a natural search process. Each search engine uses a slightly different set of algorithms to identify key phrases that match what was typed into the search box. To be listed first in an organic search requires time and effort. When a website is first launched, it will not emerge at the top of the organic search results. It takes time for the search engine to locate the site. Figure 3.13 illustrates two of these three types of search results when the search term "robotic vacuums" was typed into a search engine.

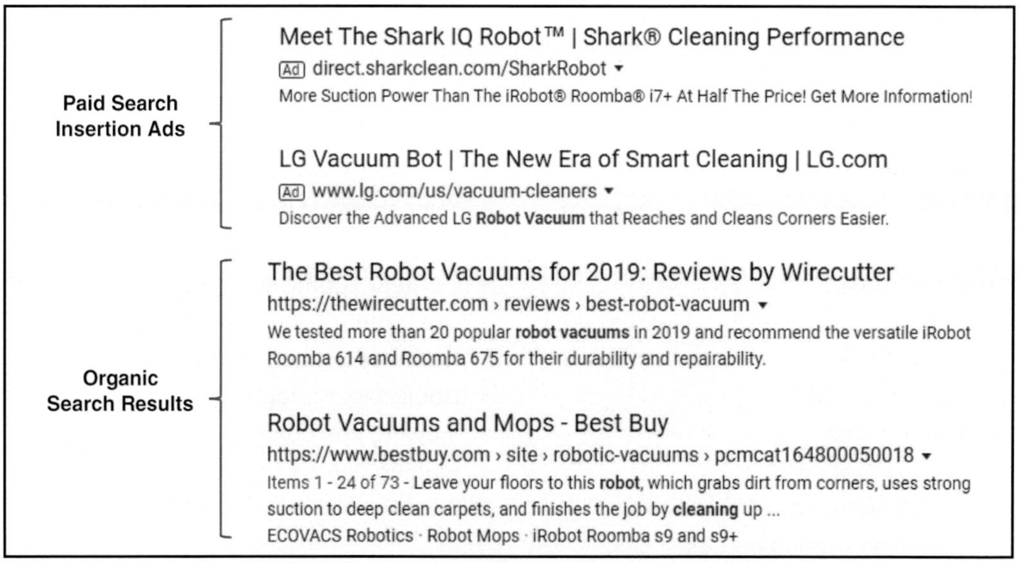

FIGURE 3.13 Illustrates the paid search insertion ads and organic search results when the search term "robotic vacuums" was typed into a search engine. Display ads typically appear at the top of the page, while text ads may be mingled between paid insertion ads and organic search results.

3.5c Published Sources of Secondary Data

LEARNING OBJECTIVE 3.5
Summarize the primary differences among the bibliographic digital databases.

In the past, when searching published sources of secondary data, it was assumed that published sources were print sources. However, the majority of published sources are now available in digital formats. Searching through digital publications is much easier and quicker, as thousands of published works can be searched within seconds by powerful computer search engines. As a result, libraries are moving away from print journals to digital databases that archive thousands of journals and can be searched through a single search engine.

The primary sources for secondary data at libraries now are **bibliographic databases**, which are databases that provide references to magazine, journal, and newspaper articles. In addition to the title and author of the article, most bibliographic databases provide summaries or abstracts and often have a PDF of the entire article. With increased computer storage capabilities and financial arrangements with journals and magazines, full-text articles are now more common. Figure 3.14 identifies some of the major bibliographic databases. Because of the high cost, libraries tend to purchase subscriptions to the databases used most frequently by their patrons rather than subscribe to all of these services.

Bibliographic databases digital databases that provide references to magazine and journal articles.

For business information, ABI/INFORM has been a reliable source. It contains full-text, abstracts, and citations of more than 1,800 academic and general business publications. LexisNexis is a firm offering several databases with full-text articles from newspapers, journals, wire services, newsletters, company reports, SEC filings, case law, public records, government documents, and transcripts of broadcasts. EBSCO is not a database, but an aggregator of full-text content. EBSCO searches over 300 different databases, which includes journals, magazines, books, monographs, reports, and other publications. ProQuest is another digital database with over 125 billion digital pages from newspapers, periodicals, dissertations, and aggregated databases. Similarly, the specialized scholar search available through Google provides access to a variety of academic journal articles, patents, and legal opinions. Using the search function is free, but full-text articles must be purchased.

The key to using bibliographic databases effectively is to develop an understanding of the search process. Each database searches by key words that are typed in by the user. It is important to remember that terminology will vary in articles and with different bibliographic search engines. Using different words or phrases will provide varying results. It is also helpful to pay attention to key words that are listed for articles of interest. These key words can be used to obtain additional related articles on the same topic. The phrasing of key words in a bibliographic database may be different than what the researcher is using. The search syntax specific to a particular database will also influence results.

3.5d Syndicated Sources of Secondary Data

LEARNING OBJECTIVE 3.6
Identify and explain the types of data available from syndicated sources.

A major source of marketing information is syndicated services. As mentioned previously, a syndicated service supplies standardized information to a number of clients. Much of the research conducted by syndicated firms is too expensive for a single company to

- **ABI/INFORM**–Full text, abstracts, and citations of more than 1,800 academic and general business publications.
- **LexisNexis**–Interdisciplinary, full-text database of over 18,000 newspapers, journals, wire services, newsletters, company reports, SEC filings, case law, government documents, and broadcast transcripts.
- **EBSCO**–Aggregator of full-text content from over 300 different databases, which includes journals, magazines, books, monographs, reports, and other publications.
- **ProQuest**–Archives of newspapers, periodicals, dissertations, and aggregated databases. Contains 125 billion digital pages.

FIGURE 3.14 Bibliographic Digital Databases

purchase. The syndicate research company can conduct the study or track the information and then sell it to a number of companies within the industry since it is more generic in nature. At the same time, the firm can collect company-specific information that is supplied only to clients that pay an additional charge.

For instance, J.D. Power and Associates collects data on an annual basis from consumers who have a home mortgage. These data are then sold to firms such as Chase Home Mortgage and other home mortgage companies. The data are standardized and apply to all home mortgage companies. During the process of collecting the data, J.D. Power will identify the financial institution that holds each individual's home mortgage. By doing this, J.D. Power can provide company-specific information, which can be compared to competitors. It is extremely valuable information to companies in the home mortgage business, like Chase Home Mortgage, because the firm can see how it ranks compared to competing firms overall and on specific attributes. Purchasing these data from J.D. Power and Associates is much cheaper for Chase Home Mortgage than if the firm hired a research company to conduct a primary study.

Syndicated services will often issue press releases that contain a nugget of information from a study or an executive summary with the primary purpose of encouraging companies to purchase the full report. The NPD Group released information from a study of the U.S. video gaming market.[35] US consumers spent over $ 9.19 billion on video games between July and September of 2019, an increase of one percent when compared to the same third quarter of the previous year. The study found that while sales declined in video game hardware, accessories and digital PC content during the first three quarters of 2019, digital console content and mobile and subscription video game spending increased, netting a 1 percent overall gain compared to the first nine months of 2018. As part of the company's ongoing tracking efforts, NPD noted that despite the decline in spending on video game accessories in the first three quarters of 2019, sales still reached the third highest total in history.

Those interested in learning more about the report are required to fill out a contact form. A sales representative will follow-up with the interested party, and encourage purchase of the fully detailed report.

Various types of syndicated data are available to companies. Some require a subscription service where data are provided on a routine basis. Others are studies performed ad hoc or periodically and provided to companies for a charge. **Figure 3.15** identifies the major categories of syndicated sources of secondary data. Because of space limitation, only a few of the primary providers will be discussed in the following sections.

Sources of Business and Corporate Information The best source for business and corporate information is Dun & Bradstreet, often referred to as D & B. One of the primary uses of the Dun & Bradstreet Business Information Report is credit information on businesses and corporations. However, the report has a number of other pieces of information that can be valuable, such as:

- Industry statistics
- Financials of the business or corporation (sales, net worth, cash, etc.)

- Sources of business and corporate information
- Sales tracking sources
- Consumer data sources
- Satisfaction and product quality
- Consumer behavior
- Media audience measurement sources
- Traditional media
- Online environment

FIGURE 3.15 Types of Syndicated Sources of Secondary Data

- Company history
- Mailing addresses
- Product and industry descriptors
- Number of employees

In addition to demographic information about a company, the Dun & Bradstreet report can be used to locate potential customers since it produces sector-based information that can be compared and contrasted with similar industries at a local, state, or regional basis. Federal agencies and the European Union have endorsed the DUNS Business Information Report as the primary identification system for international business assessment and validation throughout the world. Dun & Bradstreet has expanded their product offerings to offer data related to industry trends, and the competitive landscape. The also maintain SWOT analyses on major companies.

Sales Tracking Sources A number of research companies offer sales tracking data. The best-known syndicated sources are The NPD Group and the IRI Worldwide Group. Sales tracking is done on a continuous basis by both research firms and primarily uses scanner data from retail outlets.

The major supplier of retail sales tracking data is The NPD Group. The company was founded in 1967 and has become the leading global provider of retail tracking services at the point of sale (POS). The company has partnerships with over 1,300 retailers representing more than 300,000 retail outlets worldwide. Each store provides The NDP Group with its POS data. The data are used to generate various sales reports on a weekly basis. Other key measures include market share, pricing, and sell-through at the item level. In exchange for providing POS information, retailers can use NPD's retail market research information to guide assortment planning, merchandising, and pricing. For subscribers, NPD can provide store level information and tracking that can be used to compare the store's performance against various benchmarks.

From the data collected through POS systems, NPD produces more than 100 special market research reports that can be purchased by clients. These reports are written by NPD research analysts with in-depth knowledge of their industries and covers subjects such as:

- Category/market performance
- Trend analysis in consumer purchasing and consumption
- Consumer behavior and demographics
- Category profiles
- Retail industry trends
- Market share and segment analyses
- Brand analyses

The IRI Worldwide Group also provides sales tracking data. The IRI Group provides clients with consumer, shopper, e-commerce, retail market intelligence, loyalty data and analysis for the consumer packaged goods (CPG) industry IRI operates in 58 different countries and represents 95 percent of the Fortune Global 100 CPG, retail and health and beauty companies. Measurement services track sales across mass merchandise, drug, grocery, convenience, pet, club, military and e-commerce stores. Each week stores provide IRI with POS, ecommerce and promotional data on consumer packaged goods and beauty and health products. IRI sorts, analyzes, and verifies product price and volume and uses big data analytics and automated insights to accelerate the delivery of insights to client firms.

Consumer Data Sources In terms of measuring consumer satisfaction and product quality, the best-known syndicated service is J.D. Power and Associates. Founded in 1968, the company now conducts surveys of customer satisfaction, product quality, and buyer behavior for several industries, ranging from automobiles to electronics to travel. The company became famous for its customer-satisfaction research on new cars and then expanded into other industries, including home mortgages discussed at the beginning of this section. The company develops customer surveys and collects data from several thousand participants within each industry. The data are tabulated and then sold to clients.

Several other syndicated research firms collect consumer behavior data. In addition to retail sales tracking, the NPD Group has a consumer panel. The NPD consumer panel has 1.8 million registered adults and teens who have agreed to let NPD track their purchases via POS systems. This allows NPD to provide its clients with information on trends, purchasing, consumption, ownership, and usage by various demographic profiles. The online panel also provides customer satisfaction information that can be tied to specific brands.

Experian conducts ongoing consumer behavior and market segmentation studies. Experian serves marketers in the automotive, financial services, health, media, entertainment, restaurant, retail, travel and hospitality industries. The Experian U.S. ConsumerView database includes demographics, purchasing habits, brand preferences, interests, attitudes and lifestyle data for more than 300 million individuals, with much of the information tied to the credit data for which Experian is so well known. Data includes preferred communication channels, media habits, technology usage, and even special data points that identify new parents or movers. Experian offers several different products depending on marketer's needs. A joint venture in the syndicated research industry resulted in the launch of MRI-Simmons in 2019. MRI-Simmons is co-owned by GfK and the SymphonyAI group. Their *Survey of the American Consumer* report is the industry standard for measuring magazine ratings. It provides measures of consumer attitudes, product consumption, and media usage. Demographic, lifestyle, and psychographic data are then obtained. All of this information is then collated with consumers' product and service usage data for over 6,000 brands and 550 product categories.

MRI-Simmons' *National Consumer Study* measures over 60,000 consumer data variables, usage behavior from over 500 product categories and 8,000 brands, and in-depth psychographic, lifestyle, and attitudinal insights. The study tracks consumer usage of traditional major media, digital media, emerging media, and mobile media platforms, using data collected from 25,000 adults on a continuous basis and reported quarterly. The National Consumer Study panel members include 7,500 English and Spanish-speaking Hispanics and 4,200 English and Spanish-speaking children between the ages of 6 and 17. Data from both groups are available as separate reports. MRI-Simmons also claims to be the only syndicated data firm to have national data that provides measures of the lesbian, gay, bisexual, and transgender community. The LGBT study data are sourced from the *National Consumer Study*.

Media Audience Measurement Sources The primary provider of audience measurement data for both traditional and online media is Nielsen Media Research. The company has become the standard for audience measurement, and its statistics are used by numerous companies and media outlets. The company is most famous for its Nielsen ratings of television shows. But in addition to television, Nielsen measures audiences for radio, digital ads, some online video providers such Hulu and YouTube, and some smartphone apps for social media platforms.

The two most common television ratings are the Nielsen rating points and share, which is typically reported as "rating points/share." A single Nielsen rating point currently is equivalent to approximately 1,200,600 households. This represents one percent of the total number of 120,600.000 households in the U.S with televisions.[36] Each week the Nielsen ratings/shares are reported on the firm's website as well as other websites such as Yahoo TV. If a television show received a rating/share of 12.3/19.7, it would mean that 12.3 percent of the households in the United States were tuned to that particular television show. To find the actual number of households, the 12.3 would be multiplied by the 1,200,600 to arrive at a total of 14,767,380. The 19.7 percent share figure indicates that of the televisions that were turned on at that particular time, 19.7 percent of them were tuned into that program. Not every household in the U.S. will be watching television at any particular time. Nielsen Media Research also provides demographic information of the viewers of each television show since the Nielsen ratings influence advertising rates. The higher the Nielsen rating, the more a show's producer can charge advertisers.

Source: 360b/Shutterstock.

The Nielsen company has become the standard for audience measurement in both traditional and online media, and its statistics are used by numerous companies and media outlets.

Nielsen acquired Arbitron in late 2013, and is now the premier source for radio station ratings. In the top 48 U.S. markets, the company uses panel members who agree to wear called portable people meters that automatically track their radio listening. A diary data collection method, in which panel members record their listening behavior, is used in another 225 large and small U.S. markets. Data gathered from diaries form the basis for local radio station ratings.

With their Nielsen Mobile Performance solution, the firm collects measurements on smartphone device performance as well as consumer behaviors, attitudes, and experiences. Surveys provide attitudinal data while passive on-device metering of opt-in panel members tracks experiences, and measures device usage, data speeds and other metrics across applications and file sizes. The 45,000 member panel spans 41 cities throughout the U.S., and captures more than 400 million data points from U.S. Android smartphone users each month. The downside? IOS, the platform used by iPhone, is not part of the panel data. So, the Nielsen Mobile Performance data is not applicable to smartphone users in general. Research has shown that iPhone IOS users tend to have higher incomes, higher education levels, and spend more time per app, while Android users are less extroverted, and more likely to prefer saving money when compared to IOS users.[37] These are just a few differences between IOS and Android users. Marketers needing data specific to IOS and iPhone users would need to look elsewhere.

Nielsen offers a number of online measurement metrics. Nielsen's Digital Ad ratings provide next-day results of an online ad's audience as viewed across computers, smart phones, and any connected devices. Campaign results are available for large and small audiences at the local or national level. User demographics are matched to campaign impressions to provide reach, frequency, and gross rating point metrics. Data collection is independent of cookies, and gross ratings are comparable to Nielsen TV Ratings. Nielsen's Digital Content Ratings provide similar metrics, plus time spent on digital content viewed from computers, mobile devices, tablets, gaming platforms, videos, websites, and other connected devices. Custom reporting capabilities provide insights by (TV) program, static-web page, specific app, and through an aggregation of digital reach, audience and time spent across all platforms. Syndicated daily ratings are available for competitive benchmarking or for real-time planning. Although not as well-known as Nielsen, GfK Audience Measurement & Insights is part of one of the largest global research firms. GfK Audience Measurement & Insights tracks television, print, out-of-home, radio and digital audiences in the United States, and multiple media in over twenty other countries. In the United States, the results are not as robust as Nielsen's since the sample size is much smaller. However, it is unique in that it includes a number of different measures in all of the major media (magazines, television, radio, Internet, newspapers, and yellow pages). Combined with demographic, psychographic, and lifestyle information, GfK Audience Measurement & Insights is able to provide a rich view of consumer media consumption and how it relates to purchase behavior.

3.6 Global Concerns

Secondary data are an important source of information in international marketing research. They are often readily available at a low cost. They can provide valuable background information relating to various countries and cultures that can be used in preparing primary research. They are especially important for individuals conducting research in countries that are not native to those performing the research. The CIA World Factbook, for example, provides country profiles that describe the percent of the population who are Internet users, and basic demographic data.

When collecting secondary data in international markets, researchers need to be aware of two key issues. First, databases in other countries often do not have the detail of databases in the United States. This is especially true of government databases. The federal government in the United States collects and disseminates much more information than do governments in other countries. Second, many databases are not available in English. While many are, researchers must be aware that if they utilize only English databases they may be missing extremely valuable information.[38]

In respect to publicly available data from governmental sources, it is not unusual for data to be distorted or reported in such a way as to make the country look favorable to others. Data that reflect negatively on a country may be left out and only positively-related data reported. At other times data might be modified or collected in such a way as to make it more attractive.

Also, other countries may not collect the same types of information as in the United States, and if they do, it may not have the same relevance. For instance, in some countries individuals do not report their actual income because of fear of increased taxation by the government. In other countries, people do not report it to protect themselves from criminals and extortionists.[39]

To obtain good secondary data requires an understanding of each country's culture. It also may require the expertise of someone from that country that understands what information is valuable, what is not, and what has been modified or distorted. However, despite these cautions, secondary data are extremely important in conducting global marketing or international studies.

3.7 Marketing Research Statistics

To compare various demographics, marketing phenomena, and marketing data, researchers will often utilize index values. The Statistical Review section illustrates how index values are developed. Several questions in the Critical Thinking Exercises deal with creating and interpreting index values.

In this chapter's Statistical Reporting section, the concept of pie charts is presented. Pie charts are an effective means for presenting discrete data stemming from a single variable, but the data must add to 100 percent or 1. As with all graphs, proper labeling of the pie pieces and chart is important.

The Dealing with Data section converts a questionnaire to an SPSS file so data can be entered. Proper coding of questions is critical. Once all of the questions in a survey have been coded, then the SPSS file can be prepared.

3.7a Statistical Review

Index numbers are often used to make comparisons between periods of time, places, industries, or market segment characteristics. Index numbers offer an easy point of comparison, as they express "the difference between two measurements by designating one number as the base, giving it the value 100, and then expressing the second number as a percentage of the first."[40]

Suppose the population of your home town was 50,000 according to the 2010 census. Following the 2020 census, you find that the population size has increased to 53,000. Using the year 2010 as your time period base, its index number would be 100. Dividing the 2020 population size by the 2010 population figure shows that as of 2020, the size of your town is 106 percent of the population size in 2010; thus the index number would be 106.

It is critical to understand what index numbers mean. If the price index for HDTVs rose to 110 relative to the base year, while the price index for milk increased to 120, it simply means that the price of milk has increased twice as much in *percentage* terms as did the

Total	Total Adult U.S Population (000s)*	Frequent Diners (000s)*	Frequent Diners % of Total Pop.	Index Number
Total U.S Adult Population	225,900	27,100	12.0%	100
Education				
Did not graduate H.S.	32,300	1,650	5.1%	43
Graduated H.S.	69,800	6,300	9.0%	75
Attended college	63,000	8,650	13.7%	114
College degree	40,600	6,800	16.7%	140
Post college degree	20,200	3,700	18.3%	153
* (000s) denotes thousands. Thous 1,650 = 1,650,000 when denoted in (000s).				

FIGURE 3.16 Educational Index Numbers for Frequent Diners

price for HDTVs. It does not mean that the price of milk is more expensive, or that the absolute dollar amount of the increase in milk was greater than the dollar increase in the price of HDTVs.

Index numbers are commonly included in many forms of marketing-related secondary research as they allow users to quickly compare a characteristic of some type to its base. Consider the hypothetical data in Figure 3.16. Frequent diners for this illustration are defined as individuals who dine out at least once per week. The table shows the total adult population of the U.S. is 225,900,000. Out of the total adult population, 27,100,000 are frequent diners. Dividing the 27.1 million by the 225.9 million shows that 12.0 percent of the population are frequent diners. This 12.0 percent becomes the base to calculate the index for each of the educational demographic groups.

The fourth column in the table labeled "Freq Diners % of Total Pop" is calculated by dividing the number of frequent diners in each row by the respective total adult population. Thus, for "did not graduate high school" the 1,650 is divided by 32,300 to arrive at 5.1 percent. This means that 5.1 percent of individuals who did not graduate from high school are considered frequent diners. The corresponding index value is then calculated by dividing the 5.1 by the base of 12.0 and rounded, then multiplied by 100 to create the final index number. This same process is then used for every row of the table.

From these data, it appears that frequent diners are 40 percent more likely to have a college degree and 53 percent more likely to have obtained a postgraduate degree than the population in general. In contrast, frequent diners are 57 percent *less* likely to have not graduated from high school (100 − 43).

The essence of target marketing is to identify the characteristics which best describe the target, and more important, separate the target from other segments. The higher the index number, the more likely it is that people in the segment share that trait, compared to the population as a whole. Thus, incorporating the trait into the segment profile, and customizing a marketing campaign to such individuals, should lead to more efficient and effective campaigns. Figure 3.17 lists a few magazines and hypothetical readership for those who dine out at least once per week.

Notice the highest index number from this list of magazines is for *Cosmopolitan*, indicating frequent diners are 58 percent more likely to read this magazine than is the nation as a whole. Advertising in *Cosmopolitan* would be an efficient way to reach a significant portion of the target market while resulting in less wasted coverage.

	Total Adult U.S Population (000s)	Frequent Diners (000s)	Frequent Diners % of Total Pop.	Index Number
Total U.S Adult Population	225,900	27,100	12.0%	100
Business Week	39000	5300	13.6%	113
Cosmopolitan	***4600***	***870***	***18.9%***	***158***
Fitness	6200	890	14.4%	120
Money	7700	1300	16.9%	141
Outdoor Life	5500	550	10.0%	83
Reader's Digest	31200	4200	13.5%	112
TV Guide	17000	1500	8.8%	74

FIGURE 3.17 Selected Magazine Readership Habits of Frequent Diners

In addition to the index, it is also important to examine the number of individuals who read each magazine, which in the case of *Cosmopolitan* magazine would be 870,000 people. It is dangerous to focus exclusively on index numbers without properly considering the size of the population involved and the cost to place ads. In this case, the readership of *Cosmopolitan* is a fraction of the size of *Business Week* and *Reader's Digest*. Many individuals within the frequent diner cluster who don't care about fashion would be missed if the media selection was restricted to *Cosmopolitan*, or one of the other smaller publications. On the other hand, *Business Week* and *Reader's Digest* boast a much larger circulation base, and ads run in these publications will reach a broader cross-section of frequent diners. However, cost considerations and potential audience duplication must be considered when selecting the best media schedule.

3.7b Statistical Reporting

Pie charts are used frequently to report various statistics. Pie charts can be used under two conditions. First, the data must be discrete data. Second, the data need to add to 100 percent or 1. The pie chart represents the whole or entire data set for a particular variable. Consider the pie chart in Figure 3.18. It is a graph of forecasted U.S. advertising spending in the major media, in billions of dollars. But, it is not the actual media spending that is being graphed. It is the percent of total U.S. advertising spending in just the major media. For example, Internet spending is projected to be $87.3 billion, which represents 41 percent of the total U.S. ad spending for the major media tracked. If all of the percentages are summed around the pie, it will equal 100 percent.

Someone looking at the raw data in Figure 3.18 can see that television is second, with $67.2 billion. But the individual may want to know what percent of the total this amount is and also how it compares to other forms of advertising. The pie chart shows this relationship. Television is 32 percent of the total ad spending and is 9 percent lower in comparison to Internet. Comparing Internet to the other major media is relatively easy with this pie chart, and if someone does want to know the actual dollar value, it is supplied as well.

Figure 3.19 shows a pie chart, but with one of the slices extracted or pulled out from the pie. This is useful if a researcher wants to emphasize one particular component. In MRI-Simmons' ground-breaking study of the cannabis market, the study asked a national sample of respondents a wide variety of questions, including opinion statements related to cannabis use and legalization. The resulting data were used to form the six segments illustrated in Figure 3.19. Marijuana Mavens, the extracted slice, is the only segment

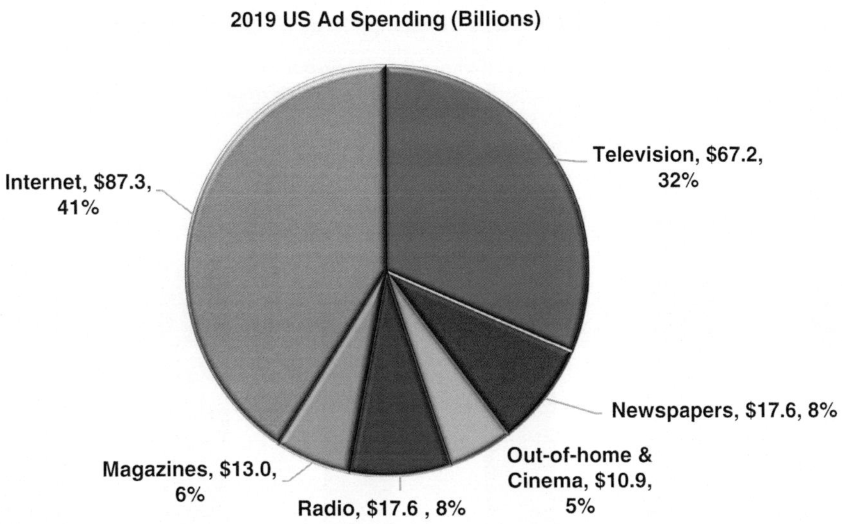

FIGURE 3.18 An Example of a Pie Chart Showing U.S. Ad Spending in the Major Media
Source: Advertising Age 2019 Marketing Fact Pack, p. 14.

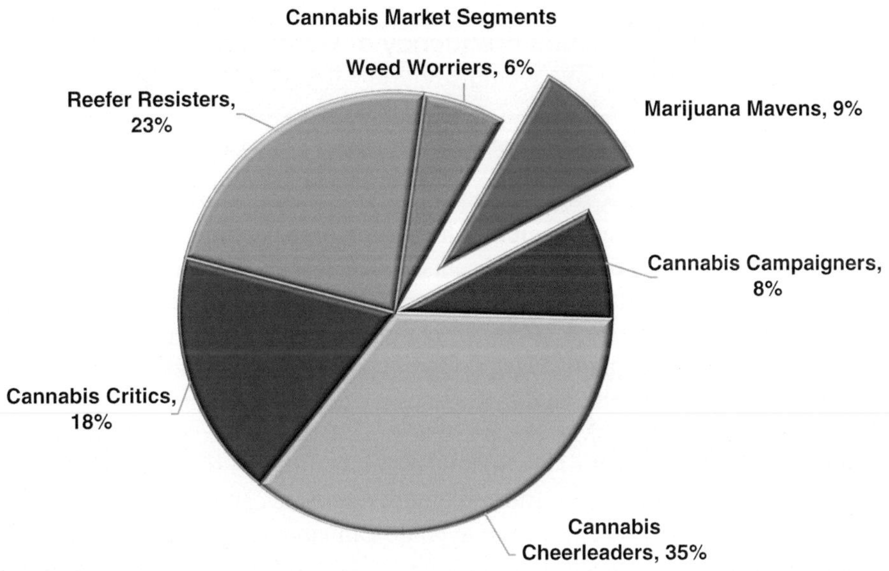

FIGURE 3.19 An Example of a Pie Chart with a Focus on One Particular Piece of the Pie
Source: Adapted from "Seven Surprising Cannabis Insights for Marketers." *MRI Simmons.* 2019.

in which all members consume cannabis for medicinal or recreational purposes. These individuals crave excitement, tend to drive luxury cars, and spend more time interacting with the Internet than watching TV. The segment has a median age of 40, and an average HH income of $72,000.[41] Many marketers would be surprised by these characteristics, as well as the data shown in Figure 3.19 as it may run counter to their intuition regarding the frequency of cannabis consumption among this segment. While all the segments are shown on the pie chart, the Marijuana Maven piece is extracted, the value is shown, and the category name and value are in black bold type for easy identification.

While legends can be used for pie charts, a wiser approach is to label the pieces of the pie with the category name as well as the value. The goal is to make the graph easy to read,

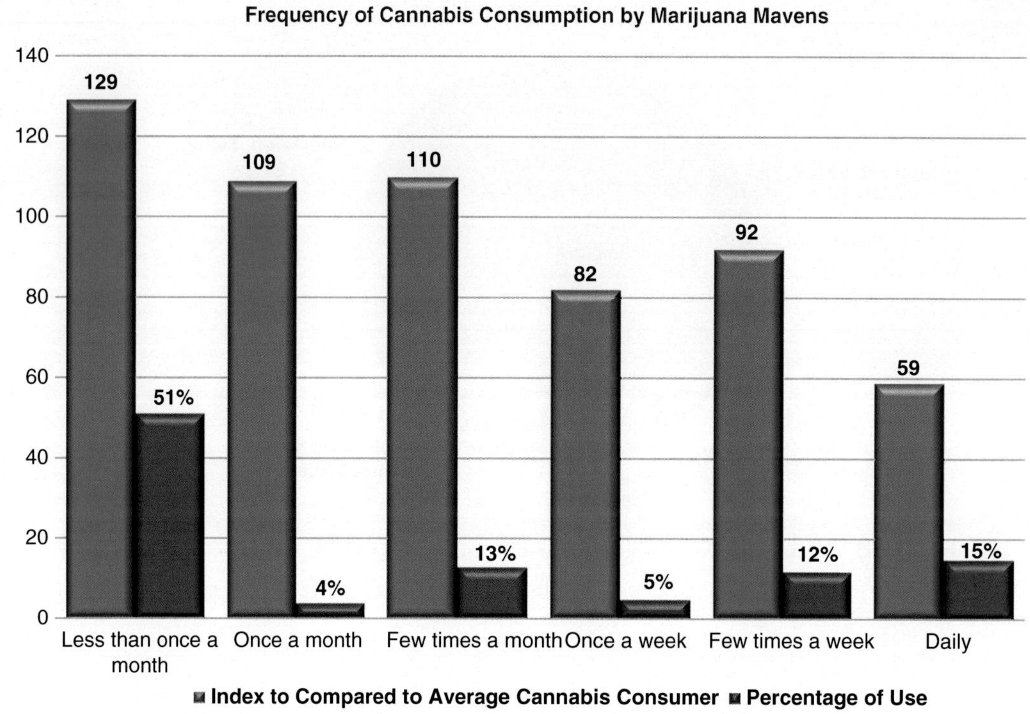

FIGURE 3.20 Marijuana Mavens Frequency of Cannabis Consumption
Source: Adapted from "Seven Surprising Cannabis Insights for Marketers." *MRI Simmons*. 2019.

easy to understand, and provide sufficient information to the audience. The title should be clear and identify what the pie chart represents.

Sometimes it is beneficial to present two-related pieces of information to present a fuller picture of the data. **Figure 3.20** uses a bar chart, rather than a pie chart, to demonstrate the percentage of Marijuana Mavens that consume cannabis at various time intervals. So, 15 percent use cannabis daily, 12 percent use it a few times a week, and so on, while the largest percentage of Mavens use cannabis less than once a month. Reviewing these percentages in the context of the matched index numbers is revealing. It would be natural to assume that Mavens were more likely to consume cannabis on daily basis. The data shows otherwise.[42] Compared to the average cannabis user, Mavens are 41 percent *less* likely to be daily users. Recall that the average is indexed at 100. So, 100 minus 59 (the index number for daily usage) equals a 41 percent lower likelihood of Mavens being daily users, compared to the group of cannabis users as a whole.

Statistical Reporting Exercise An issue that brands face in today's mobile environment is how to handle apps for cell phones. Should they sell apps with no advertising or should they give away the app or charge a low fee and include advertising? Another option is to include games that require real money purchases to score points. Use the data obtained below by Zogby Analytics to create a pie chart in Excel.[43] Give the chart a title and label each piece of the pie with the category name and value.

- Free apps with ads, 35.7%
- Free apps with games, 10.1%
- Higher cost apps, no ads, 2.7%
- Don't download apps, 39.6%
- No opinion, 11.9%

Suppose you are the marketing manager for a brand and want to convince your boss to offer free apps with advertising. Create a second pie chart in Excel based on the data from Zogby Analytics. The survey asked respondents if they had seen ads on their mobile device. Extract the piece of the pie that says "yes, often." Make sure you give the chart a title and label each piece of the pie with the category name and value.

- Yes, often—33.8%
- Yes, sometimes—38.6%
- Rarely—14.3%
- Never—13.1%

3.7c Dealing with Data

Before data can be entered into the SPSS spreadsheet, it is necessary to build the variable list. Chapter 2 reviewed the basic structure of a SPSS data file and the components of the variable portion of the data file. In this Dealing with Data exercise, the goal is to develop the variable portion of the spreadsheet so data can be entered. It may be helpful to compare the questionnaire from Chapter 2 with the SPSS data file that corresponds to the questionnaire.

Download from the textbook student website (www.clowjames.net/students.html) the file entitled Chapter 3 Dealing with Data Survey and the Chapter 3 Dealing with Data SPSS data file. Your task is to label each of the questions on the questionnaire into the SPSS data file with a variable name, variable label, and variable values. Note that the variable name cannot have spaces and should be a shortened version of the question. The variable label can have spaces and be an abbreviated version of the question that makes sense. For instance, for Question 2 the variable name might be "Q2MealsWeek" and the variable label might be "Average number of meals per week eaten at fast food restaurants."

The variable values would list the codes for the various answers. For example, for Question 1 a code of "1" would be used to represent "less than "10 percent" and a code of "2" would be "10 percent to 19 percent." Questions 2 and 3 will not have value labels since respondents are asked to write in a number. The individual recording the data will then transcribe the number on the survey sheet to the SPSS spreadsheet.

Summary

Objective 1: Discuss the advantages and disadvantages of secondary data.
Secondary research is less costly and less time consuming than conducting primary research. The ease with which information can be accessed either internally from the firm, or externally from bibliographic databases, open access sources such as the government, or even syndicated data firms is another key advantage, and one which helps to explain why secondary research is always completed prior to initiating a primary research study. Despite these obvious advantages, secondary data is often not available, or if available, can be irrelevant to the study purpose or insufficient to answer the research question. It is critical that marketers carefully evaluate the quality of secondary data by examining the data source, study purpose, sample, and overall methodology, data collection, analysis process, and interpretation.

Objective 2: Identify key uses of secondary data.
Secondary research has many uses. It complements exploratory efforts when additional insight into the research problem is needed. When designing a primary research study, a number of decisions can be influenced by relevant secondary data, including sampling procedures, data collection procedures, and measurement instruments. Secondary data is the key source of background information which can be included in both the RFP and the final research report. Secondary data is helpful to researchers seeking to identify consumer trends and industry information. In some cases, it can even be used to solve the research problem, or to answer one of the research questions. Secondary data is often instrumental in estimating demand, and can be highly beneficial when defining or selecting target markets, trade areas, or locations. Advertising agencies and other media users rely on secondary

data when selecting media for marketing campaigns, in designing behavioral advertising, and in evaluating advertising exposure via major media, such as television. Furthermore, secondary data is used to build databases which can be used in direct marketing programs. Finally, secondary data is helpful in data mining efforts, as marketers seek to discover patterns and trends in data files.

Objective 3: Explain how internal sources of data and big data can be used for secondary research.
While past marketing decisions provide information helpful when developing new campaigns, sales data is one of the most useful forms of internal information if collected and stored correctly. Sales data is helpful in profiling various customer groups, making geographic targeting decisions, and determining the best channel of communication or distribution to reach customers. Retail sales data stemming from scanners or loyalty cards help retailers develop cross-promotions, arrange items in the store, evaluate the effectiveness of point-of-purchase displays, and test marketing programs. Both accounting and marketing databases can provide useful internal information, though marketing databases typically are superior due to the large amount of consumer information that they contain. Big data encompasses this and more, including unstructured data gathered from social media websites, public records, loyalty cards, and syndicated research firms. Big data analytics can be used to discover complex patterns and consumer insights not readily available through other means. Privacy regulations and increasing demands from consumers to control access to their own data may impact internal data storage, usage, and retention policies in the future.

Objective 4: Describe the open access sources of secondary data.
Open access sources of secondary data include governmental sources, blogs, social media, web analytics, and independent websites. Governmental sources are particularly valuable due to their high data quality, and because they are free. Key governmental websites include census.gov, fedworld.gov, and stat-usa.gov. Many marketers tap into what consumers are saying about products or the competition by monitoring blogs and social media posts on a regular basis. Using multiple blogs is superior to relying on a single forum, and blogs sponsored by companies tend to more viable than blogs written by individuals. Website analytics provide valuable information regarding consumers' behavior in response to online ads. Google Analytics provides a wealth of data that can be helpful to marketers. Independent websites, though by far the most prevalent source of secondary data, are rarely relevant and must be carefully scrutinized to ascertain whether the information provided is valid.

Objective 5: Summarize the primary differences among the bibliographic digital databases.
Bibliographic databases are the primary source of published information for libraries. Some databases provide citation information along with article abstracts; others, such as ABI/Inform, contain full-text articles from academic and business publications. EBSCO is an excellent reference tool as it aggregates full-text content from over 300 different databases covering journals, magazines, industry publications, books, monographs, and reports. Similarly, ProQuest provides access to newspaper archives, dissertations, periodicals, and aggregated databases. While content overlaps between many of these databases, each usually has access to content which is unique and different from the others.

Objective 6: Identify and explain the types of data available from syndicated sources.
Syndicated data firms collect high quality data by product category, industry, media, or consumer market and sell it to data subscribers. While more costly than other forms of secondary data discussed in this chapter, standardized information is still less expensive than it would be for the firm to engage in primary research. The added time savings and high quality of the data make syndicated information a strong choice for many marketers. Various forms of syndicated data exist, and each form is characterized by multiple providers. Business and corporate information sources are found in Dun & Bradstreet. The NPD Group and IRI Group sell point-of-sale information gathered via in-store checkout scanners. While a variety of consumer data sources exist, NPD and J.D. Power and Associates are among the best known and respected firms while MRI-Simmons provides a vast amount of consumer behavioral data. Finally, Nielsen remains king of the media audience measurement sources.

Key Terms

accounting database, p. 85
behavioral targeting, p. 82
bibliographic databases, p. 91
big data, p. 85
blogs, p. 87
data minimalism, p. 86
data mining, p. 81
geo-aware ads, p. 72
geocoding, p. 80
marketing database, p. 85
metric, p. 89
network behavioral targeting, p. 82
onsite behavioral targeting, p. 82
primary research, p. 70
private labels, p. 70
programmatic advertising, p. 82

search engine optimization (SEO), p. 90
secondary data, p. 70
syndicated research service, p. 71
targeted social ads, p. 72
web analytics, p. 89

Critical Thinking Exercises

1. Suppose that the U.S. census revealed the following data about the racial profile of a zip code in North Carolina. Compute the index numbers for each line of data for the North Carolina zip code in reference to the U.S. percentages. What conclusions can you draw from this information?

	Number	Zip Code %	U.S. %	Index
One Race	30,533	98.3%	97.6%	
Two or more races	527	1.7%	2.4%	
One Race				
White	22,063	71.0%	75.1%	
Black or African American	7,418	23.9%	12.3%	
Hispanic or Latino (of any race)	993	3.2%	12.5%	
American Indian and Alaska Native	169	0.5%	0.9%	
Asian	518	1.7%	3.6%	
Native Hawaiian and Other Pacific Islander	19	0.1%	0.1%	
Some other race	346	1.1%	5.5%	

2. Visit the United States Census website at www.census.gov to investigate the profile of your zip code. Report on the gender, age, racial, and income characteristics of your zip code. Compare the index numbers of the various demographics. In what way is the population in your zip code different from the U.S. population?
3. According to an industry report, the United States restaurant industry value is $893.9 billon. Growth rates are provided for the next five years: 2021—3.5 percent; 2022—4.9 percent; 2023—4.4 percent; 2024—4.2 percent and 2025—4.0 percent. Calculate the dollar sales forecast for 2021–2025 in billions of dollars. Create a simple bar chart in Excel of the sales forecast for 2021–2025.
4. Consider your college or university. What specific forms of internal secondary data are likely to be available? As you formulate your answer, think about the types of information which might be tracked related to recruiting, the current student body, alumni, athletics and fundraising.
5. Visit Google.com and locate the "Google Scholar." Access this specialized search engine, and use it to research a topic of your choice. Conduct the same search using the same key words in the main Google window. Compare the results obtained through *Scholar* to the search from the main Google window. What similarities and differences did you see? Be sure to provide citations for the articles you use.
6. Using your preferred search engine locate the Blog Search function. Pick some type of marketing topic. Search the web for blogs on that topic. Critically evaluate at least three blogs, applying the criteria for assessing blog viability discussed in this chapter. In your evaluation, provide the URLs for the blogs you examine.
7. Visit YouTube and search for "Google Adwords Analytics". Locate the video posted by Google for beginners that describes how to use Analytics with Google Ads. Report on what you learned. Under what circumstances would the metrics discussed in these videos be considered secondary data, as opposed to primary data? Be specific.
8. Visit https://www.nielsen.com/us/en/ and locate the "Insights" tab on the home page. Select one of the sub-topics from the dropdown menu. Find a topic that interests you, and report on your findings.
9. Visit https://www.claritas.com/ and click the *Resources* tab. Select *MyBestSegments* from the menu. If you do not see a *Resources* tab, use the search feature to look for "MyBestSegments." Review the information on the page, the click the *Enter Zip Code* button. Select any five-digit zip code other than the Dallas zip code used in this chapter, and then click submit. Write a short report that lists the name of the city and zip code evaluated, the top five lifestage groups by name and number, and then describe in detail two of the five lifestage groups (with the exception of The Cosmopolitans). Note that you will only have access to the summary information. Click the name of the lifestage group to discover the details you need for your report.
10. Pick one of the following topics and conduct secondary research using one or more of the bibliographic digital databases available at your school's library. Find at least four articles that provide information on marketing of the products. Summarize your findings. In your summaries provide the full citation for each article.
    a. Advertising to teenagers
    b. Mobile phone advertising
    c. Website analytics
    d. Online privacy legislation
    e. Marketing in France

11. Pick one of the following topics or products. Conduct secondary research. Locate at least two articles from your library's bibliographic digital database, two articles or sites on the Internet in general that discuss the topic, and two blogs that provide information. Summarize your findings. Remember to cite the references in your paper and include all of your sources in a reference list at the end of your paper.
    a. Advertising to children
    b. Sports marketing
    c. Search engine optimization (SEO)
    d. Digital marketing
    e. Marketing in Japan

Lakeside Grill

(Comprehensive Student Case)

The student team of Brooke, Alexa, Juan, Destiny, and Zach collected the following information:

- Lakeside Grill sales data for the last three years aggregated by the month.
- Amount of money spent on hourly labor and food by the Lakeside Grill and the number of customers for the past three years, by month.
- Comment cards from customers spanning the last three years. The comment cards are placed in a box by diners as they leave the restaurant.
- "Restaurant and Hotel Food Trends" from this year's *Restaurant, Food & Beverage Market Research Handbook.*
- Census data for the zip code in which the restaurant is located.
- Two articles from EBSCO on trends in restaurant patronage and desired attributes of restaurants.
- A blog written by a restaurant owner in San Diego that discusses various marketing techniques that she has used for her seafood restaurant.

Critique Questions:

1. Evaluate the types of internal data obtained by the team. What other data would the owner of the Lakeside Grill be likely to have in his database which could be useful for this research project?
2. How useful are comment cards? Who tends to respond to comment cards? How can the group use this information?
3. How useful will the trend information from the *Restaurant, Food & Beverage Market Research Handbook* be to the group?
4. What can the group learn from the census data of the zip code where the restaurant is located? Is the one zip code enough? Why or why not?
5. In addition to the two articles found on EBSCO, what other topics might be of interest? Generate a list of key terms that the group could use to search for additional articles.
6. How useful is the blog information? Can blogs provide good secondary data? What is the best way to locate a blog that would be useful to the team?
7. Overall, how would you evaluate the effort of this group in locating secondary data for their Lakeside Grill project?

Notes

1. Adapted from Marshal Cohen, "How Private Label Goes Premium," NPD Group, June 2019, https://www.npd.com/wps/portal/npd/us/news/thought-leadership/2019/is-private-label-peaking/.
2. Doris Kaiser and Kristina Witzling, "Save Money—Conduct Secondary Research," *Quirk's Media* (March 2010), http://www.quirks.com/articles/2010/20100325-2.aspx?searchID=1388127914&sort=7&pg=1.
3. BIA Advisory Services, "2019 Brand and Franchisee Advertising and Marketing Insights: Ad Spending Forecast and Franchisee Survey Highlights," January 2019, https://info.vyasystems.com/franchise-market-research-data-thankyou-2019?__hstc=264539664.bea2d146fccdd542e7f5817098cce300.1560869077100.1560869077100.1560869077100.1&__hssc=264539664.2.1560869077100&submissionGuid=eaa8d7b0-0a3c-4051-a1e8-5edabdb1b781.
4. Adapted from BlogHer, "2010 Social Media Matters Study," https://www.scribd.com/document/31277666/BlogHer-iVillage-2010-Social-Media-Matters-Study.
5. Athena Rodriguez, "Researchers, You Must Stand Up for the U.S. Census," *Quirk's Media* (October 9, 2017), https://www.quirks.com/articles/researchers-you-must-stand-up-for-the-u-s-census.
6. Ibid; Athena Rodriguez, "Researchers, Are You Paying Attention to the U.S. Census?" *Quirks Media* (November19, 2018), https://www.quirks.com/articles/researchers-are-you-paying-attention-to-the-u-s-census.
7. "5 Menu Trends for 2020," *Foodservice Director*, October 29, 2019, https://www.foodservicedirector.com/5-menu-trends-2020-2019/5-menu-trends-2020.
8. "How Do US Consumers Get Their Food?" *eMarketer*, July 2019, https://chart-na2.emarketer.com/230576/

how-do-us-consumers-their-food-of-respondents-by-frequency-of-method-july-2019.
9. National Restaurant Association, "2019 State of the Restaurant Industry," 2019, https://restaurant.org/research/reports/state-of-restaurant-industry.
10. National Restaurant Association, "What's Hot Culinary Forecast," 2019, https://restaurant.org/research/reports/foodtrends.
11. National Restaurant Association, "2019 State of the Restaurant Industry," 2019, https://restaurant.org/research/reports/state-of-restaurant-industry.
12. "The QSR 50," *QSR Magazine* (2018), https://www.qsrmagazine.com/content/qsr50-2018-top-50-chart.
13. "Restaurants Industry Profile: United States," Business Source Complete, April 15, 2015.
14. "Claritas: Upscale Younger Family Mix," https://claritas360.claritas.com/mybestsegments/#segDetail/PZP/21.
15. Jon Brand, "More Than Clicks," *Quirk's Marketing Research Review* (March 2019): 42, 44–45.
16. Sophie C. Boerman, Sanne Kruikemeier, and Frederick J. Zuiderveen Borgesius, "Online Behavioral Advertising: A Literature Review," *Journal of Advertising* 24, no. 3 (2017): 363–376.
17. Michael Wlosik, "What Is Behavioral Targeting and How Does It Work?" Clearcode, July 2018, https://clearcode.cc/blog/behavioral-targeting/.
18. Ibid.
19. This section is based on Robert Allen, "How Programmatic Advertising Works," Smart Insights, July 31, 2018, https://www.smartinsights.com/internet-advertising/internet-advertising-targeting/what-is-programmatic-marketing/; and Adrian Jeffries, "The World without Ads," *Bloomberg Businessweek* (May 14, 2018): 56–59.
20. Nicole Perrin, "Consumer Attitudes on Marketing 2019," *eMarketer* (August 29, 2019), https://content-na2.emarketer.com/consumer-attitudes-on-marketing-2019.
21. Internet Innovation Alliance (IIA) and Civic Science, "Consumer Data Privacy Concerns," April 2019, https://content-na2.emarketer.com/consumer-attitudes-on-marketing-2019.
22. Adrian Jeffries, "The World without Ads," *Bloomberg Businessweek* (May 14, 2018): 56–59.
23. Jessica Santos, "The Fast-Changing Data Privacy Landscape," *Quirk's Media* (February 22, 2019), https://www.quirks.com/articles/the-fast-changing-data-privacy-landscape.
24. Michael Minelli, Michele Chambers, and Ambiga Dhiraj, *Big Data, Big Analytics* (Hoboken, NJ: John Wiley & Sons, 2013), 13.
25. Robyn Clayton, "Not Another Byte," *Quirk's Marketing Research Review* (February 2019): 32.
26. Keith Johnson, "Incorporating Big Data for a More Complete View of Consumers," *Quirk's Media* (September 13, 2017), https://www.quirks.com/articles/incorporating-big-data-for-a-more-complete-view-of-consumers.
27. Paul Neto, "Responding to Consumer Demands for Data Control," *Quirk's Media* (March 25, 2019), https://www.quirks.com/articles/responding-to-consumer-demands-for-data-control.
28. Ibid.
29. Steven MacDonald, "The Science Behind Email Open Rates (and How to Get More People to Read Your Emails," SuperOffice, https://www.superoffice.com/blog/email-open-rates/.
30. "Introduction—Background," in *2019 Email Marketing Benchmark Report*, Sign-up-to. 2019, http://www.signupto.com/wp-content/uploads/2019/03/2019BenchmarkReportR0.pdf.
31. Campaign Monitor, "Ultimate Email Marketing Benchmarks for 2019: By Industry & Day," https://www.campaignmonitor.com/resources/guides/email-marketing-benchmarks/
32. Acoustic, "2019 Marketing Benchmark Report," 2019, https://acoustic.co/files/2019/08/Acoustic-2019-Marketing-Benchmark-Report-2.pdf.
33. Ian Cain and Cassie Johnson, "Using Twitter Analysis to Drive the Creation of Real-Time Marketing Campaigns," *Quirk's Marketing Research Review* (December 2014), http://www.quirks.com/articles/2014/20141226-2.aspx? searchID=1393756166&sort=5&pg=1.
34. Pat Ahern, "SEO Stats for 2019," Junto, https://junto.digital/blog/seo-stats/.
35. "The NPD Group: U.S. Consumers Spend on Video Game Products Increased 1 Percent to $9.1 billion in 2019's Third Quarter," *NPD Group* (November 30, 2018).
36. Nielsen Company, "Nielsen Estimates 120.6 Million TV Homes in the U.S. for the 2019–2020 TV Season," 2019, https://www.nielsen.com/us/en/insights/article/2019/nielsen-estimates-120-6-million-tv-homes-in-the-u-s-for-the-2019-202-tv-season/.
37. Tyler Schmall, "iPhone and Android Users Are Completely Different People," *New York Post* (October 25, 2018), accessed from https://nypost.com/2018/10/25/iphone-and-android-users-are-completely-different-people/.
38. R. Lucas, "Issues to Consider before Starting Your Market Research Project in Eastern Europe and/or Russia," PMR Publications, 2006, http://www.research-pmr.com/a9/issues-to-consider-before-starting-your-market-research-project-in-eastern-europe-andor-russia.
39. Danuta Babinska and Aleksandra Nizielska, "International Marketing Research on the Markets of Central and Eastern Europe," *Journal of Economics & Management* 6 (2009): 5–19.

40. Statistics Canada, "Using Basic Statistical Techniques," November 2015, http://www.statcan.gc.ca/pub/11-533-x/2005001/using-utiliser/4072242-eng.htm#indexes.
41. MRI Simmons, "Seven Surprising Cannabis Insights for Marketers," April 2019, https://www.mrisimmons.com/reports/seven-surprising-cannabis-insights-marketers/.
42. Ibid.
43. "Apps for Sale! But Are People Actually Buying?" *eMarketer* (December 2014), https://www.emarketer.com/Article/Apps-Sale-People-Actually-Buying/1011636.

Qualitative Research

CHAPTER 4

Source: designer491/Shutterstock.

Chapter Outline

Learning Objectives

After studying this chapter, you should be able to:

- Explain the role of qualitative research.
- Describe the traditional focus group process.
- Explain the process of using in-depth interviews to conduct qualitative research.
- Discuss the various types of online qualitative research being used by companies.
- Enumerate the various projective techniques.

4.1 Chapter Overview

Increasingly, qualitative and quantitative studies are being used together in mixed methods research to accomplish research goals. Traditionally, qualitative research is conducted first to explore the research problem, to better understand the consumer, or to otherwise help the researchers gain information that will help them to prepare for the quantitative research phase. But, sometimes the opposite is true.

Alpine Dog Brewing Company, a craft brewery based in Denver, Colorado, used both quantitative and qualitative research in developing new labels for an upcoming craft beer release. Their goal was to involve consumers in choosing the design of the label. Alpine Dog partnered with GutCheck, a local research firm, to evaluate six very unique label designs. A sample of craft beer drinkers were targeted, and using quantitative concept testing methodology, one design emerged as a clear winner on all metrics tested. However, open-ended survey comments suggested that certain design elements lacked clarity.

Enter qualitative research. Using an online sample of 30 craft beer drinkers, GutCheck tested the top performing design in a series of online focus groups. The findings were revealing. While the "Ski Naked Wild Saison" beer name drew consumer's attention and was well-liked, other elements of the design were lost in its shadow, including the company's logo and the product information. Plus, the design was not as well-liked on the bottle as it was on the can. Based on these findings, the label was redesigned to incorporate the logo into the name rather than leaving it as a separate element, thereby simplifying the overall design. An additional color was added to the label to help certain design and informational elements standout. By using a mixed research method of quantitative and qualitative techniques, Alpine Brewery was able to refine a beer label that appealed strongly to their target market.[1]

This chapter examines various qualitative tools that are used by marketing research firms like GutCheck and many other firms. Focus groups and in-depth interviews are the two primary qualitative methods companies use. But other methods exist, such as projective techniques that can be valuable in certain situations. As with other forms of marketing research, a sizeable proportion of qualitative research studies have shifted to online methodologies.

4.2 The Role of Qualitative Research

LEARNING OBJECTIVE 4.1
Explain the role of qualitative research.

Companies often face situations that need information that cannot be sufficiently supplied through secondary research. In these situations, qualitative research may meet the need. It is not always necessary to collect quantitative data, which typically takes longer and is more expensive than qualitative data. Figure 4.1 identifies the primary ways qualitative research can be used.

Qualitative research involves unstructured data collection methods that provide results that are subjectively interpreted.

As explained in Chapter 2, **qualitative research** involves unstructured data collection methods that provide results that are subjectively interpreted. Therefore, it is an excellent means of conducting exploratory research. When companies do not understand a problem fully or want additional information about an opportunity or situation, qualitative research can be used to provide valuable insight. Focus groups can be especially helpful.

- Exploratory research
- Background for quantitative studies
- Questionnaire or research design
- Explore subconscious of consumers
- Conceptualization of concepts that are difficult to articulate
- Deeper understanding of consumer thinking
- Add richness to quantitative studies

FIGURE 4.1 Ways Qualitative Research Can Be Used

- **Sample Selection**
  - Clarifying/defining sample characteristics
  - Identifying most efficient/appropriate means for recruitment
- **Survey Design**
  - Determining criteria for screening questions
  - Identifying sample segments so skip patterns can be based on key differences in behavior/knowledge
  - Identifying relevant language and terminology for survey
- **Resolving Questions and Inconsistencies**
  - Discovering reasons/drivers of unexpected quantitative survey findings
  - Highlighting inconsistencies and contradictions
  - Refining findings and adding additional information for recommendations

FIGURE 4.2 Use of Qualitative Research at Different Stages of Quantitative Study Design

Source: Adapted from Laura Cusumano, "Can Quantitative Research Succeed with Qualitative Support?", *Quirk's Media*, (www.quirks.com), Article ID 20170505, May 3, 2017.

Qualitative research is often used as a precursor to quantitative studies, questionnaire construction, and development of the research design. Qualitative research can clarify information that is needed to execute quantitative studies and provide necessary background information. For instance, through qualitative research a company such as GE may be able to uncover what benefits consumers seek in a smart refrigerator and also how and why consumers buy them.

To verify qualitative findings, quantitative research is typically undertaken. In the past, qualitative research was perceived as inferior to quantitative studies and was used only prior to quantitative research. Now, companies use qualitative data at every stage of the research process. As **Figure 4.2** illustrates, qualitative research can be helpful in identifying the sample characteristics for a larger quantitative study, and be useful in developing survey questions. It can also be helpful in refining the research design process to ensure that the primary study objectives are met. As illustrated in our chapter opening, qualitative research can help researchers to better understand quantitative findings and help refine decisions, or help make sense of findings that seem inconsistent.

Qualitative research is often used to explore the subconscious of consumers to uncover why they act in the manner they do as consumers are often unwilling or unable to articulate reasons for their behavior. It is also an excellent means by which skilled researchers can help participants to conceptualize ideas or thoughts that are difficult to articulate. Projective techniques are especially useful in that regard. Qualitative research excels at discovering consumer motivations and can provide a deeper understanding into consumer thoughts and decision-making. All of this can add richness to quantitative studies and provide important input into management decisions.[2]

The Richards Group uses quantitative research and tracking studies to measure the effectiveness of advertising that the agency creates for various clients. But the company also uses qualitative research to understand what consumers think about its ads and how the ads are processed. A quantitative study can provide data on how an ad is doing in the marketplace, but it cannot tell the agency how the ad is being mentally processed and what is working and what is not working within the mind of the consumer. "When we read the actual comments of 150 consumers who view a particular advertisement, we get a good feel for what is going on in their minds," says Dave Snell, of The Richards Group.[3]

Figure 4.3 identifies the primary methods of conducting qualitative research. Traditionally, qualitative research was conducted through face-to-face interactions with the

- Focus groups
- In-depth interviews
- Market research online communities
- Online and mobile qualitative techniques
- Projective techniques

FIGURE 4.3 Qualitative Research Methods

market researcher or moderator. In recent years, however, companies have shifted to more online and mobile techniques. While automation is rarely a factor in qualitative research, the benefit of asynchronous communication offered by online and mobile techniques has helped marketers to reach business people and populations that are difficult to gather for in-person focus groups. Still, face-to-face focus groups and in-person in-depth interviews remain the top two most used qualitative techniques, according to research suppliers and buyers who answered the 2018 quarter 3–4 *GreenBook Research Industry Trends Report*.[4]

4.3 Focus Groups

LEARNING OBJECTIVE 4.2
Describe the traditional focus group process.

Focus groups qualitative research method in which a group of 6 to 10 individuals unknown to each other are brought together to discuss a particular topic.

Moderator trained interviewer who guides the focus group discussion, encourages respondent participation, and prepares the client report.

A widely used qualitative research method is the focus group. Typical **focus groups** consist of six to ten individuals who are brought together to discuss a particular topic led by a focus group moderator. **Moderators** are trained interviewers who guide the focus group discussion, encourage respondent participation, and prepare the client report. The primary idea behind the focus group is that the group will discuss ideas and produce insights that individuals interviewed individually might not consider. One person will feed off of a comment from another participant, generating new thoughts and ideas. Indeed, consideration of whether or not group dynamics will add to the findings is often one of the key factors considered by research professionals when determining whether to use the focus group or individual in-depth interview technique.[5]

The Richards Group used focus groups as the basis for developing the Motel 6 campaign when they first obtained the account.[6] Travelers were solicited to participate. These individuals were strangers to one another, but shared two key characteristics: they traveled frequently and stayed in motels. The participants were selected to participate in the focus group studies because all had stayed at a Motel 6. But the purpose of this study was disguised, meaning that no one knew the reason for their selection or that Motel 6 was the client behind the focus groups.

Source: Jonathan Weiss/Shutterstock.

The Richards Group, an advertising agency, used focus groups as the basis for developing the Motel 6 campaign when they first obtained the account.

In the first focus group, participants were asked to indicate what hotel they used on their last trip and why. As they went around the room various brands were mentioned, but no one mentioned Motel 6. After some discussion of how a particular hotel is chosen, the moderator asked each individual to again identify specific hotels they had patronized during recent travels other than the one they mentioned the first time. Even during the second round Motel 6 was not mentioned, which was surprising, given that all focus group participants had stayed at a Motel 6. Then, finally, one individual rather sheepishly said, "If it is really late at night, then I will stay at a Motel 6." Others in the group then admitted they had stayed at a Motel 6. Another individual stated that with the money he had saved at staying at a Motel 6 he was able to purchase a present for his grandkid. Someone else mentioned that he was able to buy a nice dinner with what he saved. The discussion then shifted to why Motel 6 was chosen.

1. Develop study parameters
2. Compose interview questions
3. Select participants
4. Conduct focus group interview
5. Debrief the client
6. Write the report

FIGURE 4.4 Steps in Conducting Focus Group Interviews

Through that initial focus group and supplemental focus groups, it became clear to The Richards Group that while Motel 6 may not have been the first choice of travelers in lodging, participants boasted and were proud of the money they had saved and how they used the money for other things. During one of the focus groups a participant commented, "You know when the lights are turned out, price doesn't make a difference and all of the motels look the same." The input from the focus groups and this key consumer insight were the genesis for the Motel 6 campaign.

In working with Motel 6, The Richards Group used a traditional focus group. Traditional focus groups are conducted in-person at the agency's place of business, or at a neutral location. The facility in which the focus group takes place should be comfortable, and seating arrangements should be considered carefully. Professional moderator Raúl Pérez notes that even the table shape can influence group dynamics "by altering distance among respondents, proximity of respondents to the moderator, respondents' ability to make eye contact with each other and the moderator's ability to visually follow respondents."[7] Similarly, the clients' ability to view focus group participants is also affected by the table design. By conducting the focus group in person, the agency is able to observe body language of participants in addition to their verbal comments. This is important, because body language cues can be used to identify when a participant might disagree with something that is being said. A good moderator will capitalize upon this opportunity by actively encouraging the participant to share thoughts. Differing points of view can stimulate the discussion and provide valuable information.

Successful focus groups are the result of careful planning. Figure 4.4 identifies the major steps in conducting a focus group.

4.3a Develop Study Parameters

The focus group interview begins by developing the study parameters. The person or agency that is conducting the focus groups needs to meet with the client to determine the study purpose and research questions, which were likely determined as part of the problem definition process. It is essential that the agency or person conducting the study understand what information is desired, what types of decisions will be made from the information, and how the results will be used. Answers to these questions will guide the focus group process.

Other study parameters that need to be decided include the timeline for conducting the interviews, the number of focus groups, the size of the focus groups, the budget, participant incentives, and whether or not client observers wish to be present or viewing by remote video. Most companies use multiple focus groups, especially when seeking input from different groups (users vs. nonusers, for example), and when the results will be used for management decisions or input into the development of marketing strategies and tactics. The number of focus group interviews will then affect the timeline and budget needed. Generally group sizes below five are avoided as too few participants are present to generate good group discussions and strong insights. Conversely, groups larger than ten make it difficult for every individual to contribute meaningful input in the allotted time-frame.

Participants in focus group interviews receive some type of remuneration for their efforts. While cash incentives work best, free merchandise, vouchers, certificates or entries into prize drawings have also been used. Participants for a focus group about airlines might receive an airline voucher, while participants for a clothing manufacturer might receive a certificate for free clothes. The key is to make certain that the incentives offered are appropriate given the time and effort expended by the participant.[8] Beverages and snacks are often provided to participants as sessions typically last between ninety minutes and two hours. To ensure unbiased results, the sponsor of the focus group is not revealed until the end of the session. Over-recruiting of one or two individuals per group is common to counteract no-shows.

The final decision to be made includes who and how many observers will be present from the client. Focus groups are typically recorded, but observers are also often present behind a one-way mirror. They can observe what is being said and the body language of the participants. Many in-person focus groups today use 360-degree cameras that are voice-activated and film each participant as they speak. This allows focus group facilities to stream focus group interviews to observers who cannot be present in person, so that they don't miss the comments, expressions, and reactions of participants in the group.[9] As a result of these observations, the client will sometimes send the interviewer a discrete message asking that a particular comment be explored in more detail, or that an additional question be addressed by the group before the focus group concludes its activities. Clients can gain valuable insights into what consumers think of their brand. However, they also must be willing to calmly listen if individuals criticize the brand. Such was the case with Dominos in the mid 2000's, as focus groups revealed people's thoughts about the brand's poor quality and cardboard-like taste. While it was difficult for Domino's leadership to hear, it provided extremely valuable insight into consumer thoughts about the brand and its pizza. As a result, Dominos made changes in their products and marketing approach.[10] They even used the results in an advertising campaign to inform consumers they had listened and modified their product. The result? A 32.2 percent increase in sales. Domino's has continued listening to customers, and combined with online and mobile marketing efforts, has become the largest pizza company in the world.[11]

4.3b Compose Interview Questions

Discussion guide series of questions that will be asked of participants by the moderator during the focus group interview.

Preparation of the **discussion guide** requires that the researcher and client work closely together to identify the series of questions which will be asked of participants during the focus group interview. Interview questions should be composed in advance, with the caveat that the moderator can modify questions and explore thoughts as the interview proceeds. Questions within the discussion guide are arranged so that more general questions are asked first, and then are followed by more specific questions. By asking general questions first, the moderator is able to encourage participants to become involved in the discussion, build rapport within the group, and stimulate in-group discussions. Then, as the session progresses, the moderator is able to ask more specific questions to guide the conversation toward fulfilling the research purpose.

Questions should probe into the thoughts and even the subconscious of participants. To do so requires open-ended questions with no right or wrong response that individuals feel free and comfortable to answer. Once the flow of information begins, additional questions can be used to probe deeper by asking "what else" or asking other participants how they feel. It is helpful to write some good probing questions in advance of the focus group to ensure the discussion goes beyond surface answers.

Questions should never imply an answer or even hint at what the answer should be. Such questioning quickly squelches open discussion. More important, it may cause participants to guard their responses and look for the "accepted" thoughts the moderator is seeking. For instance, asking participants to discuss "the impact of eating at fast food restaurants on people's health" implies fast foods are not healthy, while asking "tell me your thoughts about fast food restaurants" allows participants to freely discuss positive or negative thoughts.

Balancing questions is another technique that avoids one-sided questions that can lead to response bias. For example, asking respondents, "Do you like Brand X? Why do you like it?" is probably biasing responses as it focuses only positive aspects and forces even those who don't like the brand to think of it in more positive terms. This means that the data may not be valid. A more balanced approach to asking the question would inquire, "Do you like or dislike Brand X? Why do you say that?" Balancing questions involves mentioning both the positive and negative aspects of the concept being investigated, such as whether participants are satisfied or dissatisfied, comfortable or uncomfortable making recommendations, or whether something is an improvement or not an improvement, and then asking why they feel that way.[12]

Source: Jacob Lund/Shutterstock.

Focus group participants should be strangers as this reduces the potential for side conversations or distractions occurring during the focus group session.

4.3c Select Participants

The validity of results is highly dependent upon the selection of the focus group participants. In the situation with The Richards Group and Motel 6, both leisure and business travelers who had stayed at a Motel 6 sometime during the past year were chosen. Notice they had also stayed at other hotels, which was important for exploring the decision-making process and thoughts about Motel 6 in comparison to other motels. In most cases, participants are recruited who have used a brand or at least been exposed to it. However, a company may want to explore the thoughts of individuals who have never used a brand to see why it has never been chosen, though these individuals would most likely be included in a separate focus group. It is rare to mix users and nonusers together in a single group. Sometimes separate focus groups are also developed for different genders, ages, or some other demographic variable which has important links to attitudes or purchasing behaviors.

Participants should be strangers as this reduces the potential for side conversations or distractions occurring during the focus group session. In most instances, marketing research professionals, employees of the parent company or competing firms, and individuals who have participated in a focus group study of any type within the last six months (or longer) are not recruited as participants. Thus, recruiting from churches, work sites, or other entities in which multiple participants may have come in contact with one another can negatively affect the group dynamics and results of a focus group.

Entrepreneurs attempting DIY research should not recruit friends, or friends of friends as focus group participants. Why? First, in all likelihood, these individuals lack diversity with respect to demographic factors such as race, age, income and education. Secondly, obtaining objective opinions from friends or others in a friend's social network is unlikely to occur.[13]

The remaining criteria used for participant selection must be related to the objectives of the study. In a focus group conducted for a small regional airport, one of the research questions sought to understand why individuals chose to drive two hours to a regional airport instead of using the local facility. In order to explore this component of the interview, it was important that the participants had used the regional airport on at least one trip during the previous year and also used the local airport during the same time period. Different focus groups were used for leisure and business travelers in order to discuss topics of interest for each segment, as these interests do not always coincide.

Recruiting focus group participants is not an easy task, as professional respondents are a growing problem in all forms of qualitative research, including focus groups. **Professional respondents** are individuals who belong to multiple research panels for the purpose of participating in multiple research studies, sometimes deceitfully, in order to obtain financial

Professional respondents individuals who belong to multiple research panels for the purpose of participating in many research studies, often deceitfully, in order to obtain financial rewards or gifts.

rewards or gifts. While some professional respondents take their job seriously, and do a good job answering questions—even though they may belong to multiple panels and take a survey every single day—not all professional respondents adhere to this standard. Some professional respondents randomly select answers or barely consider a question in order to complete a study as quickly as possible. The most dangerous form of professional respondent establishes one or more false identities to participate multiple times in the *same* study or to qualify for studies on various topics for which they otherwise would not be eligible to participate. They often lie about their qualifications (such as product ownership) in order to be eligible to participate in a focus group or to take a survey. Professional respondents who engage in fraudulent behavior damage the quality of the data collected, as their lack of knowledge on certain topics often forces them to make up answers.

According to Mark Goodin, president of the Aaron-Abrams Field Support Services, the prevalence of professional respondents may be growing. There is also concern regarding fraudulent survey responses from China. Jacki Lorch, Vice President of Global Knowledge Management at SSI indicates that "a closer understanding of cultural nuances could help us separate true fraud from poor-quality data caused by our ignorance in question wording, targeting, or data interpretation."[14]

While professional respondents are certainly problematic, the Qualitative Research Consultants Association (QRCA) has published best-practice papers and other guidelines that are helpful in managing professional respondents. A sampling of the tactics that can help to eliminate professional respondents from qualitative research studies[15] are summarized in **Figure 4.5.**

1. Discontinue participant recruiting ads on Craigslist and similar sites.
2. Delete respondent databases with a history of professional respondents; start a new database from scratch.
3. Return to old-school respondent sources, such as telephone books, directories, and lists provided by clients or other sources.
4. Verify identities with background checks or Internet searches.
5. Implement high-tech respondent verification techniques, including picture IDs.
6. Use extensive screening, including online, verified by telephone or face-to-face and re-screen at check-in time.
7. Demand proof of product or service ownership when this represents a criterion for participation.
8. Alter payment practices to eliminate both instant payments and payments to professional participants (cheaters) or non-qualified respondents during or after the research study.
9. Initiate legal action against individuals who lie about their qualifications to participate in the study and who are compensated for their participation in a research study.
10. Establish and support a professional industry organization whose mission would be to combat professional fraudulent respondents globally.
11. Attempt to encrypt panel participant data into a single, verifiable and searchable profile.

FIGURE 4.5 Tactics for Minimizing Professional Respondents
Source: Adapted from Mark Goodin, "No more Mr. Nice Guy: professional respondents in qualitative research," *Quirk's Marketing Research Review*, December 2009, retrieved from https://www.quirks.com/articles/2009/20091225-2.aspx?searchID=115593271&msg=3 on September 6, 2010; Marisa L. Pope, "Qualitative Isn't Dead," *Quirk's Media*, (www.quirks.com), January 2018; Chelle Precht, "Recruiting: Looking to the Past to Determine Marketing Research's Future," *Quirk's Media*, (www.quirks.com), January 2018.

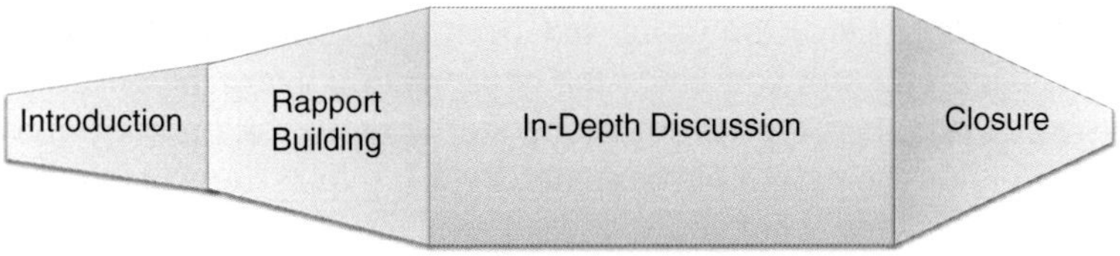

FIGURE 4.6 Stages of the Focus Group Interview

4.3d The Focus Group Session

The actual focus group interview has four distinct stages, shown in Figure 4.6. While each step is important, the bulk of information obtained will occur during the discussion phase.

Introduction During the introduction stage, the focus group participants become acquainted with each other and with the moderator. This step is important since no one in the room should have met prior to the focus group. It's important that moderators set expectations by projecting a friendly and fun attitude. Often moderators use a funny story or anecdote to set the group at ease. Others use an introductory game that cuts tension, builds synergy and the gets the group ready to participate in discussion and exercises.[16] The participants also learn more about the purpose of the focus group and any basic rules of courtesy that are expected, such as not interrupting individuals who are talking, allowing everyone to express their opinion, not talking to each other while someone else is speaking, not criticizing or making fun of a participant's response, and not being offended should the moderator need to interrupt a respondent in order to move the conversation along. If a 360 degree camera is being used, the moderator discloses that fact, and also instructs the group that they should hold any physical materials created during the session in front of them facing the camera as they discuss them with the group.[17] Laying a good foundation for the study ensures a smooth-running focus group and one that produces beneficial insights for the client.

Participants should be carefully briefed on the purpose of the focus group so the research is not compromised. For instance, if participants in the airport focus group were told at the beginning that the purpose of the focus group was to determine why individuals drive two hours to the local regional airport, a free flow of information might have been hindered, and questions not related to that objective would have seemed irrelevant. Instead, participants were told that the purpose of the focus group was to discuss their thoughts about flying and usage of airports in general. This vagueness allowed the group to explore multiple issues related to the selection of an airport and flying in general that may affect that decision. For instance, it is possible that some might drive the two hours because they don't feel comfortable (or safe) in the small planes and want to fly in large jets. Their reasons for driving to a regional airport may have nothing to do with cost savings.

During the introduction, the sponsor of the focus group is rarely identified because it can easily bias responses. If The Richards Group had told participants that the focus group described earlier was sponsored by Motel 6, then that name would have come up during the first round of questioning and participants would not have freely shared their thoughts about the hotel chain. It would have especially restricted negative thoughts about the brand.

Rapport Building As the focus group moves to the rapport-building stage, the moderator asks general questions to encourage participants to talk. The questions should be easy to answer and ones that everyone can answer. For example, it was easy for members of the motel focus group to identify what hotels they had patronized since all were selected because they had stayed in more than one hotel brand. Similarly, for the airport focus group individuals could talk about the various airports they had used since all had flown out of more airports than just the local facility. They could also talk about what they liked and disliked about the local airport as well as other airports.

In-Depth Discussion Once the group has been put at ease and become comfortable with each other, the moderator can guide the conversation using the questions developed for the discussion guide. It is typical for moderators to also ask probing questions which require deep thought on the part of participants. **Probing questions** respond to participant comments by asking "why, what, how, please explain, or tell me more." These types of questions lead to deeper thinking. During the discussion stage it is also helpful if participants begin responding to each other and not just to the moderator. Group dynamics come in to play when this free flow of information causes participants to feed off of each other's comments, which often provides valuable information. The moderator's role is to monitor the discussion and bring it back on topic if it strays too far away. However, it is not uncommon for unplanned but interesting questions to be uncovered that provide additional insight beyond what would have been captured by the original focus group questions.

Probing questions "why, what, how, please explain," or "tell me more" types of questions that will lead to deeper thinking.

In addition to answering questions, focus group participants may be asked to work in teams to brainstorm ideas, to view visual stimuli (ads or package designs, for example) and provide responses, or perform other qualitative research tasks, such as sentence completion exercises or collage building. Plus, new technological tools such as facial recognition can add additional insights from nonverbal behavior that is captured and recorded.[18]

Closure As the focus group session nears the end, the moderator should bring the interview to closure by asking participants if they have any final thoughts on the topic. It may be appropriate at this time to reveal the sponsor or provide more information about the purpose of the study. It's also a good time to gather feedback about the sessions itself to see if improvements can be made to future focus group sessions.

Moderator Characteristics The success of focus groups is highly dependent on the ability of the moderator to manage the interview process. Moderators must do their homework and fully understand several factors relevant to the focus group topic prior to beginning the interview. Examples include the market position of the client and its competition, product or market trends, brand characteristics, strengths, weaknesses and key traits of focus group participants.[19]

Managing a group of 6 to 10 individuals within an interview is not an easy task. It requires training and experience. It is also helpful if respondents can relate to the moderator. "It makes sense when doing a fashion-related group of overweight, 18–28 year-old women that the moderator be female, that the moderator not be a size two, and that the moderator be able to empathize with this segment."[20]

Perhaps the most important characteristic of a good moderator is that he or she is completely open to participant feedback, be it positive or negative. Listening in a non-judgmental manner is critical, so that participants believe that there is not a right or wrong response. Moderators must also carefully control their own body language, particularly facial expressions, as a grimace can cue respondents that the information being provided is unwelcome in some fashion, which in turn could potentially cut short the flow of valuable information. Coaxing respondent feedback from those less likely to participate, and preventing overly talkative group members from dominating the conversation are also among the most important skills possessed by experienced moderators. **Figure 4.7** summarizes the key responsibilities of moderators.

Source: Photographee.eu/Shutterstock.

Perhaps the most important characteristic of a good moderator is that he or she is completely open to participant feedback, be it positive or negative. Listening in a non-judgmental manner is critical, so that participants believe that there is not a right or wrong response.

- Establish and maintain rapport quickly
- Maintain eye contact
- Actively listen to respondents, not to confirm a hypothesis
- Provide unconditional positive regard and participant feedback; don't let personal bias or judgment get in the way
- Probe for clarity and in-depth thoughts
- Solicit input from quiet members
- Manage dominant, talkative members
- Watch for and attend to nonverbal behavior that may indicate differences of opinion
- Guide interviews to stay on topic
- Paraphrase understanding, confirm with participants
- Provide positive feedback and encouragement
- Allow and manage silence
- Manage time to ensure all topics are covered

FIGURE 4.7 Tasks of the Moderator During the Focus Group
Source: Adapted from "Two Maxims for Moderators," Marketing Research, Vol. 21, No. 2, Summer 2009, pp. 26–27; Laurie Tema-Lyn, "12 Considerations from Professional Listeners," *Quirk's Media*, (www.quirks.com), Article ID 20170507, May 4, 2017 and Naomi Henderson, "Guiding the Next Generation: Lessons Learned from Training Thousands of Moderators," *Quirk's Media*, (www.quirks.com), January 2019.

4.3e Debriefing

When the focus group is over, all of the observers and the moderator should meet to discuss what just occurred. This debriefing allows each observer and the moderator to indicate what they saw and heard. While everyone witnessed the same focus group interview, the interpretation of what was seen is likely to vary considerably. Just as eye witnesses to an auto accident can differ in their descriptions, each person might have a different account of what happened in the group. Thus, new insights are often gained that are not readily evident to the moderator. Some questions that might be asked of the observers include:[21]

- What did you hear that was a surprise, that you did not expect?
- What did you hear that confirmed what you expected?
- What new thoughts were generated by the focus group?
- How will you use the insights from the focus group?

Wyeth, which is a producer of healthcare and pharmaceutical products such as Advil, ChapStick, and Robitussin, finds debriefing extremely valuable. The company uses focus groups regularly to explore innovation opportunities, evaluations of marketing messages, and as a precursor to quantitative research. According to Tony DiMicelli, vice-president of marketing, "The fact that we're all together in the back room is important because it is a way to get everyone on the same page, to make sure the qualitative learning that is taking place is being interpreted properly."[22]

Focus group debriefing provided valuable insight for Denny's and resulted in a change in their advertising approach and positioning strategy. The participants in the focus groups did not refer to Denny's as a family restaurant. According to Frances Allen, chief marketing officer at Denny's, "People think of the brand as a diner, with great comfort food at a great price, and they feel that incredible warmth and incredible connection to the servers. There's a soul to a diner that is very authentic, very warm, and very accepting." Using the information from the focus group, Denny's was repositioned as a diner, not a family restaurant, with a new slogan. "America's diner is always open."[23]

4.3f Written Report

Once the series of focus group interviews are complete, the client will want a report. Although the sessions are recorded and can be reviewed, the moderator should capture major ideas from each session immediately upon finishing each of the sessions. This can be done by writing down "hot notes" that capture the thoughts that shout the loudest and stand out.[24] The idea is to capture these impressions immediately before they are gone. Even conversations that support the ideas can be noted, with exact wording located on the transcripts later.

If the session has been visually recorded, researchers should code and tag the video clips by keyword, brand name, research objective, or other important terms that facilitate archiving and keyword searching. It is common to include a few key clips with the report that bring to life the consumer's viewpoint, or which may summarize key thoughts or feelings on a particular topic. However, the entire video collection should be provided to the client, along with the written report.[25]

The actual report should refer back to the research purpose and specific research questions investigated by the focus group interviews. A summary of the findings should then be written in the context of these research questions. Using the hot notes, support for the various findings can then be provided. Most reports will conclude with recommendations that are based on the findings of the qualitative research.

4.3g Advantages and Disadvantages of Focus Groups

General advantages of focus groups include group dynamics that benefit the brainstorming and idea generation process, as well discussion and evaluation of concepts and ideas. The key advantage though is the richer, deeper insights that focus group data provides, especially when compared to quantitative data.

The primary disadvantage of focus groups is that each represents the opinion of only a few individuals. Even with multiple focus groups, it is still only the view of a small number of individuals in comparison to the thousands or millions of consumers who may purchase a particular product. Thus, a key disadvantage of focus groups is that the results may not represent the larger population of consumers.

Secondly, as focus groups are qualitative in nature, the results are highly subjective to the interpretation of the moderator and marketing researchers involved in the interviews. The client participants observing the sessions can also affect the results through the debriefing process, observing what they want to see rather than what actually occurred.

Group think phenomenon that occurs when individuals within the group come to a consensus on a thought or idea through the informal leadership of one or two individuals.

"Group think" is another often-cited disadvantage of focus group interviews. **Group think** occurs when individuals within the group come to a consensus on a thought or idea through the informal leadership of one or two individuals. Rather than disagree or talk about their true feelings, individuals may be swept along with the majority of consumers. It is difficult to speak up in a focus group and say "I disagree, I think . . . . ." when the majority of the group has expressed a different opinion. This is especially true for individuals who may be more introverted or too timid to talk in a group setting.

Restaurant operators have regularly used focus groups to solicit input on new menu items. But in recent years, restaurants have moved away from focus groups because they believe "group think" tended to dictate what consumers thought of new menu items. When one or two disliked it, others would agree rather than stand alone with their thoughts. Another disadvantage to these focus groups, according to Andrew Stefanovich, a senior partner at Prophet (a marketing consulting firm), "is that consumers can only react to what they're fed, and not propose something new."[26]

Executives at Quiznos, however, are strong believers in focus groups, but use them in a unique way to test new menu items. They use a speed-dining approach with as many as 25 focus groups in back-to-back sessions. The company reworks recipes based on focus group input; then re-submits the recipes to the original as well as new focus groups. This process allows Quiznos to find the right ingredients, portion sizes, and prices that consumers want.[27]

4.4 In-Depth Interviews

LEARNING OBJECTIVE 4.4
Explain the process of using in-depth interviews to conduct qualitative research.

Focus groups are excellent at probing into the thoughts of individuals, as a group. But they sometimes result in group think, where one or two individuals control the conversation or at least the direction of the discussion. Also, some participants are reluctant to speak out in a group. Others may give what they perceive as socially acceptable answers rather than reveal their true feelings. To avoid these potential pitfalls, researchers might conduct **in-depth interviews (IDIs)**, which are a qualitative research method involving one-on-one interviews conducted by a marketing research professional. The goal of the in-depth interview is to probe deeply into an individual's thoughts and ideas in an effort to better understand a person's mental activities and behaviors. For example, in journey mapping research, in-depth interviews are used to understand how consumer segments interact with a brand or marketing touchpoints, their motivations, and the process they follow. Touchpoints refers to any interaction with the brand, be it marketing communications, one or more distribution channels, customer service or sales representatives or some other brand interaction. In-depth interviews allow researchers to identify and understand the content, media, locations, technology and individuals that consumers rely on as they complete tasks desired by the marketer. Tasks can include, but are not limited to, the following:

In-Depth Interviews (IDIs) qualitative research method involving one-on-one interviews for the purpose of probing deeply into an individual's thoughts and ideas to better understand a person's mental activities and behaviors.

- Achieving purchases among new users
- Converting in-person customer service users to online or mobile customer service
- Converting users from paper to electronic communications or statements

A key benefit of in-depth interviews in the context of journey mapping is that they are very useful in highlighting touchpoints that are not performing as expected. Marketing managers can use these insights to improve the effectiveness of the touchpoints, which should improve relationships with the various consumer segments. However, IDIs alone are insufficient to complete a journey mapping study. Mixed methods research involving quantitative market segmentation studies, forecasting research, and internal marketing analytics tracking and reporting are also required.[28]

4.4a In-Depth Interview Process

Just as with the focus group, the marketing researcher will develop a list of questions for the in-depth interview. Based on input from the client, specific goals will be set that will form the basis for the questions. Probing questions or cues are also planned, though the researcher may ask unplanned questions as needed to better understand the participants' responses. But, with the in-depth interview, the researcher has an opportunity to dig deep into the thoughts and ideas of individuals in a way that is not possible with a focus group. Because it is one-to-one, individuals often feel more comfortable talking, especially about deep-seated beliefs, thoughts, and ideas.

The typical in-depth interview lasts one to two hours, which provides ample opportunity for probing deep thoughts. It also allows the researcher and the participant to become comfortable with each other so more intimate and personal reflections can be shared. Thoughts and ideas that would never be said in a group can be made to an individual, especially knowing that results of the interview will remain anonymous.

Sarah Stanley, of Missouri University of Science and Technology, used in-depth interviews to better understand why brand communities form. She attended two Jeep Jamborees and interviewed people about the Jamborees and why they attended. Through the in-depth interviews she found that the Jeep brand had a strong meaning to the participants.

Many had developed relationships with their vehicles. For instance, one person said his "Jeep was overworked that weekend and 'she' needed to go home and rest for a couple of days." Statements of personality or persona given to their vehicles were common during the interviews. Individuals felt their Jeeps stood for freedom, being able to "go anywhere—through streams and over rocks." Through story-telling and communicating with other Jeep owners, individuals developed an even stronger bond with the brand and each other.[29]

In-depth interviews can be used by marketing researchers to learn about a topic or issue prior to conducting a quantitative study. For instance, before conducting a quantitative study about digital versus traditional newspaper readership, a pair of marketing researchers conducted in-depth interviews. From these interviews they found four primary reasons individuals read newspapers: (1) to search for specific information, (2) to get updated news, (3) for leisure, and (4) as a habit. This information then served as the foundation for conducting structured quantitative research.[30]

4.4b Disadvantages of In-Depth Interviews

Because the in-depth interview process involves one-on-one interaction, it is highly subjective. The researcher not only controls the interpretation of what occurs, but also has great control over the interview itself. Interviewer rapport with the subject is critical to encouraging honest, thoughtful responses. Similar to focus group moderators, interviewers must also be careful not to bias the respondents' replies via words or actions or interviewer error will occur. Respondents may think they are "helping" an interviewer whom they like by giving responses they think that person desires to hear, rather than sharing the thoughts, feelings, and beliefs that they truly hold. Because of the length of time involved in the interview and the reporting of each interview, in-depth interviews tend to be costly to conduct, and as a result only a small set of interviews are usually undertaken. Focus groups and in-depth interviews each have their place in the research process. Ultimately, the study purpose and research questions need to be carefully considered when determining whether a focus group or in-depth interview is the appropriate methodology. More specific factors influencing the choice of focus groups versus in-depth interview methodology are summarized in **Figure 4.8**.

Use In-Depth Interviews When:	Use Focus Groups When:
• Research questions are directly related to specific respondent segments and individual behavior. • In-depth interviews reach the population of interest easier (such as in the case of small, geographically dispersed populations). • The cost-benefit ratio favors in-depth interviews. • Group think / group dynamics might be a problem. • Usability testing of a device or process is sought. • Subject matter is highly sensitive.	• Research questions seek to explore disparate views via consensus or debate. • Group dynamics are helpful in discovering information. • Topics are broad, and participants need help generating or sharing ideas. • Participant interaction is desired and helpful in stimulating discussion and discovering underlying issues. • Teamwork is desired. • Exploring common trends. • When client interaction is desirable.

FIGURE 4.8 Factors Influencing the Choice of In-Depth Interview vs. Focus Group

Source: Adapted from Carey V. Azzara, "Qualitatively Speaking: The focus group vs. in-depth interview debate," *Quirks Marketing Research Review, June 2010*, p. 16, retrieved from http://www.quirks.com/articles/2010/20100601.aspx?searchID=116421703&sort=4&pg=1 on September 6, 2010.

4.5 Online Qualitative Research

LEARNING OBJECTIVE 4.4
Discuss the various types of online qualitative research being used by companies.

In developing the concept for Burger Studio at colleges and universities, Aramark conducted online focus groups and sponsored chat rooms. The goal was to capture student thoughts about all of the elements of operation of the Burger Studio from conception to final delivery. Even the name was the result of an online contest with over 1,200 names being submitted.[31]

The qualitative research methods used by Aramark illustrate the recent trend by a number of companies and research firms relying more on online methodologies. As shown in Figure 4.9, this trend is due to a number of reasons. Reduced costs and quicker results are the primary reasons for this switch. With tighter marketing, advertising and research budgets, lower costs are a very attractive reason for using online methodologies. Just as important is the need for quicker information to make management decisions.

Advances in online and smart phone technologies have provided researchers with a number of different ways of engaging individuals in online research. Focus groups can be held via text messaging, video conferencing, or audio conferencing. It can be synchronous (done in real time) or asynchronous (spread out over longer periods of time with different people participating at different times). Discussion boards, chat rooms, and social media sites can also be used.

Online methodologies allow for geographically dispersed individuals to participate in the same research study, allowing researchers to access a broader sample of individuals more quickly, and at a lower cost compared to traditional methods. While 6 to 10 individuals are optimal for an in-person focus group, some forms of online focus groups can accommodate more individuals using asynchronous formats for discussion. Since travel is not involved, it is more convenient for participants and observers, especially if asynchronous discussions are used. Lastly, the Internet has become a primary method of communication for individuals. They share ideas and thoughts online now, so using it for qualitative research is a natural extension of this current method of communication.

4.5a Online Focus Groups

Online focus groups share many of the same characteristics as traditional focus groups, though they also differ in some important areas. Figure 4.10 provides a summary comparison of traditional and online focus groups. A key advantage shared by all online focus groups is the ability to complete the focus groups more quickly, typically in days. Traditional focus groups often require weeks to complete, especially when travel is involved.

Synchronous focus group interviews online chat, audio or video focus groups conducted in real time.

Synchronous focus group interviews are online chat, audio or video focus groups conducted in real time, usually using software purchased or leased from a vendor. Synchronous online focus groups rarely exceed eight participants as more than that becomes difficult to manage in an online environment. Sessions also tend to be shorter than traditional focus groups, lasting between 60 and 90 minutes. Moderators are able to guide the discussion just as they would if the participants were in a physical room. The compressed timeframe makes it more difficult for moderators to sufficiently probe responses from groups larger than eight people. Moderators are also more likely to stick to the discussion guide questions, and not go off-script to follow-up interesting questions, as they might

- Advancements in technology
- Availability of geographically dispersed sample
- Lower costs
- Quicker results
- Convenient for participants, clients, and researchers
- Current trend in consumer communication

FIGURE 4.9 Reasons for Conducting Qualitative Research Online

Traditional Focus Groups	Online Synchronous	Online Asynchronous
• Completion often takes weeks face-to-face • 6–10 participants per group • Longer sessions (90–120 minutes) • Group think / group dynamics might be a problem • Requires budget for transcription service of recorded audio • Participants are more focused, and pay better attention • Requires travel for moderator or observers • Allows clients to observe focus groups • Allows for observation of non-verbal behavior • Allows for collaborative exercises during session • Most expensive • Limited geographic reach	• Completion time in days • Online chat or video • Maximum of 8 participants per group • Shorter sessions (60–90) minutes • Chat-based groups can control for group think using software • Moderators can achieve group dynamics • Chat based groups provide a ready-made transcript • Participants multi-task and are less engaged • Comfortable with Internet communication • Participants may have technical problems that disrupt the entire group • No travel required • Allows for some video observation of non-verbal behavior • Some collaboration is possible • Less expensive than F2F • Diverse geographic spread	• Completion in days • Bulletin board question / response format • 30–100+ per group • Extended sessions (multiple days) • Limited group dynamics • Provides a ready-made transcript • Participants have more time to think about questions and often respond in-depth • Poor quality participants can be replaced during focus group study • Comfortable with Internet communication • No travel required • Clients can read answers as they come through or log-in. Clients can request new questions to be sent to some or all participants • Limited/non-existent non-verbal behavior • Limited potential for collaboration • Higher drop-out rates • Less expensive • Most diverse geographic spread as participants logon whenever and from wherever they wish

FIGURE 4.10 Comparison of Traditional and Online Focus Groups

Source: Adapted from Carey V. Azzara, "Qualitatively Speaking: The focus group vs. in-depth interview debate," *Quirks Marketing Research Review, June 2010*, p. 16, retrieved from http://www.quirks.com/articles/2010/20100601.aspx?searchID=116421703&sort=4&pg=1 on September 6, 2010 and Richard Clark, Online Focus Group Advantages and Disadvantages, MRQual Online Research (www.mrqual.com), October 13, 2017, retrieved from https://www.mrqual.com/2017/10/13/online-focus-group-advantages-disadvantages/, 10/15/2019.

in a face-to-face focus group. In chat-based synchronous focus groups, the moderator types in the questions and participants respond by typing their thoughts, concerns, ideas or others forms of answers.

Early attempts at online focus groups were criticized as being overly biased toward articulate respondents who could type quickly; and, since body language could not be observed in text-based sessions, the results were not considered to be the same as what could be obtained in a traditional face-to-face session. However, technology has improved and actually benefited the online focus group process in some ways. For example, many chat-based focus group software programs allow the moderator to block respondents from seeing answers to questions posted by other focus group members until they post their own response, which helps to limit group think. Plus, chat-based focus groups provide a ready-made transcript of the session immediately, whereas traditional focus groups must be sent-off to a transcript service, requiring extra time and money. Group dynamics are still present in a synchronous focus group, though it can be more difficult to achieve in a chat-based session compared to webcam/video synchronous focus group session.

High-speed internet, web cam technology, and greater bandwidth availability have led to a greater prevalence of video-based synchronous focus groups. Video-based focus groups provide an experience more closely related to a traditional focus group in that participants are able to see one another, and the moderator and observers who log on to the focus group software are able to observe at least some body language. Videos can be stored, transcribed, coded, and segmented, in a manner similar to that described with traditional focus groups that use video. However, instead of being restricted to video from a single camera, each participant's video will need to be coded and clipped individually. Plus, if the video clearly captures facial expressions, a facial coding analysis can be performed to uncover underlying emotions. And that's the trade-off. Recall that only one camera is typically used in traditional focus groups, so much of the body language and facial expressions of the rest of the group are not captured, as the 360 degree camera rotates to focus on the person currently speaking. The costs of analyzing the video content from synchronous online groups may exceed that of traditional focus groups, but the ability to uncover emotions and determine if facial expressions truly matches what people feel is often superior. Facial coding analysis will be discussed in Chapter 5.

In today's online, multitasking world, a key advantage of in-person focus groups is that the moderator enjoys the participant's full attention, assuming phones are turned off during the session. In that regard, in-person focus groups offer greater attention to detail and greater focus on the tasks at hand when compared to online synchronous groups, as online participants tend to be multi-tasking during the session, resulting in lower engagement and lower quality data. It's also easier to interpret the data for in-person focus groups than it is for online focus groups. Despite the costs, many researchers and clients believe that in-person focus groups provide greater value. Specifically, it is easier observe (in-person) the nonverbal behavior of participants that occur as a result of another's comment, or an individual's body language that occurs when viewing a package design or ad mock-up. These reactions may be at odds with what the participant says, but body language offers a truer gauge of how people really feel or think. While synchronous video captures facial expressions well, webcams are usually too close to an individual to capture their entire non-verbal behavior, and some important reactions may be missed. Plus, in-person focus groups give the appearance of offering greater security and privacy when focus group sessions deal with sensitive subjects, though in reality, asynchronous online focus groups offer the greatest privacy, as questions can be restricted to moderator view only.[32]

Drawbacks include the fact that both video and chat synchronous focus group participants often multi-task with their phones, tablets, or PCs or during the session. So participants are less engaged with tasks and questions than are participants in face-to-face focus groups. The remaining advantages and disadvantages outlined in Figure 4.10 are self-explanatory. Time and cost savings are key advantages of online synchronous groups, as is access to a more geographically diverse group.[33]

J.C. Penney used an online focus group to investigate cross-channel shopping behaviors. The study began with an online survey that asked broad questions about shopping behaviors and attitudes. Heavy cross-channel shoppers were gleaned from the survey to be participants for an online focus group. Each participant was given $50 to go shopping. The shoppers were then asked to share via the online focus group venue what they purchased, where they purchased it, their feelings about the shopping experience, and why they bought what they did. As J.C. Penney observed the interactions among the participants, the company was surprised that cross-channel shopping was not limited to a specific demographic group, age, or income. The company also learned that shopping can begin with any of the three channels—the physical store, online store, or catalog.[34]

The trend in online focus groups, however, is moving away from real-time to asynchronous communication. **Asynchronous online focus groups** take place over several days, allowing participants to login and off at their convenience. With this format focus groups tend to run over a few days to as long as two weeks. Respondents log on at their convenience, make comments, reply to questions or queries, and interact with other respondents. While asynchronous online focus groups share the benefits common to all online methodologies, group think and other negative personality influences associated with traditional focus groups are often minimized with this format. According to Katie Harris of Zebra Research, "You're providing respondents with a relatively safe and anonymous environment, conducive to deep thought and honesty. You're giving them thinking time. You're giving them air time. It's a level playing field where everyone looks the same.

Asynchronous online focus groups take place over several days, allowing participants to login and off at their convenience.

[Online focus groups] mirror the way people voice opinions and communicate with each other, including corporations, in the real world."[35]

Questions are posted one at a time, and answered in a sequential order. Group sizes include 30 or more individuals with some topping over 100 participants, so data can be gathered more quickly. The format is similar to a chat-based focus group, though participants have more time to think about the questions and to post their responses. Because respondents login when it is convenient for them to do so, they are more engaged in the task compared to participants in synchronous focus groups. As a result, they often post detailed, in-depth responses to questions.[36]

It is common for moderators to request that participants upload videos or images as part of their responses, which helps researchers to understand the written responses. Furthermore, the imagery and video clips help bring the final report to life for the client. Most platforms allow moderators to control for group think by requiring posts before respondents can read the responses of others in the group. Additionally, some software allow for notifications when someone has responded to a post, so that the original poster can read the reply and respond to further the discussion. Client observation is easier and more convenient compared to both face-to-face and synchronous focus groups. With asynchronous focus groups, clients can receive and read responses when they are posted, or they can login and read them at a time of their own choosing. The asynchronous online focus group format more easily incorporates suggestions, questions, or probes offered by the client, compared to traditional or synchronous groups. For example, new questions can be inserted easily into the discussion, or a client can tell the moderator to direct that certain questions or new probes be sent to only one or some of the participants. An additional benefit is that poor quality respondents can be replaced while the research is underway, as a replacement participant would simply begin by answering the first question, and then move forward with the remaining questions. Finally, asynchronous focus groups allow for the greatest geographic diversity as participants login and off at their own convenience from anywhere in the world, and they often are the least expensive type of focus group to complete.[37]

Asynchronous focus groups are not with disadvantages. Achieving meaningful group dynamics is difficult due to the asynchronous nature of the group. Non-verbal behavior is typically non-existent, unless the participant submits a video interview showing his or her face answering questions (which is atypical). Collaboration among focus group participants is most difficult with this type of group. Higher dropout-rates are common, because of the multi-day format. But, for many situations, especially those involving sensitive subjects or requiring detailed, thoughtful answers, the benefits outweigh these advangages.[38]

Source: Andrey_Popov/Shutterstock.

High-speed internet, web cam technology, and greater bandwidth availability have led to a greater prevalence of video-based synchronous focus groups.

The market research firm Decision Analyst offers potential clients a bulletin board format for their asynchronous online focus groups, which they label "Time Extended™ Online Discussion Forums." Moderators facilitate discussions among 12 to 15 participants who have been recruited for a specific study. Follow-up questions encouraging detailed, thoughtful responses are posted by the moderator, targeting either the group as a whole, or a specific individual. The result is very rich, highly detailed information. Decision Analysts believes that this key benefit of the extended format stems from the fact that "the extra time available to the moderator (and to the clients) allows them to ask more reflective and insightful follow-up questions than would be practical in other types of qualitative research."[39]

For researchers on a budget, FocusGroupIt (https://www.focusgroupit.com/) is a free software platform that can be used for asynchronous focus groups of up to ten people (moderator included). Videos, PDF files, and graphic files can be attached to focus group questions created by the moderator, enabling ad testing, concept testing, and participation in other qualitative research activities. FocusGroupIt is primarily a chat-based platform, so responses are generally typed, but participants can also share video answers less than three minutes in length. When creating questions, settings allow for a question to be private, meaning that only the moderator (and observers) see a respondent's answer, which is preferred when asking sensitive questions. Respondent's names can be used, or they can be assigned an avatar, or alias, to ensure anonymity. Clients can login and review the focus group responses at any time, and they can leave private comments for the moderator. However, clients cannot directly interact with the respondents. New questions can be added at any time.[40]

4.5b Online In-Depth Interviews

In-depth interviews can also be conducted online or through mobile devices. It can be a text-based interview or a video interview. Either way, a trained moderator is typically involved in the process. Online interviews further reduce the costs since no travel is required. It is good way to conduct interviews about sensitive topics that may be embarrassing to individuals. This is especially true for the text-only approaches where the interviewer cannot see the respondent. While online in-depth interviews may be as short as 30 minutes, research firm Decision Analysts offers a time-extended version of the in-depth interview which varies in length from as little as two days to as long as one week. Key advantages of the time-extended format include 1) richer content and deeper, more meaningful consumer insights; 2) real-time transcript viewing by clients, and a correspondingly greater opportunity for clients to interact with the facilitator; and 3) ability to ask more detailed, insightful follow-up questions, compared to other forms of qualitative research. Decision Analysts also offers Time-Extended Close-Ups™ in which respondents reply to fewer questions in a single posting. Time-Extended™ Concept Reactions gather participants immediate reactions to new concepts as well as suggestions for improvement.[41]

4.5c Market Research Online Communities (MROC)

Market Research Online Communities (MROCs) remain the most popular emerging methodology for research industry professionals. A recent *GreenBook Research Industry Trends Report* found that 59 percent of the market research suppliers and clients who responded to the survey indicated they currently use online communities, while another 21 percent were considering adoption.[42] A MROC is an online group of either brand advocates or highly involved individuals who agree to participate in research related to an activity or brand that is of interest to the researcher. MROCs are proprietary to the recruiting firm, which may be a brand manufacturer or a market research firm specializing in qualitative research. MROCs can take the form of an instant community that is recruited for a specific project, then disbanded when finished, a pop-up group, in which members are only called upon intermittently throughout the year, or may instead serve as an ongoing branded community that is used on a long-term basis. This latter form of MROC works well when attempting to understand the target audience's attitudes, interest and usage patterns, or when testing marketing communications messages with the target audience.[43]

Market Research Online Community (MROC) online group of either brand advocates or highly involved individuals who agree to participate in research related to an activity or brand that is of interest to the researcher.

MROCs are especially effective with younger consumers who are already tech savvy, and branded MROCS allow researchers to better understand opinions over time. For example, Roxy is a manufacturer of footwear that strives to stay in touch with the latest fashion happenings of the teen and immediate post-teen market. To do so, Roxy has established an ongoing branded MROC called the Style Squad, which consists of thousands of girls from across the United States. Birgit Klett, designer for Roxy, posts questions and styles online to get Style Squad members' reactions and feedback. Since feedback is quick and anonymous, Klett is able to obtain input much more quickly than through traditional means such as focus groups. She is also able to obtain feedback from a much larger sample. While it is still subjective information and should not be subjected to any type of quantitative analysis, it does provide input into what styles of shoes are "in" and what will be acceptable to her target market.[44]

Ongoing branded MROCs do an excellent job of providing quick responses and reactions to specific questions, especially when an issue pops up unexpectedly. They can also be used to crowdsource innovative ideas, services or products and to tap into the target market's stream of consciousness. Concept validation, service quality improvement, and advertising refinement are a few additional uses of MROCs.[45]

MROCs offer firms the ability to reduce research costs compared to traditional in-depth qualitative studies, while providing faster results due to the continuous nature of the insights generated. For example, a major office supply chain decided to forgo its typical research plan of approximately seven independent projects in favor of a MROC. One-hundred office supply chain purchasing agents were recruited to participate in the MROC, and the research agency worked together with the client to develop a continuous stream of research projects. For example, one week half of the panel was asked to complete a purchase diary and discuss their purchasing needs in a MROC forum. The next week, just a few customers were asked to provide interactive feedback, via webcam, on a new concept of interest to purchasing agents.[46]

MROCs make use of a variety of technologies. Chat-based bulletin boards are used for interactive discussions among members, while blog tools serve as a platform for journals or diaries, and allow for video uploads. Surveys and mini-polls are also possible, though researchers should never use this as a substitute for true quantitative research. Usually, open-ended questions are included in the surveys along with simple multiple choice questions, and the purpose is simply to get a quick read on a situation, product, or idea. Angelfish Fieldwork offers a MROC software solution called Shoal Mates. In addition to the technologies previously mentioned, it offers an Ideastorm tool that allows participants to submit ideas or concepts in text, photo or video format related to an assignment, then rate the submissions made by others. Photo sharing technologies help to accumulate pictures quickly, and can be used for collage activities or semiotic studies when participants are asked to caption each photo submitted. Finally, the MarkUp tool allows participants to view an ad or concept, and drop pins in areas of interest. Pins are explained using text answers or emoticons, and heat maps are generated for client review.[47]

To be effective, branded MROCs require a high level of resource commitment and dedicated personnel to manage the community. IT security is paramount, and a steady stream of new recruits will be necessary to replace churn. Using a variety of research topics and methodologies helps to keep participants engaged. MROCs work best when a company representative engages directly with community members as the "human face" of the brand. Specifically, representatives should follow-up with consumers and give them feedback on what the firm is doing as a result of their input. Participants want to know that their opinions matter and are valued. Branded MROCs are best used when a firm has both longitudinal research objectives and a continuous stream of stimuli to present to MROC participants. They work well with niche target markets that may be difficult to recruit from research panels. The speed with which data can be delivered is a primary advantage, but it should not be the only factor driving selection of a MROC. Let the research objectives drive the research; budget pressure is not a sufficient reason to disengage from existing qualitative research studies unless you truly believe that MROCs can accomplish the same research objectives.[48] Key considerations for setting up a branded MROC are displayed in **Figure 4.11.**

Instant MROCs offer an excellent and cost-efficient way to obtain quick, gut-level feelings about a topic, issue, or concept, assuming the stimuli presented to the group are fairly straightforward and simple. Data can usually be collected in a few hours either asynchronously or synchronously, especially through panels of pre-established participants who are often selected from a larger branded MROC based on demographic profiles or other criteria.

- Create a 12 month interaction plan including topics and types of interactions
- Personalize notifications to members' specific interests to increase engagement
- Recognize highly engaged members with points, titles or discounts on merchandise
- Make participation fun through gamification by maximizing interaction and visual elements.
- Give participants the option to remain anonymous when they sign-up

FIGURE 4.11 Recommendations When Setting Up a MROC
Source: Adapted from Alex Osbaldeston, "Are You Embracing the Increase in Consumers Willing to Participate in MROCs?" *Quirk's Media*, (www.quirks.com), Article ID 2016076-2, July 2016.

4.5d Chat Rooms, Bulletin Boards

When firms lack the resources to recruit participants or to host an ongoing or instant MROC, an alternative method of data collection occurs when a researcher creates a forum on a free bulletin board or chat room. Recruiting participants can be challenging, as they must articulate their thoughts clearly in order to contribute meaningfully to the discussion. Moderators ask for feedback or pose questions that can elicit interesting information. However, the ethical researcher should follow the Word-of-Mouth Marketing Association's guidelines, and not misrepresent themselves as regular consumers, but instead identify their company affiliation. The use of live chat rooms unaffiliated with MROCs or research panels is now fairly rare.

Some firms still use bulletin boards for qualitative research. Predominantly text-based, bulletin boards function as asynchronous chat rooms that require an experienced moderator to keep the ensuing discussion on track. Bulletin boards offer a more relaxed, less expensive and less complicated method of collecting qualitative data, and are best used when the topic generates strong, diverse, and passionate opinions. Data are collected over a few days, rather than a few hours as with MROCs, but the bulletin boards allow for deeper thinking and participation at the respondent's convenience. Questions are posed by the moderator and participants are asked to comment. Interaction among participants is quick to develop, especially since each person is anonymous. The inherent difficulty lies in the recruitment of subjects, as participants must be extremely articulate to express insightful opinions. The lack of visual stimuli is also problematic, and for these reasons, instant MROCs and other asynchronous methods have largely replaced bulletin boards in recent years.[49]

However, recent research suggests that mobile chat apps may have a future in qualitative research. In a presentation at the 21st annual ESOMAR Global Qualitative conference, representatives from InSites Consulting and Heineken discussed the results of a study in which they tested the WhatsApp and Messenger chat apps as qualitative research alternatives to traditional forums. The apps generated better quality data, including more examples and better insights. Participants were more comfortable conversing on Apps compared to the forum, resulting in increased levels of conversation. Automated chat bots, which used artificial intelligence in place of interviewers, were also tested. These bots asked questions, and probed responses. Interestingly, the bots came to the same research conclusions as did the human

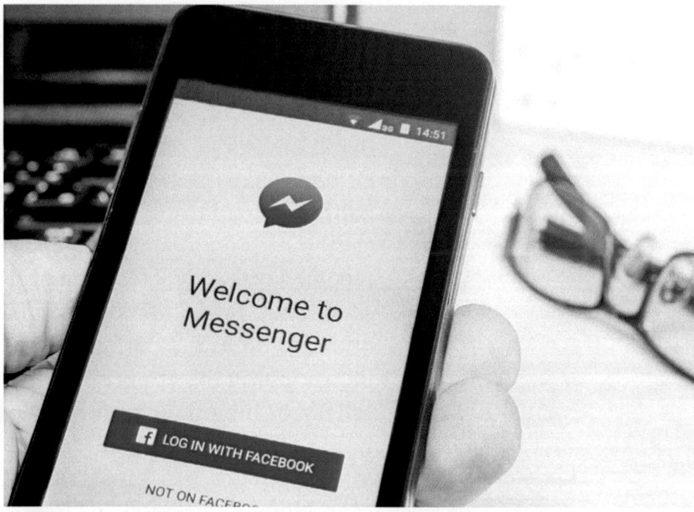

Source: Jakraphong Photography/Shutterstock.

Mobile chat apps such as Messenger and WhatsApp may have a future in qualitative research, as one study found that the apps generated better quality data, including more examples and better insights when compared to bulletin board forums.

moderators, but in a much more timely fashion. The bots were able to complete the analysis in just 20 percent of the time required by humans, which allowed Heineken to test all 60 concepts using the bot-moderated chat app.[50]

While the idea of integrating bots into qualitative research based on this study's results is enticing, these findings are based on only a single study, and may not be valid in other research scenarios. The ability of bots to save time seems reasonable, but many researchers do not believe that artificial intelligence can truly replace people in focus groups or in-depth interviews, as machine's lack empathy, a key trait shared by the best moderators and interviewers. "Empathy may even serve the qualitative research process before the respondent begins answering, as it is used to make the respondents feel comfortable,"[51] noted marketing strategist Evelyn Starr. Empathy builds respondent rapport, which in turn influences what and how much people are willing to say when responding to questions. Furthermore, without the empathetic ability to truly understand and share the feelings of another, bots are incapable of "reading between the lines" and integrating not only what people say but they how say it, and cannot connect with consumers in a manner that allows for an understanding of deeply held needs and wants. A very valid concern is that qualitative research conducted with today's bots may fail to uncover needs and wants that requires creativity, interpretation, and empathy, or possibly fail to gather surface information if the bot is not able to establish rapport and trust with respondents. Still, artificial intelligence is improving, and the research industry will likely continue to experiment with bots in qualitative research. Widespread adoption in the immediate future is unlikely though.[52]

4.5e Mobile Qualitative

Usage of mobile qualitative data collection has remained steady for the past few years, as respondents the *GreenBook Industry Research Trends Report* indicates that mobile qualitative is in use among 43 percent of the client and research suppliers answering the survey, while another 26 percent are considering adoption.[53] As Internet bandwidth and speed continue to improve, data transmission of video and photo files has become easier, less expensive and less time-consuming than in the past, opening up demographic profiles in the U.S. and abroad. The earliest forms of mobile qualitative research posted a question via a text message to an individual's phone. The participant then used his/her phone to post a reply to a message board. As technology advanced, software became available that could schedule text messages at specific times, such as at 5:00 P.M., when a researcher might wish to post a question asking about dinner plans or other activities the individual may be engaged in. The prevalence of mobile qualitative grew because memory recall errors are no longer a factor in the behaviors and thoughts that are recorded by participants when questions are posted in real-time. The ability of mobile qualitative to gather data in-the-moment, which might not otherwise be recalled later during a focus group or in-depth interview, remains a key advantage today.

Mobile qualitative continues to evolve and now is commonly employed as an effective method of capturing real-time feedback during a shopping experience, allowing for easy testing of products, messages or services already on the market. Geofencing technology recognizes the GPS location of participants' smartphones and can transmit that data to the researcher, for example, when participants enter a store. Software can send an automatic notification to the participant, asking that he or she answer a few short questions about the shopping experience, such as whether the product was easy to locate, and how they felt about the product once they saw it on the shelf or inspected it in greater detail.[54] The in-the-moment nature of data collection is made possible by smart phone features such as sound recorders, cameras, scanner apps, and video that capture consumer actions and even facial expressions as they respond to questions or are prompted to complete tasks. Mobile easily allows for stimuli such as TV, online, and print ads to be seen by study participants, or may be an integral aspect of a usage study in which consumers are directed to a test website and asked to perform various task on their mobile device.[55]

The evolution of mobile qualitative is spurring the growth of "mixed-mode" research that involves multiple modes of interaction between the researcher and the respondent. Mobile qualitative integrates ethnographic observation research (such as photos and videos) with stream of consciousness commentary or responses to qualitative questions. Geolocation provides additional observation data on the consumer's locations and travel patterns. Mobile analytics can also be tapped for various data. Using these mixed-mode research methods allows researchers to put the consumer's thoughts and feelings into context and gain greater insight into consumers' minds.[56]

4.6 Projective Techniques

LEARNING OBJECTIVE 4.5
Enumerate the various projective techniques.

Researchers, especially psychologists, believe that respondents tend to give answers they believe the researcher wants to hear and that are socially acceptable. Too often, respondents are unwilling to offer negative answers, and respondents typically avoid giving any responses that might reflect negatively on their own behavior, beliefs, attitudes, or values. In some situations, respondents may not consciously even understand the reasons or motivations behind their actions and thoughts, and thus are prevented from articulating those reasons with researchers. Because of these theories, psychologists have developed alternative approaches that allow respondents to project beliefs and ideas outside of themselves. These **projective techniques** are indirect methods of qualitative research using ambiguous stimuli that allow respondents to project their emotions, feelings, thoughts, attitudes, and beliefs onto third-parties or inanimate objects.

Projective techniques indirect methods of qualitative research using ambiguous stimuli that allow respondents to project their emotions, feelings, thoughts, attitudes, and beliefs onto third-party or inanimate objects.

Projective techniques work especially well in situations where respondents cannot or will not respond truthfully to direct questioning. Projective techniques are based on the principle of free association, as respondents are not asked questions that in any way limit or inhibit their reactions. Instead, individuals are asked to share immediate thoughts that are generated by stimuli provided by a researcher. Quite often the goal is to stimulate the subconscious and to uncover emotions, feelings, and thoughts that respondents may not even consciously be aware of, but which become evident to a trained psychologist. The most common projective techniques are shown in Figure 4.12.

4.6a Sentence Completion

With **sentence completion**, respondents are given a partial sentence and asked to complete it with the first thoughts that come to mind. For a study about motorcycles, some examples may be:

Sentence completion projective technique in which respondents are given a partial sentence and asked to complete it with the first thoughts that come to mind.

- People who ride motorcycles are ......
- Women ride motorcycles because ......
- Men who ride motorcycles ......
- Women who own their own motorcycle are .....

The purpose of the sentence completion projective technique is to solicit an individual's thoughts without inhibiting their answers, so most sentences are written in the third person or projected toward someone else. Responses are recorded word-for-word and

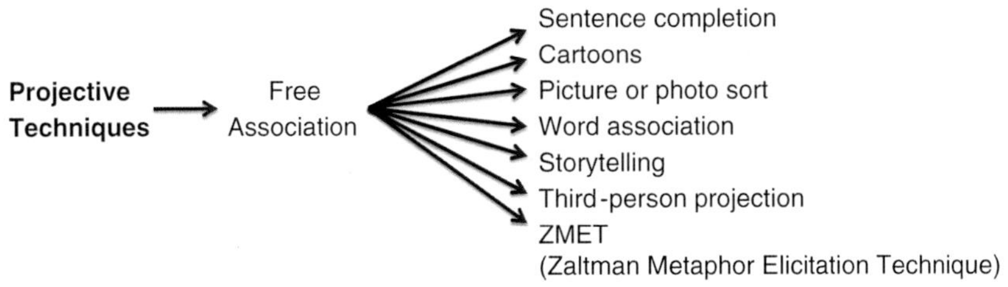

FIGURE 4.12 Projective Techniques

later analyzed in conjunction with the individual's other answers and in comparison to other respondents. While qualitative research involves subjective interpretations, sentence completion is less subjective than some of the other techniques. Consider the following responses from three different respondents to the first question:

- People who ride motorcycles are *scary and are usually criminals or at least in some type of gang or something.*
- People who ride motorcycles are *free, independent people who enjoy the outdoors and doing things.*
- People who ride motorcycles are *a lot of times professionals, like lawyers, doctors, businesspeople, not people you would normally think of as being bikers.*

The way each person answered the question provides a rich insight into that person's thoughts about motorcycles and the types of individuals who ride motorcycles. As the person answers additional questions, researchers gain a deeper insight into the respondent's thoughts and attitudes.

In developing questions, researchers have to be careful not to guide the individual's answers or convey the purpose of the study. Suppose the purpose of the above study was to better understand why women ride motorcycles, both as passengers and as drivers. If only questions about women were asked, the purpose of the study would become obvious and, as a result, might influence the response patterns. Similarly, careful attention must be paid to the order in which sentences appear, so that information contained in a one sentence doesn't serve as a cue, which in turn might influence responses to sentences asked later.

4.6b Cartoon Tests

Cartoon tests projective technique in which respondents are asked to fill in a dialogue bubble of a cartoon illustration in which one or more characters are present.

Cartoon tests are very similar to sentence completion tasks and serve much the same purpose. **Cartoon tests** show a cartoon illustration, in which one or more characters are present. At least one of the characters has an empty dialogue bubble. The respondent is asked to project his or her feelings and thoughts by filling in the character dialogue. A cartoon test might show a man and a woman in a showroom examining a motorcycle. The man's character may be shown as saying, "What do you think?" while the female's dialogue bubble is left empty for the respondent to fill in. When used in a focus group setting, cartoon tests help group members to relax, and have a little fun.[57]

4.6c Picture Sorts

Picture sort projective technique requiring participants to sort through a stack of cards containing images or photos and select those that are representative of the topic of interest.

Picture sorts require that participants sort through a stack of cards containing images or photos, and select or rank those that are representative of the topic of interest. Picture sorts can be used as part of an in-depth interview or focus group. Respondents in a motorcycle study may be given a stack of cards featuring photos of individuals from all walks of life. Gender, age, ethnicity, and dress would vary. The images selected by the participant as representative of Harley-Davidson riders might still reflect the leather-clad, tough, long-haired, bearded biker image that was long their norm, though as a group this portion of Harvey-Davidson's market is relatively small today. Alternatively, the same individual might select photos of young men in casual clothes or business apparel as indicative of Honda riders.

Picture sorts are often performed on brands or products and are helpful in understanding usage situations, how consumers think or feel, or to clarify brand positioning perceptions.[58] For example, the motorcycle study participants could be told to arrange the logos of different motorcycle brands from best to worst based on a purchase criteria such as reliability.

Word association qualitative projective research technique where respondents are given a series of words and asked to respond with the first word that comes to mind.

4.6d Word Association

Word association is a qualitative projective research technique where respondents are read a series of words and asked to respond with the first word that comes to mind. In developing the list of words, the researcher will add neutral words that have nothing to do with the study in order to disguise the study's purpose. For the study on motorcycles, stimulus words that might be given are *motorcycles, biker, bike, leather jacket, and Harley Davidson*. Neutral words mixed in might include *food, blue jeans, red, mobile phones, and shopping*. Word association can be very helpful in understanding the various associations (positive or negative) that people form toward brand names, retail stores, product categories, ad slogans, or spokespeople.

As with sentence completion, responses are recorded word for word, and the length of time between the word and the answer is recorded. Analysis identifies what types of associations the person makes with each of the words being studied. The goal is to dig into the subconscious or at least the attitudes that might be below the surface. Also, with a topic such as females and motorcycles, individuals may try to hide their true feelings and thoughts about female bikers because they feel they may be perceived as being prejudiced. Projective techniques are designed to uncover a person's true feelings without them realizing it.

When analyzing word associations, researchers tend to look at three things. First, the researcher examines the frequency with which a particular word is given by different respondents or even by the same respondent to different stimulus words. When a stimulus word reflects a product category, and a large proportion of responses reflect a particular brand name, the results reflect strong top-of-the-mind awareness of that brand. Similarly, if a stimulus word is a brand name, high-frequency responses reflecting key benefits such as "low prices" indicate that marketing communications are successful in portraying this benefit.

Second, the amount of time that lapses before a response is given indicates whether it is a top-of-mind response, or if the individual is thinking about a response perhaps because they do not want to state the first word that comes to mind. For instance, when responding to the word "biker" the first thought by a female respondent may be rape. But, the respondent doesn't want to say that because it may appear she has a negative attitude or is fearful of bikers, so she pauses to think of a different word. This pause is an indicator that the individual may be hiding some underlying thoughts or attitudes.

Lastly, researchers will look at words where individuals did not give a response within the stated amount of time, usually three seconds. Again, this can be an indicator of hidden thoughts, but it can also indicate a neutral position or weakly held beliefs and attitudes which make it difficult for the respondent to think of anything to say.

In developing the study, the selection of stimulus words and neutral words is critically important. Also, the order of words can affect the responses. Even with neutral filler words, respondents may see a pattern that reflects sequential thinking. For example, if "Harvey-Davidson" preceded the word "motorcycle," responses to the second stimulus word may be colored by perceptions of Harley-Davidson, specifically. Depending on the purpose of the research, this may not always be a negative aspect of the study, but the order of stimulus words should always be reviewed for potential problems that might cause bias.

Compared to sentence completion, word association is more difficult for the researcher to analyze. It involves more subjective analysis since the researcher has to piece together the responses to understand the individual's thoughts. But, it also has the potential to reveal deeper hidden attitudes and beliefs.

4.6e Storytelling

The **storytelling** approach involves showing respondents a picture or series of pictures and asking them to tell a story about what they see, who is saying what, and what might happen next. Instead of pictures, researchers can use cartoons or cartoon-type characters. With the storytelling approach, respondents might be shown a picture of a couple riding a motorcycle through the mountains and be asked to describe what they see or who the couple is—in other words, to tell a story about the picture. Additional pictures can be shown that display specific elements of a study to gather more details and understanding. For example, the couple may be shown stopped at a gas station, with a service bay in the

Storytelling qualitative projective approach that involves showing respondents a picture, cartoon, or series of pictures and asking them to tell a story about what they see.

background. Stories may reveal thoughts about gas mileage, comfort, or even the reliability of the motorcycle brand.

Like the other methods, this projective technique allows respondents to convey their thoughts without any type of restriction. While deep-seated, hidden beliefs and attitudes may surface, it is more difficult to get at these because the respondent can provide a story about a single picture that is socially acceptable. Thus, by using a series of pictures a researcher is better able to uncover a person's real thoughts about the topic. It is more likely he or she will make statements that reflect inner thoughts rather than provide the socially acceptable answer.

4.6f Third-Person Technique

We as individuals are very protective of our self-image and especially the image of ourselves we want other people to see. We guard this image by attempting to control the environment around us, including the words we speak. This defense mechanism may make it difficult for the researcher to gather accurate information from respondents, especially about sensitive subjects that in some way might negatively affect a person's image or that might be seen as socially unacceptable. To get around this defense, researchers can use a **third-person technique**, which involves asking individuals how someone else (a third person) would react to the situation, or what that person's attitudes, beliefs, and actions might be.

Third-person technique qualitative projective technique that involves asking individuals how someone else (a third person) would react to the situation, or what his/her attitude, beliefs, and actions might be.

To understand how this technique is used and the importance of it, consider a college educator who wants to examine student cheating on homework. When asked directly about cheating, almost all students would deny they have cheated and become defensive about the topic. But, when asked in the third person, the student might freely talk about cheating, why students cheat, how it is done, the ethical views of students who do cheat, and even ethics of society in general. By projecting all of their thoughts on a third person, defensive self-protection mechanisms are bypassed.

The challenge for the researcher is interpreting the results. Are these individuals expressing their own thoughts about cheating? Or are they expressions from conversations with other students and projections on why they think others cheat? To separate these two, researchers will watch the respondent's body language closely. While not a foolproof indicator, it does provide some indication of which it might be. A better technique is to ask probing questions and keep the individual talking. The more the respondent talks, the more likely the person will reveal his or her own thoughts about cheating.

4.6g ZMET (Zaltman Metaphor Elicitation Technique)

ZMET qualitative projective technique that uses an in-depth interview to uncover emotional and subconscious beliefs and attitudes over a two- or three-week period of time.

ZMET, which stands for Zaltman metaphor elicitation technique, is a qualitative projective technique that uses an in-depth interview to uncover emotions and subconscious beliefs and attitudes. The technique was developed and patented by Olson Zaltman Associates. Gerald Zaltman explains, "Consumers can't tell you what they think because they just don't know. Their deepest thoughts, the ones that account for their behavior in the marketplace, are unconscious."[59]

With the ZMET method, participants are told the topic of the study, such as motorcycle riding, or it can even be more specific, such as females and motorcycles. Respondents are then asked to collect 10–15 pictures or images that in some way reflect the topic. During the in-depth interview respondents are asked to talk about each picture. They are also asked to project what else the picture might contain if it could be enlarged. Once participants have talked about all of the pictures, they are asked to string them together in a mini-movie, discussing the sequence and how they all fit together. At the end of the interview, respondents are asked to summarize their feelings about the topic.

A major advantage of the ZMET methodology is that it allows individuals time, usually one to two weeks, to think about a topic and collect images or photographs that reflect their thoughts. Coupled with the in-depth interview, the ZMET method elicits thoughts that often are not part of a typical in-depth interview and may not surface using one of the other projective techniques. It is a good method of extracting deep-seated thoughts that individuals may not have even realized they possessed.[60]

Source: Proxima Studio/Shutterstock.

A variation of the ZMET methodology is the digital collage, in which participants are directed to create a collage of images taken from stock-or fee-based photo sites or other sources. Digital collages can be created more quickly and the process is simple and more engaging for the participant.

4.6h Digital Collages

A variation of the ZMET methodology is the digital collage, in which participants are directed to create a collage of images taken from stock- or fee-based photo sites or other sources. Digital collages are easily created by pasting images into a document or by using Google's Picasa. The digital collage can be assigned in advance of a focus group or in-depth interview and serves as the basis for discussion during the actual research session.

There are several advantages to using digital collages compared to cutting and pasting together physical collages. Digital collages can be created more quickly, saving both respondents and researchers time, a key benefit given research client demands for faster results. The process is simple and more engaging for the participant, reducing the need for financial incentives typically paid when "homework" prior to a focus group or IDI is required. The final product is of higher quality and offers greater insight into the consumer's thoughts, as the web provides access to a large number of extremely diverse images. The digital nature of the finished product makes sharing with multiple parties easy via email or FTP upload, and sample collages can be incorporated into research reports, providing greater value to clients.[61]

4.7 Global Concerns

Understanding the various cultures throughout the world is important for conducting qualitative research. For instance, in western cultures individualism tends to be dominant, which allows for greater freedom to discuss opinions and ideas in focus groups and in-depth interviews. But in eastern cultures, collectivism tends to be dominant. **Collectivism** refers to the extent an individual's life is intertwined with the lives of others and society. Individuals living in these societies see their life as part of a larger group and the needs of society as being more important than the needs of individuals. Thus, in focus groups and in-depth interviews they tend not to express opinions that will differ from others or what they believe the moderator is seeking.

Another facet of eastern cultures is that they tend to take a long-term orientation versus the short-term orientation found in western cultures. With a long-term orientation, it is important for individuals to take time to become acquainted with each other before consummating any type of business transaction, or before engaging in marketing research. Long-term orientation also puts a higher priority on future rewards over short-term rewards and values thriftiness and perseverance towards goals. In contrast, societies with a short-term orientation place emphasis on the now and present. As a result, they are very time conscious and want to move immediately into the research and get it finished so they can move onto other things. Taking time to become acquainted first is not necessary and is often viewed as a waste of time and money.

A number of multinational firms, like Kimberly-Clark Professional, have developed online message boards to gather input from consumers within various countries. In a recent qualitative study, Kimberly-Clark Professional developed ten message boards in ten different countries with a total of 120 respondents speaking seven different languages. Each board lasted two weeks and involved moderators probing daily respondents for country-specific information as well as globally-important information. The boards were asynchronous, which provided opportunities for respondents to give thoughtful feedback and moderators to guide conversations. In addition to text, respondents could add photos and videos, increasing the richness of the information. The advantage of running the boards in ten countries simultaneously is that company researchers could examine input that was both globally relevant and country specific.[62]

4.8 Marketing Research Statistics

A basic statistic used by researchers is a frequency count and corresponding measures of central tendency. The *Statistical Review* section examines this topic and how the central measures of the mean, mode, and median are calculated. The *Statistical Reporting* section presents information on graphing frequency counts, what it means, and if the actual frequency value or the percentage of each value should be reported. The *Dealing with Data* section explains how the means and frequencies are obtained in SPSS.

4.8a Statistical Review

Frequency distributions are perhaps the most simplistic method of compiling and presenting data. *Frequencies* are computed by counting the number of times a particular response is recorded for a particular variable. *Frequency tables* compile this data. Percentages are normally computed to make the data easier to understand and allow for cross-category comparisons. Frequency tables, similar to the one shown in **Figure 4.13**, might be included within the body of a research report, or within the appendix of a study.

Interpreting Frequency Table Information The last row of the table shows a total frequency of 85, which in this case represents the total number of research subjects who

Respondent's Age					
		Frequency	Percent	Valid Percent	Cumulative Percent
Valid	18–22	37	43.5	53.6	53.6
	23–29	23	27.1	33.3	87.0
	30–49	6	7.1	8.7	95.7
	50+	3	3.5	4.3	100.0
	Total	69	81.2	100.0	
Missing	System	16	18.8		
	Total	85	100.0		

FIGURE 4.13 Frequency Report

were asked this question. Unfortunately, age is one of the more sensitive demographic questions, and 16 people, representing 18.8 percent of the sample, did not supply an answer. These numbers can be found in the *Missing* row, under the *Frequency* and *Percent* columns. The remaining frequency counts are specific to those individuals who did answer the question. Of these 69 individuals who responded, 37 were between the ages of 18 and 22, 23 were between 23 and 29, 6 were 30 to 39 years of age, and 3 were 50 or older.

The last three columns show percentages. The key to understanding the difference between the three columns is to understand what number was used as the denominator in the percentage calculation. The denominator used in computing the *Percent* column figures includes both people who did (69) and did not (16) answer the question. The *Valid Percent* column and the *Cumulative Percent* column calculate percentages on the basis of those who provided a response. In examining the 23 to 29 age bracket, 27.1 percent of the total sample was this age. Of those who provided a response to the age question, 33.3 percent were 23 to 29. For the cumulative percent, 87 percent of the respondents are 18 to 29 years old. Note the cumulative percentage grows progressively larger for each row of data, as each successive line in the table adds the valid percent for that row to the cumulative percentage shown on the previous line.

Measures of Central Tendency Measures of central tendency include the mean, median, and mode. *Means* are frequently calculated in marketing research when numerical data representing actual quantities are collected. For example, a fill-in-the blank question might ask respondents to indicate the number of radio ads they could actually recall hearing during their drive to work, the number of times they ate at a particular restaurant during the last week, or the number of jeans they purchased on their last shopping trip. For this type of data, calculating a mean would be appropriate.

For the purpose of reviewing measures of central tendency, suppose 10 individuals answered the question about hearing radio ads as shown below:

0, 0, 0, 1, 1, 1, 2, 2, 3, 9

The number of ads recalled by different respondents could be averaged, meaning that the values would first be summed, and then divided by the number of respondents answering the question. In this instance, the sum of these responses (19) was divided by the number of responses (10), to compute a mean of 1.9. Notice three people could not recall a single ad, although they had been listening to the radio, thus the value of zero. If the respondent had left the question blank, the researcher cannot assume the response is zero. It must be recorded as a missing value.

It is important to remember that means should not be calculated for all data. For instance, the values 1 through 4 are used in the data file to represent the ages of respondents in Figure 4.13. These numbers in and of themselves do not represent quantities—they are used strictly for classification purposes. Therefore, averages cannot be calculated since the values do not represent actual ages.

The *median* is the value within a frequency distribution that marks the midway point in an ordered frequency distribution, in that half of the observations within the frequency distribution fall below the median value and half are above the median value. Review of the cumulative percentage column can often help to identify this value. While the use of median data is inappropriate for classification variables such as age and gender, it can be used with other types of data. The median is particularly helpful in better understanding the central tendency of a variable when extreme observations, called outliers, are present. For the radio ad data, the median is "1". The median in this case offers a better understanding of the central tendency for this variable than does the mean, as the mean was artificially inflated by the outlier value of 9.

The final measure of central tendency is called the *mode*, a term used to describe the value that occurs most frequently. The mode is the only measure of central tendency that can be used with classification data. Reviewing the age frequency table presented in Figure 4.13 shows the highest frequency is 37, for the 18–22 age bracket. On the other hand, the radio recall data does not demonstrate a single mode, as both "0" and "3" occur 3 times. However, with larger samples, as is common in most research studies, a single mode usually emerges.

4.8b Statistical Reporting

An owner of a company that specializes in building decks decided to market his company towards DIY (do-it-yourselfers) through offering a video on how to build a deck. While the video did provide instructions on building a deck, it also offered viewers two options: 1) have the company build the entire deck for them or 2) provide assistance or "mentor building" where the company supplied an individual to work with the DIY person. The owner, Chris Bauer, felt that by offering this instructional video it would build his credibility. He also believed that while some people would use the video to build their own decks, others would end up hiring his firm to either assist or build the entire deck.

The video was promoted through digital ads and social media. After the 90-day campaign, Chris downloaded the web statistics on the number of visits to his website from each of the sources. These data are provided in **Figure 4.14**. He also obtained engagement data. The engagement data consisted of pageviews, which is the number of pages visited on the website, the average number of pages viewed per visit, and the percent of total pageviews generated by each digital ad or social media source.

In graphing the website visits, Chris has two options. He can graph the percentage of visits from each of the sources, shown in **Figure 4.15**, or he can graph the raw numbers, the frequency, as shown in **Figure 4.16**. Both are correct ways to graph the data, and appropriate. The difference lies in the information that he wants to convey. By graphing the percentages in Figure 4.15, Chris is able to compare the various digital and social media sources. Clearly, Pinterest generated the highest percentage of visits to the website, 25.4 percent. But, this graph does not give Chris any idea of the actual number of website visits, although it could be calculated from the total, which was 406 visits.

Suppose this was the first time that Chris had ever used digital and social media to promote a video and the first time he has targeted DIY. He then might be interested to know how many actual visitors came from each of the sources. Figure 4.15 displays this information.

Figure 4.15 tells Chris that 103 people saw his post on Pinterest and visited the company's website. Chris doesn't know from the graph what percentage that is, but he can

	Website Visits		Engagement		
	Frequency	Percent	Pageviews	Avg. Pages per Visit	Percent of Total Pageviews
Display ad	47	11.6%	147	3.13	13.5%
Local search ad	72	17.7%	182	2.53	16.7%
Facebook	62	15.3%	114	1.84	10.5%
Twitter	35	8.6%	149	4.26	13.7%
Instagram	66	16.3%	133	2.02	12.2%
YouTube	21	5.2%	37	1.76	3.4%
Pinterest	103	25.4%	328	3.18	30.1%
Totals	406		1090		

FIGURE 4.14 Analytical Data of Digital Campaign for Evergreen Decks

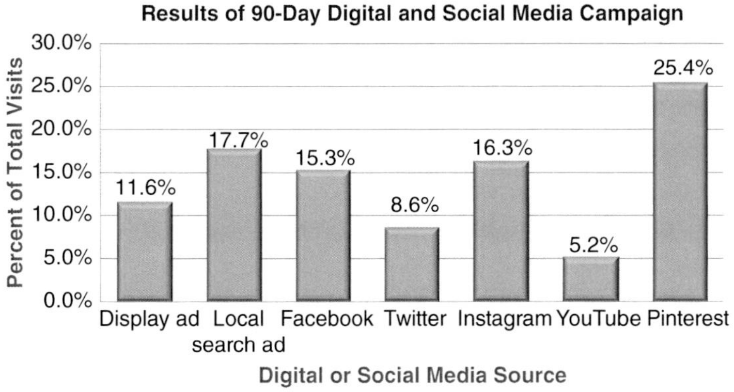

FIGURE 4.15 A bar graph showing the percentage of total visits to Evergreen Deck's website generated from each of the digital and social media sources.

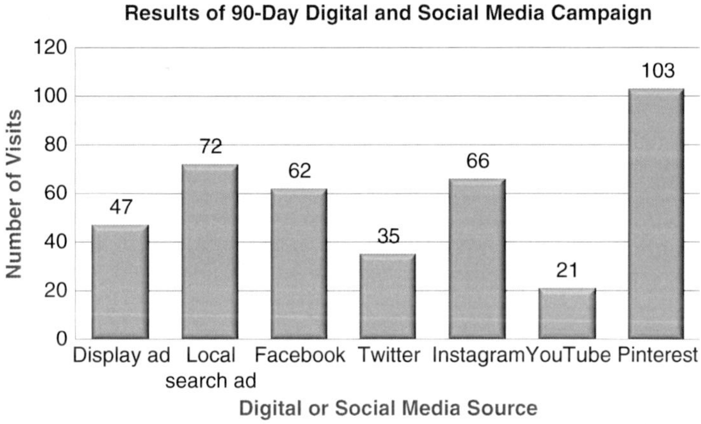

FIGURE 4.16 A bar graph showing the actual number (frequency) of visits to Evergreen Deck's website generated from each of the digital and social media sources.

still tell it is the highest percentage. The size of the bars are the same on both graphs. The difference is in graphing the frequency versus the percentages.

Statistical Reporting Exercise: Use the information provided in Figure 4.14 for Evergreen Decks. Create bar graphs of the last three columns dealing with engagement: pageviews, average pages viewed per visit, and percent of total pageviews. Provide each graph with an appropriate title as well as label the x-axis and y-axis. Explain the information each graph provides and how it is different from the other two graphs. If Chris wanted to narrow the sources through which his video was promoted down to the top three, which three would you recommend? Explain why by using the graphs to justify your decision.

4.8c Dealing with Data

The SPSS software simplifies the process of preparing frequency tables. It also makes it possible to recode existing data into new variables. For this exercise you will need to download the SPSS word association data entitled *Chapter 4 Dealing with Data* found at the student website, www.clowjames.net/students.html. This data file was created from a word association exercise. Students viewed a word and were told to write down the first word that came to mind. A total of 85 students completed the word association exercise within the specified time limit, four seconds for each stimulus word. (Detailed step-by-step instructions for using the SPSS software are provided at the same textbook student website, www.clowjames.net/students.html)

Exercise One: Frequency Counts

Using SPSS, run a frequency count of all of the variables except the first variable, which is just the code number for each case. Based on the output, answer the following questions. The frequency command is located under the descriptive statistics menu button.

1. Select four of the stimulus words from "insurance" through "money" and identify the top five responses, with the frequency and valid percent for each stimulus word you selected.
2. Identify the demographic profile of the sample by providing the frequency, percent and valid percent for gender and race. How many individuals did not provide their gender or race?
3. What is the mode for the four stimulus words chosen in step 1 of this exercise?
4. What is the median for student credit hours completed and age?
5. Use the valid percentage values to create a column or bar chart for the four stimulus words selected in Question 1. Graph the top seven responses. Be sure to provide a title for each graph and titles for the x-axis and y-axis. It is also helpful to place values above each of the bars so it can be read easily by managers.
6. For gender, create a pie chart. Include the percentage of females, males, and missing values, i.e., the percent of no responses. Be sure to provide a title for the graph and label each section of the pie with the variable name and value.

Exercise Two: Mean

Use SPSS to calculate a mean for "time to complete exercise" and "age." The mean command is found under the "Descriptive" menu in SPSS. What is the mean for each of these variables?

Exercise Three: Recoding

Researchers will sometimes want to recode variables for either reporting purposes or to conduct additional analysis. For this exercise recode the "student credit hours completed" variable into a new variable using the following categories. It is always wise to use a new variable when recoding so you never lose the original data.

Category 1: Less than 30

Category 2: 30 to 59

Category 3: 60 to 89

Category 4: 90+

Now recode the age variable into a new variable using the following categories.

Category 1: 19–20

Category 2: 21–22

Category 3: 23+

Once the two variables are recoded, run a frequency count of your new variables. Answer the following questions using the output file of these two variables.

1. *What is the frequency count and valid percent for each of the two new variables?*
2. *What is the mode for each of the two new variables?*

Summary

Objective 1: Explain the role of qualitative research.
Qualitative research provides valuable insights into consumer motives, attitudes, and feelings. Commonly used in exploratory studies, findings from qualitative research can be used to refine research questions, aid in questionnaire or research design, and develop background information for quantitative studies. Furthermore, the deep understanding of consumer behavior made possible via qualitative research provides richness to quantitative studies. Qualitative research is particularly helpful in exploring the consumer's subconscious when they cannot or will not answer direct questions.

Objective 2: Describe the traditional focus group process.
Focus groups are useful when group dynamics produce new insights or thoughts that might not otherwise be discovered via in-depth interviews. The focus group process begins with the development of the study parameters, during which decisions related to the research questions, study timeline, number of focus groups, budget, stipends, and level of client participation are made. The interview questions and probes are developed next for the discussion guide. Prior to recruiting participants, criteria for participant selection should be developed. Care should be taken to avoid professional respondents. The moderator conducts the focus group in four stages: 1) introduction, 2) rapport building, 3) in-depth discussion, and 4) closure. Immediately following each focus group session, the observers and moderators meet to debrief. Once all sessions have been conducted, the moderator writes and submits a written report to the client. While focus groups are very popular, they suffer from three disadvantages: 1) results are not definitive and cannot be generalized to the population; 2) results are highly subjective; and 3) group think may intimidate some respondents and prevent them from sharing their opinions.

Objective 3: Explain the process of using in-depth interviews to conduct qualitative research.
In-depth interviews conducted one-on-one probe deeply into an individual's thoughts, ideas, and motives using a prepared list of questions asked by a professional interviewer. Often, interviews are conducted prior to a quantitative study. Respondents normally feel more comfortable discussing sensitive issues or deep-seated beliefs in a one-on-one scenario. Richer data is gathered, compared to focus groups. Interpretation is highly subjective and entirely dependent upon the interviewer, because, unlike focus groups, clients do not observe in-depth interviews. In-depth interviews can also be conducted online, in text or video format. Online interviews are especially useful when the subject is sensitive or potentially embarrassing to the respondent.

Objective 4: Discuss the various types of online qualitative research being used by companies.
Online qualitative research offers reduced costs and quicker results, leading to widespread adoption of online techniques. Focus groups can be held using chat rooms, discussion boards, social media sites, websites, or videoconferencing. Market research online communities and mobile qualitative are increasingly being used to gather data. The trend toward asynchronous communication methods maximizes participant convenience and often results in better probing and richer responses.

Objective 5: Enumerate the various projective techniques.
Respondents are often unwilling to respond truthfully to direct questions regarding sensitive issues or behaviors, and at other times are unable to articulate their motives or why they behaved in a given fashion. Projective techniques use indirect motives to discover feelings, thoughts, attitudes, and the motives that underlie respondent behavior. Based on the principle of free association, projective techniques include word association, sentence completion, cartoon tests, picture and photo sorts, storytelling, third-person techniques, ZMET and digital collages.

Key Terms

asynchronous online focus groups, p. 123
cartoon tests, p. 130
discussion guide, p. 112
focus groups, p. 110
group think, p. 118
in-depth interviews (IDIs), p. 119
market research online community (MROC), p. 125
moderator, p. 110
picture sort, p. 130
probing questions, p. 116
professional respondents, p. 113
projective techniques, p. 129
qualitative research, p. 108
sentence completion, p. 129
storytelling, p. 131
synchronous focus group interviews, p. 121
third-person technique, p. 132
word association, p. 130
ZMET, p. 132

Critical Thinking Exercises

1. You have been asked to investigate college students' attitudes toward and usage of various social media, as well as their thoughts about the use of social media for marketing purposes. What type of qualitative research technique would you use? Would it be appropriate to combine multiple techniques? Justify your recommendations.
2. A snack food company that markets various types and flavors of chips is interested in better understanding consumer attitudes toward snack foods, including how and when snack foods are consumed and positive and negative perceptions of snack foods. Develop a focus group discussion guide to investigate this topic.
3. Develop a set of stimulus (test) words and neutral words for a client, such as Domino's Pizza restaurants. Your list should contain a minimum of five stimulus words. Administer your word association test to ten students not enrolled in your class and summarize the results.
4. Develop a series of ten sentence completion exercises for the purpose of investigating college students' attitudes toward and usage of various social media, as well as businesses' use of social media for marketing purposes. Administer your sentence completion exercises to ten college students who are not currently enrolled in your research class. Take care to select an equal number of males and females. Summarize the results, being careful to note any common themes that emerge, as well differences that appear to be gender specific.
5. Develop a series of ten sentence completion exercises, for the purpose of investigating college students' attitudes toward and usage of credit cards. Administer your sentence completion exercises to ten college students who are not currently enrolled in your research class. Take care to select an equal number of males and females. Summarize the results, being careful to note any common themes that emerge, as well differences that appear to be gender specific.
6. Using the following series of questions and probes, interview three people who are not enrolled in your marketing research class. Summarize your findings.
   a. Describe a typical morning from the time you get out of bed until the time you leave the house and arrive at either work or school.
      i. Probe: Explain how breakfast fits into your morning routine.
      ii. Probe: Does your breakfast routine vary on those days you don't leave your residence in the morning for school or work? If so, how?
   b. What type of food do you eat for breakfast?
      i. Probe: Under what circumstances are you likely to eat breakfast out at a fast food restaurant? At a sit-down restaurant?
   c. Tell me your thoughts about cereal.
      i. Probe: What cereals do you like or dislike. Why?
      ii. Probe: Do you eat cereal at any time other than breakfast, or use it as an ingredient when cooking something else? Explain.
7. Using the following series of questions and probes, conduct a mini-focus group with four or five people who are not enrolled in your marketing research course. Summarize your findings.
   a. Describe a typical morning from the time you get out of bed until the time you leave the house and arrive at either work or school.
      i. Probe: Explain how breakfast fits into your morning routine.
      ii. Probe: Does your breakfast routine vary on those days you don't leave your residence in the morning for school or work? If so, how?
   b. What type of food do you eat for breakfast?
      i. Probe: Under what circumstances are you likely to eat breakfast out at a fast food restaurant? At a sit-down restaurant?
   c. Tell me your thoughts about cereal.
      i. Probe: What cereals do you like or dislike. Why?
      ii. Probe: Do you eat cereal at any time other than breakfast, or use it as an ingredient when cooking something else? Explain.
8. Conduct a 30-minute in-depth interview on the topic of your choice. Submit a copy of your questions and probes, as well as a summary of your results.
9. Suppose you have been assigned the task of determining which brands are perceived as being trendy and "in" (e.g., "cool") by teenagers. Could a photo sort exercise be used for this purpose? Explain. What other type of qualitative research method could be used? Explain why.

Lakeside Grill

(Comprehensive Student Case)

The AMA student team held a focus group at the university in a meeting room that had a two-way mirror along one side of the room. Lakeside Grill owner Mr. Zito supplied free beverages and appetizers to the participants and observed from behind the mirror along with the members of the student project group. The focus group was moderated by one of the college professors with experience in focus group research, and was assisted by Brooke Redding, one of the student team members. Prior to the focus group, the team composed the following interview questions:

1. How often do you eat at a dine-in restaurant?
2. What are some of the dine-in restaurants you have patronized in the last two weeks?
3. Suppose you were going to eat out tonight, how would you decide on the restaurant?
4. What criteria are important in selecting a restaurant?
   Probe: What is the one most important thing? Why?
5. In terms of the food, what is most important to you—quality, variety, something else?
6. What about service? How important is it?
   Probe: What constitutes good service? What constitutes bad service?
7. Let's go back to some of the restaurants you have mentioned. How many have been to? (pick a restaurant that several have already mentioned, but not Lakeside Grill) Tell me about your experience.
   Probe: What did you like? What did you not like? Why?
8. Okay, let's talk about another restaurant, Lakeside Grill. How many have been there? Tell me about the last time you were there.
   Probe: What did you like? What did you not like? Why?
9. Let's think about a restaurant that you have patronized, but for some reason have never gone back. What happened?
   Probe: Why have you never gone back?
10. Okay, let's think about one of your favorite restaurants. One that you really enjoy going to. Why is it your favorite? What makes it different?
11. Let's suppose that your significant other or someone close to you said, "You know let's eat out tonight. What about going to the Lakeside Grill (or pick a restaurant that has been mentioned by several people)?" Which would you pick?
    Probe: Why?
12. As we close our focus group, is there anything you would like to add to our discussion about eating at dine-in restaurants?

The local Chamber of Commerce assisted the group in locating participants for the focus group. An e-mail was sent to the Chamber's membership asking the recipient at each business to pass the e-mail invitation to participate on to their employees. The e-mail contained a link to a qualifying questionnaire that asked for demographic information and a qualifying question that listed 20 local restaurants that were randomly selected each time a different person logged on to the online questionnaire. For each restaurant, participants were asked if they had eaten at the restaurant and if so, approximately when was the last time. From the 42 replies received, 10 were selected randomly.

While Brooke assisted with the focus group, Alexa and another marketing faculty member conducted four in-depth interviews. To provide consistency, the same set of questions used in the focus group was also used for the in-depth interviews.

Since the Chamber of Commerce had received 42 replies to their email, Juan decided to utilize a sentence completion exercise with the 28 individuals who were not selected for the focus group or for the in-depth interviews. The 28 individuals were sent an email and asked to go to a survey website to complete the exercise. Detailed instructions were given before they began. The following sentence completion exercise was developed with the help of the other group members:

- The Lakeside Grill is ______________________.
- My favorite place to eat seafood is ______________.
- People who eat at Lakeside Grill are ____________.
- The service at Lakeside Grill is ______________.
- The food at Lakeside Grill is _______________.
- Eating out is ______________________.
- The restaurant that is most like the Lakeside Grill is ________________________________.
- The Lakeside Grill's menu is _______________.
- The reason I eat at the Lakeside Grill is _________.
- I would eat at the Lakeside Grill more often if ________________________________.
- If the Lakeside Grill were a person, I would describe it as ________________________________.

Critique Questions:

1. Evaluate the list of questions and the sequence in which they are used for the focus group. What changes would you suggest? Does it allow for a free flow of information?
2. Critique the process the group used to obtain focus group participants—what did they do well, what did they do poorly? How could it be improved?
3. Is selecting participants randomly the best process, or should some type of approach be used to ensure gender, age, income, and ethnic diversity?
4. From the 42 replies, 7 had never eaten at Lakeside Grill. Should these be eliminated from the pool of potential focus group participants? Why or why not?
5. Should the same questions be used for the focus group as for the in-depth interviews? Why or why not?
6. Evaluate the sentence completion exercise the group designed. Which statements should the group eliminate? Why? What additional statements should be added? Should the order in which these statements are presented be changed, and if so, how?
7. Evaluate Juan's decision to contact the 28 remaining individuals from the Chamber of Commerce via an email request for the sentence completion exercise.
8. What are the pros and cons of conducting the sentence completion exercise online?

Notes

1. Brooke Patton, "Brewery Turns to Research for Label Design," *Quirk's Media* (May 21, 2018), https://www.quirks.com/articles/brewery-turns-to-research-for-label-design.
2. Hemnabh Varia, Monika Mahto, and Susan K. Hogan, "Trying to Understand Respondent Behavior? Take Your Research Back to the '90s," *Quirk's Media* (July 23, 2018), https://www.quirks.com/articles/trying-to-understand-respondent-behavior-take-your-research-back-to-the-90s.
3. Interview with Dave Snell, The Richards Group, May 11, 2010.
4. "Usage of Traditional Methodologies," in *GRIT Report: GreenBook Research Industry Trends Report, Quarters 3–4, 2018* (New York: GreenBook, 2018), 33–36.
5. Carey V. Azzara, "Qualitatively Speaking: The Focus Group vs. In-Depth Interview Debate," *Quirks Marketing Research Review* (June 2010), https://www.quirks.com/articles/qualitatively-speaking-the-focus-group-vs-in-depth-interview-debate; Lisa Boughton, "Focus Groups: A Beginner's Guide," *Quirk's Media* (August 20, 2019), https://www.quirks.com/articles/focus-groups-a-beginner-s-guide.
6. Based on an interview with Stan Richards, The Richards Group, February 5, 2010.
7. Raúl Pérez, "What Effect Does Tabletop Shape Have on Focus Group Dynamics and Client Viewing?" *Quirk's Marketing Research Review* (May 2010), https://www.quirks.com/articles/what-effect-does-tabletop-shape-have-on-focus-group-dynamics-and-client-viewing.
8. Lisa Boughton, "Focus Groups: A Beginner's Guide," *Quirk's Media* (August 20, 2019), https://www.quirks.com/articles/focus-groups-a-beginner-s-guide.
9. Jasmin Brazil, "How Video Tech Is Changing In-Person Focus Groups," *Quirk's Media* (May 22, 2017), https://www.quirks.com/articles/how-video-tech-is-changing-in-person-focus-groups.
10. Barbara Lippert, "Domino's Delivers," *MediaWeek* 20, no. 21 (May 24, 2010): 22.
11. "How Digital Marketing Crowned Domino's the King of Pizza," Online Marketing Institute, May 22, 2018, https://medium.com/online-marketing-institute/how-digital-marketing-crowned-dominos-the-king-of-pizza-3d327d7350f8.
12. Mark A. Wheeler, "Small Changes Can Make a Big Difference," *Quirk's Media* (December 2018), https://www.quirks.com/articles/how-to-avoid-asking-leading-questions.
13. Mario X. Carrasco, "No Your Friends Are Not a Focus Group," *Quirk's Media* (September 25, 2019), https://www.quirks.com/articles/no-your-friends-are-not-a-focus-group.
14. Joseph Rudholm, "We Are Optimistic But Our Industry Needs to Keep Evolving," *Quirk's Marketing Research Review* (January 2015), https://www.quirks.com/articles/we-are-optimistic-but-our-industry-needs-to-keep-evolving.
15. Mark Goodin, "No More Mr. Nice Guy: Professional Respondents in Qualitative Research," *Quirk's Marketing Research Review* (December 2009), https://www.quirks.com/articles/no-more-mr-nice-guy-professional-respondents-in-qualitative-research.
16. Michelle Lenzen, "Building Synergy in Focus Groups with Applied Improvisation," *Quirk's Media* (May 21, 2018) https://www.quirks.com/articles/building-synergy-in-focus-groups-with-applied-improvisation.
17. Jasmin Brazil, "How Video Tech Is Changing In-Person Focus Groups," *Quirk's Media* (May 22, 2017), https://www.quirks.com/articles/how-video-tech-is-changing-in-person-focus-groups.
18. Lianna Willoughby, "5 Reasons Why Focus Groups Will Never Disappear," *Quirk's Media* (September 29, 2016), https://www.quirks.com/articles/5-reasons-focus-groups-will-never-disappear.
19. Jennifer Schranz, "Tips from a Market Research Bond Girl," *Quirk's Marketing Research Review* (July 2015), https://www.quirks.com/articles/tips-from-a-market-research-bond-girl.
20. Rhoda Schild, "Qualitatively Speaking: Communication Keeps Focus Groups Divine Not Dreadful," *Quirk's Marketing Research Review* (May 2009), https://www.quirks.com/articles/qualitatively-speaking-communication-keeps-focus-groups-divine-not-dreadful.
21. Naomi Henderson, "Invisible Gold Mines: Unseen Opportunities Exist Just Outside the Focus Group," *Marketing Research* 21, no. 3 (Fall 2009): 26–27.
22. Piet Levy, "In with the Old, In Spite of the New," *Marketing News* 43, no. 9 (May 30, 2009): 19.
23. Andrew Adam Newman, "Yes, the Diner's Open. How about a Seat at the Counter?" *The New York Times* (February 1, 2011), http://www.nytimes.com/2011/02/02/business/media/02adco.html.
24. Naomi Henderson, "Hot Notes: Capture What Shouts Loudest," *Marketing Research* 21, no. 4 (Winter 2009): 28–29.
25. Jasmin Brazil, "How Video Tech Is Changing In-Person Focus Groups," *Quirk's Media* (May 22, 2017), https://www.quirks.com/articles/how-video-tech-is-changing-in-person-focus-groups.

26. Michael Arndt, "Damn! Torpedoes Get Quiznos Back on Track," *Business Week* 4164 (January 25, 2010): 54–55
27. Ibid.
28. James Rohde, "The Role of the Journey Map," *Quirk's Media* (October 2017), https://www.quirks.com/articles/the-role-of-the-journey-map.
29. Interview with Sarah Stanley, University of Wisconsin–Oshkosh, July 28, 2010.
30. Carlos Flavian and Raquel Gurrea, "Digital versus Traditional Newspapers," *International Journal of Market Research* 51, no. 5 (2009): 635–657.
31. "Aramark Launches Student-Created Burger Studio on College Campuses," *Foodservice Equipment & Supplies* 62, no. 11 (November 2009): 8.
32. This section is based on Lianna Willoughby, "5 Reasons Why Focus Groups Will Never Disappear," *Quirk's Media* (September 29, 2016), https://www.quirks.com/articles/5-reasons-focus-groups-will-never-disappear; Lisa Boughton, "Will Traditional Focus Groups Become a Thing of the Past?" *Quirk's Media* (November 3, 2017), https://www.quirks.com/articles/will-traditional-focus-groups-become-a-thing-of-the-past; and Richard Clark, "Online Focus Group Advantages and Disadvantages," MRQual Online Research, October 13, 2017, https://www.mrqual.com/2017/10/13/online-focus-group-advantages-disadvantages/.
33. Adapted from Carey V. Azzara, "Qualitatively Speaking: The Focus Group vs. In-Depth Interview Debate," *Quirks Marketing Research Review* (June 2010), http://www.quirks.com/articles/2010/20100601.aspx?searchID=116421703&sort=4&pg=1; and Richard Clark, "Online Focus Group Advantages and Disadvantages," MRQual Online Research, October 13, 2017, https://www.mrqual.com/2017/10/13/online-focus-group-advantages-disadvantages/.
34. Nikki Hopewell, "Online Group Messaging," *Marketing News* 41, no. 14 (September 1, 2007): 22.
35. Katie Harris, "Qualitative Research: Quo Vadis?" *B&T Magazine* 56, no. 2660 (May 30, 2008): 15.
36. Richard Clark, "The Two Types of Online Focus Group Software Platform or Tool," MRQual Online Research, December 2, 2017, https://www.mrqual.com/2017/12/02/types-of-online-focus-group-software/.
37. Richard Clark, "Online Focus Group Advantages and Disadvantages," MRQual Online Research, October 13, 2017, https://www.mrqual.com/2017/10/13/online-focus-group-advantages-disadvantages/.
38. Ibid.
39. "Online Qualitative Research," Decision Analyst, https://www.decisionanalyst.com/qualitative/onlinequalitative/.
40. "Watch a 5 Minute Demo," https://www.focusgroupit.com/.
41. "Online Qualitative Research," Decision Analyst, https://www.decisionanalyst.com/qualitative/onlinequalitative/.
42. "Adoption of Emerging Methods," in *GRIT: GreenBook Research Industry Trends Report, Quarters 3–4, 2018* (New York: GreenBook, 2018), 20.
43. Nicole M. Freund, "Thoughts on Using the New Online Qualitative Tools," *Quirk's Marketing Research Review* (May 2013), https://www.quirks.com/articles/thoughts-on-using-the-new-online-qualitative-tools; Maxim Schram, "Market Research Online Communities (MROCs) Explained," May 15, 2018, https://www.cmnty.com/blog/mroc-market-research-online-community/.
44. Lindsay E. Sammon, "Roxy Lady," *Footwear News* 65, no. 6 (February 9, 2009): 84.
45. Jon Lo, "What to Consider before You Build an Insight Community," *Quirk's Media* (June 24, 2019), https://www.quirks.com/articles/what-to-consider-before-you-build-an-insight-community.
46. Isaac Rogers, "Leveraging Online Qualitative for Fast Delivery of Insights," *Quirk's Media* (January 2017), https://www.quirks.com/articles/leveraging-online-qualitative-for-fast-delivery-of-insights.
47. "Shoal Mates," Angelfish Fieldwork, https://info.angelfishfieldwork.com/shoal-mates-market-research-online-communities.
48. Mike Stevens, "How to Build a Great Insight Community," May 31, 2019, https://www.insightsassociation.org/article/how-build-great-insight-community.
49. This section is based on Nicole M. Freund, "Thoughts on Using the New Online Qualitative Tools," *Quirk's Marketing Research Review* (May 2013), https://www.quirks.com/articles/thoughts-on-using-the-new-online-qualitative-tools.
50. Julie Aebersold, "Quallies Take Tech Risks to Get Closer to Consumers," *Quirk's Media* (November 20, 2017), https://www.quirks.com/articles/quallies-take-tech-risks-to-get-closer-to-consumers.
51. Nana T. Baffour-Awuah, "Empathy, AI and the Future of Qualitative," *Quirk's Marketing Research Review* (June/July 2019), https://www.quirks.com/articles/empathy-ai-and-the-future-of-qualitative.
52. Ibid.
53. "Adoption of Emerging Methods," in *GRIT" GreenBook Research Industry Trends Report, Quarters 3–4, 2018* (New York: GreenBook, 2018), 21.
54. Julie Aebersold, "Quallies Take Tech Risks to Get Closer to Consumers," *Quirk's Media* (November 20,2017),https://www.quirks.com/articles/quallies-take-tech-risks-to-get-closer-to-consumers.
55. Nicole M. Freund, "Thoughts on Using the New Online Qualitative Tools," *Quirk's Marketing Research Review* (May 2013), https://www.quirks

.com/articles/thoughts-on-using-the-new-online-qualitative-tools.
56. Carl Van Ostrand, "The 4 New Qualitative Evolutions You Need to Know About," *Quirk's Marketing Research* (July 2014), https://www.quirks.com/articles/the-4-new-qualitative-evolutions-you-need-to-know-about.
57. Frank Hines, "Creative Exercises in Qualitative Market Research," http://www.hinesandlee.com/sites/default/files/Hines%2BLee-CreativeExercises.pdf .
58. Ibid.
59. Emily Eakin, "Penetrating the Mind by Metaphor," *New York Times* (February 23, 2002), p. B11.
60. Catheryn Khoo-Lattimore, Maree Thyne, and Kirsten Robertson, "The ZMET Method: Using Projective Technique to Understand Consumer Home Choice," *The Marketing Review* 9, no. 2 (2009): 139–154.
61. Carey Rellis, "A Guide to Adding Digital Collage to Your Qualitative Research," *Quirks Marketing Research Review* (December 2010), https://www.quirks.com/articles/a-guide-to-adding-digital-collage-to-your-qualitative-research.
62. Janet Ziffer and Mike Mabey, "Experiences in Global Online Qualitative," *Quirk's Marketing Research Review* (November 2013), https://www.quirks.com/articles/experiences-in-global-online-qualitative.

Observation Research

CHAPTER 5

Source: metamorworks/Shutterstock.

Chapter Outline

Learning Objectives

After studying this chapter, you should be able to:

- Identify the conditions for observation research.
- Describe the dimensions of observation research.
- Discuss the various human observation methods.
- Describe the various online observation methods.
- Describe how mechanical devices can be used for observation research.

5.1 Chapter Overview

The previous chapter highlighted qualitative methods of conducting research. Rather than investigate subconscious thoughts, ideas, and beliefs, researchers might choose to study actual behavior. The idea behind this approach is that the ultimate goal of marketing is to influence actions, primarily purchases. Thus, rather than study what people think, it is sometimes better to just observe their actions in the marketplace.

This chapter will present three primary methods of observation: human observation, mechanical observation, and online observation. Human observation involves people watching people or some type of marketing phenomenon. Mechanical observation uses various devices to track human actions and behavior. Online observation utilizes web metrics and other online tracking devices to map human movement on the web and within a particular website.

To illustrate the last method of observation research, consider the following case study. Online shopping volume continues to grow, and the product page elements on a retail website can make or break sales. To study shopping page elements in more detail, EyeSee Research partnered with Lightspeed to sample 300 online shoppers. Shoppers viewed the product pages for Colgate or Tide from either Walmart, Amazon or Target's website. Mechanical observation research using eye-tracking technology followed the eye movement of shoppers as they viewed the web page, and recorded the amount of time spent looking at different web page elements. **Figure 5.1** highlights a few of the findings.

Advertisers know that photos both attract attention and convey important information about the product. So it's not surprising that shoppers spent more time viewing the product image than any other element on the web page. Given this finding, it makes sense to use a better resolution photo that potentially offers multiple angles of product viewing, illustrates the product in multiple colors, or offers the opportunity for enlargement. Photo size may be important as well. Walmart's photos were noticeably larger than either Target's or Amazon's product images.

Overall, 14 percent of shoppers' time was spent viewing the check-out information, though variances occurred between retailers. While 92 percent of study participants

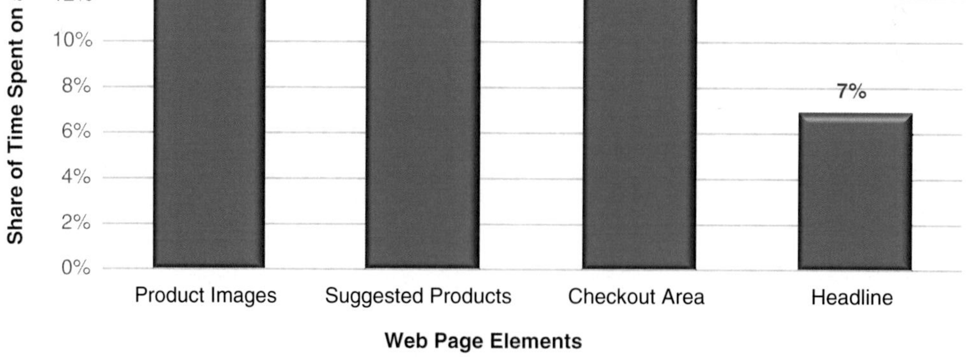

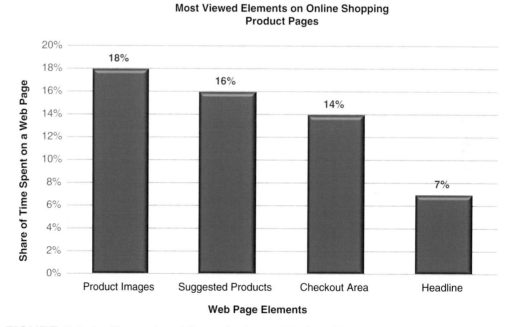

FIGURE 5.1 An Example of Data Gathered Using Observation Research
Source: Adapted from Miljkovic, M., Djuric, M., and O. Tilleuil. (2018), "Which Elements Matter Most on a Web Shopping Page?" *Quirk's Media*, (www.quirks.com), July 2018, Article ID 20180708.

noticed the check-out information on Walmart's website, only 34 percent spent any time looking at this information on Target's website. Perhaps this was because the price, delivery information, quantity, and add to cart information are easily located right next to the product image on Walmart's product pages. Walmart's shopping information area is large, and features easy to read print and larger buttons.

The study also asked participants to indicate whether they would be interested in buying the product (via an online question). The purchase intention measure was highest for Walmart (53 percent) when averaged for Colgate and Tide, compared to Amazon (47 percent) and Target (46 percent). The time spent looking at the product image also correlated positively with purchase intentions.[1] While tracking actual purchases would have provided better quality data consistent with observation research, this study demonstrates how researchers are increasingly mixing observation techniques with quantitative and qualitative data collection.

5.2 Observation Research Conditions

LEARNING OBJECTIVE 5.1
Identify the conditions for observation research.

Observation research systematic process of recording the behaviors or the results of behaviors of people, objects, and occurrences.

Baby animals learn from watching adult animals. Children learn from watching adults and other children. Considerable learning occurs from simply observing the actions of human beings as well as animals, and even objects such as a car engine or an airplane in flight. It is not surprising, then, that marketing researchers use observation as a means of collecting data. Within the context of marketing research, **observation research** is defined as the systematic process of recording the behaviors or the results of behaviors of people, objects, and occurrences. A key advantage of observation research is accuracy, especially when compared to survey research. Many questioning techniques ask consumers to recall past behaviors that ultimately are not accurately reported. Often this is because of time lapses, or because a choice or behavior was based on routine, intuition, or emotion, and was simply not memorable. Observation research provides greater detail and accuracy when investigating behavior than will surveys, focus groups, or interviews.

Observation research cannot be used to explain consumers' motivations, attitudes, or reasoning behind the behaviors. At the same time, while respondents can lie or just not reveal their inner thoughts on a survey or in focus groups, deceit is less likely when actual actions can be recorded via observation research. Individuals may say that sex in advertising does not affect them at all, but eye tracking devices or brain waves, as well as products that are actually purchased, may indicate otherwise. While understanding motivations, attitudes, and thoughts are important to marketers, equally important are the actions of consumers. Thinking about purchasing a product or even liking a particular brand does not generate revenue. Only the actual purchase of the product produces sales.

5.2a Conditions for Using Observation Research

Figure 5.2 highlights conditions where observation research can be used to collect data. First, the action or behavior must be observable, or the results must be observable. Individuals shopping in a mall or examining a point-of-purchase display are observable. So are the facial expressions and verbal comments made to employees in a retail store. Trash cans reveal the products and brands that households purchase. The number of visits to a website listed on an advertisement can be measured. However, what occurs in the privacy of a home is typically not observable; nor could marketers ethically or legally observe behavior in store dressing rooms.

- Action or behavior is observable or results are observable
- Action or behavior must be repetitive or occur frequently
- Action or behavior must be of short duration

FIGURE 5.2 Conditions for Observation Research

Source: Prostock-studio/Shutterstock.

Actions or behaviors for observation must be repetitive or occur frequently enough to produce usable results. One example is observing the number of people who stop to view a store window display.

The second condition for observation research is that the behavior or action must be repetitive or frequent in nature. Observing pedestrians walking down the street to see how many look at a store display or stop and read a sign is repetitive in nature and occurs frequently enough to produce usable results. However, observing how many times a particular individual looks at new cars on a car dealer lot during nonbusiness hours before coming back to talk to a salesperson is difficult because the actions are not frequent and repetitive. An individual may look more than once, but it may be several weeks apart.

Actions or behaviors need to be of a short duration. Observing a consumer's browser and mouse movements on a company website is of short duration and can be easily measured. So can the reactions of children to a new toy. But, more difficult would be the changes in how children play with a toy over a year or the impact of a new over-the-counter drug to reduce the signs of aging on skin. Shorter duration behaviors are necessary in order to complete research projects in a timely manner and to minimize the cost of conducting the research.

5.3 Dimensions of Observation Research

LEARNING OBJECTIVE 5.2
Describe the dimensions of observation research.

In using observation research, marketers have a number of options created by the various dimensions of the research procedure. Figure 5.3 identifies five dimensions that must be considered. Each dimension has its own set of advantages and disadvantages. The best approach is dependent on the objectives of the research and the types of decisions management must make. The quality of data needed and the budget available will also affect the choice of observation method.

5.3a Natural versus Contrived Setting

Natural setting observation individuals are observed in their natural environment where they may or may not know they are being observed.

Contrived setting individuals are studied in a controlled or laboratory setting where they know they are being observed.

Researchers can observe consumers in a **natural setting**, such as at home, in a store or at work. They *may* or *may not* know they are being observed. With a **contrived setting**, individuals are studied in a controlled location, such as a laboratory. With this approach, subjects know they are being observed and have agreed to participate in the research study. In the chapter opening example, study participants viewed the retail websites in a natural setting, using their own computer or laptop.

A company such as Hallmark could use a natural setting approach to observe how customers use an in-store kiosk to create a personalized greeting card. A fast food restaurant could watch customers' reactions to a new automated ordering system, menu display board, or point-of-purchase display. The primary advantage of using a natural setting is

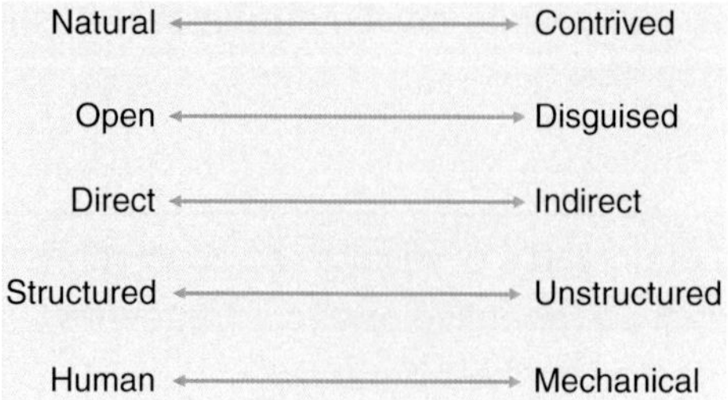

FIGURE 5.3 Dimensions of Observation Research

that researchers do not interfere with customers, and thus observations are natural reactions. Even if consumers know they are being watched, they will still tend to act more naturally than they might in a laboratory or contrived setting.

The major disadvantage is that researchers must wait until the behavior occurs. Also, other factors may affect the consumer's behavior. For example, suppose researchers are measuring the amount of time Burger King customers look at the menu display before making a decision. A friend of the customer might walk in and distract the customer by spending time talking. It would then be difficult to know exactly how long the customer examined the menu before making a decision, as he or she might look at it several times in the process of carrying on a conversation with the other person.

Source: TY Lim/Shutterstock.

McDonald's could watch customer's reactions to a new screen-based electronic ordering system with credit and debit payment options. Study results may help to clarify instructions or suggest a different location for the ordering system within the store.

To control for extraneous variables such as these affecting or confounding the results, researchers can use a contrived environment. An approach used by consumer packaged goods manufacturers is the simulated supermarket. Researchers can observe consumers as they interact with the supermarket, displays, and other items placed in the simulated store. Frito-Lay, for example, created a 15,000 square foot facility to study how different merchandising tactics influence shopper behavior, particularly impulse purchasing. Rob Clancy is the group manager of consumer strategy and insights with Frito-Lay North America. According to Clancy, "The key thing we struggled with in the past was how shoppers would react when they were actually in that environment. You can observe them in stores, but this was the first time we could do it on our own. We could create whatever we wanted to. We could change the merchandising, the product, or whatever we wanted."[2]

An alternative to using a physical facility or lab is conducting the research online using computer simulations and virtual displays or virtual reality store simulations. While the participant knows he or she is being studied, researchers have the advantage of being able to control the setting to prevent extraneous variables. In a natural setting, extraneous variables such as competitive coupon offerings, in-store circulars, and other factors can complicate consumers' decision-making process and potentially interfere with accomplishing the research purpose. Such factors can be controlled in both simulated and virtual environments.

The primary disadvantage of a contrived environment is that it is artificial. Participants may act differently than they would in a natural setting. Therefore, the results may not be applicable to real-world situations. But, this may not be a significant problem depending on the research purpose. Often it is used as a precursor to a quantitative study or to more fully understand the results obtained from a previously conducted quantitative study.

5.3b Open versus Disguised Observation

In **open observation** (or undisguised observation) individuals know they are being observed. The online shoppers recruited from Lightspeed's panel knew they would be observed when asked to participate in the product webpage research project described earlier. In the Hallmark kiosk example, the researcher could ask the customer for permission to observe and then encourage the individual to interact with the kiosk as he or she normally would. The same may be true of an observation study undertaken in a fast food restaurant, except in that setting the customer may not know exactly what the researcher is observing, just that he or she is being watched. This approach may help encourage the customer to act normally and not be affected by the researcher's presence (though some

Open (or undisguised) observation individuals know they are being observed.

individuals might alter their behavior or choices specifically because they know they are being watched). An alternative for open observation in the retail and service sector is to inform customers as they enter the facility that researchers are observing customers, and encourage them to go ahead and shop as they normally would. Unless researchers walk around in a suit with a clipboard, customers may not notice the researchers and quickly forget they are being observed.

Disguised observation participants do not know they are being observed.

With the **disguised observation** approach participants do not know they are being observed. This can be done through video cameras, one-way mirrors, online tracking software, passive measurement devices such as geolocation devices associated with smart phones, for example, or even via human observers who look and act like another customer or one of the employees. The major advantage of the disguised approach is that the participants' behaviors are not affected by knowledge of being observed. They also are not affected by the physical presence of a researcher. Having a researcher standing close to customers using a kiosk may affect how they use it, make them more nervous, or even influence them to use it in a way they believe the researcher wants.

A major disadvantage of the disguised observation approach is that researchers cannot gather any demographic or additional information about the participants. While they can see the person's gender and may be able to approximate the individual's age or race, that is about all they know about the individual. If the open observation method is used, the researcher can request demographic information from each of the participants. Or, in the case of panel members, the information is already available to the researcher. Additional information could even be gathered that might relate to the study. For example, with the fast food study the researcher could find out what other fast food restaurants the participant had visited, how often they visit the one being studied, and even what other menu items they have purchased in the past. Additional information allows the researcher to group the participants by different variables related to the behaviors under study, such as gender, age, or income, and then see how behaviors differ among these groups.

5.3c Direct versus Indirect Observation

Direct observation researchers watch participants as the behavior takes place.

Indirect observation observing the results of consumer actions rather than the action itself.

Most observation research is **direct observation**, which involves researchers (or machines) watching participants as the behavior is taking place. For example, a grocery store shopper may pick up a plum, squeeze it, wrinkle her nose, then put it down and select a different plum. This approach not only allows researchers to observe the behavior, but also any words spoken, facial expressions and even body language. Eye-tracking technology tracks what consumers are viewing, when, and for how long. **Indirect observation** involves observing the results of consumer actions rather than the action itself. Online observations often fall into this category since the research examines the results of the behavior, such as the amount of time spent on a website, the number of pages visited, and whether items placed into a shopping cart were purchased. The same would be true for using point-of-sales data to measure the impact of an end-of-aisle display at a retail store.

5.3d Unstructured versus Structured Observation

Unstructured observation research researchers watch participants and record behaviors they feel are relevant to the study being conducted.

Unstructured observation research involves researchers watching participants and recording behaviors they feel are relevant to the study being conducted. Observers have considerable latitude and freedom on what to record and how to record it. As such, the data is subjective in nature. This research method is better suited for exploratory research where the research problem is not clearly understood.

The primary advantage of unstructured observation lies in the freedom to observe and record whatever data the researcher believes to be important. Essentially, the researcher can note anything that is relevant or might appear to be relevant. For exploratory studies, this advantage can be instrumental in understanding problems a company or brand might be facing.

The disadvantage is that not all relevant behaviors might be recorded, or adequately categorized, because the observer is watching too much to be able to notice fine details.

This problem might be especially apparent if more than one individual was being observed simultaneously. It could even occur when only one person is being observed if that person is with other individuals. Furthermore, when multiple observers are involved in the same study, each observer might actually judge different behaviors as important; behaviors deemed important by one observer might be ignored entirely by another.

With **structured observation research** the problem has been sufficiently defined, which allows researchers to know beforehand what behaviors they can expect and even the various categories or options within each behavior to be tracked. Data collection usually involves the use of a checklist form, which tells the researcher exactly which actions should be recorded. All other behaviors are ignored. Structured observations work well with descriptive research studies because researchers have specific objectives they want to accomplish and may even have hypotheses related to the behaviors expected. Most online and many mechanical methods of observation are structured.

Structured observation research researchers know beforehand what behaviors to expect and even the various categories or options within each behavior that should be recorded.

Referring back to the fast food example, with structured observation the researcher would have the menu categories listed on their data collection form and would check the one that is ordered. There could be a place to record the number of seconds or minutes the customer looked at the menu board, or special display, the time it took for the counter worker to greet the customer, or whatever else is being studied. The researcher could even record the number of times the customer looks away and then back at the menu, which might indicate indecisiveness. With structured observation the checklist form is prepared in advance, and the researcher simply checks off or records the behaviors under study.

Because observation research often relies upon multiple individuals to collect data, structured observation studies offer the advantage of being more objective, which increases the reliability of the findings. Less bias is introduced since the researcher checks or records behaviors that have been specified prior to undertaking the observation research. Individual observers are not placed in the position of deciding what is and is not important enough to record. In many cases this allows for comparisons and parametric analysis procedures since it produces more objective, quantitative data.

5.3e Human versus Mechanical Observation

The last dimension that differentiates observation methods is whether the observation is undertaken by humans or some type of mechanical device. Humans have the advantage of being able to observe another person's entire repertoire of behaviors, from actions to body language to words spoken. Significant data could be missed if a mechanical device were used. However, that ability to fully observe could also result in failure to accurately notice various behaviors if the actions occur too rapidly or the researcher is distracted by another person, the environment, or even the subject's actions that are not part of the study. In addition, human observation tends be subjective in nature, which may be okay for exploratory research, but would not be as appropriate for more quantitative studies, unless a structured observation method was also used.

Mechanical devices and software used in observation research can vary from scanner data at retail stores to smartphones, web tracking software, social listening software, eye-tracking devices and facial recognition software, to name just a few. A major advantage of mechanical devices and related software is data accuracy. Unless the machine is malfunctioning or out of proper calibration, it will measure the phenomena being studied accurately, assuming any associated software has been programmed correctly. Imagine the difficulty that a human observer might have in counting the number of vehicles travelling through an intersection during rush hour. Mechanical traffic counters aren't subject to fatigue or other factors that may detract from a human observer's accuracy, and can easily be used 24 hours a day. On the other hand, additional behaviors that might provide valuable information can be missed since the machine is programmed to measure a specific set of limited behaviors or results of behaviors. For instance, despite the advances made in text analytics, artificial intelligence has not reached the point where computers can comprehend unstructured text to the same degree as humans.

Source: Extarz/Shutterstock.

Watching how long a customer looks at various brands will be more accurate than asking individuals how much time they spent examining the available brands.

5.4 Overview of Observation Research

Observing actual behavior may be more accurate than data obtained from surveys that ask people to report what they did. To illustrate, one researcher electronically monitored the use of printers in a large office, and also asked individual users how much they were printing. In comparing the results, he learned that the *closest* people were able to estimate their usage was +/− 50 percent of their actual volume.[3] It follows then that a scanner record of customer purchases will be more accurate than asking consumers what they purchased on their last trip to the store since consumers often have difficulty recalling information if a number of items were purchased. There may be no intention of being deceptive or untruthful. They may not have paid attention to their purchases, or they may simply have forgotten. This is particularly true for shopping trips involving the purchase of routine items or those in which many items were purchased. Furthermore, the likelihood of forgetting increases as the time between the study and shopping trip lengthens.

Similarly, watching how long a customer looks at various brands of packaged goods will be more accurate than asking individuals how much time they spent examining the available brands. This fact is particularly important for customer service studies, as participants almost universally overestimate the amount of time they spend waiting to be seated, or acknowledged by a server, for instance.

Sometimes survey participants may be reluctant to share specific information related to particular types of purchases or behaviors. For instance, in a study about gambling, individuals may not want to admit they gamble or go to casinos. If they do, they will almost always under-estimate the amount of money gambled in a desire to avoid being thought of as a habitual gambler, or looking bad in front of the researcher.

Children are often studied through observation research methods not only due to accuracy issues, but also because children lack reasoning skills, and are typically not capable of answering questions on a survey. A three-year-old child cannot explain how she or he feels a toy should be used. But, through observation, researchers can watch a child play with the toy and often attain this type of information.

The primary disadvantage of pure observation research is that only observed behaviors or observed characteristics can be reported. Researchers are not able to discern motives, attitudes, beliefs, or feelings of the participants. They may learn what the person did, but not why the individual acted in a particular manner. This is a serious disadvantage, since understanding why certain actions were taken is often more important than learning what was done. In addition, current actions may not be a good predictor of future behaviors. Increasingly, the trend is to include observation research as part of a larger research study that may also include a quantitative survey, focus groups, in-depth interviews, or some other type of qualitative research technique that is helpful in understanding consumer motivations.

A second disadvantage is that only public or observable behaviors or results of behaviors can be researched. What occurs in private, before or after the observation session, cannot be seen. The before actions may be important in explaining a participant's behavior. For instance, researchers watching individuals shop for clothes may notice that a number of participants spend little time walking around the store and looking at clothes. They find the item quickly and then move to the checkout. The reason for such quick purchase behavior may be that they were on the Internet and had already picked out the clothes they

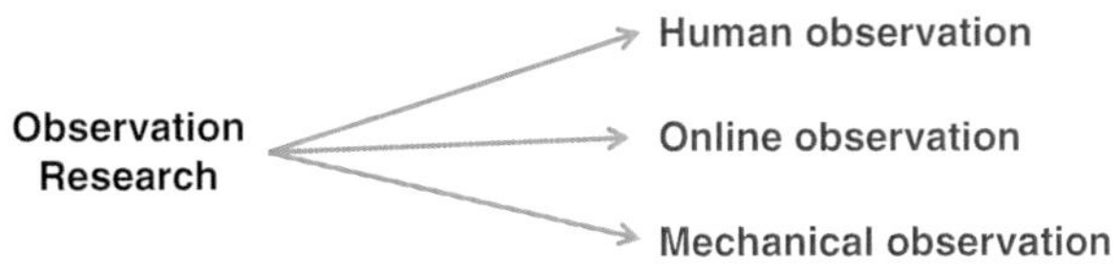

FIGURE 5.4 Observation Research Categories

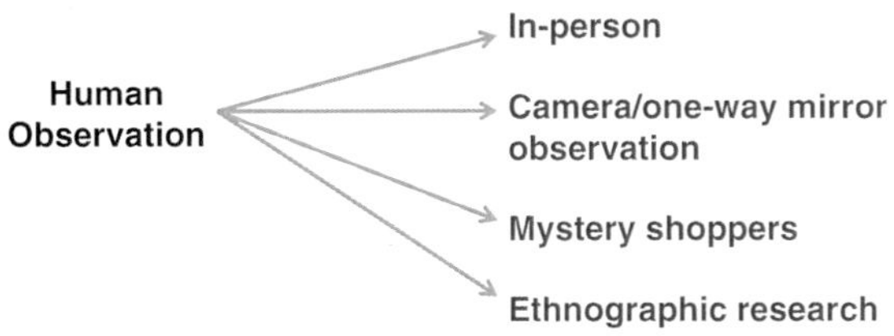

FIGURE 5.5 Human Observation Research Techniques

wanted, or they may have been at the store the day before and later decided to come back and purchase the items.

As shown in **Figure 5.4**, observation research can be divided into three main categories: human observation, online observation, and mechanical observation. While these three often overlap in terms of characteristics and design, for the sake of studying observation research it is useful to think along these three categories.

5.5 Human Observation

LEARNING OBJECTIVE 5.3
Discuss the various human observation methods.

Human observation provides an opportunity to watch the behaviors of people. A tremendous amount of learning can take place from careful observation. **Figure 5.5** identifies the four primary methods researchers use for human observation.

5.5a In-Person Observation

Using humans to observe consumers is a form of ethnographic research discussed later in this chapter. In pure observation research, no interaction takes place with the participants during the observation period. The researcher may ask for demographic and other types of information at the conclusion of the observation, but does not interact with the person being studied in any way as the behavior being recorded takes place.

Moniek Buijzen and Patti Valkenburg used human observation to study parent-child communication as it related to purchasing behavior.[4] They wanted to observe the actual communication as it occurred in real, everyday life and not rely on memory recall. They also felt that direct observation would be more accurate in determining how parents and children communicated during the purchase process in the retail store.

The study was conducted in ten supermarkets and five toy stores in the Netherlands. A total of 269 parent-child dyads were observed. The children ranged from ages of less than a year to 12 years old. The parent-child dyad was observed from the time they entered the store until after they had passed through the checkout having made their purchase. The researchers wrote down all of the behaviors they observed as well as the interactions between the children and parents. After the purchase was made and the individuals were leaving the store, the researchers approached them and told them about the study and asked for their permission to use the data they had just collected through observation. The parent was then asked to fill out a questionnaire that requested for demographic information, the child's television viewing habits, and family communication patterns.

While the researchers were free to write down any behavior or interaction they thought was relevant, the researchers had also developed a coding sheet that required looking for specific behaviors and interactions. By structuring the majority of the observation cues in advance, they were more diligent in looking for specific behaviors and communication interactions. This allowed the two researchers to work independently observing different parent-child dyads, yet produce data that were compatible.

In the study by Buijzen and Valkenborg, the observers did not identify themselves until the parents had left the store. This procedure allowed for the individuals to act normally since they had no idea someone was watching them. Some researchers feel this approach borders on being unethical and an invasion of privacy, so they stop individuals prior to entering the store to solicit permission to watch them. The danger of this approach is that the individuals being watched may not act normally, but act instead in a way they think the researcher wants. However, companies that use this approach say that most consumers forget within minutes they are being watched and soon act normally.

5.5b Camera or One-Way Mirror Observation

In situations where in-person observation may bias the behaviors of the participants, researchers can observe via cameras or one-way mirrors. Most retail stores have security cameras that can be used for observation research, and plug-and-play wi-fi enabled cameras are so inexpensive that they provide a reasonable alternative. Participants can be studied as they interact with special displays or shop for merchandise. The primary concern with using cameras is that it may be considered an invasion of privacy. However, if consumers are asked for permission, then the rationale for using cameras is defeated.

Research firms such as Envirosell (https://envirosell.com) use first person and video observation studies to capture store traffic patterns as well as other behaviors. One advantage of recording activity in-store is that researchers have multiple opportunities to observe and code behavior, as the video can be reviewed multiple times. An additional advantage of video footage is that video is often instrumental when reporting results, as video clips can help demonstrate key findings.

Noldus Information Technology used an experimental design featuring video-based observations to test whether elderly patients in a nursing home would increase their food consumption if dining conditions were optimized. First, residents were placed in either a control group or the experimental group. People in both groups were observed two days a week over a 12-week period. During the first four weeks, nothing changed. At the beginning of week five, the experimental group began receiving, 1) better quality food; 2) improved ambience (white table clothes and candles; and 3) higher quality staff interaction. The control group received the standard meal, in the standard setting, with the standard level of staff interaction. Key behaviors observed included the meal duration, food intake, and body weight. While the time spent eating, and the type of foods consumed were observed and coded from the video, body weight was measured separately before and after the experiment. The results indicated that the experimental group spent more time eating, ate more vegetables, potatoes, and pasta, and increased their body weight under the optimal dining conditions when compared to the control group.[5]

One-way mirrors are often used for observing children. Companies, such as Mattel, have play rooms where children can play with toys. Researchers can watch from behind one-way glass to see which toys the children choose and how they play with them. Having an adult in the room taking notes may change the children's behavior. Children often want to please an adult or let them see what they are doing so the actions may not be natural without the use of a one-way mirror.

5.5c Mystery Shoppers

Mystery shoppers are used by a large number of companies, and are particularly popular in the retail, service and restaurant industries. Mystery shoppers are typically used to evaluate customer service. But mystery shoppers can also be used to investigate the appearance of a retail store, the cleanliness of a facility, and other elements of a business décor or customer amenities. Some companies will have mystery shoppers visit the competition in order to make benchmark comparisons.

While companies strive to gather feedback from customers via 800 numbers, email, or website comment forms, such feedback tends to be polarized. The good customers are happy to talk about the great service, the great products, or the wonderful employees. The unhappy customers are often even more eager to be heard. Unfortunately, it is the group of consumers in between these two extremes that is usually silent, which is troubling since this group makes up the largest percentage of a firm's customer base. For this reason, mystery shoppers are used to provide a better gauge of how all customers see a firm.

According to Marshall Cohen of market research firm NPD Group, "It [using mystery shoppers] doesn't just help you understand how customers see the display of merchandise and determine the ease of finding products; it can also measure employees' willingness to give help within the store. Is the shopper treated as a guest or the enemy? Are employees more interested in cleaning the store than they are in saying hello to the customer? Service is very much a part of the value equation today, and mystery shopping lets you gauge it more effectively than many other channels."[6]

While mystery shoppers are trained to observe and record whatever they see, they also typically use a structured, specific code sheet to record information. The code sheet is based on the company's operational standards and goals. For instance, a mystery shopper at a restaurant would note the time it takes to be seated, the time it takes the server to bring a menu or ask for a drink order, the time it takes to get the food, and the appearance of the food when it arrives. They would also take notes on the server's appearance, demeanor, and quality of service. Other elements that might be recorded are the type of music playing, loudness of music, and cleanliness of the facility. By posing as a customer, a mystery shopper is able to obtain very detailed information about a firm's operation. This information can be used for training programs, staff motivational programs, communication strategies, and branch or site evaluations.

As marketers become increasingly concerned about the customer's experience with different forms of marketing communications, mystery shopping is now moving beyond its roots in retail. Mystery shoppers are often used now to evaluate the accessibility of e-commerce websites across different device types and browsers. Navigation, searching, ease-of-checkout, and the delivery/return process are investigated by mystery shoppers who look for problems during the purchase process. Mobile apps, online chat tools and consumer/company email contacts are another area where mystery shopping would be beneficial. While customer contact centers can help strengthen a customer's relationship with a brand if problems are successfully addressed, long wait times, insufficient answers, and poor service may do just the opposite. Mystery shoppers can help gauge critical wait/hold time metrics, agent helpfulness/friendliness, and knowledgeability.[7]

Mystery shopping studies vary in complexity. Some studies involve minimal interaction with employees, while others are designed to test the depth and accuracy of employee knowledge. Mystery shopping does not have to be conducted in person at a physical facility. For example, an automotive company used telephone mystery shopping to determine whether dealer associates were correctly informing callers about two promotions that were available to those seeking information about tires. Mystery shoppers initiated the phone call at random times, and listened to determine if employees mentioned both promotions. If the associate was successful, he or she received congratulations and a gift card incentive inside a customized card carrier that was sent to his or her home address. Reports gave management insight into how well associates provided information about the promotions at different locations, as well as the number of calls that were transferred by associates. In this instance, the mystery shopping firm Confero, also managed the implementation of the rewards, saving the client time.[8]

Another component of mystery shopping programs is a competitive audit. With competitive audits, mystery shoppers visit competitors. The visits provide an opportunity to collect comparative data. A firm can see how well it performs in relation to its competitors.

Source: nd3000/Shutterstock.

Icon Health and Fitness used ethnographic research to examine how consumers used treadmills for exercising. The firm realized they would need to redesign the machines to hold items consumers accessed while working out.

In addition, the data can serve as a benchmark against a company's own performance levels. The value in the data is that it is from the customer's perspective since the mystery shopper is posing as a customer. It provides more accurate information than would be obtained from interviewing actual customers from competing firms. Depending on the level of loyalty to the brand, customers of competing firms tend to be biased toward their favorite brands, which makes it difficult to objectively compare brands.

5.5d Ethnographic Research

Ethnographic research observing individuals in their natural settings using a combination of direct observation and video and/or audio recordings.

Ethnographic research involves observing individuals in their natural settings using a combination of direct observation and video and/or audio recordings. Adopted from the field of anthropology, ethnographic research allows researchers to study individuals through observing their behaviors, emotions, and responses to the environment where they live, use products, or shop. Instead of asking consumers how they use various products as part of a focus group, ethnographers can observe the products being used in the home or business and interact with individuals during the consumption process. Many researchers believe that people will be more open in their home than in a focus group facility, and that richer insights can be obtained regarding things such as how and where products are stored, and how consumers interact with packaging.[9] Ethnography offers an excellent opportunity to understand consumer behavior prior to developing a quantitative segmentation study, and can clear away misleading assumptions. It is also a helpful technique when developing marketing communications, as ethnography often discovers the emotions aroused by products in different use contexts. Finally, ethnography is essential to understanding unarticulated consumer needs that could be met through innovation or product redesigns.[10]

Icon Health and Fitness decided to use ethnographic research to examine how consumers used treadmills for exercising. The researcher observed individuals using treadmills in their homes as well as in fitness centers. The observer noticed that individuals came to the treadmill with a variety of personal items such as towels, water bottles, keys, cell phones, magazines, and books. They would search the floor for a place to put items or try to find something to put on the treadmill to hold their items, especially the magazines and books. It might be some old plastic piece, an old magazine rack, or something that they could wedge or tie or hang onto the treadmill so they could read while walking. During the workout the individuals would slide the reading material to the side to see their time or read other measurements on the display. During a typical workout they would use the display panel for five minutes, but then use it as a magazine or book holder the remaining 25 minutes. After analyzing the observation data and session video recordings, the company realized it needed to redesign its treadmill so it would be able to accommodate how individuals used it.[11]

Typically, ethnographic research involves the researcher working primarily from the background as an observer having little interaction with the consumer being studied. An alternative is to become engaged with the consumer and become their "instant" friend. This process may produce insights, with the consumer talking about things he or she does and explaining the reason for behaviors. The concept behind this approach is that in addition to the observation, the ethnographic researcher is gaining valuable understandings of motivations through the trust and friendship that has been built.[12]

Traditional ethnographic research is quite expensive and time consuming, as it involves multiple days of study and multiple locations. Rarely can researchers afford to study more than one or two geographic areas. One variation that has become more popular is the ethnographic immersion. An **immersion** is an ethnographic study that last hours, not days, and involves prompting by the researcher. Whereas traditional ethnographic researchers would simply observe activity as it takes place in the kitchen, a researcher in an immersive study might say, "Would you mind showing me how you prep and cook vegetables?" Immersive ethnography is best used when exploring specific topics or lines of inquiry, or when testing hypotheses.[13]

Immersion an ethnographic study that last hours, not days, and involves prompting by the researcher.

Digital ethnography is becoming more popular, and can take many forms. One variation combines video diaries and in-person interviews. Prescreened participants are sent video cameras with instructions or a checklist on what to film. For example, the instructions might read, "Please film the preparation and consumption of a typical weekday evening meal in your home. Please film the interior of your freezer, each shelf of your refrigerator, and any other storage area where food is kept." Completed videos are returned to the research firm for review. Follow-up interviews are conducted in-person to uncover the reasons behind key behaviors identified by researchers who viewed a video.[14]

A video-based ethnography process called "Echo" was used to learn about the "Game of Thrones" (GOT) TV series. First, a sample of fans answered a series of questions about the show and its characters. Video responses were recorded via smartphones and submitted to researchers, who compiled responses into a short film. This film was shown to a larger fan group, who accessed it via a media-testing app on their video camera-enabled smartphones or tablets. Fans responded in real-time to questions about what they were viewing, and were encouraged to rate or comment on the video. Ultimately, the study found that GOT fans highly valued characters' complexity and ambiguity. Fans watched the show because of the vibrant magical setting, the depth of characters, and the unpredictability of the plot twists. Based on this information, researchers suggested that brands can connect with fans if the brand resonates with a character or plot thread.[15]

Video-based ethnography can also use cameras to record passive behaviors without the presence of a researcher. For example, a camera may be positioned to capture how often the microwave, refrigerator, washer, dryer or some other appliance is used, as well as how consumers make use of the appliance. Are microwave users making snacks, such as popcorn, or preparing meals?[16] The advantage of passive video-based ethnography is that the cameras can record behaviors at all hours of the day and over a longer period of time. Behavior is natural and uninterrupted, especially as users tend to forget the camera's presence. Researchers would send the camera(s) to the participants, and either install the camera or instruct the recipient how and where to position the camera. Often a wi-fi modem would be preconfigured to work with the cameras and stream the video signals.

Finally, "in-the-moment" mobile ethnography is gaining traction. One variation is the shop along, which combines open observation of willing subjects with attitudinal research gained via personal interviews. Researchers either accompany a shopper throughout the store, recording their activities with a smartphone, and interviewing them about their behaviors as they happen, or, the shoppers record their activities on their own smartphone and stream it to the researcher in real-time. Researchers watching the shopping experience as it happens can question the shopper to determine how he or she feels about the product. Open-ended questions starting with "Why" and "What" yield a wealth of data that can be analyzed by human coders, or imported into text analytics software programs. Sentiment neutral questions help to elicit quality data. For example, in the parking lot prior to entering the store, an interviewer might ask, "Please describe your last trip to Whole Foods."[17]

In some variations of mobile ethnography, consumers simply record their experience and upload it to a website. Kraft Foods sought to better understand the process of hosting self-catered parties, and used mobile video ethnography. Twenty-eight participants were recruited from different regional boards of CraigsList. A different meal was served at each party, in a variety of party contexts. Video and photos documented event preparation, shopping, day of event activities, the actual party, and cleanup. Kraft discovered that despite the stress involved in entertaining, hosts found it to be a very rewarding activity. Kraft's proprietary research uncovered many consumer insights and discovered several

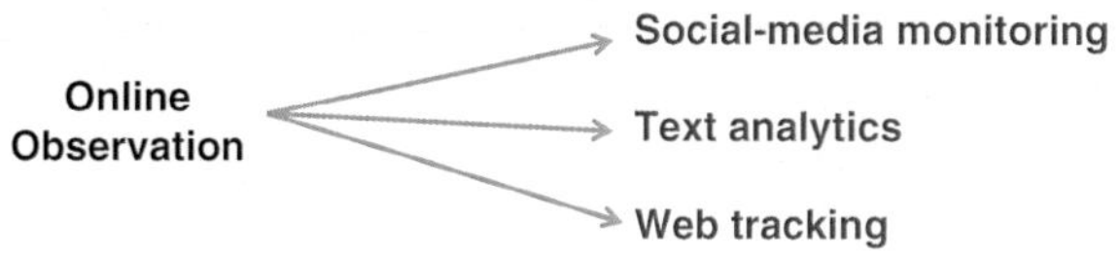

FIGURE 5.6 Online Observation Research Techniques

new product ideas during the process. While mobile ethnography can yield consumer insights and is much less costly than traditional ethnographic research, a potential disadvantage is that it allows the consumer to edit the video, so the researcher may not really see what happens in the moment and important information may be lost. In the Kraft study, it was often difficult for participants to film every action, especially when two hands were needed to complete a task.[18]

Digital and mobile ethnography offer cost and time savings, while bringing together participants and researchers who may be geographically dispersed. Passive video ethnography allows for extended observations without disrupting participant's daily lives. These techniques are particularly effective with Generation Z and Generation Y, who are used to sharing their thoughts and feelings via video on social media.

5.6 Online Observation

LEARNING OBJECTIVE 5.4
Describe the various online observation methods.

With consumers spending more time online and making greater use of the Internet in the purchase decision process, it is important for marketing researchers to examine ways of studying online behavior. Online observation includes social-media monitoring, text analytics and web tracking, as outlined in **Figure 5.6**. Online observation research offers a number of advantages and disadvantages,[19] as shown in **Figure 5.7**.

Because of the large number of people on the Internet, the number of potential participants for research studies is almost limitless. The Internet is increasingly representative of the U.S. population. For example, as of 2019, one-hundred percent of adults 18–29 use the Internet, while 97 percent of those aged 30–49 use the Internet. Similarly, 88 percent and 73 percent of those aged 50–64 and 65 and older use the Internet, respectively.[20] This easier access to participants means costs are lower and collecting data is faster than with conventional human observation methods of research, especially when smartphones are used. Participants do not have to travel to a central site, retail store, or other location. The same is true for the researchers. They can conduct the study from their office or company headquarters.

Computers leave a digital trail that improves data accuracy. Researchers can go back and track data. They can use the computer to tally and track activities and movement on the Internet. The research is not dependent on humans carefully observing behavior and trying to accurately record everything that occurs, when it occurs. This digital trail also means there is greater flexibility in the types of research that can be conducted.

- **Advantages**
  - –Access to large group of potential participants
  - –Lower costs
  - –Faster data collection
  - –Digital trail
  - –Greater flexibility in observation methods
- **Disadvantages**
  - –Lack of auditory and visual cues
  - –Extreme difficult establishing respondent authenticity
  - –Rambling and unfocused content complicates task
  - –Profile of online users may not be representative

FIGURE 5.7 Advantages and Disadvantages of Online Observation

On the downside, online researchers cannot see any visual cues, such as facial expressions and body language of the person at the computer. They cannot hear verbal tones or inflections. The same words can be written online by two individuals, yet have totally different meanings based on auditory cues or body language. It is not always easy to interpret what is meant by individuals from written communications.

Researchers cannot always be sure the individual on the Internet is who he or she purports to be. It is extremely difficult and often impossible to authenticate identity. With anonymous online observation identity authentication is virtually impossible. Someone who appears to be a female may actually be an underage person or even a male.

Blogs, chat rooms, and even websites can provide valuable opportunities for online research, but they may also contain considerable rambling and unfocused content. With a focus group or interview, individuals can be kept on track. With human observations, participants tend to stay on task. That does not always occur online. Individuals tend to vent emotions, share ideas, and just share thoughts. Some may be of value, others may not. Researchers may have to sort out what is relevant and what is not.

Last, online users may not always be representative of the population. Low income and under-educated individuals tend to have less computer and online access, although this is less of a problem than it was even three or four years ago. If they do use a public access computer at a library or other facility, the individuals are less likely to be part of chat rooms or blogs.

A major concern facing online observation research is the issue of privacy. Consumers are concerned that current technology allows companies to track their movements and online activities. Congress and other government entities have discussed this issue and are still considering legislation that may restrict what companies can and cannot do in terms of web tracking. Such legislation would have an impact on how online research is conducted, especially in situations where individuals are being studied without their knowledge. The impact of the European Union's General Data Protection Regulation which took effect in 2018 has already been felt by market researchers. Recall that the GDPR affects any business that collects or handles personal information from someone residing inside of the European Union. In April of 2018, Facebook restricted U.S. firms' (as well as firms in other countries) access to Instagram's public comments, post content, profile pictures, user names, and more. Now Instagram users must explicitly agree to provide this information to researchers; simple observation methods alone will not do.[21]

Certainly the GDPR presents challenges for researchers moving forward. Facebook may be the first of many to implement similar policies. Without knowing who is or is not a member of the European Union, researchers must proceed with caution in collecting personally identifiable information and would be wise to follow the GDPR rules as a general principle. Respecting consumer's right to see *all* data a company has recorded and linked to their name, and deleting information upon request or once it has served its purpose are two other mandates outlined in the GDPR which should certainly be respected.[22]

As Figure 5.7 demonstrates, marketing researchers have a number of online observation research methods that can be used. The best method will depend on the research problem and research objectives. It will also depend on the information that is needed and the location of that data on the web.

The rise in the popularity of e-commerce, online TV, online radio, social media, and the Internet in general has provided market researchers with an opportunity to study a wide variety of topics. Marketing researchers can observe online chatter, customer reviews, communications, and some social media postings without participants ever knowing they are present, which allows them to capture real thoughts of individuals in natural online settings. Even in situations where researchers identify themselves, the online environment offers participants a high level of confidentiality, and they may not be identified at all. Participants often feel more comfortable sharing thoughts online compared to focus groups or personal interviews. Social media monitoring tools help make sense of this information, and more complex text analytic software solutions are also available. Analyzing information found throughout the Internet is challenging though, due to its

Unstructured data text-dominant data that is not organized in a predefined manner when input by the source, nor does it have a pre-defined data model.

unstructured nature. **Unstructured data** is not organized in a predefined manner when input by the source, nor does it have a pre-defined data model. Social media information is an example of unstructured data, as are comments on product review or e-commerce websites. While some forms of social media allow tags to be used, this data is still unstructured as tags are not systematically used in an identical fashion by everyone posting information. Unstructured data is primarily composed of text though it may also contain dates or numbers. Answers to open-ended survey questions and transcribed video content are considered unstructured data, as is offline data such as content gathered from telephone or online customer service centers.

5.6a Social Media Monitoring

In social media observation, researchers utilize a variety of online sources such as social media sites, Twitter, blogs, chat rooms or chat logs from customer service centers, customer reviews, and even websites. Most information will be written, but a number of blogs and websites will also contain videos. These videos can be as insightful as written material, but may be more difficult to interpret. The choice of online sources will depend on the research purpose and research questions being addressed. Locating postings about topics of interest may not be the researcher's greatest challenge. Locating a single software solution or multiple software solutions to help make sense of the data is critical. While many social media monitoring software solutions exist, they aren't equally capable of tracking different sources of data, and the power of their text analytics software varies widely.

Unlike with human observation, researchers can download text from the Internet and take more time to analyze what is written. The information is almost always asynchronous, except for live chat rooms. By downloading the textual information, researchers can use computer programs to locate key words or phrases. They can also pull out postings by a single individual and study changes in communication and or behavior over time.

Marketing research firms have become interested in mining the vast number of visuals that make up the majority of social media content. Many consumers, especially millennials, communicate using images rather than words, perhaps because the human brain processes visual information faster than text. Pinterest, Instagram, Tumblr and Snapchat are image repositories that speak volumes about consumers' dreams and aspirations as well as how they perceive brands. A visual audit of what's being pinned to a Pinterest site can be revealing. What keywords are being used to describe consumers' pins? What ideas are customers illustrating? Where are posted brand pins being repinned? Answering these and other questions can influence future marketing efforts. For instance, a 2016 study of over 15.75 million brand-related Pinterest posts found that Mondays and Tuesdays were the most popular days for posting on Pinterest, by a slight margin, though Mondays and Saturdays were the top days for user engagement. Interestingly, the top nine words used on Pinterest to describe images or what users thought about images were 1) make, 2) design, 3) logo, 4) new, 5) love, 6) get, 7) one, 8) free, 9) day. Based on these and other study results, recommendations to marketers included offering a free resource to Pinterest followers, sharing new and creative pins, experimenting with the content posting schedule to gauge the best days for engagement and repins for the marketer's brand, and using fewer words to describe pins.[23]

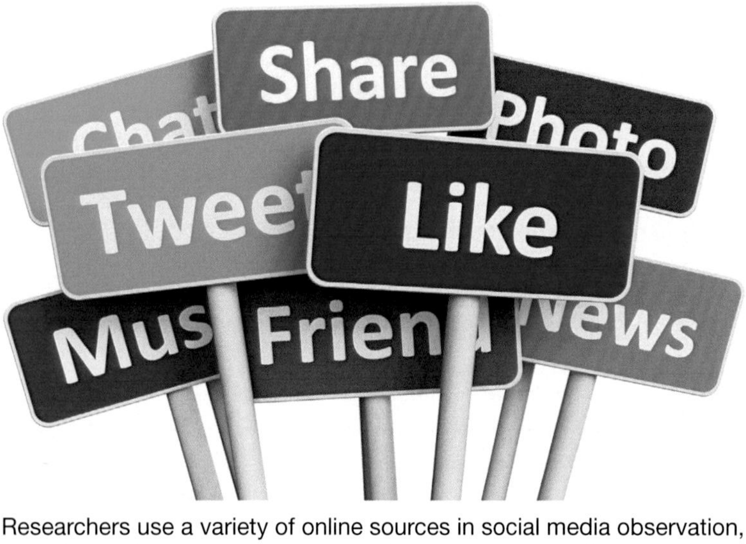

Source: Oleksiy Mark/Shutterstock.

Researchers use a variety of online sources in social media observation, including Twitter, blogs, review web sites, and social media sites.

Social media research can be used by companies in a number of ways. It can be used for exploratory research to gain a better understanding of a particular topic or to investigate potential problems a company or brand may be facing. While it is not a true assessment of word-of-mouth communications, it is an excellent method of learning what consumers think about a brand and what they are telling others as well as what triggers them to discuss brands online. It can also be used to help frame messaging strategies. Social media research can be used in conjunction with descriptive research to provide a better understanding of particular findings and provide personal insights into thoughts and feelings of consumers.

Because of their large size and easy access, social media sites can be used as research samples. In addition to monitoring chatter, researchers can post questions on social media sites. Responses come almost instantaneously. If the research is carefully crafted, important information can be gathered. Asking "why" instead of "what" questions elicits longer comments and richer data.[24] But it is important to remember that the sample being used is not likely to be representative of the population being studied. The results, therefore, are not likely to be applicable to the population as whole. Despite this disadvantage, using social media as a sample for marketing research can provide useful data.

During the 2019 Super Bowl game, Crimson Hexagon, a provider of social media listening software that has now merged with Brandwatch, monitored social media conversations to measure people's opinions of ads and to rank the brands being advertised. The first step was to tally the number of social media mentions for each brand. A sentiment score was calculated by subtracting the number of negative mentions from the number of positive mentions, then dividing that result by the total number of mentions. Bubly, Avocados from Mexico, and Audi all had positive net sentiment scores of 56 percent or more, while Turbotax's ad performed the worst, with a net sentiment of −43 percent, followed by Mint Mobile, at −31 percent. Interestingly, none of these brands were among the top five in terms of overall social media mentions. This type of data provides advertisers with an idea of what individuals who watched the Super Bowl thought about the ads. It also indicates how a particular brand's ads compared to other brands. Since the social media mentions occurred during and immediately after the game, it was a quick, easy, and relatively inexpensive way to evaluate the impact of Super Bowl ads and to measure the buzz created by the ads.[25]

5.6b Text Analytics

Computer software technologies have been developed that allow advanced forms of text analysis to be incorporated into Social Media Listening software, and artificial intelligence is improving the quality of text analytics on a daily basis. Text analytics are generally used for one of two broad purposes. **Descriptive text analytics** look for word associations, the frequency of word counts, words that are in proximity to one another, or other patterns. **Predictive text analytics** use text to predict the outcome of a target variable, such as ratings, purchases, or recommendations.[26] **Figure 5.8** identifies some of the

Descriptive text analytics look for word associations, the frequency of word counts, words that are in proximity to one another, or other patterns.

Predictive text analytics use text to predict the outcome of a target variable.

- Keyword analysis
- Natural language processing
  - –Named entity recognition
  - –Targeted event extraction
  - –Exhaustive fact extraction
- Machine Learning

FIGURE 5.8 Forms of Text Analytics

Source: Based on Eric Weight, "What can text analytics teach us?" *Quirk's Marketing Research Review*, August 2011, Article ID 20110807, pp. 58, 60–62 and "How to Apply AI to Your Social Media Listening in 2019: An Essential Users Guide," accessed August 2, 2019, https://converson.com/wp-content/uploads/2018/11/Social-Listening-White-Paper.pdf

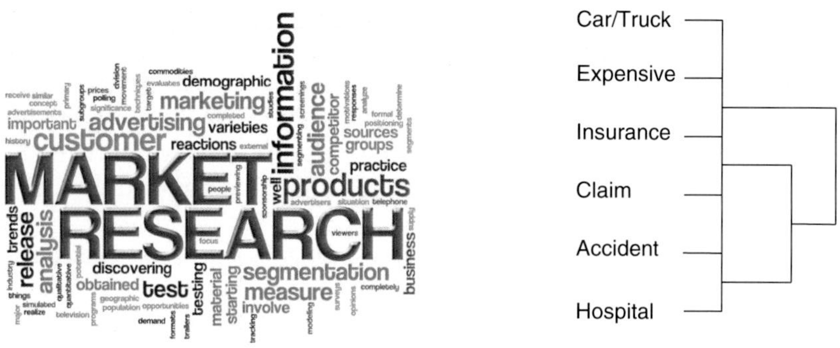

A Word Cloud for "Marketing Research"

A Word Clustering Diagram

FIGURE 5.9 Displaying Results of Keyword Analysis
Source: nasirkhan/Shutterstock.

text mining technologies that are now being used by marketing research firms.[27] While text mining is used in other disciplines, such as medicine, government, and education, the most promise is in the field of business. It is being used to research competitors, a firm's own customers, and to develop marketing and advertising strategies.

Keyword analysis form of text analytics that looks for predefined sequences in text through analyzing unstructured text and identifying key phrases and relationships.

Keyword analysis looks for predefined sequences in text through analyzing unstructured data and identifying key phrases and relationships. For instance, when studying iced coffee, the software would look for text that would mention "iced coffee" and other key words such as "purchase," "buy," and "like." The key to its use is defining the key words and phrases to be analyzed, and it is important that the researcher consider acronyms, pluralities, codes, hashtags and "text talk" when creating definitions. Keyword analysis is fast and efficient and can help to identify trends, suggestions for improvement, a need for customer contact, or product issues. Results are often displayed in a word cloud, such as the one shown in Figure 5.9. The larger the size of the words surrounding "marketing research", the more frequently these terms were mentioned. Word clustering is another method of displaying the results of keyword analysis. Word clusters create a diagram that shows the relationship of words within a document. In the example shown in Figure 5.9, shorter lines indicate that words are more closely related. Other variations of word clusters map words spatially to show distance and closeness, or use other techniques to display relationships. Multidimensional scaling, a topic beyond the scope of this text, can be used to help create even more complex representations of the relationships between various words, and help in defining groupings.[28] However, it should be noted that most keyword analysis software is not capable of discerning the meaning of words. Depending on the width and breadth of data being processed, searches on the word "scale" would likely turn up conversations related to fish, as scale can be a noun (i.e., fish scales) or a verb (i.e., "to scale" means to remove the scales from a fish). It may also find "scale" discussions related to weight-loss, or marketing research questions, as scale in both situations relates to a form of measurement. Many free social media monitoring tools exist that can assist with keyword analysis, including Hootsuite and Social Mention.

Natural language processing (NLP) technologies that require training a software program to understand language and the way it is used by people.

Natural language processing (NLP) technologies involve training a software program to understand language and the way it is used by people. This is not an easy task. Fortunately, advances in computer programming, machine learning, and artificial intelligence have advanced the field, though no single software program currently approaches the level of accuracy of human coding. To understand the challenges involved, it might be helpful to understand the process. First, an understanding of grammar and word forms such as nouns, verbs, adjectives and prepositions must be developed. The vast majority of commercial text analytic software solutions have accomplished this basic step. However, challenges still exist as computers cannot comprehend or struggle to understand sarcasm, slang, misused words, indirect phrasing, and poor grammar. There may come a time when artificial intelligence is "smart enough" to grasp these concepts, but human intervention is typically still necessary in the training process. Once trained, the software can often derive the true meaning of words and phrases in context.[29] There are three advanced forms of NLP-based analytics: named entry recognition, targeted event extraction, and exhaustive fact extraction.

Named entity recognition identifies and extracts classes of entities (such as people, brands, firms, products, or locations) and related information. It is only feasible when the researcher already knows the entities to be extracted and the classification to which they should be assigned. The software is able to distinguish between nouns and verbs, which helps eliminate irrelevant comments. Many free social media monitoring tools or off-the-shelf text analytic software programs are sufficient for this purpose, though buyers should select a program that allows the user to input additional classifications. **Sentiment analysis**, which identifies a brand or business, then extracts and classifies words as positive, negative, or neutral, is a common application of named entity recognition. A sentiment score is computed by subtracting the number of positive words from the number of negative words, and then dividing the result by the total words (excluding neutral words) to form a net percentage score. Positive scores indicate positive feelings, or sentiment, while negative scores indicate the reverse. Named entity recognition is the simplest form of text analytics, and often struggles with the challenges identified earlier in the natural language processing discussion. Most research firms are now seeking higher quality text analytic solutions.

Named entity recognition identifies and extracts classes of entities (e.g., people, brands, firms, products, locations) and related information.

Sentiment analysis a form of named entity recognition which identifies a brand or business, then extracts and classifies words as positive, negative, or neutral.

Targeted event extraction occurs when complex rules for finding and grouping data are initiated based on specific trigger words. The rules often describe contextual words or attributes which must be present if the information is to be grouped and reported. For example, "bass" can be a type of freshwater fish, or a musical term. If searching for comments about the fish, related attributes might include "bait," "boat," "fishing," "tournament," "casting," or others. Thus, targeted event extraction can further narrow search results by recognizing **homonyms**, or words that have multiple meanings, and only select comments for analysis pertaining to the desired word meaning. The advantage of this approach is that it weeds out the meaningless comments and clutter that plague social media today. Industry or application specific text analytic programs are preprogrammed with specific terms or categories applicable to the situation or industry, saving businesses time.

Targeted event extraction occurs when complex rules for finding and grouping data are initiated based on specific trigger words.

Homonyms words that have multiple meanings.

For instance, **emotion language analysis (ELA)** is form of targeted event extraction text analytics that identifies both surface feelings and the deeper emotions that consumers feel toward brands or other topics. ELA overcomes some of the difficulties in interpreting emotions measured by mechanical means, such fMRIs and biometric evaluations, which are discussed later in the chapter. ELA is also more scalable than mechanical measurements conducted in laboratories, allowing for larger sample sizes. The analytics software used in ELA contains a 10,000 word emotion dictionary and linguistics algorithms that categorize words into "emotion channels." The benefit of this process is that it allows the researcher to better understand consumer's interest, engagement, and even passion toward the subject matter. For example, an ELA study examined consumer's feelings toward handwashing. Initial results were positive, as both women and men reported pleasant emotions. Women's feelings remained positive throughout the study. However, when asked to elaborate on other words associated with handwashing, the language used by men indicated that they found handwashing annoying, as the chore was associated with feelings of anger and dread. As a result, the research client segmented the market by gender and featured the time-saving nature of touch-free soap dispensers when targeting men, while focusing on fragrance and skincare benefits when targeting women. Thus ELA can be helpful in determining marketing communications, understanding the emotions consumers associate with brands or competitors, and determining whether a brand's image is emotionally positive. It is also helpful in understanding the touchpoints where consumers develop emotions toward the brand during their customer experience.[30]

Emotion language analysis (ELA) a form of targeted event extraction text analytics that identifies both surface feelings and the deeper emotions that consumers feel toward brands or other topics.

Many text analytic solutions for target event extraction offer users the ability to further customize the software to meet their individual needs, which is often necessary to train the software properly. Still, it is not appropriate for all situations. Despite its advantages over named recognition processes, targeted event extraction algorithms typically do not understand the *semantics* of a sentence. Most humans would understand the frustration underlying the following comment, "I spent my entire lunch hour trying to get more information about builder's risk insurance." However, the comment contains no words or groups of words that would stand out in helping to discern the negative feelings underlying this comment. A more complex form of text analytics is needed to comprehend the logic and true meaning behind this sentence.

Exhaustive fact extraction computer-based linguistic problem-solving techniques to identify, pattern, and refine key facts and concepts within the source data.

Exhaustive fact extraction is an advanced form of natural language processing that uses computer-based linguistic problem-solving techniques to identify, pattern, and continually refine key facts and concepts within the source data. Once recognized, these patterns can be applied to multiple forms of text data found internally within the company or elsewhere on the Internet, offering real-time reporting of data. For example, KitchenAid faced a dilemma when social media users stopped engaging with the company and instead forwarded technical media requests through social media channels. Their solution was to use Clarabridge Engage, a social media listening and text analytics program. Engage's dashboard featured trends in customer feedback, and allowed departments across the company to engage with customers easily via one platform. As a result, KitchenAid's customer response time increased, and they experienced a 90 percent increase in its social media fan base, a 143 percent increase in social interactions, and an 85 percent growth in engagement. The detailed information provided by the text analytics helped inform the product design team of potential new product ideas or desired improvements, and the customer care staff gained a great deal of insight as well.[31]

Other types of exhaustive fact extraction combine text analytics with financial data or purchase transaction data. Banks and credit card companies do so to gain a better understanding of their customers. In addition to analyzing the financial data of a customer, the software will analyze call and e-mail logs associated with each customer. It can also reach into the Internet and locate web chatter, blogs, social media, and other places where customers might be talking. Plus, predictive text analytic tools forecast the likelihood of customer defection, of purchase, or receiving a certain rating, or other target variables that are collected outside of the text itself. Often these variables are located near the text, such as star ratings being near comments. These text mining analyses can also be combined with financial data analysis to look at such things as spending patterns and best-customer profiles.

Machine learning a form of artificial intelligence that uses statistical processes to help computers "learn" from data, without being explicitly programmed.

Finally, researchers are more readily adopting text analytic solutions that feature machine learning. **Machine learning** is a form of artificial intelligence (AI) that uses statistical processes to help computers "learn" from data, without being explicitly programmed. The more data an AI is exposed to, the faster it learns. Machine learning saves training time on the part of the researcher, assuming the firm has a large enough set of unstructured data available to "train" the software, though supervision by experts is necessary when designing or customizing the initial model. Accuracy grows over time, as the AI is exposed to more information. Additionally, more complex models allow for unstructured data from sources beyond the Internet to be analyzed, including recorded telephone calls, and open-ended surveys. With unstructured data growing at exponential rates, the analytical abilities and accuracy of text analytics software is exceedingly important due to the tremendous time and cost savings involved.[32] **Figure 5.10** lists several criteria researchers should consider when selecting a text analytics or social media listening software provider.

5.6c Web Tracking

Web tracking involves studying human actions and movement on the Internet. It can be performed using historical data generated by computer tracking software or it can be observed live as it is happening. In both cases, the research can take place anonymously in the background without participants knowing it is occurring. This procedure prevents any potential changes in behavior due to the subject knowing he or she is being watched.

Web tracking observation research is valuable in assessing website traffic and the effectiveness of web content and banner or search engine advertising. Web tracking can be

- **Industry and business function adaptability.** Different words have different meanings in different domains. While "thin" is a desired outcome for diet products, "thin" walls in a motel are undesirable.
- **Customization ability.** Either you or the provider must be able to customize and train the software to understand brands, products, and distinctive language used in the product context.
- **Data sources handled.** Some software will not track all types of information, and some options are better than others at analyzing data from particular forms of social media.
- **Languages supported.** Not all software handles multiple languages.
- **Analysis functions provided.** Will the software perform the desired analysis at the topic, entity, and attribute level? What type of analyses do you need?
- **Accuracy.** Precision and relevance of results at a granular level are desired.
- **High performance.** Speed, throughput and reliability are key.
- **Established provider.** Look for a strong track record, sound financial condition, and excellent market position.
- **Cost.** Price and licensing terms vary widely; shop around, try before you buy.

FIGURE 5.10 Criteria to Consider When Selecting a Text or Social Analytics Provider

Source: Adapted from Seth Grimes, "12 Criteria You Should Consider When Looking for a Text or Social Analytics Provider" *Quirk's Media*, February 19, 2016.

used to identify the page where individuals enter a website, the referring site visited directly before they entered the site, or if, instead, a QR code was used to access the site on a mobile device, where they go and how long they stay on the site, and what they do. Even activities such as mousing over a button can be detected. Often researchers will begin with a specific action or result of the visit (such as adding an item to the online shopping cart) and track backward to see where the individual had been on the site, perhaps what drove the action, and how they entered the website. Researchers can even trace prior activity to see what other sites the individual visited and if they used a search engine to initiate the process.

An extremely important research agenda for web tracking is to detect "leaky" or "drop-off" points. These are the places were web visitors leave a website. In addition to identifying the place where the person leaves, researchers are able to construct the clickstream that occurred prior to the person leaving. This type of research is valuable in identifying potential negative points in the website, though additional research may be required to learn why people abandoned their shopping cart or did not place an order.

Because of cookies that identify unique visitors to a website, it is possible to track the activities of individuals over time. This can be valuable in terms of discerning what drives various activities, such as making a purchase, signing-up for a newsletter or requesting additional information. One danger of tracking visitors over multiple visits is that the cookie is tied to a particular computer. It is possible that different members of the family may be using the computer and thus the web tracking that is done may be confounded and not provide an accurate picture of a single individual. Alternately, many households now have multiple computers, tablets or smartphones, and some consumers shop online at lunch from work. Thus, it is equally possible that a given individual may complete some activities on one device, but finish their transaction on another.

Web tracking research does not have to be disguised. Valuable information can be gained from recruiting individuals to participate in a study, then watching their online actions. Honda UK used this approach to better understand how consumers interact with a used-car website. Participants were recruited, then given a single task or set of online tasks to perform using their home computers. With software downloaded by the participants, researchers were able to watch participants as they carried out the tasks on Honda's used-car website. Watching how participants carried out the tasks provided information to Honda UK on how to redesign the website to make it more user-friendly and meet the needs of customers.[33]

Measuring digital advertising campaign effectiveness is an important application of web tracking, especially in light of the following facts. Nielsen's advanced web tracking research has shown that 56 percent of digital ad spending is wasted on invalid ad impressions. Invalid impressions occur when digital ads are viewed by bots, spiders, adware, competitors or other "off-target" groups.[34] The problem is so widespread that in 2018, when surveyed, 74 percent of chief marketing officers indicated little to no confidence in their ability to measure digital advertising campaign effectiveness.[35] Nielsen now offers a single-source solution that combines their Qualified Ad Audience service with web tracking observation, to provide a better picture of digital advertising performance.[36]

- First, Nielsen records whether the source viewing the ad was on-target, meaning the viewer's demographics matched the target audience as defined by the client. These numbers are tallied and divided by the total number of impressions to obtain an on-target percentage that is compared between ad campaigns and over time.
- Second, Nielsen's service determines if the ad was "viewable." Here, the client sets parameters that determine what "viewable" means. For a display ad, it may mean that 75 percent, 85 percent or 100 percent of the ad's pixels were on screen for at least one or two seconds. For a video ad, it may require the entire ad be played to count as an impression, or that the ad play for a certain length of time. Dividing the number of viewable ads by the number of impressions determines the viewable rate.
- Third, Nielsen's service counts the qualifying seconds the ads were seen. For video ads, this offers the opportunity to weight impressions by dividing the qualifying seconds by the viewable impression. Higher weights indicated better quality views. Marketers can experiment with creating ads of different lengths to determine optimal ad length.

5.7 Mechanical Observation

LEARNING OBJECTIVE 5.5
Describe how mechanical devices can be used for observation research.

Marketing research can be conducted using some type of mechanical device, as shown in Figure 5.11. The most common mechanical forms of observation are market basket analysis, radio and television monitoring, and eye tracking. The newest technique that is rapidly gaining adherents because of its potential is cognitive neuroscience. The physiological measures are still being used, but less frequently, as the accuracy of the other methods increases. Increasingly, mechanical forms of observation are being integrated with qualitative research or quantitative surveys.

Market basket analysis modeling and analysis of items purchased by households on shopping trips to retail stores or e-commerce websites.

5.7a Market Basket Analysis

Using scanner-generated data, **market basket analysis** involves analysis and modeling of items purchased by households on shopping trips to retail stores or e-commerce websites. In-store research typically utilizes store loyalty cards to tie purchases to demographic

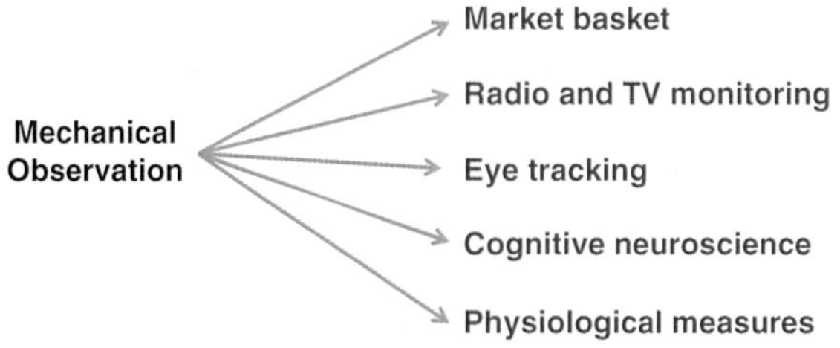

FIGURE 5.11 Mechanical Observation Research Techniques

profiles, while online purchases are easily linked to geographic data, and may be expanded to include demographic information from other databases. Market basket analysis can be used in a number of ways by members of the distribution channel to enhance marketing decisions.

Market basket analysis begins by analyzing the various items that are purchased by a consumer on a shopping trip. Through this analysis, companies can identify:

- how often consumers purchase a product
- how much of it they purchase per trip
- where they purchase the item
- what other products that are purchased with the item
- whether coupons or other incentives were used in the purchase of the item

This information can be used for cross-promotions by a manufacturer or in-store product placement by a retailer. It makes sense that if two items are typically purchased together, they should be placed in close proximity to encourage the purchase of both. The importance of promotions, such as coupons, in the purchase decision process can also be determined, particularly when household behaviors are tracked over time.

Because most basket analysis uses loyalty cards, researchers can tie demographic profiles to the basket analysis. Retail stores, casinos, and other businesses that use electronic loyalty cards require that consumers fill out an application to secure the card. Demographic and psychographic data are collected in this manner. When this data are combined with behavioral data, marketers can identify the consumer profile of users of a product. Regular users can be identified and compared to occasional users to see if there is a difference in their profiles. Marketers can also see if there is a difference in the basket composition of occasional versus heavy or regular users of a product.

Researchers can look for differences in the content of a market basket between stores, regions, and types of retailers. These differences may be just as important as commonalities. Because market basket analysis will not typically tell researchers why there is a difference, further research may be needed. If it is a difference between retail stores within the same retail chain, for instance, store audits or observation research may be needed to uncover what is causing the difference. It could be the types of customers at each store, the appearance of the stores, or even the type of customer service being offered.

It is interesting to speculate about the future of scanner-based data and the possibilities it presents for an enhanced understanding of shopping behavior. Large grocery chains often provide loyalty-card shoppers with *handheld scanners* that allow the shopper to prescan their purchases as they place them in the cart, as this allows the consumer to fast-track the checkout process. Incorporating GPS and time-keeping chips into the scanner would allow retailers to go beyond market basket analysis, and use the data to reveal the customer's path through the store. By examining how consumers move through the store, bottlenecks or underutilized areas may be discovered, and suggest changes to the store layout that may help trigger impulse buys, or streamline consumers purchase path. The order in which items are scanned and the time lapse between scans could be indicative of items that are difficult to find. GPS enhanced scanner data would also be useful in illustrating to suppliers how many people actually walked by a product display or promotion. [37] The technology exists, and it may be that GPS enabled scanners are already in use in your favorite grocery store.

A related form of research involves tracing the shopper's journey as the make their way toward a purchase, and even afterwards when they interact with the brand or company. While market basket analysis is part of this process, journey mapping is much broader, and is highly relevant given the impact that mobile phones have had on product research and shopping habits.

Journey mapping studies identify different stages in the shopping process, as well as the customer's relationship with a brand over time, and across different distribution channels or communication touchpoints. While not everyone follows the same path

Journey mapping studies identify different stages in the shopping process, as well as the customer's relationship with a brand over time, and across different distribution channels or communication touchpoints.

to purchase or learns about a brand through the same touchpoints, patterns do emerge that can be tied to segments with different demographics or psychographics, allowing for better targeting.[38] One study for a breakfast item found that it was critical to reach Hispanic shoppers *before* they get to the store. Hispanics' shopping experience is more structured and less likely to be influenced by point-of-purchase materials than is the case with other breakfast item consumers.[39] It should be noted that it is now more common for journey-mapping studies to employ multiple research methods, including direct observation, ethnography, in-person interviewing, surveys, online tracking, diaries, and potentially other methodologies.

5.7b Radio and Television Monitoring

Ratings a form of audience measurement that represent the percentage of a base population that is watching a television program or listening to a particular radio station at a given time.

Ratings are a form of audience measurement that represent the percentage of a base population that is watching a television program or listening to a particular radio station at a given time. Ratings are important, because they historically have served as the basis for setting advertising prices charged to marketers. Syndicated data research firms such as Arbitron (now part of Nielsen) and Nielsen historically relied upon research subjects to self-report their radio station listening and television viewing habits via media "diaries." Diary data were used by Arbitron to compile ratings of radio stations in various markets; similarly, data provided by Nielsen families historically served as the basis of television program ratings. Concerns about the accuracy of the diary data have led both firms to implement mechanical observation methods.

Arbitron and the audio Portable People Meter (PPM™) technology were acquired by Nielsen in 2013. Unveiled in 2019, the PPM wearable device options now include wristbands, pendants, or clothing clip mounts which are worn by consumers throughout the day. A companion app assists with data collection outside of the home.[40] These devices recognize unique identification codes that are embedded in broadcast transmissions that are heard by the consumer in the home, car, work place, or other location. At the end of the day, the consumer syncs the PPM to its base station, which sends the data collected by the device to the household hub. The hub collects the codes from all of the base stations corresponding to family members' PPMs and transmits the data back to the firm.[41] This methodology allows Nielsen to issue reports on a monthly basis. However, Nielsen still uses diary data to determine radio station ratings in 225 large and small markets. Diary panelists record their listening behavior in one-week increments, and reports are issued to local markets either twice a year, quarterly, or monthly. In responses to changes in listening habits, Nielsen has expanded its mechanical audio measurement systems to include audio streaming. App or media player usage by Nielsen's panel members is mechanically tracked, and media information is integrated with census and demographic data to profile listeners. Nielsen also uses streaming measurement methods to track podcast consumption, and combines this data with detailed demographic and qualitative profiles. Even more impressive is Nielsen's RADAR service, which matches the time commercials air with PPM and diary data to discover the characteristics of those who truly hear specific ads, on specific stations, at specific times.[42]

Nielsen's television rating system now relies solely on proprietary mechanical technology for data collection; diaries are no longer used. The rating system has expanded to capture in-home and out-of-home viewing, and viewing through computers and mobile devices. Mobile and computer viewing information is collected from panel members.

People meters devices that log who is watching television and what content is being viewed.

Nielsen Families provide data for in-home and out-of-home television viewing. Nielsen Families are recruited to represent segments of the population at both the national and local levels, which allows demographic and geographic data to be linked to television ratings. Once recruited, people meters are installed on every television set or cable/satellite box within the Nielsen Family household. **People meters** are devices that log who is watching television and the specific television show being viewed. The device senses people as they enter and exit rooms, and prompts them to login or logout as appropriate. People meters track specific television shows by identifying unique sounds that are inaudible to the human ear, known as watermarks. Fortunately, watermarks exist in nearly all television programming, and people meters capture signals every two seconds to ensure that channel changes are accurately recorded. The technology is also capable of distinguishing live viewing from DVR recorded viewing. Portable people meters are provided to Nielsen family members so that television viewing in bars, hotels, gyms, and other out-of-home locations can be measured.[43]

While many believe that mechanical observation methods of assessing television ratings offer substantial improvement over the diary method, critics contend that accuracy is still a problem. Nielsen's in-home device requires that panel members actively sign in and sign out when entering and exiting the room. Too often, panel members become bored and stop participating, forget to sign in or out, or refuse to do so, especially when leaving the room for only a few minutes.

TV viewing habits are also changing. To account for other forms of viewership, Nielsen uses panel members to track those who are increasingly using tablets or smartphones to view programming from online subscription services or TV channel websites. Of course, the system is not perfect. Audiences who do watch their television set are often distracted, as one study found that almost half were simultaneously using a phone or tablet to answer email, engage in social media, research information, or shop online.

Nielsen has also launched a cross-platform advertising campaign measurement system that seeks to span the entire TV and digital advertising universe. The enhanced system is deeply rooted in mechanical observation research methodology. The unduplicated audience data will provide media buyers with insights about ad viewing behavior by mobile phones, tablets, computers, and television. For the first time, ad views from YouTube will also be included.[44]

5.7c Voice Pitch Analysis

Voice-pitch analysis focuses on subtle, involuntary physiological changes and anomalies in a respondent's voice because these changes are believed to reflect various emotions, stress, truth, or deception. Channel M2's Voice Analysis service uses specialized software to analyze responses to open-ended questions either live or via recording. Each subject answers several warm-up questions that the software uses for calibration purposes, and as a point of comparison when analyzing responses to open-ended questions. Voice analysis can serve as a supplemental technique when researching brands, customer satisfaction, customer motives, consumers' evaluations of package designs or responses to advertisements, and may also be helpful in analyzing ethnographic information. According to Channel M2, their technology produces accuracy levels of 90 percent or greater in the identification of emotions.[45]

Voice-pitch analysis focuses on subtle, involuntary physiological changes and anomalies in respondent's voice to reflect various emotions, stress, truth, or deception.

5.7d Neuromarketing Techniques

Neuromarketing refers to the measurement of consumers' physiological and neural signals to gain insight into their motivations, preferences, and decisions. Popular techniques include eye-tracking, functional magnetic resonance imaging (fMRI), electroencephalogram (EEG), pupilometry, biometrics, and facial coding. Academics have been fascinated with the possibilities presented by neuromarketing measurement, as different techniques can help inform creative advertising decisions, or assist in pricing, product development, package design, and shelf placement of products within the store. While some techniques, such as eye-tracking research, are commonplace, marketers have been less inclined to adopt other methods, such as the expensive fMRI technology.[46]

Neuromarketing the measurement of consumers' physiological and neural signals to gain insight into their motivations, preferences, and decisions.

5.7e Eye Tracking

Eye tracking analysis involves analyzing the movement of the eye. Most eye tracking uses infrared technology to show where the pupil is by reflecting off of the eye's retina. The sensors can be placed in a computer monitor, head gear that is worn by the participant

Eye tracking analysis infrared technology that shows where the pupil is tracking by reflecting off of the eye's retina.

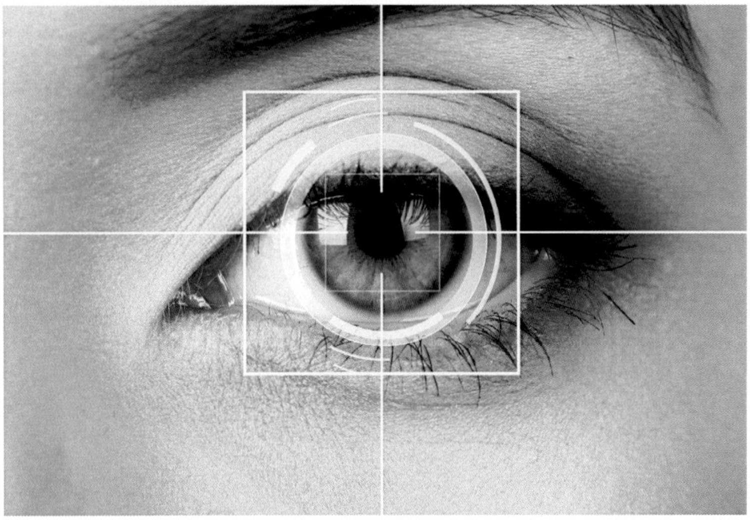
Source: MaximP/Shutterstock.

Eye-tracking analysis involves analyzing the movement of the eye, and is used to study advertising, package design, in-store signage, and shelving decisions.

while the perform normal shopping behavior, or a special eye-glass apparatus. Eye tracking research is being used to study advertising in various forms such as print, television, outdoor and on the Internet. It is used to study package design and in-store signage and shelving. It has also been used to study price sensitivity in an in-store environment.[47]

Eye-tracking studies are beneficial because they show the spots in an advertisement, store or marketing piece where people focus. So it shows what ad elements grab consumers attention, their speed of recognition of brands or packaging, and also what portions of the ad or store layout confuses them.[48] For television ads it will show this focus through sequential scenes in the advertisement. When the results from multiple consumers are placed on a perceptual-type map, it gives advertisers a good picture of what individuals notice in an ad, potential hot spots that attract a lot of attention, and areas that tend to be ignored. Shopping studies often result in gaze plots or heat maps showing where the eye focuses on the shelf or throughout the store. Eye-tracking glasses have been enhanced by lightweight designs featuring high-resolution miniature cameras. Proponents argue that this form of wearable technology results in more natural in-store shopping behavior, which enhances the validity of the results and credibility of research insights.[49]

Eye-tracking studies are relatively quick, easy and inexpensive to administer. Eye-tracking does not measure emotions, and it is often used in conjunction with other research techniques, such as biometrics or surveys.[50] In eye-tracking studies, it is important to realize that catching a person's attention may not always be positive. A negative visceral reaction can grab attention, but not enhance the selling of a product or a consumer's attitude toward the advertisement being studied. Thus, with eye-tracking research it is always a good idea to include other types of observation, quantitative, or qualitative research.

Tobii Pro Insight, a leading firm in eye-tracking research, conducted a study of more than 3,000 television ads. Participants from 150 households living in seven cities wore eye-tracking glasses while watching 30-90 minutes of TV in their home. No attitudinal or recall data were collected by means of survey; the study focused only on observation data. Some of the key findings of the study are shown below:[51]

- People pay attention on average to only the first 6 seconds of a 15 second ad.
  - *Implication*: State your message clearly, concisely, and early!
- People pay less attention to ads that run later during a commercial break.
  - *Implication*: Advertisers can pay extra for a premium position near the front of a commercial break. This finding suggests it may be worthwhile to do so.
- Attention to ads grows as the TV show progresses.
  - *Implication*: Fewer distractions occur as viewers become engaged with the TV show content, so buying space in commercial breaks scheduled in the latter portion of the show makes sense.
- Music in TV ads can help or hinder attention.
  - *Implication*: Surprisingly, ad specific jingles did more harm than good, as brand jingles resulted in a loss of 22 percent attention, compared to the average view time. Perhaps jingles annoy today's jaded consumers, and signal a sales pitch.

- *Implication*: Rock (9.4 percent) and classical (14.2 percent) music resulted in above average view times, compared to the norm. If these genres work for your product or service, consider using music as a way to engage readers.
- Celebrity athletes and surprise endings or reveals are the most effective commercial elements in terms of increasing the average time spent viewing.
  - *Implication*: While celebrity athletes increased the average time spent viewing by 18.5 percent, the tremendous costs associated with celebrity endorsers and the fit between the endorser and the product must be carefully considered.
  - *Implication*: Intriguing the audience is a less expensive, and more effective creative alternative as average viewing time increased by 27.6 percent.

5.7f Cognitive Neuroscience

Cognitive neuroscience includes EEG and fMRI techniques that measure brain activity. **Functional magnetic resonance imaging (fMRI)** is a brain-image measurement process that tracks the flow and movement of electrical currents in the brain associated with increased neural activity. fMRI was used to verify a preference for Coke or Pepsi. According to Justin Meaux, a neuroscientist, "Preference has measurable correlates in the brain; you can see it." Another neuroscientist, Richard Siberstein from Australia, was able to show through brain activity that successful ads tend to generate higher levels of emotional engagement and long-term memory coding.[52]

Functional Magnetic Resonance Imaging (fMRI) a brain-image measurement process that tracks the flow and movement of electrical currents in the brain associated with increased neural activity.

In terms of marketing research, fMRI is being used in pricing research and in advertising to measure consumer reactions and detailed emotional responses to various advertisements, their level of engagement, and their advertising recall.[53] With certain ads, such as ones that may contain sexually provocative material, individuals may not be honest about how an ad affects them using standard survey testing procedures. Members of a focus group may cover up their true feelings and reactions to the ad by stating that the ad is sexist and inappropriate. This is more likely to occur if someone in the focus group has already expressed a negative opinion of the ad, or if individuals detect the moderator feels that way. The negative stigma attached to sex in advertising often affects self-reported reactions. Such reactions cannot be faked using cognitive neuroscience.

Many marketing researchers believe physiological tests that measure body reactions or brain activity are more accurate than self-reported tests, because physiological reactions cannot be easily faked.[54] It can't be denied that fMRI's ability to measure emotions is important, as emotions drive purchasing behavior. So by testing emotional responses to advertising, marketers can better understand advertising's impact on consumer behavior. However, fMRI's must be performed in a laboratory setting, and it is the most expensive mechanical observation method. It is also the most invasive, and many researchers find it less detailed than the EEG for measuring *specific* emotions.[55]

Frito-Lay used neuroscience research to test product packaging. The company discovered that matte beige bags of potato chips picturing potatoes and other healthier ingredients did not trigger guilt feelings as much as shiny potato chip bags. Ann Mukherjee, Frito-Lay's chief marketing officer, said, "Brain-imaging tests can be more accurate than focus groups." A Cheetos advertisement that was rejected by a focus group for its "mean-spirited" content was tested using neuroscience. The neuroscience test showed women loved the commercial.[56]

The power of fMRI is that it reveals physiological reactions to a message. It shows where brain activity occurs and to a certain degree the level of that activity. It can identify times when a test subject becomes enthralled with a marketing message. It also indicates when the person merely focuses on the logo, an attractive person, or some other component of the commercial. The methodology identifies positive and negative emotions and the intensity of the emotions by the amount of neurons that are firing. This research method allows marketers to better understand how marketing messages are being processed, where it is processed in the brain, and how the individual reacts to an ad or marketing piece. Although marketers have been slow to adopt fMRI technology due to need for conducting studies in laboratories, the high cost, and the resulting small samples, fMRI does offer great potential for evaluating advertising and marketing.

Electroencephalogram (EEG) records signals on the scalp from neurons firing inside of the brain.

A related cognitive neuroscience technique is the **electroencephalogram**, or EEG. The EEG places pads on the scalp and records signals from neurons firing inside of the brain. Similar to the fMRI, the EEG can help researchers understand a consumer's advertisement recall, and their level of engagement. Results can be used to improve branding and ads. Unfortunately, it is not as precise as the fMRI, but it can measure changes over smaller increments of time. EEG tests are typically performed in a lab; as such, they are invasive and more expensive than all but the fMRI neuromarketing techniques.[57]

5.7g Facial Coding and Body Language Analysis

Facial coding and body language analysis fall under the umbrella of neuromarketing. Mechanical observation occurs when subject's facial expressions and body language are digitally recorded as they watch an ad or are exposed to some other type of stimulus. Proponents of facial coding and body language analysis argue that these unfiltered reactions reveal consumers' true feelings toward ads or other stimuli. Facial coding is strongly tied to emotion research, and has been gaining traction with those who believe emotions are at the heart of consumer behavior. Facial movements are categorized according to an existing well-tested emotional classification scheme by trained coders or professional software. Body language is analyzed similarly, as a well-documented classification model exists. These techniques are relatively inexpensive, and very good at revealing general emotional responses such as surprise, fear, happiness, and the like.[58]

5.7h Other Biometric Measures

fMRI and eye-tracking techniques are often supplemented by long-standing biometric measures. Muscle tension, heart rate, skin conductance, respiration, and pupil dilation are a few of the biometric measures that are commonly used. Biometrics supplement many forms of advertising research. In general, these measures help to determine the level of engagement, and whether a subject's response to a stimulus is positive or negative. Additional information on two specific types of biometric devices—galvanometers and pupilometers—demonstrates why these devices are used in conjunction with other methods and not as standalone methods.

Galvanometer measures changes in the electric resistance in the skin that results from a subject's exposure to stimuli.

Pupilometer measures the degree of pupil dilation which occurs in response to stimuli.

Galvanometers measure changes in the electrical resistance in the skin in response to a subject's exposure to stimuli, such as a television commercial. The resulting galvanic skin responses (GSR) were originally deemed important to marketers because GSR is strongly linked to emotions. Unfortunately, in and of itself, GSR measures are of limited use to researchers, as these measures cannot identify what emotion has been stimulated or changed.

Pupilometers measure pupil dilation, as cognitive activity will cause pupils to change in response to visual stimuli when other factors are held constant. While the device can note changes in the size of the pupil, the pupilometer cannot identify the reason behind pupil changes, although it is able to identify rather accurately if the emotion is positive or negative. Anger or negative emotion typically causes the pupil to get smaller, while positive or pleasurable scenes cause the pupil to get larger.

5.8 Global Concerns

Compared to other forms of marketing research, observation research can be used in global markets with fewer problems. The method of observation may be altered due to local customs and culture, but the overall techniques can be used. Human observation, online observation, and mechanical observation are all viable methods of research throughout the world. As with other forms of research, hiring a local native of the country to assist in the planning and execution of observation reach is important. Major problems can be easily prevented.

Open human observation in some cultures may yield biased results since individuals may alter their behavior in an effort to please the observing researcher. In some countries, especially in the Middle East, the gender of the observer is very important. It would be unacceptable for a male researcher to observe or interact with a female consumer without the husband's presence. In fact, observing females in general is more difficult because of their role within the culture.

For observation research to be successful, researchers must understand the culture being studied. The demand for ethnographic research of Hispanics has recently increased as more companies focus marketing efforts on this ethnic group. However, to be successful, researcher companies need to understand the importance of the family to Hispanics and allow extra time to become acquainted with the Hispanic subjects. It is important to be conscious of their customs and beliefs. In general, Hispanics are less forthcoming with information than the general population. They also tend to be more positive about companies or brands. Again, these differences highlight the need for having someone who fully understands the culture of the group being studied.[59]

5.9 Marketing Research Statistics

A marketing researcher can collect a large volume of data through the various observation techniques presented in this chapter. To understand the data, researchers will often want to compare results based on one or more variables. A useful technique is cross-tabulation. The Statistical Review, Statistical Reporting, and Dealing with Data sections examine the cross-tabulation methodology and how researchers can use it.

5.9a Statistical Review

Cross-tabulations are used to describe the relationship between two variables when one or more of these variables is a classification variable. Classification variables contain category data. Examples would be gender (1=male and 2=female), race (1=Caucasian, 2=African-American, and 3=Hispanic), brands (1=Ford, 2=Chevrolet, 3=Toyota, 4=Nissan, 5=Dodge, and so forth), or day of the week (Sunday through Saturday with each day of the week being assigned a number from 1 to 7).

A clothing store conducted an observation study to examine how customers interacted with various display racks. Cross-tabulation analyses can provide insights into the relationship between the type of display table or rack and demographic variables such as gender, age and income. The most basic form of cross-tabulation analysis shows data counts through combining frequency tables of two or more variables. As shown in Figure 5.12, the dependent variable of interest (in this case type of rack/table) is displayed in rows and the classification variable of gender is displayed in columns. The output

		Gender		
		Male	Female	Total
First rack/ display approached	Display Table	6	25	31
	Sales Rack	5	11	16
	Featured Brand Rack	7	6	13
	Regular Jeans Rack/ Area	7	5	12
	Total	25	47	72

FIGURE 5.12 Cross-Tabulation from SPSS
An example showing the first rack/display approached, by respondent's gender.

			Gender		
			Male	Female	Total
First rack/ display approached	Display Table	Count	6	25	31
		% within Gender	24.0%	53.2%	43.1%
	Sales Rack	Count	5	11	16
		% within Gender	20.0%	23.4%	22.2%
	Featured Brand Rack	Count	7	6	13
		% within Gender	28.0%	12.8%	18.1%
	Regular Jeans Rack/ Area	Count	7	5	12
		% within Gender	28.0%	10.6%	16.7%
	Total	Count	25	47	72
		% within Gender	100.0%	100.0%	100.0%

FIGURE 5.13 Cross-Tabulation from SPSS

An example showing the "First Rack/Display Approached" by the respondent's gender with actual frequency counts and percentages.

shows a total of 72 people were observed, 25 males and 47 females. Of the 47 females, 25 stopped at the display table first, 11 stopped at the sales rack first, 6 went to the featured brand rack first, and 5 went to the regular jeans rack first.

Usually, marketers find it more beneficial to display data as percentages, rather than counts in the cross-tabulation. Figure 5.13 includes the percentages of males and females and which table or rack they went to first. It is normally easier to make comparisons when using percentages rather than raw numbers. For instance, when examining the raw numbers for the featured brand rack, 7 males went there first compared to 6 females. It would appear there is not much of a difference. But, when looking at the percent, 28 percent of the males went to the featured brand rack first compared to only 12.8 percent of the females. Rather than putting these data into a table, a researcher may want to show it graphically, as shown in Figure 5.14.

Note that cross-tabulations cannot be used to prove causality. The only statistical test appropriate for cross-tabulation data is the chi-square, which tests the goodness-of-fit of the observed data with that which would be expected under the null hypothesis of no difference. SPSS provides for a chi-square test. Figure 5.15 shows the chi-square test output for the cross-tabulation of the first rack/display approached and the respondent's gender.

The Pearson Chi-Square value is 8.364 with 3 degrees of freedom. The significance level (or p-value) is .039. If the statistical test was being conducted at the 95 percent confidence level, then any p-value equal to or below .05 would indicate a rejection of the null hypothesis. Recall from Chapter 2 that a null hypothesis would state there is "no difference regarding which table/rack is approached first based on the respondent's gender." Since the p-value is .039, which is less than the .05 test p-value, the null hypothesis would be rejected. Therefore, we can assume there is a significant difference between males and females in which table/rack is approached first upon entering the store. The chi-square value does not tell us where the difference is, but only that there is a difference. Examination of the table in Figure 5.11 and the graph in Figure 5.12 would show that females are more likely to go to the display first than males, and are less likely to go to the featured brand rack or the regular brand rack first.

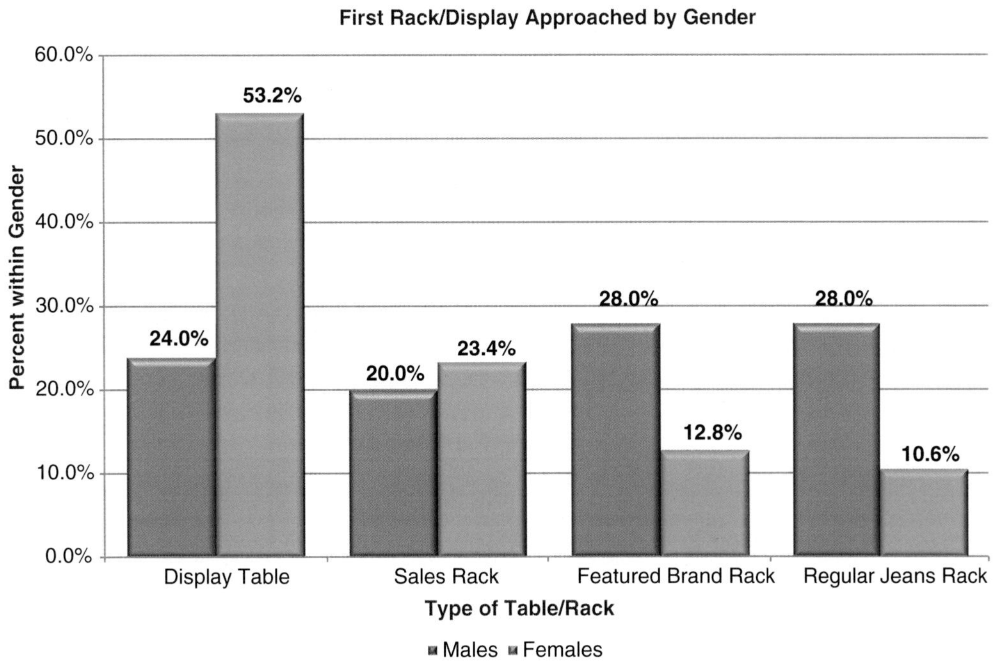

FIGURE 5.14 A Graphical Presentation
An example showing the "First Rack/Display Approached" by the respondent's gender.

	Value	df	Asymp. Sig. (2-sided)
Pearson Chi-Square	8.364	3	.039
Likelihood Ratio	8.400	3	.038
Linear-by-Linear Association	7.933	1	.005
N of Valid Cases	72		

FIGURE 5.15 Chi-Square Test Results of First Rack/Display Approached by the Respondent's Gender

Another way to look at the p-value is to think about it as a percent, or probability. In this case, the probability of the researcher being wrong in stating there is a difference between males and females in which table they approached first is only 3.9 percent. Alternatively, the researcher is 96.1 percent (100−03.9=96.1) confident there is a significant difference in the population based on gender.

5.9b Statistical Reporting

Cross-tabulation are used frequently in marketing research statistics because it allows for comparisons between groups. Figure 5.16 is a bar graph showing the percentages of females and males and which rack or display was approached first. Because the graph is showing two different groups (males and females) it is necessary to have a legend indicating each group. The bars will also need to be a different color or design to clearly distinguish the two groups. The figure allows an individual to quickly see the differences between males and females and is easier to grasp than the data put into a table.

A local restaurant in Dallas accessed online metrics obtained from a mobile geo-targeting ad campaign around a Dallas Mavericks basketball game. Individuals were sent a

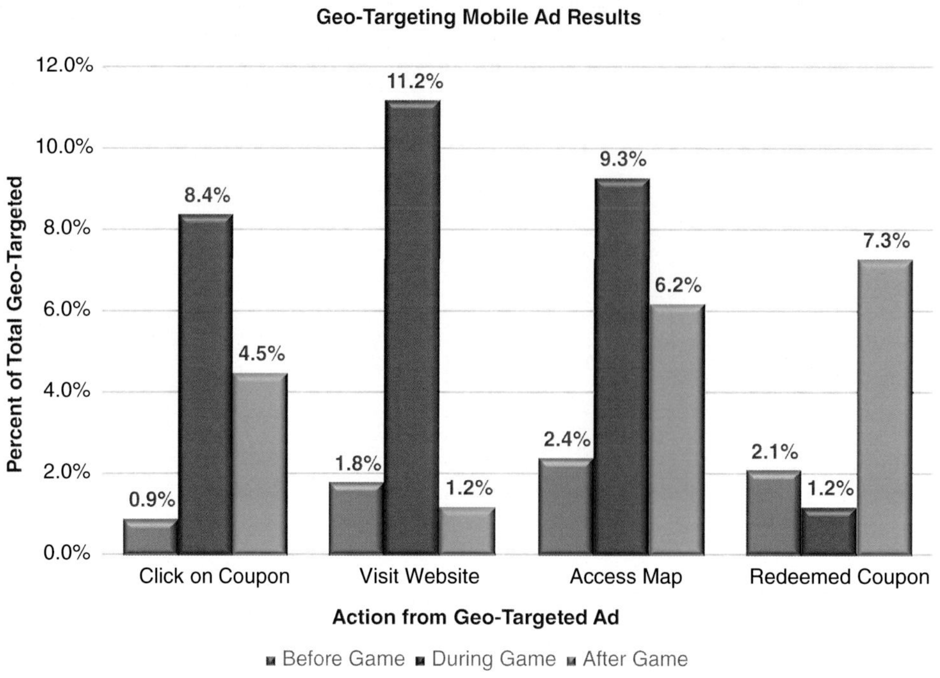

FIGURE 5.16 Graph of a Cross-Tabulation of Responses to a Geo-Targeting Mobile Advertising Campaign

Marketing Method	Before Game	During Game	After Game
Geo-targeting	3.6%	2.1%	18.4%
E-Mail	7.4%	8.7%	6.8%
Street handouts	0.4%	2.4%	20.8%
Search ads	19.4%	1.7%	8.3%

FIGURE 5.17 Results of Four Different Marketing Campaigns and the Percentage of Patrons before, during, and after the Game

coupon for 10 percent off of a meal to their mobile phones three hours before game time. The restaurant was located two blocks from the arena. Figure 5.15 shows the results of the campaign. Cross-tabulation was used to compare actions consumers took before the game, during the game, and after the game. The data provided insights into when individuals accessed the coupon information, visited the restaurant's website, accessed a location map to the restaurant in reference to the arena, and redeemed the coupon. The graph clearly indicated that most of the actions were taken during the game or after the game.

Statistical Reporting Exercise: The restaurant owner used four different marketing methods during the first half of the Maverick's basketball season. She used mobile geo-targeting of individuals attending the game, an e-mail campaign, local college students passing out flyers before, during, and after the game, and online search ads. Patrons were asked by the wait staff when they ordered their meals how they heard about the restaurant and why they came. The results are shown in Figure 5.17.

Use the data provided in Figure 5.15 to create two graphs. The first graph should use the row heading: before, during, and after the game as the primary grouping variables and the marketing method as the legend. The second graph should be the reverse: the primary grouping variable should be the marketing method with the before, during, after games as the legend. Interpret each graph. Discuss the similarities and differences in the two graphs. Be specific about the message each sends to someone looking at the graph. Make sure you provide appropriate titles for the x-axis, y-axis, legend, and chart.

5.9c Dealing with Data

Observation data is often well-suited for cross-tabulation analysis. The data set *Chapter 05 Dealing with Data* was generated at a retail clothing store by an observer. The retailer wanted to examine the difference between a display table, sales rack, featured brand rack, and regular jean racks. The data that was collected are shown in the file *Chapter 05 Dealing with Data Instrument*. It is helpful to review the various data that were collected and the SPSS data file before beginning the following exercises. The data files and step-by-step instructions for using SPSS are available on the textbook website (www.clowjames.net/students.html).

Exercise One: Frequency Counts

Using SPSS generate frequency counts and percentages for all of the following variables that deal with the display table.

- *Did customer stop at display table?*
- *How much time at display table?*
- *Number of jeans examined?*
- *Number of jeans tried on?*
- *Number of jeans purchased?*

Based on the output, answer the following questions.

1. What percentage of the customers stopped at the *display table*?
2. What was the median and mode for each of the four sub-variables: *how much time at display table, number of jeans examined, number of jeans tried on,* and *number of jeans purchased?*
3. Create a bar graph of the *number of jeans tried on* from the *display table*. Be sure to provide a graph title, label the x-axis, y-axis, and provide value labels above the bars. Use the valid percent for the graph.

Exercise Two: Means

Using SPSS, calculate the mean for each of the following variables under each of the types of racks or displays. That is, obtain a mean for *number of jeans examined* under the *display table* variable, the *sales rack* variable, the *featured brand rack* variable, and the *regular jeans rack* variable. Do the same for *number of jeans tried on* and *number of jeans purchased*.

Use the SPSS output file to create three different bar graphs. First, graph the means obtained for *number of jeans examined* for each of the four types of racks or displays. Next create graphs for each of the other two variables. Based on the graphs and output, answer the following questions.

1. At which table or display do customers appear to examine the most jeans?
2. At which table or display do customers appear to try on the most jeans?
3. At which table or display do customers appear to purchase the most jeans?

Exercise Three: Compare First Table Approached to the Respondent's Age

An important research question posed by the retailer was, "Did the respondent's age influence what table/rack the customer approached first?" Perform a cross-tabulation using the SPSS variable *first rack/display approached* for the row variable and *age* as the column variable. In order to better understand the results, ask for column percentages and run the chi-square test. Based on the chi-square results at a 95 percent confidence level, did the respondent's age make any difference on which table/rack was approached first? If it did, explain what differences were observed.

Summary

Objective 1: Identify the conditions for observation research.
Observation research is useful when researchers are interested in tracking behaviors, but it cannot be used to explain why people behave the way they do. Observation research is only appropriate when the behavior or action: 1) is observable, or the results are observable; 2) occurs frequently or is repetitive in nature; and 3) is of short duration.

Objective 2: Describe the dimensions of observation research.
Approaches to observation research vary across five key dimensions, each of which has its distinct advantages and disadvantages. Observation research can 1) occur in a natural or contrived setting; 2) be openly conducted or disguised so subjects are unaware; 3) directly observe the behavior or instead use indirect observation to assess the results of the behavior; 4) rely on the observer to record important actions in an unstructured manner, or require that all observers look for the same behavior in a structured fashion, and 5) use humans or machines to observe the behavior as it takes place.

Objective 3: Discuss the various human observation methods.
Human observation of behavior may take place in-person, through one-way mirrors, or remotely, by viewing video footage. Mystery shoppers are frequently used in the retail and service industries to gauge employee knowledge, friendliness, and a host of other factors. While most mystery shopping occurs in-person, mystery shopping telephone calls are also useful. Ethnographic researchers watch consumers in their home or whatever setting is natural for the use of the product under study, and supplements observation data with in-depth interviews designed to reveal deeper consumer insights.

Objective 4: Describe the various online observation methods.
Social media monitoring of tweets, blogs, online community postings, and other venues is one of the fastest growing forms of online observation. Text mining of online conversations is a specific form of social media monitoring, but can also involve other online postings. Text analytics can be used to perform keyword analysis of online communications. Natural language processing techniques of text analytics include named entity recognition, targeted event extraction, and exhaustive fact extraction. Machine learning is the future of text analytics, with constant improvements occurring. Computer software can track web traffic patterns within web sites, as well as between sites, advertising campaigns, and users.

Objective 5: Elaborate on how mechanical devices can be used for observation research.
Scanner data provides the mechanism for advanced market basket studies that tie consumer purchases to shopper card data files. Nielsen uses metering technology and other mechanical methods to track television viewing in home, out-of-home, and across platforms, while personal people meters and diaries are used for radio audience measurement. Mechanical devices also measure physiological responses to stimuli via eye-tracking, voice-pitch analysis, cognitive neuroscience, and fMRI. Cognitive neuroscience and eye-tracking technology are supplemented by biometric measurements.

Key Terms

contrived setting, p. 148
descriptive text analytics, p. 161
direct observation, p. 150
disguised observation, p. 150
electroencephalogram (EEG), p. 172
emotion language analysis (ELA), p. 163
ethnographic research, p. 156
exhaustive fact extraction, p. 164
eye tracking analysis, p. 169
functional magnetic resonance imaging (fMRI), p. 171
galvanometers, p. 172
homonyms, p. 163
immersion, p. 157
indirect observation, p. 150
journey mapping studies, p. 167
keyword analysis, p. 162
machine learning, p. 164
market basket analysis, p. 166
named entity recognition, p. 163
natural language processing (NLP), p. 162
natural setting, p. 148
neuromarketing, p. 169
observation research, p. 147
open observation, p. 149
people meters, p. 168
predictive text analytics, p. 161
pupilometers, p. 172
ratings, p. 168
sentiment analysis, p. 163
structured observation research, p. 151
targeted event extraction, p. 163
unstructured data, p. 160
unstructured observation research, p. 150
voice-pitch analysis, p. 169

Critical Thinking Exercises

1. Visit the Nielsen web site at http://www.nielsen.com and report on the top ten ratings for either television, mobile, or sports. The "Top Ten" are typically found under the "Insights" text menu. How could a consumer goods marketer use this information? Did any of the top 10 entries for your chosen category surprise you? Why or why not?
2. Why are diary methods of recording radio listening behavior less accurate than information collected via the Personal People Meter? Explain.
3. Access Tobaii Pro at www.tobaipro.com and search for "Videos" using the site search function. Click on the "Videos" link and select either the " reality with eye tracking changes the landscape of market research," "Eye Tracking in Reading Behavior and Media Consumption Research," or "Display Advertising Eye Tracking Study" links. Alternately, select videos not listed that are related to marketing, consumer behavior, or advertising. Watch at least two videos that interest you. Write a summary of your findings.
4. Del Monte has commissioned an observation research study for the purpose of better understanding the actions undertaken by consumers when buying canned fruit. Explain how you would implement the study. Would you recommend a virtual shopping observation study, or one conducted within the actual grocery store? Should human or mechanical observers be used? Should the observation be open or disguised? Structured or unstructured? Justify your decisions.
5. While Twitter is commonly used to build relationships with business clients, it can also be used as a research tool to track conversations about brands, companies, ads, and celebrity endorsers in real time. Visit twitter.com/search-home and review the different operators for advanced searching. Search for tweets on 1) a company that has recently made news 2) a well-advertised brand that has recently introduced a new advertising campaign. Review a minimum of 20 tweets for each. Summarize the relevant findings.
6. Describe your television viewing habits with respect to the type of devices you use, whether you subscribe to a video service such as NetFlix, and how frequently you view programs at times other than when they are broadcast. Now suppose your viewing habits are representative of an entire market segment. What are the implications for marketers who are trying to reach that segment? How might it affect their media planning? Explain in detail.
7. A consumer goods manufacturer is interested in learning more about meal preparation in the homes of dual career couples. Specific topics to be investigated include factors influencing the choice and usage of fresh ingredients versus those that are frozen, canned, or freeze dried; the relative importance of nutrition and healthy food factors vs. convenience; and the situations or factors that influence whether meals are cooked and consumed at home, picked up from restaurants and eaten at home, or eaten out at restaurants. What type of observation research study would you recommend? Why? List the specific actions, behaviors, questions, etc., that you would investigate, and how this information would be recorded.
8. Leapfrog, a manufacturer of educational toys, is interested in seeing how five to eight-year-old children react to and play with several new toy prototypes. What type of observation research technique would you recommend? Why?
9. Design a mystery shopper observation form to evaluate facility and signage aspects of a retail store environment. Do not include observations related to employees, such as customer service interactions.
10. Suppose you were interested in learning how consumers used smartphones in a shopping environment. What type of observation research study would you recommend? What research questions would you propose? What types of behavior should be observed in order to answer these research questions?

Lakeside Grill

(Comprehensive Student Case)

The student team of Alexa, Brooke, Zach, Juan, and Destiny decided to use human observation to study the Lakeside Grill. The following decisions were made in regard to the dimensions:

- Natural setting
- Disguised format
- Direct observation
- Structured observation form
- Human observers

Each member of the team participated in the observation. Since the Lakeside Grill was open for two meals, each student observed a lunch meal and a dinner meal over a two week period. "Because the employees had seen all of us in there," Zach explained, "we got a copy of Mr. Zito's financial report and would pretend to be working on tabulating it. We thought if the wait staff knew we were observing that it would alter their behavior." Before conducting the research, the group developed the observation form that follows.

Lakeside Grill Observation Research Form

Observer name: ____________________ Date: ____________________

1. Meal: Lunch ________________ Dinner ________________ 2. Time of arrival: ________________

Upon arrival

3. Number of tables with customers: ________________ 4. Number of total customers: ________________
5. Number of wait staff: ________________ 6. Table number where you sat: ________________

Observation (Complete for each table you observe)

7. Number of people at the table: ________________
8. Time between being seated and server greeting: ________________
9. Demeanor of wait person: unhappy ______|______|______|______|______|______ cheerful
10. Demeanor of customers: unhappy ______|______|______|______|______|______ cheerful
11. Time between taking drink order and bringing drinks: ________________
12. Was drink order correct? Yes: ________________ No: ________________
13. If No, why not? ________________
14. Did customers place order when drinks arrived? Yes: ________________ No: ________________
15. If No, time between wait staff leaving and returning to take order: ________________
16. Time between placing food order and arrival of food: ________________
17. Number of times wait staff checked on customers between order and arrival of food: ________________
18. Was food prepared correctly? Yes: ________________ No: ________________
19. If No, what was wrong? ________________
20. Response of wait staff: ________________
21. Number of times wait staff checked on customers from delivering food to leaving ticket: ________________
22. Time between customers finishing food and arrival of ticket: ________________
23. Time between customer leaving payment and waiter picking up ticket: ________________
24. Time between picking up payment and return of ticket: ________________
25. Relevant comments made by customers during the time wait staff was present.
26. Relevant comments made by customers when wait staff was not present.

Critique Questions:

1. For each of the five observation research dimensions, identify the specific variation chosen for this study. Do you feel these were the best choices? Why or why not? Explain.
2. Consider Zach's comment, "We got a copy of Mr. Zito's financial report and would pretend to be working on tabulating it. We thought if the wait staff knew we were observing that it would alter their behavior." Do you agree with this statement? Why or why not?
3. Do you think it is likely the wait staff figured out they were being observed anyway? Why or why not? How could the group use human observation and be sure that their observation did not change the wait staff behavior?
4. Although the group obtained some good observation data, they do not know anything about the customers and whether they were satisfied. Brooke had suggested waiting for customers to finish the meal, then going to their table, introducing themselves, explaining their research project, and then asking customers questions about the food, service, and level of satisfaction. Is this a good idea or not? What are the pros and cons?
5. What about using mystery shoppers? What would have been the pros and cons? How would the group obtain mystery shoppers since they had an extremely small budget for the research project?
6. Critique the observation form. What suggestions would you make?

Notes

1. M. Miljkovic, M. Djuric, and O. Tilleuil, "Which Elements Matter Most on a Web Shopping Page?" *Quirk's Media* (July 2018), https://www.quirks.com/articles/which-elements-matter-most-on-a-web-shopping-page.
2. John Karelefski, "Simulated Supermarket Helps Frito-Lay Understand Shopper Behavior," Shopper Insights, August 2008, retrieved from http://www.cpgmatters.com/ShopperInsights0808.html.
3. Ed Crowley, "Will IoT and Advanced Analytics Be the Death of Traditional MR?" *Quirk's Media* (June 12, 2017), https://www.quirks.com/articles/will-iot-and-advanced-analytics-be-the-death-of-traditional-mr.
4. Moniek Buijzen and Patti M. Valkenburg, "Observing Purchase-Related Parent-Child Communication in Retail Environments: A Development and Socialization Perspective," *Human Communications Research* 34, no. 1 (January 2008): 50–69.
5. Leanne W. S. Loijens, "Quantitative Tools for Measuring Consumer Reactions and Behavior," *Quirk's Media* (June 2017), https://www.quirks.com/articles/quantitative-tools-for-measuring-consumer-reactions-and-behavior.
6. Paula Andruss, "The Case of the Missing Research Insights," *Marketing News* 44, no. 7 (2010): 23–25.
7. Jeff Hall, "Mystery Shopping in an Omnichannel World," *Quirk's Media* (January 2018), https://www.quirks.com/articles/mystery-shopping-in-an-omnichannel-world.
8. "Mystery Shopping and Customer Experience Research Case Studies: Telephone Mystery Shopping with Incentives, Rewards on a Budget," Confero, https://www.conferoinc.com/case-studies/.
9. Michael Carlon, "Qualitatively Speaking: Evolving Ethnography," *Quirks Marketing Research Review* (April 2008): 18, 20.
10. Karin O'Neill and Liza Walworth, "Which Ethnographic Approach Is Right for You?" *Quirk's Media* (December 2017), https://www.quirks.com/articles/which-ethnographic-approach-is-right-for-you.
11. Paul Skaggs, "Ethnography in Product Design: Looking for Compensatory Behaviors," *Journal of Management & Marketing Research* 3 (January 2010): 1–6.
12. Bill Abrams, "The Irreplaceable On-Site Ethnographer," *Quirk's Marketing Research Review* (February 2012): 20–22.
13. Karin O'Neill and Liza Walworth, "Which Ethnographic Approach is Right for You?" *Quirk's Media* (December 2017), https://www.quirks.com/articles/which-ethnographic-approach-is-right-for-you, Article ID 20171209.
14. Michael Carlon, "Qualitatively Speaking: Evolving Ethnography," *Quirks Marketing Research Review* (April 2008): 18, 20.
15. Kadley Gosselin and Ian Schutte, "Exploring the Game of Thrones Audience Using Video-Based Ethnography," *Quirk's Marketing Research Review* (December 2014): 38, 40–42.
16. Karin O'Neill and Liza Walworth, "Which Ethnographic Approach is Right for You?" *Quirk's Media* (December 2, 2017), https://www.quirks.com/articles/which-ethnographic-approach-is-right-for-you, Article ID 20171209.
17. Miguel Ramos, "Tips for Leveraging Video Feedback," *Quirk's Media* (March 12, 2018), https://www.quirks.com/articles/tips-for-leveraging-video-feedback.
18. This section is based on Karin O'Neill and Liza Walworth, "Which Ethnographic Approach is Right for You?" *Quirk's Media* (December 2, 2017), https://www.quirks.com/articles/which-ethnographic-approach-is-right-for-you, Article ID 20171209; Alex Hunt, "Mobile Ethnography Let Kraft Capture the Highs and Lows of Party Planning and Hosting," *Quirk's Media* (December 2014), https://www.quirks.com/articles/mobile-ethnography-let-kraft-capture-the-highs-and-lows-of-party-planning-and-hosting.
19. Jiyao Xun and Jonathan Reynolds, "Applying Netnography to Market Research: The Case of the Online Forum," *Journal of Targeting, Measurement, and Analysis for Marketing* 18, no. 1 (March 2010): 1731; and Nikhilesh Dholakia and Dong Zhang, "Online Qualitative Research in the Age of E-Commerce: Data Sources and Approaches, *Forum Qualitative Sozialforshung/Forum: Qualitative Social Research* 5, no. 2 (May 2004): Article 29.
20. Pew Research Center, "Share of Adults in the United States Who Use the Internet in 2019, by Age Group," Statista, https://www.statista.com/statistics/266587/percentage-of-internet-users-by-age-groups-in-the-us/
21. Ryan Griffith, "Using Social Data in 2018," *Quirk's Media* (August 22, 2018), https://www.quirks.com/articles/using-social-data-in-2018.
22. Ibid.
23. Hailley Griffis, "What 1.5M Pins Taught Us about Pinterest Marketing: Common Words, Popular Times, Plus 4 Experiments to Try," Pinterest Marketing Study, https://buffer.com/resources/pinterest-marketing-study.
24. Carolyn Lindquist, "By the Numbers: For Better Insights from Text Analytics, Elicit Better Comments," *Quirk's Marketing Research Review* (April 2012): 24, 26.

25. "By the Numbers: Super Bowl 2019," https://www.marketingdive.com/news/super-bowl-2019-by-the-numbers/547612/, 2019.
26. Steven Struhl, "A Look at Predictive and Descriptive Text Analytics," *Quirk's Media* (January 2017), https://www.quirks.com/articles/a-look-at-predictive-and-descriptive-text-analytics.
27. Eric Weight, "What Can Text Analytics Teach Us?" *Quirk's Marketing Research Review* (August 2011): 58, 60–62.
28. Steven Struhl, "Applying Descriptive Text Analytics," *Quirk's Media* (February 2017), https://www.quirks.com/articles/applying-descriptive-text-analytics.
29. Steven Struhl, "A Look at Predictive and Descriptive Text Analytics," *Quirk's Media* (January 2017), https://www.quirks.com/articles/a-look-at-predictive-and-descriptive-text-analytics.
30. Chuck Bean, "How Language-Based Emotion Research Can Uncover Customers' Feelings," *Quirk's Media* (October 2017), https://www.quirks.com/articles/how-language-based-emotion-research-can-uncover-customers-feelings.
31. "KitchenAid Improves Speed of Response, Driving 85% Growth in Social Engagement," Clarabridge, https://www.clarabridge.com/resources-support/resources/case-study/kitchenaid-improves-speed-of-response-driving-85-growth-in-social-engagement, 2019.
32. This section is based on Rick Kelly, "Fit for Purpose: Online Qualitative, Certainty-Cost Trade-Offs and Machine Learning," *Quirk's Media* (January 2019), https://www.quirks.com/articles/fit-for-purpose-online-qualitative-certainty-cost-trade-offs-and-machine-learning; and Rob Key, "How to Apply AI to Your Social Media Listening in 2019: An Essential Users Guide," *Quirk's Media* (December 2018), https://www.quirks.com/articles/how-to-apply-ai-to-your-social-listening-in-2019-an-essential-user-guide.
33. Matt Schroder, "Watch Me as I Buy. How Online Observational Techniques Help Qualitative Researchers Keep Pace with the Speed of Consumers," *Quirk's Marketing Research Review* (February 2010): 32, 34–35.
34. *Measurement Breakthroughs. Keeping Up with Digital Advertising Challenges* (Chicago: The Nielsen Company, 2019).
35. *The Nielsen CMO Report 2018* (Chicago: The Nielsen Company, 2018).
36. Samuel Carter, "I Hope Supermarkets Are Stalking Me," *Quirk's Media* (October 7, 2016), https://www.quirks.com/articles/i-hope-supermarkets-are-stalking-me.
37. This section is based on *Measurement Breakthroughs. Keeping Up with Digital Advertising Challenges*.
38. James Rohde, "The Role of the Journey Map," *Quirk's Media* (October 2017), https://www.quirks.com/articles/the-role-of-the-journey-map.
39. Russ Rubin, "The Value of Tracing the Shopper's Path to Purchase," *Quirk's Marketing Research Review* (July 2012): 46, 48–51.
40. "Nielsen Showcases New Media Measurement Technology and Expertise at NAB Show 2019," http://sites.nielsen.com/newscenter/nielsen-showcases-new-media-measurement-technology-expertise-nab-show-2019/, The Nielsen Company, 2019.
41. "New Age for Radio—Electronic Audience Measurement with the Portable People Meter™ System," http://www.arbitron.com/portable_people_meters/ppm_service.htm, 2010.
42. "Nielsen Audio," The Nielsen Company, https://www.nielsen.com/us/en/solutions/capabilities/audio/, 2019.
43. This section is based on information obtained from ratingsacademy.nielsen.com/.
44. "Nielsen Launches Enhanced Cross-Platform Campaign Measurement across TV and Digital Ads," https://www.nielsen.com/us/en/press-releases/2019/nielsen-launches-enhanced-cross-platform-campaign-measurement-ac/, 2019.
45. http://www.channelm2.com/M2VoiceAnalysis%20-%20Considerations.html.
46. Eben Harrell, "Neuromarketing: What You Need to Know," *Harvard Business Review* (January 23, 2019), https://hbr.org/2019/01/neuromarketing-what-you-need-to-know.
47. Joey Goldberg, "La Croix Owes Success to Packaging Research," *Quirk's Media*, February 6, 2018 https://www.quirks.com/articles/la-croix-owes-success-to-packaging-research; and Kirk Hendrickson, "Using Eye-Tracking to Understand Price Sensitivity," *Quirk's Media* (October 10, 2016), https://www.quirks.com/articles/using-eye-tracking-to-understand-price-sensitivity.
48. Eben Harrell, "Neuromarketing: What You Need to Know," *Harvard Business Review* (January 23, 2019), https://hbr.org/2019/01/neuromarketing-what-you-need-to-know.
49. Mike Bartels, "How Improvements in Eye-Tracking Methodology Have Improved the Method's Deliverables," *Quirk's Marketing Research Review* (July 2015): 46, 48–51.
50. Eben Harrell, "Neuromarketing: What You Need to Know," *Harvard Business Review* (January 23, 2019), https://hbr.org/2019/01/neuromarketing-what-you-need-to-know.
51. "Maximizing Results in Television Advertising," TobaiiPro/Insight, https://www.tobiipro.com/insight/landing-page/maximize-results-television-advertising-pdf/, 2018.
52. Bruce F. Hall, "On Measuring the Power of Communications," *Journal of Advertising Research* 44, no. 2 (June 2004): 181–88.

53. Eben Harrell, "Neuromarketing: What You Need to Know," *Harvard Business Review* (January 23, 2019), https://hbr.org/2019/01/neuromarketing-what-you-need-to-know.
54. Bruce F. Hall, "On Measuring the Power of Communications," *Journal of Advertising Research* 44, no. 2 (June 2004): 181–188.
55. Rob Riester, "Understanding Limitations: Non-conscious vs. Conscious Marketing Research," *Quirk's Media* (July 10, 2018), https://www.quirks.com/articles/understanding-limitations-non-conscious-vs-conscious-marketing-research; and Eben Harrell, "Neuromarketing: What You Need to Know," *Harvard Business Review* (January 23, 2019), https://hbr.org/2019/01/neuromarketing-what-you-need-to-know.
56. Laurie Burkitt, "Battle for the Brain," *Forbes* 184, no. 9 (November 16, 2009): 76–78.
57. Eben Harrell, "Neuromarketing: What You Need to Know," *Harvard Business Review* (January 23, 2019), https://hbr.org/2019/01/neuromarketing-what-you-need-to-know.
58. Eben Harrell, "Neuromarketing: What You Need to Know," *Harvard Business Review* (January 23, 2019), https://hbr.org/2019/01/neuromarketing-what-you-need-to-know; and Curt Fedder and Meagan Peters, "Using Facial Coding and Body Language Analysis to Research Consumer Emotions," *Quirk's Media* (May 2016), https://www.quirks.com/articles/using-facial-coding-and-body-language-analysis-to-research-consumer-emotions.
59. Pablo Flores and Jennifer Karsh, "Getting to Know You," *Quirk's Marketing Research Review* (February 2012): 36–39.

Survey Research

CHAPTER 6

Source: Rawpixel.com/Shutterstock.

Chapter Outline

Learning Objectives

After studying this chapter, you should be able to:

- Discuss why survey research is used.
- Identify the two time frames for survey research.
- Describe the various types of errors that can occur with survey research.
- Discuss the advantages and disadvantages of each of the data collection alternatives.
- Discuss each of the survey selection considerations as they apply to the various data collection alternatives.

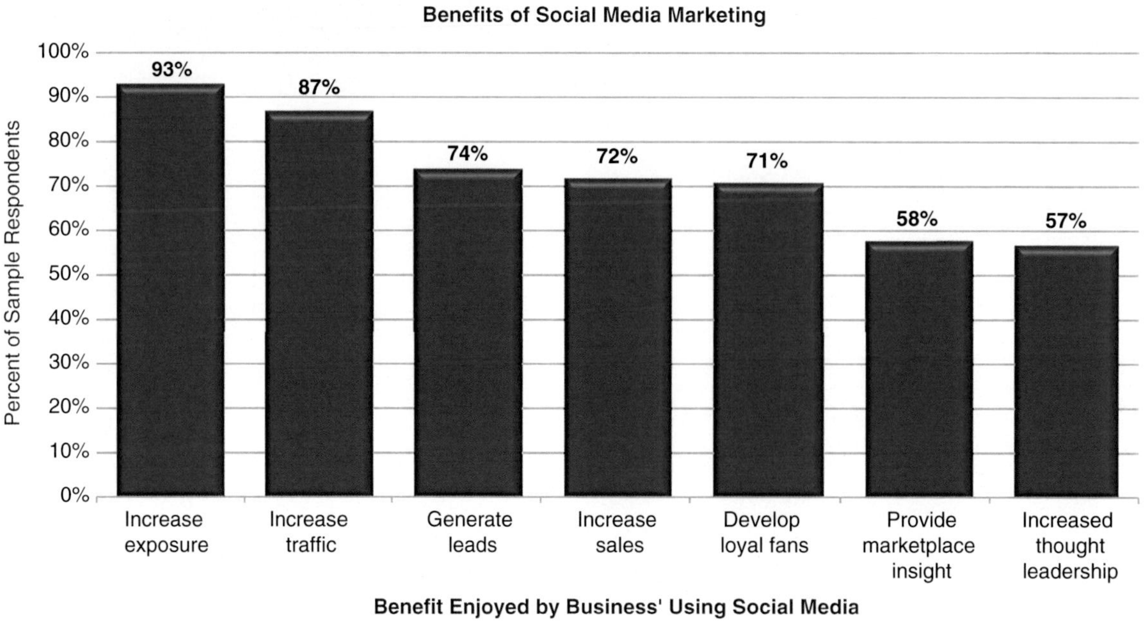

FIGURE 6.1 Bar Graph Showing the Benefits of Social Media Marketing
Source: Michael A. Stelzner, Adapted from "2019 Social Media Marketing Industry Report," *Social Media Examiner*, 2019, p. 7.

6.1 Chapter Overview

Social media consultants from companies such as Zen Media (formally known as the Marketing Zen Group) often hear clients discuss the need to be on Facebook and other social media sites. Many companies feel the need to post on Twitter. But, as Shama Kabini of the Zen Media has advised, "You need a strategy and a purpose. Just being there won't get you more customers."[1] *Social Media Examiner* has tracked social media marketing industry practices for over a decade. Their 2019 study surveyed 4,800 marketers about their usage of social media to grow and promote business. One of the questions on the survey asked the marketers to identify the benefits of social media marketing. Results are shown in Figure 6.1. The top two benefits of social media marketing were to increase exposure of the brand and to increase traffic to the business's website and other social media platforms. Of the top seven benefits, sales was in the middle with 72 percent relating social media marketing to increased sales. While respondents reported that social media efforts increased benefits in every area compared to the previous year, sales showed the largest gain, improving 19 percentage points from the 53 percent reported in 2018.[2]

This chapter presents information about survey research and various data collection methods such as telephone, mail, personal interviews, online, and mobile. The types of survey error are discussed, and methods for minimizing error in survey research are highlighted. The chapter concludes with a discussion of the criteria marketing managers need to consider in selecting the appropriate survey method.

6.2 Why Use Survey Research

LEARNING OBJECTIVE 6.1
Discuss why survey research is used.

Survey research remains one of the most popular forms of marketing research. Through surveys companies can gather the information needed to make good business decisions. Survey research tends to be used for descriptive purposes. The results can be used to describe situations, target markets, and other phenomena. Survey research is an effective means of providing answers to the "W" questions—who, when, where, what, and why. The information is very important in making optimal marketing decisions because it tends to be quantitative in nature. While qualitative questions may be part of survey research, they tend to be a minor component and used more for exploration purposes or in the early stages of questionnaire development as part of the survey instrument pretest.

In recent years the methods of collecting survey information have changed with the increased usage of digital media and digital communications. While the traditional methods of telephone and mail data collection are still used, they are being quickly replaced by cheaper and faster methods of surveying individuals and businesses.

Source: Andrey_Popov/Shutterstock

Survey research results can be used to describe situations, target markets, and other phenomena. Recently, the methods of collecting survey information have changed as online surveys are cheaper and faster than mail and telephone survey alternatives.

6.3 Survey Research Time Frame

Survey research can be conducted using two different time frames: cross-sectional or longitudinal. **Cross-sectional studies** are conducted at a single point in time and thus provide a snapshot of the subject or topic being studied at that particular time. The study by *Social Media Examiner* on the benefits of social media (see Figure 6.1) was a cross-sectional study. Most marketing research survey studies are cross-sectional in nature as marketing mangers seek information to solve a particular problem or to develop specific marketing strategies.

LEARNING OBJECTIVE 6.2
Identify the two time frames for survey research.

Cross-sectional studies research conducted at a single point in time that provides a snapshot of the subject or topic being studied at that particular time.

Longitudinal study research study over time in which the same questions are asked at different points in time.

An alternative to cross-sectional studies is a **longitudinal study**, which is a study that asks the same questions at multiple points in time. Typically, a longitudinal study will involve retaining the same respondents, although it is not absolutely necessary. Longitudinal studies are an excellent method of identifying and tracking trends; a key purpose of longitudinal studies is to examine the change or continuity of responses over time. If the same respondents are used, then it is easier to verify whether a change in behavior or responses has actually occurred. If different respondents are used, then there is a possibility that any differences found may be due to differences in the sample respondents (old vs. new) rather than being due to true changes in behaviors, attitudes, opinions, or whatever is being measured.

The Gallup polls that are used during political seasons are a type of longitudinal study. Gallup polls tend to measure voter reactions to issues and candidates through the weeks leading up to the election. Different respondents are identified for each polling period, but comparisons are made since the Gallup organization uses very strict sampling procedures and a large sample size.

In marketing, tracking studies are a type of longitudinal study. Marketing research firms such as Nielsen use tracking studies to measure the impact of advertising and branding campaigns over time. Through the data collected, Nielsen is able to determine when an advertising campaign takes off or connects with the intended audience, or conversely, when it begins to wear out and needs to be changed.

Source: Rawpixel.com/Shutterstock.

Consumer panels are composed of individuals that have been recruited by a marketing research firm to participate in various studies over time. Consumer panels can be used to study consumer behavior, consumer attitudes, or media behavior over time using longitudinal studies.

Another source for longitudinal studies is the consumer panel. These are individuals that have been recruited by a marketing research firm to participate in various studies over time. Nielsen uses a consumer panel to determine television viewership and, thus, the Nielsen television ratings. Other firms, such as MRI-Simmons, uses consumer panels to study

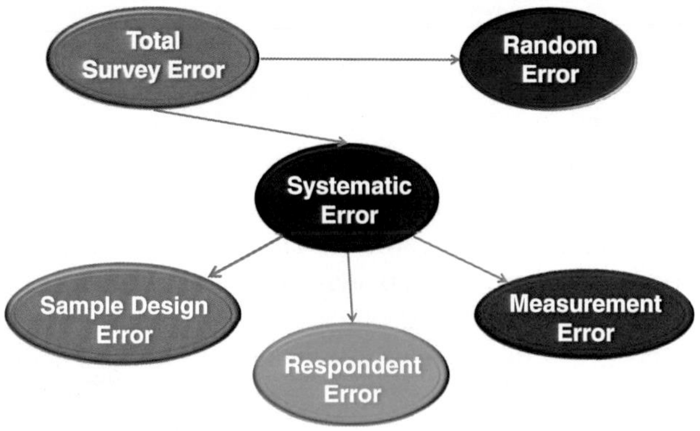

FIGURE 6.2 Types of Errors

consumer behavior and consumer attitudes. Using such panels allows the research firm to avoid seeking new study participants each time a study is conducted. But, since the studies ask the same questions and seek the same information, using a panel allows companies like MRI-Simmons to measure changes that occur over time. These data can be examined by marketing researchers to identify trends and, in some cases, predict the future or at least theorize about what might happen in the future.

6.4 Types of Errors in Survey Research

LEARNING OBJECTIVE 6.3
Describe the various types of errors that can occur with survey research.

Random error results from chance variation between the sample surveyed, and the population that they represent.

Systematic error mistake or problem in the research design or the research process.

The goal of marketing research is to collect useful, accurate information that is free of errors. In reality, however, that is extremely unlikely. Errors will occur that can affect the quality of the data gathered. As shown in Figure 6.2, research errors can be divided into two broad groups: random error and systematic errors. **Random error** results from chance variation between the subjects surveyed and the population, or group, they are chosen to represent. As will be discussed in Chapter 8 on sampling, researchers can reduce random error simply by increasing the sample size. Generally speaking, the more people that are surveyed, the less impact random error will have on the data.

Systematic error results from a mistake or problem in the research design or the research process. For example, suppose on a questionnaire respondents were asked if they were:

1. Single
2. Married
3. Single, but living with someone.

Option 3 is unclear. Does it mean living with a roommate, or a significant other, or does it mean living with one's family? Thus, when a "3" is recorded in the data, the researcher has no idea which situation best fits the respondent. In this case, increasing the sample size may compound the systematic error that has resulted from a problem in the measurement process.

While reducing random error is important, systematic error is of greater concern. By careful attention to the research design and the research process, the occurrence of systematic error can be significantly reduced. As was shown in Figure 6.2, there are three broad categories of systematic errors: sample design error, respondent error, and measurement error.

6.4a Sample Design Error

It is rare that in a research study every person in the study population can be surveyed, so marketing researchers will typically select, or "sample" individuals within the population to complete the survey. In this process several different types of systematic errors may

- Population specification error
- Frame error
- Selection error

FIGURE 6.3 Sample Design Errors

occur. These include population specification error, frame error, and selection error (see Figure 6.3).

The initial step in the sample design process is to specify the population, or group of subjects that is to be studied. Most populations are composed of individuals, though sometimes stores or companies may form the population. **Population specification error** occurs when the population is incorrectly identified. Suppose a company defines the population as all users of Facebook. The study is conducted. Then in meeting with the client, the client mentions that the population should have been all individuals who use social media. The population was incorrectly specified since individuals who use social media sites other than Facebook did not participate in the study. This creates error in the data if the responses of the individuals who were missed were different from the responses of Facebook users. A study flawed in this manner would yield results that cannot be extrapolated, or generalized, to the larger category of social media users. It would be applicable to Facebook users only. Another example of population specification error occurs during longitudinal studies of customer satisfaction. What happens over time is that unhappy customers stop buying the product, and are dropped from the study as they are no longer part of the customer population. This can be dangerous as the survey results may give management the mistaken impression that satisfaction is improving and that everything is fine. However, as the population does not include recent customers, the dissatisfaction that is driving customers away from the firm is not present in the data, and management may be missing critical insights that could help explain why customer numbers are dropping despite an increase in satisfaction ratings.[3] Thus, it is very important to consider the characteristics that define the population. Should it be current customers only? Those who have purchased and used the product within the last 3 months? The answer lies with the purpose behind the customer satisfaction study, though marketers would do well to remain cognizant of the point previously mentioned. Minimizing population specification error requires that the researcher sit down with the client and carefully discuss the specific characteristics that describe the population that will be studied, as well as any characteristics that will cause potential respondents to be excluded from the study. It is also helpful if the researcher puts things into perspective for the client. In the first example, the population specification error could have been avoided had the researcher said, "So you understand that any results we gather from this study can only be inferred about Facebook users, and not about users of Linked In, Twitter, Instagram, or other social media?"

Population specification error population is incorrectly identified.

If the population is defined correctly, then a second type of error that can occur relates to the choice of sample frame. The **sample frame** is the list of population members or elements from which the sample will be selected. **Frame error** occurs when an incorrect or incomplete sample frame is used to choose study participants. Suppose a bank such as J.P. Morgan Chase wanted to survey their customers and defined the population as all of its customers. Now suppose that all credit card and/or checking account holders were used as the sample frame. Has frame error occurred? Almost certainly! Chase most likely has customers who have neither type of account, but instead maintain a savings account, Christmas club account, home equity line of credit, vehicle loan, or home mortgage with the bank. Frame error occurs because these individuals did not have the opportunity to participate in the study as they were not even included in the sample frame. The results of the study could be misleading if the opinions of those who were not part of the sample frame differ significantly from the opinions of those who were. Minimizing frame error requires diligence on the part of the researcher. For this reason, many firms that conduct

Sample frame list of population members or elements from which the sample will be selected.

Frame error use of an incorrect sample frame.

Source: MOZCO Mateusz Szymanski/Shutterstock.

Suppose a bank such as J.P. Morgan Chase wanted to survey their customers and defined the population as all of its customers. If only credit card and checking account holders were used as the sample frame, sample frame error would occur as customers who have Chase accounts other than these types would not have the opportunity to participate in the study. The results of the study could be misleading if the opinions of those who were not part of the sample frame differed significantly from the opinions of those who were.

research online use intermediaries such as sample aggregators to assist with the sample selection process. Sample aggregators have access to multiple sample panels and lists from multiple providers, which enhances the breadth of the sample frame and reduces frame error. Sample aggregators assist in the quality control process, which helps to ensure better quality data and a more representative sample. Still, frame error will occur. Even if the population is defined as online users, not every online user is a panel member, or has opted-in to a list that provides sample aggregators with demographic details and email contact information.

The last type of sample design error occurs as part of the selection process. **Selection error** occurs when the sampling procedures are not followed or are not clearly defined. Suppose research interviewers using a mall intercept approach are told to interview every fourteenth person. If an interviewer counts off and sees a fourteenth person, but decides that individual looks too busy, and instead just skips to the fifteenth or sixteenth person, then selection error has occurred. This error becomes worse if the interviewer continues self-selecting respondents based on looks or what is perceived to be willingness to participate based on appearance. Minimizing this type of selection error requires that interviewers be properly trained and supervised in the field.

Selection error sampling procedures are not followed or are not clearly defined.

Another example of sampling procedures not being followed occurs when programmers are careless in creating screening questions, and mistakenly screen out those who should be included in the study. For example, suppose respondents need to be 21 years of age to answer an online questionnaire about tobacco advertising. The survey asks them to enter their birth year. Behind the scenes, the survey software computes their age by subtracting the birth year from the current year. But, the online survey logic is incorrectly programmed, so that those who are 21 years of age or older are told they don't qualify to take the survey, while those under the age of 21 are passed through to the survey questions. Careful pretesting of the online survey *prior* to implementation should catch these types of errors before the survey is released. However, it would also be a good idea to have a categorical age question, with one response option reading, "under 21." Obviously, if all respondents fall into that category, the researcher would know (after the fact) that selection error had occurred.

Selection error can also result from incomplete instructions. Going back to the mall intercept study, suppose the fourteenth individual happens to be a child thirteen years old, and the study requires all participants to be 21 or over. What should the interviewer do? Should they go to the next person, the fifteenth, or do they count off another fourteen? What if the fourteenth person is identified, but declines to participate in the study? Should the interviewers choose the very next person, or do they count off another fourteen? To ensure consistency among interviewers and to prevent selection errors, it is important to have clear instructions on how to handle these situations as well as others that may occur.

6.4b Respondent Error

As shown in Figure 6.4 respondent errors fall into two categories: non-response bias (or error) and response bias (or error). **Non-response bias** occurs when there is a difference between the responses of those who participate in a study and those who do not. Suppose Twitter is used to send a survey concerning the use of coupons offered by businesses through Twitter. It would be a logical way of conducting the survey since the purpose

Non-response bias difference between the responses of those who participate in a study and those who do not participate in the study.

- Non-response bias
- Response error or bias
  - Deliberate falsification
  - Unconscious error, omission or bias

FIGURE 6.4 Respondent Error

of the study is to examine how effective coupon issuance is with Twitter users. Suppose 300 people respond to the survey. The question in terms of non-response bias would be whether there is a significant difference in the attitudes of the 300 who responded and the attitudes of individuals who did not respond. Is it possible that the 300 who responded are heavy users of coupons and actively watch for coupons issued through Twitter? If so, their attitudes are likely to be more favorable than are the attitudes of those who make little or no use of coupons. It is very likely that if those who did not respond to the original survey were contacted and questioned, their responses to the survey question would be quite different.

The response rate of a study gives some indication of the potential for nonresponse bias. The **response rate** is simply the percentage of individuals who complete a study from among those who are contacted and asked to participate. For example, the response rate to a mail study may be 1.7 percent, meaning that 98.3 percent of those contacted did not respond.

Response rate the percentage of individuals who complete a study from among those who are contacted and asked to participate.

Individuals do not respond to surveys for three primary reasons. First, the individual cannot be contacted at the particular time of the study. Suppose a bank identifies 500 of their customers randomly to receive a mail survey. If a particular customer happens to be out of the country for an extended period of time, then he or she may not be available to participate in the study. Alternatively, an individual may be away from home, or engaged in outdoor activities when called to participate in a telephone survey.

The second situation occurs when the individual is contacted but cannot participate in the study at that particular time. He or she may be ill, involved in a complex business deal, or have another reason for not being able to participate at the particular time the study is being conducted. Time is a precious commodity for consumers today. Again, telephone surveys that interrupt an evening meal, putting children to bed, or watching a favorite television program may suffer from this form of non-response bias. The perception that surveys are long and complicated, and people's busy lifestyles have contributed greatly to lower response rates. Consumers no longer feel special or valued when asked for their opinion. Instead, the proliferation of surveys had led many individuals to feel hassled.[4]

Minimizing non-response bias in either of the first two cases may require sending multiple email or survey mailings, making multiple attempts to call the household at different times, or sending pre-notifications or reminders designed to encourage the individual to complete the survey. Online surveys generally send three invitations, spread-out over a week, so that one invitation is sent on the weekend. A recent poll by Branded Research, a firm that provides businesses access to online samples, as well brand tracking, advertising, and product development research, found that rewards were the primary reason why respondents took surveys. The poll results are displayed in **Figure 6.5**.[5] Short surveys delivered by means of mobile devices and incentives can be helpful in improving survey response rates. Incentives may take the form of cash, points that can be redeemed for cash or merchandise, coupons, product discounts, charitable contributions, gift cards, movie tickets, or entry into a drawing for a substantial prize.[6] Research has shown that monetary incentives generate the highest response rates, and a strong quality of responses.[7] For mail surveys, dollar bills sent with the survey request generate higher response rates than do promises of larger rewards upon return of the survey. Instant cash, or points can be used with online recipients. Smaller incentives are also preferred as they are less likely to bias survey results, either by encouraging an over representation of lower-income respondents

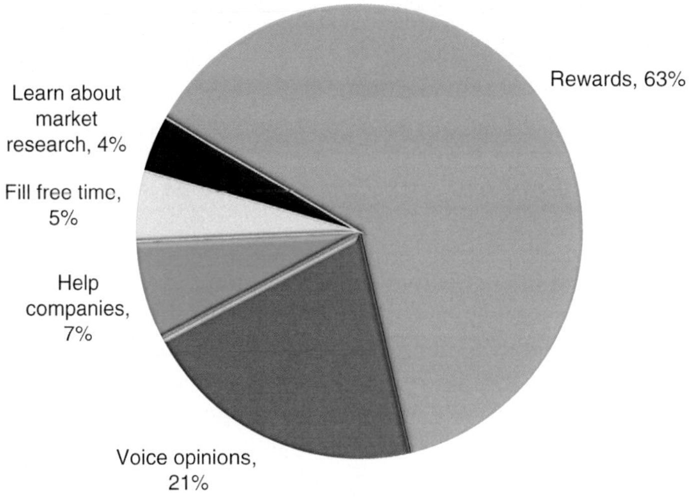

FIGURE 6.5 Primary Reasons Why People Take Surveys
Source: Adapted from Kirsten Miles, "Survey Participants Are Motivated by Rewards," *Quirk's Media*, (**www.quirks.com**), March 12, 2019, accessed August 28, 2019.

or people who just answer the survey for the money, and may or may not otherwise provide quality responses.[8]

The final type of non-response bias occurs when the individual is contacted, but just refuses to participate. They are not interested. It may be because they have been duped before by promises of short surveys that turned into sales calls or longer surveys, or for fear of being putting on mail, email, or phone-lists. Potential loss of privacy is also impacting individual's willingness to respond.[9] Whatever the underlying cause, refusal to participate, unfortunately, has become more common and may have the greatest impact on nonresponse bias. Since they refuse to participate it is difficult to know if their response would have been different from those who did participate. Incentives can help to minimize outright refusals somewhat. Sometimes assuring respondents of anonymity can help improve response rates among this group, particularly when dealing with those who fear a loss of privacy, or who worry their contact information will be sold for marketing or research purposes. Anonymity can also increase response rates for studies into sensitive subjects, or when sampling employees or other groups over whom the surveying entity holds power.[10] However, there will always be a portion of the sample that refuses to participate in the study.

The only way to measure non-response bias is to conduct a second wave, which involves sending the survey to those who did not respond the first time. With the second wave, it is highly likely that individuals from the first two groups will respond—those who could not be contacted and those who were unable to participate. But, individuals in the third group will still likely refuse to participate. By comparing the responses of the first wave and second wave, it is possible to get a feel for any type of non-response bias. Unfortunately, it will never be possible to compare the answers of the respondents to the group who refuse to participate.

Deliberate falsification an individual provides false answers on purpose.

Response bias (or error) can occur under two circumstances: deliberate falsification and unconscious error. **Deliberate falsification** occurs when an individual provides false answers, purposely. There may be a number of different reasons why individuals are not truthful. If a question is potentially embarrassing or makes a person look foolish or bad, particularly in personal interview situations, then the respondent may provide a false answer. If a question is too personal and the respondent doesn't want to answer, the person might lie rather than not respond. Also, the respondent may want to appear intelligent, frugal, or display some other desirable characteristic and thus provide a false answer. Sometimes respondents are in a hurry and provide the answer they think will end the survey most quickly. Other times they offer the interviewer the answer they think the researcher wants to hear. Some respondents just want the incentive and randomly answer questions without reading them. Often respondents will answer in a way that is socially desirable, meaning in way that fits with social norms or expectations.

In cases where respondents answer but are not truthful due to privacy concerns, privacy disclaimers and instructions that explain why the data are needed, how it will be reported, how participants can delete or change their personal information and whether responses will be confidential and anonymous can deter some people from providing false answers. Also, rotating the order in which questions appear on the survey can help to statistically "even out" such biases, especially when due to fatigue or time pressure. Some measurement error occurs because the researcher assumes that participants can answer a question, when respondents have little understanding of the topic being studied. To minimize error, "don't know," "no opinion," or "not applicable" response options should be included when there is a legitimate chance the respondent may lack the knowledge to answer questions.

The second type of response bias is an unintentional error. It may be placing a checkmark by the third response item when they meant to check the second item in the list. It may be due to a faulty memory. When asked how many times an individual accessed a particular website over the last month, the respondent may respond it was four, when it was actually lower. In fact, research consistently finds that people overstate numbers, particular those related to purchase. Depending on the price of the item and the time-period consumers are asked to recall, consumers responding to a survey may list double or quadruple the number of purchases made, compared to their actual behavior over the same time-period.[11] The response was not intentionally false. The problem lies with memory and an inability to recall accurately. Shortening the recall period, from a month to a week, or even from a week to "yesterday" can minimize memory errors and improve the quality of data. Consumers also overstate their likelihood of purchase, again, not intentionally. Many experienced research firms make adjustments for potentially overstated data during the interpretation phrase,[12] though the process used is proprietary to each firm.

Including quality control questions is essential to combat both forms of response bias. A west coast bakery chain commissioned a nationwide study to determine awareness of its brand and seven regional competitors. Researchers included two ghost (fictitious) brands to help identify the anticipated one to three percent of the sample who honestly thought they had heard of one of the brands that didn't exist. Researchers were shocked when analysis revealed awareness levels of 9 percent and 12 percent for the ghost brands and a much higher than expected 16 percent for the client brand. Worried about data accuracy, the researchers found that 3 percent of respondents indicated awareness of all 10 brands when the researchers expected sample members to be aware of one or two brands at the most. These fraudulent responses were eliminated.[13]

6.4c Measurement Error

Figure 6.6 identifies three types of measurement error: processing error, interviewer error, and measurement instrument error. **Measurement error** is the difference between the responses that are obtained and the true responses that were sought. By paying close attention to the design of the survey instrument, the measurement process, and the data entry procedure, measurement error can be reduced.

Measurement error difference between the responses that are obtained and the true responses that were sought.

- Processing error
- Interviewer error or bias
- Measurement instrument error or bias

FIGURE 6.6 Measurement Error

Process error when data from a survey instrument are incorrectly entered into the computer program that is being used to tally the data and to analyze it.

Process errors occur when data from a survey instrument are either incorrectly coded or incorrectly entered into the computer program that is being used to tally the data and to analyze results. If humans are coding data on a paper survey, different response categories are represented by a particular number. An employee coding gender as a "1" to represent a male respondent when males are supposed to be coded as "2" would be a processing error. In transferring data from a paper survey sheet into Excel or SPSS, processing errors can occur when the wrong number or data is entered. For instance, a survey response may be 23 but the data processing person mistakenly typed 32 or accidentally hit a "4" instead of a "3" resulting in 24 instead of 23. If the survey question answers are being machine scored, the machine may be out of calibration or the scantron was not clearly marked and the machine could not pick up the answer.

To check for process errors, researchers can randomly select 10 percent of the surveys and proofread the coding process and data entry process. If a large number of errors are found in the coding process, all surveys may be proofread for errors. Frequency tables and double data entry can be used to identify process errors resulting from the data input process as well. A frequency table that shows a value above or below the legitimate range for a variable indicates that process error has occurred. In double data entry, one individual enters the data for the study. A separate set of variables that mimic those entered are created, and a second individual reenters the data into these new variables. Correlation analysis between the first and second data set will identify any discrepancies when a particular variable does not have 100 percent correlation. The researcher can then examine the original survey data and both data entries to see which is correct.

Interviewer error or bias when an interviewer influences a respondent to give erroneous answers, either intentionally or unintentionally.

Interviewer error or bias occurs when an interviewer influences a respondent to give erroneous answers, either intentionally or unintentionally. Respondents who like an interviewer may provide the answer they think the interviewer wants to hear. Others often agree with interviewers or evaluate concepts more positively because they perceive the interviewer as an expert.[14] The tone of voice or the way an interviewer asks a question can influence a respondent's answer. Interviewers who say, "Ok" or "Uh-huh" after a question is answered unintentionally offer cues to the "right" response or may be interpreted as disapproving of the participant's answer. Interviewers should adjust their rate of speech to match that of the participant to enhance rapport.[15] Body language of the interviewer can have an effect on the respondent. For example, an interviewer who refuses to make eye contact and who speaks in a quick, clipped tone of voice may receive short, non-descriptive answers from study participants. In addition, such things as the interviewer's age, gender, and even what he or she is wearing can affect how respondents answer. To reduce interviewer errors it is important that all interviewers be properly trained so they do not have any impact on how respondents answer questions. It is important that questions be read verbatim since even small changes in phrasing can alter the question meaning. Imagine how changing the word "would" to "could" might introduce error into the data. When respondents answer questions in their own words, it is critical that the interviewer evaluate the answer for clarity and completeness, then ask probing questions if necessary. It is also important that the interviewers follow instructions and are monitored to ensure interviewer errors are kept to a minimum.

Measurement instrument error or bias errors caused by the questionnaire or instrument being used for measurement.

Order bias occurs when respondents are influenced to select a certain response or set of responses based on the order in which they appear in the survey.

Measurement instrument error or bias occurs with the questionnaire itself. Chapter 11 presents questionnaire development and issues that may affect the quality of data. As a single question can influence answers to later questions by providing a context, frame of reference, or focal point, careful consideration must be given to the order in which questions appear. **Order bias** occurs when respondents are influenced to select a certain response or set of responses based on the order in which they appear in the survey. If two new product ideas are being evaluated, the one shown first is generally preferred over the second. In questions with a long list of brand names or other possible responses, options toward the top of the list are chosen more often than are those toward the bottom of the list. In both examples, order bias has occurred. The best way to minimize order bias is to randomize the presentation of questions within a section, and randomize the order of question responses, when possible. Researchers must be careful about how questions are worded to avoid leading respondents to an answer or confusing them as to what is being asked. Questions should be clear, not ambiguous, and avoid suggestions, implications or justifications that may subtly influence the respondent to answer in a certain fashion. In transitioning from one subject to another, the change must be noticeable so that respondents realize they are evaluating a new product category, brand, or topic. Pretesting is essential, as questions that are clear to a researcher may not be clear to individuals responding to the survey. Response categories should be mutually exclusive (meaning responses fit into only one category) and categorically exhaustive (meaning every response has a category into which it fits). Often this means that response options should include a "Don't Know," "Not Sure," "Not Applicable," or "Other" with a fill-in-the-blank response option. When possible, response categories within a question are randomly ordered to help eliminate order bias, though this is not possible with types of questions, such as rating scales. Questions with similar response options, especially scaled response or rating questions, should be grouped together within a section. Consistency is key. Error would occur if one set of questions used a rating scale with response options ranging from "Strongly Disagree" to "Strongly Agree" while other questions reversed the scale and listed response options ranging from "Strongly Agree" to Strongly Disagree." It would be far too easy for even the most attentive respondent to miss the alteration in response formats, especially as these questions are typically presented in a grid format, with the top of the column labelled with the response option. By paying careful attention to the design of the questionnaire and pretesting the survey instrument with individuals who are similar to the survey sample, potential problems can be detected and corrected before data collection begins, thus minimizing measurement instrument error.[16]

While systematic error cannot be completely eliminated, it can be reduced by paying close attention to the research design and the research process. It is also helpful to know the types of errors that can occur and thus guard against them. Therefore, it is important to take steps to reduce systematic errors when designing the research and also during the survey collection process.

6.5 Data Collection Alternatives

LEARNING OBJECTIVE 6.4
Discuss the advantages and disadvantages of each of the data collection alternatives.

Figure 6.7 identifies the various data collection alternatives for survey research. Each method has its own set of advantages and disadvantages. The traditional methods of telephone and mail surveys have been steadily declining in usage in favor of online, mobile, and mixed modes methods. The 2018 *GRIT: Greenbook Industry Trends Report* asked those working in the research industry to rank the top three data collection methods used in 2018. Online surveys were ranked first by 59 percent of respondents, while mobile, computer-assisted telephone interviewing (CATI), and other forms of data collection methods were ranked first by 6 percent or less of the respondents. Figure 6.8 shows the percent of respondents who ranked various data collection alternatives among the top three forms of data collection used during 2018. Online is most popular, followed by mobile, CATI, face-to-face interviewing, computer assisted interviewing (CAPI), and mail.[17] Cost and speed of response have been major reasons behind the shift, but other factors such as response rates and changes in technology have also influenced the shift. For example, telephone survey response rates have plunged from an average of 28 percent in 2001 to just 6 percent in 2018.[18]

- Telephone (CATI/CAPI)
- Mail
- Face-to-face personal interviews/Intercept
- Internet (online, email, social media, mobile, MORC)
- Mixed modes

FIGURE 6.7 Data Collection Alternatives

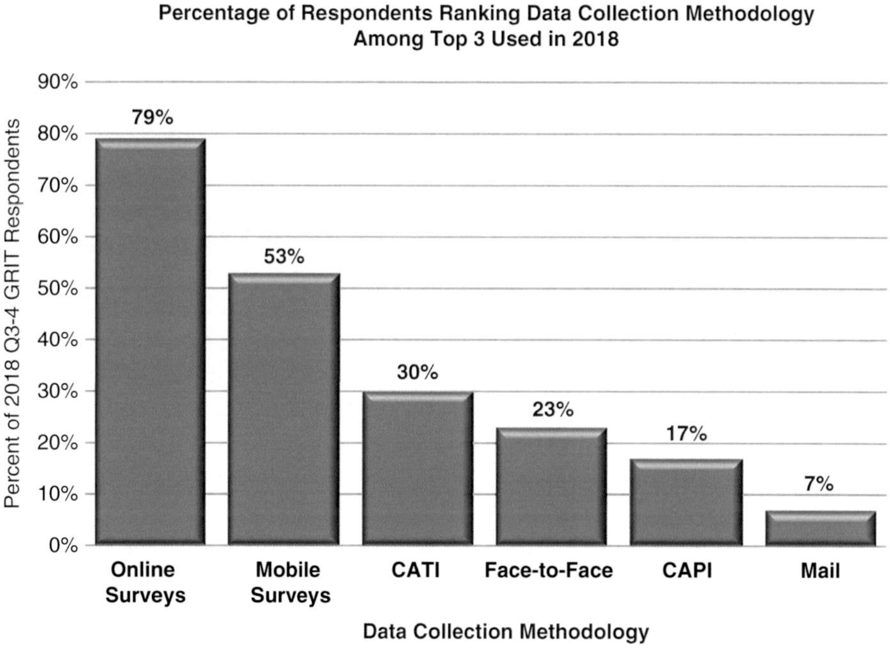

FIGURE 6.8 Percent of GRIT Survey Respondents Ranking Data Collection Methodologies Among Top 3 Used in 2018
Source: Adapted from "Usage of Traditional Methodologies," in *GRIT Report: Greenbook Research Industry Trends Report, Quarters 3–4, 2018* (New York: GreenBook, 2018).

6.5a Telephone Surveys

Before the 1990s and the rise in popularity of cell phones, land line telephone research was the most popular method of conducting survey research. It was less costly than other methods, had a higher response rate, and was a quick way to collect data. It was an efficient method of conducting research and provided usable, valuable data.

Telephone interviewing became especially effective with the development of random-digit dialing. Researchers no longer had to rely on telephone directories. Homes could be dialed randomly, producing a good sample and, in most cases, a sample with a relatively high response rate. The technology allowed for the elimination of business phones so only residences were contacted.

Source: Cecilia Lim H M/Shutterstock.

Telephone survey research is still used today for a large number of studies and is particularly effective in business-to-business interactions where customer satisfaction is assessed.

Telephone survey research is still used today for a large number of studies. In the *2019 Global Market Research* study, ESOMAR reports that in the United States, 15 percent of the money spent on market research in 2018 was devoted to telephone interviews, a substantial portion of researchers overall budget.[19] Telephone research is particularly effective in business-to–business interactions where customer satisfaction is assessed. For instance, Toshiba sells expensive medical imaging devices to hospitals and clinics. Data is first collected six to eight months after the equipment is installed via a lengthy phone survey that targets administrators, physicians, and technicians. Customer satisfaction with the installation, training, maintenance, and equipment performance are assessed. The post-installation survey serves as an

Advantages	Disadvantages
• Fairly low cost • Faster than mail surveys • CATI minimizes some forms of process errors • CATI easily uses skip patterns	• Limited types of information • Shorter surveys • Screening devices • Declining number of land line phones • Declining response rate • Sample distortion / sample design error

FIGURE 6.9 Advantages | Disadvantages of Telephone Research

early warning indicator and allows the company to address problems or dissatisfactions before they become critical. The same survey is repeated two years after the installation to identify changes in satisfaction levels for particular customers, as well as trends in overall satisfaction for groups of customers.[20]

The advantages and disadvantages of using landline telephones for research are identified in Figure 6.9.

Computer-assisted telephone interviewing (CATI) interviewers read questions and response options from a computer screen over the telephone and select the answer indicated by the respondent.

Computer-assisted telephone interviewing (CATI) is the norm. With CATI, interviewers read questions and response options from a computer screen and select the answer indicated by the respondent. CATI interviewing provides results more quickly and at a lower cost when compared to mail surveys, though online and mobile surveys now provide data more quickly and faster than any other data collection technique. Process error that often occurs with mail surveys when data is transferred from survey to spreadsheet is minimized because the responses are already programmed into the survey, so no additional data entry is required. CATI surveys can be programmed to accept data within a given range so that an interviewer who erroneously enters five digits for a respondent's birth year would be alerted to the error before moving on to the next survey question. But, it cannot eliminate all error, particularly if the interview selects the wrong answer choice. CATI software may be programmed to automatically skip over irrelevant questions based on a respondent's previous answers. For example, if certain questions are contingent upon owning a specific item in a product category, respondents who don't own qualifying products would not be asked questions. This makes administering the survey easier for the interviewer who does not have to remember to follow complicated skipping instructions, and respondents are not plagued with irrelevant questions that may irritate them and result in an incomplete survey.

Still, for many firms, the disadvantages outweigh the benefits, or firms may choose to incorporate telephone surveys as part of mixed mode approach to surveying. The types of research information that can be collected by telephone are limited to respondent behaviors, attitudes, and opinions about topics that do not require visualization. With traditional telephone surveys, respondents cannot be shown an advertisement, marketing brochure, or even a product. It is difficult to ask certain questions over the phone, such as those that require respondents to choose from a set of scaled responses such as very satisfied, satisfied, somewhat satisfied, somewhat dissatisfied, dissatisfied, or very dissatisfied. Because these response options would need to be read for each question using these categories, the number of questions that could be asked on the survey would be very limited. Furthermore, some respondents might become impatient and terminate the survey early. In general, telephone surveys are most suitable for shorter surveys. However, even with these limitations, a large number of topics cannot be researched through telephone surveys.

The last four disadvantages are inter-related and have occurred simultaneously. Consumers increasingly started using answering machines and caller ID to screen calls, initially to screen out telemarketers. Automated telemarketing has exploded, with the *New York Times* reporting more than 3.4 billion automated calls to both cellular and traditional phone lines in a single month of 2018.[21] With increased screening came a declining response rate and a higher level of refusals to participate, even when individuals could be reached. The rise in the popularity of cell phones reduced the number of landlines. As of 2018, 55 percent of U.S. households rely solely on cell phones. This trend, however, is not equal across all demographic groups. It is primarily the younger and middle-aged consumers who have moved to cell only households, while older consumers who own their homes have maintained landlines.[22] Taken together, these factors create a distorted sample frame for landline telephone research, which contributes to sample design error.

For companies who want to utilize landline telephone surveys, mailing a letter or postcard in advance increases the response rate. This alerts the potential respondent that a phone call survey will be coming and solicits their support.

Using an advance letter requires identification of the sample in advance, so random digit dialing cannot be used. This in turn means that households whose phone numbers are unlisted are not included, resulting in higher levels of frame error. But, for certain types of research this is acceptable. For instance, suppose a company such as Toyota wants to survey individuals who have purchased a new Toyota within the last year. By sending a letter to a sample of these customers, they will be more likely to participate in the telephone survey even though Toyota will use a marketing research firm to do the actual data collection.

Cell Phones In 2017 the Census Bureau conducted an experiment to examine the impact of integrating cell phone households into their *American Community Survey (ACS)*, which previously had used landline only telephone samples as part of a multi-mode research method. The study surveyed two groups using CATI. The control group contained landline only households and the experimental group contained a mixture of landline and cell phone households. **Contact rates**, or the percent of sample phone numbers reached by an interviewer, and survey completion rates were higher for the experimental group. Plus, researchers were successful in reaching a younger, more ethnically diverse population. They also reached households that rented, rather than owned homes in the experimental group. These findings were attributed to the inclusion of the cell phone only households. As the resulting sample was more representative of the population under study, sample design error was reduced.[23]

Contact rates the percent of sample phone numbers reached by an interviewer.

The Census Bureau is not the only entity that has recognized the importance of including cell phone only households. According to one source, over 50 percent of CATI research today combines both cell phone households and landline households in the hope of creating a more representative sample.[24] Yet using cell phones for surveys in which an interviewer is involved has its challenges.

Source: Gil C/Shutterstock.

In 2017 the Census Bureau conducted an experiment to examine the impact of integrating cell phone households into their *American Community Survey (ACS)*, which previously had used landline only telephone samples as part of a multi-mode research method. The experimental group containing cell phone households resulted in higher contact rates, higher survey completion rates, and a more representative sample.

In examining cell phone survey research a number of factors must be considered. These factors are listed in Figure 6.10.

Currently, there are legal restrictions that apply to cell phones that do not apply to land lines. Specifically, research companies cannot use random digit dialer technology to contact a cell phone user without the individual's prior consent, according to the Telephone Consumers Protection Act. To obtain such consent is costly, time consuming, and practically impossible. Therefore, each number has to be dialed individually by the researcher, which increases the costs and time needed to complete the study. The Marketing Research Insights Association estimates that including cell phone users in studies costs 2 to 4 times as much as a landline study.[25] Also, because cell phones are viewed as personal, many individuals feel that receiving a phone call from a research company is an invasion of their privacy. As new privacy regulations begin to permeate throughout the United

- Legal restrictions
- Costs
- Sample frame error
  - Cell phone owner vs. cell phone user
  - Work vs. home cell phones
  - Cell phone area codes may not indicate location
- Mobility of respondent when answering may influence completion
- Length of survey must be short

FIGURE 6.10 Factors in Cell Phone Survey Research

States, special care must be taken to abide by state laws related to privacy, data storage, and the treatment of private information. Phone numbers are considered personally identifiable information. When possible, they should be hidden from people who don't need to see the information, and only exposed to interviewers when dialing. The General Data Protection Regulation (GDPR) put in place by the European Union already ensures that any firm surveying citizens from the EU must take great care with personally identifiable information. Strict rules for data handling and storage are required, and if sound recordings are taken, the respondent must be informed. In the United States, consumers who have listed their cell numbers on the Do Not Call list are typically unaware that marketing research is exempt from the DNC provisions, and often refuse to participate as a result. Firms may wish to develop an internal DNC list based on opt-out requests from consumers.

The owner and user of cell phones may be two different individuals. Many cell phones are used by children, but owned by parents. With a land line, researchers know that there will be an adult in the home, even if a child answers the phone. Such is not the case with cell phones. Similarly, adults may have a work phone and a personal phone, which increases the likelihood of sample frame error, since some individuals may have a greater chance of being selected to participate in research than others.

Also, because of the transitory nature of individuals with mobile phones, the phone number area code does not indicate where the person lives. People don't change their cell phone number just because they move from one state to another. The individual can be anywhere in the United States. For national studies, this would be okay. But for any type of study limited to a specific geographic area, it would be a problem when area codes are used to define the sampling frame. A screener question would be needed to determine if the person answering the phone lived in the desired location. Contact lists tying cell phone numbers to physical addresses could be purchased to capture some households with cell phone area codes from other outside of the local area.

Another challenge with cell phones is that the person answering the phone may be anywhere and engaged in any number of activities. The person may be at work, at a restaurant, shopping, or driving a vehicle. These circumstances may prevent the subject from completing a survey. Even if they consent to the survey, it may be a distraction, especially if the survey is longer than the respondent anticipated.

In most cases, surveys using cell phones must be shorter than those using a traditional land line phone, for a number of reasons. First, the location of the respondent may dictate they cannot or should not spend very much time on the phone. Second, many individuals see a phone call to their cell phone as invasive and thus may answer a few questions, but not want to participate in a lengthy survey. Third, the individual may be engaged in activities, such as driving or working, or using smart phone apps. As a result, the subject may not fully concentrate on the questions, or may give hurried answers, incomplete answers, or wrong answers, or just discontinue the survey prior to completion.

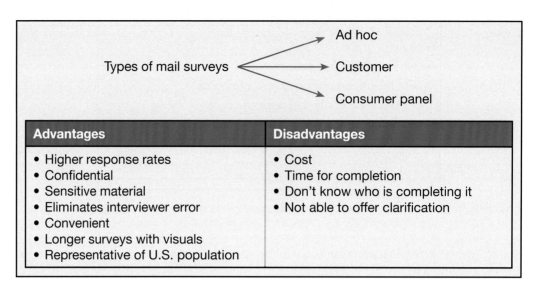

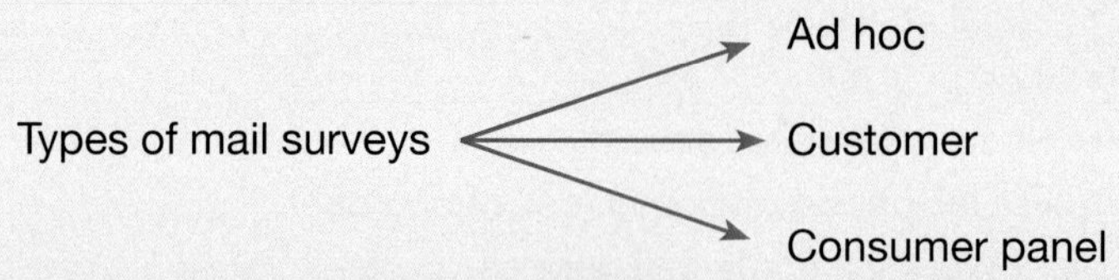

Advantages	Disadvantages
• Higher response rates	• Cost
• Confidential	• Time for completion
• Sensitive material	• Don't know who is completing it
• Eliminates interviewer error	• Not able to offer clarification
• Convenient	
• Longer surveys with visuals	
• Representative of U.S. population	

FIGURE 6.11 Mail Survey Research

6.5b Mail Surveys

Mail survey research has been around a long time, but, just like telephone research, has declined in recent years for a variety of reasons. As shown in **Figure 6.11**, mail survey research can be divided into three types. Ad hoc surveys are sent to individuals at random or through some type of selection process from a database. The individuals have not been notified in advance. They may have been selected from a database based on a demographic or psychographic profile requested by the client. Other than meeting the pre-determined criteria, nothing else is known about the individual receiving the survey. Of the three forms of mail surveys, ad-hoc surveys have the lowest response rates. Most ad-hoc surveys have been replaced by online surveys or mixed methods research which may use some combination of online, telephone, mobile, and mail.

The second type of mail survey is with a firm's customers. Normally, these surveys are sent by marketing research firms, but they are mailed to specific individuals who have purchased a particular brand. Companies like to use surveys to follow up on purchases to learn more about who purchased the product and why. They may also survey individuals one, two, or even more years after the initial purchase to gauge the level of satisfaction and to evaluate any difficulties with the product or need for repair. This information is especially important in making product changes and discovering weak parts or defective areas. It also serves as a reminder that it may be time to make another purchase or trade the old product in for a new one. The last type of mail survey is sent to consumer panels. These are individuals who have agreed to participate in research studies. They are either paid a small fee for participating or their names are put into a lottery for a gift card or some other prize that is given to participants on a random basis. Consumer panels vary across research firms, but participating in three or four studies per year is common.

As indicated in Figure 6.11, mail survey research has some specific advantages and disadvantages. For many years mail surveys were plagued by low response rates. Lately, response rates have increased, with rules of thumb for a "good response rate" ranging from 15 percent for a single survey mailing, to between 30 and 40 percent for a series of mailings including a pre-notification postcard, survey mailing with incentive, and a follow-survey or reminder.[26] Numerous factors influence the response rate, including the type of mail survey, the use of incentives, whether prenotification and reminders are used, personalization, and additional factors listed in **Figure 6.12**. All things being equal, ad hoc studies have the lowest response rates, while rates are higher for customer surveys. The challenge, however, with customer surveys is that customers who have had a positive experience and those who have had a negative experience will be most likely to complete

- Teaser on the outside of the envelope to encourage individuals to open the letter
- Pre-notification letter or postcard before the survey
- Incentives
  - Unconditional incentive regardless of whether survey is completed (based on reciprocity and guilt)
  - Non-monetary incentives such as prizes through a lottery
- Provide opportunity to see results (online)
- Send second copy of questionnaire to non-respondents
- University or non-profit sponsorship of the survey
- Provide a stamped and preaddressed return envelope
- Send reminder postcard

FIGURE 6.12 Suggestions for Improving Mail Surveys
Source: Adapted from Neil G. Connon, "Improving Postal Questionnaire Response Rates," *The Marketing Review*, Vol. 8, No. 2, 2008, pp. 113–134.

the survey. Since the product or experience was neither good nor bad, those who are neutral often feel there is nothing worthwhile to report in a survey and typically don't participate. Finally, because panel participants have agreed in advance to participate in surveys, the response rate for this type of mail survey is the highest.

A second major advantage of mail surveys is confidentiality. Respondents can answer questions in the privacy of their homes and without any interviewers present in person or on the telephone. This allows for survey questions involving sensitive or potentially embarrassing topics that individuals would otherwise find difficult to answer in the presence of an interviewer, and eliminates interview error. Because the respondent can complete the survey any time that is convenient, it allows for longer surveys. Unlike telephone surveys, visuals can be sent in the mail or placed on a website that individuals can view before or during the survey. Finally, mail surveys have the potential to be representative of the U.S. population as a whole as mail is delivered to over 159 million addresses. Not everyone uses the Internet, and the difficulties with telephone survey samples have been previously discussed.

Despite these advantages only 1 percent of the money invested in surveys by U.S. market researchers during 2018 was specifically spent on mail surveys.[27] Mail surveys are very expensive, due to postage, paper, envelopes, incentives, and labor costs related to entering data into the analysis software. Also, researchers typically send pre-notification postcards, a second survey mailing, and a reminder postcard, adding more postage and paper costs. Finally, firms must send more surveys then they expect to have returned, based on the anticipated response rate. For example, if a research firm expected a 33 percent response rate, and sought a final sample size of 1,000, a total of 3,000 surveys would need to be mailed with each containing an incentive ranging from $1 to $5, though a lottery option might be substituted instead. Of course the study would also require 3,000 pre-notification letters or postcards, a second survey mailing (without an additional incentive), and potentially a final mailing of postcard reminders. The number of surveys and postcards sent after the first mailing would depend upon whether or not the returned surveys were truly anonymous. If they could not be matched with specific addresses, then each household would require a repeat mailing, even if they had previously answered the survey. The vast majority of these costs evaporate when online and mobile surveys are used in place of mail.

Mail survey studies also take much longer to complete, particularly when compared to online and mobile surveys. They take longer to analyze than do other forms of research, as the data must be transferred from questionnaires into the data analysis program. The longer time to completion is a serious disadvantage, as clients today expect research results and insights more quickly than ever before. When time is of the essence, mail surveys are a poor choice.

Another problem with mail surveys is that the researcher doesn't really know who is completing it, even if it is addressed to a specific person. A spouse, significant other, roommate, or even a child might complete the survey and mail it back. Researchers have to rely on the honesty of individuals that the demographic information provided and the responses given are indeed the responses of the individual and not of someone else.

Lastly, mail surveys offer no opportunity for clarification of a question. With telephone and personal interview surveys, explanations can be given. While doing so can possibly bias the response, it is often better than an individual guessing at what they think a question means. In instances where the question is not understood, measurement instrument error occurs, but the researcher has no idea it is present. They assume if a question has a response, that the respondent fully understood what was being asked.

6.5c Personal Interviews and Intercept Studies

Personal interviews can be used to conduct survey research. The questionnaire might be given to the respondent to complete with the interviewer nearby ready to answer questions or provide information, or the interviewer can read the questions and record the respondent's answers. The personal interview can occur in respondents' homes, at respondents' businesses, at a client's business or at some neutral location. When the latter is used, quite often research companies will use an intercept approach where they intercept individuals at random, or according to a sampling plan. Intercept studies pertaining to special events such as county fairs, sporting events, and tourist sites are commonly used to assess economic impact and customer satisfaction, though they can also be used for other purposes. **Computer-assisted personal interviewing (CAPI)** allows the interviewer or respondent to record the answers to questions on an electronic device, such as a phone, tablet or laptop during a face-to-face interview. CAPI is commonly used in many forms of Intercept Studies.

Computer-assisted personal interviewing (CAPI) allows the interviewer or respondent to record the answers to questions on an electronic device, such as a phone, tablet, or laptop, during a face-to-face interview.

The advantages and disadvantages of personal interview and intercept studies are shown in Figure 6.13. Because the interviewer is present when the questionnaire is completed, there is an opportunity to clarify questions or instructions. This can occur even when respondents are completing the questionnaire on their own. Interviewer presence can also reduce non-response to particular questions by offering explanations, clarifications of the question, or relating why it is important. With self-administered questionnaires, the interviewer can examine the completed survey prior to the respondent leaving to ensure all of the questions have been answered. CAPI interviews completed by respondents can be programmed to require answers to key questions. As a result, personal interviews and intercept surveys tend to have the highest percentage of completed answers.

In most cases, personal interviews allow for longer surveys than would be possible with the telephone, the Internet, mobile and other electronic modes. The only possible exception might be mail surveys. But, the problem with mail surveys is that if the respondent thinks a survey is too long they are likely to quit and never finish. With personal interviews, respondents can often be encouraged to answer just a few more questions.

Visual aids can be used. It may be something as simple as a print advertisement, or as large as an automobile. It is even possible to have short demonstrations or to show a short

Advantages	Disadvantages
• Question clarification • Lower item non-response • More complete answers • Longer interviews • Visual aids • Higher participation	• Mall intercepts are not representative • Lack of respondent anonymity • Poor for sensitive topics • Interviewer bias • Higher costs

FIGURE 6.13 Advantages | Disadvantages of Personal Interviews

video or television commercial. Personal interviews offer the researcher considerable latitude in the types of visuals that can be used.

Because the interviewer asks individuals to participate, the response rate is higher. It is more difficult for someone to say "no" when they are confronted in person by the interviewer than when contacted by phone or mail. The one exception may be at malls, where individuals are busy shopping and do not want to take time for a survey, especially a lengthy survey. Mall intercepts have largely fallen out of favor because mall shoppers are not representative of those who live in a given area, and results cannot be generalized beyond the population of shoppers for the particular mall where the study took place.

A primary drawback of personal interviews is that the respondent is not anonymous. The interviewer knows who he or she is, and often names, email addresses, or other personally identifiable information are recorded as part of the survey. While answers can be confidential, respondents may not feel comfortable providing honest answers to all of the questions on the survey. This happens more for surveys that are read by the interviewer than for those that are self-administered. Sensitive topics or potentially embarrassing questions are difficult to administer with personal interviews. Individuals will either become embarrassed or give socially acceptable answers rather than their true feelings.

Another concern that has already been discussed is interviewer bias, especially if the interviewer conducts the survey. Tone of voice, body language, and other characteristics of the interviewer can influence a respondent's answers. Even with training and supervision, it is difficult for the interviewer not to display reactions to respondent answers. Self-administered surveys that the interviewer collects and reviews are less subject to interviewer influence.

The last disadvantage of personal interviews and intercept studies is cost. Individuals must be hired and trained to conduct the research. Because of the personal nature of the interviews, only one interview can be conducted at a time, and if the interviewer reads the questions, it normally takes longer than if it is self-administered. Coding and analyzing the data can also be costly, particularly if some questions require open-ended responses.

6.5d Online Surveys

Online survey research is now the leading survey research methodology, primarily because it is faster and cheaper than any of the alternatives. According to the U.S. Census Bureau, approximately 85 percent of the U.S. population now has access to the Internet from their home,[28] while a greater percentage has access through their workplace and public institutions. In fact, the United States' Internet penetration rate of 95 percent as of early 2019 was matched only by Northern Europe.[29] In the U.S., smartphone ownership is on the rise, with the Pew Research Center reporting that 81 percent of Americans owned a smartphone in 2019, a drastic increase from the 35 percent who reported ownership in 2011. Smartphones are so prevalent that 37 percent of U.S. adults reported using their phone as their primary means of connecting to the Internet, though percentages among age groups varied dramatically as illustrated in **Figure 6.14**.[30] Still, it is clear that all ages are increasingly using smartphones as their primary means to access the Internet. This has important implications for mobile research, a topic that will discussed later in the chapter.

Online surveys can be conducted in a variety of ways, as indicated in **Figure 6.15**. The survey can be placed on a website and visitors to the site can be asked to complete it. Surveys can be sent through an e-mail, though this is rare now, or a web link can be provided in an email that will take individuals to the survey. Social networking sites such as Twitter or Facebook can also be used to conduct research or to recruit participants for online studies. Survey research can be conducted through mobile devices such as smartphones and tablets, which allow researchers to utilize voice and texting in addition to a web link. Finally, market research online communities (MROCs) can used with caution for some forms of survey research.

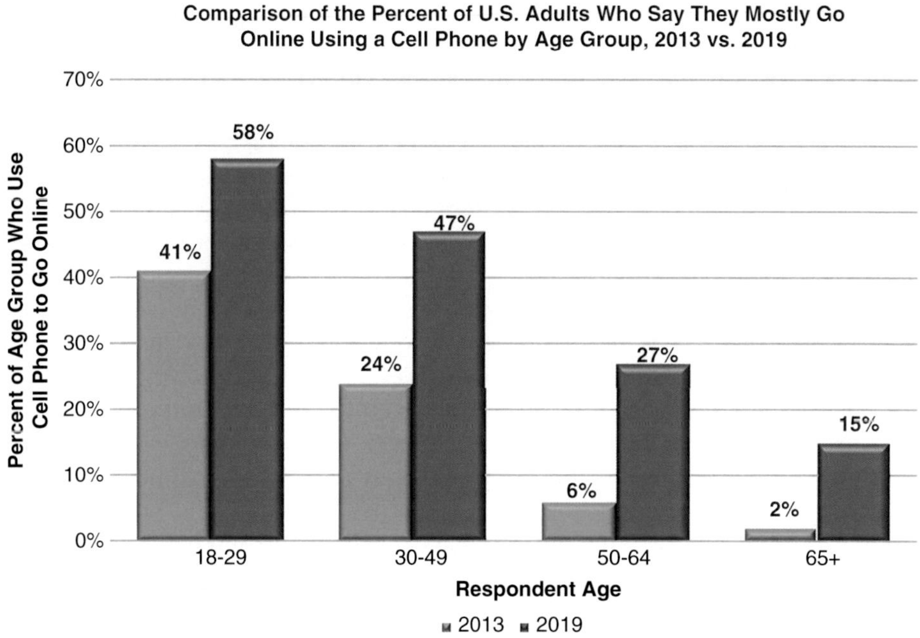

FIGURE 6.14 A Clustered Bar Chart Comparing the Percent of U.S. Adults Who Say They Mostly Go Online Using a Cell Phone by Age Group, 2013 vs. 2019

Source: Adapted from Monica Anderson, "Mobile Technology and Home Broadband 2019," (pewinternet.org), June13, 2019, retrieved on August 21, 2019 from https://www.pewinternet.org/2019/06/13/mobile-technology-and-home-broadband-2019/.

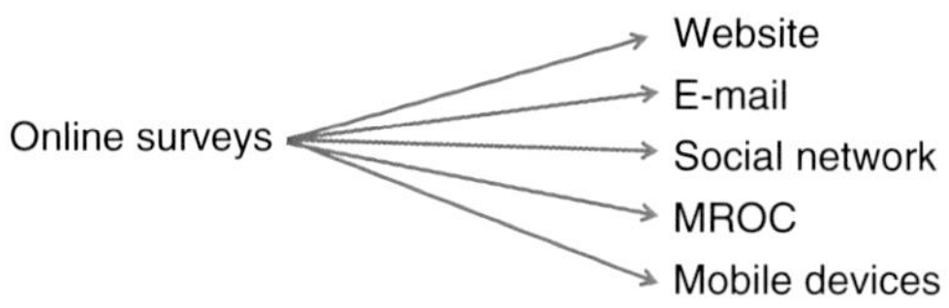

FIGURE 6.15 Types of Online Surveys

Advantages of Online Research Online research has a number of advantages and disadvantages, as shown in Figure 6.16. As cited earlier, individuals enjoy a high level of access to the Internet and that number continues to grow each year. Lower costs and the speed of survey completion are major advantages, as the majority of online surveys are answered within 24 hours of the invitation receipt. Thousands of email surveys can be sent to potential respondents simultaneously (though it is often better to batch email surveys to avoid spam filters that flag mass emails). Surveys can be completed in just days or even hours in some cases at a very low cost. Results are almost in real-time. This is particularly true when mobile surveys are used for "in-the-moment" research studies that respondents participate in while they are completing a task or shopping. Another advantage is that researchers do not have to wait until all of the surveys are received to tabulate results. Specialized survey software instantly transforms responses into spreadsheets and graphs so at any time researchers can examine the results. Survey software also minimizes item non-response by forcing subjects to answer key questions before they can go to the next question.

The web allows for more sophisticated surveys as well as the use of visuals. Videos, 3-D images, and virtual illustrations can be used with online surveys. Realistic and complex visuals can illustrate various features of a product or marketing materials. Tasks

Advantages	Disadvantages
• High level of accessibility • Lower costs • Speed • Real-time results • Personalization • More sophisticated surveys • Use of visuals	• Location of respondent • Sample representativeness • Data quality • Spam and clutter • Panel member response bias • Hardware/software capabilities • Screen size adaptation • Respondents take surveys on device of their choice

FIGURE 6.16 Advantages | Disadvantages of Online Research

that would be difficult to do with other survey modes can be programmed into an online survey.

Two techniques available with online surveys are piping and branching. **Piping** occurs when the answer to one question is incorporated into the text of sequential questions. For instance, a question might ask a respondent to select their favorite restaurant from a drop down menu. If "Olive Garden" is selected, that answer can be piped into a subsequent question, such as "How would you rate Olive Garden's restaurant on the following characteristics?"

Piping occurs in online surveys when the answer to one question is incorporated into the text of sequential questions.

Branching is the process whereby the answer to a multiple-choice question indicates the next survey question to be asked. Responses to branching questions automatically route the survey software to the appropriate next question. For instance, if a respondent says the majority of their clothes are purchased at boutiques, then a series of questions about clothing boutiques would appear. If the respondent chooses department stores instead, then the questions would relate to department stores.

Branching a process by which the answer to a multiple-choice question indicates the next survey question to be asked.

Branching questions can be used to screen out those who should not answer the survey, and also allows for non-relevant questions to be skipped entirely. For example, if respondent says price is not important in the decision process, then questions about pricing can be skipped entirely. Branching can allow researchers to word questions that match a person's purchase behavior, gender, or other characteristics. The language and tone of a question used with teens answering a survey can be different from those used with retirees. Thus an age question asked near the beginning of the survey could be used to customize the survey as appropriate.

Disadvantages of Online Research Although online research offers a number of advantages, it does have some disadvantages. First is in identifying the location of the respondent. If the respondent is using a computer, the location can be identified through the IP address. However, if a mobile device is being used, it becomes more difficult. In addition, the person might live in Ohio but be in Florida attending college, working, or just on vacation when the survey is completed.

There is some concern about how representative online survey respondents are of the population in general. This concern has diminished in recent years as more people gain access to the Internet. Still, if results are to be generalized to the population as a whole, telephone or mail surveys can be used to supplement online surveys.

Another concern is that many online researchers rely on volunteers to complete the survey, or they utilize an online panel. While the general population is becoming less willing to complete online surveys, a small percentage of individuals have become "professional respondents," completing surveys for a number of different research firms and organizations. Because these individuals are paid or rewarded in some manner for completing surveys, they might complete as many as 15 to 20 a month.

It should be pointed out that not all professional respondents are bad. Some individuals like giving their opinion. They are thoughtful and take time to answer questions carefully. They only respond to surveys on topics where they are knowledgeable. While these individuals might be called professional respondents because they participate in multiple surveys, their motivation is different. It is not to earn credits, prizes, or money. It is to share their opinion on various topics. They also tend to answer fewer surveys than other professional respondents, perhaps only one or two per month.[31]

The greater concern relates to "negative" professional respondents who answer surveys simply for the rewards. Often these individuals will create fake personas to maximize the likelihood of passing screener questions, and thus increase the probability they will be chosen to respond to surveys. The speed of data collection and the rise of the negative professional respondents have led to another concern—data quality. The less time individuals spend in completing a survey, usually the poorer the data quality. Respondents will answer questions without thoroughly reading the question and without spending time thinking about the best response. The rate of honest or random errors will also increase where respondents mark the wrong answer, not on purpose but because they rush through the survey. For those negative professional respondents who do 15 to 20 surveys a month, quality of data is a major concern because the individual's goal often is to complete the survey, not to provide valuable data for the research study.

Research companies and data collection firms, such as Research Now and ReRez, have methods in place to check data quality. Computer programs can check for "straight liners." These are individuals that just go down a survey and answer "C" or some other response for all of the questions. The program also checks for "speeders," individuals who take only five minutes to answer a survey that should take 30. Leaving the survey open for 30 minutes just to make it appear that it took that long, when the person only spent five minutes checking responses, can also be detected because it will look at actual time spent between clicking various responses. Questionnaires will also have feedback or check questions called "traps" that have obvious wrong answers and may have nothing to do with the survey just to see if the person is even reading the question. Other forms of quality control questions include completion checks for open-ended questions, grid checks in which respondents are told to select a particular answer, and fake brand names inserted into awareness questions. Researchers can use IP address location checking and digital fingerprinting to identify respondents with multiple registrations using fake identities and profiles, and ID verification at the time of registration with the panel. Most research panels have a policy of "Three strikes and you're out" in an attempt to eliminate the bad professional respondent. [32]

In an effort to better understand the types of people who exhibit these characteristics, MarketTools conducted multiple comprehensive studies with large data sets to identify these "unengaged" negative professional respondents. Their findings indicate that they tend to be males, primarily between the ages of 25–44, though those most likely to be chronically disengaged are 35 or younger. Disturbingly, these professional respondents are more likely to select the "definitely would buy" response for a purchase intent question than are engaged respondents, and also rate the quality of the survey higher, thus skewing the data. Most unengaged professsional respondents select neutral answers when asked attitudinal questions, though there is a subset that habitually selects the most positive answer. All of these issues negatively affect the quality of data.[33]

Despite concerns about data quality, research studies have shown that *qualitative data* obtained through online surveys is comparable to data obtained from telephone and mail surveys.[34] Similar studies have validated the quality of the data.[35] Obtaining quality data requires careful attention to research design, the research process, and the sample selection. Such attention will increase costs, but greatly increases the usability of the data.

Spam and online clutter has increased, which has had a negative impact on people participating in ad hoc online survey research. Just as with the other survey alternatives, it is becoming more difficult to obtain a good sample of respondents from the general population. As a result, companies are increasingly using third party or specialist research panels and firms that have built large consumer and business-to-business research panels. While this practice encourages higher response rates, it may also result in response bias if those who participate in panels are systematically different from those who do not.

Because of smartphones and various forms of computer Internet connections, hardware and software capabilities vary widely. Some individuals have high-speed Internet connections; others must rely on satellite or phone connections. Also, software and hardware varies widely. If videos, visuals, and other more sophisticated aids are used, not all Internet users will be able to view the materials because of older computers that lack memory or video cards. Differences in screen size are of particular importance, as answering grid-based questions becomes very difficult on smartphones. Research has shown that respondents will take a survey on the device of their choosing, even when specifically told to use a particular device, such as a computer.[36] Surveys that are not specifically designed for mobile devices, or optimized for mobile suffer from lower response rates due to their inability to adapt the questionnaire format to the smaller screen size.

Advantages of Mobile Device Currently, surveys designed specifically for mobile devices are the second most heavily used quantitative research method, behind only online surveys[37] and mobile survey usage will only increase over time. With the growth in mobile devices, the percent of online respondents attempting to answer a website-based online survey on their mobile device has increased from 6.7 percent in 2011 to 35 percent or more, according to FocusVision, as of 2016,[38] and the growth rate shows no sign of abating. Research has indicated that tablets are more likely to be used at home when answering surveys than are laptops or computers.[39]

The ability to receive and *send* pictures and videos as answers to questions is a key advantage of mobile devices, particularly for research conducted "in-the-moment" such as while shopping in the store. Photos and videos not only provide richer data for the researcher, they also are more engaging tasks for respondents and help to reduce the likelihood that they will abandon the survey. Mobile's ability to integrate barcode scanning into survey responses is invaluable for studying purchasing behavior and helps to minimize memory errors, leading to higher data quality for "in-the-moment" studies.[40] Time and date stamps with mobile devices allows for tracking of results and tracking when each question was answered. Researchers can use GPS to identify the location of the respondent, if the respondent grants permission. More important, GPS allows researchers to target and intercept respondents based on location.[41] While responses are confidential, respondents can choose to be anonymous by hiding their personal data in the results database. If participants do not respond, a reminder can be sent via a text message, email, or phone call.[42]

One of the major advantages of mobile research is speed of responses. Tests by Lightspeed Research with their mobile panel found that 60 percent of the usable, completed surveys were returned within 15 minutes of distribution and 90 percent were returned within an hour. Fly Research had similar response rates. Approximately 85 percent of surveys are completed and returned within two hours with its 18–25-year-old mobile panel.[43] Multiple studies have found that the speed of response to mobile surveys surpasses even that of online computer surveys.[44]

Another unique aspect of mobile research is that individuals are more likely to respond to "private, personal, or sensitive" questions on a cell phone or tablet than in telephone or personal interviews. They are also happy to send photographs or videos of themselves, brands, events, advertisements, in-store displays, and other phenomena. Because smartphones and tablets are viewed as personal devices by consumers, they are willing to provide these more intimate thoughts and views of personal situations, which allows researchers a deeper understanding of consumer behavior than is possible with the other survey methods.[45]

Disadvantages of Mobile Devices In terms of mobile phones, screen size is the root cause of most disadvantages because it can affect response rates, time needed to complete the survey, respondent satisfaction with the survey process, and data quality. Figure 6.17 summarizes the advantages and disadvantages of using mobile devices for research.

Advantages	Disadvantages
• "In the moment" studies – Send/receive images/bar codes – Richer data – Higher respondent engagement – Better data quality • Tracking time/location • Location-based targeting • Fastest response time • Respond to sensitive questions	• Screen size – Task difficulty – Completion time – Survey abandonment • Short survey length • Most mobile surveys are completed at home

FIGURE 6.17 Advantages | Disadvantages of Mobile Devices

Mobile users value speed and ease of use. Surveys that are simply smaller versions of a traditional web page are unfriendly to mobile users, and often require scrolling both horizontally and vertically to read page content. Respondents answering a grid scale question with seven responses could easily forget to scroll, and thus base their answer on five categories instead of seven, damaging data quality. The small font size and tiny selection buttons are difficult to read or select, requiring respondents to zoom in on these elements or risk selecting the wrong answer. Grid-type questions are particularly difficult for respondents to answer. By contrast, mobile optimized surveys render properly on different screen sizes. Text and selection elements are large and easy to read or use while horizontal scrolling is eliminated. Unnecessary elements are eliminated to optimize survey layout. Finally, grid questions are shown as multiple single answer questions on a smartphone, while those taking a survey on a tablet or PC see the traditional grid format.[46] The need to break down grid questions in this manner limits the number of questions that can be asked in mobile-optimized surveys, as responding to grids using computers is typically faster than responding to individual questions on smartphones (requiring individual page loads and reiteration of the basic question). To determine how survey design affected respondent behavior, SSI sampled 1,869 mobile phone respondents, 1,435 tablet respondents, and 2,197 laptop/desktop respondents. The results are shown in Figure 6.18. Using mobile-optimized surveys increased response rates among smartphone and tablet users, as fewer individuals quit the survey before finishing. The time needed to complete the survey also declined for smartphone and tablet users, while respondents to the mobile-optimized survey were more satisfied with the survey experience compared to those who answered the mobile unfriendly version. Interestingly, data quality did not significantly differ by device used to answer the survey.[47]

Today, many firms have moved beyond mobile-optimized surveys and now practice mobile-first design. The details of mobile-first survey design are discussed later in Chapter 11, but as the name suggests, it involves improving the mobile respondent's survey experience and putting their needs first to reduce manual effort, limit cognitive effort (without compromising the research purpose), and make the survey motivating.[48]

Additional studies have confirmed that time is a precious commodity for mobile participants and surveys must be short. Ideally, the completion time for mobile surveys should be 10 minutes or less, according to a presentation made to the Advertising Research Foundation.[49] This is especially true for surveys targeting Millennial respondents. A sharp break-off (or survey abandonment) rate was noted at the 13-minute mark when custom research studies conducted over the past two years were analyzed by research firm YPulse, Inc. The fact that studies were conducted among panel members who had agreed in advance to participate in research underscores the importance of keeping mobile surveys short.[50]

Survey Abandonment

Type of Survey	Mobile Unfriendly	Mobile Optimized
Mobile phone	21%	11%
Tablet	9%	7%
Laptop / Desktop	4%	4%

Length of Interview

Type of Survey	Mobile Unfriendly	Mobile Optimized
Mobile phone	13.25 minutes	10.99minutes
Tablet	10.15 minutes	9.60 minutes
Laptop / Desktop	7.02 minutes	7.02 minutes

Satisfaction with Survey Experience

Type of Survey	Mobile Unfriendly	Mobile Optimized
Not satisfied	4%	1%
Somewhat satisfied	35%	24%
Satisfied	61%	74%

FIGURE 6.18 Itemizing the Impact of Survey Design on Respondents' Behaviors for Mobile Unfriendly and Mobile Optimized Surveys
Source: Adapted from Nicole Mitchell, "When it comes to mobile respondent experience and data quality, survey design matters," *Quirk's Marketing Research Review*, (www.quirks.com), August 2014, Article ID 20140825-3.

Finally, there is evidence to suggest that mobile may not be living up to its potential with regard to "in-the-moment" research studies. Multiple studies have found that the majority of mobile surveys are completed at home. More troubling, one study related to purchase behavior discovered that what should have been "in-the-moment" mobile surveys were actually completed at a location other than the store.[51] Fortunately, GPS, geofencing, and time and date stamps can be used to weed out responses that are not taking place on-site or "in-the-moment."

Advantages of MROCs Many companies have developed marketing research online communities composed of customers who are highly engaged with the brand. While these communities are most often used for qualitative research purposes, some companies do undertake quantitative research studies on a regular and systematic basis. The advantages and disadvantages of using MROCs are displayed in Figure 6.19. Engaged customers can provide valuable feedback on many brand topics, including product ideation and co-creation, new product concept validation, product feature development, service improvement, marketing communications campaign refinement, and strategy definition and refinement.[52]

Once a MROC is in place, research studies can be quickly deployed as the sample recruitment phase is eliminated, saving both time and money. This allows for on-demand data collection, with one source indicating that data are collected at a tenth of the cost of traditional online surveys, and in half of the time.

MROC members typically fill out a profile sheet when they first opt-in to joining the community. The data profile contains a variety of demographic information and other data that can be linked to survey responses to provide an in-depth understanding of customers' relationships with a brand or firm. A business can collect data at key times during the customer's lifecycle, such as after a brand has suffered negative publicity, or after

Advantages	Disadvantages
• Engaged customer based familiar with brand • Valuable feedback on many topics • Less costly, faster deployment • In-depth understanding of customer/ brand relationship • Discover key insights	• Not representative of the population • Cost • Ongoing commitment and communication • Not useful for certain types of research topics

FIGURE 6.19 Advantages and Disadvantages of MROCs

launching a new product. Studying the collective interactions and experiences of loyal consumers assists marketers in finding insights that can help in building true consumer advocates. It can also undercover problems that are eroding core customers.

Disadvantages of MROCs While commonly used for qualitative research, many firms shy away from MROCs as a quantitative sample frame because they are neither representative of the general population, nor the brand's consumers. MROC members self-select to join the group, and research has shown that their perceptions are positively skewed toward the firm, indicating response bias. Some businesses have methods of adjusting for this bias and take it into account when interpreting the data. But attempting to generalize the results beyond the population of current customers would likely result in substantial sampling error.[53] Building and maintaining a MROC can be costly. The software is generally based off a licensed cloud-based SaaS technology that requires ongoing subscription fees. Different "modules" within the MROC, such as forums, surveys, and other features, require additional expenses, and the initial costs of panel member recruitment are substantial. Incentives are generally required to reward panel members as well.

MROCs require a level of commitment that many firms are not willing to provide. Regular communication with MROC members is necessary, as they want to know what actions have been taken as a result of their feedback. Regular surveys that offer interesting topics help keep panel members engaged, and a well-run MROC uses more than just surveys to collect data, as was discussed in Chapter 4.

Finally, there are certain types of research that would be inappropriate to collect from a MROC-based sample, including any form of research that requires random probability-based sampling. Institutional program evaluation, forecasting or demand estimation, awareness tracking, or attempts to collect performance metrics are also inappropriate topics of research.

6.5e Mixed Modes

For some research studies, using multiple modes provides better results. For instance, using both land line telephones and cell phones can increase the response rate and ensure the sample is more representative of the U.S. population. With online research, multiple forms may be used combining the posting of a survey on a firm's website with e-mailing a link to individuals in its database. The government commonly mixes modes to ensure an adequate representation of the population. For example, the 2020 census data collection methodology involved first sending a postcard to all verified home addresses with an invitation to complete the census online using the device of the respondent's choice. Online surveys were optimized for mobile devices to help maximize completion rates. Paper questionnaires with prepaid reply envelopes were mailed to areas of the country with low Internet penetration rates or poor bandwidth, as well as to those individuals who do not respond to the initial postcard mailing. Individuals also had the option to telephone a number and answer the survey over the phone by interacting with a call center representative.

The final phase of data collection involved fieldwork by census interviewers who visited households and conducted personal interviewers among those who did not respond to other methods, or who could otherwise not be reached. Throughout the data collection period, a variety of ads in many different media encouraged people to complete the census and provided information on how to do so.[54]

Source: Fotazdymak/Shutterstock.

Coca-Cola utilized a mixed mode approach to track emotional responses to its products in retail stores and its advertisements.

Coca-Cola utilized a mixed mode approach to track emotional responses to its products in retail stores and its advertisements. The first stage of the research involved online questionnaires designed to understand an individual's relationships with various brands. The second stage used mobile phones. Individuals were asked to text whenever they came into contact with one of the brands indicated in the first stage of the research. The individual was to text where they saw the brand, how they felt about the venue or medium where it was displayed, and how it influenced their purchase decision. By using mobile phones, Coca-Cola was able to collect data in real time, at the touch-point when it occurred. Respondents did not have to rely on memory. Many of the respondents attached photos to their messages, and GPS technology allowed the researchers to identify the location where the interaction occurred.

6.6 Survey Selection Considerations

LEARNING OBJECTIVE 6.5
Discuss each of the survey selection considerations as they apply to the various data collection alternatives.

A number of factors must be considered when deciding which survey alternative to use. These factors are highlighted in Figure 6.20. In discussing these factors, it is important to know that they are interrelated, and a decision on one factor will affect other factors. None can be considered in isolation.

6.6a Budget, Time Frame, and Precision

The level of data precision or accuracy that is desired is inversely related to the research budget and the time frame. The greater the desired precision, the more costly the research and the longer it will take to collect the data. If a company is in a time crunch to make a decision and needs data quickly, it will sacrifice precision and accuracy. The type of decision to be made and the monetary value connected with that decision will largely determine the level of precision that is needed. Decisions involving millions of dollars will require much greater accuracy than decisions that involve thousands of dollars.

In terms of the survey research methods, the level of precision or accuracy is determined more by research design, costs, time frame, and the research process than it is by the data collection method. All of the alternatives, from telephone to the Internet, can provide high quality data if careful attention is paid to the research design and its

- Cost
- Time frame
- Level of precision or accuracy
- Questionnaire length
- Questionnaire structure
- Incidence rate
- Sample characteristics

FIGURE 6.20 Survey Selection Considerations

implementation. Alternatively, poor quality data is often obtained when corners are cut to save money and time, or the research design is poorly developed or not followed.

Because companies have finite budgets for research, cost is an important consideration. Costs can vary widely within each data collection alternative depending on the depth of the research design, the desired sample size, and the time frame for the study. Increasing sample size increases costs and also lengthens the time frame for the study. So does developing a comprehensive research design that has a large number of steps to ensure low systematic error.

Of the different modes for survey data collection, the least costly tends to be online research, especially online panels. The major costs for an online survey are hosting the survey questionnaire, survey design, and data tabulation. Sending out thousands of e-mails with a survey attached or survey link is no more costly than sending out hundreds. Mobile surveys are slightly more expensive because administration may require the creation of a special app, or because of programming costs associated with optimizing the survey design or creating a mobile first design.

The most expensive methodology on a per contact basis are personal interviews and intercepts. Interviewers can do only one interview at a time, which limits the number of interviews that a single individual can do within a specified time frame. Most research involving personal interviews and intercepts will have multiple interviewers. So in addition to the cost of the interviewers, there are additional costs for training, supervision, and travel. The costs are only slightly reduced if the questionnaires are given to respondents for self-administration.

Telephone interviews tend to fall in the middle in terms of costs. With land line survey research, interviewers are required to read the questions. However, the system is computerized and the automatic dialing increases the number of interviews that can be conducted per hour. Data is automatically recorded into the computer, saving the data recording process required for personal interviews and mail surveys.

Costs for cell phone research vary depending on how it is conducted and the length of the survey questionnaire. Text surveys can be pre-typed and sent to potential respondents, thousands at a time, very much like e-mail. Additional costs may be incurred if visuals, videos, or photos are used as part of the research study and need to be mailed in advance. Personal interviewing on cell phones would require the same costs as land line telephone surveys, with the exception of travel.

Mail surveys tend to be more costly than telephone primarily because of the high non-response rate and the cost of materials, labor, and incentives. Each survey questionnaire has to be mailed, which requires postage. Often, sample names are purchased from a database research firm, which adds to the costs. Also, return postage is either pre-paid or stamps are placed on return envelopes. Labor costs are incurred in the envelope stuffing process and then in coding and recording the data into a spreadsheet. While mail surveys can be used to generate a larger sample than personal interviews, they are still very costly to field.

The time frame allotted for a study can affect which one is used. Tablets, smartphones, and cell phones tend to have very quick response rates. Online surveys also are fast, with most responses coming with 48 hours of posting either online or in an e-mail. The slowest method is mail since research firms have no control over when individuals complete the survey and mail it back. Responses will often trickle in for weeks after the initial mailing. In addition, firms often send a follow-up letter or second wave mailing to individuals who have not responded, which lengthens the amount of time to complete the study.

6.6b Questionnaire Length and Structure

Questionnaire length and questionnaire structure are important considerations when choosing the best survey method. Mail surveys are good for long questionnaires. In some cases personal interviews can also work well for long questionnaires. Telephone surveys cannot be as long and mobile surveys typically are even shorter, especially text surveys. Online surveys can vary greatly in length depending on the sample and how it is administered. However, if online surveys are too long respondents either stop reading the questionnaire thoroughly and just quickly fill in answers, quit taking the survey, or speed through it without giving any thought to what is being asked. One advantage to online surveys is that responses can be saved so that individuals who leave a survey before finishing it can return to the exact location where they left off.

Online surveys provide the greatest flexibility in terms of questionnaire structure. Branching and piping can be used. Videos, photos, and other visuals can be incorporated as part of the study. Other modes, such as mail and telephone, have less flexibility.

6.6c Incidence Rate

Another important factor is the **incidence** rate, which is the percentage of individuals, households, or businesses in the population that would be qualified as potential respondents in a particular study. Not everyone meets the criteria for a study. For instance, a firm may define as its population Chinese, Korean, Japanese, and Vietnamese immigrants who were born outside of the United States. The incidence rate for this type of study would be very low because only a small percentage of the population meets the criteria.

Incidence percentage of individuals, households, or businesses in the population that would be qualified as potential respondents in a particular study.

Researchers must search the population for individuals that meet the criteria set forth in the research design. Mail surveys typically have a high incidence rate since individuals are pre-screened based on mailing list characteristics and only individuals that meet the criteria are sent the questionnaire. The same can be true for telephone and mobile research, though not always.

The incidence rate for personal interviews and intercepts can be quite low depending on the method of selection. Using a shopping mall is convenient, but may not exactly meet the sample selection criteria for the study. To increase the incidence rate for personal interviews, pre-screening can be done. But, this process also increases the **search cost**, which is the cost to locate individuals that meet the sample criteria for a study.

Search costs costs associated with locating individuals that meet the sample criteria for a study.

The incidence rate for online research tends to be higher because respondents can be pre-screened through cookies, tracking software, or a series of qualifying questions. Cookies and tracking software can quickly exclude individuals that do not meet the requirements for the study. If these technologies cannot be used or are not available, then individuals can be asked questions prior to the research to determine if they qualify. If individuals are part of a research panel, then their profile can be used as means of selecting the correct respondents and those that meet the research sample criteria.

6.6d Sample Characteristics

The selection of the survey method may be affected by the characteristics of the desired sample. For example, the 65 and older age bracket is growing at a fast rate, and represents a major market for health care products. Using an online survey as the sole form of data collection would be unwise, as Pew Research reports that nearly a quarter of this senior-aged group does not use the Internet. Some have health issues that make reading a screen difficult, or chronic arthritis that limits their mobility and usage of computers, tablets, or smart phones. Plus, many older adults simply don't trust that their information will be secure or anonymous on the Internet. A healthcare provider who limited data collection to the Internet would end up with a skewed sample. At a minimum, a mixed mode technique that also incorporated landline telephone sampling would be superior, as landline phones would reach many seniors who own their own homes. Telephone interviewing would also be helpful in determining whether or not respondents understood the questions.[55] Thus, in making a decision about the survey method, researchers must look at the sample characteristics and choose the method that will produce the most representative sample.

6.7 Global Concerns

Because of culture and language differences, systematic error is a greater concern with international marketing research. It is important to carefully plan the research to reduce sample design error, respondent error, and measurement error. Using native interviewers and translators is essential. Although an individual may be able to speak multiple languages, he or she is not likely to understand the nuances of the various cultures and common idioms used by each nationality and culture. For example, someone from Mexico can speak Spanish, but it is not the same Spanish that is spoken in Puerto Rico, Cuba, or Argentina. Idioms and meanings of words will vary, just as they do in English-speaking countries such as the United States and England.

In conducting a telephone or personal interview in the United States it is customary to use an assumptive approach. After saying hello, the interviewer will normally launch directly into the study's introduction and then move onto the first question. In some cultures, this approach would be considered rude and unacceptable. After saying hello, the interviewer is expected to engage in small talk before asking the interviewee for his or her cooperation.[56]

In Middle Eastern countries, it is important to understand the differences between the status of men and women, especially married women. Before interviewing a female, the interviewer must ask permission from the husband. It is also not unusual that, to be granted permission, the interviewer must also be female. For Orthodox Muslims, it would be unacceptable for a male interviewer to conduct an interview with a female respondent, especially a personal interview. It is also common for the male to be present during the interview process.

The types of visuals that can be used and even the types of questions that can be asked will vary across cultures. Again, in Middle Eastern countries visuals that display any type of sexual situation or even show affection between males and females would not be acceptable. Discussing personal sexual situations and even products related to sex or personal hygiene is often taboo.

Emerging markets create a special challenge for researchers, as data shows that landlines are often limited and desktop PCs are not widely available. While in the past, research has been conducted face-to-face, the growth in smartphone adoption and mobile Internet usage offers researchers a new venue to reach individuals in Latin America, Africa, other emerging markets. As many emerging markets have multiple languages and hundreds of regional dialects, using the most common languages in the specific region of study is critical. Short questionnaires of 15 or fewer questions that take 10 minutes or less to answer will maximize response rates. Photo and video sharing is not recommended, as the high cost of mobile data in emerging markets must be considered when asking respondents to complete these tasks. Mobile airtime credits are popular forms of compensation that often equate to around $ 0.50 for a short mobile survey.[57]

6.8 Marketing Research Statistics

All marketing research studies will have error. The goal is to minimize the error so that results obtained from a sample can be applied to the population being studied. This chapter's marketing research statistics examine the concepts of margin of error, confidence levels, and confidence intervals. One method of graphically showing confidence intervals is through a floating bar chart, which is illustrated in the Statistical Reporting section. The Dealing with Data section involves using SPSS to test for significance difference at different confidence levels and then calculating the confidence interval.

6.8a Statistics Review

Understanding the margin of error, confidence intervals, and the confidence level associated with research studies is critical to comprehending the accuracy of the results based on sample data. Many organizations use public opinion polls or surveys with "yes" and "no" or "approve" and "disapprove" type answers to track attitudes toward various issues. Gallup might track the percentage of people who approve or disapprove of the President's job performance on a weekly basis using a random telephone sample of over 3,500 adults. A Gallup report stated that, compared to the previous week, the President's job approval rating had declined from 50 percent to 46 percent. The article explained, "For results based on the total sample of national adults, one can say with 95 percent confidence that the maximum margin of sampling error is ± 2 percentage points."[58]

Margin of Error The margin of error determines how close the results obtained from a sample are compared to what you might find if you surveyed the entire population. In the case of the President's job approval rating, this means that the real approval rating of the U.S. population as a whole could have been anywhere between 44 percent (46 percent minus 2 percent margin of error) and 48 percent (46 percent plus 2 percent margin or error). Because the same margin of error characterizes all of Gallup's' Presidential job approval polls, it also means that the President's job approval rating may not have slipped at all! The 50 percent rating reported during the first week may have been two percent higher than what would have been found if Gallup had surveyed the entire population, while the 46 percent rating found during the second week (using a different random sample) might have underestimated the population's approval of the President by two percent.

Minimizing the level of sampling error associated with a research study can be critical, especially in instances in which opinions are fairly evenly divided. On the other hand, if a survey found that 85 percent of a sample answered "Yes" to a question while only 15 percent answered "No" or were undecided, a higher level of sampling error, such as ± 5%, or even ± 10% could still provide useful information.

Confidence Levels The Gallup poll stated that, "one can say with 95 percent confidence that the maximum margin of sampling error is ± 2 percentage points."[59] Confidence levels are best explained in the following manner. Suppose Gallup conducted a new study to determine the approval ratings (in percentage terms) of the President pertaining to his handling of 20 specific issues, such as the deficit, higher education funding, the economy, and so forth. At the 95 percent confidence level, one would expect that for 1 of the 20 questions (5 percent of the data), the percent of people who answered "yes" to that question would be *more* than the margin of error *away* from the true answer, which would only be found if the entire population was surveyed. Thus, the confidence level simply indicates the degree to which the researcher can be assured that the results obtained from sample data are truly representative of the population, and not due to random chance.

Confidence Intervals Confidence intervals estimate the range of values that are likely to include the true population value for a particular variable, at a given confidence level. In this regard, they are very similar to the margin of error. The difference is that confidence intervals are calculated for means, rather than proportions.

Suppose a local retailer was considering buying an ad package through the Fox affiliate for the upcoming NFL season. Though expensive, this would allow the retailer to run a 30 second commercial in the local market during each NFL game broadcast by Fox. The price of the ad campaign is contingent upon the local population watching, on average, fourteen NFL games a year. Figure 6.21 shows the results of a two-sample t-test using sample data gathered from shoppers in the local market.

The first table in Figure 6.18 demonstrates that the average number of professional football games watched in a year by the sample is 12.0052. The second table shows the results of the one-sample t-test using a 95 percent confidence level. The null hypothesis of equality being tested is that the population watches, on average, 14 NFL games a year. The number found under the Sig. (2-tailed) column indicates the exact probability the mean of the sample (12.00052) is equal to 14 in the population. The Sig. (2-tailed) value is .009, which is less than the alpha value of .05, indicating that the null hypothesis should

One-Sample Statistics

	N	Mean	Std. Deviation	Std. Error Mean
Number of professional football games watched in a year	573	12.0052	18.23281	.76169

One-Sample Statistics

	Test Value = 14					
					95% Confidence Interval of the Difference	
	t	df	Sig. (2-tailed)	Mean Difference	Lower	Upper
Number of professional football games watched in a year	–2.619	572	.009	–1.99476	–3.4908	–.4987

FIGURE 6.21 Results of One-Sample T-Test

be rejected. As a result, the retailer can be 95 percent confident that the true number of games watched by the population is *not* 14.

But what is the actual confidence interval? While SPSS does not provide the confidence interval, it can be computed by using the "Lower" and "Upper" columns of the 95 percent confidence interval of the difference. The difference between the test value of 14 and the sample mean of 12.0052 is –1.99476. The lower boundary of difference is 3.4908 and the upper boundary of difference is –0.4987. Subtracting these values from the test value of 14, respectively, yields a lower boundary of 10.5092 and an upper boundary of 13.5013. Thus, the researcher can be 95 percent confident the actual number of professional games watched is between 10.5 and 13.5, which is lower than the 14 that was stated in the hypothesis. Again, the null hypothesis can be rejected.

Thinking that race may well be related to the number of NFL games watched in the local market, a researcher can utilize an ANOVA analysis. Race is designated as the grouping variable. The results of this analysis are shown in Figure 6.22.

The null hypothesis being tested is that there is no difference in the mean number of NFL games watched by African-Americans, Caucasians, and people of other races. The tables shown in Figure 6.22 suggest that this is not the case, as the p-value found in the Sig. column of the second table is less than .05, indicating that the null hypothesis should be rejected. Of greater importance to the retailer though, are the numbers shown under the "lower boundary" and "upper boundary" columns of the 95 percent confidence interval of the mean. Unlike the one-sample t-test that listed the confidence interval of the difference (between the mean and test value), the column in the ANOVA table shows the actual confidence interval. Using this information, the retailer now realizes that he can be 95 percent confident that the true number of games watched by Caucasians in the population falls within the range of 11.4922 to 16.1065. When confidence intervals are desired for the means of different groups, ANOVA can be used.

If the main ANOVA test sig. value indicates that the null hypothesis of no difference should be rejected, the next step is to determine which groups differ significantly from one another. The ANOVA test is repeated, though this time a post-hoc comparison test is selected. Post-hoc tests compare each group individually against each other group to determine whether the numerical differences found in the sample means are likely to occur within the population. Figure 6.23 illustrates the results of a Duncan post-hoc comparison test.

Descriptive

Number of professional football games watched in a year

					95% Confidence Interval for Mean			
	N	Mean	Std. Deviation	Std. Error	Lower Bound	Upper Bound	Minimum	Maximum
African American	189	10.8360	16.45948	1.19725	8.4742	13.1978	.00	100.00
Caucasian	309	13.7994	20.61093	1.17251	11.4922	16.1065	.00	250.00
Other	71	7.1972	8.31800	.98717	5.2283	9.1660	.00	50.00
Total	569	11.9912	18.26598	.76575	10.4872	13.4953	.00	250.00

ANOVA

Number of professional football games watched in a year

	Sum of Squares	df	Mean Square	F	Sig.
Between Groups	2894.241	2	1447.121	4.389	.013
Within Groups	186616.715	566	329.712		
Total	189510.956	568			

FIGURE 6.22 Results of ANOVA Analysis

Number of Professional Football Games Watched in a Year

Duncan[a,b]

		Subset for alpha = 0.05	
Race	N	1	2
Other	71	7.1972	
African American	189	10.8360	10.8360
Caucasian	309		13.7994
Sig.		.103	.184

Means for groups in homogeneous subsets are displayed.

[a] Uses Harmonic Mean Sample Size = 132.674

[b] The group sizes are unequal. The harmonic mean of the group sizes is used. Type I error levels are not guaranteed

FIGURE 6.23 Results of ANOVA Post-Hoc Comparison Test

In interpreting the Duncan test results, it is important to understand that means listed within the same column are not significantly different from one another. When testing the null hypothesis that African-Americans watch an equal number of football games compared to people of other races, the sig. value of .103 is greater than .05, indicating that the null hypothesis cannot be rejected. While the sample means appear to be different, we cannot be 95 percent confident that these differences would be found throughout the population. The observed differences may simply be due to random sampling error. However, when mean values are found exclusively in different columns, the null hypothesis of equality can be rejected. So the results indicate that one can be 95 percent confident that Caucasians watch significantly more NFL games than do those grouped under the "Other" race category, since the mean number of games watched by Caucasians is 13.7994 compared to 7.1972 for "Others."

6.8b Statistics Reporting

England Oaks is interested in developing a social media marketing campaign. But, the company wants to invest in the social media that is used by the majority of the company's target market. To determine which social media platforms to use, England Oaks surveyed their customers, asking them which social media channels they used regularly. The results of this survey are shown in Figure 6.24.

If England Oaks set the cutoff at 50 percent, then Facebook and Instagram would be the two social media channels selected. But, if confidence intervals are considered, would other channels reach the 50 percent level? Based on the results of one-sample t-tests, confidence intervals were calculated for each of the social media channels, shown in Figure 6.25. An examination of the table shows the mean for Snapchat is between 44.5 percent and 53.0 percent. For Pinterest, the mean is between 40.7 percent and 51.6 percent. Thus, based on the criteria stated by England Oaks, Snapchat, and Pinterest also meet the 50 percent cutoff since the mean of both could be above 50 percent.

If England Oaks wanted to present the results graphically, a floating column chart can be used. Figure 6.26 shows the confidence interval for each of the social media platforms. The column, or bar, starts at the lower boundary and ends at the upper boundary. By inserting a solid line at the 50 percent level, it is easy to see that Facebook, Snapchat, Instagram, and Pinterest all meet the 50 percent cutoff point.

Social Media Channel	Mean
Facebook	51.4%
Snapchat	48.8%
Instagram	58.2%
Pinterest	46.2%
Twitter	37.1%
YouTube	43.3%

FIGURE 6.24 Average Percent of the Sample Drawn from England Oak's Customers that Use Each of the Social Media Channels

Social Media Platform	Lower Bound	Upper Bound
Facebook	46.3%	56.5%
Google+	44.6%	53.0%
Instagram	54.3%	62.1%
Pinterest	40.7%	51.6%
Twitter	32.5%	41.7%
YouTube	39.7%	46.8%

FIGURE 6.25 Table Showing the Upper and Lower Boundaries for Confidence Intervals for Each of the Social Media Channels

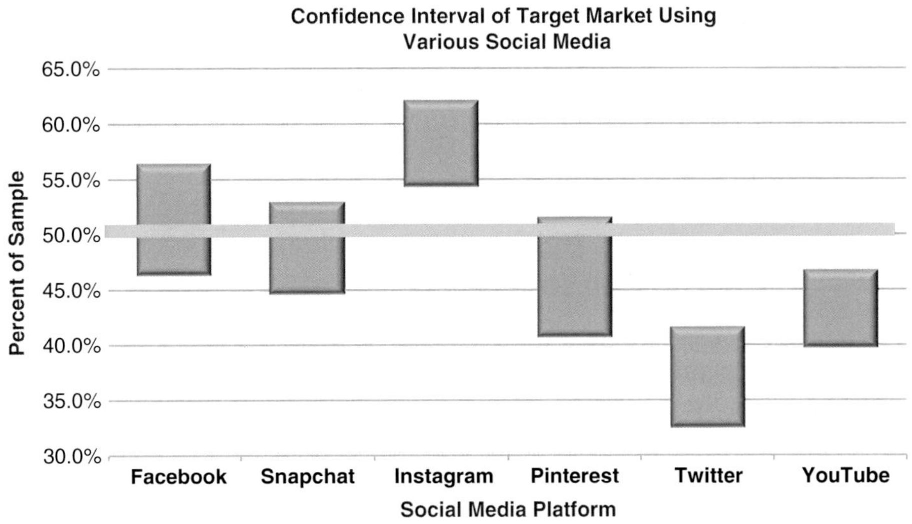

FIGURE 6.26 A Floating Bar Chart Showing the Confidence Interval for Each of the Social Media Channels

Social Media Channel	Mean	Lower Bound	Upper Bound
Facebook	9.3	7.3	11.2
Google+	8.3	6.2	10.3
Instagram	7.7	5.8	9.6
Pinterest	7.0	5.2	8.8
Twitter	4.5	3.7	5.2
YouTube	9.0	6.5	11.4

FIGURE 6.27 Table Showing the Mean and Confidence Interval for Number of Hours Spent with Each of the Social Media Platforms

Statistical Reporting Exercise In the same survey, England Oaks asked respondents to estimate how much time they spent with each social media platform per week. The results are shown in Figure 6.27. The second column is the mean number of hours per week. The third column is the lower bound for the confidence interval and the last column is the upper bound.

Create a floating bar chart showing the lower and upper bounds for each of the social media channels. If you have not done a floating column chart, go to the authors' website at www.clowjames.net/students.html for instructions. Be sure to properly label the x-axis, y-axis, and chart.

Suppose England Oaks stated the cutoff would be 10 hours per week. Based only on the mean, which social media channels meet the minimum cutoff of 10 hours per week? Based on the floating column chart of the confidence intervals, which social media channels include the 10 hours per week? Explain why examining confidence intervals is important and changes your response.

6.8c Dealing with Data

Visit the textbook website and download the files needed to complete this exercise. The questionnaire is entitled *Chapter 06 Dealing with Data Survey* and the data file is entitled *Chapter 06 Dealing with Data*. The files and step-by-step instructions are also available on the textbook website: www.clowjames.net/students.html.

A local businesswoman is considering purchasing a package of television spots that will run during college football game broadcasts during the upcoming season. However, she is not willing to invest in this marketing effort at the price quoted unless the population watches, on average, 15 college football games a year. If the population watches fewer than 15 games per year, she wants the television station to reduce the price.

1. Run one-sample t-tests at the .90, .95, and .99 level. Compute confidence intervals for each analysis. Use the confidence intervals to create a floating column chart. Report the results of the analysis. Based on this data, would you recommend that she invest in the college football advertising package at the quoted price, or should she attempt to renegotiate the price?
2. Suppose the majority of her clientele are African-Americans. Perform an ANOVA using Race as the grouping variable. Create a floating column chart and run a post-hoc analysis if the overall ANOVA results are significant. Based on this analysis, do you still believe she should invest in the collegiate football advertising package at the price quoted? Why or why not? Justify your decision based on the results of the analysis.

Summary

Objective 1: Discuss why survey research is used.
The results of survey research are used to describe situations, target market profiles, attitudes toward brands, endorsers, and ads, as well as other phenomena. Survey research provides answers to questions about who, when, where, what, and why.

Objective 2: Identify the two time frames for survey research.
Cross-sectional research studies provide a snapshot of the subject being investigated because they take place at a single point in time. Longitudinal studies are effective for tracking trends since they ask the same question, to essentially the same respondents, at multiple points in time. Longitudinal studies are typically conducted by syndicated research firms and often make use of consumer panels to track branding campaigns, media consumption, and advertising impact.

Objective 3: Describe the various types of errors that can occur with survey research.
Random error is unavoidable, and can be reduced only by increasing sample size. Systematic error results from problems in the research process related to the sample design, measurement process, or respondents. Sample design error may result from population specification error, frame error, or selection error. Measurement error may occur as a result of interviewer error or bias, measurement instrument error or bias, or processing error. Respondent error takes the form of non-response bias and response error or bias that occurs deliberately or unconsciously. Various strategies exist for minimizing each type of error.

Objective 4: Discuss the advantages and disadvantages of each of the data collection alternatives.
While data collection via telephone can be completed quickly, at a low cost and with minimal processing error only limited information can be collected, surveys must be shorter and visuals cannot be used. Answering machines, sample distortion, and declines in both the number of households that have landlines and response rates are key disadvantages of phone surveys that often result in sample distortion. Other issues apply to mobile phone survey research. Mail surveys suffer from high costs, long completion time frame, an inability to clarify questions that respondents may have about the survey, and lack of knowledge as to who is completing the questionnaire. However, mail surveys are good for sensitive material and longer surveys, and offer greater convenience to respondents along with confidentiality. Response rates have improved compared to the past, and visuals can be used with mail surveys. Personal interviews allow the researcher to clarify questions respondents may have, and stimulate more complete answers, lower item non-response, and higher participation. Personal interviews are useful for longer interviews and those requiring the use of visual aids. Disadvantages include lack of respondent anonymity, interviewer bias, higher per-respondent costs, and poorer data quality for sensitive topics. The advantages of online research are many and include fast, real-time results, lower costs, the ability to personalize and use more sophisticated surveys that may include visuals, and a high level of access. Disadvantages exist related to respondent locations, sample representativeness, data quality, spam and clutter, panel member response bias, and hardware/software capabilities. Mobile surveys are the superior choice for "in-the-moment" research, and the ability to track time and location aids in targeting surveys. Mobile has the fastest response time and is a great choice for surveys with sensitive questions. The small screen size leads to greater task difficulty, higher abandonment rates, and longer completion

times when surveys are not kept short and optimized or designed specifically for mobile. MROC surveys should never be used when the goal is to represent the population, all customers, or any type of random sample. MROCs are costly to create and maintain, in terms of time and money. However, MROCs do offer valuable feedback from engaged customers who are familiar with the brand, often in a fraction of the time and at a lower cost than other forms on online research. Insights stemming from the customer / brand relationship can be helpful.

Objective 5: Discuss each of the survey selection considerations as they apply to the various data collection alternatives.
When selecting a data collection method, researchers must consider a number of factors, including the level of precision or accuracy desired, cost, time frame available to complete the study, questionnaire length and structure, the incidence rate, and sample characteristics. The level of precision is influenced more by the research design, budget available and projected costs, time frame, and research process than it is by the data collection method. Online data collection is the least costly, while personal interviews and intercepts cost the most. Online and mobile surveys and those targeting cell phone users have fast response times, while mail surveys may take weeks to collect. Personal interviews, mail surveys, and some types of online surveys are appropriate for long questionnaires, while telephone surveys must be shorter and are among the least flexible with respect to questionnaire structure. Online surveys provide the greatest flexibility in this area.

Key Terms

branching, p. 205
computer-assisted personal interviewing (CAPI), p. 202
computer-assisted telephone interviewing (CATI), p. 197
contact rates, p. 198
cross-section studies, p. 187
deliberate falsification, p. 192
frame error, p. 189
incidence, p. 213
interviewer error or bias, p. 194
longitudinal study, p. 187
measurement error, p. 193
measurement instrument error or bias, p. 194
non-response bias, p. 190
order bias, p. 194
piping, p. 205
population specification error, p. 189
process error, p. 194
random error, p. 188
response rate, p. 191
sample frame, p. 189
search costs, p. 213
selection error, p. 190
systematic error, p. 188

Critical Thinking Exercises

1. Identify the type of error found in each of the following scenarios and discuss what actions could be taken to minimize future errors of this type:
   a. An interviewer frowns and blinks her eyes upon hearing the response offered by a study participant.
   b. The researcher in charge of programming the random digit dialer for a telephone survey forgets to enter two area codes for the population being studied.
   c. The data entry clerk's finger slips and he enters a "2" for a variable coded as "3."
   d. An individual forgets to fill out a mail survey by the due date.
   e. A survey to estimate demand for refrigerators includes a screening question that disqualifies anyone from taking the survey who has purchased a refrigerator in the last four years.
2. A local heating and air conditioning firm that traditionally targeted the construction trade needs to look for other revenue sources, as the faltering economy has led to a sharp decline in new housing construction. While the firm provides maintenance for some business and residential AC/heating units, it must expand its presence within these markets if the business is to survive. The firm is willing to invest in marketing research and is in the process of developing a questionnaire. Specifically, the firm wants to learn how important the AC/heating unit brand name is to business owners and residential consumers when purchasing a replacement unit. They also want to know what criteria both groups use when selecting a heating and A/C firm to provide maintenance for existing units. Finally, the firm wants to understand how aware consumers and businesses are of their firm, and how their image is perceived by each group. What survey method would you recommend to gather this data? Why? Should the same data collection method be used for residential consumers and businesses? Why or why not?
3. A minor league baseball team has developed a questionnaire that will be administered to people who attend the game scheduled on July 4th. This date was chosen because the team expects to fill every seat in the stadium. The purpose of the survey is to determine

how satisfied attendees are with the ballpark in terms of parking, food service, and other amenities. Is this an effective method of data collection? Why or why not? How can it be improved? How can the baseball team get feedback from fans that visited the ballpark and watched a game in the past, but never returned?

4. Suppose a bank is considering surveying its customers to determine their awareness of a new service that was recently introduced. Compare and contrast the pros and cons of surveying via mobile phones versus land lines versus mail surveys. Evaluate each method against the selection criteria discussed in the text. Which method would you recommend? Why?
5. A fast food franchisee with multiple restaurant locations throughout the designated market area has chosen the mall intercept approach to collect data. What types of systematic error are to be expected with this technique? Give examples to clarify your answer. What steps can the researchers take to minimize systematic error in the mall intercept study?
6. The state congressman for your area has chosen to survey constituents via telephone to better understand their views on higher education funding. What types of systematic error are to be expected with this technique? Give examples to clarify your answer. What steps can the researchers take to minimize systematic error when data is collected via telephone?
7. A national music store chain has chosen an online survey methodology to collect data regarding attitudes toward purchasing music online compared to purchasing in the store. They also want to understand consumer perceptions of the chain's strengths and weaknesses. What types of systematic error are to be expected with this technique? Give examples to clarify your answer. What steps can the researchers take to minimize systematic error when data is collected online?
8. A university researcher is using mail surveys to study the type of business-to-business marketing techniques employed by firms within a variety of industries. What types of systematic error are to be expected with this technique? Give examples to clarify your answer. What steps can the researchers take to minimize systematic error when data is collected by mail?
9. Create a table in which the method of data collection is listed at the head of each column. List a different type of systematic error at the beginning of each row. For each data collection method and error type combination, identify whether the error type is a major concern, minor concern, or of no concern by filling in the table with the appropriate label.

The Lakeside Grill

(Comprehensive Student Case)

The student team studying the Lakeside Grill wants to use an intercept approach for the survey component of their research. As Juan explains, "Since we were dealing with a local restaurant that most people had either been to or had at least heard about, we thought an intercept approach would work well." To ensure a more 'unbiased sample' the team is considering the intercept in two places. First, the students will survey customers in the Lakeside Grill as they are eating. Second, they will survey people at the local mall on two different weekends. The rationale for the mall intercept is to reach people who haven't eaten at the Lakeside Grill or haven't eaten there lately for some reason, such as, possibly, having had a bad experience.

The group spent a long time debating whether or not they should read the questions to participants. The alternative being considered was to give the survey questionnaire to individuals, let them fill it out on their own and just collect it later when they were finished. The group decided on the latter. "Especially since people would be eating, we didn't feel that it would be appropriate to sit down and ask them the questions," Brooke explains. "Also, we thought people would be more honest if they wrote down their answers themselves instead of giving them to us. It completely eliminates any interviewer error!"

Not everyone in the group was in agreement with the survey approach chosen. According to Zach, "Using telephones and cell phones would be better. We will get a lot of refusals, especially at the mall because people are busy shopping and don't want to complete the survey. I really think the non-response bias will be lower with a telephone survey and I also think response error will be less because you don't have somebody watching you fill out the questionnaire. People tend to be more honest on the phone than in person."

Critique Questions:

1. How would you evaluate the approach the student team chose? Do you think it is the best survey approach? Why or why not?
2. What about Zach's statement that "people tend to be more honest on the phone than in person?" Do you agree or disagree? Why?
3. Do you agree or disagree with Zach's statement that "non-response bias would be lower with a telephone survey than the intercept approach that was used?" Why?
4. Consider Brooke's statement, "We thought people would be more honest if they wrote down their answers themselves instead of giving them to us?" Do you agree or disagree? Why?
5. Brooke made the statement that by having respondents complete the survey themselves, "it completely eliminates any interviewer error?" Do you agree or disagree with this statement? Why?

6. What types of systematic errors would be a concern with the intercept approach used by the students?
7. Instead of an intercept approach, what other survey method could the team use? How would it compare to the intercept approach in terms of systematic error? What about the survey selection considerations listed in the chapter? How would the selection factors compare?

Notes

1. Interview with Shama Kabini, Marketing Zen Group, February 20, 2010.
2. Adapted from Michael A. Stelzner, "2019 Social Media Marketing Industry Report," *Social Media Examiner* (2019): 7.
3. Jerry Thomas, "Moving Beyond Standard Error," *Quirk's Marketing Research Review* (March 2019), https://www.quirks.com/articles/moving-beyond-standard-error.
4. David Ensing, "Response Rates: Part I: Looking at Cost-Benefit Decisions," *Quirk's Media* (July 17, 2017), https://www.quirks.com/articles/response-rates-part-i-looking-at-cost-benefit-decisions.
5. Kristen Miles, "Survey Participants Are Motivated by Rewards" *Quirk's Media* (March 12, 2019), https://www.quirks.com/articles/survey-participants-are-motivated-by-rewards.
6. Archana Narayanan, "Impact of Reward Type on Survey Response Rate and Quality," *2017 Winter AMA Proceedings*, American Marketing Association, pp. B22–B27; David Ensing, "Response Rates: Part II: Using Monetary Incentives," *Quirk's Media* (July 19, 2017), https://www.quirks.com/articles/response-rates-part-ii-using-monetary-incentives; "Sponsored Content: 11 Easy Ways to Improve Your Survey Response Rates," *Quirk's Marketing Research Review* (January 2012): Article ID 20100398.
7. Archana Narayanan, "Impact of Reward Type on Survey Response Rate and Quality," in *2017 Winter AMA Proceedings* (Chicago, IL: American Marketing Association), B22–B27.
8. David Ensing, "Response Rates: Part II: Using Monetary Incentives," *Quirk's Media* (July 19, 2017), https://www.quirks.com/articles/response-rates-part-ii-using-monetary-incentives.
9. David Ensing, "Response Rates: Part I: Looking at Cost-Benefit Decisions," *Quirk's Media* (July 17, 2017), https://www.quirks.com/articles/response-rates-part-i-looking-at-cost-benefit-decisions.
10. Keith Brady, "Methods of Diminishing Total Survey Error by Eliminating Bias," *Quirk's Marketing Research Review* (February 2016): pp. 26, 28–29.
11. Ibid.
12. Ibid.
13. Peter Gold, "When Fake Brands Are Used to Get Real Data. Were Respondents Lying or Trying Not to Look Stupid?" *Quirk's Marketing Research Review* (November 2013): 42, 44–47.
14. Rebecca Sarniak, "9 Types of Research Bias and How to Avoid Them," *Quirk's Media* (August 2015), https://www.quirks.com/articles/9-types-of-research-bias-and-how-to-avoid-them.
15. John C. Stevens, "Back to Basics: Six Essential Skills for Telephone Interviewing," *Quirk's Marketing Research Review* (April 22, 2013): Article ID 20130426-3.
16. This section is based on Rebecca Sarniak, "9 Types of Research Bias and How to Avoid Them," *Quirk's Media* (August 2015), https://www.quirks.com/articles/9-types-of-research-bias-and-how-to-avoid-them; Jerry Thomas, "Moving beyond Standard Error," *Quirk's Marketing Research Review* (March 2019): Article ID 20190305, pp. 21–23; and Keith Brady, "Methods of Diminishing Total Survey Error by Eliminating Bias," *Quirk's Marketing Research Review* (February 2016): Article ID 20160205, pp. 26, 28–29.
17. "Usage of Traditional Methodologies," in *GRIT Report: Greenbook Research Industry Trends Report, Quarters 3–4, 2018* (New York: GreenBook, 2018).
18. Courtney Kennedy and Hannah Hartig, "Response Rates in Telephone Surveys Have Resumed Their Decline," Pew Research Center, February 27, 2019, https://www.pewresearch.org/fact-tank/2019/02/27/response-rates-in-telephone-surveys-have-resumed-their-decline/.
19. ESOMAR, "Distribution of Market Research Spending in the United States in 2018, by Method of Survey," Statista, September 4, 2019, https://www.statista.com/statistics/492156/market-research-revnue-survey-method-usa/
20. Catherine M. Wolfe, "For Toshiba America Medical Systems, Satisfaction Research Removes Uncertainty from Customer Relationships," *Quirk's Marketing Research Review* (October 2010): Article ID 20101005, pp. 40–44, 46.
21. Tara Siegel Bernard, "Yes, It's Ad. Robocalls, and Their Scams, Are Surging," *New York Times* (May 6, 2018), https://www.nytimes.com/2018/05/06/your-money/robocalls-rise-illegal.html
22. This section is based on Felix Richter, "Landline Phones Are a Dying Breed," Statista, May 17, 2019, https://www.statista.com/chart/2072/landline-phones-in-the-united-states/; and William E. Gibson, "Most U.S. Households Do without Landline Phones," AARP, January 10, 2018, https://www.aarp.org/home-family/personal-technology/info-2018/landline-phones-fd.html.

23. Gregory J. Mills, "Investigating the Use of Cellular Telephone Numbers for the Computer-Assisted Telephone Interview Operation in the American Community Survey," United States Census Bureau, November 6, 2017, https://www.census.gov/content/dam/Census/library/working-papers/2017/acs/2017_Mills_01.pdf.
24. Paula Vincente, "Exploring Fieldwork Effects in a Mobile CATI Survey," *International Journal of Market Research* 59, no. 1 (2017): 57–76.
25. Marketing Research Insights Association, "The Telephone Consumer Protection Act (TCPA) and Calling Cell Phones," July 12, 2017, https://www.insightsassociation.org/legal-article/tcpa-restrictions-using-autodialers-call-cell-phones.
26. Readex Research, "Mail Survey Response Rate,"http://www.readexresearch.com/mail-survey-response-rate/; Nigel Lindemann, "What's the Average Survey Response Rate? [2019 Benchmark]," Surveyanyplace.com, August 8, 2019, https://surveyanyplace.com/average-survey-response-rate/.
27. ESOMAR, "Distribution of Market Research Spending in the United States in 2018, by Method of Survey," Statista, September 4, 2019, https://www.statista.com/statistics/492156/market-research-revnue-survey-method-usa/
28. U.S. Census Bureau, "Percentage of Households with Internet Use in the United States from 1997 to 2018, Statista, September 26, 2019, from https://www.statista.com/statistics/189349/us-households-home-internet-connection-subscription/.
29. "Global Internet Penetration Rate as of January 2019, by Region." Statista, January 31, 2019, https://www.statista.com/statistics/269329/penetration-rate-of-the-internet-by-region/.
30. Monica Anderson, "Mobile Technology and Home Broadband 2019," pewinternet.org, June 13, 2019, https://www.pewinternet.org/2019/06/13/mobile-technology-and-home-broadband-2019/.
31. Interview with Debbie Peternana, ReRez Research, February 25, 2011.
32. This section is based on Interview with Debbie Peternana, ReRez Research, February 25, 2011; Joe Hopper, "Fight the Good Fight," *Quirk's Marketing Research Review* (January 2019): Article ID 20190108, pp. 66, 68; Brook Patton, "6 Survey Respondents to Avoid," *Quirk's Media* (April 9, 2019), https://www.quirks.com/articles/6-survey-respondents-to-avoid; Tim Macer and Sheila Wilson, "A Report on the Confirmit Market Research Software Survey," *Quirk's Marketing Research Review* (June 2013): Article ID 20130609, pp. 50, 52–57; and Keith Phillips, "Data Use; An Evaluation of Quality-Control Questions," *Quirk's Marketing Research Review* (December 2013): Article ID 20131205, pp. 26, 28–31.
33. Nallen Suresh, "Who Are the Unengaged and What Do They Mean for Our Data?" *Quirk's Marketing Research Review* (November 2011): Article ID 20111108, pp. 46, 48–53.
34. Francois Coderre, Natalie St. Laurent, Anne Mathieu, "Comparison of the Quality of Qualitative Data through Telephone, Postal and Email Surveys," *International Journal of Marketing Research* 46, no. 3, quarter 3 (2004): 347–357.
35. Michael Hesser, "Each Has Its Strengths and Weaknesses," *Quirk's Marketing Research Review* (January 2008): Article ID 20080101, pp. 26–28.
36. Tom Wells, "What Market Researchers Should Know about Mobile Surveys," *International Journal of Marketing Research* 57, no. 4 (2015): 521–532.
37. "Usage of Traditional Methodologies," in *GRIT Report: Greenbook Research Industry Trends Report, Quarters 3–4, 2018* (New York: GreenBook, 2018), p. 34.
38. Charles Young, "How the iPad Is Impacting Advertising Research," *Quirk's Marketing Research Review* (March 2014): Article ID 20140308, pp. 36, 38–40.
39. Tanja Pferdekaemper, "Mobile Research Offers Speed, Immediacy," *Quirk's Marketing Research Review* (June 2010): Article ID 20100607, pp. 52, 54, 56, 58–59.
40. Tom Wells, "What Market Researchers Should Know about Mobile Surveys," *International Journal of Marketing Research* 57, no. 4 (2015): 521–532.
41. Kurt Knapton, "Why Respondents Suffer IF You Are Not Mobile-Ready," *Quirk's Marketing Research Review* (October 28, 2013): Article ID 20131026-2.
42. Tanja Pferdekaemper, "Mobile Research Offers Speed, Immediacy," *Quirk's Marketing Research Review* (June 2010): Article ID 20100607, pp. 52, 54, 56, 58–59.
43. Ibid.
44. C. Antoun, "Nonresponse in a Mobile-Web Survey: A Look at the Causes and the Performance of Different Predictive Models," paper presented at the American Association for Public Opinion Research, Anaheim, California, 15–18 May 2014; J. A. Cunningham, C. Neighbors, N. Bertholet, and C. D. Hendershot, "Use of Mobile Devices to Answer Online Surveys: Implications for Research," *BMC Research Notes* (2013): 6, note 258; and "Research on Research into Mobile Market Research: Three Paper Review," Vision Critical University Whitepaper, http://vcu.visioncritical.com.
45. Tanja Pferdekaemper, "Mobile Research Offers Speed, Immediacy," *Quirk's Marketing Research Review* (June 2010): Article ID 20100607, pp. 52, 54, 56, 58–59.
46. Nicole Mitchell, "When It Comes to Mobile Respondent Experience and Data Quality, Survey Design Matters," *Quirk's Marketing Research Review* (August 2014): Article ID 20140825-3.
47. Ibid.

48. Randall K. Thomas and Frances M. Barlas, "Best Practices in Mobile-First Design," GfK Whitepaper, January 2018, https://www.gfk.com/fileadmin/user_upload/dyna_content/US/documents/GfK_Whitepaper_-_Best_Practices_in_Mobile-First_Design.pdf.
49. C. Bacon, "Mobile Research Quality Checklist," paper presented at the Advertising Research Foundation's Re: Think 2016 Conference, New York, March 14–16, 2016.
50. Dan Coates, MaryLeigh Bliss, and Xavier Vivar, "Ain't Nobody Got Time for That," *Quirk's Marketing Research Review* (February 2016): Article ID 20160210, pp. 46, 47–48.
51. Tom Wells, "What Market Researchers Should Know about Mobile Surveys," *International Journal of Marketing Research* 7, no. 4 (2015): 521–532.
52. This section based on John Lo, "What to Consider before You Build an Insight Community," *Quirk's Media* (June 24, 2019), https://www.quirks.com/articles/what-to-consider-before-you-build-an-insight-community.
53. Ibid.
54. U.S. Census Bureau, "2020 Census Operational Plan, version 4.0," December 2018, https://www2.census.gov/programs-surveys/decennial/2020/program-management/planning-docs/2020-oper-plan4.pdf.
55. Mary McDougall, "Survey Tips: Reading Adults Age 65 and Older," *Quirk's Media* (March 24, 2017), https://www.quirks.com/articles/survey-tips-reaching-adults-age-65-and-older.
56. Pam Bruns, "By the Numbers: Make Your International Phone Interviews Successful in Any Language," *Quirk's Marketing Research Review* (December 2009): Article ID 20091202, pp. 20, 22.
57. Roxana Elliott, "Tips for Collecting Data in Emerging Markets," *Quirk's Media* (May 3, 2018), https://www.quirks.com/articles/tips-for-collecting-data-in-emerging-markets.
58. Jeffrey M. Jones, "Obama Approval Rally Largely Over," June 15, 2011, http://www.gallup.com/poll/148046/Obama-Approval-Rally-Largely.aspx on June 15, 2011.
59. Ibid.

Experimental Research

CHAPTER 7

Source: Shine Nucha/Shutterstock.

Chapter Outline

Learning Objectives

After studying this chapter, you should be able to:

- Explain the concepts of internal and external validity.
- Identify the three conditions that must be present to prove causation.
- Discuss the extraneous factors that can affect internal and external validity.
- Explain the basic notation used in experimental design.
- Describe the various types of pre-experimental designs.
- Describe the various types of true experimental designs.
- Describe the various types of quasi-experimental designs.
- Discuss the concept of test markets and field studies.
- Identify ethical practices with experimental research.

7.1 Chapter Overview

Color influences perceptions of product attributes and benefits, including size, weight, quality and other factors, as well as the consumers' willingness to pay.[1] Research has also found that blue lighting favorably influences the perceptions of wine quality and can increase the time people spend browsing in stores.

A recent study examined how blue light influenced preferences for hedonic and utilitarian goods. In this experiment, 220 students at an Italian University were asked to make purchase decisions for 10 items using their mobile device. The students were randomly assigned to one of two treatment conditions. Half of the students were shown a specific shade of blue light in the background called actinic blue when they viewed each item on their phone. The other students viewed each item against a white light background. Students who saw the blue light background demonstrated higher purchase intentions of hedonic products (specific brands of lingerie, sunglasses, watches, chocolate creams, and clothing) when compared to purchase intentions for utilitarian products (such as detergent, toothpaste, toilet paper, shampoo and calculators). Interestingly, there was no difference in the purchase intentions for hedonic goods vs. utilitarian goods among those students who were exposed to the white light treatment.

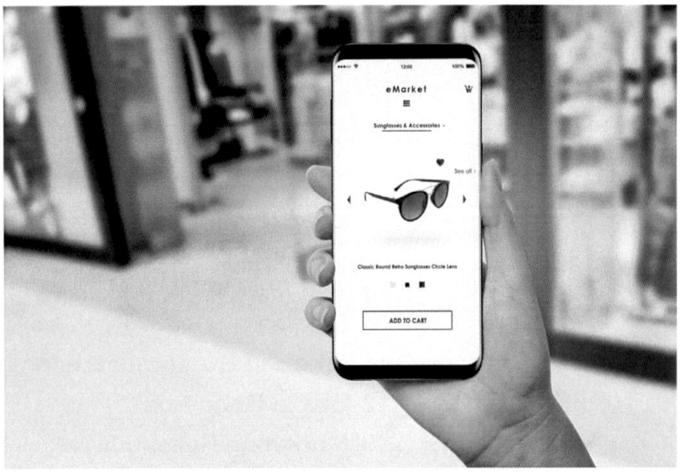

Source: Nikola Stanisic/Shutterstock.

Experiments manipulate variables to find a cause and effect. An experiment found higher purchase intentions for sunglasses and other hedonic products when they were viewed against a blue background, versus a white background. The bottom line? Color influences perceptions.

What does this mean for marketing? "The use of blue light in ambient and mobile displays could increase consumers' level of arousal when watching Web promotions, using an app or sending viral messages—at least when hedonic products or services are involved," says Professor Gianluigi Guido, of the University of Salento, who developed the study. "Managers could also implement blue light as part of Web site customization, allowing users to alter the online atmosphere with a click."[2]

Chapter 7 explores the topic of experimental research. Various experimental designs can be used by marketing researchers. Because of its high cost and the need to have tight controls on the variables being studied, experimental design is not used as much in the commercial marketing research industry as are other forms of research. However, it is important to understand how experimental research is conducted and how it can be used.

OBJECTIVE 7.1
Explain the concepts of internal and external validity.

7.2 Research Validity

Dependent variable outcome variable of the experiment that the independent variable seeks to influence, the *effect* component of a cause-and-effect relationship.

Independent variables variables that are manipulated, or changed, in order to observe the effect on the dependent variable, the *cause* element in the cause-and-effect relationship.

Treatment change or manipulation in the independent variable.

Before discussing the concept of research validity, it is necessary to define the basic components of experiments—the dependent variable, independent variables, treatment, and subjects. The **dependent variable** is the outcome variable of the experiment that the researcher measures and is most interested in studying, i.e., the *effect* component of the cause-and-effect relationship that is being studied. In the previous example, the independent variable was purchase intentions towards different types of products. **Independent variables** are those variables that are manipulated, or changed, in the experiment in order to observe the impact they may have on the dependent variable. They are the *cause* element in the cause-and-effect relationship. To ensure causality, researchers will manipulate only one independent variable at a time and hold the other independent variables constant. The manipulation of an independent variable is called the **treatment,** and the individuals involved in the experiment are called **subjects** rather than respondents. In the opening vignette, the background color for an ad viewed on a mobile device was manipulated, and student subjects were randomly assigned to either the actinic blue light (experimental treatment group) or white light (control group). The **control group** is the group of subjects who were not exposed to the treatment. While all subjects were shown the same ten ads, half of the ads were for hedonistic products and the other half were for utilitarian products. Thus the type of product represented a second type of independent variable that was held constant for both groups. This allowed the researchers to compare purchase intentions for each of these types of products (utilitarian vs. hedonistic) within each treatment condition.

Researchers conduct experiments because they have the potential to have a high degree of validity. **Validity** refers to the degree to which an experiment (or research study) measures what it is supposed to measure. An experiment designed to measure brand image has a high degree of validity if indeed brand image is being measured and not something else, such as product attractiveness, attitude toward an ad, or even brand preference.

Validity consists of both internal and external validity. **Internal validity** is the extent to which a particular treatment in an experiment produces the sole effect on the dependent variable being studied. Obtaining a high level of internal validity requires ruling out any other possible extraneous effect or influence that may have contributed to the change in the dependent variable. Otherwise, these extraneous effects represent competing explanations for the dependent variable change that **confound**, or call into question, the results of the study.

External validity refers to the extent the findings of an experiment (or research study) can be generalized to the population as a whole or to the specific population being studied. External validity depends on how well the sample selected for the study represents the population to which it is projected. If the population under study is college students, then to obtain external validity the sample needs to be representative of college students in terms of characteristics such as major, class status, age, gender, and race.

Subjects participants in an experimental research study.

Control group group of experimental subjects who are not exposed to the treatment or manipulation of the independent variable.

Validity refers to the degree to which an experiment (or research study) measures what it is supposed to measure.

Internal validity the extent to which a particular treatment in an experiment produced the sole effect observed in the dependent variable.

Confounds (results) occurs when extraneous effects that represent competing explanations for the dependent variable call into question the results of the study.

External validity the extent to which the findings of an experiment (or research study) can be generalized to the population as whole, or to the particular population being studied.

7.3 Nature of Causal Research

Experimental research is important to marketing researchers because it is the only type of research that can actually show cause-and-effect. Thus, experimental research is often referred to as causal research. Many make the mistake of thinking that descriptive research, which can be used to determine if two variables vary (or correlate) together, provides proof of causation. For instance, an increase in a firm's advertising budget might be followed by an increase in sales for the item that was advertised. While it would appear that advertising might be the cause of the increase in sales, descriptive research of this nature cannot prove that the budget increase actually was the cause. A number of other factors may have also contributed to the increase in sales, such as a price drop by the manufacturer (or price increase by a competitor), issuance of coupons, changes in the economy, changes in product quality perceptions, or a lack of competition. The only way to prove a cause-and-effect relationship between advertising and sales is to conduct some type of experimental research in which other alternative explanations are eliminated or held constant. To demonstrate a causal relationship, three conditions must be met: concomitant variation, time order of occurrence, and elimination of extraneous factors (see **Figure 7.1**).

OBJECTIVE 7.2
Identify the three conditions that must be present to prove causation.

In examining causation, it is important to understand the current, popular view held by most marketing researchers and the scientific view. When conducting causal research, the *popular view* is that if *X* causes *Y*, then the relationship always holds true and changes in *X* will always cause corresponding changes in *Y*. The *scientific view* holds that one can never prove beyond a shadow of doubt that *X* causes *Y*. There is always a possibility that an extraneous variable was present that contributed to the change in *Y*, and because of

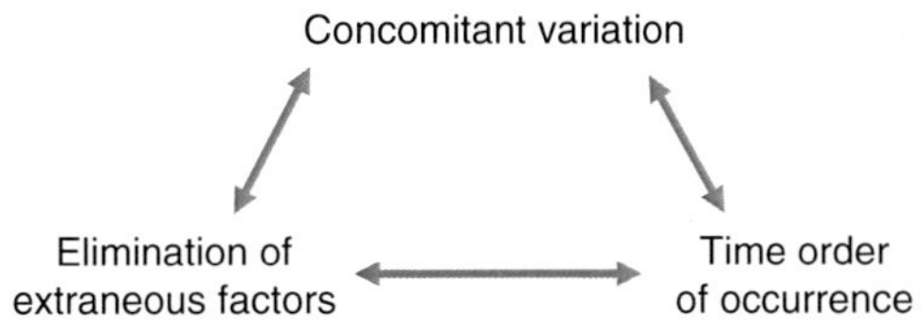

FIGURE 7.1 Conditions for Causal Relationships

this possibility, all researchers can do is infer that *X* causes *Y*. Further, the relationship between X and Y is not perpetual as relationships may change over time. However, one can reasonably infer the relationship exists and that there is a high probability that any changes in *X* will cause corresponding changes in *Y*.

7.3a Concomitant Variation

Concomitant variation condition for causality in which two variables are either positively or inversely correlated and vary together in a predictable manner.

The first condition that must be met for causation is **concomitant variation**, which means two variables are correlated and will vary together in a predictable manner. The correlation can be positive or inverse. With a positive correlation, as *X* increases, *Y* increases. The reverse is also true in that decreases in *X* correlate with decreases in *Y*. With an inverse correlation, the opposite occurs, meaning that as *X* increases *Y* decreases and as *X* decreases *Y* increases. For example, a recent study proposed a relationship between lunch order timing in a corporate office setting and calorie consumption. Specifically, calorie consumption (X) was believed to increase as the time gap between meal ordering and meal pick-up (Y) shortened.[3]

The second component of concomitant variation is the predictability of the variation as it must occur in a predictable manner. This means that if the correlation between *X* and *Y* is such that for every one-unit increase in *X* there is a corresponding three-unit increase in *Y*, then a two-unit increase in *X* should produce a six-unit increase in *Y*. The relationship between variables in the lunch order timing study was based on a series of academic research studies that essentially found that people who made food choices for immediate consumption chose higher calorie, or unhealthier foods.[4]

Spurious correlation a coincidental correlation between variables that does not indicate causality.

It is also important to realize that just because two variables are correlated it does not mean a true causal relationship exists. The correlation between these variables can be a **spurious correlation**, that is, coincidental. For instance, the number of snow shovels and snow blowers sold is highly, but inversely correlated with the average winter temperatures of a region. More snow shovels and snow blowers are sold in states with lower average winter temperatures, such as Minnesota and New York, than in states with higher average winter temperatures, such as Florida and Texas. But, it is not the temperature that makes the difference. It is the amount of snow. New York receives more snow than Texas and as a result more snow equipment is sold in New York than in Texas. While the temperature is a factor, it is not the cause. People buy snow shovels and snow blowers to remove snow, and what they buy is directly related to the amount of snow they anticipate. Thus, correlation alone does not prove causation, and, though necessary for causation to occur, the presence of a predictable correlation alone is insufficient. Demonstrating a true cause-and-effect relationship requires that two other conditions be satisfied as well.

7.3b Time Order of Occurrence

For causation to be present, *X* must occur before or simultaneously with *Y*. To say issuing coupons caused an increase in sales means the coupons must have been issued before sales increased. If the coupons were issued after the increase in sales, then it does not meet the time order of occurrence condition. In the lunch order timing experiment, participants were randomly assigned to one of two treatment conditions. The first group was told that they must order their lunch online from their corporate dining facility before 10 am (advance order treatment condition). The second was required to order their lunch between 11 am and 2 pm (lunchtime condition). Both treatment conditions met the time order of occurrence requirement as orders preceded or occurred concurrently with lunch pick-up, available between 11 am and 2 pm.[5]

Just as mentioned with concomitant variation, meeting the time order of occurrence does not prove a cause-and-effect relationship. Coupons for pizza may have been distributed just before the Super Bowl football game, and during the evening of the game sales of pizza may have doubled or tripled. However, the large increase is more likely due to the

Super Bowl game and the prevalence of Super Bowl parties and not the issuance of coupons, especially if competitors also issued coupons or offered other promotional deals.

7.3c Elimination of Extraneous Factors

The most difficult condition for a causal relationship is the elimination of extraneous factors. To meet all three conditions, researchers often use experiments where variables can be controlled, meaning that they are kept the same as different treatments are administered and measured, and only the one variable that is under study is manipulated to see if it does have an impact. To prove that *X* indeed causes *Y*, a researcher must eliminate all other variables that could possibly have an impact on *Y*. For that reason, most experimental research studies are conducted in a laboratory or tightly controlled environment where everything but the variable under study can be controlled.

While field studies can be used for causal research, it is much more difficult to control extraneous variables, and results are not as conclusive as those obtained in a lab setting. Extraneous factors influence both participation in the experiment—particularly field experiments—and interaction with the dependent variable. For example, research has shown that people are more likely to spend after receiving their paycheck because they feel "richer."[6] The implication is that over the course of the four-week lunch-timing field experiment, some subjects may buy their lunch from the cafeteria some days, but not others. Alternatives include skipping lunch or opting to bring lunch from home. Further, many positions within a firm, such as account representatives or managers, take clients to lunch as part of their job. Obviously, business lunches do not take place in the corporate cafeteria, so subject's availability to participate may vary any given week depending upon their business lunch commitments. Finally, if the daily menu changes, that would also be an extraneous factor as not everyone likes meatloaf (or the special of the day), and thus might be inclined to order a less healthy alternative not due to timing, but because of the menu choices available. Similarly, with respect to another one of our examples, most marketers would agree that advertising does have an impact on sales, but so does hiring new salespeople, and issuing coupons. Plus, advertising has a lag effect that influences sales after the campaign has finished running. To show cause-and-effect during a field study, it would be necessary to isolate all of the variables except the one being studied. Such a task would be impossible in an actual marketplace (field) setting! However, it is often possible to track and statistically control for some extraneous variables when analyzing the data.

7.4 Extraneous Variables

OBJECTIVE 7.3
Discuss the extraneous factors that can affect internal and external validity.

To prove causation or even to assert causation, it is important to control for any extraneous variable that may have an impact on the dependent variable, because the presence of extraneous variables provides an alternative reason, or competing explanation, for any changes observed in the dependent variable. Controlling these extraneous factors is easier in a laboratory setting than in field studies. Figure 7.2 identifies the primary extraneous variables or factors that can affect experimental research.[7] Controlling these factors increases the validity of an experiment. The elimination of competing explanations for the study findings allows the researcher to have confidence in asserting that the change in the dependent variable was due to the treatment, and not to the presence of one or more extraneous variables.

- History
- Maturation
- Testing
- Instrumentation
- Selection
- Attrition

FIGURE 7.2 Extraneous Factors in Experimental Research

7.4a History

History effects occur when some external event takes place between the beginning and end of an experiment that changes the outcome of the event.

History effects occur when some external event takes place between the beginning and end of an experiment that changes the outcome of the event. Internal validity is affected by history effects since the change in the dependent variable is due to something other than the treatment. In field studies, a large number of events can affect the results, such as actions by competitors, changes in the economy, and a catastrophic event such as a tornado or hurricane. Changes to the product or competition's pricing, shelf location, point-of-purchase displays, promotions or advertising that occur during a field experiment such as a test market are history effects. The longer the experiment lasts, the more likely history will affect the results. Researchers should record small or large variation in the experimental setting and carefully consider how it might influence the dependent variable and confound the study results. This is especially true for field studies. For example, suppose a researcher conducted a "pay what you want" experiment for homemade ice cream at a local farmer's market every weekend in July. If three of the weeks averaged temperatures in the high nineties, and one was marred by thunderstorms and temperatures in the low 70's, it is very likely that people would be less willing to buy ice cream, and that those that did would be willing to pay less on stormy days. The savvy researcher would seriously consider deleting this data to control for the extreme temperature and weather variation.[8] Conducting experiments in a laboratory reduces the chances of history effects, especially if there is a *short time* between the beginning and end of the experiment. If the experiment is administered multiple times, minimizing changes to room lighting, room location, noise levels, people administering the experiment, equipment used, time of day, day of week or other extraneous factors within the laboratory setting can also help to minimize history effects.

7.4b Maturation

Maturation changes in the subject over time that can affect the results of an experiment.

While the history effect involves some event that changes the results of an experiment, **maturation** involves changes in the subject over time that can affect the results of the experiment. Times series studies, which take place over weeks or months, are particularly prone to this effect. Maturation often occurs when subjects become fatigued or tired, hungry, or simply due to maturing (i.e., "growing up") over time.

If an experiment lasts several hours, subjects may get tired or hungry and hurriedly answer questions after the treatment without paying much attention to what they are reading, or without thinking through the answer. In this case, the results that are attributed to the experiment may be caused by the subject's fatigue rather than exposure to the treatment. Experiments that last several weeks or months are often affected by subject maturation. The person just gets older and with age comes greater life experiences, different priorities, and changes to the mind and body. The subject's mood can also vary from one time period to the next. As a result of any or all of these factors, the subject's views may change, which in turn affects the results and damages the internal validity of the experiment. The longer an experiment runs, the more likely maturation effects will occur.

Source: Dean Drobot/Shutterstock

Experiments seek to control extraneous factors that may confound the study results. Maturation occurs when subjects become fatigued, tired, hungry, or after several measurements have been taken in a time-series study. Shorter experiments are less likely to experience maturation.

Randomly assigning subjects to treatment and control groups is one method by which researchers can control for maturation effects. By randomly assigning subjects, the laws of probability allow the researcher to assume that maturation effects will be evenly spread out between treatment conditions. This is an important assumption. It means that the negative impact due to maturation will in fact "cancel out" in the final analysis since what affects one group affects all equally.[9] (The same random procedure can be used to reduce history effects.)

7.4c Testing

Testing effects occur when subjects become sensitized to the measurement instrument or experiment through the pretest in a way that affects the results of the experiment. Testing effects occur in two different ways. First, when the pretest and posttest are identical, subjects have already seen the questions, so they know how to answer. Some subjects choose to answer the same as they did on the pretest to demonstrate consistency, regardless of whether or not their actual attitudes or reactions have changed. Others will provide different answers to the posttest based on what they think the researcher wants them to say, rather than how they really feel, because exposure to the pretest and experiment has given them a clue as to the topic being studied.

Testing effects occur when exposure to a pretest sensitizes subjects to the test or experiment in a manner that affects the results of the experiment.

The second way testing effects occur is it sensitizes the subjects to the experiment. They pay closer attention than normal. For instance, a common experiment in advertising research begins with a pretest in which subjects are asked their thoughts about several brands. Questions that are not relevant to the true purpose of the study are also interspersed throughout the survey to disguise the researcher's intent. Subjects then watch an online video or a television show with ads or product placements embedded. When it is over, subjects are asked about the brands again, though the purpose of the posttest is disguised in some fashion. The researcher might claim to have accidentally left one or more brands off of the list, or the researcher might state that they are interested in respondents' reactions to the television show they have just viewed. However, the process of participating in the experiment may cause the subjects to pay more attention to the ads and product placements than they would in "real life." Suppose Coca-Cola was one of the brands. When the subject sees the actor drinking the Coke, it is noticed, where in normal circumstances the subject may never have noticed it.

Several methods are used to reduce testing effects with the measurement component of an experiment. Random assignment of subjects is often used, and as mentioned previously, the purpose of the study is typically disguised in some fashion. Claiming the intent of the study is to assess attitudes toward the TV show, rather than toward advertisements, is not unethical, unless the researcher fails to debrief participants afterwards. Including multiple ads for different brands in addition to the test ad(s) helps to disguise which brand is being studied. Furthermore, researchers will often modify the measurement process by changing 1) the order of the questions, 2) the names of brands that have been added to disguise the true brand being studied, or 3) the wording of the questions themselves. Finally, the posttest often includes a question asking subjects to identify the purpose of the study. If the subject answers in a way that indicates knowledge of the specific topic and brand, the researcher often chooses to exclude that individual from the sample.

7.4d Instrumentation

It was just mentioned that researchers often modify the measurement process to reduce the impact of testing effects. Doing so, however, creates the possibility of **instrumentation effect**, which is caused by a change in the measurement instrument, its calibration, or other procedures used to measure the dependent variable.

Instrumentation effects occur when a change in the measurement instrument or other procedures used to measure the dependent variable cause an unwarranted change in the dependent variable.

Changing the wording of questions used on the posttest is one way of reducing testing effects. However, changing the wording raises the possibility of instrumentation effect since the change in the dependent variable may be due to the way the posttest questions were phrased and not due to the experiment itself. Thus researchers have to be careful when they use a pretest and posttest to ensure any changes between the two measurement instruments is not due to the instrument itself.

If human interviewers are used, then instrumentation effect can also occur. First, if different interviewers are used for the pre- and posttest, then the effect on the dependent variable may be due to the differences in the interviewers and not the experiment. If the same interviewer is used and if he/she asks the questions in a different way, with different words, different body language, and a different tone of voice, then instrumentation error can occur.

So researchers face a dilemma. To reduce testing effects, the researcher wants to modify the posttest from the pretest. But doing so increases the likelihood of instrumentation effects. The solution is to find a method that is the least likely to produce error and as a result increase internal validity.

7.4e Selection

Selection effects occurs when the sample selected for a study is not representative of the population or the samples selected for different groups within the study are not statistically the same.

Selection effect occurs when the sample selected for a study is not representative of the population being studied or the samples selected for different groups within the study are not statistically the same prior to being exposed to treatments. If the study sample is not representative of the population then external validity is threatened as the results of the experiment cannot be generalized to the population.

If the samples within the study differ, then the internal validity of the experiment is threatened. For instance, if an experiment uses a control group and a treatment group, then both samples need to be similar and both need to be representative of the population under study. When the control or treatment sample is different, any results obtained in the experiment may be due to the differences in the two samples rather than the treatment. For example, if the treatment group has statistically more females than are present in the control group, then the results may be due to the larger percentage of females in the treatment group rather than the treatment itself, as it is likely that females' attitudes towards shampoo differ from those of males. While it is possible to "match" samples between groups on one or possibly two important characteristics, researchers typically rely on two methods of controlling for selection effects. First, subjects who match the population's characteristics are randomly assigned to the treatment or control condition. Second, during the data analysis stage, various statistical techniques can be used to control for the influence of important characteristics—such as gender in the example above, which may not otherwise be evenly distributed among treatment conditions, even when randomly assigned.

7.4f Attrition

Attrition the loss of subjects during the time the experiment is being conducted (also called mortality).

Sample **attrition**, also called *mortality*, is the loss of subjects during the time the experiment is being conducted. As would be expected, the longer the experiment lasts, the more likely it is that individuals will drop out of the study. The impact of attrition depends on the size of the sample. If the sample size is sufficiently large and only a few drop out of the study, it is unlikely to affect the overall results of the study. But if a larger number drop out of the study, there is concern that those who drop out may in some way be different from those who completed the experiment, resulting in a non-response bias. In this case the results would be affected by the attrition.

Controlling for attrition is difficult. The ethical marketing researcher must respect the subject's right to terminate participation in an experiment at any time, for any reason. Forcing subjects to complete an experiment via coercion or "guilt-tripping," is unethical and should not be used.

Randomly assigning subjects to treatment conditions is again recommended as a means of evening out the influence of attrition between experimental and control groups. Alerting subjects ahead of time to the amount of time needed to complete the study may help to stave off some attrition. Providing incentives for participation that are given only to those who complete the experiment may also be helpful. Recruiting participants from research panels may result in a sample that is less subject to attrition than one recruited by the researcher via other means. Of course the shorter the experiment, the less likely attrition will occur, so the pre- and posttest measurement instrument should be kept as short as possible, while still accommodating "dummy" questions that help to disguise the research purpose.

It is important for marketing researchers to be aware of all seven extraneous factors that can affect both internal and external validity. While completely eliminating these factors may not be possible, being aware of each one can help researchers reduce their impact. At the same time researchers must be aware of the potential tradeoffs between internal and external validity. By tightening experimental controls, researchers can increase the internal validity of the findings. However, in so doing they may decrease the realism of the study and detract from the findings' external validity. Such an outcome would defeat the real purpose of the study—being able to generalize the findings to the population.[10]

7.5 Experimental Design Notation

OBJECTIVE 7:4
Explain the basic notation used in experimental design.

A standard system of notation has been developed for experiments consisting of *X* and *O*, with subscripts included to note the time period. ***X*** denotes the application of a treatment to a variable or group of subjects. ***O*** represents a measurement, or **observation** of a variable or group of subjects. When written in a horizontal line, these notations represent different periods of time. Consider the following example:

Observation measurement of a variable or group of participants during an experiment.

$$O_1 \quad X \quad O_2$$

The notation can be interpreted in the following fashion. The experiment began with an observation or measurement of the dependent variable(s). The experiment took place with some type of treatment. Then a second observation or measurement of the dependent variable took place. This type of experiment includes a pre- and posttest. To illustrate, suppose a company wanted to test the impact of a product placement in a movie. Subjects could be recruited and, before seeing the movie, be asked to complete a survey on their attitude toward various brands (O_1). They watch the movie that includes a product placement for the test brand, which is the treatment (X). Then at the end, they take the same survey again (O_2). The attitude toward the test brand before the movie is compared to the attitude toward the brand after the movie to see if the product placement had any effect (or change) on their attitude towards the target brand. This impact, known as the **experimental effect**, is calculated by means of this simple formula: $O_2 - O_1$. In order for researchers to repeat the survey without the subjects being suspicious, they are typically told that one or more brands were inadvertently left out of the original survey and subjects are requested to take the survey again.

There are times that a researcher will have more than one test group of subjects, each of which receives a different type of treatment. In the above example, one group might see the primary actor using the brand and mentioning the brand's name in the movie. The second group might see the brand being used by the actor, but the brand name itself is not mentioned. Assuming a pre- and post-survey, the notation for this experiment would appear as:

$$\begin{array}{cccc} (R) & O_1 & X_1 & O_2 \\ (R) & O_3 & X_2 & O_4 \end{array}$$

X_1 would denote the first treatment group, the one where the actor used and also mentioned the brand name. X_2 would denote the second treatment group that saw the product being used by the actor, but made no verbal mention of the brand name. The symbol **(R)** means that subjects have been randomly assigned to either the first or second treatment condition, a process called **randomization**.

Randomization process by which subjects are randomly assigned to treatment and control groups.

To prove causation, the three conditions mentioned earlier all must occur. To be certain the results were from the treatment and not some other extraneous variable, researchers will use a control group. The control group receives the same measurement process as the test subjects, but is not exposed to any treatment. For the product placement in the movie, the control group would be surveyed before and after the movie just as the treatment

Source: mindscanner/Shutterstock.

To test the effectiveness of product placement in a movie, test subjects would be assigned to experimental and control group conditions. Both groups would watch the movie, but only the experimental condition would see the movie version containing the product placements (dependent variable). Pre- and postests would assess attitudes towards this brand (independent variables) and other brands, and would allow the researcher to see if attitudes changed in the experimental group. There should be no change in the control group as they were not exposed to the product placement.

group. But, the movie watched by the control group would not contain the product placement at all. Thus, their attitude toward the brand should not change. By comparing the results of the experiment of the test group with those found in the control group, researchers can determine if the product placement did indeed have an impact on attitudes toward the brand. If the test subjects indicated a more positive attitude and the control group showed no change in attitude, then researchers can assert that the product placement did have an impact on consumer attitudes toward the product placement brand since that was the only difference in the movies being watched by the two groups.

In terms of notation, this type of experiment would be denoted in the following manner:

$$\begin{array}{ccc} O_1 & X_1 & O_2 \\ O_3 & & O_4 \end{array}$$

The first line denotes the treatment group, and X_1 is the product placement episode in the movie. The second line is the control group. Notice the control experiences both measurement processes, but is not exposed to the product placement (although they do view the movie). Keep in mind that the treatment is the product placement, not the movie. The movie is just the vehicle that researchers use for the experiment.

7.6 Experimental Designs

As shown in Figure 7.3, experimental designs can be divided into three broad groups: pre-experimental designs, true experimental designs, and quasi-experimental designs. The difference in the designs is based on the way researchers handle the treatment, extraneous variables, and the presence of a control group.

7.7 Pre-Experimental Designs

OBJECTIVE 7.5
Describe the various types of pre-experimental designs.

Pre-experimental designs offer little or no control over extraneous variables and no randomization of subjects.

Pre-experimental designs are characterized by little or no control over extraneous variables and no randomization of subjects (see Figure 7.4). Pre-experimental designs tend to be used in field tests where the researcher has no or little control over factors that may affect the dependent variable. Thus, pre-experimental designs lack both internal and external validity.

- Pre-experimental designs
- True experimental designs
- Quasi-experimental designs

FIGURE 7.3 Types of Experimental Designs

One-shot pre-experimental design pre-experimental design that exposes test subjects to a treatment variable that is then followed by a measurement of the dependent variable.

7.7a One-Shot Pre-Experimental Design

With the **one-shot pre-experimental design,** test subjects are exposed to a treatment variable followed by a measurement of the dependent variable. It does not have any type

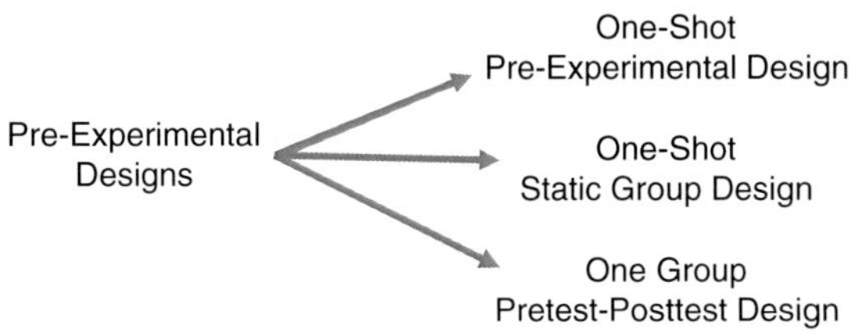

FIGURE 7.4 Pre-Experimental Designs

of control group, nor is there a pretest prior to exposure to the treatment variable. In terms of experimental notation, it would be shown as:

$$X \quad O_1$$

Because there is no control group, researchers cannot say with any degree of certainty that a change in the dependent variable was due to the treatment effect. Further, with no pretest, it is impossible to determine whether or not a change actually occurred. Thus, the one-shot pre-experimental design lacks both internal and external validity.

The one-shot experimental approach is often used with the introduction of new products, or a change to the product's pricing strategy. No past data exists so there is no way a company can obtain pretest measures. Thus, the new product is placed in select markets, select stores, or offered for sale on a company's website. After a pre-specified time, sales are measured to determine if the new product has potential and should be launched nationally.

Komal Nagar used the one-shot pre-experimental design to examine the effect of deceptive advertising on claim recall. Respondents in the experiment were told the study was concerned with the effectiveness of advertising in print media. Each was then given a print ad of a fictitious brand of oral antiseptic that had both true claims and deceptive claims (the treatment, ***X***). After the participants had time to look at and study the ad, it was returned to the researcher. The participants were then asked to recall as many of the claims as possible and to list them on a blank sheet of paper (the measurement, ***O***). It was found that true claims were recalled with a higher frequency than deceptive claims.[11]

7.7b One-Shot Static Group Design

With the **one-shot static group design,** measurements are also taken after the experiment. However, this design differs from the one-shot pre-experimental design in that it includes a control group for comparison purposes. But, it does not include any pretesting of subjects. In terms of notation, the one-shot static group design would be written as:

One-shot static group design pre-experimental design that uses a control group for comparison purposes and takes measurements after the experimental treatment.

$$\begin{matrix} X & O_1 \\ & O_2 \end{matrix}$$

The first row indicates the treatment group and contains the treatment and observation. The second row is the control group that consists of only a measurement. The experimental effect is calculated by subtracting the measurement of the control group from the posttest results of the treatment group, $O_2 - O_1$.

The major validity problem with this design is the comparison of the two groups: the experimental group to the control group. For results to be valid, the two groups must have been equal prior to the experiment. Since no pretest was conducted and subjects were not randomly assigned to conditions, researchers have no way of knowing if the two groups were indeed equal. It is possible that the difference in regard to the dependent variable was already present prior to the experiment and that the experiment itself did not cause any change in the test group.

The one-shot static group design is sometimes used in the testing of new products. For instance, a company might conduct an experiment to test a new software program that allows salespeople to track their activities. Suppose the software is distributed to half of the salespeople in a company. After using the software, the research company measures satisfaction of the salespeople with the software they used. Half used the new software (the experiment); the other half continued using the old software (the control). By comparing the two groups, the research company can determine if there is a higher level of satisfaction with the new software.

While the results provide an indication of how effective the software was in increasing satisfaction, two problems exist. First, it is possible there were differences already between the two groups and that the new software had nothing to do with the treatment group's higher scores. Second, since no pretest was taken the researcher has no idea if there was a change in satisfaction. It is even possible that the level of satisfaction with the old software was higher and that using the new software resulted in a decrease in satisfaction.

7.7c One-Group, Pretest-Posttest Design

One-group pretest-posttest design pre-experimental design in which measurements of the dependent variable are taken prior to the experiment and again after the experiment.

With the **one-group pretest-posttest design**, observation measurements are taken prior to the experiment and again after the experiment. Taking a pretest measurement is certainly an advantage over the one-shot design, but still lacks a control group. In terms of notation, it would be:

$$O_1 \quad X \quad O_2$$

To measure the impact of the treatment, researchers calculate the experimental effect by $O_2 - O_1$, which is the difference between the posttest results and the pretest measurement.

This approach would measure subjects prior to the experiment and then after the experiment to see if any differences occurred. Kraft may want to test the impact of a new digital end-of-aisle display with their Planters breakfast bars. The company has weekly sales data for the breakfast bars already. Suppose the company obtains the cooperation of 25 different grocery stores to test the new digital display for 4 weeks. Kraft is able to access their database for the exact sales for each of the 25 stores, which would be the pretest score. Kraft can monitor the sales of Planters breakfast bars that are placed on the display of the 25 stores and after the four-week period is up, compare sales for the four-week period with the digital display to the four weeks prior to the special display.

While it seems that the one-group pretest-posttest design is an excellent research method, it suffers from some internal validity issues. The history effect is especially a problem with field studies, such as the one with the breakfast bars. If sales increased in the stores with the digital display, it is conceivable that the increase may have been due to other factors, such as actions by competitors, advertising, and promotions. If sales did not increase, it could also be due to competitive coupons, sales, or other actions.

7.8 True Experimental Designs

OBJECTIVE 7.6
Describe the various types of true experimental designs.

True experimental designs experiments in which subjects are randomly assigned to treatment conditions from a pool of subjects.

Pretest-posttest control group design true experimental design in which subjects who have been randomly assigned to experimental and control groups take a pretest, followed by exposure to the treatment in the experimental group, then both groups take a posttest.

With **true experimental designs**, subjects are randomly assigned from a pool of subjects. The sample size needed for each cell (treatment or control group) can be influenced by a variety of factors. For instance, in pricing research it is common to have sample sizes that range from 200 to as many as 400 subjects per group. Variables that influence the exact sample size per cell might include the number of brands involved in the study or the number of price points being tested.[12] Whereas in pre-experimental designs subjects were not randomized, randomization is a key component shared by all true experimental designs. Randomizing reduces the selection effect since probability theory tells us that groups within an experimental design should not differ due to the individual random assignment of members to the groups. Figure 7.5 identifies the two primary experimental designs.

7.8a Pretest-Posttest Control Group Design

In the **pretest-posttest control group design**, subjects are randomly assigned to experimental and control groups. Both groups are then pretested. The experiment is conducted with only the experimental group being exposed to the treatment. Once the treatment is

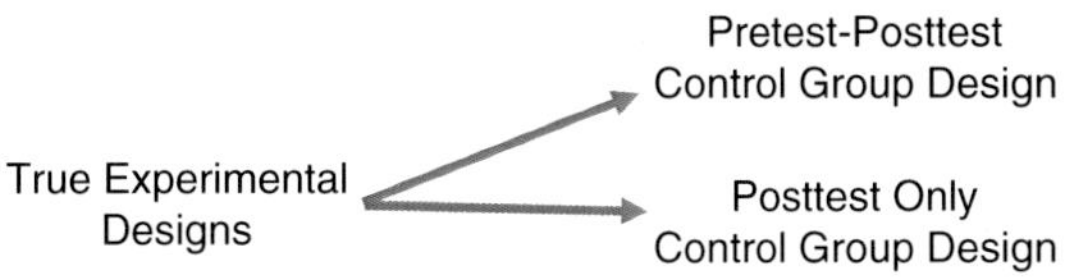

FIGURE 7.5 True Experimental Designs

over both the experimental and control group are measured again, which is the posttest. The notation used for the pretest-posttest control group design is:

$$\begin{array}{cccc} \textbf{(R)} & O_1 & X & O_2 \\ \textbf{(R)} & O_3 & & O_4 \end{array}$$

Suppose advertising researchers wanted to test an advertisement that had been developed for the Super Bowl. Assume 400 individuals were recruited to participate in the study. They are not told the purpose of the research, only that they will be watching a new television show with advertisements as it would appear on television during sweeps week. The subjects are randomly assigned, with half being selected for the experimental group and the other half for the control group. During the television show, both groups see ten different ads. The experimental group is exposed to the newly designed Super Bowl ad, the control group is not. Test measures are taken by both groups before watching the television show and again after the show is over.

To determine the experimental effect, or impact of the experiment, it is necessary to subtract the pretest scores from the posttest scores then compare the treatment group difference to the control group difference. In notation language, it would be written as:

$$(O_2 - O_1) - (O_4 - O_3)$$

To illustrate, suppose the treatment variable is brand awareness. Before the experiment 42 percent of the experimental group was aware of the test brand compared to 40 percent awareness among the control group. After the experiment, awareness of the test brand in the experimental group who were shown the new Super Bowl ad rose to 54 percent, compared to 43 percent for the control group. The difference in the experimental group was 14 percent (54 percent minus 42 percent) and the difference in the control group was three percent (43 percent minus 40 percent). Thus, the treatment effect was 11 percent (14 percent minus 3 percent).

The benefit of a true experimental design is that the extraneous variables discussed earlier would have the same effect on both the experimental and control groups. Therefore, these factors would not affect the validity of the research. It is the randomization process that allows researchers to make this claim. History, maturation, instrumentation, selection, and attrition, if present, would have the same impact on both the treatment and control groups.

The one extraneous variable that might decrease internal validity is testing effect. By asking subjects to identify their awareness before the experiment, the subjects could become more sensitized to watching ads during the television show and pay more attention to ads featuring the brands named in the questions. No matter how the posttest questionnaire is worded, the results of the posttest could have been biased because they had already been exposed to the questionnaire or survey before the television show. In the preceding example, the increase in brand awareness of the test brand in the control group may be an indicator that testing effect was present. Theoretically, the difference in awareness should have been zero.

Posttest only control group design experimental design in which subjects are randomly assigned to experimental and control groups, followed by exposure to the treatment in the experimental group, after which both groups take a posttest, with no pretest.

7.8b Posttest Only Control Group Design

The **posttest only control group design** looks very similar to the one-shot static group pre-experimental design. The only difference is the randomization of the subjects, which makes the design a true experiment rather than a pre-experimental design. The notation would be:

$$\begin{array}{lll} (R) & X & O_1 \\ (R) & & O_2 \end{array}$$

Subjects are randomly assigned to either the experimental or control group. The experimental group is exposed to the treatment variable. Then both groups are measured. The treatment effect is the difference between the experimental group posttest score and the control group posttest score, $O_2 - O_1$.

The posttest only control group design is often used to study the effect of new products. Suppose Skin So Soft developed a new skin lotion with a medicated compound that is designed to help soothe the itch in dermatitis. Subjects selected for the study are randomly assigned to the treatment group and the control group. The treatment group receives the skin solution with the new anti-itch compound, and the control group receives the product without the anti-itch compound. Both groups use the lotion and are then asked a series of questions about the itch of the dermatitis. If the treatment group indicates less itching when using the new product than the control group, then it would indicate that the decline in itching is likely due to the anti-itch compound.

Because only a posttest is used, the potential for testing and instrumentation effect are eliminated. The other extraneous variables, history, maturation, selection, and attrition, are not factors since the subjects were randomly assigned to the two groups.

7.9 Quasi-Experimental Designs

Quasi-experimental designs type of research design in which researchers are unable to randomly assign subjects to group or lack control of when the treatment occurs.

While true experimental designs can be used for marketing research, the use of these designs requires an appropriate laboratory setting, and time, which is often a scarce commodity. More often, marketing research is conducted using either one of the pre-experimental designs or one of the quasi-experimental designs. With **quasi-experimental designs**, researchers lack control of when the treatment occurs or they cannot randomly assign subjects to groups. Quasi-experimental designs work well for field studies where marketers have limited control of the environment. Figure 7.6 identifies the two primary quasi-experimental designs.

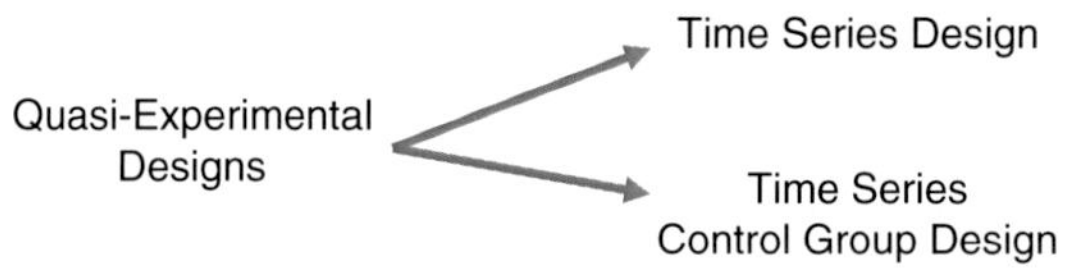

FIGURE 7.6 Quasi-Experimental Designs

7.9a Time Series Design

OBJECTIVE 7.7
Describe the various types of quasi-experimental designs.

Time series design quasi-experimental design in which several pretests are conducted over time prior to exposure to the treatment, followed by several posttests over time.

While individual Super Bowl ads can be tested in a laboratory setting, the impact of an actual Super Bowl ad is a different situation. One method that marketing researchers can use is a **time series design**. Notation for the time series design might be:

$$O_1 \quad O_2 \quad O_3 \quad X \quad O_4 \quad O_5 \quad O_6$$

In studying Super Bowl ads, researchers cannot have a control group since they cannot control who watches the Super Bowl and who does not. Also, they cannot control which ads individuals watch and which ads they do not see due to extraneous factors such as snack breaks and conversations with friends.

Because advertising tends to have a lag effect, researchers can use multiple observations to measure any trend that may occur. Suppose Bridgestone wants to measure the impact of being the Super Bowl half-time sponsor and their corresponding Super Bowl ads. A single pretest on awareness of Bridgestone or even attitudes toward Bridgestone may not be accurate. So researchers could measure Bridgestone awareness, attitude, and image several times prior to the Super Bowl. Then the company can measure awareness, attitude, and image several times after the Super Bowl.

By comparing before and after scores, Bridgestone can determine how much of an impact the Super Bowl half-time sponsorship and ads may have had on consumers. They can also see if any trends exist and how long the Super Bowl advertising carried over. A single measurement of the dependent variable(s) before and after the Super Bowl would not be as accurate as multiple measurements. It also helps to offset the fact that the researchers are not able to have much control on the extraneous variables that affect validity of the study.

7.9b Time Series Control Group Design

Researchers can improve the validity of time series studies through adding a control group. However, not all time series situations allow for a control group. The notation for the **time series control group design** is:

Time series control group design time series design that includes a control group that includes both a pretest and posttest at the same intervals as the treatment group.

Treatment Group:	O_1	O_2	O_3	X	O_4	O_5	O_6
Control Group:	O_1	O_2	O_3		O_4	O_5	O_6

With this quasi-experimental design researchers have no control on whether the subjects are part of the treatment or control group. In some situations individuals might self-select to be part of the treatment, while in other situations it might be a random event.

Consider a study to measure the impact of a new advertising campaign. Instead of launching the ad campaign nationally, the advertising agency might launch the campaign in a selected city, such as New York City or Chicago, or in a specific region, such as the Northeastern or Southwestern part of the United States. In either situation, sporadic measures of the brand, such as awareness, image, and attitude, can be obtained prior to the campaign from individuals in the area where the campaign will be launched and in the area where it will not be launched. Measures can then be taken again after the campaign. Scores for the treatment group can then be compared to the control group.

7.10 Test Markets and Field Studies

OBJECTIVE 7.8
Discuss the concept of test markets and field studies.

Marketing researchers will often use test markets to study various facets of marketing. **Test marketing** involves using pre-experimental or quasi-experimental designs to test new product introductions as well as changes to components of an existing product's marketing mix. Commonly called **field studies,** these pre-experimental and quasi-experimental designs take place outside of a laboratory setting and study behavior rather than intentions or attitudes. So the field experiments related to test marketing help to gauge how changes to advertising, promotions, pricing, the product, customer service and distribution will impact sales, recommendations, click-thrus, churn or other behavior-oriented dependent variables. While it is common to think of test markets as being appropriate for consumer goods typically sold in grocery or mass merchandise stores, test marketing is also used by service providers, restaurant chains, and business-to-business firms.

Test marketing uses pre-experimental or quasi-experimental designs to test new product introductions and various aspects of the marketing mix.

Field studies pre-experimental and quasi-experimental designs that take place outside of a laboratory setting and study behavior rather intentions or attitudes.

Test markets and field studies serve three primary functions. First, test markets help a company to introduce a new product. Based on the results of the test market, national estimates can be made in terms of sales and marketing costs. These estimates also allow the manufacturer to kill a brand that fails its test market before incurring the enormous expense of a national launch. Second, test markets allow a firm to make modifications in the marketing mix of a new product before a national launch. Again, making those modifications on a small scale is less costly and less damaging to the brand's image than doing it at a national level. Finally, marketers can use test markets and field studies to modify elements in the marketing mix of a current product in a local market, or to learn how current customers will respond to a proposed change in the marketing mix prior to implementing the change nationwide. Netflix made a strategic error in 2011 when they divided their unlimited streaming and DVD rental membership plan into two separate plans, each costing $7.99. What essentially resulted in a 60 percent price increase to maintain equivalent service prior to the plan separation outraged consumers, and Netflix's market value fell by over $11 billion in 3 months as customers dropped their Netflix subscriptions in protest. Had Netflix conducted a field experiment with a sample of their current customers, they would have learned of consumers' reaction to the new pricing plan, and gained insight into the level of churn it would generate. The ramifications for revenue, profit, market value and negative publicity could have been considered as part of a well-informed decision-making process prior to implementing changes. The information would have been all the more valuable, being based on actual behavior, rather than stated intentions which might otherwise have been gathered via surveys.[13]

Test markets provide managers with valuable information that can be used in making better marketing decisions. They can take place in stores, on e-commerce websites, in digital advertising environments, via direct mail executions, or in the workplace. Researchers may include randomization of subjects in the treatment conditions when possible, in order to help control for extraneous factors and improve internal validity. While this isn't always possible, technology has made it easier to randomize subjects in field studies/test markets related to digital advertising or search engine marketing.

7.10a Types of Test Markets

Standard test markets typically used when companies introduce a new product and wish to test every element of the marketing mix in a small number of representative test cities.

Three types of test markets exist: standard, controlled and simulated test markets.[14] **Standard test markets** are the most costly and time-consuming, and are generally used when companies introduce a new or severely redesigned product. Marketers opting for standard test markets typically wish to test every element of the marketing mix in a small number of representative test cities. It is also common for changes to be made to various elements of the marketing mix throughout the test market time-period in any one (or more) of the following areas: positioning strategy, advertising, pricing, distribution, branding, packaging, and budgeting. Product sales are tracked over time, and consumers, retailers, and distributors are interviewed and surveyed at multiple times during the test market.

Academics also seek to partner with small, medium and large businesses to obtain behavioral data for their academic research. Normally these field studies seek only to manipulate one or two variables, and as such are scaled-down versions of standard test markets. Academic and business partnerships can be beneficial to both groups. Academics develop a research plan that minimizes the influence of extraneous variables through every aspect of the research design (to the extent possible), enhancing the validity of the data for the firm's decision-making purposes. Ultimately, well-informed decisions can lead to improved promotional effectiveness and increased sales and profits. A key benefit is that firms learn the ramifications of decisions, and what choices work well (or not) under different conditions or circumstances. From the academics standpoint, actual customer behavioral data provides a superior opportunity to test theory when compared to survey data that is restricted to willingness-to-buy and other attitudinal measures. Still, convincing firms to partner with academics is not easy. Concerns include time and money costs, and legal or reputational problems which could stem from the study. Facebook was highly criticized for their part in an emotional manipulation experiment undertaken in partnership with academic researchers, for example. For their part, academics are concerned about a firm's potential interference with the methodology, as often business leaders won't embrace recommended actions designed to enhance the internal validity of the study due to extra cost or other factors.[15]

Traditional controlled test markets panels of stores who have agreed to participate, for a fee, in test markets maintained by professional research firms carry new products and provide sales or other data to the research firm.

Traditional controlled test markets collect data from stores who have agreed to participate, for a fee, in test markets maintained by professional research firm panels such as AC Nielsen's Scantrack or Information Resources Inc's (IRI) Behavior Scan. The test market is less subject to some changes in extraneous variables controlled by the store as the shelf position, pricing, POP displays and the number of product facings are held constant throughout the test. Data can be gathered in as little as three weeks. Sales are measured at the checkout, and the impact of local advertising and promotions may also be evaluated during the test. Sometimes consumers are interviewed to provide qualitative data related to the product. Controlled test markets are generally quicker and less expensive to use than are standard test markets.

Lately, field studies that act as a scaled down and less expensive alternative to controlled test markets have become more practical for smaller businesses that wish to test variations in online advertising or search engine marketing. Google Analytics provides behavioral data that helps to evaluate the effectiveness of various ads or key words, without the need to pay for help from professional research firms.

Simulated test markets attempt to imitate real-life consumer behavior in a simulated environment, such as a laboratory, virtual setting or in-home use test. For example, an artificial grocery store may be set-up in a room or modelled in a virtual reality setting. Subjects are given a budget to shop for items, and as they work their way through the retail environment, they encounter point-of-purchase displays, ads, packages, and prices for the brand being tested, as well as other products. Different subjects may be assigned to different treatment conditions and be exposed to different displays, ads, packages, or prices depending upon the element of the marketing mix that is being evaluated. Virtual reality simulations offer multiple benefits over creating mock physical environments. Virtual reality testing is less expensive, and is easily combined with eye-tracking technology or focus groups. Changing stimuli (POP displays, ads, shopping environments) is quick, and easily accomplished. Subjects can experience a variety of shopping environments at a single facility, which saves costs associated with staff or participant travel to different locations with physical mock-ups of different shopping environments. The technology is intuitive to use, and involves gloves that record a subject's movements, and a headset screen that projects the virtual environment to the subject's eyes. Virtual reality simulations can also be used online by supplying respondents with plug-in equipment for their computer. The advantage is that subjects may come from a wider geographic range, and that it is easier to engage working professionals tied to their office.[16] Explorer Research and Tobii Pro are two research companies that specialize in virtual reality research.[17]

Simulated test markets attempt to imitate real-life consumer behavior in a simulated purchase or usage environment, such as a laboratory setting or in-home use test.

Alternately, consumers may receive an actual product to evaluate as part of a simulated test market. In August of 2018, Nielsen launched the BASES Product Quick Use service, "a new in-home use product testing solution aimed at helping marketers quickly and

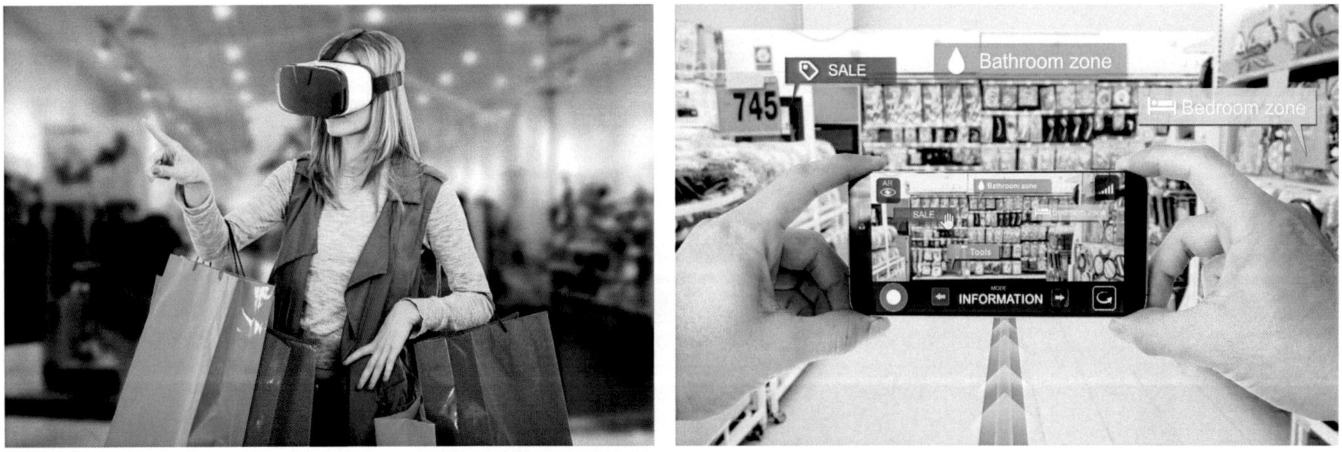

Virtual reality simulations are easily combined with eye-tracking technology, and are intuitive to use. The headset screen projects the virtual environment into the subject's eyes.

Sources: (left) Pop Paul-Catalin/Shutterstock *(right)* buffaloboy/Shutterstock.

accurately simulate a consumer's true product experience prior to launch."[18] Consumers who are part of the panel and meet the target market requirements are sent a product for use, and then answer a series of questions after having experienced the brand.

While also quicker and less costly than the standard test market, simulated test markets have the additional advantages of being exempt from the influence of extraneous variables or competitive reactions, simply because the environment is simulated or limited to the consumer's home. However, the results of these tests have the lowest external validity of the three types of test markets discussed. After all, it is easy to spend virtual money in a simulated shopping environment when it doesn't really come out of your bank account. It is also easier to read ads, product labels, or notice package designs when your two-year old is not screaming at you from his seat in the shopping cart.

7.10b Challenges of Test Markets

As shown in **Figure 7.7**, conducting a test market poses a number of challenges. The degree to which some of these challenges vary between standard, controlled, and simulated test markets is illustrated in **Figure 7.8**. Cost and time are two major challenges. It took Chick-fil-A six years of test marketing before they deemed their chargrilled barbecue chicken sandwich ready for a national rollout[19] and it is not uncommon for standard test marketing to last 3 or more years. The length of the test market is a major decision that has ramifications, good and bad. The longer the test market, the more it will cost. Longer standard test markets also provide the competition with insight on new products and give them more time to develop their own new brand, if desired. Conversely, a major advantage of simulated test markets is that the competition does not gain knowledge of product changes or new products under development. While the competition does learn about new products in controlled test markets, the shorter time frame of these types of test markets leaves less time available for competitors to react.

- Cost
- Time (length of test market)
- Competitive reactions
- Controlling extraneous variables
- Measuring results
- Novel versus normal behavior

FIGURE 7.7 Challenges of Test Markets

Standard Test Market	Controlled Test Market	Simulated Test Market
Most costly	Moderately costly	Varies, depending upon simulated elements
Most time-consuming	May be completed relatively quickly	May be completed relatively quickly
No control over extraneous validity—lowest internal validity	Minor control over a few extraneous store-related variables—low-medium internal validity	Strong control over most extraneous variables—high internal validity
High likelihood of competitive reactions	Moderate—low likelihood of competitive reactions	Low—no likelihood of competitive reactions
May provide more reliable/accurate results and greater predictability	May provide a moderate level of predictability depending on the sample	Lowest level of external validity and predictability

FIGURE 7.8 Test Market Type Comparison

However, on the positive side, longer test markets may provide more reliable and accurate results, which offer greater predictive power, assuming that the competition's actions do not grossly skew sales. The size, location and quality of the sample will influence the accuracy of the results of controlled test markets, and because of the artificial conditions under which they are conducted, simulated test markets suffer from the lowest level of external validity and predictive power. Managers must carefully weigh the advantages of test marketing against the disadvantages to determine how long they want to run the test market.

It is very costly to set up a standard test market. A new product or modified current product requires setting up a new distribution system in a standard test market or making arrangements with the current distribution system members to stock the new product. Then promotional materials have to be prepared. This may include point-of-purchase materials, advertising, promotions, and, of course, packaging. The idea behind a test market is that the product and the marketing communications should resemble that which will be used in the national market as much as possible. Thus, all of the costs that go into marketing a national product are incurred, but on a smaller scale for the test market. It is not unusual for a test market to cost in the millions of dollars. While a controlled test market can save the hassle and cost of setting up a specialized distribution system, marketers must still pay the research firm, who in turn pays fees to participating retailers. Other costs may remain the same for a new product, though they may be much lower if the controlled test market is only being used to test a new package design or a point-of-purchase display. Simulated test markets are not necessarily the cheapest option. Creating a "Shopping Space" that replicates a grocery store—either in real-life or virtually—can be more expensive than you might think. Even in-home use tests require mailing, packaging, and product development/sampling costs, in addition to research expenses related to data recording and analysis. Because of the costs involved, managers must weigh the benefit of a test market against the costs.

In terms of experimentation, a major challenge of test markets is controlling extraneous variables that affect the validity of the test market. Almost all of the extraneous variables discussed earlier can affect a test market. Since standard test markets are conducted in the real world, researchers have little control on events that might affect the results, though controlled test markets do allow for minor control by limiting the potential for history effects such as changing the shelf space, shelf facings, pricing, and POP displays, as mentioned in the previous section. The advantage, however, is that the product is in the store and marketers can gauge the reactions of consumers to the new product or a change in the marketing mix of an existing product. If done correctly, the test market can be an accurate predictor of what would occur on a larger, national scale. It is more difficult to expand the findings to an international scope because of differences in culture and consumers throughout the world. Simulated test markets offer very strong control over extraneous variables, but at the same time, lack the real-world element and predictive power that many marketers seek from a test market. As mentioned earlier, being given fake money to spend in a virtual store is not as predictive of future behavior as consumer's actual shopping behavior in a real store.

Measuring the results of a test market can offer challenges. It is easy to measure sales or coupon usage, but other perceptual measures are more difficult. Measures such as consumer awareness, brand and product image, and consumer attitude offer greater challenges as the researcher must approach consumers, obtain their consent to participate, and administer a survey. If surveyed prior to the shopping experience, consumers may act differently if they believe they are being observed. Still, these measures may be important as they will provide additional information for marketing managers to make good decisions. Researchers will often use one of the quasi-experimental methods to obtain these measurements. Not only does it provide multiple measures, but it will also provide trend results. Marketers need to know if purchases are due to the novelty of the item and if repeat purchases occur. One-time trial purchases are important, but will those purchases continue? That is a very important measurement.

• Offer consumer promotions	• Reverse engineer a new product
• Increase advertising	• Develop a competitive version
• Do nothing	• Prepare a national counter campaign

FIGURE 7.9 Competitive Reactions in Test Markets

7.10c Competitive Reactions

One of the primary disadvantages of test markets is competitive knowledge of what a company is doing. Most companies are engaged in collecting competitive information on a continual basis. If the test market runs long enough to obtain multiple measures and to obtain information that is valuable, the competitors will learn about it. Competitors can react in a number of ways, as identified in Figure 7.9.

One reaction competitors can carry out immediately is to offer consumer promotions on its own brands. Coupons, premiums, and price-offs are the easiest and quickest to offer. Such offers can alter consumer actions in a test market and can easily skew sales figures by undermining the sales potential of the new product. Proctor and Gamble test marketed a new color-safe, low-temperature bleach named Vibrant in Portland, Maine. Clorox learned of the test market, and went to the extreme length of giving every household in Portland a free gallon of Clorox bleach. Vibrant never went to market; the competitive actions undertaken by Clorox trumped the P&G's advertising, couponing, and sampling efforts during the test market.[20] If a test market is about pricing, promotions, or some other component of the marketing mix, competitors offering special deals are still likely to affect the test market results.

For longer test markets, competitors can alter their advertising budget and even the content of their advertising. Competitors are not likely to take this approach unless they feel that whatever is being test marketed can have a significant impact on their market share. Competitors do not want to lose customers and do not want to lose any of their market share, so advertising is a long-term approach to protect themselves. This strategy can also be taken if a company believes that whatever is being test marketed will be launched nationally. Rather than wait on the national launch, competitors can be one step ahead with an advertising campaign aimed at countering the national launch even before it happens.

Competitors might choose to do nothing. This approach is used for two reasons, primarily. First, competitors do not believe whatever is being test marketed will succeed in the marketplace. So by doing nothing competitors are saving resources, but also possibly giving the test market effort a false hope. That is, the test market results will look good for the company conducting it and the company will go ahead with the national launch, only to have the new product or change in marketing mix fail.

The second reason a competitor may do nothing is just the opposite. They believe the new product or whatever is being test marketed is a major threat. Rather than combat it in the test market, resources are gathered and a marketing plan is developed to counter the national launch. The longer the test market lasts, the more time it gives competitors to build a counter marketing campaign.

For new products, companies will certainly pursue reverse engineering. They will purchase the new product and tear it apart, trying to find out exactly how it is made. Competitors will then take this information and look at ways of improving their own products. Thus, by the time the test market is finished and a national launch is made of the new product, competitors may have already developed a competitive version. The longer the test market, again, the more time competitors have to develop their own version of the new product with identical, similar or superior features. This in turn enhances the likelihood that competitors will counter the launch with national advertising campaigns of their own.

The challenge for planners of test markets is to properly interpret competitive reactions. If competitors react during the test market, marketing managers have to decide if these reactions would be consistent with a national launch. If so, then the test market

• New products	• Pricing
• Brand extensions	• Advertising and communications
• Consumer promotions	• Distribution elements

FIGURE 7.10 Marketing Elements That Can Be Test Marketed

results would be a good predictor of future sales potential and consumer reactions. If marketing managers feel that competitors have intentionally reacted to sabotage the test market, then the results of the test market are much more difficult to interpret.

7.10d Novel versus Normal Behavior

Another facet of test markets that researchers must consider is novel versus normal behavior. For a new product, individuals may make an initial purchase because of its novelty. The same can occur with a test market involving advertising, special promotion, pricing, or another marketing test variable. The novelty or uniqueness may trigger a purchase by a consumer. But, will the consumer purchase the product once the novelty is gone?

Marketers must be able to distinguish between novel and normal behavior. Novelty can result in initial signs of success, but spell doom in a national launch. To ensure long-term success it is critical that normal behavior occurs during the test market. One way of ensuring this occurs is to lengthen the time for the test market. Doing so, however, invites competitor reactions that further complicate the situation.

7.10e Test Market Opportunities

Test markets offer a number of opportunities for companies because of the wide range of marketing phenomena that can be manipulated in a test market. Figure 7.10 provides an idea of some of the marketing elements that can be part of a test market. New products are a natural opportunity for test markets and have already been discussed. So are brand extensions. A new flavor of oatmeal, a new type of potato chip, and a new cosmetic extension can be tested to gauge consumer reactions.

A major advantage of test marketing a brand extension is to measure the level of cannibalization. The primary goal of a brand extension is to gain new customers. But instead, what can happen is that current customers switch to the new extension. So the firm does not gain new customers. The brand extension just cannibalizes sales from current versions of the product. If this occurs, launching the brand extension will increase costs but not increase sales. The only way a company should go ahead with the brand extension is to counter competitive actions. If a competitor is introducing a similar brand extension or is anticipated to introduce it, then moving ahead with the extension is a good decision.

Test markets can be used for a variety of consumer promotions and pricing points. A company can develop a special coupon offer and have it distributed in the test market. Using the code on the coupon, researchers can easily measure the redemption rate in the test market. It is possible to have multiple markets, each with a different type of coupon or a coupon with varying face values. Test markets can be used to examine different pricing points. The ideal would be to have one test market at a special price point and then compare the results to markets with the standard price. However, to save money and time, marketers might develop several test markets, each with a different price point.

Advertising and communications programs can be evaluated through test markets. The challenge with advertising and communications campaigns is the lag effect in marketing communications, meaning that advertising does not usually have an immediate impact. So to measure the impact it is necessary to run the test market for several months and maybe even up to a year. During that time a number of the extraneous variables can alter the treatment effects.

Test markets can be used for a number of distribution decisions. Various retail displays, shelf locations, and even channels of distribution can be evaluated with test markets. Before developing an entire distribution channel, a company can use a test market to see how a product would sell first. The restaurant chain El Pollo Loco used test marketing when it participated in the ten-day Taste of Chicago festival in order to gauge consumer acceptance and demand of their menu items before going to the expense of building an actual restaurant. At that point no locations existed in the Chicago area.[21]

7.10f Issues in Selecting a Test Market

Projecting results from a test market to the national level requires careful consideration of which markets should be selected for the test. Figure 7.11 identifies the primary issues that are to be considered when selecting a test market location. Foremost are the population characteristics. It must be of sufficient size to obtain reasonable results. If the area is too large, it drives up costs and often does not provide any better results than a smaller test market. However, if the test market is too small, it is difficult to generalize any results to the population as whole.

In addition to size, the test market population needs to represent the population as a whole, or at least the target market of the product that is being tested. Test markets should be "a microcosm that matches the larger market. The two should be functionally equivalent on all variables that might affect the criterion measure."[22] Thus, demographic composition in terms of gender, age, income, ethnicity, and education should be representative of the population. It is also helpful if the psychographic profile also matches the population. For most national products, the test market population should resemble the U.S. population. However, if a product in the test market has a target market that consists primarily of senior citizens, then test marketing in areas that have a high density of seniors, such as locations in Florida or Arizona, may be appropriate. Figure 7.12 lists eleven U.S. cities that strongly resemble the U.S. population, based on economic, demographic, social, and housing factors. These cities would be strong contenders for test markets.[23]

In light of these characteristics, it may be somewhat surprising to learn that some test markets have recently taken place in Montreal, Canada. "The rationale is that Quebec's relative cultural isolation—its language barrier prevents much outside media from seeping in, and vice-versa—makes it an ideal place for U.S.-based marketers to experiment with new ideas and approaches before rolling them out to wider audiences."[24] While such an approach has the advantage of limiting competitive knowledge of the test market, careful consideration of the factors discussed in the previous paragraph should ultimately govern the choice of a test market.

The market situation in the test market needs to match as closely as possible the marketing situation the company will face when the product is launched. Especially important are competitors. The test market needs to represent the same situation that consumers will face with the national launch in terms of choosing among competing brands. If the test market is done where the major competing brands are not fully represented, the test market will not provide accurate results.

- Population
  - Size
  - Demographic composition
- Market situation
- Media options
- Distribution options

FIGURE 7.11 Issues in Selecting Test Markets

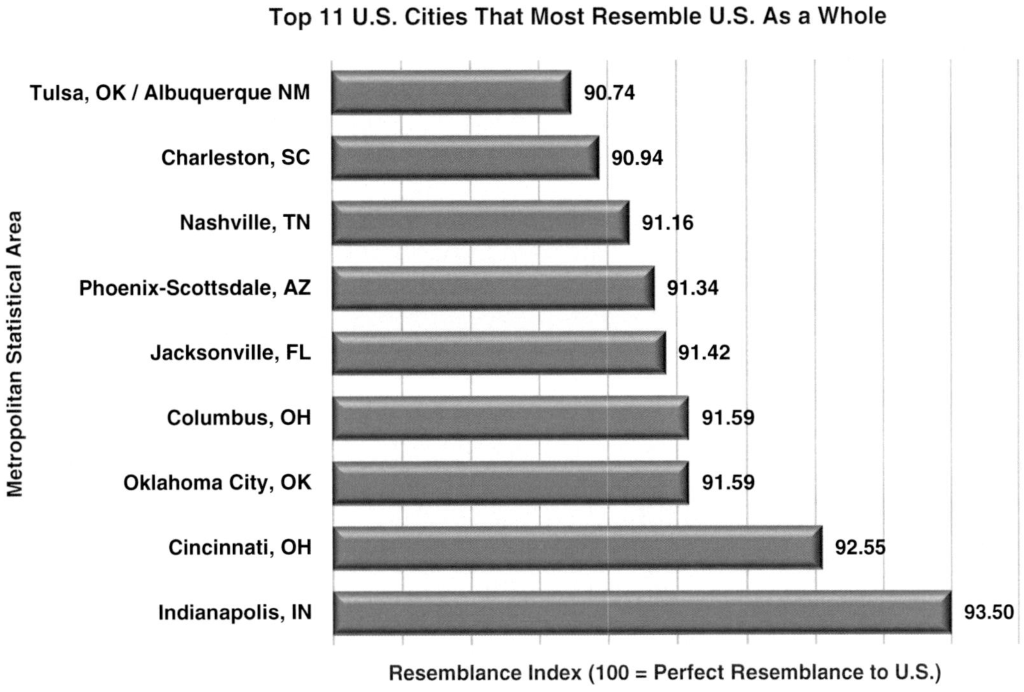

FIGURE 7.12 Potential Test Market MSAs
Source: Adapted from Bernardo, Richie. "2016's Metro Areas That Most and Least Resemble the U.S." https://wallethub.com/edu/metro-areas-that-most-and-least-resemble-the-us/6109/, June 15, 2016, retrieved June 19, 2019.

Media options are important if any type of advertising or marketing communications are part of the test market. But, it is also important that the media not cover an area that is exceptionally larger than the target market. For example, suppose Dallas, Texas is chosen as a test market location. If television and radio stations in Dallas cover an area much larger than Dallas, then not only is money wasted (since the product is not available in areas outside of Dallas) but it may also affect the results of the study.

For new products, a more difficult issue is distribution. What options does a company have in moving the product to the test area? If the test market lasts several weeks (or months) the company must ensure there is a distribution channel to handle it. For companies with an established distribution channel, this is not an issue normally. But, it can add extra costs to the test market.

7.11 Ethics in Experimentation

OBJECTIVE 7.9
Identify ethical practices with experimental research.

Administering an experiment requires careful attention to detail and ethical conduct by the researcher (see **Figure 7.13**). First and foremost, participants should never be put at risk of physical or mental harm. Laboratory experimental subjects should always be informed of their right to withdraw from the experiment at any time for any reason. Subjects also have the right to know how the data will be used, and whether the information they provide is confidential and anonymous. Normally this information is provided in an "Informed Consent" document that researchers ask participants to sign. Field studies may not involve an informed consent document, as behavior is often tracked by gross sales dollars or coupon redemptions not tied to specific individuals (but rather groups of individuals). It is not always possible to obtain consent as the researcher may not know who is participating in the experiment. However, if participants were selected from a database or research panel, it should be possible to secure an informed consent as a condition of participation.

The purpose of the experiment or the exact nature of the experimental treatment itself is often disguised by the researcher in order to minimize bias on the part of the respondent.

- No physical or mental risk
- Right to withdraw
- Knowledge of how data will be used
- Information confidential or anonymous
- Debriefing

FIGURE 7.13 Ethical Considerations in Experimental Research

When a disguise of some type is used, the ethical researcher should debrief participants once the experiment is concluded. Debriefing entails explaining the true purpose of the study, what variables were being manipulated, and why.

7.12 Global Concerns

Experimental designs become more challenging in global markets because they transcend countries and cultures. Experimental designs involve more than just translating languages. They require understanding the culture of the region so an experiment can be designed properly to accomplish the intended objectives. Unfortunately, results obtained in one country or region are not always transferrable to other regions of the world.

Researchers have to pay close attention to nonverbal communication aspects of experimental design, such as concepts of time, mannerisms, body language, space, etiquette and relationships. For instance, in most western countries time is important, and an experiment set for 2:00 pm is expected to start right at 2:00 pm. However, in some countries, especially in Spanish-speaking countries, time is not so formal. Also, afternoon siestas are part of the culture. Personal space is another issue. Some individuals and cultures feel uncomfortable if another person is too close to them. In other cultures it is acceptable. Etiquette varies greatly between countries. In countries such as Japan etiquette and behavior, especially toward elders, is more formal than in the United States. Because of these types of differences, it is important to hire a research company that understands the customs and culture of a region, or to involve someone who has this level of understanding to assist in designing experiments.

Test marketing presents a unique challenge for global companies. The greatest challenge relates to deciding where the product should first be introduced, since results in one country may not be indicative of whether the product will succeed or fail if marketed globally. Coca-Cola used New Zealand to test a raspberry version of its Coca-Cola. The final decision to launch the flavor globally was based on the results of the New Zealand test market.[25] In deciding where to test market a new product or brand extension, marketers have to think about which country would be most like the global markets it is seeking for expansion. Even then, separate in-country testing may be required for some elements of the marketing mix that be seen as offensive, or not be understood, due to cultural differences.

7.13 Marketing Research Statistics

Statistical tests for experiments vary greatly due to the various types of experimental designs that can be used and the types of data that can be collected. The Statistical Review section examines two common procedures used in analyzing experiments: independent sample t-tests and paired sample t-tests. The Statistical Reporting section provides information on possible ways to graphically illustrate results of an experiment. The Dealing with Data section provides data through the authors' website www.clowjames.net/students.html that can be tested using both the independent t-test and the paired sample t-test.

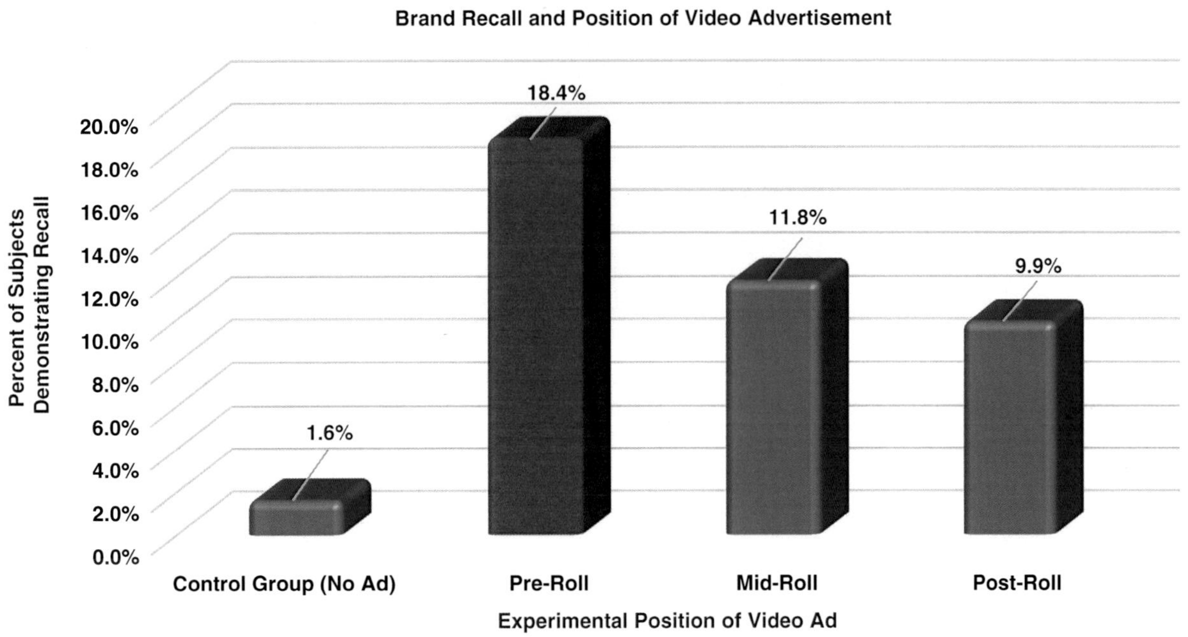

FIGURE 7.17 Graphed Results of Posttest only Group Design

Treatment	Pretest	Posttest
Test Ad	5.23	5.87
Control Group	5.28	5.31

FIGURE 7.18 Results from a Pretest-Posttest Control Group Experiment

different locations representing three treatments. Pre-roll ads are at the beginning of a video, mid-roll ads appear in the middle of the video and post-roll ads at the end. A posttest only control group design was used. Subjects were randomly assigned to the three treatments or the control group. After the subjects watched the video they were asked questions about the video and to name the brand in the advertisement. The results, shown in Figure 7.17, indicate the highest recall percentage was for the pre-roll location, 18.4 percent.

Statistical Reporting Exercise. Figure 7.18 shows the results of a pretest-posttest control group experimental design. Brand awareness was measured before the experiment and again after watching a television show with the test ad embedded. The control group watched the same television show, but without the test ad. Graph the results of the experiment. Be sure the pretest and posttest for the brand awareness are grouped close together. Do the same for the control group.

Figure 7.19 shows the results of additional measures that were taken before and after watching the advertisement. Create a second graph of the three treatments: brand image, likeliness to recommend, and purchase intentions. As with your first graph, group the pretest and posttest scores for each variable together. You will not have the control groups on this graph so place a footnote at the bottom of the graph indicating that the control groups indicated no significant differences between pretest and posttest scores. Create a chart title and label both the x-axis and y-axis properly.

Treatment	Pretest	Posttest
Brand Image	6.21	6.77
Likely to Recommend	4.82	5.43
Purchase Intentions	4.02	4.77

FIGURE 7.19 SPSS Results from a Pretest-Posttest Control Group Experiment

7.13c Dealing with Data

A retailing chain is interested in determining whether a digital point-of-purchase display would stimulate higher sales for an advertised brand than would a standard point-of-purchase display. To test this, a one shot-static group design experiment was conducted over a four-week period in 100 different stores. Fifty stores were assigned to the control treatment and 50 stores were assigned to the experimental treatment. Every store used a display for the same product. Sales were measured at the end of the four weeks for both the control group (standard display) and the experimental group (digital display). The data are in the SPSS files entitled Chapter 7 Dealing with Data 1 (www.clowjames.net/students.html). Compare the sales of the control group (standard POP) to the experimental group (digital POP) using an independent sample t-test. Based on your output, answer the following questions.

1. What were the average sales for the standard POP display (control group)? What about the digital display (experimental group)?
2. What is the mean difference in sales between the experimental group and the control group?
3. At a 95 percent confidence level, was the difference significant? Explain why or why not?
4. Should the manager of the retail chain install new digital displays? Justify your answer. What other factors should the manager consider before making the decision?
5. What extraneous factors could have impacted sales, positively or negatively, at any time over the course of the 8-week experiment?

Another retail outlet tested a digital point-of-purchase display using a one-group pretest-posttest design. The data are in the file Chapter 7 Dealing with Data 2 (www.clowjames.net/students.html). With this experiment, the retailer measured the sales of a regular point-of-purchase display for four weeks prior to the experiment. The standard POP display was replaced with the digital display in 59 stores and sales were measured after another four weeks. Again, the POP displays were all focused on the same product. Use a paired sample t-test to compare sales before and after the new digital display. Based on your output, answer the following questions.

1. What were the average sales for the four weeks prior to the experiment?
2. What were the sales during the four weeks when the stores used the digital display?
3. What is the mean difference in sales?
4. At a 95 percent significance level, was the difference significant? Explain why or why not?
5. Should the manager of the retail chain install new digital displays? Justify your answer.

Summary

Objective 1: Explain the concepts of internal and external validity.

Validity refers to the degree to which an experiment (or research study) measures what is supposed to measure. Validity consists of both internal and external validity. Internal validity is the extent to which a particular treatment in an experiment produces the sole effect on the dependent variable being studied. Obtaining a high level of internal validity requires ruling out any other possible extraneous effects. External validity refers to the extent the findings of an experiment (or research study) can be generalized to the population as a whole or to the specific population being studied.

Objective 2: Identify the three conditions that must be present to prove causation.

Experimental research, also known as causal research, is the form of research that can actually prove cause and effect. Proving causation requires three conditions be met: 1) concomitant variation between X and Y; 2) time order of occurrence, in that X occurs prior (or simultaneously) to Y; and 3) elimination or control of extraneous factors that might otherwise be responsible for causing a change in Y. Most experiments take place in a laboratory setting instead of the field in order to control the influence of extraneous factors.

Objective 3: Discuss the extraneous factors that can affect internal and external validity.

Extraneous factors may confound the results of an experiment by offering a competing explanation for any changes noted in the dependent variable(s). This damages the internal and external validity of the experimental results. Extraneous factors include: history effects, maturation, testing effects, instrumentation, selection effects, and attrition.

Objective 4: Explain the basic notation used in experimental design.

Three notation symbols are used to identify actions undertaken within control groups or treatments. The notion **(R)** is used to designate the fact that subjects have been randomly assigned to a group. Exposure to the treatment, or experimental stimuli, is designated by the ***X*** notation. Observations, during which measurements of the subject groups are undertaken, are denoted by the symbol ***O***. Observations occurring at different times or among different treatments and multiple treatments are followed by a subscript number.

Objective 5: Describe the various types of pre-experimental designs.

Pre-experimental designs have low internal and external validity because they do not randomly assign subjects to groups and offer little or no control over extraneous variables. The one-shot pre-experimental design exposes subjects to the treatment, then measures the dependent variable. The one-shot static group design expands this design to include a control group. The one group pretest-posttest design has the advantage of measuring the dependent variable before the treatment occurs, as well as after, though no control group is used.

Objective 6: Describe the various types of true experimental designs.

True experimental designs are characterized by the randomization of subjects, which controls for the influence of extraneous variables, thereby resulting in greater internal validity. True experimental designs include the pretest-posttest control group design and the posttest only control group design.

Objective 7: Describe the various types of quasi-experimental designs.

Quasi-experimental designs lack internal validity because they do not allow for subject randomization. They tend to be used in field studies that limit the researcher's control over extraneous variables and when the treatment actually occurs. To compensate for these weaknesses, the time series design and time series control design both take multiple measurements of the dependent variable both before and after the treatment occurs.

Objective 8: Discuss the concept of test markets and field studies.

Marketers use test markets to evaluate new products and aspects of the marketing mix. Field studies used in test markets occur outside of the laboratory and track behaviors rather than attitudes. Standard, controlled or simulated test market studies can be used. Academics may partner with businesses in running limited test markets via field studies. Test markets are time-consuming and costly, and it is difficult to control for extraneous variables. Furthermore, competitive reactions can interfere with the test market or the national rollout of a product that passes this test. Selecting a test market requires consideration of the population, market situation, media options, and distribution options. Global test markets present a special challenge.

Objective 9: Identify ethical practices with experimental research.

Participants in experiments should never be put at risk of physical or mental harm. Experimental subjects should be informed of their right to withdraw from the experiment at any time, for any reason. Subjects also have the right to know how the data will be used, and whether the information they provide is confidential and anonymous. Researchers should debrief participants once the experiment is concluded.

Key Terms

attrition, p. 234
concomitant variation, p. 230
confounds (results), p. 229
control group, p. 229
dependent variable, p. 228
external validity, p. 229
field studies, p. 241
history effects, p. 232
independent variables, p. 228
instrumentation effect, p. 233
internal validity, p. 229
maturation, p. 232
observation, p. 235
one-group pretest-posttest design, p. 238
one-shot pre-experimental design, p. 236
one-shot static group design, p. 237
posttest only control group design, p. 239
pre-experimental designs, p. 236
pretest-posttest control group design, p. 238
quasi-experimental designs, p. 240
randomization, p. 235
selection effect, p. 234
simulated test markets, p. 243
spurious correlation, p. 230
standard test markets, p. 242
subjects, p. 229
test marketing, p. 241
testing effects, p. 233
time series control group design, p. 241
time series design, p. 240
traditional controlled test markets, p. 242
treatment, p. 228
true experimental designs, p. 238
validity, p. 229

Critical Thinking Exercises

1. A consumer goods manufacturer recently conducted an experiment in which coupon formats were tested in different variations, classified as high, moderate, or low value. The face value of the high, medium, and low value cents-off coupon treatments were 75 cents, 50 cents, and 25 cents, respectively. Similarly, buy one get one free, buy two get one free, and buy three get one free treatments were classified as high, moderate, and low value treatment conditions for the second coupon type. Redemption rates for each coupon treatment are shown in the table:

	COUPON REDEMPTION RATE		
Type of Coupon	High value	Moderate Value	Low Value
Cents-off	1.5%	2%	1.5%
Buy X, Get 1 Free	4%	2%	.5%

   Do the results shown in this table provide evidence of concomitant variation? Why or why not? Interpret these results. What conclusions can be drawn regarding the relationship between the type of coupon and the coupon redemption rate in this experiment? What other factors should be considered when interpreting the data?
2. Suppose your supervisor is interested in determining whether or not a sweepstakes program should be used to promote your brand. Identify potential independent variables, dependent variables, and treatments. What type of experimental design would you recommend? Why?
3. Knowing that you are a college student majoring in marketing at the local university, your supervisor at the local pizza parlor has asked for your input regarding a research study. She wants to determine which of three new pizza toppings should be added to the menu: broccoli, spam, or pineapple. She plans on promoting broccoli in February, spam in March, and pineapple in April, and using the number of pizzas ordered with each topping to make her decision. List and briefly describe the extraneous factors that may interfere with the results of her study.
4. A researcher was trying to determine the impact that placing a branded product in a movie has on brand attitudes. In the pretest **(O_1)** and posttest **(O_2)** measurement process, a single question is used to assess attitude toward the brand, asking respondents to rate how favorable their attitude is by selecting one of five responses: very unfavorable (1), unfavorable (2), neutral (3), favorable (4), and very favorable (5). In between the pretest and posttest measurements, subjects watch a movie in which the hero conspicuously consumes the branded product while commenting favorably on its attributes. In both the pretest and posttest, subjects' responses to the question are assigned the value shown in parentheses above. These values are averaged across all subjects for the pretest and averaged again for the post. The results are as follows: Pretest: 2.57 Posttest: 4.21. What is the experimental effect? How would you interpret this information? What does it mean? What statistical test

would be needed to determine whether the experimental effect may simply have occurred by chance?

5. A researcher has designed an experiment in which three groups of subjects are first surveyed regarding their attitudes toward various brands of snack food in general, and potato chips in particular. Each group is then told to "shop" for products they would purchase for a Super Bowl party if they were hosting such an event. Shopping takes place in a simulated super market environment controlled by the researcher, which is designed to mimic an actual grocery store. In the chip aisle, two of the three subject groups walk past a point-of-purchase display for Frito-Lay products, though the display shown differs for each group. Everything else in the store is the same. After completing the shopping exercise, the group is told that a brand was inadvertently left off of the survey, and asked to complete it again. Identify the following: 1) independent variable(s); 2) dependent variable(s); 3) treatment; 4) experimental notation depicting this experiment; 5) the formula for calculating the experimental effect.
6. Suppose Procter and Gamble is interested in updating the package design for one of their laundry detergents. Design an experiment to help with this task, clearly identifying the dependent variable(s), the independent variable, and the treatment(s) and how the experiment should be administered to control for extraneous factors. Defend your choice of experimental design.
7. A manufacturer of plug-in air fresheners is curious to learn whether consumers rely more on brand name or the scent of the air freshener when making their purchase decision. Design an experiment to help with this task, clearly identifying the dependent variable(s), the independent variable, the treatment(s) and the experimental design that should be used. Justify your choice of experimental design.
8. Suppose a brewery was considering introducing a new packaging alternative—plastic bottles. Would experimentation designed to test consumers' preference of packaging materials be the first step undertaken by the company in researching this potential opportunity? Why or why not? Justify your answer.
9. As a student worker in the Marketing Department, one of your professors has assigned you the task of randomly assigning members of a sample to either the control group, or one of two treatment conditions. Explain the process and tactics you would use in completing this assignment.
10. Suppose that the mass merchandiser Target wanted to test a digital point-of-purchase display. How should Target choose the stores to be part of the test market? What type of experimental design would you recommend? Why? What treatments should be used? What dependent variables would be measured? Explain and justify your answer.

The Lakeside Grill

(Comprehensive Student Case)

Making a decision about experimental research was challenging for the student team researching the Lakeside Grill. While ideas were generated, there were doubts if experiments could be conducted with the restaurant. They felt the inability to control extraneous variables would dilute any results that might be obtained. Here are some of the ideas that were generated by the group.

1. Some of the other area restaurants served bread or chips and dip to customers while they waited for their meal. Destiny suggested using a one-shot pre-experimental design where a free loaf of bread would be given to guests for a two-week time period. Overall restaurant sales would be measured to see if the bread caused an increase in sales. Alexa suggested a different dependent variable. She thought customers should be surveyed to see if the free bread would affect their decision to return.
2. In comparing Lakeside Grill's menu with other restaurants and the results of the focus group, Juan suggested the restaurant offer three new appetizers not currently on the menu. A new menu would be printed containing the three new appetizers but otherwise it would look identical to the current menu. Half of the customers would receive the new menu with the new appetizers and the other half would receive the old menu and serve as the control group. (Everyone in a party at a table would receive the same menu.). This one-shot static group design would allow the student team to see if adding new appetizers would affect the number of orders for appetizers by comparing the control group orders with the experimental group orders.
3. The last suggestion dealt with wait staff. Approximately three-fourths of the wait staff were male. However, the focus group results suggested that having more female servers might enhance the image of the restaurant. Brooke suggested scheduling more females to work over a three-week period so the ratio was closer to 50/50, and that wait staff be randomly assigned to customers. At the conclusion of the meal, each customer would be given a card asking them to rate the quality of service and the likelihood of their return. For the control group, Zach suggested that during the next three weeks they keep the 75/25 ratio of male to female waiters and again use the feedback card. The results of the control group could then be compared to the experimental group. "Comparing

males and females is not a one-shot static group design," he added.

Critique Questions:

1. Evaluate the three experimental design suggestions. Do they fit the criteria for pre-experimental designs?
2. Is Zach statement correct that "comparing males and females is not a one-shot static group design"?
3. For the free bread experiment, what extraneous variables would be of concern? What can be done to control for each of the extraneous variables?
4. For the free bread experiment, which observation variable is the best, sales or future purchase intentions? Why?
5. For the second experiment, the three new appetizers, what extraneous variables would be of concern? What can be done to control for each of the extraneous variables?
6. For the third experiment, the new male/female staff ratio, what extraneous variables would be of concern? What can be done to control for each of the extraneous variables?
7. Which experimental design would you recommend for the Fantastic Five? Why?
8. Do you have any other suggestions in terms of experiments or different ways of designing the ones suggested? Elaborate.

Notes

1. Information in this section is based on H. Hagtvedt and S. A. Brasel, "Color Saturation Increases Perceived Product Size," *Journal of Consumer Research* 44, no. 2 (2017): 396–413; P. Walker, B. J. Francis, and L. Walker, "The Brightness-Weight Illusion: Darker Objects Look Heavier but Feel Lighter," *Experimental Psychology* 57, no. 6 (2010): 462–469.
2. Gianluigi Guido, Luigia Piper, M. Irene Prete, Antonio Mileti, and Carla M. Trisolini, "Effects of Blue Lighting in Ambient and Mobile Settings on the Intention to Buy Hedonic and Utilitarian Products," *Psychology & Marketing* 34, no. 2 (2017): 215–226.
3. Eric M. Vanepps, Julie S. Downs, and George Loewenstein, "Advance Ordering for Healthier Eating? Field Experiments on the Relationship between the Meal Order–Consumption Time Delay and Meal Content," *Journal of Marketing Research* 53, no. 3 (2016): 369–380.
4. Daniel Read, Shane Frederick, and Mara Airoldi, "Four Days Later in Cincinnati: Longitudinal Tests of Hyperbolic Discounting," *Acta Psychologica* 140, no. 2 (2012): 177–185; Tabea Bucher-Koenen and Carsten Schmidt, "Time (In)Consistent Food Choice of Children and Teenagers," *SSRN Electronic Journal* (2011); Andrew S. Hanks, David R. Just, and Brian Wansink, "Preordering School Lunch Encourages Better Food Choices by Children," *JAMA Pediatrics* 167, no. 7 (2013): 673.
5. Eric M. Vanepps, Julie S. Downs, and George Loewenstein, "Advance Ordering for Healthier Eating? Field Experiments on the Relationship between the Meal Order–Consumption Time Delay and Meal Content," *Journal of Marketing Research* 53, no. 3 (2016): 369–380.
6. Nathan M. Fong, Zheng Fang, and Xueming Luo, "Geo Conquesting: Competitive Locational Targeting of Mobile Promotions," *Journal of Marketing Research* 52, no. 5 (2015): 726–735.
7. Information in this section is based on Donald T. Campbell and Julian C. Stanley, *Experimental and Quasi-Experimental Designs for Research* (Boston, MA: Houghton Mifflin Company, 1963), 5–12.
8. Ayelet Gneezy, "Field Experimentation in Marketing Research," *Journal of Marketing Research* 54, no. 1 (2017): 140–143.
9. Paul E. Spector, *Research Designs* (Beverly Hills, CA: Sage Publications, 1981), 16–17.
10. Marla B. Royne, "Cautions and Concerns in Experimental Research on the Consumer Interest," *Journal of Consumer Affairs* 42, no. 3 (2008): 478–483.
11. Komal Nagar, "Effect of Deceptive Advertising on Claim Recall: An Experimental Research," *Journal of Services Research* 9, no. 2 (October 2009): 105–122.
12. Keith Chrzan, "Data Use: An Overview of Pricing Research," *Quirk's Marketing Research Review* (July/August 2006): 24, 26–29.
13. Ayelet Gneezy, "Field Experimentation in Marketing Research," *Journal of Marketing Research* 54, no. 1 (2017): 140–143.
14. Information in this section is taken from Sallie B. Middlebrook, "Basics of Product Test Marketing," ToughNickel, January 17, 2017, https://toughnickel.com/industries/Product-Test-Marketing; Kevin J. Clancy, Peter C. Kreig, and Marianne McGarry Wolf, *Market New Products Successfully* (Lanham, MD: Lexington Books, 2006), 19–38.
15. Ayelet Gneezy, "Field Experimentation in Marketing Research," *Journal of Marketing Research* 54, no. 1 (2017): 140–143.
16. "Virtual Reality Research," Explorer Research, 2019, https://explorerresearch.com/learn/consumer-research-techniques/virtual-reality-market-research/.
17. "Top Marketing Research Companies Specializing in Virtual Reality," *Quirk's Media* (2019), https://www.quirks.com/directories/sourcebook/specialties/virtual-reality.

18. “Nielsen Bases Debuts Faster In-Home Product Testing Solution for Fast-Moving Consumer Goods,” Nielsen Company, August 22, 2018, https://www.nielsen.com/us/en/press-room/2018/nielsen-bases-debuts-faster-in-home-product-testing-solution-for-fmcg.html.
19. Milford Prewitt, “R&D Executives Find Testing New Products, Designs Costly but Necessary,” *National's Restaurant Business* 40, no. 49 (December 4, 2006): 1, 46.
20. Karen Dillon, “I Think of My Failures as Gifts,” *Harvard Business Review* 89, no. 4 (April 2011): 86–89.
21. Prewitt, “R&D Executives Find Testing New Products, Designs Costly but Necessary.”
22. Robert Zimmerman, “Problems Inherent in Using a Test Market,” *Quirk's Marketing Research Review* (August 1988): 12.
23. Richie Bernardo, “2016's Metro Areas That Most and Least Resemble the U.S.,” WalletHub, 2016, https://wallethub.com/edu/metro-areas-that-most-and-least-resemble-the-us/6109/.
24. Jerry Mullman, “The Next Hot Spot for U.S. Test Market Is in Canada,” *Advertising Age* 80, no. 38 (November 9, 2009): 4, 33.
25. “Coca-Cola Soft Drink—Raspberry,” *MarketWatch: Drinks* 4, no. 9 (September 2005): 6.

PART III

Sampling and Measurement

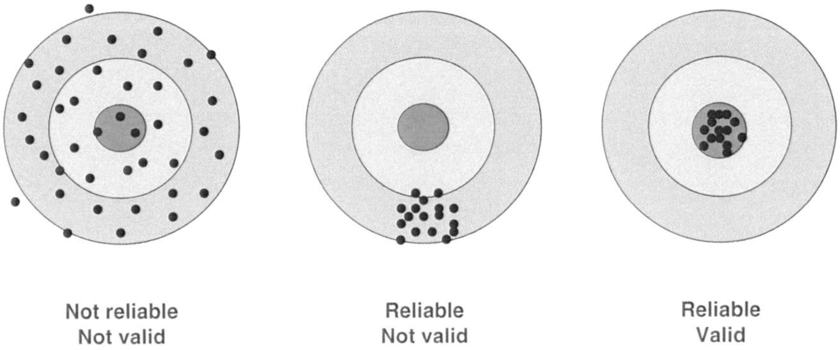

Source: Artem Twin/Shutterstock.

Sampling Procedures

CHAPTER 8

Source: Mr. Whiskey/Shutterstock.

Chapter Outline

Learning Objectives

After studying this chapter, you should be able to:

- Explain the difference between a population and a sample.
- Discuss the steps involved in selecting a sample.
- Identify and describe the four nonprobability sampling methods.
- Identify and describe the four probability sampling methods.
- Describe the various methods of determining sample size.
- Discuss the benefits and issues related to online research panels.

8.1 Chapter Overview

The Pew Research Center published a study in 2018 that reported social media usage among various age groups, genders, and ethnicities.[1] A sample of 500 adults aged 18 years or older living in all United States and the District of Columbia were randomly selected using random digit dialing to participate in landline telephone surveys. An additional sample of 1,502 individuals were selected for cell phone interviews.

Consider the unweighted age of the sample listed in Figure 8.1, the 2017 population estimate based on the U.S. Census data, the difference between the sample and population percentages, and the margin of error based on a 95 percent confidence level. While the overall margin of error was 2.4 percent for the total study based on the total sample size, in terms of age, the 18–24 and 25–29 age groups exhibited high margins of error in the unweighted sample. In recognition of this problem, Pew Researchers weighted the final sample by age, gender, race, and Hispanic origin characteristics. This tactic helps to reduce error, ensuring that the results of the study are more representative of the U.S. population.

The survey examined social media usage in the United States, the growth of different social media platforms, how usage varies by age, and other factors. A key question asked respondents to identify the social media platforms they followed online or via cell phone. Figure 8.2 shows the results. YouTube and Facebook were the leading social media sites, at nearly double that of the other social media sites. Additional data revealed that 73 percent of the sample used more than one of the social media platforms investigated, with greater usage being more prevalent among younger age groups.

By using a sample that was carefully selected, the Pew Research Center is able to project their findings to the U.S. national population. This chapter examines the procedure companies and research firms would use in selecting a sample to survey. Probability and nonprobability sampling methods are discussed as well as methods of determining the size of the sample. The chapter concludes with a discussion of online research panels since they have become such a prominent means of soliciting respondents for marketing studies.

8.2 Introduction to Sampling

LEARNING OBJECTIVE 8.1
Explain the difference between the population and a sample.

Sampling process of choosing the group of individuals to survey.

Sample group of individuals chosen to survey.

In a previous chapter, the various methods of survey research were presented. Most involved surveying individuals in some manner. The process of choosing the group of individuals to survey is called **sampling** and the group of individuals chosen is the **sample.**

Age Category	Percent of Sample	Percent of Population (US Census)	Difference	Margin of Error (95% Confidence)
Age 18–24	10.3%	12.36%	-2.06%	+/-7.7%
Age 25–29	7.7%	9.18%	+1.48%	+/-8.8%
Age 30–49	27.0%	33.35%	-6.35%	+/-4.7%
Age 50–64	27.9%	25.37%	+2.53%	+/-4.7%
Age 65+	27.1%	19.74%	+7.32%	+/-4.7%

FIGURE 8.1 Comparison of Age to Population Characteristics
Sources: Adapted from "Social Media Use in 2018," Pew Research Center, Washington, D.C., (March 1, 2018), http://www.pewinternet.org/2018/03/01/social-media-use-in-2018/ and United States Census Bureau. "Table S0101: Age and Sex, 2017 American Community Survey 1-Year," *American Community Survey*. U.S. Census Bureau. Washington D.C.: U.S. Census Bureau, 2017.

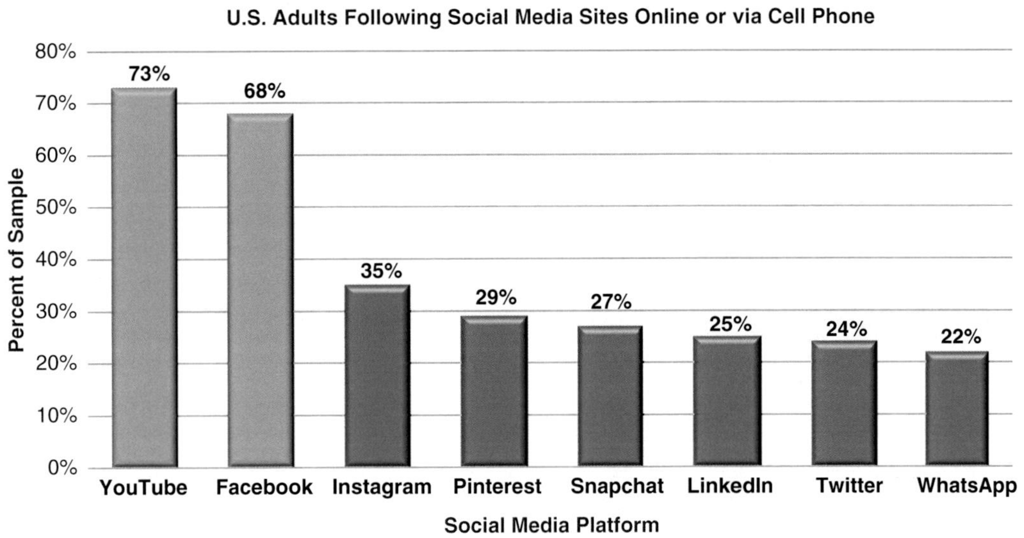

FIGURE 8.2 A Graph Showing the Percentage of U.S. Adults Following Social Media Platforms Online or via Cell Phone
Source: Adapted from "Social Media Use in 2018," Pew Research Center, Washington, D.C., (March 1, 2018), http://www.pewinternet.org/2018/03/01/social-media-use-in-2018/.

It is important to keep in mind that a sample can also refer to objects, such as retail stores, websites, and products. Sampling does not always have to involve people, although it is the most common form of sampling used in marketing.

The group from which the sample is drawn is called the **population**. The population can vary widely. It can be all of the individuals in the United States, all of the individuals in a specific state, all of the employees of a company such as Kraft Foods, or the individuals in a small, private college graduating class. It can also be all individuals who own a certain type of product or who suffer from a particular medical condition. It can range from millions of people or objects to just a few.

Population group from which a sample is drawn and which is the target of the research study.

Sampling is used because in most cases it is not practical to survey an entire population, unless the population size is small. Surveying all of the parents of seventh grade students at a local school that has 75 children is feasible. Surveying all the members in a local advertising club or Lion's organization makes sense. A business-to-business firm that has only 40 clients can survey all of their customers. When the entire population is surveyed, then it is called a **census**.

Census survey of the entire population.

In most cases, sampling an entire population is not practical, for two reasons. First, if the population is large the cost and time to conduct the survey would be prohibitive. For instance, *Socialmediaexaminer.com* implemented its 10th annual study to understand how social media is used to grow and promote businesses. The sample consisted of more than 5,700 social media marketing professionals. When asked about the key benefits of social media marketing, the percentage of respondents who agreed with each of the following is shown below in parentheses:

- increased exposure (87%)
- increased traffic (78%)
- lead generation (64%)
- developing loyal fans (63%)
- providing marketplace insight (54%)
- improving sales (53%)[2]

The second reason to use surveys rather than a census is accuracy. If a sample of a population is properly selected, the survey can provide results that accurately reflect the entire population within an acceptable degree of error. In some cases, the sample may even be

Source: Yaoinlove/Shutterstock.

Adding sample restrictions, such as (1) individuals must be married, (2) of Asian ethnicity, (3) have a non-working spouse and, (4) at least one child, lowers the incidence rate. This means a smaller percentage of the population will qualify to participate in a survey. Inserting screening questions into a survey can help determine if a person meets the eligibility criteria. Or, a sampling firm can recruit participants who meet the restrictions.

more accurate than an attempted census. After all, it would be extremely difficult to locate everyone in a population, much less ensure their participation, which leads to the possibility of non-response bias. In addition, surveying an entire population would require a large staff of individuals to conduct the surveys, which compounds the likelihood of interviewer error. It is not necessary to survey an entire population as long as the sample adequately represents the population.

8.3 The Sampling Process

Obtaining a good sample does not happen by accident. It takes careful planning and execution. **Figure 8.3** outlines the steps involved in selecting a sample.

8.3a Define the Population

LEARNING OBJECTIVE 8.2
Discuss the steps involved in selecting a sample.

The first step is to define the target population. While it sounds easy to do, for many marketing studies it can be a challenge. In addition to defining who to include, limitations or boundaries of exclusion must also be part of the definition. Most commercial market research firms exclude marketing research professionals or those who work in the marketing industry for fear of bias. Individuals who work within the product segment may also be excluded, or, depending on the study purpose, they may be the population under study. Keep in mind that a population can be stores, businesses, households, institutions, and even purchase transactions.

StrongMail Systems, Inc. is a provider of marketing solutions for businesses seeking assistance in e-mail and social media marketing. The company joined with the Relevancy Group to conduct research in the travel and hospitality industry. Before selecting a sample, the researchers had to define the target market of the research. The company defined the population as marketing executives in the United States and in the United Kingdom within three industries—retail, travel, and media/publishing. The definition also contained an exclusion or boundary. Companies that sent less than one million e-mail messages per month were excluded.[3] By carefully defining the population, StrongMail Systems and Relevancy Group were able to locate e-mail marketers that met the criteria to be part of their sample.

The simpler the population definition, the higher the incidence and the less costly it will be to locate an appropriate sample. Recall from Chapter 7 that *incidence* refers to the percentage of individuals, households, or businesses in the population that would be qualified as potential respondents in a particular study. Incidence is important because it provides clues to the level of effort that will be required to find eligible respondents. The more restrictions or exclusions that are included, the more difficult it will be to locate sample respondents because a lower percentage of the population will meet all of the criteria. Consider a population defined as males aged 20 to 40 with incomes between \$50,000 and \$100,000. If further restrictions are added, such as married with at least one

1. Define the population
2. Identify the sample frame
3. Choose a sampling procedure
4. Decide on the sample size
5. Select the sample

FIGURE 8.3 Steps in Selecting a Sample

child and a spouse who does not work, then incidence is reduced, which means a smaller percentage of the population now qualify. These additional criteria require that screening questions related to the number of children, marital status, and spousal employment be included in the survey to determine eligibility.

A similar situation occurs for studies involving objects, such as retail stores. If the population is defined as individual retail clothing stores with sales of $2 million or more, the population is rather simple and broadly defined. A large number of stores would meet this definition. If the researcher wants to examine only stores that sell female clothing and that are not part of a major retail chain, then the definition becomes more complex and incidence will be reduced. Notice to define the population, the term "major retail chain" will also have to be defined. Does that mean a company with more than 50 stores, 100 stores, or 500 stores? Defining "major retail chain" will have a significant impact on the size of the population and the incidence.

8.3b Identify the Sample Frame

Once the population has been defined, the next challenge is to identify the **sample frame**, which is the listing of people or objects from which the sample will be drawn. In some cases identifying the sample frame is rather easy, but in other situations it is very difficult. For example, suppose a business wanted to survey its customers. If it is a B2B firm, it is very likely the company has a listing of every customer who has made a purchase. Thus, the sample frame would be drawn from the customer database. But, if a company such as Reebok wanted to survey its customers, there is no listing of all individuals who have purchased Reebok shoes. Identifying a sample frame would be more challenging. Sampling only those who have ordered online would result in frame error if the intent is to represent all consumers who purchase Reebok shoes.

Source: Kheng Guan Toh/Shutterstock.

Random digit dialing is a superior method of sampling used for telephone surveys. However, mobile phone users must grant prior consent for contact, or fines of up to $1500 per phone call can be levied against marketers.

Suppose a researcher wanted a sample drawn from the city of Atlanta. In the past, a telephone directory could be used as a sample frame since most individuals living in the city had a landline telephone that was listed in the directory. Now, a large percentage of individuals with landlines have unlisted phone numbers and an even greater and growing problem is that many individuals have discontinued landline telephone service. Cell phones have replaced landlines in 54.9 percent of U.S. households as of 2018, and that number has been steadily increasing since 2004.[4] Furthermore, no free directory exists for cell phones that can be used for sampling purposes.

Sample frame the listing of people or objects from which the sample will be drawn.

Random digit dialing (RDD), is a technique in which area codes and phone prefix numbers are entered into an auto-dialer that then randomly generates the remaining digits, and automatically dials the phone number. While this works fine for landlines as it generates unlisted phone numbers, the Telephone Consumer Protection Act (TCPA) requires cell phone users to grant *prior consent* before they can be contacted by an autodialer. Fines of up to $ 1,500 *per telephone call* violation are being enforced to the point where Gallup reached a $12 million dollar settlement agreement in a TCPA class action lawsuit.[5] In 2015, one of the new TCPA rules approved by the FTC made it even easier for consumers to revoke their consent to receive calls and texts messages from autodialers.[6] While this provision makes it more difficult for marketers to conduct telephone surveys on their own, many marketers now purchase samples from professional research firms such as Survey Sampling. Survey Sampling maintains millions of landline and wireless mobile numbers often linked to verified names, addresses, and demographic variables that can be used as part of a dual frame RDD telephone interview methodology. Still, while the telephone sample will include unlisted numbers, it most likely will not include all cell households, or landlines that have placed on the "Do Not Call" list at DNC.gov. Plus, there is the additional problem that many individuals who moved into a geographic area, such as Atlanta, already owned cell phones whose area codes and prefixes do not correspond with existing Atlanta area codes and prefixes, and as such would not be generated by an auto-dialer. For

Random digit dialing (RDD) a probability sampling technique in which area codes and phone prefix numbers are entered in an auto-dialer, which then randomly generates the remaining phone number digits and then dials the phone number.

Source: Sorbis/Shutterstock.

In developing their sampling frame, Reebok might obtain information from stores that sold Reebok products in the last year. This approach would capture credit card customers, loyalty card holders, and others who were in the stores' databases. It would not include cash customers since their information is not included in the stores' databases.

these reasons, random digit dialing and the use of sampling firms will provide a sample that is still not completely representative of the entire Atlanta population.

Seldom will a sample frame match a target population perfectly. Therefore, the researcher's goal is to develop a sample frame that will include most elements of a population and be representative of the population. For Reebok, a sample frame might consist of individuals who have logged into the company's website during the last 90 days, who "like" Reebok on Facebook, and who follow Reebok on Twitter. This sample frame would exclude the part of the population that had purchased Reebok shoes, but did not engage in any of the online activities mentioned. An alternative sample frame could be to obtain customer information from stores that sold Reebok shoes and obtain a listing of individuals who had purchased Reebok shoes within the last year. This approach would work for credit card customers, loyalty card holders, and others that were in the stores' databases. It would not include cash customers since no information about the individuals would be in the retailers' databases.

As can be seen, identifying a sample frame is difficult, and researchers have to use a process that would include the largest percentage of a target population. Sometimes this includes combining multiple sources and purging duplicate entries. Magazine subscription lists can be used as part of the sampling frame when the magazines in question feature a lifestyle activity that is related to the purpose of the study or the manufacturer's brand. For example, Reebok might have included subscribers to *Runner's World, Running Times,* and *Fitness & Men's Fitness* magazines. Because some households may subscribe to more than one of these publications, duplicates would need to be eliminated from the sample frame list. Of course, Reebok manufactures more than just running shoes, so other magazines might be appropriate as well. An efficient method of selection may be to access the syndicated data provided by a research firm such as GfK, which provides brand-specific information related to the demographics and media habits of product users. Reebok might also purchase opt-in email lists or telephone numbers of those who enjoy running, walking, cross-training and related activities from a provider such as InfoUSA.

In terms of national or even regional U.S. household samples, telephone surveys were the staple approach in the past. With random-digit dialing, fairly robust samples of households could historically be generated. In recent years, the increase in cell phone only households, increased difficulty in making contact with consumers and the decrease in willingness of consumers to respond to telephone surveys has caused a number of research companies to shift to online surveying, address-based mail sampling, or some combination of dual or multi-frame sampling which may (or may not) including telephone/cell phone samples. Furthermore, the average response rate to telephone surveys dropped from 28 percent in 1997 to just seven percent in 2017, according to research conducted by the American Association of Public Opinion Research,[7] while address-based sampling averaged response rates of 50 percent in 2016.[8] The United States Postal Service (USPS) maintains a computerized delivery sequence file (DSF2) that contains every delivery point in the United States linked to a specific address (some rural and post office boxes are excluded). The second generation database (DSF2) is the most comprehensive list of addresses available, with over 162 million addresses.[9] The USPS also offers address validation and completeness services allowing a research firm to maintain accurate mailing addresses. Marketers can combine geographic and demographic data from other public and commercial databases and append them to the database files.[10] This makes the DSF2 a feasible sample frame for national surveys. However, the *Greenbook Research Industry Trends Report* indicates that in 2017, only two percent of quantitative research projects were mail-based, while telephone surveys comprised 9 percent and online surveys 56 percent.[11] Why? Address-based mail sampling takes much longer to complete than online surveying and is much more costly.

In recent years, there has been a shift to using online samples and online research panels. Both of these topics are discussed later in this chapter. The online sample has dramatically changed the way samples are built and even the way companies conduct research. The online methodologies allow companies to obtain samples more quickly and cheaply than other traditional methods, though data quality may be a problem.

8.3c Choose a Sampling Procedure

Choosing a sampling procedure is closely related to identifying the sample frame. Typically, both decisions are made at the same time. The next section discusses the various sampling methods and approaches that can be used. Researchers have two broad categories from which to choose: probability and nonprobability samples. With a **probability sample** each member of the target population has a known and nonzero chance of being selected. The probability of each member being selected may not be equal, but the probability for each member is known. The exact probability is determined by the process used to select the sample. A key advantage of using a probability sample is that sampling error can be computed, allowing the researcher to determine the degree of accuracy of his or her results. **Sampling error** refers to the amount of error that the researcher is willing to accept as a result of the sampling process. This allows the results of the study to be generalized to the larger population within some degree of confidence.

Probability sample each member of the target population has a known and nonzero chance of being selected.

Sampling error refers to the amount of error that the researcher is willing to accept as a result of the sampling process.

With a **nonprobability sample** the probability or chance of someone being selected is not known and cannot be determined. Nonprobability samples rely on the judgment of the researcher. For instance, a researcher might identify the students at the University of Tennessee as the target population. Suppose the researcher staged individuals at three different points on campus to intercept students as they walked by. The chance of a particular student of the university being selected is not known and cannot be determined. Only students who are on campus the day the research is being conducted, and only those who happen to go past one of the three researchers have a chance of being selected. Thus, only a portion of the university student body has a chance of being selected making this a non-probability sample. The concern is that there is no guarantee that those who are selected to participate are representative of those who were not selected. Technically, this means that the results of such studies should not be generalized to the population, as

Nonprobability sample the chance or probability of someone being selected within a target population is not known and cannot be determined.

- The correct sample size increases the probability the findings will accurately reflect the target population.
- Sample should be large enough to reveal important patterns.
- Sample should be large enough to show significant differences between segments being studied.
- The method for obtaining the sample is as important as the sample size.

FIGURE 8.4 Considerations in Deciding the Sample Size
Source: Adapted from Bonnie W. Eisenfeld, "Qualitatively Speaking: Sampling for Qualitative Researchers," *Quirk's Marketing Research Review*, March 2007, Article 20070308, www.quirks.com/articles/2007/0308.aspx, accessed January 4, 2011.

sampling error cannot be computed, and the researcher has no way of knowing how much confidence can be placed in the study results.

8.3d Decide on the Sample Size

The next step in the process is to decide on the sample size needed. Statistical methods for determining sample size are discussed later in this chapter. However, what is statistically desired and what the budget will allow may not coincide. The marketing research project must be conducted within the time frame and budget that is allocated. Unfortunately, this may require using a smaller sample than is statistically desirable. Caution must be exercised, however, for if the sample is too small the research project may not reach any valid conclusions and the funds that are spent will have been wasted. Figure 8.4 identifies some principles of sample size that are important to consider, whether selecting a sample for qualitative or quantitative research.

First, and most important, it is important to understand that using the correct sample size does not guarantee that the findings of the research will accurately reflect the target population. It does, however, increase the probability. The sample has to be large enough to reveal important patterns in the data. If the sample is too small, patterns may not appear. If the study involves comparing various segments of the population, then the sample must be large enough to show if significant differences are present between segments. The more segments that are being compared, the larger the sample that is needed. Last, the method for obtaining the sample is just as important as the sample size.[12] The old maxim, "Garbage In, Garbage Out" holds true.

Fixed sample sample size is determined prior to conducting the research.

Sequential sample sample is selected in stages or sequences, stopping when sample size is sufficient for research purpose.

Most research projects use a **fixed sample**, which means the sample size is determined prior to conducting the research. Occasionally, researchers will use a **sequential sample**, which involves surveying a sample; if enough respondents are obtained then the research moves into the analysis stage. If there are not enough respondents or the evidence is not conclusive to draw any inferences, then another set of sample elements are chosen for a second round of research. The sequential sampling is also used in situations where obtaining samples is very expensive, or an object being evaluated by study participants is destroyed or used up in the process of conducting the research study.

Surveying CEOs or vice-presidents of corporations using personal interviews would be very costly. In addition to the costs of the interviewer's time, a substantial incentive may be required for these corporate executives in order to help garner their participation. A research firm might select a sample of 50 to survey. If a sufficient number did not respond or refused to participate, then another sample of 50 might be selected. The sequential process would continue until the research firm had enough responses to meet their client's needs.

8.3e Select the Sample

The last step in the process is the actual selection of the sample. The next section of the chapter presents methods that can be used. In selecting the sample, the goal is to have a sample that represents the target population. Thus, if the target population is females in the 18 to 34 age group, then the sample needs to consist of females aged 18 to 34.

- Convenience sample
- Judgment sample
- Quota sample
- Snowball sample

FIGURE 8.5 Nonprobability Sampling Methods

8.4 Nonprobability Sampling Methods

LEARNING OBJECTIVE 8.3
Identify and describe the four nonprobability sampling methods.

With nonprobability samples, the probability of being selected for the sample is unknown and not all members of the population have an equal or known chance of being selected. The process of selecting the sample is often based on the judgment of the researcher. Figure 8.5 identifies four methods that can be used.

8.4a Convenience Sample

Convenience sample nonprobability sample method where individuals or objects are chosen based on convenience.

As the name implies, **convenience samples** are individuals or objects that are convenient for the researcher to survey. It can also involve individuals self-selecting to be part of a research project (for example, clicking on a website link to take a survey). The challenge with convenience sampling is collecting a representative sample. It is even more difficult with self-selection. Convenience samples are seldom representative of the target population. The convenience sampling method is more appropriate for exploratory research or the early stages of a descriptive study than for more definitive studies.

To understand challenges with a convenience sample, suppose a minor league baseball team wanted to conduct a survey of fans. A convenience sample might be individuals who attended games over a two-week period. Each person 18 and over who entered the park would be given a survey and asked to complete it and then drop it off at any number of drop boxes throughout the baseball stadium. This method raises several questions concerning the validity of the sample. First, are the views of those who complete the survey the same as those who do not? Often individuals who love the stadium and those who have complaints or strongly negative opinions complete surveys. Individuals whose feelings are somewhat in the middle or neutral tend to neglect the request, and those that don't have complaints, but who don't love the facility will probably not complete the survey either. If this happens, management may think there is a significant dislike of an amenity, such as concessions, when in fact it is only a small minority who hold that opinion. To illustrate, suppose 1,200 out of the 2,750 completed surveys received rate concessions as poor or extremely poor. It would appear that 44 percent of the respondents had a negative opinion of concessions and that management needs to make some changes. But, what about the 12,000 fans who did not complete the survey? If only 1,200 out of the 14,750 fans in attendance felt concessions were bad, that is around 8 percent (1,200/14,750), not 44 percent. Alternatively, perhaps those that did not answer the survey shared the opinion that concessions are bad. In this worst case scenario, as much as 89 percent (13,200/14,750) could believe that the concessions are poor. Which is correct? We just don't know. The problem is that the researcher has no way of estimating the confidence level for the results found because a probability sampling process was not used.

A second factor that must be considered with this example is how representative the sample is during the two weeks the survey is distributed. Are survey participants the same as the individuals who attended games the rest of the minor league baseball season? Without conducting some type of spot or random check with fans at other times during the season, it would be difficult for management to know.

Finally, the time of year when the survey was undertaken would need to be considered. Were the two weeks of the study scheduled at the beginning of the season, when fans are happy and hopeful about the team's chances, or did it take place at the end of a losing season, when fans are disappointed, and only the die-hard season ticket holders are attending games? Attitudes toward the team and their performance could be a mitigating factor that influences attitudes toward the concessions to some degree. The type of individual (season ticket holder vs. groups, or families, or causal visitors) could also be linked to variations in attitudes.

Crowdsourcing distributes tasks to a large number of people via a flexible, open call.

Crowdsourced Convenience Samples Many do-it-your-self researchers and academics experimented with crowdsourced samples in recent years by posting surveys to platforms such as Amazon's Mechanical Turk (MTurk). **Crowdsourcing** distributes tasks to a large number of people via a flexible, open call. "Turkers" sign-up to complete a variety of simple tasks, such as identifying which photos feature cars vs. trucks, or answering surveys. Samples drawn from M-Turk are pure convenience samples. MTurk members "self-select" which, if any, research projects they will complete. Furthermore, the population of Turkers is probably not representative of the U.S. population. While the majority of the MTurk population are U.S. citizens or from India, little else is known for certain as Amazon refuses to share demographic information about the Turker workforce, including how many Turkers exist (the figure on their website has not been updated for years), and how many Turkers are currently active. However, multiple studies have examined the characteristics of Turkers. Findings suggest that African-Americans and Hispanics are under-represented, while European- and Asian-Americans are over-represented. Evidence seems to indicate that a large portion of MTurkers are underemployed Millennials living with their parents, and that they are less likely to be married than the general population, though those who are married are more likely to have step-children. MTurkers are also more likely to identify as lesbian, gay, bisexual, transgender, or queer compared to the general population.[13]

Compared to other forms of convenience samples, MTurk samples were found to be more representative of U.S. workers than were college students, community samples from college towns, and in one 2010 study, online convenience samples. As would be expected of any convenience sample, the MTurk sample was less representative than an online sample selected using a probability technique.[14]

Bots computer programs that attempt to mimic human behavior automatically.

In 2018, MTurk came under fire as researchers noted a sharp decline in data quality. One researcher reported on Facebook that almost 50 percent of the responses to his open-ended question contained nonsense answers. Others soon echoed this complaint, and many concluded that **bots**, computer programs that attempt to mimic human behavior automatically, were the culprit. Bots are currently not sophisticated enough to truly understand an open-ended question and generate a legitimate response, and instead insert meaningless words. Amazon's terms of use allow bots, and many Turkers had used them in the past to find the highest paying tasks. Some Turkers took bots a step further, and attempted to use them to answer surveys. The use of bots by cheaters is not limited to MTurk, as you will learn later in the chapter.[15]

Yet the use of bots to answer surveys automatically may not have been the only culprit to impact data quality. The low value incentives paid by companies who use MTurk have been widely criticized as sub-minimum-wage payments. For example, a recent survey-related task paid only 80 cents to read a review and complete a survey. Forty-five minutes were allotted for task completion. Currently, most crowdsourcing sites are largely unregulated so these low payments don't violate the minimum wage law. However, one could certainly argue that treating respondents in this fashion is unethical, and the greater problem is that poor incentives typically lead to poor data quality. Plus, the experience of taking the survey for so little reward may be so unpleasant that the Turker decides not to participate in future research studies. Unless payment policies change in the future, and the use of bots is controlled, MTurk is likely to become a less attractive vehicle for online convenience sampling.[16]

When using convenience samples, researchers should to strive to make it representative of the target population. Careful planning and careful execution of the sampling process can aid in producing a good convenience sample. However, care should be taken when making decisions. Interesting results from convenience samples should be further researched using a probability sample that allows for the computation of margin of error, and the ability to generalize results to the population.

Judgment sample nonprobability sample method where researchers use personal judgment to select the sample.

8.4b Judgment Sample

With a **judgment sample**, researchers use their personal judgment to select a sample they believe can provide useful information or which they believe reflects the population being studied. Suppose someone in education wanted to survey the student population at a university about their attitudes toward online education versus traditional classroom education. In using a judgment sample approach, the researcher could go through the list of online classes offered by the university and handpick the classes the researcher thinks would provide valuable input and be representative of the student population. The same process could be followed for the traditional classroom portion of the sample. This approach produces a judgment sample since the classes selected were based on the judgment of the researcher conducting the study.

The key to using a judgment sample is to choose individuals or objects that will mirror the population being studied. In the case above, if the demographic profile of the sample reflects the makeup of the university student population, it can be a good sample for the study, though issues of respondent duplication may arise if a respondent is enrolled in multiple courses chosen to be part of the sample.

Unfortunately, judgment samples often are not representative of the population being studied. A mall interceptor might decide not to select an individual to interview who otherwise fits the qualifications for the study because he or she thinks the individual "looks" scary, mean, stupid, too smart, impatient, unlikely to participate, or any one of a number of factors that may in fact not be true. When personal bias gets in the way of collecting data, the information obtained will not be representative of the population. Furthermore, restricting the sample to a mall would only appropriate if the survey was related to the mall or one of its stores. Mall surveys are not representative of the geographic region surrounding the mall as so many people choose to shop elsewhere, including online.

8.4c Quota Sample

In order to produce a nonprobability sample that is more representative of the population under study, researchers will often use a **quota sample**. The concept behind the quota sample is to ensure that the sample contains the same proportion of characteristics specified by the researcher as is evident in the population being examined.

Quota sample nonprobability sample method of selecting a sample based on the target population's characteristics or criteria specified by the researcher.

Suppose a medical facility hired a research firm to survey patients about their level of satisfaction with the medical care received and the effectiveness of treatment. Figure 8.6 shows the demographic composition of the patients that have used the facility during the last two years broken down by gender, age, and primary physician. The fourth column indicates the percent within each category. For instance 56.9 percent of the patients are female and 43.1 percent are male. In terms of age, 8.6 percent of the patients are ages 18 to 24, 12.2 percent are 25 to 34, and so forth. The last few rows show the number of patients for each attending physician.

The last three columns in Figure 8.6 indicate how many individuals would need to be interviewed within each group to create a quota sample of 200, 400, and 600 individuals. For a quota sample of 200, the sample would need to contain 114 females and 86 males. For a quota sample of 400, it would be necessary to interview 228 female patients and 172 male patients. Looking further down the table at the sample of 600, the sample needs to include 108 patients from Dr. Cook, 130 from Dr. Dempster, 118 from Dr. Millwood, and so on.

Suppose to conduct the study the research firm sent interviewers to the medical facility to talk to patients as they waited for their appointment to see their primary care physician. Each interviewer would be given a quota. For example, Andrea might be sent to the clinic and told to interview the following 20 individuals:

- 12 females and 8 males
- 5 patients 18-24, 5 patients 25 to 34, 5 patients 35 to 44, and 5 patients 45 to 54
- 10 patients of Dr. Cook and 10 patients of Dr. Dempster

It should be noted that Andrea is seeking to complete interviews with a total of 20 patients, though she may end up speaking with many more, only to find out that they do not fit the remaining quota categories. For example, the first qualifying patient may be a patient of Dr. Cook, who is 18 to 24 years old, and female. This individual checks

Demographic Variable		Number	Percent	Sample Size		
				200	400	600
Gender	Female	4,332	56.9%	114	228	342
	Male	3,275	43.1%	86	172	258
Age	18–24	653	8.6%	17	34	52
	25–34	926	12.2%	24	49	73
	35–44	1,638	21.5%	43	86	129
	45–54	1,145	15.1%	30	60	90
	55–65	1,814	23.8%	48	95	143
	66+	1,431	18.8%	38	75	113
Physician	Cook	1,363	17.9%	36	72	108
	Dempster	1,647	21.7%	43	87	130
	Millwood	1,502	19.7%	39	79	118
	Rogers	1,755	23.1%	46	92	138
	Sanchez	1,340	17.6%	35	70	106
Total number of patients		7,607	100.0%			

FIGURE 8.6 Quota Sample for Medical Facility

off three of the required characteristics. After the fifth female (or male) 18 to 24 year old patient of Dr. Cook has been interviewed, no more female (or male) patients of Dr. Cook in this age range will be selected for interviewing. That quota category is complete.

Notice that Andrea's quota does not match the quota percents shown in Figure 8.6. Andrea is not going to interview patients of Millwood, Rogers, or Sanchez. It is not necessary for each interviewer to have a quota that matches the overall sample quota as long as the total sample matches the population characteristics specified in the quota plan.

The quota sampling method is a nonprobability approach since not every patient has a known chance of being selected. It is really up to the judgment of the interviewer. Andrea can pick any of the patients in the waiting room that fit her quota. As a result, the sample may not truly reflect the opinion of all patients. Andrea might look around the room and pick patients that look as if they would be willing to answer questions. Thus, her sample might be biased toward patients who have a positive attitude toward the medical facility. Other interviewers might use a different approach to select patients to meet their quotas, but it could also produce a biased sample. Also, once a particular quota is filled, say males aged 18 to 24, no other individuals exhibiting these characteristics will be interviewed regardless of who their physician might be. Using a quota sample does not guarantee a sample that truly reflects the opinion of the population. What it does do is produce a sample that more closely mirrors the population based on the demographic or behavioral characteristics identified by the researcher.

It may surprise you to learn that even large professional research firms such Nielsen use non-probability sampling techniques, especially quota sampling. For example, in May of 2018, Nielsen conducted an online Global Connected Commerce Study of more than 30,000 consumers in 64 countries worldwide. Because quotas were imposed on the basis of age, sex and country, sampling error could not be computed.[17] There is no guarantee that the sample accurately reflects global opinions of individuals with online access, as the attitudes of those who chose to participate may differ from those who chose not to answer the survey (or who could not answer because the quota was full). Remember, sample size alone does not guarantee accuracy.

8.4d Snowball Sample

A unique nonprobability sampling technique is the **snowball sample**. The research begins with one or a few individuals who have been identified as good subjects for the research. Then each of these individuals is asked for names of others who would be good candidates for the study. This approach is used in situations where it is difficult to identify individuals who meet specific criteria needed for the research project, such as those characterized by low incidence rates.

Source: Bascar/Shutterstock.

The snowball sample approach might be used by companies such as Whitetail Gear, Danner, or Wolverine that sell equipment and supplies to avid deer hunters.

The snowball sample approach might be used by companies such as Whitetail Gear, Danner, or Wolverine that sell equipment and supplies to avid deer hunters. While other sampling approaches might work, the snowball approach could be used to locate avid deer hunters who spend considerable time and money on the sport. Hunters often hunt together and know other avid deer hunters. Starting with a few names, a researcher would be able to get contact information for other avid hunters. The personal reference from a friend who hunts would increase the probability of each hunter participating in the research. A sequential approach could be used until the research company obtained a sufficient sample size.

Snowball sample nonprobability sample method of selecting a few respondents to participate in a study, then asking each respondent for names of additional individuals to participate.

The disadvantage of the snowball approach is that the views of the sample obtained may not truly represent all avid deer hunters. The researcher has little control over the composition of the sample since he or she is relying on hunters to provide names of other hunters. It is possible the sample would be largely composed of individuals who hunt using rifles. Hunters who use a bow and arrow may be underrepresented in the final sample since the season for bow hunting occurs at a different time of year than rifle hunting, reducing the likelihood that rifle and bow hunters would know one another. Furthermore, hunters who hunt with a rifle may subconsciously forget to provide the names of those who bow hunt due to their different hunting technique. The advantage to snowball sampling is that most who are contacted are likely to participate in the study, so the cost and time involved in obtaining the sample are reduced.

However, in some instances snowball sampling can yield helpful results. In gathering data for the Q1–Q2 *Greenbook Research Industry Trends Report*, respondents were recruited directly by Greenbook and through snowball sampling. Key partner firms and organizations, such as ESOMAR, Survey Sampling, Lightspeed and others helped to recruit both marketing research clients and marketing research suppliers. The final sample contained data from more client firms and research suppliers than Greenbook would have been able to recruit on their own. In this instance, marketing research firm suppliers such as Lightspeed were able to encourage their clients to participate, while professional organizations such as ESOMAR were able to email research firms who were members of their organization and ask them to participate. The added credibility of these intermediaries helped to improve the overall response rate to the survey reducing non-response bias, as more than 3,930 firms responded to the 2018 survey, compared to only 1,533 for Q3–Q4 in 2017 and 2,637 in Q1–Q2 of 2017.[18]

8.4e Nonprobability Studies in Practice

Earlier, it was mentioned that the results of nonprobability studies should not be generalized to the population because nonprobability samples typically do not represent the population and because it is not possible to ascertain a confidence interval for the results that would allow the user to understand the margin of error associated with the results. In actual practice, however, researchers might make inferences to the population on the basis of data drawn from nonprobability samples. They often justify their actions by incorporating some element of random selection into the sampling process. For example, many studies make use of online samples and randomly select participants from online panels to participate in the research. The random selection of participants doesn't negate the fact that not all members of the population are part of the panel, even if the population is defined as broadly as individuals who have online access. Thus, the data is in effect drawn from a convenience sample.

Given that firms might draw inferences from nonprobability data, it is absolutely critical that researchers strive to ensure that the sample accurately reflects the target population as much as possible. The more the sample reflects the makeup of the target population, the higher the generalizability of the results to the population being studied.

8.5 Probability Sampling Methods

LEARNING OBJECTIVE 8.4
Identify and describe the four probability sampling methods.

With a probability sample, every person or object in the population has a known and nonzero chance of being selected. Researchers can actually calculate what that probability is since subjects are selected objectively and not subjectively by individuals. Because of the objective nature of selection, it is possible to determine the reliability of the sample and the amount of sampling error that is likely to occur. Probability sampling does not guarantee the sample will be representative of the population. It is highly likely to be, but there is no guarantee. It is possible, although unlikely, that a nonprobability sample would produce a more representative sample than a probability sample. Researchers have several options for probability sampling, as shown in **Figure 8.7.**

8.5a Simple Random Sample

Simple random sample probability sample method where each element of the population has a known and equal chance of being selected.

With a **simple random sample** each element in the population has a known and equal chance of being selected. If a small business has 5,000 customers and wants a sample of 500, then with simple random sampling each customer would have a 10 percent chance of being selected for the sample (500/5,000). By using a random process, such as a random number generator on a computer, every customer has the same chance of being selected.

Generating a simple random sample begins with numbering every element in the population. Students at a university, members of a non-profit organizations, stores in a retail chain, and employees of an organization can all be listed and given numbers since each is known and can be identified. Furthermore, there can be no duplicate listings. This would become important when surveying adult households, if the names of both members of a married couple appeared on a list. Such households would have twice the chance of being surveyed as would households headed by unmarried adults. The next step is to use a random number generator or random number table to generate a list of random numbers. The elements of the population that correspond to those random numbers are then selected to be part of the sample.

- Simple random sample
- Systematic random sample
- Stratified sample
- Cluster sample

FIGURE 8.7 Probability Sampling Methods

A simple random sample is ideal for marketing research because every element has a known and equal chance of being selected. However, for many studies it is not possible to use the simple random approach because not every element can be identified. For example, suppose a firm wanted to study males ages 20 to 50 in the city of Detroit. There is no way to generate a list of every male who lives in Detroit in that age group. Whatever sample frame is suggested would leave some males out. Similarly, there is no way to generate a list of all email addresses associated with people who have Internet access in the U.S. Thus a random sample of U.S. Internet users is not possible using email. For this reason, researchers tend to use one of the other methods of generating a sample.

8.5b Systematic Random Sample

The difference between the systematic random sample and a simple random sample is found in the process of how the elements are selected. With both sampling methods, members of the population have an equal and known chance of being selected. Rather than using a random number generator or table, a **systematic random sample** uses some type of systematic process to select participants.

Systematic random sample probability sample method that involves randomly selecting the first respondent, then selecting each Nth element of the population.

With the systematic random sample approach individuals in the population must be arranged in some type of order or list. A random starting point is selected. Then every "Nth" element is chosen. To determine the "Nth" number, the total population is divided by the number of elements desired in the sample. The resulting number is called the **skip interval**. So if a sample of 300 is desired out of a population of 4800, then every 16th element would be selected after the random starting point is determined. The process would begin by generating a random number between 1 and 16. Suppose it was 4. The 4th element would then be chosen from the list for the sample followed by the 20th element, the 36th element, the 52nd element, and so forth.

Skip interval the total population is divided by the number of elements desired in the sample to yield the "Nth" number of elements skipped when implementing systematic sampling.

Systematic random sampling is used often in direct marketing campaigns for testing direct marketing offers. Almost all direct mail, database, and CRM (customer relationship management) software has capabilities to sort based on a systematic random sampling. The problem is that many researchers mistakenly begin with the first record, which means that the sample selection is no longer random. To be random, it is critical that the first element be chosen through a random process using either a random number table or random number generator.[19]

8.5c Stratified Sample

A simple or systematic random sample works best for studies involving one population. It does not work well in situations where researchers want to make comparisons between segments of a population. For instance, researchers may want to test a new type of digital point-of-purchase retail display and want to compare stores with the new display to those without the new display. Alternatively, a company may want to compare the sales of a particular brand of a product at discount stores versus specialty stores or mass merchandise stores. It may even be a case where a university wants to evaluate the attitude of students concerning online classes and compare the traditional students to the nontraditional students. In all of these cases, a simple or systematic random sample will probably not produce a sample that will represent both or multiple groups equally or proportionately.

The **stratified sample** involves dividing the population into mutually exclusive and categorically exhaustive groups that are related to the behavior (or variables) of interest, then randomly selecting elements independently from within each group. In the case with the new digital POP display, stores would be divided into two groups, those that were using the new digital display and those that were not. Then from each group a random sample would be chosen either using the simple random sample approach or the systematic sample approach. This process ensures the researcher will have sufficient subjects in each group to make valid comparisons. The same process would be used for comparing discount, specialty, and mass merchandise stores.

Stratified sample probability sampling method that requires dividing the population into mutually exclusive and categorically exhaustive groups related to the behavior or variables of interest, then randomly selecting elements independently from within each group.

The criteria used to divide the population into groups are based on the research objectives of the study and the discretion of the researcher. However, there are usually two key criteria: Every member of the population must be in one of the groups, and no member can be in two or more groups. The division must be mutually exclusive and categorically exhaustive.

On occasions, stratified sampling is confused with quota sampling. With both approaches, the population is divided into groups. The key difference is in how the subjects are selected for the sample. With the stratified sample, some type of random process is used. With the quota sample, subjects are chosen based on the judgment of the researcher. In the example of the medical facility discussed in the section on quota sampling, recall that interviewers were given quotas but they could use their personal judgment in selecting who to interview. With a stratified sample approach, the patients would be divided into mutually exclusive and categorically exhaustive groups and then selected randomly.

8.5d Cluster Sample

Cluster sample probability sample method that involves dividing the population into mutually exclusive and categorically exhaustive groups or subsets where each group or subset is assumed to be representative of the population, then randomly selecting elements from within each group or subset.

Clusters sample groups that are assumed to be representative of the population as a whole rather than homogenous groups based on some criterion.

One-stage cluster sample probability cluster sample method that involves randomly selecting clusters, then surveying all of the elements within the clusters that are selected.

Two-stage cluster sample probability cluster sample method that involves randomly selecting clusters, then randomly selecting elements within the clusters that were selected.

Cluster samples are very similar to stratified samples. With a **cluster sample** the population is divided into mutually exclusive and categorically exhaustive groups, or subsets, called clusters. **Clusters** are sample groups assumed to be representative of the population as a whole rather than homogenous groups based on some criterion as with the stratified sample approach. Once the clusters are formed, then elements can be chosen through some type of random approach.

To illustrate, suppose a state board of higher education wanted to interview faculty at its state-supported universities about impending legislation concerning higher education in the state. With the cluster approach, each of the state's universities would be considered a cluster. Suppose there are 18 universities in the state. With a **one-stage cluster sample** a certain number of universities are selected, such as two, three or four, and then all of the faculty members at the selected universities are interviewed. To be random, the selection of the universities must be chosen through a random process.

Instead of interviewing all faculty members at the chosen universities, a **two-stage cluster sample** could be used, which involves randomly selecting faculty within the university clusters that were chosen in the first stage of the sample selection process.

A popular form of cluster sampling that is used by research firms is area sampling. A research company might want to study the marketing efforts of independent retail clothing stores. It could use a cluster sample since obtaining a listing of all independent retail clothing stores for the United States would be difficult. And if it were obtained, the cost of sending interviewers to retail stores all over the United States would be quite high. Costs and time can be greatly reduced by using a cluster approach.

The research firm could begin with the U.S. Census Bureau data and create clusters based on the 384 metropolitan statistical areas (MSAs). From the 384 MSAs, the research firm could choose a specific number of MSAs. The number chosen would depend on whether a one-stage or two-stage approach is used. With the one-stage approach, the research firm might choose 10 MSAs, then interview managers/owners of all of the independent retail clothing stores within each chosen MSA. For large MSAs such as New York, Houston, and Chicago, that might be quite cumbersome. So instead of the one-stage approach, the firm might use a two-stage approach and select 30 MSAs. Then within each MSA the research firm might randomly select 10 independent retail clothing stores. To be a cluster sample approach the MSAs must be chosen randomly, and with the two-stage approach the retail clothing stores must also be chosen randomly.

From a cost and time perspective sending research personnel to 10 or even 30 MSAs would be considerably cheaper than sending staff to 300 different retail clothing stores scattered throughout the United States. Also, it requires obtaining a listing of independent retail clothing stores for only a few MSAs rather than for the entire United States. If conducted properly, the cluster approach would yield results that would be as valid as a simple random sample, at a much lower cost.

- General practice
- Previous studies
- Statistical formula
- Sample size calculator
- Sample size table

FIGURE 8.8 Methods of Determining Sample Size

With increased pressure from clients and marketing research firms to obtain results quickly and as inexpensively as possible, researchers can be tempted to reduce the number of clusters and increase the sample size within each cluster to maintain the same overall sample size. Doing so risks a loss of precision and statistical reliability. It is better to increase the number of clusters and reduce the sample size within each cluster.[20] From the previous example, surveying 30 stores in 10 MSAs will yield a sample of 300. But, depending on how those 10 MSAs are chosen, it could be a biased sample. To increase precision and reliability of the study, it would be better to survey 10 stores in 30 MSAs. Even 30 MSAs out of 384 is a very small percentage of MSAs being represented. It would increase costs, but surveying five stores out of 60 MSAs would increase the reliability and precision of the study and ensure it more accurately reflects what is happening in all 384 MSAs.

8.6 Determining the Sample Size

LEARNING OBJECTIVE 8.5
Describe the various methods of determining sample size.

Sample size is an important issue because clients would like to ensure study results are accurate. But, as sample size increases, so does the cost to conduct the research. So in every research project there is a balance between the desired or adequate sample size and costs. Remember, **sample size** refers to the number of usable responses needed by the client, not the number of invitations or surveys which must be distributed to ensure the desired sample size is met. **Figure 8.8** lists the most common methods for determining sample size.

Sample size the number of usable responses needed by the client.

8.6a General Practice

In practice, most companies consider a sample of 1,000 to 2,000 respondents to be sufficient for national surveys, though larger samples may be needed when smaller margins of error are desired or a large number of items need to be rated. For example, Nielsen interviewed 1,058 U.S. residents aged 18 and older when studying the shopping habits of America's Millennials.

The National Retail Federation, on the other hand, surveyed 7,516 individuals about their Thanksgiving shopping plans for 2018. The sample yielded results with a margin of error of plus or minus 1.2 percentage points. Comparisons were made between different age groups, and the large overall sample size ensured that each subgroup was adequately represented.[21] In summary, the key to such samples being interpreted as the view of the general population of the United States is obtaining a sample that is representative of the population. If the data is not representative of the target market, then sample size doesn't mean anything. Sampling 50,000 people would still not yield results that could be generalized to the target population.

Source: Pressmaster/Shutterstock.

The National Retail Federation surveyed 7,516 individuals about their Thanksgiving shopping, which includes retail's busiest day, "Black Friday". The key to being able to generalize findings nationwide is obtaining a sample that is representative of the United States population. If the data is not representative of the target market, then sample size doesn't mean anything.

8.6b Previous Studies

Another approach to sample size is looking at previous studies that are similar to the one being proposed. If a previous study sampled 800 respondents, then the current study could sample the same number, assuming similarities exist between the population being studied and the number of groups being compared. The primary motivation behind using this approach is often cost. The client requesting the study often has a limited budget and may request the same sample size as a previously completed study to ensure costs are close to the same. If a previous study was utilized for decision-making and the results were positive, there would not be an urgent need on the part of management to increase the sample size. However, if the new study required comparing a greater number of subgroups, the sample size would likely need to be increased. Furthermore, if the recommendations garnered from the previous study were implemented and failed, management may feel the need to increase the sample size.

8.6c Statistical Formula

From a statistical standpoint, the necessary sample size can be calculated if a probability sampling approach is used. If one of the nonprobability sampling approaches is used to obtain a sample, then sample size cannot be statistically calculated. One of the other methods would have to be used instead.

Sample size can be calculated in a number of ways. Each will yield a slightly different sample size. One of the simplest methods is to calculate the sample size using a formula based on the desired level of confidence, the allowable or acceptable margin of error, and the variability of the population characteristic being studied. The more variability that is present in a population characteristic, the larger the sample that will be needed. The formula for calculating sample size using these three variables is:

$$\text{Sample size} = \frac{Z^2\, pq}{e^2}$$

The value for Z is based on the level of confidence, or accuracy that is desired. For example, a 95 percent confidence level means the researcher is willing to tolerate only a 5 percent chance that the confidence interval for a variable does not include the true value of the population. Z values for various confidence levels are obtained from a Z-table. If a 95 percent confidence level is desired, then the Z value would be 1.96. For a 99 percent confidence level, $Z = 2.58$ and for the 90 percent confidence level, $Z = 1.64$. The estimated proportion of an attribute that is present in a population is designated in the formula as p. In most studies, p is not known, therefore researchers will often use a value of $p = 0.5$. That means there is a 50/50 chance that the population will have the characteristic being studied, which is the maximum level of variability within a population. The value q is equal to $1\text{-}p$. The last value e is the margin of error that the researcher is willing to accept. For example, .03 would indicate a plus or minus ($\pm$) 3 percent margin of error. Margin of error determines the level of precision that the study results provide. (Margin of error, confidence levels, and confidence intervals were discussed in greater detail as part of the Statistical Review section of chapter 6.)

Suppose a researcher wants to know the sample size needed at the 95 percent confidence level, the variability of the population is unknown, and the desired precision is $\pm$ 3 percent. The sample size would be 1,067. The calculation would be:

$$\text{Sample size} = \frac{(1.96)^2\,(.5 * .5)}{(.03)^2} = \frac{(3.8416)\,(.25)}{(.0009)} = \frac{.9604}{.0009} = 1{,}067$$

If the researcher wants a higher level of precision, meaning a lower margin of error, or a higher level of confidence in the results, then a larger sample would be needed. If the confidence level is increased to 99 percent, then sample size would have to be increased to 1,849.

If instead the researcher wants a lower margin of error, such as ± 2 percent, then a sample size of 2,401 would be necessary to yield a 95 percent confidence level when $p = 0.5$.

Assigning p a value of 0.5 always results in the most generous estimate of sample size for a given confidence level and margin of error, ensuring that the sample size is adequate. If p is any other value, the sample that is needed would be less. Consider a situation where in a previous study the percentage of youth who used cell phones was 78 percent. Suppose that researchers want to see if this percentage has changed since the original study was conducted. Assuming a 95 percent confidence level, a relatively high precision level featuring a margin of error of ± 3 percent, and a p value of $= 0.78$, then $q = 0.22$. When the numbers are plugged into the formula, the size of the sample needed would be 732, instead of 1,067.

8.6d Sample Size Calculators

A number of online sample size calculators are available for researchers. Usually, all that is needed is to type in the level of confidence desired, the precision (or margin of error) desired, and the variability. The calculator will provide the necessary sample size. Some calculators make adjustments based on the size of the population. These adjustments are necessary when a smaller-sized population exists (for example, when surveying organizations that belong to a particular trade association). More advanced calculators take into account the anticipated survey response rate so that the researcher knows how many people must be contacted in order to achieve the desired number of completed surveys. Sample size calculators are convenient when a client requests the necessary sample size for various levels of confidence, precision, or variability, and when other factors, such as small population sizes and survey response rates, come into play.

8.6e Sample Size Tables

The formula and simple calculator methods of determining sample size assume an infinite or a large population, such as that of a country like the United States. For a finite population, the formula has to be corrected slightly. While some sample size calculators can be used for this purpose, a number of useful tables also exist, such as the one displayed in **Figure 8.9**. This table provides sample sizes for finite populations for a confidence level of 95 percent and precision levels of ±5 percent, ±3 percent, and ±1 percent.

	Confidence Level of 95%		
Population Size	+/-5%	+/-3%	+/-1%
100	80	92	99
300	169	234	291
500	217	341	475
1,000	278	516	906
5,000	357	866	3,288
10,000	370	964	4,899
50,000	381	1,056	8,056
100,000	383	1,064	8,762
500,000	384	1,065	9,423
1,000,000	384	1,066	9,512

FIGURE 8.9 Table for Determining Sample Size

Notice that for a population of 100, it would take a sample of 80 for a precision level of ±5 percent and a sample size of 99 if the precision level was increased to ±1 percent. For a small population, researchers often will conduct a census and attempt to survey everyone in the population. For a precision of ±5 percent, it would take 357 for a population of 5,000, but only 384 for a population of one million, assuming that no groups were being compared. Notice after a population reaches 50,000, the sample size does not change much.

Earlier, it was stated that for national samples the general practice was to survey 1,000 to 2,000 individuals. Notice that surveying slightly over 1,000 individuals would produce a 95 percent confidence level and a precision of ±3 percent. The general practice that a sample of at least 1,000 is needed was actually based on tables such as this and calculations illustrated in the previous sections.

8.6f Size of Invitation Pool

Prior to mailing surveys or issuing email invitations to participate in a study, researchers generally try to estimate the number of contact attempts needed to achieve the desired sample size. The simplest method is to divide the desired sample size by the anticipated response rate. If there is reason to believe that response rates will differ between groups in a stratified sample, then separate calculations should be performed for each group. Response rate estimates can come from prior studies, industry trade data, or be based on a researcher's gut instinct. As response rates are typically much higher among panel members, many commercial research firms have adopted their use, especially for mobile and online surveys.

8.7 Online Research Panels

LEARNING OBJECTIVE 8.6
Discuss the benefits and issues related to online research panels.

A number of firms provide research panels for the purpose of conducting marketing research. Most are online panels, in which members have agreed to participate in research studies. Online panels may contain thousands or millions of members. For instance, Dynata, formally known as Research Now SSI, has a worldwide research consumer panel of more than 11 million people, and a Healthcare specialty panel that reaches over 180,000 healthcare professionals. Dynata tracks over 1,100 panel profile attributes, allowing clients to request samples that participate in particular lifestyle activities, or who consume certain types of products. They also have a panel composed of B2B members. All panel members are recruited using a "By-Invitation-Only" recruitment process. The company has panels in 39 countries.[22] Syndicated research firms may use panels for tracking studies, such as NPD's "Dining Out" panel, while custom research or sampling firms many select samples matching the client's specifications for surveys or shorter term research projects.

Panel Member Recruitment Recruiting members for a research panel is done in a number of ways. One of the most common is "By-Invitation Only." A typical technique is to obtain names from partnering firms such as Best Buy, British Airways, Hilton Honors program, and Pizza Hut or other partner firms or global communities. Based on demographic, behavioral, or ownership characteristics that are needed for the panel, individuals are sent an e-mail or letter with a request to be a part of the research panel. Those who choose to "opt-in" are added to the panel.

Some companies, such as Valient Market Research and Pacific Market Research, use open-source recruiting to publicly solicit participants through websites or Facebook. Open-source recruiting allows individuals to openly enroll and be part of the panel.

For their automobile panel, J.D. Power and Associates uses a "By-Invitation only" recruitment process based on both information from an independent party that has access to state motor vehicle registrations and contact information provided by their automotive clients.[23] While in the past J.D. Powers allowed open enrollment, this practice was discontinued in order to improve data quality. Still, some firms, such as Dynata, supplement their "By-Invitation Only" panel with open enrollment members who are subjected to strict identity verification and deep profiling. Tracking hundreds of characteristics per panel member makes it easy for Dynata to identify low incidence populations and to identify key sample characteristics desired by their clients.[24]

Panel Member Management The number of surveys each panelist will complete varies by research company and each person's profile. Most reputable research firms that use panels will send no more than one to two surveys per month to panelists on topics in which they have knowledge, experience, or interest and that fit the demographic or ownership profile requested by the client. A few firms allow panelists to select surveys they want to complete. Typically, panelists will receive cash, gift cards, or points for each finished survey. Points can be accumulated and redeemed for prizes, cash payments, or gift cards and other merchandise. Other incentives include donations to a good cause or entry into sweepstakes or lotteries.[25]

When using a panel for research, clients should request some basic validation metrics from the supplier to ensure quality. Basic metrics that can be supplied by companies are listed in **Figure 8.10**. Sample providers should disclose is the sample is representative of the population. The percentage of panelists who have verified or updated their profile within the last month, three months, or six months provides an indication of the currency of a research firm's panel. People move, change jobs, and change other aspects in their personal lives. To ensure the sample selected meets the client's demographic and even psychographic profiles, updating of profile information on a regular basis is important.

Panelists' activities are monitored. Individuals who do not respond to surveys or who submit surveys that are not properly completed are dropped from panels by reputable research firms that manage panel data. Individuals can also opt-out of the panel at any time, and many do so. For most panels, the annual attrition rate is between 10 and 50 percent per year. Unfortunately, poor sample management practices and overly long surveys are often the reason why. Recent research reported by the *Greenbook Research Industry Trends Report* found that only 25 percent of research subjects were satisfied with their experience while participating in research. The same study found that clients and research suppliers placed a very low priority on whether subjects thought well of their research experience, were compensated fairly, or had a positive impression of Market Research after the study was completed.[26] These findings are troubling, as they coincide with declining response rates and declining data quality. Improving data quality, and improving relationships with panel members, has become a priority for many in the research industry.[27]

Reputable sample companies should cross-reference and validate panel member information using other databases to help verify identities. This practice can help to protect against professional respondents who create multiple fake identities. Data quality can be protected by assigning a unique respondent ID so that only those invited can complete the survey. The best panel providers are those who enforce participation limits among their panel members. Sample quality is critical, as research clients and suppliers increasingly

- Sample providers should disclose if sample is representative of the population
- Percentage of panelists who have verified or updated their profile
- Attrition rate
- Panelist response rates
- Panelist activity rates
- Device fingerprinting
- Geo-IP reviews

FIGURE 8.10 Validation Metrics for Sample Panels

expect to be told whether the samples provided by a panel are representative of the population.[28] Finally, clients should examine the drop-out rate for each study, and each question within a study, as "the rate at which people abandon a study is a direct indication of the quality of the responses you will receive."[29] However, it should be noted that the drop rate is often an indicator of problems in the survey design, rather than a problem with the panel members. Long surveys, open-ended questions, and unclear questions are just some of the factors that lead to higher dropout rates.

The panel attrition rate provides an idea of why people join a particular panel and how the research firm handles the panel. A panel with a high attrition rate would indicate potential problems in either recruiting legitimate members, treating panel members fairly, or maintaining their interest in completing surveys. Inability to maintain members can be due to a low reward structure, lack of interest in survey topics, insufficient number for surveys to hold their interest, router bouncing, being sent too many surveys or otherwise abusing respondents in some fashion.

Programmatic sampling automates the buying and selling of a sample and automatically directs respondents into survey projects.

Programmatic sampling automates the buying and selling of a sample and automatically directs respondents into survey projects. One of the problems inherent with programmatic sampling is that it can lead to respondent abuse, which in turn influences both survey response rates and panel attrition. For example, some sample vendors allow their respondent pool to be automatically bounced from router to router, where they are passed from one survey to the next and asked over and over to provide basic qualification characteristics such gender, race or age until they find a survey for which they qualify. Router bouncing, as it is called, creates a terrible experience for the research participant, and is unnecessary as the nature of programmatic sampling makes it possible for the characteristics of the panel member to be automatically compared to the study qualifiers of a properly programmed survey *prior* to sending the participant to the survey website. The challenge that sampling companies face is developing an automated system that can recognize how each variable is coded by different companies, because different firms store data in different ways. This is true of both client firms seeking to collect data, and the different sources used by sample aggregators. For example, one firm may use a variable called "sex" while another may use a variable called "gender" to store the same data.

Sending respondents to surveys where quotas matching the respondent's characteristics have already been filled, or where respondents answer twenty questions before finding they don't qualify for compensation are other examples of respondent abuse that impact panel attrition.[30]

The panelist response rates provide an average completion rate for panel members. The panelist activity rates refer to the range and mean number of surveys completed by panelists within the last month, or three months, or six months. A wide range may indicate some members are being overused while others are not being used enough. A high mean may indicate individuals are in the panel just for the rewards and not because they have an interest in providing their opinions. Too many surveys can result in people just filling in answers and not taking time to read or think about the information being requested.

Digital fingerprinting occurs when a panel provider creates and tracks a unique ID for a panel member's computer, tablet or smartphone.

Digital fingerprinting occurs when a panel provider creates and tracks a unique ID for a respondent's computer, tablet, or smartphone. This allows for detection of whether more than one respondent participated in a survey on the same computer and is helpful in catching professional respondents who create fake identities in order to participate in multiple surveys. Geo-IP validation reviews the IP address of the respondent's computer and compares it to the targeted survey location. Discrepancies result in respondents being blocked from the survey.

8.7a Benefits of Online Research Panels

Online panels provide researchers with a number of benefits, listed in **Figure 8.11**. Collecting data is faster since the panels already exist. This is especially true as much of online sampling has become automated. Programmatic sampling automates the buying and selling of a sample and directs respondents into survey projects with the click of a

- Faster data collection
- Cost effective
- More efficient targeting of low-incidence groups
- Higher response rates
- Use of graphics, videos, and audio
- Automated data entry
- Automated data validation
- Real-time results

FIGURE 8.11 Benefits of Online Research Panels

button, meaning the marketing research client does not have to wait for an email to be sent, or for a supplier to select and "drop" the sample. Furthermore, there is less reliance on interactions with people in another country or time zone because the process is automated. This speeds the process of data collection and because the survey is fielded more quickly, data can be gathered, analyzed, and reported more quickly. For groups that have a low-incidence rate, a sufficient sample can usually be selected since many of these panels consist of a million or more individuals.[31]

A key benefit of using online research panels is that response rates tend to be higher than for online survey invitations sent to individuals who have not agreed to be part of a research panel. Being online, researchers can use graphics, videos, and audio with the survey. The online feature allows for automated data entry into a spreadsheet, reducing data entry errors that can occur when employees transfer a paper survey to a computer spreadsheet. Online surveys can also have some automated data validation procedures to ensure that people are reading the questions and that the panelist is completing the survey and not someone else. For instance, the same question worded differently at two different spots on the survey can be automated to check to see if the person provides the same reply, or if he or she is just filling in blanks. Finally, special software allows clients to check basic results while the survey is stilll in progress.

8.7b Concerns with Online Research Panels

A major concern with online research panels is the recruitment process. Recruitment can occur through "open enrollment" (also called open-source recruitment) or "by-invitation only," as previously described. Open-source recruitment allows individuals to self-select to be on a research panel. They may see an advertisement on a search engine or on the Internet and respond, search for sample firms that offer open enrollment, or hear from a friend about the research panel. Which method is used is not the issue. The issue is that the individual has chosen to be part of the research panel and in some cases has actively searched for research panels to join. Amazon's M-Turk is composed entirely of open enrollment members.

The danger of open-source recruiting is that it is likely to produce a biased sample. While it can result in millions joining the panel, it can create a sample that is biased toward Internet-savvy people who like giving their opinion, who respond to online ads, and who want to earn money or rewards. In some cases these individuals participate in a number of online panels and complete large numbers of surveys. These individuals are known in the industry as "professional survey takers" or "professional respondents". Not all professional survey takers are bad. There are some who enjoy giving their opinion, take the survey seriously, and take their time in answering the questions.

The danger with most professional survey takers is that they tend to give false and misleading information in order to qualify for surveys or to complete surveys quickly. They may read questions, but will give little thought to the answers. They may even use different profiles and email addresses in order to take the same survey several times, thus saving time and effort. They often are members of multiple online research panels. While Chapter 6 discussed a variety of methods that can be used to help identify professional respondents, increasingly, firms are using background checks, profile questionnaires that may contain hundreds of questions, validation checks against databases and a telephone follow-up to verify a respondent's identity prior to adding them to a panel. Often profile characteristics are checked against respondent's answers in surveys, and if key characteristics do not match (e.g., gender) or change randomly to fit a study's qualification parameters, respondents are dropped from the panel, and in some cases, black-listed and shared with other research firms. This is part of the panel management process.

The marketing research industry is deeply concerned about the quality of the data it has been collecting. Correspondingly, an essential element of panel management is eliminating panel members who provide poor quality data. Everyone has an off day, so typically a panel member will not be removed for a single violation, but rather a pattern of behavior. Respondents who provide poor quality data generally fall into one of six categories of behavior.

"Rule breakers" don't follow directions, either intentionally, or simply because they aren't paying adequate attention. A good panel manager will be certain to check responses to open-ended questions—rule breakers often skip such questions or provide vague answers that are of no use to the client. Screening questions that require careful reading before the respondent can move forward in a survey can also help to identify rule breakers.[32]

"Speeders" were discussed in chapter six. Technology now makes it very easy to define the acceptable minimum survey completion time; a response under this parameter can be eliminated from a particular study. Respondents with multiple "speeding" violations should be dropped from the panel as they are often professional respondents who randomly assign answers to questions simply to obtain rewards.

"Straightliners" provide either overly positive or overly negative answers on a survey, in some cases without reading the questions. Catching these individuals is very easy if a few questions are phrased in a both a positive and negative fashion. For example, one question might say, "I love shopping in the mall." A second question later in the survey may state, "I hate shopping in the mall." A person selecting "Strongly Agree" to both statements is obviously not reading the questions. His or her data should be eliminated from the study, and the individual should be dropped from the panel when multiple violations occur.

"Cheaters" are the most dangerous type of problematic respondent. Just as technology has made it easier to automate sampling, so has technology made it easier for professional respondents to take advantage of online market research opportunities. Bots, which attempt to mimic humans and answer surveys for rewards (sent to their programmer), are problematic not only for MTurk, but also for professional sample firms and commercial market research entities. Fortunately, technology can help to identify most bots. Captcha—little boxes that require the participant to enter the alphanumeric characters shown in an image—can help to identify bots, particularly when the captchas are introduced at random places in the survey and not just at the beginning where a human may see them prior to letting the bot take over the rest of the survey. Because the characters are shown in an image, the bot cannot "read" and identify the letters. Other mechanical methods help to identify bots and cheaters, and one of the easiest methods is to use open-ended questions. Machines can't answer open-ended questions well and typically insert words that don't make sense. Cheaters with multiple accounts often use the same open-ended answers over and over, and can be statistically identified in this fashion, especially when paired with IP address, and device fingerprinting. It should be noted though that the rise of artificial intelligence may make it easier for a new generation of bots to defraud the marketing research industry.

The presence of negative professional survey takers is more pronounced with international samples. For instance, in India companies offer seminars to individuals on how they can locate research panels and how to complete surveys. For these individuals, completing surveys is a way of life. They are often a member of multiple online research panels and may even do so under a number of different profiles. They may be a 25-year-old college graduate working for an international firm for one survey and a 40-year-old female homemaker for another. While companies strive to locate and eliminate these individuals from their research panels, they are difficult to identify.[33]

Invitation-only recruiting is a closed system where individuals are requested to be part of the online research panels. Most often, these panels are developed through purchasing rights to a large company's database, such as Hilton Hotels or Nielsen. Individuals are then selected based on their demographic profile. Individuals are sent a request to participate in the research panel. Using this type of method allows a research company to have much tighter control over who becomes a member of a panel. While it does not eliminate the professional survey taker, it greatly reduces the number that will be on the panel. The attempt is made to recruit individuals who truly want to share their opinions as opposed to those whose sole goal is to earn money or prizes.

Another problem with online research, in general, is the representativeness of the sample. Although over 88 percent of the U.S. adult population use the Internet and have access to it, Internet users still tend to be a little different from the general population. Internet users tend to be younger, more educated, and have higher incomes than non-Internet users.[34] While this may not be a problem for some industries, such as electronics, it can pose a problem for others, such as food product manufacturers.

8.8 Global Concerns

Issues that concern marketing researchers in the United States regarding samples are present in other countries as well. In addition, issues with translation and cultural differences add to the challenge of conducting global studies. While survey questions can be translated into a different language, the meaning may still be different depending on the culture of that country.

Research panels can be used, but it creates unique problems in terms of global research. While the differences between online users and non-online users in the United States are not that great, in other countries the differences can be much larger. It may be that only a small part of a country's population has access to the Internet. For instance, only 34 percent of the 1.3 billon individuals living in India use the Internet, while 56.7 percent of China's 1.4 billion people have access to the Internet. By contrast, 93.3 percent of the more than 127 million individuals living in Japan have access. Hong Kong (87 percent), Taiwan (87.9 percent), and South Korea (92.6 percent) also have widespread Internet penetration throughout their countries.[35] The differences in income and education between Internet users and non-users can be much greater, especially in third world countries.

Most people would think that online studies in China and India would closely resemble online studies conducted in the United States. Such is not the case. While the overall number of Internet users is high (due to the large populations), the composition is skewed toward urban areas and large cities. In countries such as the United Arab Emirates the floating population is high, which means the profiles of locals versus expatriates varies greatly. For these countries, updating profiles on a regular basis is important. Respondents in Japan and France are very sensitive to how they are treated, so survey quality is highly dependent on effective communications with panel members.

Another facet of global samples is that in western countries, such as the United States, many individuals do not want to be part of a research panel. Even for invitation-only panels, the refusal rate to participate is high. However, in other countries where the Internet is new and online survey research is in its infancy, being part of a research panel is exciting and novel. It can even be a status symbol for those who participate. As a result, the views of people in these countries may differ considerably from the views in a country where it is difficult to recruit panel members.[36]

8.9 Marketing Research Statistics

The Statistics Review section discusses how the chi-square test can be used to check the degree to which a sample represents the population with respect to key demographic traits. The Dealing with Data assignment offers the opportunity to apply this knowledge. Stacked bar charts are one method of displaying sample characteristics, and are discussed in the Statistical Reporting section.

8.9a Statistics Review

To be able to make inferences to a population, the sample needs to be representative of the population being studied. A statistical method to check for representativeness is the chi-square test. The test can be used to compare sample characteristics to population characteristics to see if they are statistically the same.

Consider Figure 8.12, which compares the gender of the sample to the gender of a target population. In this situation, the target population consists of 50 percent males and 50 percent females. Thus, the 1,024 responses should be split equally between males and females. The sample, however, has 563 females and 491 males, a ratio of 53.4 percent to 46.6 percent. The question that must be considered is whether the difference in gender between the population and sample is significant at the 95 percent confidence level. For this to be true, the p-value of the chi-square test must be below .05. If it is, then it would indicate a significant difference between the population and sample. As a result the sample would not be truly representative of the population, at least with respect to gender.

Before examining the chi-square test statistic, examine the table in the bottom left entitled "Demographic—Gender." Since the target population is split equally between males and females, in the sample of 1,054 the chi-square test assumes an expected frequency of 527 females and 527 males. The observed N is 563 females and 491 males. The residual shows the sample has 36 more females than it should (563–527) and has 36 fewer males than is expected (491–527).

The table on the bottom right shows the chi-square value is 4.918. The p-value, or significance level, is designated as "Asymp. Sig." in the table, and shows a p-value of .027. This is below the test value of .05, which means there is a significant difference between the gender makeup of the sample and what was expected for the population. Thus, the sample is not representative of the population in terms of gender. It has too many females and not enough males.

Demographic-Gender

		Frequency	Percent	Valid Percent	Cumulative Percent
Valid	Female	563	52.8	53.4	53.4
	Male	491	46.1	46.6	100.0
	Total	1054	98.9	100.0	
Missing	System	12	1.1		
Total		1066	100.0		

Demographic-Gender

	Observed N	Expected N	Residual
Female	563	527.0	36.0
Male	491	527.0	-36.0
Total	1054		

Test Statistics

	Demographic-Gender
Chi-square	4.918[a]
df	1
Asymp. Sig.	.027

a. 0 cells (.0%) have expected frequencies less than 5. The minimum expected cell frequency is 527.0.

FIGURE 8.12 Chi-Square Test; Gender

Population—Age	
18–22	68%
23–29	25%
30–39	5%
40+	2%

Demographic—Age					
		Frequency	Percent	Valid Percent	Cumulative Percent
Valid	18–22	723	67.8	68.3	68.3
	23–29	274	25.7	25.9	94.2
	30–39	44	4.1	4.2	98.4
	40+	17	1.6	1.6	100.0
	Total	1058	99.2	100.0	
Missing	System	8	.8		
Total		1066	100.0		

Demographic—Age			
	Observed N	Expected N	Residual
18–22	723	719.4	3.6
23–29	274	264.5	9.5
30–39	44	52.9	-8.9
40+	17	21.2	-4.2
Total	1058		

Test Statistics	
	Demographic—Age
Chi-square	2.674[a]
df	3
Asymp. Sig.	.445

a. 0 cells (.0%) have expected frequencies less than 5. The minimum expected cell frequency is 21.2.

FIGURE 8.13 Chi-Square Test: Age

Figure 8.13 shows a chi-square test for age. The top left table shows the target population's age composition. In the target population, 68 percent are ages 18 to 22, 25 percent are 23 to 29, 5 percent are 30 to 39, and the remaining 2 percent are 40 or older. The top right table shows the sample's age breakdown. Does the sample adequately represent the target population? The bottom left table shows the observed N from the sample, the expected N calculated from the sample characteristics, and the residual difference. The chi-square test in the bottom right table shows a chi-square value of 2.674 and a p-value of 0.445. Since the p-value is greater than .05, there is not a significant difference between the age composition of the sample and the age composition of the target population. Thus, in terms of age, the sample is representative of the population for this research study.

The greatest difficulty in determining the representativeness of the sample is locating the appropriate target population parameters. Data from the U.S. census can be helpful when surveys attempt to represent the population of the U.S. as a whole, a particular state, city, or zip code. Marketing studies may sample college students at a particular university. Characteristics of a university's student population are usually made available by the institutional research department, and can typically be found on the university's website. Customer databases that include demographic profiles can be compared against those of the sample when studies targeting current customers are used. In situations in which no customer database is present, an alternative source that approximates these characteristics may have to be used. If Reebok conducted a survey drawn from the population of individuals who purchased athletic shoes in the last six months, they could use the demographic characteristics contained in the data available from syndicated research firms such as Mediamark. Of course Mediamark's data are also based on a sampling procedure, but at least it is a large national sample and as such would likely be close to the population of Reebok purchasers.

8.9b Statistical Reporting

When data are in tabular form, stacked bar charts are often used. Stacked bar charts allow a researcher to illustrate volume or size while at the same time showing relationships among entities. Consider the stacked bar shown in **Figure 8.14**. The graph shows for each social media platform the percentage of users within the designated age groups. Thus, for Snapchat, 37 percent of Snapchat users are 18 to 24 compared to 15 percent for Facebook. For Pinterest, the largest age group is 30 to 49 year olds, 39 percent. The graph allows for easy comparisons among the five social media platforms in terms of the age of users within each platform. Note the percentages in Figure 8.14 all add to 100 percent for each of the social media platforms.

Another form of stacked bar chart is shown in **Figure 8.15**. This graph allows for comparisons among the age groups and also indicates the relative size of each social media

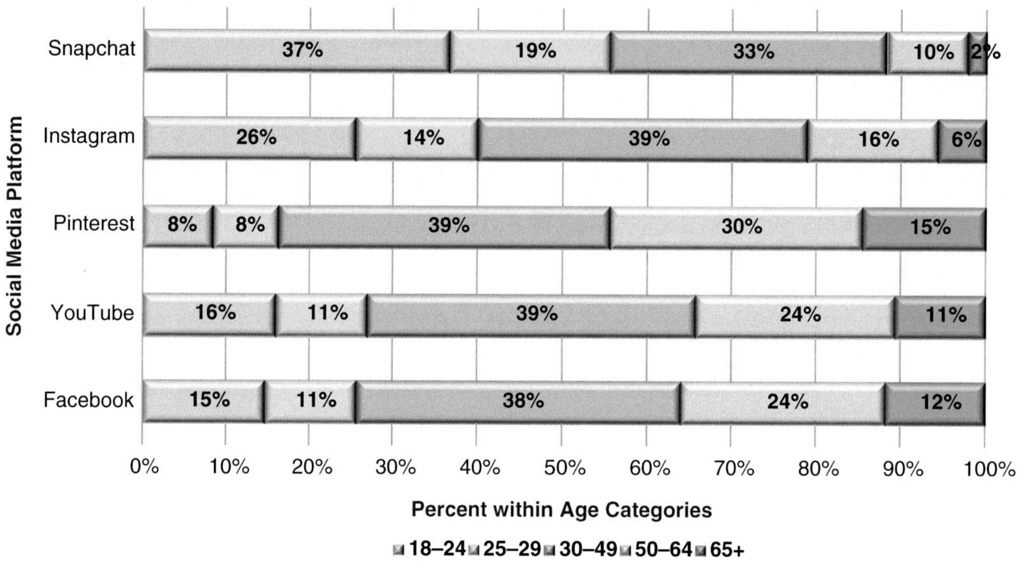

FIGURE 8.14 Age Composition of Social Media Users
Source: Adapted from "Social Media Use in 2018," Pew Research Center, Washington, D.C., (March 1, 2018), http://www.pewinternet.org/2018/03/01/social-media-use-in-2018/.

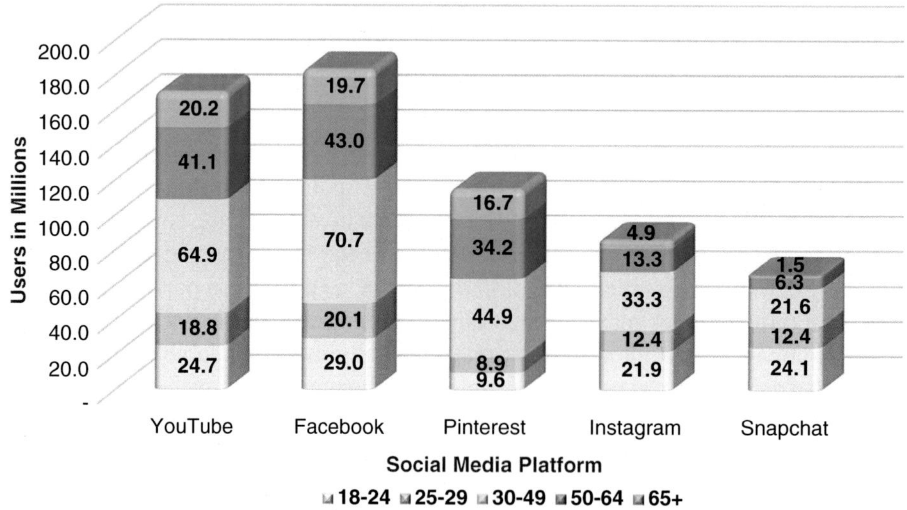

FIGURE 8.15 Social Media Platform Users by Ages
Source: Adapted from "Social Media Use in 2018," Pew Research Center, Washington, D.C., (March 1, 2018), http://www.pewinternet.org/2018/03/01/social-media-use-in-2018/.

platform. The graph indicates the number of users (in millions) for five age categories within the 18 to 65 and older bracket. For Facebook, 29 million users are from the age of 18 to 24, 20.1 million are from 28 to 29, and 70.7 million are from 30 to 49, 43 million are 50 to 64 and 16.7 million are 65 years of age or older. While the graph maintains the relative size for each age group for each social media platform, it also shows the relative size of each social media platform. It is easy to see that the total number of users of Snapchat is smaller than any of the other social media platforms.

The type of stacked bar chart that should be used depends on the information the researcher wants to convey. Figure 8.14 allows the researcher to examine the age make-up of users for each platform. Figure 8.15 takes into consideration the total number of users, as well as the age breakdown.

Statistical Reporting Exercise: Walker Hunting Supplies has launched an aggressive social media campaign on Facebook, Snapchat, Instagram, Pinterest, and Twitter. The company's advertising agency designed a coupon offer, a contest, a sweepstakes, and offered a free sample. These promotions were randomly displayed on each of the social media sites whenever someone would log on. After the three-month campaign, the data in **Figure 8.16** was collected. The table shows the number of purchases originating from each type of sales promotion from each of the social media platforms. Create a stacked bar graph showing the results of the campaign. Explain what the graph conveys.

Figure 8.17 shows the percentage of each sales promotion associated with purchases based on the social media platform. Each row adds to 100 percent. Thus, for Facebook 39 percent of purchases that originated from Facebook were through the coupon offer, 17.7 percent from a contest, 14.6 percent from a sweepstakes, and 27.8 percent from an offer for a free sample. Create a stacked bar graph of the data in Figure 8.17. Interpret the results.

Social Media/ Sales Promotion	Coupon	Contest	Sweepstakes	Sample
Facebook	63	28	23	44
Twitter	19	13	30	15
Instagram	50	17	21	14
Pinterest	24	5	27	11
Snapchat	29	17	49	26

FIGURE 8.16 Number of Purchases at Walker Hunting Supplies from Each of the Sales Promotions by the Social Media Platform

Social Media/ Sales Promotion	Coupon	Contest	Sweepstakes	Sample
Facebook	39.9%	17.7%	14.6%	27.8%
Twitter	24.7%	16.9%	39.0%	19.5%
Instagram	49.0%	16.7%	20.6%	13.7%
Pinterest	35.8%	7.5%	40.3%	16.4%
Snapchat	24.0%	14.0%	40.5%	21.5%

FIGURE 8.17 Percentages of Purchases at Walker Hunting Supplies from Each of the Sales Promotions by the Social Media Platform

8.9c Dealing with Data

A marketing professor has surveyed the students at her university concerning the use of PowerPoint slides. To be able to make inferences to the entire student body, the sample drawn needs to represent the university's student population. Figure 8.18 shows five student demographic variables. The professor found the breakdown of the overall student population along the five dimensions in the university's fact book posted online.

The questionnaire used for this study is located at www.clowjames.net/ students.html and is entitled Chapter 08 Dealing with Data Survey. The SPSS data file is entitled Chapter 08 Dealing with Data. Use the chi-square test found under the nonparametric menu button in SPSS. Test the sample demographics against the population percentages shown in Figure 8.18. Remember, each variable will have to be tested separately. After running the five chi-square tests, answer the following questions:

1. Based on the chi-square test, which sample variables adequately represent the university's student population and which ones do not? Support your answer by providing the p-value of the chi-square test and explaining what it means.
2. Using the results from question 1, make recommendations for adjusting the sample. For example, which categories have too many respondents and which ones do not have enough?
3. Based on the five chi-square tests, is this sample representative of the student population? Why or why not? Can the professor make inferences to the student population about the use of PowerPoint slides by students? Why or why not?
4. Can the professor make inferences to college students in general, i.e., for all college students in the United States? Why or why not?
5. Are any important population characteristics missing from this study? If so, what are they? Why do you feel that they would be relevant?

Variable	Category	Population Percent
Gender	Female	64%
	Male	36%
Tradition/Nontraditional	Traditional	66%
	Nontraditional	20%
	Other	14%
Race/Ethnicity	African-American	25%
	Caucasian	66%
	Other	9%
Full Time/Part Time	Full Time	63%
	Part Time	37%
College	Arts & Sciences	34%
	Business	25%
	Education	26%
	Health Sciences	15%

FIGURE 8.18 Population Characteristics

Summary

Objective 1: Explain the difference between a population and and a sample.
A population is the set of people, websites, stores, or other objects the researcher wants to study and from whom the researcher wishes to collect data. A sample is a subset of the population that should provide a representative cross-section of the people, stores, websites, or objects that exist in the population.

Objective 2: Discuss the steps involved in selecting a sample.
The sample selection process begins with a definition of the characteristics that describe the sample, as well as characteristics that should exclude participants from being part of the sample. Next, the sample frame is identified and developed. Sometimes multiple sources are used in this process. The next step requires that the researcher make a choice between probability sampling and nonprobability sampling. This step is followed by determination of the sample size. Finally, the specific sampling technique used to select sample elements is selected and implemented.

Objective 3: Identify and describe the four nonprobability sampling methods.
Convenience samples choose sample elements based on convenience factors, such as ease of access or availability during the surveying period. The personal judgment of the researcher determines who is and is not selected to be a member of a judgment sample. Quota samples attempt to ensure some level of representativeness of the population in the sample based on one or more characteristics of the target population, or some other factor specified by the researcher. Most appropriate for populations with low incidence rates, snowball samples are formed when a few respondents who initially participate in a study agree to provide the researcher with the names of additional individuals who share some key characteristic.

Objective 4: Identify and describe the four probability sampling methods.
Random sample elements are randomly selected from a numbered list using a random number generator or some other random selection process. A skip interval is used to select members of a systematic random sample, following the random selection of a starting place on an ordered list of sample frame elements. Stratified samples first create mutually exclusive and categorically exhaustive groups for one of the characteristics of the sample or behavior of interest to the study. Subjects are randomly selected from within each group to ensure that the population is adequately represented. Cluster samples divide populations into mutually exclusive and categorically exhaustive groups, or clusters where each cluster is assumed to be representative of the population as a whole. One-stage cluster samples randomly select clusters, then survey all elements within the cluster. Two-stage cluster samples begin by randomly selecting clusters, then randomly selecting elements within the clusters to be part of the sample.

Objective 5: Describe the various methods of determining sample size.
Methods of determining sample size include using general practice rules of thumb, sample sizes found in previous studies, the sample size statistical formula, sample size calculators found on the web, and sample size tables.

Objective 6: Discuss the benefits and issues related to online research panels.
Online research panels allow data to be collected faster and in a more cost-effective manner. It can be especially beneficial in targeting low-incidence populations. Online panels allow for graphic, video, and audio stimuli and panel response rates are superior to non-panel online surveys. Plus results can be viewed in real-time. Data quality is enhanced by the automated data entry and validation aspects associated with online software, as well captchas and checks of open-ended question responses. When using panels, marketers should check a variety of validation metrics to ensure data quality. Open recruitment practices, problems stemming from programmatic sampling, respondent abuse, and professional respondents and bots damage the quality of data available via online panels. Furthermore, online panels are not truly representative of the general population. However, as more individuals gain access to the Internet, online panels are becoming more representative.

Key Terms

bots, p. 272
census, p. 265
cluster sample, p. 278
clusters, p. 278
convenience samples, p. 271
crowdsourcing, p. 272
digital fingerprinting, p. 284
fixed sample, p. 270
judgment sample, p. 272
nonprobability sample, p. 269
one-stage cluster sample, p. 278
population, p. 265
probability sample, p. 269
programmatic sampling, p. 284

quota sample, p. 273
random digit dialing (RDD), p. 267
sample, p. 264
sample frame, p. 267
sample size, p. 279
sampling, p. 264
sampling error, p. 269
sequential sample, p. 270
simple random sample, p. 276
skip interval, p. 277
snowball sample, p. 275
stratified sample, p. 277
systematic random sample, p. 277
two-stage cluster sample, p. 278

Critical Thinking Exercises

1. Topal is a whitening toothpaste that is known for its ability to clean tough stains while controlling tartar and fighting plaque. Suppose the manufacturer of Topal was interested in surveying both current consumers of the product, as well as those who don't use it but who would benefit from Topal's superior whitening ability. Define the population characteristics for the study. Remember to include exclusionary factors that are relevant.
2. A manufacturer of fishing equipment and supplies would like to sample people who participate in fishing activities on a regular basis. Define the population characteristics in greater detail. Assume that you have been tasked with building a sampling frame list of individuals who are part of this population. What sources would you use to build this list? Your goal is to develop a sampling frame that is as representative as is possible.
3. Under what circumstances would a stratified sample be preferable to a random sample? Explain. List one or more products or services where stratification would be especially helpful. Why do you feel that at stratified sample would be best?
4. Identify the type of sampling technique used in the following studies:
   a. A telephone surveyor calls people listed in the phone book in alphabetical order. The survey is administered to the first 100 African-American men and 100 African-American women who agree to participate.
   b. A pest control company uses a random number generator to select 100 current customers from their customer database to survey regarding their satisfaction with the firm's services.
   c. The state of Texas randomly selects 10 school districts in the state, then randomly selects five middle schools within each district to participate in a survey.
5. You have been asked to conduct a study of students who attend your university. Unfortunately, you are restricted to using one of the non-probability sampling techniques discussed in this chapter. Which would you choose? Why? Explain how you would implement your sampling plan and the tactics you would use to try to make your sample as representative of the student population as you can.
6. Describe the differences between systematic samples, cluster samples, and stratified samples. Give examples of each that differ from those described in the textbook.
7. Calculate the skip interval to be used in a systematic random sample if the population size is 5000 and a sample of 350 individuals is required to provide the desired confidence level and margin of error.
8. Suppose a researcher wanted to know the sample size needed at the 99 percent confidence level for a pharmaceutical drug study in which the variability of the population is unknown and the acceptable margin of error is ± 1 percent. Use the statistical formula discussed earlier in this chapter to calculate the sample size needed. What if the researcher were willing to drop the confidence level to 95 percent? What sample size would be needed under these conditions? Show your work for both sets of calculations.
9. A trade association with 3500 members needs to know how many members should be sent email invitations to participate in a study. The variability of the population is unknown, and the trade association wants to be 95 percent confident that the sample results fall within a margin of error of ± 3 percent. Find an online sample calculator that takes into account the population size in addition to confidence level, variability of the population, and margin of error. Calculate the sample size needed and provide the URL of the sample size calculator used.
10. Go to your university's website and locate the page or document that describes the population characteristics of the student body. This information may be listed in a document titled, "Fact Book", "Fast Facts", "Student Profiles" or something similar. Typically the information is provided by the division or department of institutional research. Some Universities provide access to this information from web pages that target parents or families, community members or media, or new students. This information should be publicly available, so if you don't find it on the website, visit your University's library and speak to a reference librarian. Once you have located the population characteristics, prepare a report of what you've found. Make certain that you paraphrase the information (don't cut and paste directly from the website), and cite your source appropriately.

Lakeside Grill

(Comprehensive Student Case)

After considerable discussion, Brooke, Alexa, Juan, Destiny and Zach arrived at a sampling plan, shown in Figure 8.19. Based on information from the owner of the Lakeside Grill, secondary research, and a focus group, the team defined the population as households within a five-mile radius of the grill. They believed that most of the patrons of the restaurant came from within that distance. A couple of the group members, Juan and Brooke, had argued that a five-mile radius was too far and that they should concentrate on a two or three mile radius.

Since the target population was defined as households within a five-mile radius, the sampling frame was designated as all homes and apartments within that area. That decision was easy. The liveliest discussion occurred over the sampling procedure. The group finally decided on a cluster approach. While some argued for a one-stage approach, others argued for a two-stage approach.

In support of the one-stage approach, Destiny argued, "I think the best way for us to do this is to randomly select blocks within our sampling frame. Then we should deliver a questionnaire to every house and apartment on that block. That will be easier than just going to some of the homes on that block. It will get really confusing I think to do the two-stage approach."

In contrast, Zach argues, "I must say I disagree with Destiny. While it may be easier to use that approach, I feel strongly it needs to be a two-stage approach. After we identify the blocks then we need to randomly select the homes or apartment buildings. This will ensure a better random sample."

- Population—households within five miles
- Sampling frame—homes within five mile radius
- Sampling procedure—cluster sampling
  - –One stage
  - –Two stage
- Sample size—300

FIGURE 8.19: Sampling Plan for Lakeside Grill

Critique Questions:

1. Do you agree with the group's definition of the target population? Why or why not?
2. Is the sampling frame defined properly? Why or why not?
3. What is your evaluation of the one-stage cluster approach? What is your evaluation of the two-stage cluster approach? Which should be used? Justify your answer.
4. What other methods of sampling could the group use? What would be the pros and cons?
5. Go through each method of sampling and discuss its feasibility for this student research project with the Lakeside Grill.
6. The group decided on a sample size of 300. Is this enough? Is this realistic?

Notes

1. This section is based on information from "Social Media Use in 2018," Pew Research Center, March 1, 2018, http://www.pewinternet.org/2018/03/01/social-media-use-in-2018/; and United States Census Bureau, "Table S0101: Age and Sex, 2017 American Community Survey 1-Year," *American Community Survey*, 2017, https://factfinder.census.gov/faces/tableservices/jsf/pages/productview.xhtml?pid=ACS_17_1YR_S0101&prodType=table.
2. Michael A. Stelzner, "2018 Social Media Marketing Industry Report," Social Media Examiner, May 7, 2018, https://www.socialmediaexaminer.com/social-media-marketing-industry-report-2018/.
3. "Travel and Hospitality Study Reveals Top Email Marketing Challenges and Priorities," Yahoo! Finance, May 6, 2010, http://finance.yahoo.com/news/travel-and-hospitality-study-iw-3461419906.html .
4. Felix Richter, "Landline Phones Are a Dying Breed," Statista Infographics, May 17, 2019, http://www.statista.com/chart/2072/landline-phones-in-the-united-states/.
5. Howard Fienberg, "New U.S. Restrictions on Telephone Research Prompt Risk Management Debate: Do the New TCPA Rules Mean You Should Junk Your Autodialer?" Alert!, August 3, 2015, http://www.marketingresearch.org/article/new-us-restrictions-telephone-research- prompt-risk-management-debate-do-new-tcpa-rules-mean.
6. "FCC Approves New TCPA Rules—Telephone Consumer Protection Act," *The National Law Review* (June 18, 2015).
7. "Telephone Survey Response Rates," Marketing Charts, June 12, 2018, https://www.marketingcharts.com/industries/market-research-81996/attachment/gallup-telephone-survey-response-rates-1997-2017-jan2018.
8. Scott Keeter, Nick Hatley, Courtney Kennedy, and Arnold Lau, "What Low Response Rates Mean for Telephone Surveys," Pew Research, June 1, 2018, http://www.pewresearch.org/methods/2017/05/15/what-low-response-rates-mean-for-telephone-surveys/on.

9. "Delivery Sequence File (DSF2)," Anchor Computing, October 15, 2018, http://www.anchorcomputer.com/index.php/dsf2/.
10. Dennis Dalbey and Ashley Hyon, "Why Address-Based Sampling Is Much More than Just Addresses," *Quirk's Media* 30, no. 7 (July 2016): 50, 52, 53.
11. "Usage of Traditional Methodologies," in *GRIT Report: GreenBook Research Industry Trends Report, Quarters 3–4, 2017* (New York: GreenBook, 2017), https://www.greenbook.org/grit/grit-archive.
12. Bonnie W. Eisenfeld, "Qualitatively Speaking: Sampling for Qualitative Researchers," *Quirk's Marketing Research Review* (March 2007): Article ID 20070308.
13. Jerry Chandler and Danielle Shapiro, "Conducting Clinical Research Using Crowdsourced Convenience Samples," *Annual Review of Clinical Psychology* 12 (2016): 53–81.
14. Ibid.
15. Emily Dreyfyss, "A Bot Panic Hits Amazon's Mechanical Turk," *Wired* (August 17, 2018), https://www.wired.com/story/amazon-mechanical-turk-bot-panic/.
16. Alana Semuels, "The Internet Is Enabling a New Kind of Poorly Paid Hell," *The Atlantic* (January 23, 2018), https://www.theatlantic.com/business/archive/2018/01/amazon-mechanical-turk/551192/.
17. "Connected Commerce," The Nielsen Company, November 2018, https://www.nielsen.com/content/dam/corporate/us/en/reports-downloads/2018-reports/connected-commerce-report.pdf.
18. "Methodology and Sample," in *GRIT Report: GreenBook Research Industry Trends Report, Quarters 3–4, 2017* (New York: GreenBook, 2017), https://www.greenbook.org/grit/grit-archive.
19. Joe DeCosmo, "Nth-ing to Consider," *Direct* 15, no. 7 (May 15, 2003): 29–31.
20. Andrew Zelin and Roger Stubbs, "Cluster Sampling: A False Economy?" *International Journal of Market Research* 47, no. 5 (2005): 503–524.
21. "Millennials on Millennials," The Nielsen Company, 2018, https://www.nielsen.com/content/dam/corporate/us/en/reports-downloads/2018-reports/millennials-on-millennials-shopping-insights-report.pdf; "NRF Survey Says More than 164 Million Consumers Plan to Shop over Five-Day Thanksgiving Weekend," November 16, 2018, https://nrf.com/media-center/press-releases/nrf-survey-says-more-164-million-consumers-plan-shop-over-five-day.
22. "Research Now Panel Book," Research Now, 2017, https://www.researchnow.com/wp-content/uploads/2017/11/Panel-Book-10-17-WEB-1.pdf.
23. "Survey Help & FAQ," J.D. Power, 2019, https://www.jdpower.com/business/about-us/surveyhelpdesk.
24. Ryan Jantz, "The Foundational Stepping Stone to Quality Research: Panel Recruitment and Panel Management," June 23, 2017, https://www.researchnow.com/blog/foundational-stepping-stone-quality-research-panel-recruitment-and-panel-management/.
25. Tim Macer and Sheila Wilson, "A Report on the Confirmit Market Research Software Survey," *Quirk's Marketing Research Review* (June 2013): 50, 52–61.
26. "Consumer Participation in Research" [Addendum], in *GRIT Report: GreenBook Research Industry Trends Report, Quarters 1–2, 2017* (New York: GreenBook, 2017), https://www.greenbook.org/grit/grit-archive.
27. "The Future of Sampling," in *GRIT Report: GreenBook Research Industry Trends Report, Quarters 1–2, 2018* (New York: GreenBook, 2018), https://www.greenbook.org/grit/grit-archive).
28. This section is based on Debbie Balch, Kara Carroll, Joey Torretto, and Cailee Osterman, "Beating the Cheaters of Qual and Quant Research" [Webinar recording], *Quirks Media* (December 2017), https://www.greenbook.org/marketing-research/Webinar-recording-Beating-the-Cheaters-of-Qual-and-Quant-Research, and "The Future of Sampling," *GRIT Report*, p. 26.
29. J. D. Deitch, "Sample Companies Step Up: Quality and Engagement Have Become Our Job," *Quirks Media* (January 2018), https://www.quirks.com/articles/sample-companies-step-up-quality-and-engagement-have-become-our-job.
30. Ibid.
31. Nikhil Lobo, "What's Programmatic Sampling—And Why Should You Care?" CMS Wire (May 2, 2016), https://www.cmswire.com/analytics/whats-programmatic-sampling-and-why-should-you-care/.
32. This section is based on Brooke Patton, "6 Survey Respondents to Avoid," *Quirks Media* (April 9 2018), https://www.quirks.com/articles/6-survey-respondents-to-avoid; and Mathijs de Jong, "Using New Technologies to Mitigate Fraud in Online Research," RW Connect, April 12, 2018, https://rwconnect.esomar.org.
33. Interview with Debbie Peternana and Carrie Bellerive, ReRez, February 25, 2011.
34. "Internet/Broadband Fact Sheet," Pew Research Center, http://www.pewinternet.org/fact-sheet/internet-broadband/.
35. "Asia Internet Use, Population Data and Facebook Statistics—June 30, 2018," https://www.internetworldstats.com/stats3.htm.
36. Chuck Miller and Suresh Subbiah, "Methods of Ensuring Online Sample Quality around the World," *Quirk's Marketing Research Review* (January 2011): 34, 36, 38.

Measurement Methods

CHAPTER 9

Chapter Outline

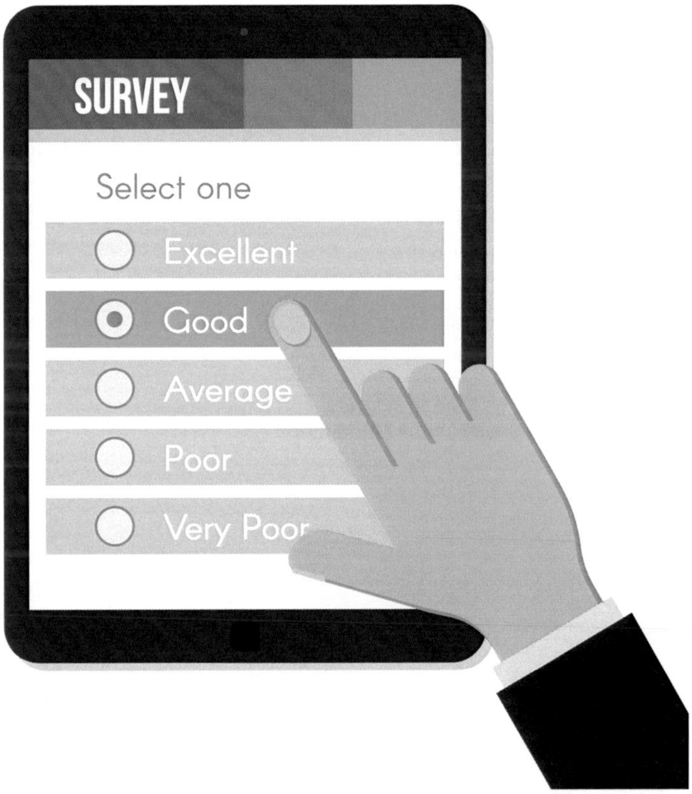

Source: EgudinKa/Shutterstock.

Learning Objectives

After studying this chapter, you should be able to:

- Explain the concept of measurement.
- Describe the characteristics and give examples of nominal scales.
- Describe the characteristics and give examples of ordinal scales.
- Describe the characteristics and give examples of interval scales.
- Describe the characteristics and give examples of ratio scales.
- Discuss methods for assessing reliability.
- Elaborate on methods of evaluating validity.

9.1 Chapter Overview

Advertising dollars continue to be shifted toward social media marketing because of its ability to engage with consumers. It started with Facebook and has grown to other social media platforms. Michael Stelzner of the *Social Media Examiner* recently surveyed over 5,700 marketers about their company's use of social media and their attitudes toward social media. One question asked the marketers to identify the platforms currently being used by their companies. Results from this question are shown in **Figure 9.1**. It is not surprising that the most frequently used social media platform is Facebook, at 94 percent.

This chapter addresses the concept of measurement and how marketers can determine if the measures are reliable and valid. For instance, with social media marketing, researchers have several options. They can provide the list of responses shown in Figure 9.1 and ask respondents to check all that apply, as was the case in the survey data shown in Figure 9.1. Alternately, they could provide the list and ask respondents to rank them in various ways such as by importance, by usage, or even by level of benefit. The researchers could have provided the list and asked which option or options generated the highest sales or had the highest level of engagement or click-through rate. The bottom line is that researchers have a number of ways of asking a question. Each way could yield a different type of data that will in turn affect the ways the data can be analyzed. Chapter 9 begins with a discussion of the four types of scales and then provides information on how to decide the best scale to use.

The last part of the chapter examines the issues of reliability and validity. Obtaining responses to questions is only part of the researcher's task. The marketing research must also ensure that the responses accurately measure what they are supposed to measure. In addition, the researcher must take steps to minimize errors from adversely affecting the results of the marketing study.

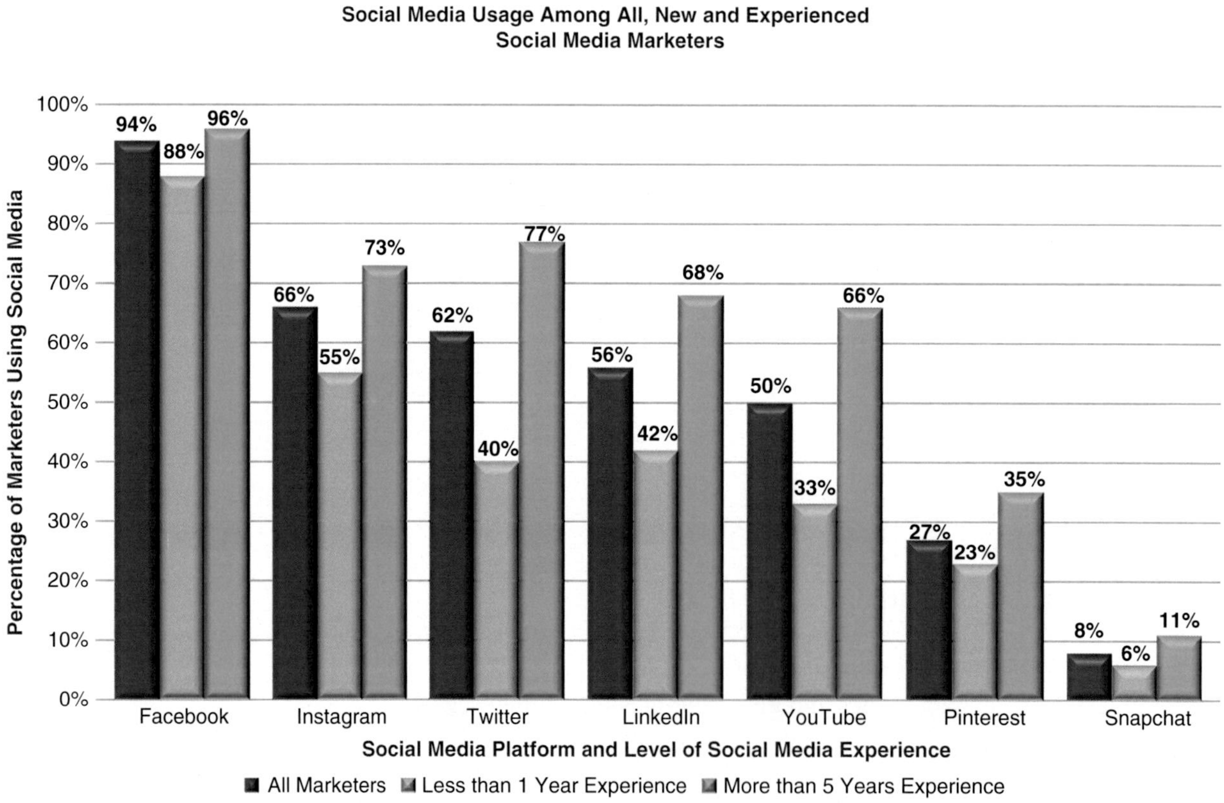

FIGURE 9.1 A Graph Indicating which Social Media Platforms Are Being Used by All, New and Experienced Social Media Marketers

Source: Adapted from Michael A. Stelzner, "2018 Social Media Marketing Industry Report," *Social Media Examiner*, 2018.

9.2 The Concept of Measurement

LEARNING OBJECTIVE 9.1
Explain the concept of measurement.

Measurement process of assigning numbers or labels to phenomena or characteristics.

Managers seek information from marketing research in order to make intelligent decisions. To obtain the necessary information, marketers are often engaged in measuring various phenomena or characteristics of a respondent or entity. These might include demographic characteristics, product ownership characteristics, and attitudes toward various things. **Measurement** is the process of assigning numbers or labels to these phenomena or characteristics. It can be individuals, objects, or events.

The numbers must be assigned according to specific rules or guidelines to ensure the numbers are meaningful and consistent. **Figure 9.2** provides several examples. For instance, the number 1 might be assigned to females and the number 2 to males. Numbers can also be assigned to more abstract concepts such as brand attitude or brand loyalty. Researchers could use a range of numbers from 1 to 5 to indicate the strength and direction of a person's attitude. A "5" might represent a very positive attitude and "1" a very negative attitude. A "3" might be a neutral attitude with "4" being slightly positive and "2" being slightly negative. The key to measurement is to specify the rule or process for assigning numbers to whatever is being measured.

The process of measurement involves two important concepts. First, it is not the person, object, or event that is being measured. It is an attribute or characteristic, such as the income of an individual, sales produced by an advertising campaign, or degree of willingness of a person to purchase a product. Second, the numbers are assigned by rules or a process specified by the researcher. While the way the numbers are assigned can affect the types of analyses that can be done, the process of assigning values is determined by the researcher. For instance, the number 1 does not have to be assigned to females and 2 to males. It can be the reverse; or the numbers 33 and 45 can be used, or whatever numbers the researcher designates, because these numbers do nothing other than group respondents with similar characteristics together. So long as all females are designated by the same number, and that number differs from the one assigned to males, the actual numbers used are irrelevant for nominal scales.

Respondent or Entity	Characteristic/ Phenomena	Measurement Designations
Survey respondent	Gender	Female = 1 Male = 2
	Attitude toward brand	1 = very unfavorable 2 = unfavorable 3 = neutral 4 = favorable 5 = very favorable
	Brand usage	1 = current user of brand 2 = former user of brand 3 = never used brand
Store	Type	1 = Convenience 2 = Grocery or supermarket 3 = Mass merchandise 4 = Discount 5 = Department store 6 = Boutique 7 = Other

FIGURE 9.2 The Process of Measurement

Source: Sorbis/Shutterstock.

Measurement assigns numbers or labels to represent characteristics of individuals, objects, or events. According to Figure 9.2, the store in this photo would be assigned the number "1" to identify it as a convenience store.

Researchers have four different types of scales that can be used for measurements: nominal, ordinal, interval, and ratio (see **Figure 9.3**). The characteristics of each scale determine the types of data analyses that can be performed. Nominal scales are considered to be the lowest or most restrictive type of scale and ratio the highest order scale.

9.2a Nominal Scales

LEARNING OBJECTIVE 9.2
Describe the characteristics and give examples of nominal scales.

Nominal scales scale in which numbers are assigned to objects or sets of objects for the purpose of identification.

With **nominal scales** numbers are assigned to objects or sets of objects for the purpose of identification and classification. It is the lowest order of the four scales since the numbers have no meaning other than identifying a particular characteristic. The number used for each object or set is entirely up to the discretion of the researcher. Examples of nominal scales are:

Gender: (1) Female (2) Male

Preferred Fast Food: (1) McDonald's (2) Burger King (3) Wendy's (4) Taco Bell (5) KFC

How did you hear about our business? (Check all that apply):

______________ Yellow Pages
______________ Radio
______________ TV
______________ Newspaper
______________ Internet
______________ Friend
______________ Relative
______________ Other (please specify): ______________

Notice the numbers assigned in the first two examples have no real meaning other than they provide a process for coding each respondent's answer and grouping together those with similar characteristics. No numbers are provided in the third example. Instead, respondents are asked to check the blank next to each answer that applies. While this may be confusing at first glance, this type of question does collect nominal data. Each potential response (yellow pages, radio, and the like) is treated as an individual question or variable, the responses to which would be coded as 0 = no (not checked) and 1 = yes (checked). Thus, the response options implied by the "Friend" variable are, "Yes, I heard of the business {from a friend}" or "No, I did not hear of the business {from a friend}."

Mutually exclusive each response category is uniquely different from others and respondents either fit into one category or another, but cannot belong to multiple categories.

Categorically exhaustive all possible responses are included in the answer categories.

In developing nominal scales, it is highly desirable for the scale choices to be **mutually exclusive** and **categorically exhaustive**. Mutually exclusive means that each response is uniquely different from other possible responses. Thus, respondents either fit into one category or another, but cannot belong to multiple categories. This is why the third question creates separate variables for each possible checked response. Categorically exhaustive means that all possible responses are included in the answer categories. With gender, that may be evident, assuming the population is one in which transgender individuals are

- Nominal scales
- Ordinal scales
- Interval scales
- Ratio scales

FIGURE 9.3 Types of Measurement Scales

not present or it is not important to distinguish this group from males or females. But, for the fast food preference, suppose an individual wanted to select Hardees. It is not listed, so while the scale is mutually exclusive, it is not collectively exhaustive. In case a choice is left out, researchers often include as the last item "other" and allow the respondent to write in their own response. These "other" responses can then be coded into separate categories later before analysis; or, if it is a small number of responses, the researcher might leave it as "other." When preferences or consumption habits are being surveyed, researchers may also wish to include additional categories, such as "no preference" or "do not eat fast food." Doing so would avoid forcing respondents to make a selection that otherwise would introduce error into the data.

The nominal scale is considered the lowest scale form since the only analysis that can be conducted is to obtain a frequency count and percentage of responses. For instance, researchers can count how many males and females are in a sample and even assign a percentage, such as 63 percent females and 37 percent males. For the fast food item, it is possible to count how many respondents indicated each choice and then calculate a percentage. **Figure 9.4** shows the type of results that might be obtained from the fast food item. The table shows 74 individuals preferred McDonald's, which was 21.7 percent of the sample. The least preferred fast food for this sample was Taco Bell with 44, or 12.9 percent. The table indicates 17 individuals, or 4.88 percent, checked "other." These 17 could be listed in the table if the researcher deemed it important. Otherwise, they can be left in the "other" category since it was only about 5 percent of the responses.

Source: Black Salmon/Shutterstock.

The Internet offers consumers many sources of information. Online review websites such as Angie's List and the Better Business Bureau provide reviews for local businesses. Many e-commerce websites, such as Amazon, allow verified customers to rate products after purchase. Social media, blogs, and YouTube videos offer other outlets to consumers who wish to share their opinions.

Ordinal scales scale in which numbers are assigned for the purpose of identification, but also have the property of being arranged in some type of array or order.

9.2b Ordinal Scales

LEARNING OBJECTIVE 9.3
Describe the characteristics and give examples of ordinal scales.

With **ordinal scales** numbers are assigned for the purpose of identification, but also have the property of being arranged in some type of order. As with nominal scales, response options should be mutually exclusive and categorically exhaustive. The sequence of numbers means something in terms of one response category being larger or better than another.

Preferred Restaurant	Number of Respondents	Percent of Total
McDonald's	74	21.70%
Burger King	82	24.05%
Wendy's	51	14.95%
Taco Bell	44	12.90%
KFC	68	19.94%
Other	17	4.99%
None/don't eat fast food	5	1.47%
Total	341	100%

FIGURE 9.4 Results from Using a Nominal Scale

However, the basic mathematical functions of adding, subtracting, multiplying or dividing cannot be used with ordinal scales. Consider the following examples of ordinal scales:

1. Age: (1) 18–24 (2) 25–34 (3) 35–44 (4) 45–54 (5) 55+
2. Number of websites visited: (0) None (1) 1 or 2 (2) 3 to 5 (3) 6 to 9 (4) 10 or more
3. Please rank the following search engines in terms of your personal preference with 1 indicting your first choice, 2 indicating your second choice, 3 indicating your third choice and 4 indicating fourth choice.

   Bing: ____________
   Google: ____________
   Ask.com: ____________
   Yahoo: ____________

Notice with the first ordinal scale, age, the values given range from "1" for individuals 18 to 24 to "5" for individuals 55 and over. The reason ordinal scales are used for age is that many individuals will not write down their age if asked directly, but will normally check one of the brackets to indicate their age group. There is an order to the sequence in which numbers are assigned to categories. Specifically, the larger the number used to represent a response category, the older the respondent. However, ordinal scales do not allow the researcher to compare numbers using mathematical operations. You cannot say that individuals in category 4 are twice as old as those in category 2, or four times older than those in category 1. All the numbers can be used to indicate is the category to which the respondent belongs, and whether a given respondent is older or younger than other respondents.

The same properties hold true for the second ordinal item dealing with the number of websites visited. In this case, the researcher chose to use a "0" to represent an answer of "none." The researcher could actually have used any number for this response as well as any other response. The only stipulation is that whatever numbers are chosen, an ascending order must be maintained. Instead of using codes of 0 through 4, the researcher could have chosen 10, 20, 30, 40, and 50 or even 5, 22, 36, 41, and 78. Ordinal scales do not imply the existence of equal intervals, as the last example makes clear.

The last ordinal example asked respondents to rank four search engines based on their personal preferences, with a "1" indicating their first choice, a "2" their second choice, a "3" their third choice and a "4" for their last choice. Order is still maintained with numbers from 1 to 4. However, with this coding the lower the number, the more preferred the search engine is among the respondents that were interviewed. There is no rule that says the greater a quantity, the higher the code number must be. It is common to do so, but not absolutely necessary. More often, ranking questions use the format of "1" for the first choice, "2" for the second choice and so on. This is common because that is the way consumers would think when asked to indicate their preferences.

Figure 9.5 shows one method for reporting the age variable. The pie chart can be used since the categories are mutually exclusive and collectively exhaustive and the groups together add to 100 percent (since only those 18 years of age or older were surveyed). The graph shows that the largest category of respondents is in the 25 to 44 year old age category. It consisted of 144 respondents, or 40 percent of the sample.

Figure 9.6 provides another way for reporting ordinal data. The 3-D column chart shows the number of respondents who indicated each answer. The raw numbers are presented in this graph. The researcher could have reported the percentages instead, or reported both numbers. Most people (218) visited three to five websites.

Figure 9.7 reports the results of the last question, the ranking of the four search engines. Notice for this table, the researcher has chosen to report the percentages for each category. Google was ranked as first choice by 48 percent of the respondents, Bing was ranked first by 31 percent, Yahoo was ranked first by 17 percent, and Ask.com was ranked first by only 4 percent. The mode, or most frequently occurring number, could also be

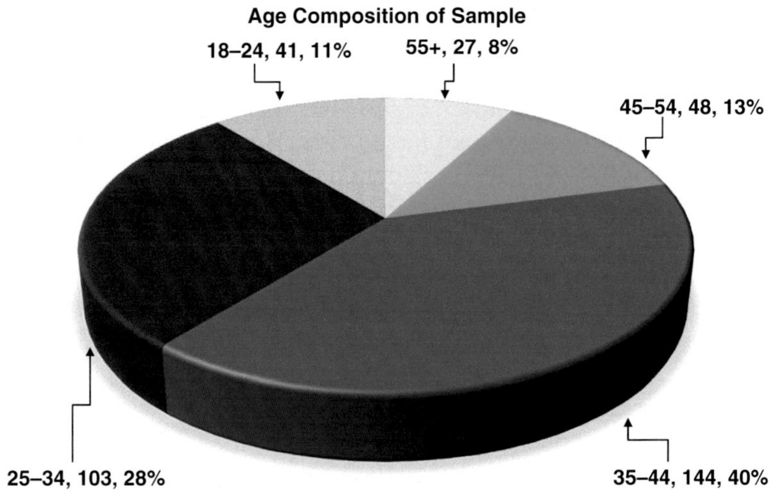

FIGURE 9.5 Pie Charts Can Be Used to Graph Ordinal Data When the Total Adds to 100 Percent

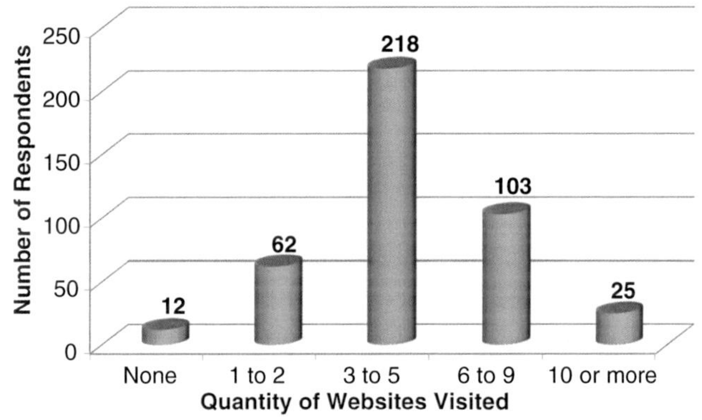

FIGURE 9.6 Number of Websites Visited by Respondents

Search Engine	First Choice	Second Choice	Third Choice	Fourth Choice
Bing	31%	36%	22%	11%
Google	48%	33%	15%	4%
Ask.com	4%	13%	23%	60%
Yahoo	17%	18%	40%	25%

FIGURE 9.7 Ordinal Scale—Ranking of Search Engines

reported. Note how each row adds up to 100 percent, and how each column adds to 100 percent.

It would be tempting to calculate a mean for the ranking question to determine a relative ranking among the four search engines. While some researchers might do this, such a calculation violates the characteristics of an ordinal scale. Recall that with ordinal scales, numbers signify order but do not possess mathematical properties. The numbers merely indicate group membership or classification. Instead of using numbers 1 through 4, the researcher could have used the numbers 1, 3, 6, and 10, or any other numbers.

To understand ordinal scales and why mathematical operations such as means are inappropriate, it also helps to consider how different individuals might go through the process of ranking the four search engines. Suppose Chelsea ranks Google as her first choice, but had a really difficult time because she also likes to use Bing just about as much. But she finally decides to rank Google first, Bing second, and for her, Yahoo is a distant third. She doesn't even like Ask.com and so gives it a "4" but in her mind it wouldn't even rank in her choice of search engines. Furthermore, one of her favorite search engines isn't even shown on the list. Now consider Codie, who has the same order for the four search engines. But Google is his first and ONLY choice as the other three aren't even a consideration. Instead, he had a hard time ranking the 2nd and 3rd and 4th choice in search engines as in his mind those three search engines are about equal. While Chelsea and Codie ranked the engines in the same order, the distance or interval between the rankings was quite different in their minds. For Chelsea first and second were very close. For Codie they were not close at all.

Unlike nominal scales, ordinal scales that ask respondents to rank order items cannot include an "other" option. For the data to have meaning, all respondents must rank the same items. Allowing people to enter an "other" choice would result in different people potentially ranking different search engines since Person A might enter "DuckDuckGo" in the other category while Person B might enter "AOL." This is further complicated by the fact that Person C's rankings may have differed if either DuckDuckGo or AOL had been originally listed as part of the ranking question. To avoid this problem, it is critical that all potential options be presented within ranking questions.

9.2c Interval Scales

LEARNING OBJECTIVE 9.4
Describe the characteristics and give examples of interval scales.

Interval scales scale in which numbers are assigned for the purpose of identification, the numbers indicate order, and the distances between the numbers assigned are considered to be equal.

With **interval scales** the distance, or space, between the numbers assigned to objects or sets of objects is considered to be equal. So if a scale from 1 to 5 is being used, then the distance between 1 and 2 is the same as between 2 and 3 as well as any other set of consecutive numbers that are chosen. Interval scales subsume the properties of both the nominal and ordinal scales in that numbers are assigned to objects or sets of objects and the numbers chosen represent an ordered progression. With ordinal scales the distance between scale points cannot be assumed to be equal, while with interval scales this assumption does hold true. While an ordinal ranking question can tell us that something is ranked more favorably than something else, we don't know by how much. The advantage of interval scales is that they allow us to determine the degree to which something is preferred, or the level of agreement that is being expressed via calculations of means and standard deviations. For this reason, interval scales are the scale of choice when measuring attitudes. The following are examples of interval scales:

Please evaluate each of the following appetizers served at the Riverfront Grill on a scale of 1 to 5 according to how well you like the appetizer.

Cheese sticks	Dislike a lot_1_|_2_|_3_|_4_|_5_Like a lot
Coconut shrimp	Dislike a lot_1_|_2_|_3_|_4_|_5_Like a lot
Chicken fingers	Dislike a lot_1_|_2_|_3_|_4_|_5_Like a lot
Potato skins	Dislike a lot_1_|_2_|_3_|_4_|_5_Like a lot
Egg rolls	Dislike a lot_1_|_2_|_3_|_4_|_5_Like a lot

Please indicate your level of agreement with the following statements.

I like to eat Mexican food.	Strongly Disagree _1_|_2_|_3_|_4_|_5_Strongly Agree
I eat only healthy food.	Strongly Disagree _1_|_2_|_3_|_4_|_5_Strongly Agree
The quality of service is excellent.	Strongly Disagree _1_|_2_|_3_|_4_|_5_Strongly Agree

Appetizer	Mean
Cheese sticks	3.79*
Coconut shrimp	3.11*
Chicken fingers	4.13*
Potato skins	4.27*
Egg rolls	3.37*
Statement	**Mean**
I like to eat Mexican food	3.88**
I eat only healthy food	2.75**
The quality of service is excellent	4.03**

FIGURE 9.8 Interval Scale—Sample Report

* Items were evaluated on a scale of 1 to 5, where 1 = dislike a lot and 5 = like a lot

** Items were evaluated on a scale of 1 to 5, where 1 = strongly disagree and 5 = strongly agree

Both scales use five intervals or **points**, but the number of points used on an interval scale is up to the researcher. It could be three points, four points, seven points, or any number that the researcher feels would be the best for collecting the information needed. Because the distances between the scale points are equal, it is possible to calculate a mean and standard deviation and to compare differences among the items within each question using more advanced statistical techniques. Figure 9.8 shows a common method of reporting the results from interval scales.

Points number of intervals in a scale.

For each item, the mean or average is computed. The results show that potato skins are the most liked, followed by chicken fingers. The least liked appetizer is coconut shrimp. In terms of agreement or disagreement with the statements, the statement "the quality of service is excellent" shows a rather high level of agreement, while the statement "I eat only healthy food" shows a lower level of agreement.

Because interval scales do not have an **absolute zero point**, in which "0" indicates a total absence of the property being measured, we cannot compare means and say that one is twice as much as another. For instance, if the mean for one appetizer was 4.0 and the mean for another one was 2.0, we can't say the one is liked twice as much as the other. While the distances on an interval scale are assumed to be equal distance, the absence of an absolute zero prevents such comparisons.

Absolute zero point measurement designation of "0" indicates a total absence of the property being measured.

Comparisons of means between various groups can also be conducted. Suppose the researcher would like to see if there is a difference between males and females in terms of how much they like the various appetizers. Figure 9.9 shows this comparison in graphical form using a clustered bar chart.

From the graph of this survey question results, it would appear that males like chicken fingers and potato skins more than females, while females like egg rolls and coconut shrimp more than males. There is not much difference between males and females in regard to cheese sticks.

In addition to calculating a mean, interval scales allow researchers to conduct more advanced tests such as t-tests and ANOVA. These tests can help to determine if the difference in preference for potato skins or any other appetizer is significant and real, or merely due to random error. In addition to gender, the researcher could see if there were any differences based on other factors, such as age or if the person was a college student or not.

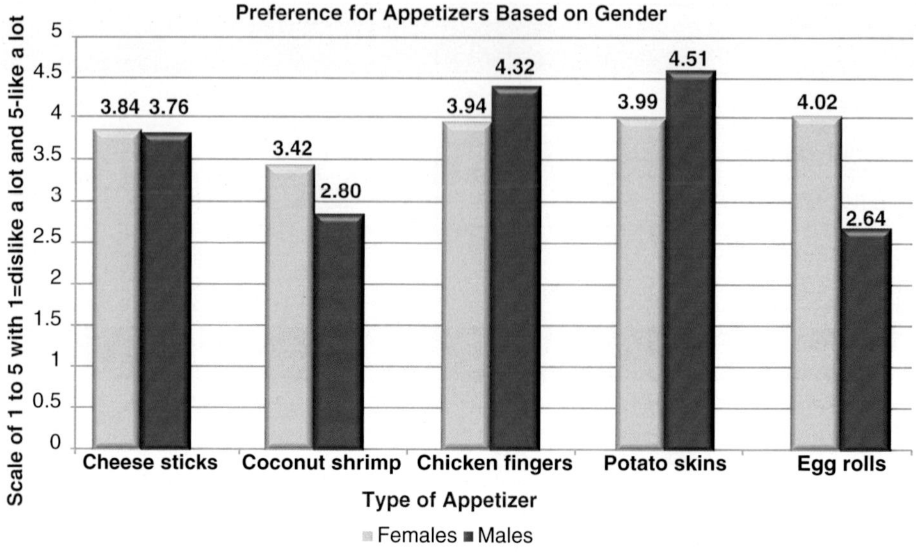

FIGURE 9.9 Preference for Appetizers Based on Gender

9.2d Ratio Scales

LEARNING OBJECTIVE 9.5
Describe the characteristics and give examples of ratio scales.

Ratio scale scale in which numbers are assigned for the purpose of identification, the numbers indicate order, the distances between the numbers are equal, and the scale has an absolute zero.

The highest order scale is a **ratio scale**. It has all of the properties of the interval scale plus the attribute of having an absolute zero point. The numbers entered as data represent actual quantities of the variable in question. Examples would be open-ended questions asking for income or distance travelled. A zero would signify none, or absence of the variable in question. Zero income means no income and zero distance means no distance. The presence of the absolute zero point allows the numbers to have ratio properties, meaning that numbers can be divided, multiplied, subtracted, or added. An income of $50,000 is twice as much as an income of $25,000 and five times greater than an income of $10,000. A distance of 20 feet is half the distance of 40 feet and one-fifth the distance of 100 feet. Examples of ratio scales follow:

For each of the following quick service restaurants, indicate how many times you have eaten there during the last two weeks.

McDonald's: __________ Burger King: __________Wendy's: __________
Taco Bell: __________ KFC: __________

On the average, how much do you spend dining out each week at all types of restaurants?

____

What year were you born? __________

Notice that no coding scale is indicated on the questions because the respondent will write in his/her response. For instance, Tim may record the following answers:

For each of the following quick service restaurants, indicate how many times you have eaten there during the last two weeks.

McDonald's: ____**3**____ Burger King: ____**6**____ Wendy's: ____**2**____
Taco Bell: ____**2**____ KFC: ____**0**____

On the average, how much do you spend dining out each month at all types of restaurants? $125

What year were you born? 1995

Notice the answers have ratio properties. Ratio scales have an absolute zero indicating an absence of a characteristic. We can say Tim has not eaten at KFC during the last month. We can also say that he has eaten at Burger King three times more than he has at Taco

Bell. In terms of average expenditures dining out, Tim's answer of $125 can be compared to other individuals, or the average amount of money spent by males can be compared to the average spent by females. Comparisons can be made based on age and any other variable the researcher feels might affect the amount of money spent on dining out.

The last item asks for the year the respondent was born. People are often reluctant to provide how old they are on a survey and will often leave it blank. Researchers can use a scale, like the one that was under the ordinal scale discussion, or they can ask for the year of birth. Amazingly, people who will not write down their age will often give their year of birth. All a researcher has to do then is to subtract it from the current year to obtain the person's age. As with the other questions, someone who is 40 is twice as old as someone 20.

Results from the ratio scales are shown in the table in Figure 9.10. Of the quick service restaurants listed, respondents eat at Taco Bell the most, an average of 4.82 times per month. That is over twice as much for KFC (2.06) and Wendy's (1.78). In terms of how much money is spent each month dining out at all types of establishments, the mean or average was $147.16. The average age of the sample was 26.45. Note that age collected as ratio data can always be recoded into categories by creating a new variable, thus allowing for pie charts or frequency tables, if desired.

Figure 9.11 is an example of using a bar graph to present ratio data. Notice that for individuals 18–24, the average was 6.27 times per month compared to only 1.22 for individuals 55 and over. From the graph, it is easy to see that as individuals get older they eat at Taco Bell less.

Fast Food Restaurant	Mean Response
McDonald's	3.21
Burger King	2.95
Wendy's	1.78
Taco Bell	4.82
KFC	2.06
Variable	**Mean**
Expenditures per month dining out	$147.16
Average age	26.45

FIGURE 9.10 Ratio Scale—Sample Report

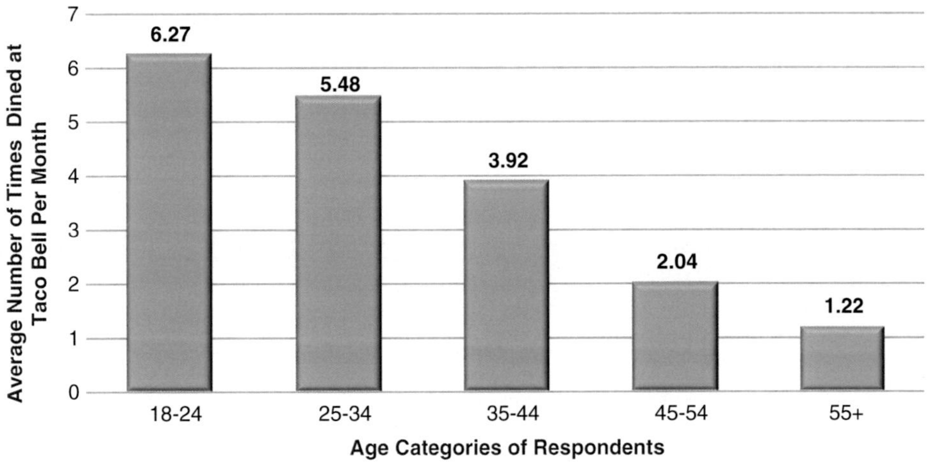

FIGURE 9.11 Differences in Dining Out at Taco Bell Based on Age

9.2e Deciding Which Scale to Use

In some situations, researchers do not have a choice on which scale to use. For instance, gender will always be a nominal scale. So will ethnicity and the college or university you are now attending. But, for other questions, researchers may have a choice. When they do, it is advisable to use higher order scales to increase the types of analyses that can be conducted.

Suppose a researcher wants to investigate consumer use of coupons. Figure 9.12 shows four ways researchers could ask a question about coupon usage, each using a different type of scale. With the nominal scale, all the researcher can determine is what percentage of the sample has used coupons within the last 30 days. No information about frequency or quantity is available. With the ordinal scale, the researcher can determine what percentage of the sample does not use coupons at all, what percent uses them occasionally, what percent uses them sometimes, and what percent uses them frequently. Thus, the ordinal scale provides more information than the nominal scale in terms of coupon usage.

With the interval scale, a mean can be calculated which provides researchers with an indication of how frequently consumers use coupons. Comparisons can also be made among different types of consumers by comparing the means of each group, which gives the researcher more analytical options. With the ratio question, researchers can determine how many coupons are redeemed without having to rely on the concept of frequency. The problem with using the scale indicator of "frequently" is that one respondent may have used five coupons and considered that "frequently," while another may have used the same quantity but marked it "sometimes." They may also have checked different boxes in the interval scale. Plus, someone who does not use coupons would be forced to answer "very infrequently" unless an option of "do not use coupons" was presented off to the side of the interval scale (but not as a part of it). Because "frequently" has different meanings to people, the results are not as accurate as having the actual number that is produced with the ratio scale. Also, the ratio scale allows for the highest order data analysis.

When developing questions for a survey, it is advisable to use the highest scale possible. This allows for higher order analyses. It also provides more in-depth information. Data can be reduced to lower levels, but cannot be increased to higher scale levels. For instance, the responses from the ratio scale data in Figure 9.13 can be grouped to provide additional information beyond the mean. The mean response was 4.6. The table shown in Figure 9.13 indicates that more than 28 percent of the respondents did not use coupons within the last 30 days and that 31 percent used only one to four coupons. Only about 10 percent of the sample appears to be heavy users of coupons, using 10 or more during the last 30 days. However, having the mean also allows for better comparisons among groups. For instance, the mean for males was 3.15 while the mean for females was 6.04.

9.3 Validity and Reliability

The purpose of marketing research is to provide decision makers with information. If that information is correct, timely, and accurate, then more intelligent decisions can be made. The challenge for researchers is to collect data that is both correct and accurate. The difficulty is that errors creep into the measurement process. Recall from Chapter 6 that two types of

Nominal ⟶ Have you used coupons within the last 30 days? Yes_____ No_____

Ordinal ⟶ In the last 30 days, how often have you used coupons?
Not at all______ occasionally_____ sometimes ______frequently____

Interval ⟶ In the last 30 days, how frequently did you use coupons?
Very infrequently _____|_____|_____|_____|_____ Very frequently

Ratio ⟶ In the last 30 days, approximately how many coupons have you used?
____

FIGURE 9.12 Coupon Usage and the Four Types of Scales

Coupons Used	Number of Respondents	Percent of Total
None	98	28.74%
1 to 4	106	31.09%
5 to 9	64	18.77%
10 to 19	33	9.68%
20 or more	11	3.23%
Total	312	

FIGURE 9.13 Coupon Usage

errors were identified: systematic error and random error. Both can affect the accuracy and correctness of the measurement process. Random error can be reduced by increasing the sample size and by paying careful attention to the research process. Systematic error, however, increases with sample size, so researchers need to carefully guard against any type of systematic error that will have a significant impact on the results. While systematic error cannot be completely eliminated, it can be reduced to a point where its impact is minimal.

Validity and reliability address the issues of measurement and error. Validity deals with systematic error while reliability deals with random error. Both approaches are important to ensure the lowest possible total error.

9.4 Reliability

LEARNING OBJECTIVE 9.6
Discuss methods for assessing reliability.

A measurement instrument that provides the same results time and time again is said to be reliable. Scales that show an object weighs 150 pounds is reliable if, every time the object is weighed on the scale, it indicates it is 150 pounds. One reason researchers like to use mechanical measuring instruments is that they tend to be more accurate, and also more reliable, than human measurements. However, with most marketing research, non-mechanical methods have to be used, such as questionnaires and observation. So from a marketing perspective, **reliability** is defined as the degree to which a measurement is free from error and provides consistent results over time. Reliability can be evaluated using three different approaches: test-retest, equivalent forms, and internal consistency (see Figure 9.14).

Reliability the degree to which a measurement is free from error and provides consistent results over time.

9.4a Test-Retest Reliability

One method to evaluate reliability is to repeat the measurement process with the same instrument and the same set of subjects, which is called **test–retest reliability**. For instance, suppose a survey was administered to a group of retail store managers. Then four weeks later the same survey is administered to the same set of store managers. Scores for the two surveys are then compared. If there is a high level of correlation (or similarity) between the two, then the survey is believed to have a high level of reliability. Since the same measurement instrument was used with the same subjects, the answers should be the same. Differences should be due to random error and not to deficiencies in the testing instrument.

Test-retest reliability method to evaluate reliability by repeating the measurement process with the same instrument with the same set of subjects.

Using the test-retest reliability method poses three potential problems, as indicated in Figure 9.15. As discussed in the chapter on experimentation, exposing individuals to the

- Test-retest
- Equivalent forms
- Internal consistency

FIGURE 9.14 Methods of Assessing Reliability

- Testing effects
- Environmental changes
- Locating same subjects

FIGURE 9.15 Potential Problems with Test-Retest Reliability

survey or measurement instrument during the first measurement may have an impact on their responses to the second survey. The longer the researcher waits between the first and second administrations, the less likely testing effect will occur. However, from a practical standpoint, researchers have a limited time and budget to prepare a measurement instrument and collect the data.

The second problem is changes in the environment that can alter the responses of the subjects. It can be personal factors, such as mood or health. It can be a wide range of external factors depending on the type of measurements. For retail stores, sales may be down, the weather could be poor, or the manager was extremely busy and rushed through the survey. Any number of environmental factors could affect the responses given.

The third potential problem may be in locating the same subjects. If it is retail store managers, this would not be a major concern. There may have been some attrition, but most will still be in their positions and available for the second survey. But if the subjects were consumers, then locating each one would be more difficult.

9.4b Equivalent Form Reliability

Equivalent form reliability method to evaluate reliability in which a second measurement instrument is developed that is equivalent to the first and then administered to the same subjects.

With **equivalent form reliability** a second measurement instrument is developed that is equivalent to the first and then administered to the same subjects. Suppose researchers wanted to measure brand attitude toward soft drinks. Two separate surveys would be developed with questions that are similar and believed to measure the same thing. The first survey would be given; then at a later time the second would be given, just as was done with the test-retest approach. Sometimes both are given at the same time because of the difficulty in locating the same set of subjects. However, researchers feel giving the two tests at the same time is not as reliable as using two different time periods.

Some of the same problems occur with the equivalent form reliability approach, such as environmental changes and locating the same subjects. However, testing effects are not present since the survey or measurement instruments are different. The challenge is in creating a second survey using different questions that will produce the same results. Some believe it is impossible to do. Others see it as extremely difficult and not worth the time and money required to do so.

9.4c Internal Consistency Reliability

Internal consistency reliability method to evaluate reliability that involves using one measuring instrument and assessing its reliability through using different samples or different items within each scale.

Split-half technique method to evaluate reliability through randomly splitting items designed to measure a construct into two groups and then measuring the correlation between the two groups.

Internal consistency reliability involves using one measuring instrument and assessing its reliability through using different samples or different items within each scale. This method eliminates the problems that can occur with a second administration of a survey instrument. The internal consistency reliability method is used more frequently than test-retest or equivalent forms techniques and can be assessed in three different ways.

The first is to administer the survey to a group of test subjects. The subjects are then randomly split into two groups. If the instrument is reliable, the scores between each group should be highly correlated. This approach is used in judging Olympic events and beauty pageants with multiple judges. The idea is that a more reliable score should be obtained when several judges evaluate the same performance since they are looking at the same set of criteria.

The second approach is called the **split-half technique** and is used with scales that have multiple measures. For example, to measure brand loyalty a researcher may have a set of eight questions, or to measure attitude toward a brand, a set of 10 questions might be used. The items are randomly split into two groups. If the items are measuring the same construct, then there should be a high correlation between the two groups or sets of questions. In practice, though, reliability may vary considerably depending upon which items are assigned to each group. This occurs because each item is supposed to measure a part of the overall construct that is uniquely different in some way from the other items.

The most popular internal consistency reliability method is a test called **Cronbach alpha**, which produces a reliability coefficient for all possible combinations of a set of items within a scale. The higher the Cronbach alpha score, the more reliable is the measure. A major advantage of the Cronbach alpha procedure is that if one of the items within the construct is not a good measure, it will have a low correlation with the other items. Researchers can then discard the item and retest the construct for reliability. This is particularly helpful when researchers are creating a new measurement scale, though Cronbach alpha is also frequently calculated with scales that exist and have been used in prior research.

Source: Sergey Nivens/Shutterstock.

Multiple judges are often used to assess an ice-skating performance, as multiple judgments based on the same criteria should be correlated, enhancing reliability. Similarly, in marketing research, internal consistency reliability may be assessed by randomly dividing subjects who have taken a survey into two groups. If the measurement instrument is reliable, scores between the two groups should correlate highly.

The internal consistency reliability method avoids the problems discussed with the other two approaches since it is not administered at two different times or with two different measuring instruments. But it does have a potentially serious problem—it measures reliability with just one exposure. There is no guarantee that, if a different set of subjects are used or if the instrument is used at a future point in time with the same subjects, the same results will occur. Thus, many researchers review the literature for the purpose of identifying prior studies where the measure may have been used. This allows the researcher to see whether the Cronbach alpha achieved in the current study is consistent with those reported in other research studies.

Cronbach alpha internal consistency reliability method that produces a reliability coefficient for all possible combinations of a set of items within a scale.

9.5 Validity

LEARNING OBJECTIVE 9.7
Elaborate on methods of evaluating validity.

Validity refers to the ability of a measurement scale to measure what it proposes to measure and the degree to which it is free of both systematic and random error. Thus, for a measurement to be valid, it must be reliable. However, the opposite is not true. A measurement instrument may be reliable yet still not be valid if it does not measure what it is supposed to measure. For example, it may be designed to measure customer satisfaction, but instead measures customer loyalty. In such cases the results are erroneous and, if used to make a decision, may result in a poor or even incorrect decision. Researchers have four ways to evaluate validity, identified in **Figure 9.16**.

Validity ability of a measurement instrument to measure what it proposes to measure and is free of both systematic and random error.

9.5a Face Validity

Face validity is present when it is the opinion of the researcher or experts that an instrument measures what it is intended to measure. It is the weakest form of validity since it

Face validity opinion of the researcher or experts that an instrument measures what it is intended to measure.

- Face validity
- Content validity
- Predictive validity
- Construct validity

FIGURE 9.16 Methods of Assessing Validity

is the subjective opinion of the individual designing the instrument or of other experts in marketing research. Some items on a survey are easy to evaluate as being valid, such as requesting demographic information like gender, age, income, and ethnicity. Even for the following questions, marketing researchers would agree they are valid questions and measure what is intended.

Have you purchased a new lawn mower within the last six months? How much did you spend on your last trip to purchase groceries?

Which brand of computer do you currently own?

Many concepts marketers want to measure are more complicated and cannot be easily measured, such as brand attitude, brand loyalty, brand image, service quality, and purchase intentions. Since these concepts are more abstract, researchers often develop a series of questions to measure the construct, or idea. On the surface, that is, in terms of face validity, the questions may appear to be measuring the construct that is intended. But they also may be measuring something else. That is why researchers look to one of the other forms of validity to assess a survey instrument and its measurement scales.

9.5b Content Validity

Content validity systematic process to evaluate validity by assessing the adequacy of the items used to measure a concept or construct.

Scale item (or item) a question or statement that needs to be evaluated.

With **content validity** researchers use a systematic process to assess the adequacy of the items used to measure a concept or construct. A **scale item (or item)** is simply a question or statement that needs to be evaluated. The steps involved in the process are identified in Figure 9.17. The process begins with a literature review to identify how other marketing researchers measured the concept. If brand image is being measured, then researching how other people measured brand image will identify questions, phrases, or words that have been used. A list is compiled that includes all items that have been used, with notation of those that have been used the most frequently. The second step then involves using a panel of marketing research experts to assess the list of items, eliminating items that may not fit with what is being measured and adding new items that may not have been identified with the literature review.

The third step is to pretest the instrument using all of the items that have been identified in the first two steps by administering the instrument to a sample similar to the intended target audience. In addition, an open-ended question is added allowing the respondent to identify any idea or concept that should be included that was not. Sometimes study participants are also asked questions related to item phrasing and their comprehension of various items. The last step is to reduce the number of items through data analysis to determine which items have a high correlation with each other. This can be done through a process called factor analysis and through the reliability measure of Cronbach alpha discussed earlier. When the process is finished, the researcher should have a smaller number of highly correlated questions, phrases, or words that can be used to measure the construct. The resulting high correlation of the construct items yields content validity.

With this process a researcher might start with a list of 15 items to measure brand image of a company such as Shell Oil or Delta Airlines. After the literature review another 10 to 15 items might be added. Then in the second step the panel of experts might either add more items or delete some from the list that do not appear to be relevant for the current study. The list of items is then pretested with a sample similar to the target audience with an open-ended question at the end in case the respondent thought of an item that

1. Literature review
2. Panel of experts
3. Pre-test with open-ended question
4. Scale reduction through data analysis

FIGURE 9.17 Steps in Developing Content Validity

was not included. If a number of new items are identified with the open-ended question, they would be added to the list and another pretest would be conducted. Changes in phrasing would also be considered based on participant feedback. The next step would be to do a factor analysis to reduce the items to a smaller subset of highly correlated items. These items would then be tested using Cronbach alpha to determine their level of inter-correlations. Those achieving inter-correlations of 0.7 or higher are generally retained within the scale. The end result will be a smaller list of items that can be used to measure the company image of Shell Oil or Delta Airlines.

9.5c Predictive Validity

Predictive validity assesses how well a measurement can predict future actions or behavior. For instance, attitude toward an advertisement should influence attitude toward the brand being advertised, and the attitude toward the brand should influence purchase intentions and purchase behavior. If this occurs, then each of the scales is said to have predictive validity. Another example would be the SAT that everyone takes to enter college. It is believed to be a predictor of how well an individual will do in college and the person's potential to learn.

Predictive validity measure of validity that assesses how well a measurement can predict future actions or behavior.

9.5d Construct Validity

Construct validity is the most difficult to achieve and exists more in theory than it does in actual practice with marketing research companies. **Construct validity** assesses how well the measurement captures the construct or concept under consideration and how well it logically connects to underlying theories. In addition to the measuring instrument capturing the construct it is supposed to measure, it also must be based on theories that are accepted by research experts. While such discussions are part of the academic world, they are seldom addressed in the practical business world of marketing research.

Construct validity method of evaluating validity by assessing how well the measurement captures the construct or concept under consideration and how well it logically connects to underlying theories.

Construct validity can be demonstrated by finding that a measure has both convergent validity and discriminant validity. Both apply to constructs that have multiple dimensions, such as the SERVQUAL measure developed by Parasuraman, Berry, and Ziethmal[1] to measure service quality. **Convergent validity** refers to the degree of correlation among constructs and tests whether constructs that should be related actually are. For example, a great deal of academic research has demonstrated that attitude toward the ad should influence brand attitudes, which in turn should influence purchase intentions. There should be a high level of correlation among these constructs as determined by theory and prior research.

Convergent validity refers to the degree of correlation among constructs, and tests whether constructs which should be related actually are related.

Discriminant validity means the items designed to measure one construct, such as attitude toward the ad, have a low correlation with items that measure a different construct that should be unrelated to the first, such as social desirability bias. While the statistical techniques used to assess convergent and discriminant validity are beyond the scope of an introductory marketing research textbook, using valid measures is a key consideration in research. For this reason, many researchers choose to use existing measures that have been validated by previous researchers. Many classic measures still useful for consumer behavior and advertising research can be found in the various editions of the *Marketing Scales Handbook*, along with a history of the scale usage, reliabilities reported in previous studies, and the manner in which scale validity was assessed.[2]

Discriminant validity items designed to measure one construct have a low correlation with items that measure a different construct.

9.6 Relationship of Validity and Reliability

Figure 9.18 highlights the relationship between validity and reliability. An analogy that has often been used is target practice with a bow and arrow or a gun. The figure on the left illustrates an instrument that has neither validity nor reliability. The shots (or data points in this case) are all over the target. A loose site on a gun that moves every time the gun is fired would produce these types of results even though the person firing the gun always aimed at the center of the target.

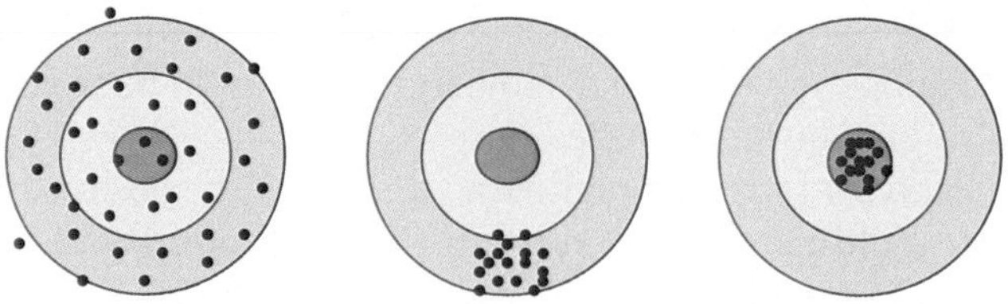

FIGURE 9.18 Relationship between Validity and Reliability

The middle picture shows what happens when the site on the gun is adjusted improperly. The person firing the gun is aiming at the center of the target, but the bullet always lands below the center. It is very reliable because it always hits in the same area, but is not valid since it does not hit in the center. This would be a good representation of survey results achieved when a great deal of systematic error is present. The only way a measurement can be valid is for the instrument to measure what it is supposed to measure. For a gun or bow, that means when you aim at the center of the target, the bullet or arrow hits the center of the target, not above, below, or to one of the sides. Similarly, a research instrument can be reliable, in that it consistently measures something, but not valid if the construct being measured is not what the researcher is trying to measure. However, a research instrument can never be valid if it isn't also reliable.

The last picture shows the gunshots or arrows hitting the center of the target. The site is properly adjusted and hitting where it is supposed to hit. In terms of marketing research, it is measuring what the instrument proposes to measure and is doing so in a reliable manner. It is both valid and reliable.

9.7 Global Concerns

While the four types of scales are universal, how they are used will vary depending on the culture of a particular region. People in Pacific Rim countries such as Japan tend to be more modest, which may reflect the way scales are developed. Instead of using a ratio scale to reveal their absolute level of income, Japanese respondents may be more comfortable responding to an ordinal scale that lists income in ascending categories.

Scale responses are often influenced by cultural norms. In the Philippines, respondents tend to give positive answers rather than negative answers. One research study found that using more scale points helped to mitigate this skewing effect. Instead of using the more traditional five-point scale, this cross-cultural segmentation study adopted a 10-point scale, which ultimately yielded nine segments after the data were analyzed.

Asian consumers are also more likely to give positive responses compared to U.S. consumers. To combat this positivity bias, response options are typically reversed, meaning that the answer choices begin with "Strongly Disagree", followed by "Disagree", "Neutral", "Agree" and "Strongly Agree."[3]

9.8 Marketing Research Statistics

Nominal, ordinal, interval, and ratio scales are used extensively in marketing research. Therefore, the Statistics Review, Statistical Reporting, and Dealing with Data sections examine some of the issues involved with these measurement scales. Understanding these scales is critical to advanced statistical procedures discussed in future chapters.

9.8a Statistics Review

The type of data that survey questions yield determines both the type of descriptive measures that are needed as well as the type of analyses that can be performed. Figure 9.19 summarizes the type of descriptive measures that can be used with each type of scale and

Type of Scale	Descriptive Measure	Difference Test
Nominal	Frequency	Chi-square
Ordinal	Frequency	Chi-square
Interval	Mean standard deviation	T-test, Z-test or ANOVA
Ratio	Mean standard deviation	T-test, Z-test or ANOVA

FIGURE 9.19 Descriptive and Difference Tests and Type of Scale

the type of analyses that would be used to test for differences in means or in frequency counts.

With both nominal and ordinal scales, the appropriate descriptive measure is a frequency count. The appropriate test for differences would be a chi-square test. For interval and ratio scales, the appropriate descriptive measure is the mean and standard deviation. The standard deviation is a *measure of dispersion* indicating how variable, or spread out, the data points are around the mean. Suppose the following statements were evaluated using a five-point scale where 1 = strongly disagree and 5 = strongly agree.

Mean		Standard Deviation
Fast food is convenient	3.82	.55
Fast food tastes great	3.75	1.63

While the means are quite similar, the standard deviations vary widely. In the case of the first statement, the majority of respondents rated the convenience aspect of fast food similarly, as evidenced by the small standard deviation, or spread, in the data. In fact, a frequency analysis would reveal that most respondents answered "3" or "4" to this question. However, opinions related to the taste of fast food were much more diverse, as evidenced by the large standard deviation. Frequency counts in this instance would show more people answering toward the extreme ends of the scales (e.g., "1" or "5") than in the case of the first statement. In fact, the mean alone may be misleading as the large standard deviation suggests that the taste of fast food may be a subject on which people's opinions are polarized.

The tests that can be used for differences in means would be a T-Test, Z-Test, or ANOVA, depending on the number of categories in the grouping variable and the sample size in each cell. If the analysis involves only two categories, such as gender, then the T-Test would be used if the sample contained fewer than 30 subjects of each gender, while the Z-Test would be appropriate if 30 or more subjects represented each gender. Programs such as SPSS automatically adjust the testing procedure to reflect the proper technique, even though users choose the "t-test" option. If a test for difference in means involved three or more categories, then the One-Way ANOVA can be used so long as each cell, or category, contains at least 30 subjects. All tests assume that the data was drawn from a normal population.[4]

9.8b Statistics Reporting

The two most common methods of graphing nominal data are pie charts and bar charts. However, there are occasions when there are too many categories to show on one chart, or some of the categories are too small to be easily visible. In these situations a useful method is the pie of pie chart or the bar of pie chart. This type of chart is also useful for emphasizing one particular section of the pie that has multiple components. A bar of pie chart of nominal data is shown in Figure 9.20.

Statistical Reporting Exercise: A business located in Shreveport, Louisiana draws from a four-state area. The percentages for each state are shown in Figure 9.21.

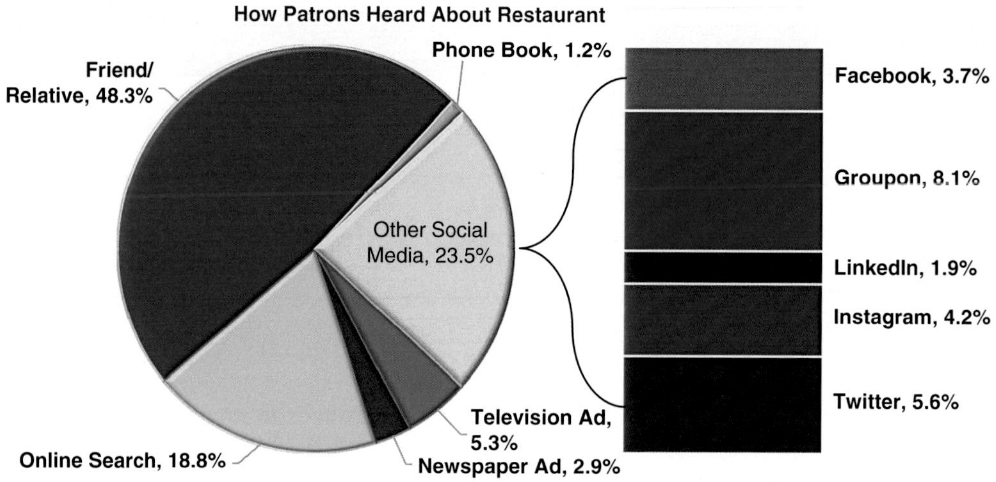

FIGURE 9.20 A Bar of Pie Chart Showing How Patrons Heard About a Restaurant

State Locations	Percent	Louisiana Locations	Percent
Arkansas	6.2%	Alexandria	12.2%
Oklahoma	2.4%	Baton Rouge	7.1%
Texas	24.3%	Lafayette	8.8%
Louisiana	67.1%	Monroe	16.1%
		Shreveport	22.9%

FIGURE 9.21 Location of Customers for a Business in Shreveport, Louisiana

Within Louisiana the percentages of customers from five metropolitan areas are also shown. Use the data provided in Figure 9.21 to create either a pie of a pie chart or a bar of a pie chart. If you do not know how to create the chart in Excel, see the website (www.clowjames.net/students.html) for instructions. The pie or bar that is shown extracted from the state percentages will be for Louisiana.

9.8c Dealing with Data

Data were collected from 184 individuals concerning their patronage and attitudes toward fast food restaurants, and five fast food restaurants in particular. The data are in the SPSS file Chapter 09 Dealing with Data. The corresponding questionnaire that was used is entitled Chapter 09 Dealing with Data Survey. Both files can be downloaded from the text website (www.clowjames.net/students.html).

Create a table similar to the one in Figure 9.22. Identify the type of scale for each question, then determine the appropriate descriptive measure and difference tests. Once your table has been completed, use SPSS to run the appropriate frequency count or mean. Answer the following questions or create the appropriate graph.

1. What percent of the respondents ranked Arby's (Q4) as the most desirable?
2. What percent of the sample ranked Burger King (Q4) as the most desirable?
3. Create a column graph showing the ranking of McDonald's (Q4).
4. Based on the frequency counts of Question 4, which fast food was ranked the most desirable by the most people? Which fast food was ranked the least desirable by the most people?

Question	Type of Scale	Descriptive Measure	Difference Test
Q1	Ratio	Mean, standard deviation	T-test, Z-test or ANOVA
Q2			
Q3			
Q4			
Q5			
Q6			
Q7			
Q8			
Q9			
Q10			

FIGURE 9.22 Sample Table for Dealing with Data Exercise

5. What was the average number of times respondents ate at fast food restaurants in a typical week (Q1)?
6. Examine the means for the statements in Question 3. Which one had the highest level of agreement? What was the mean? Which one had the lowest level of agreement? What was the mean?
7. Examine the standard deviations for the statements in Question 3. Which one had the highest variability of responses? What was the standard deviation? Which one had the least variability in responses? What was the standard deviation?
8. For Question 5, which fast food restaurant had the highest mean? What was the mean?
9. For Question 6, which fast food restaurant had the highest level of customer service? What was the mean response? Which restaurant had the lowest level of customer service? What was the mean? Which fast food restaurant had the greatest variability in responses? What was the standard deviation?

Using the table you created for this exercise and SPSS, run either a T-test or ANOVA test for Questions 1 and 2 based on the respondent's gender, age, income, and race. Answer the following questions or create the appropriate graph.

1. At the 95 percent confidence level, did gender have an impact on either Question 1 or 2? If so, what was the mean and standard deviation for each gender?
2. At the 95 percent confidence level, did age have an impact on either Question 1 or 2? If so, what was the mean and standard deviation for each age group?
3. Create a column graph showing the results from SPSS for Question 2 by the respondent's age. Which age group had the highest percentage of dollars spent at fast food restaurants? Which age group had the lowest percentage?
4. At the 95 percent confidence level, did income have an impact on either how many times a fast food restaurant was patronized (Question1) or the percentage of money spent dining out that is allocated to fast food restaurants (Question 2)? If so, what was the mean and standard deviation for Question 1 or 2 for each income bracket?
5. At the 95 percent confidence level, did race have an impact on either Question 1 or 2? If so, what was the mean and standard deviation for each question by racial category?

Summary

Objective 1: Explain the concept of measurement.
Measurement is the process by which rules and guidelines are used to assign numbers to represent characteristics of respondents, brands, or other objects.

Objective 2: Describe the characteristics and give examples of nominal scales.
Nominal scales provide only limited information and are useful when the purpose of a question is to classify objects or respondents as having a certain characteristic (or not) or belonging to a particular group (or not). The numbers used to represent each category have no inherent meaning other than to separate those who share a characteristic from those who do not. For this reason, it is critical that the response options in nominal scales be mutually exclusive and categorically exhaustive. Data analysis options for nominal data are limited to frequency counts and percentages. Many demographic questions, such as gender, education, and ethnicity, are examples of nominal scales.

Objective 3: Describe the characteristics and give examples of ordinal scales.
Ordinal scales are those in which the response categories are ordered, or which allow the respondent to rank items on the basis of some factor, such as preference. Ordinal scales maintain the classification properties of nominal scales, but also allow subjects to show that a certain category of response is greater than or less than another. Frequency counts, percentages, and modes can be computed using ordinal data. However, because there is no guarantee that the interval between ordered item choices is the same, means and standard deviations cannot be computed for this type of data. Questions that provide categories for income or age in ascending order are examples of ordinal questions, as are those that provide categories related to frequency of use, frequency of purchase, or amount spent.

Objective 4: Describe the characteristics and give examples of interval scales.
Although interval scales contain the classification and order characteristics of lower level scales, the data provided is more valuable because the interval between choices is equal. This allows the researcher to compute means and standard deviations and to run more advanced statistical analyses to compare the differences in means between groups using t-tests, z-tests, and ANOVA. The majority of questions devised to measure attitudes use interval scales.

Objective 5: Describe the characteristics and give examples of ratio scales.
Ratio scales are the most powerful since they contain an absolute zero point in addition to all the scale properties discussed for lower-level scales. The numbers recorded represent actual quantities of the variable in question. While means and standard deviations can be computed, ratio level data can also be subjected to basic empirical operations such as division, multiplication, subtraction, and addition. Ratio scale questions are typically asked in an open-ended format so that respondents can enter the exact number that best describes their answer. The year an individual was born, the number of children living at home, frequency of patronage, weight, and a variety of other questions can be formulated as ratio scales. Generally speaking, higher level scales should be used, when possible, due to the richness of the data provided.

Objective 6: Discuss methods for assessing reliability.
It is important that measurement instruments be reliable, and thus free from error, so that consistent results can be achieved over time. The degree to which a measure is reliable can be assessed using the test-retest method, the equivalent forms technique, and the internal consistency method. Problems inherent in the test-retest and equivalent forms techniques have influenced the popularity of the internal consistency method. While three methods of measuring internal consistency exist, the Cronbach alpha method is used most frequently.

Objective 7: Elaborate on methods of evaluating validity.
Valid measurement instruments measure what they are designed to measure and are relatively free of systematic and random error. Four methods of validity assessment exist. The weakest form of validity, and the form that is simplest to assess, is known as face validity. Measures with face validity appear to measure what they are supposed to in the opinion of the researcher or experts. Content validity ensures that a concept or construct is accurately measured via a four-step process that ultimately evaluates the quality and completeness of the items used to measure the construct. Predictive validity is demonstrated by showing how well the measure predicts future actions or behavior. Construct validity assesses how well the measure captures the construct and its relationship to theory. This is the most difficult form to achieve because it requires that the researcher demonstrate two validity subtypes: convergent validity and discriminant validity. Convergent validity is exemplified when a measure correlates with another construct to which it is theoretically related. Conversely, discriminant validity assures that a measure does not vary, or correlate, with constructs to which it has no theoretical relationship.

Key Terms

absolute zero point, p. 305
categorically exhaustive, p. 300
construct validity, p. 313
content validity, p. 312
convergent validity, p. 313
Cronbach alpha, p. 311
discriminant validity, p. 313
equivalent form reliability, p. 310
face validity, p. 311
internal consistency reliability, p. 310
interval scales, p. 304
measurement, p. 299
mutually exclusive, p. 300
nominal scales, p. 300
ordinal scales, p. 301
points, p. 305
predictive validity, p. 313
ratio scale, p. 306
reliability, p. 309
scale item (or item), p. 312
split-half technique, p. 310
test-retest reliability, p. 309
validity, p. 311

Critical Thinking Exercises

1. Your firm is conducting a study in which the key dependent variable is annual sales. The firm plans to compare sales among different types of customers with whom the firm does business. What type of scale should be used to measure annual sales? Why?
2. Identify the type of scale shown below. Then critique the scale in terms of whether or not the response options are mutually exclusive and categorically exhaustive. Be specific in pointing out any flaws that exist.

> What is your household annual income from all sources?
> (1) Less than $ 25,000 (2) $ 25,000 $ 50,000
> (3) $ 50,000 – $ 75,000 (4) $ 75,000 – $ 100,000
> (5) $ 100,000 and above

3. Identify the type of scale shown below. Then critique the scale in terms of whether or not the response options are mutually exclusive and categorically exhaustive. Be specific in pointing out any flaws that exist.

> Which of the following mass merchandise stores have you shopped at in the past week (check all that apply)?
> ______Wal-Mart______Kmart______Target______
> Sam's Club______Costco

4. Identify the type of scale shown below. Justify your answer. What types of analyses could be performed with these data?

> Please rate your university's financial aid office on the following items using a scale ranging from poor to outstanding.

	Poor	Fair	Good	Excellent	Outstanding
Friendliness of staff	1	2	3	4	5
Helpfulness of staff	1	2	3	4	5
Speed of service	1	2	3	4	5

5. Suppose a pet store is interested in surveying its customers and learning more about customers' pet ownership, their attitudes toward various types of pet products, basic demographic information, and spending habits. Develop a measurement instrument in which at least one example of the different types of measurement instruments (nominal, ordinal, interval, and ratio) can be found. At a minimum, your survey will contain four questions. Restrict your survey to no more than 10 questions. Make certain that the questions you create are your own work and do not duplicate questions found in this chapter. Where appropriate, check to be certain that response choices are mutually exclusive and categorically exhaustive.
6. Refer back to the measurement instrument you developed in question 5.
   a. Critique each question. Was the type of data collected optimal, or would it have been better to collect information using a higher level of measure instrument? Why or why not?
   b. What type of descriptive statistics would be obtained for each question?
   c. What types of analyses would you recommend for each question?
   d. How should the data be presented to the client?
7. In reading the executive summary of a research report, you note that the researcher concluded that men are twice as likely to watch sports on television as are women. With respect to sports viewership on TV, was the data collected nominal, ratio, interval, or ordinal? Justify your answer.
8. You have been asked to develop a measurement instrument capable of assessing people's attitudes toward Betty Crocker cakes mixes. Construct a multi-item measure that has face validity. Justify why you feel the items you selected capture people's attitudes toward Betty Crocker cake mixes.

9. A researcher has attempted to create a measurement instrument capable of assessing college students' attitudes toward online classes. Review the following items and determine if they have face validity. Are any items missing that you recommend be added? Justify your decision.

Indicate your level of agreement or disagreement with each of the statements shown below using the following scale 1 = Strongly Disagree (SD); 2 = Disagree (D); 3 = Neither Agree nor Disagree (N); 4 = Agree (A); 5 = Strongly Agree (SA):

	SD	D	N	A	SA
Online classes are easy.	1	2	3	4	5
It takes less time to complete a face-to-face class than it does one that is offered in a	1	2	3	4	5
100 percent online format.					
I like online classes because they free up my time so that I can work more hours.	1	2	3	4	5
Online classes let me do school work when it is convenient for me to do so.	1	2	3	4	5

10. A friend of yours has just completed a one-group pretest, posttest experiment. (Refer back to Chapter 7 if you need to refresh your memory on the types of experimental designs.) He told you that he plans to assess the reliability of the key dependent measure using the test-retest method, since he was able to collect interval level data for the measure using the same sample at two different points in time. Would you recommend that he follow through this plan? Why or why not? If not, how would you suggest he evaluate the reliability of his key dependent variable? Justify your decision.

Lakeside Grill

(Comprehensive Student Case)

Figure 9.23 shows the demographic measures the team developed. Brooke had unsuccessfully argued that two additional demographic questions should be added that would ask how far the person lived and worked from Lakeside Grill. While the other students understood why such a question would be beneficial, they didn't believe it would yield any additional information that could be used in developing recommendations and action plans for the restaurant since any marketing tactic developed could not be restricted to a specific distance from the restaurant.

Figure 9.24 shows the patronage measures developed by the student team. The item that generated considerable discussion and disagreement was Question 4. Some students argued the information was not necessary since it asked for percentages for overall dining out and wasn't specific to Lakeside Grill. Others argued since Lakeside Grill didn't serve breakfast, including it in the question was not a good idea.

The scale used to evaluate the Lakeside Grill is shown in Figure 9.25. Discussion generated by this scale centered on two concerns: the four-point scale, and if it was

Scale	Question Item
Nominal	Gender: Female____ Male____
Ordinal	Age: 18–22____ 23–29____ 30–39____ 40–49____ 50+____
Ordinal	Income: $0–$19,999____ $20,000–$39,999____ $40,000–$59,999____ $60,000–79,999____ $80,000+____
Nominal	Ethnicity: African-American____ Caucasian____ Asian-American____ Hispanic____ Other____
Ordinal	Education: High School____, Some college____, 2-year college degree____ 4-year college degree____, Post-graduate____

FIGURE 9.23 Demographic Measures

Scale	Question Item
Ratio	1. How many times have you eaten at the Lakeside Grill during the last month? ______
Ordinal	2. On the average, how much do you spend per month dining out? $0–$49____ $50–$99____ $100–$149_____ $150–$199_____ $200+_____
Interval	3. In terms of your total eating out, how frequently do you eat at each of the following? Fast food restaurant.......... Never____|____|____|____|____|____ Always Delivery or pickup.............. Never____|____|____|____|____|____ Always Casual dine-in restaurant.... Never____|____|____|____|____|____ Always
Ratio	4. In terms of eating out, what percentage of your expenditures fall into each of the following categories? (the percentages should add to 100) Breakfast ____Lunch____ Dinner____ Other_____

FIGURE 9.24 Patronage Measures

Scale	Question Item				
	Please rate Lakeside Grill on each of the following items using a scale from poor to excellent.				
		Poor	Fair	Good	Excellent
	Food quality	1	2	3	4
	Food quantity	1	2	3	4
	Food taste	1	2	3	4
	Value for the money	1	2	3	4
Interval	Food presentation	1	2	3	4
	Speed of service	1	2	3	4
	Customer satisfaction	1	2	3	4
	Restaurant appearance	1	2	3	4
	Restaurant atmosphere	1	2	3	4
	Location	1	2	3	4
	Parking	1	2	3	4
	Overall rating	**1**	**2**	**3**	**4**

FIGURE 9.25 Restaurant Evaluation Measures

interval or ordinal data. Some of the students thought it should be a seven-point scale. In terms of type of data, the group was split between the question yielding interval or ordinal data.

To measure reliability, Zach suggested they use Cronbach alpha. While this could be used for items that had scales, it would not work for the non-scaled items. So the team decided a test-retest with a sample of students could measure the entire questionnaire's reliability. For validity, the team discussed using either face validity or content validity. Zach argued for content validity, saying, "We don't have the experience and knowledge to do construct validity and we are not trying to predict anything so that method is out. Besides, I think content validity is the best anyway."

Critique Questions:

1. Evaluate the demographic, patronage, and restaurant evaluation measures in terms of types of scales. Has the group used the best scales? Why or why not? What changes would you suggest? Why?
2. Zach had argued instead of using a scale for age they should just ask respondents their age. By so doing, they could obtain ratio data instead of ordinal data. Is this a good idea? Why or why not?
3. Should a question about distance from the Lakeside Grill be added to the demographics? Why or why not?
4. Discuss Question 4 of the patronage measures (Figure 9.22). Should it be included? Why or why not? Should it be modified or a different question asked? Why?

5. As it is written now, are the restaurant evaluation measures (Figure 9.23) truly an interval scale? Why or why not?
6. Is the four-point scale optimal for this research project or should it be a seven-point scale? Why or why not? What other options does the team have in terms of number of points in the scale?
7. Discuss each of the methods of assessing reliability as it relates to the Lakeside Grill project.
8. Which method do you think is the best for assessing reliability for the Lakeside Grill project: test-retest or internal consistency using Cronbach alpha? Why?
9. Discuss each of the methods of assessing validity as it relates to the Lakeside Grill project.
10. Do you agree with Zach's statement about validity: "We don't have the experience and knowledge to do construct validity and we are not trying to predict anything so that method is out. Besides, I think content validity is the best anyway." Why or why not?

Notes

1. A. Parasuraman, Valerie A. Zeithaml, and Leonard L. Berry, "SERVQUAL: A Multiple-Item Scale for Measuring Customer Perceptions of Service Quality," *Journal of Retailing* 67 (Winter 1988): 420–450.
2. Gordon C. Bruner, II, Karen E. James, and Paul J. Hensel, *Marketing Scales Handbook: A Compilation of Multi-Item Measures,* Vol. III (Chicago, IL: American Marketing Association, 2001); and Gordon C. Bruner, II, Paul J. Hensel, and Karen E. James, *Marketing Scales Handbook: A Compilation of Multi-Item Measures for Consumer Behavior & Advertising, 1998–2001,* Vol. IV, Mason, OH: Texere, an imprint of Thomson/South-Western, 2005).
3. Sarah Faulkner, "Tips on Conducting International Research," *Quirk's Marketing Research Review* (November 2016): Article ID 20161107.
4. Julia Lin, "Does the Rating Scale Make a Difference in Factor Analysis?" *Quirk's Marketing Research Review* (April 2008): 22, http://www.quirks.com/articles/2008/20080409.aspx?searchID=186762791&sort=4&pg=2.

Marketing Scales

CHAPTER 10

Source: antoniodiaz/Shutterstock.

Chapter Outline

Learning Objectives

After studying this chapter, you should be able to:

- Discuss the concept of attitude measurement.
- Explain the concept of using scales for attitude measurement.
- Identify and describe the various comparative scales.
- Identify and describe the various non-comparative scales.
- Identify and describe scales that can be either comparative or non-comparative.
- Discuss the considerations involved in selecting marketing scales.
- Explain ways researchers can ensure the reliability and validity of scales.

10.1 Chapter Overview

Marketing scales are used extensively by marketing researchers to measure a wide array of beliefs, attitudes, and behaviors. They can be used to measure beliefs individuals have about brands, people, or objects. They can be used to measure people's feelings. They can also be used to measure past or current behavior as well as future intentions. **Figure 10.1** shows the result of a single item marketing scale that was used to measure how much time members of Generation Z spend on their phone daily. In April of 2018, out of the sample of 1,000 respondents aged 13–22, 95 percent owned a smartphone. As Figure 10.1 shows, over half of Gen Z smartphone owners use their phone five or more hours a day while over 26 percent use it 10 hours a day or more! Even more surprising—less than 3 percent used their phone less than an hour.

While scales can be used to measure behavior, they are especially important in the measurement of consumer attitudes since attitudes cannot be observed. Various types of scales are presented in this chapter. Some scales ask individuals to make comparisons, while other scales do not. The chapter concludes with a discussion of how to ensure reliability and validity of marketing scales.

10.2 Measuring Attitudes

LEARNING OBJECTIVE 10.1
Discuss the concept of attitude measurement.

Attitudes relatively enduring predispositions to respond to an object in a consistent fashion.

Attitudes are relatively enduring predispositions to respond to an object—such as a brand, spokesperson, advertisement, event or store—in a consistent fashion. You may recall from a study of consumer behavior that an attitude consists of three components: cognitive, affective, and behavioral. The cognitive component represents the belief and knowledge part of attitude. Examples of items designed to measure beliefs or knowledge may be "The Ford Fusion was rated Motor Trends mid-size car of the year" or "Pepsi has a sweeter taste than Coke." The affective component of attitude is the feelings and emotions. Statements such as "I love my new Dell computer" or "I hate the taste of grapefruit" reflect the affective or feeling component of attitude. The behavioral component is the action or intentions aspect of attitude. It may involve measuring the intent to purchase a pair of Guess jeans at a retail store or the actual purchase of a Mounds candy bar.

Counting the number of shirts sold from a point-of-purchase (POP) display is easy to do. So is comparing sales from different types of displays, different POP locations, and among stores using different types and locations of POP displays. Measuring consumer attitudes that influence those purchase decisions is more problematic. Since attitudes cannot be seen and exist only in the minds of consumers, researchers have to look

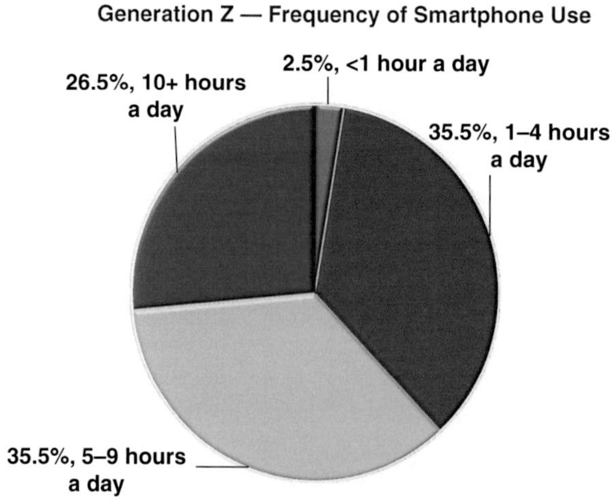

FIGURE 10.1 Graph of a Behavioral Marketing Scale
Source: "Gen Z and Their Smart Phones," *The State of Gen Z 2018*, The Center for Generational Kinetics (GenHq.com), Fall, 2018.

at alternative methods of measurement. A common method is to use some type of scale. Some scales contain a single item, such as the one in Figure 10.1, while others contain multiple items. While ordinal scales are often used, researchers would prefer using interval scales since they produce higher-order data that can be subjected to more robust statistical tests. However, attitude scales that produce interval data are more difficult to construct.

Because an attitude consists of multiple dimensions, is abstract, is nonobservable, and rests in the minds of consumers, measuring an attitude is challenging. To do so, researchers develop attitude constructs and measurement scales. How individuals respond to the items or questions constituting the scale provides an understanding of a person's attitude.

10.3 Scale Development

LEARNING OBJECTIVE 10.2
Explain the concept of using scales for attitude measurement.

Since consumer attitudes cannot be observed, researchers develop scales to measure it. **Scaling** is the process of assigning numerical values or properties to subjective or abstract concepts. Attitude might be measured along a continuum using a seven-point scale with 7 indicating a very positive attitude and 1 indicating a very negative attitude. Thus, a value of 5 would indicate a more positive attitude than a value of 4, 3, 2, or 1. Alternatively, customer satisfaction attitudes might be assessed by selecting from among "Very Dissatisfied," "Dissatisfied," "Neutral," "Satisfied," and "Very Satisfied" scaled response categories.

Scaling the process of assigning numerical values or properties to subjective or abstract concepts.

Scales can be unidimensional or multidimensional. **Unidimensional scales** measure only one attribute or concept, such as a general attitude toward an advertisement. A researcher may use several items to measure the construct, but all of the items in a unidimensional scale measure a single concept. **Multidimensional scales** are designed to measure multiple dimensions or facets of a concept, idea, or attitude. Measuring store image involves multiple dimensions, such as atmospherics, aesthetics, product selection, and price.

Unidimensional scale measures only one attribute or concept.

Multidimensional scale measures multiple dimensions or facets of a concept, idea, or attitude.

Developing or using good existing scales is important if a concept, such as attitude or customer satisfaction, is going to be measured with any degree of precision. Figure 10.2 identifies some of the characteristics of a good scale.

Scales should be relatively easy for respondents to understand. Wording is important. It is advisable to use language that is used by respondents, but also important to ensure the scale items are clear and concise. Clarity and language familiarity are important because these factors help to ensure that respondents understand the question and interpret it correctly, thus minimizing measurement error. The scale needs to provide useful data, so in addition to being clear and concise, the items need to discriminate well among different attitudes held by respondents. If a five-point scale is used to measure attitude toward a brand and if 95 percent of the respondents check the same response category, then the

- Relatively easy for respondents to understand
- Clear and concise
- Provides useful data
- Discriminates well
- Limited response bias
- Valid and reliable

FIGURE 10.2 Characteristics of a Good Scale

Source: Vinko93/Shutterstock.

Avid Apple users are very likely to rate the Apple brand as a 5 on a five-point rating scale. In the United States, higher numbers are associated with "better" characteristics, such as excellence.

question does not discriminate adequately because it doesn't identify differences in attitudes. Scale items can be developed or borrowed from existing scales that produce a wide range of responses. In rare cases when a given scale does not discriminate well among respondents, the problem may not be with the scale but with the sample selected. For instance, if avid Apple users are surveyed, they are very likely to rate the Apple brand as a 5 on a five-point rating scale.

Good scales limit response bias. Asking individuals to evaluate fast-food restaurants in terms of food quality may produce response bias because respondents know the food is not the healthiest, even though they really like eating at fast-food restaurants. Thus, they may provide answers that are not completely honest. The reverse can also occur. If the survey is being taken in Japan and the respondents think the interviewer or survey sponsor wants to show the positive side of American food served in Japan, they may respond with a more positive attitude than they really have.

Last, scales need to be valid and reliable. The validity and reliability tests discussed in Chapter 9 can be used to ensure a scale is valid and reliable. Alternatively, researchers can use scales that have already been established by prior researchers and that have been validated through proper research methods. It must be kept in mind, however, that if well-established scales are modified, used with a unique sample that is different than the general population, or used in a context that is significantly different, they may not produce valid and reliable results.

LEARNING OBJECTIVE 10.3
Identify and describe the various comparative scales.

10.4 Marketing Scales

Scales can be divided into two primary categories: comparative scales and non-comparative scales. With **comparative scales** respondents are asked to evaluate or rate a brand, product, object, concept, or person relative to other brands, products, objects, concepts, or individuals or to an ideal item. **Non-comparative scales** involve respondents making judgments about a brand, product, object, concept, or person without reference to another or ideal item. Figure 10.3 identifies the most common scales used by marketing researchers. Typical comparative scales include rank-order, Q-sort, paired comparison, and constant sum. Common non-comparative scales are graphical rating and itemized rating. The semantic differential and Likert scales can be either comparative or non-comparative depending on how the question is worded.

Comparative scale respondents are asked to evaluate or rate a brand, product, object, concept, or person relative to other brands, products, objects, concepts, or individuals or to an ideal item.

Non-comparative scale respondents make judgments about a brand, product, object, concept, or person without reference to another or ideal item.

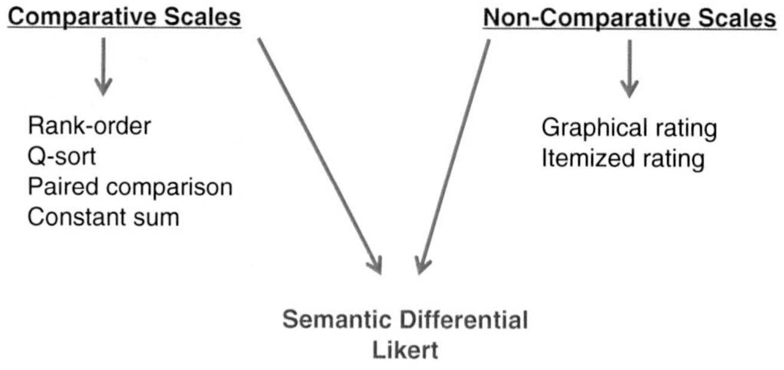

FIGURE 10.3 Frequently Used Marketing Scales

10.4a Rank-Order Scales

When researchers want to evaluate brands in relation to competing brands, rank-order scales are often used. **Rank-order scales** involve respondents comparing two or more objects, concepts, or persons and ranking them in some type of order sequence. Because respondents are asked to make comparisons, rank-order scales are classified as comparative scales. They are relatively easy for respondents to answer and tend to mimic reality somewhat because consumers often will rank brands, products or attributes mentally when faced with purchase decisions. Figure 10.4 illustrates a typical rank-order question.

While rank-order scales are relatively easy to administer, they do have some disadvantages (see Figure 10.5). First, the list of alternatives may not be categorically exhaustive. In the case of the sample question shown in Figure 10.4, a researcher can identify all of the restaurants in the Oakview Mall area fairly easily, so this is not a problem. But if respondents were asked instead to rank computer brands, a brand that a consumer prefers may not be on the list because it is much more difficult to identify all brands of computers. Ranking attributes or criteria used in making purchase decisions is even more difficult in terms of including all possible items. If the key criterion used by a consumer in making a decision is not listed, and thus not ranked, the resulting data is biased. It is also important to understand that for ranking data to be meaningful, all respondents must rank the exact same items relative to one another. This means that an "other" option with a fill-in-the-blank next to it cannot be used in a ranking question.

A second disadvantage is that a consumer may have no experience with one or more items in the list to be ranked, and as a result is unable to make meaningful evaluations. With the sample scale shown, a respondent may have no experience with Jade Garden or Pueblo Viejo and may only have eaten at an Olive Garden in another town. Thus, ranking those three restaurants could produce meaningless data.

A third disadvantage occurs in paper and pen surveys when respondents don't follow instructions. They may rank only a few items, or assign the same numbers to two or more items. While these rankings may represent a truer representation of their attitudes, the

All of the following restaurants are located in the Oakview Mall area. Please rank the restaurants in terms of your personal preference from "1" being your most preferred, "2" being your second most preferred, and so forth to "7" being your least preferred. Each number can only be used once, and each restaurant listed below must be ranked.

_____ Chili's
_____ Jade Garden
_____ Longhorn Steakhouse
_____ O'Charleys
_____ Olive Garden
_____ Pueblo Viejo
_____ Red Lobster

FIGURE 10.4 Sample Rank-Order Scale

- List may not be categorically exhaustive
- Respondent may not have knowledge or experience with all items listed
- Respondents don't follow instructions
- Difficult to rank middle items in a long list
- Criteria used in the ranking may not be clear
- Produces ordinal data, not interval

FIGURE 10.5 Disadvantages of Rank-Order Scales

data cannot be reconciled with existing ranking data, and ultimately must be deleted from the data set.[1] The fourth disadvantage typically occurs when individuals are asked to rank a long list of items. The longer the list, the more difficult it is for individuals to distinguish between those items in the middle. Consumers know what they love, they know what they hate, but differentiating between ranked items toward which they are relatively neutral in a meaningful way is difficult.

Fifth, ranking data is often of limited value because researchers do not have any knowledge of why the restaurants were ranked in a specific order. It could be based on price, on personal experiences, or on what someone told them about a particular restaurant. Thus, rank-order questions may result in significant measurement error. More important, the reason behind the rankings may provide more insight than the rankings themselves.

The last disadvantage relates to the type of data produced by rank-order scales—ordinal data. While ordinal data indicates an order, it does not indicate the distance between the rankings. Suppose both Maria and Josh ranked Red Lobster as 1 and Olive Garden as 2. Suppose for Maria, the two were very close and she had a difficult time deciding which to rank 1 and which to rank 2. But, for Josh, the decision was easy. In his mind there was a large gap between Red Lobster and Olive Garden. The magnitude of this difference in preference is not captured by ordinal data. Similarly, ranking questions force individuals to rank items they may not consider to be viable alternatives. Thus, while Josh may have ranked Jade Garden as 5, he may have no intention of ever eating at any of the restaurants ranked 5 through 7. The forced nature of ranking questions can be misleading in terms of gauging preferences.

Rank-order questions are best used in situations in which the respondent is highly familiar with all items to be ranked and when the number of items to be ranked is relatively small. Ranking questions featuring five items or fewer tends to be optimal. Questions with more than five items to rank become challenging for the respondent. In many cases, an itemized rating question or constant sum scale will yield more useful information and should be considered as viable alternatives.

In terms of reporting results of a rank-order scale, **Figure 10.6** shows the rankings for Olive Garden for a survey of 180 respondents. Notice that the highest percentage, 25 percent, ranked Olive Garden as their second-most preferred. It was ranked either first or second by a combined 46.7 percent of the respondents, indicating it is a popular choice for dining in the Oakview Mall area. Very few ranked Olive Garden near the bottom at sixth or seventh.

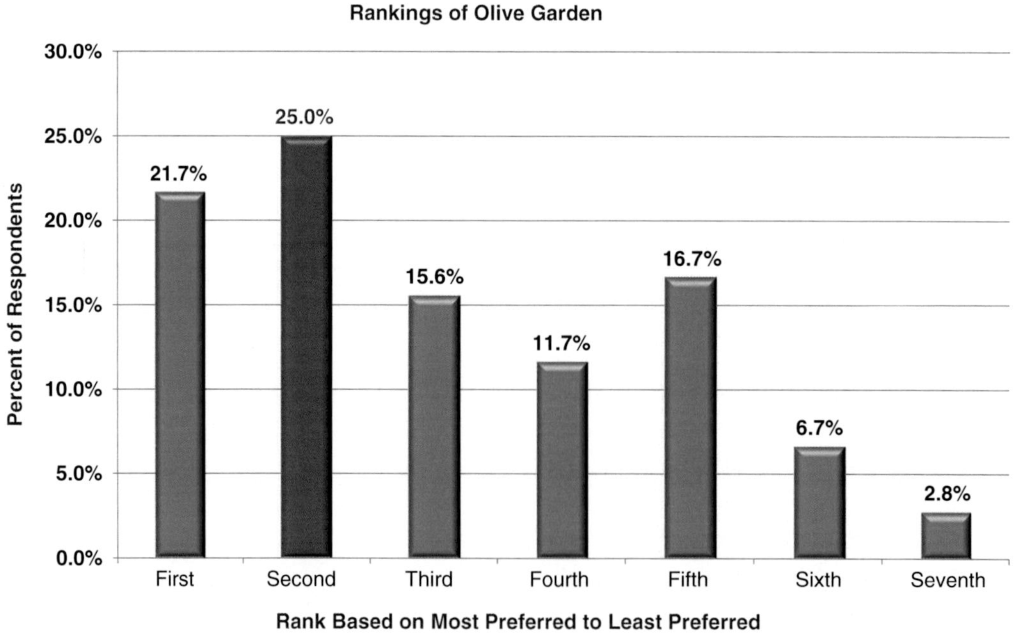

FIGURE 10.6 A Sample Graph of Ordinal Data

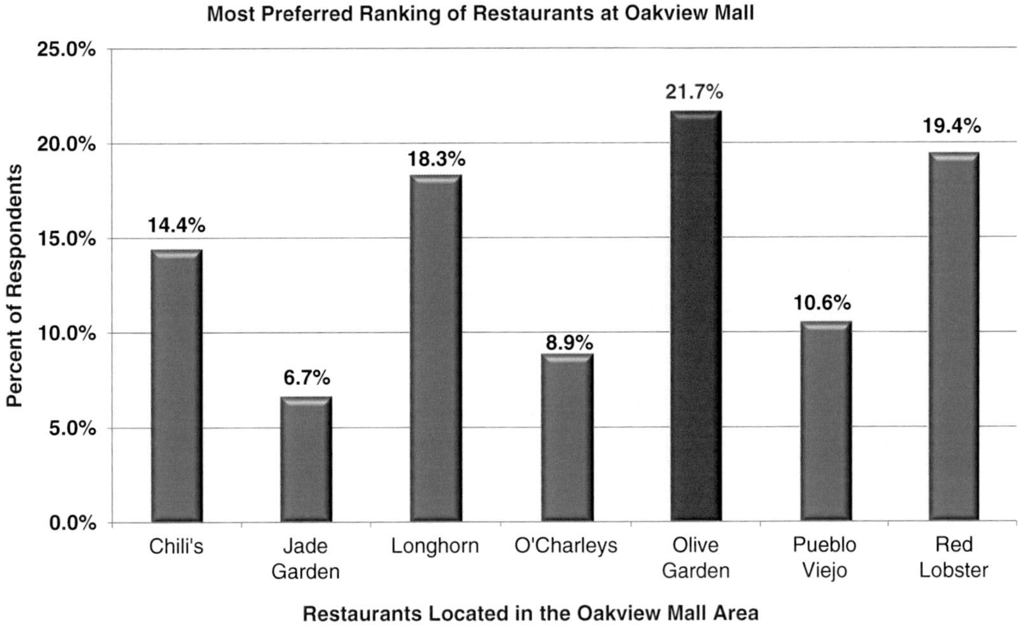

FIGURE 10.7 A Graph Showing the Top Choice Ranking for a Selection of Restaurants

Another way for the researcher to report the findings is to identify the top choice. Based on the graph in Figure 10.6, it would be easy to conclude that Olive Garden is the second-most preferred restaurant in the Oakview Mall area. The manager of Olive Garden would likely be interested in which restaurant ranked first. **Figure 10.7** shows the percent of respondents who ranked each of the restaurants as their "most preferred." Surprisingly, Olive Garden was ranked as the most preferred by the highest number of individuals, 21.7 percent. Red Lobster was second at 19.4 percent and Longhorn Steakhouse was third at 18.3 percent. In examining results of rank-order scales and ordinal data, it is important for researchers to analyze the data in multiple ways. Frequencies, percentages, mode, and median can be used.

10.4b Q-Sort

Q-sorting is a comparative technique whereby respondents rank a set of objects into a prespecified number of categories along a particular attribute or criteria. Rank-order scales are good for a small number of items, while Q-sorting works better for a large group of items, such as 50 to 100. Ranking 50 items using rank-ordering would be impossible for an individual to do, but can be done using Q-sorting. With this method, individuals are asked to place the items in piles based on some criteria.

Q-sort a comparative technique whereby respondents rank a set of objects into a prespecified number of categories along a particular attribute or criterion.

Suppose Oscar Mayer wanted to test three new print ads that have been designed by its advertising agency. It gathers a large number of print ads from recent issues of magazines that fit the Oscar Mayer target market. The three new Oscar Mayer ads are placed in a stack randomly with 57 other ads, making 60 ads total. Respondents are asked not to study the ads, but just look at each as if they were thumbing through a magazine. In the first sorting round, they would begin by picking the top five—the "great" ads. Next, they would be instructed to select the five "poorest" ads from the remaining pile. In the second stage, respondents would first select the 10 next-best ads and place them in the "good" ad pile, then identify the 10 next-worst ads, which would be placed in the "not-so-good" pile. The 30 ads that remain after the second stage sort would be left in a fifth "OK ad" pile. Switching from one extreme to the other makes the sorting task easier and faster than sorting great, good, OK, not-so-good, and poor ads in order. It is likely that the ads placed in the "great" pile would be ads which caused them to stop and look closer. The ads in the "worst" pile would be those which were quickly ignored or were offensive

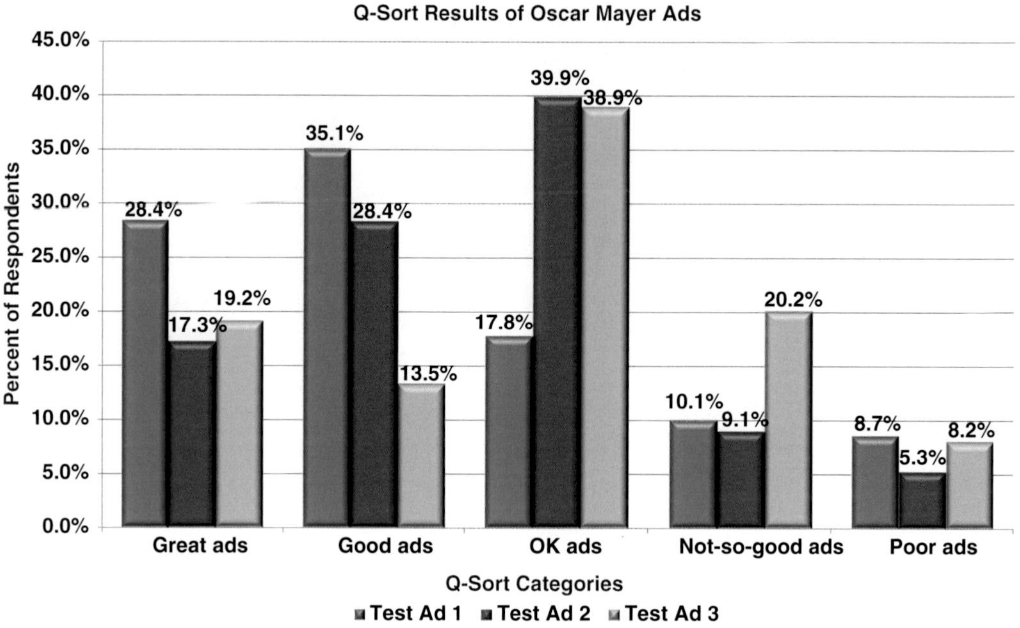

FIGURE 10.8 Graph Showing the Results of the Oscar Mayer Test Ads

in some fashion. The stacks between the two extremes would indicate some degree of interest. Using this method, a respondent could quickly evaluate 60 ads. Researchers with Oscar Mayer would be able to see how their test ads ranked compared to ads currently in circulated magazines.

Like rank order scales, Q-sort scales produce ordinal data. The results of the Oscar Mayer Q-sort are shown in Figure 10.8. Test ad 1 was placed in the first stack by 28.4 percent of the respondents and in the second stack by 35.1 percent. So about 63 percent of the respondents saw test ad 1 as either great or good, compared to the other 59 print ads they sorted. Notice test ads 2 and 3 did not produce results as good as test ad 1. Less than 50 percent of the respondents placed the ads in the great or good groups. Clearly, test ad 1 is the one that Oscar Mayer should use based on this research, though other ad pretesting measures may be appropriate before making the final decision.

With a Q-sort, the results tend to display a normal distribution curve. However, instructions given by the researcher, the types of items being sorted, and the category specifications can alter the data distribution. For example, respondents in the Oscar Mayer test could have been instructed to select all of the "great" ads—regardless of the number—and so on, rather than forcing respondents to fill preset quotas for great, good, OK, not-so-good, and poor categories. Had this been the case, the total distribution of ads for the Oscar Mayer Q-sort experiment could be similar to that shown in Figure 10.9, in which the distribution is skewed slightly positive. This information is beneficial to researchers since it tells them that, as a group, the respondents ranked more ads in the great and good categories than would be typical for a normal distribution curve.

10.4c Paired Comparisons

Paired comparison scale asks respondents to choose one of two items in a set based on some specific criterion or attribute.

Rather than ask individuals to rank-order a set of items, researchers can use a series of paired comparisons. With the **paired comparison scale**, respondents choose one of two items in a set based on some specific criterion or attribute. Figure 10.10 illustrates a paired comparison scale examining four criteria consumers use in purchasing a laptop computer. The key advantage of the paired comparison scale is that it is typically easier for respondents to choose between two items than it is to rank a series of items. The paired comparison scale also tends to overcome order bias that can be created in listing the items

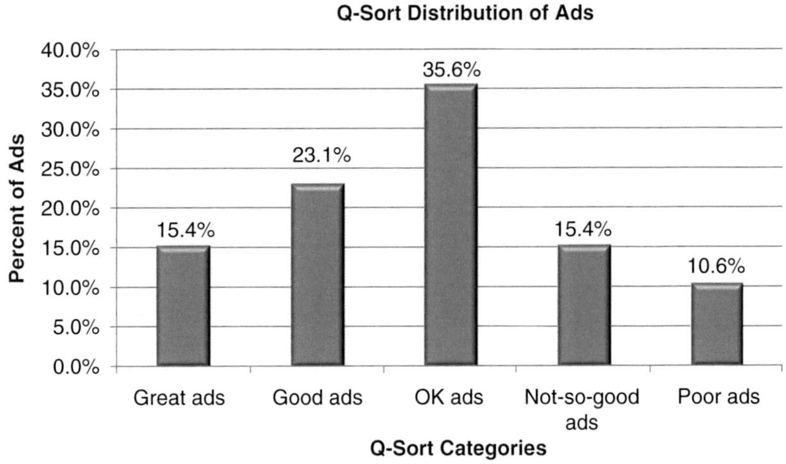

FIGURE 10.9 Graph Showing the Distribution of Ads in Each of the Q-Sort Categories

For each of the following pairs of criteria in purchasing a laptop computer, indicate which item in each pair is more important to you by placing a checkmark on the appropriate line.

_____ Price or Size of computer _____
_____ Physical appearance or Technical specifications _____
_____ Price or Physical appearance _____
_____ Physical appearance or Size of computer ____
_____ Technical specifications or Price _____
_____ Size of computer or Technical specifications _____

FIGURE 10.10 Sample Paired Comparison Scales

for a rank-order scale. Respondents may be influenced by the order items are listed in the rank-order scale, even if the list is alphabetical.

A major problem with the paired comparison scale is that all possible combinations must be listed. For a small set of items, such as the four used in Figure 10.10, only six paired combinations are needed. But as the number of items to be evaluated increases, the number of paired combinations increases geometrically according to the following formula, $[(n)*(n-1)/2]$. For instance, for five items it would take 10 pairs, for six items it would take 15 pairs, and for seven items it would take 21 pairs. Evaluating 15 or 21 pairs of items can be quite taxing, producing respondent fatigue. By the end of the exercise, respondents may start checking responses and not spend much time thinking about the paired items being evaluated.

While ordinal data is produced from a paired comparison scale, reporting the results can be challenging. Figure 10.11 provides the results of the sample comparison scale on the four purchase criteria for laptop computers. Of the 240 respondents who completed the exercise, 80 percent said that price was more important than the size of the computer, 65 percent said price was more important than the physical appearance of the computer, and 76.7 percent indicated that price was more important than technical specifications. Clearly, price is important. The size of the computer may be the least important since it was selected less than the other three comparison alternatives. Physical appearance was more important than either size or technical specifications. Last, technical specifications was more important than size.

Purchase Criteria*	Price	Size	Appearance	Specs
Price		80.0%	65.0%	76.7%
Size of computer	24.2%		42.9%	38.8%
Physical appearance	35.0%	57.1%		60.4%
Technical specifications	23.3%	61.3%	39.6%	

* Percentages indicate percent of sample that chose the row criterion over the column criterion.

FIGURE 10.11 Results from a Paired Comparison Scale

Listed below are the restaurants located in the Oakview Mall area. Please allocate 100 points among the seven restaurants based on your overall preference for each restaurant. The more points you assign to a restaurant, the higher the overall preference. The lower the points, the lower the overall preference. A restaurant that is preferred twice as much as another restaurant should have twice as many points. It is possible to assign zero points to a restaurant if it is not at all preferred. The total number of points should add to 100.

Chili's	_____
Jade Garden	_____
Longhorn Steakhouse	_____
O'Charleys	_____
Olive Garden	_____
Pueblo Viejo	_____
Red Lobster	_____
Total number of points	100

FIGURE 10.12 Example of a Constant Sum Scale

10.4d Constant Sum

Constant sum scale asks respondents to allocate points among various alternatives so the total sums to a specified amount designated by the researcher.

With the rank-order, Q-sort, and paired comparisons, relative distance between rankings cannot be determined and can vary substantially among respondents. To overcome this disadvantage, researchers can use a constant sum comparative scale. The **constant sum scale** asks respondents to allocate points among various attributes or brands to indicate their importance or preference relative to one another. Typically, researchers will ask respondents to divide 100 points, but any number of points can be used, such as 10 or 20. Because the total points must add to 100 (or another specified number) the number of items to be ranked must remain small. **Figure 10.12** illustrates a constant sum scale for evaluating the set of restaurants in the Oakview Mall area.

The primary advantage of the constant sum scale over rank order and the other comparative scales is that the relative distance between rankings can be determined. Refer back to the example of both Maria and Josh ranking Red Lobster and Olive Garden 1 and 2 using the rank-order scale. Recall that for Maria, the two restaurants were very close while for Josh they were not. Using the constant sum scale, Maria might give Red Lobster a rating

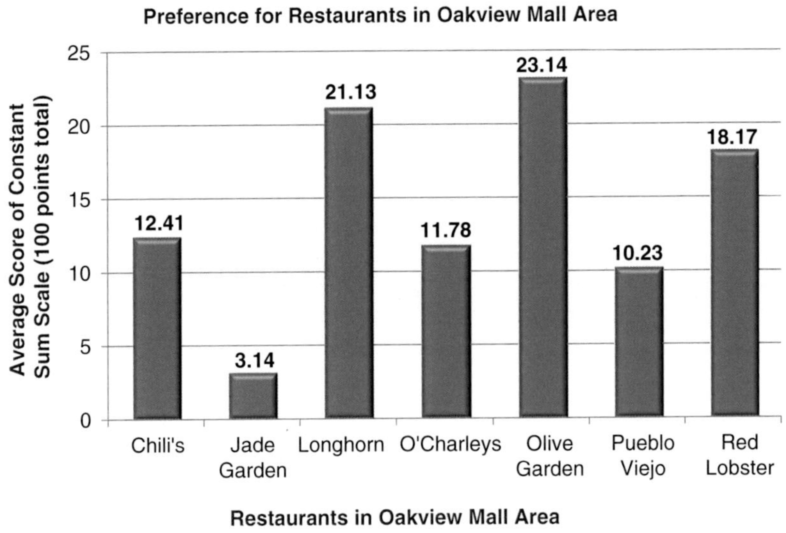

FIGURE 10.13 Constant Sum Scale Results

of 30 and Olive Garden a 28. Josh, on the other hand, might give Red Lobster a 35 and Olive Garden a 20. With the constant sum it is even possible to give the same number to two items. If Maria really could not decide between Red Lobster and Olive Garden, she could give them both the same score.

Another advantage of constant sum scales is that they produce ratio data, which is the highest order data. In addition to rankings, researchers can compare the relative magnitude of the rankings. Suppose instead of using a rank-order scale researchers had used a constant sum scale to evaluate the seven restaurants in the Oakview Mall area. Figure 10.13 shows the results.

Results are very similar to the rank-order scale in Figure 10.7, but now relative magnitude can be compared. Notice that Olive Garden is still rated the highest, but using the constant sum scale, Longhorn Steakhouse was second and Red Lobster was third. Because ratio data is produced, it is possible to say that the respondents, overall evaluation of Olive Garden was about twice as high as Chili's (23.14 compared to 12.41). The overall evaluation of Olive Garden is about seven times greater than for Jade Garden, a local Chinese restaurant. The low ranking for Jade Garden reflects the fact that constant sum scales allow respondents to assign a zero to items that are not at all preferred. Similarly, if asked to evaluate the relative importance of factors influencing a purchase decision, the constant sum scale would allow consumers to indicate the relative magnitude of the factors.

While the constant sum scale offers the advantage of producing ratio data and allows researchers to see relative distances between rankings, its primary disadvantage is the proper allocation of the points. Respondents may find it difficult to allocate 100 points among seven different choices. Unless the exercise is done on a computer that automatically adds the scores, respondents can easily make a mistake resulting in a total that does not add to 100. Using a smaller scale such as 10 is easier for respondents to add the values, but a scale of 10 does not allow as much discrimination among choices as would 100.

Graphical rating scale non-comparative scale that allows respondents to place a response anywhere on a continuous line.

10.4e Graphical Rating Scales

LEARNING OBJECTIVE 10.4 Identify and describe the various non-comparative scales.

Graphical rating scales are a non-comparative scale that allows respondents to place a response anywhere on a continuous line. Respondents are not making any comparisons, but are asked to make a judgment or evaluation. The scale is normally anchored at each end with antonyms or words with highly different meanings, such as poor and excellent or friendly and unfriendly. Figure 10.14 illustrates two different types of graphical rating scales. In the first example, respondents can place an "X" anywhere on the line that they

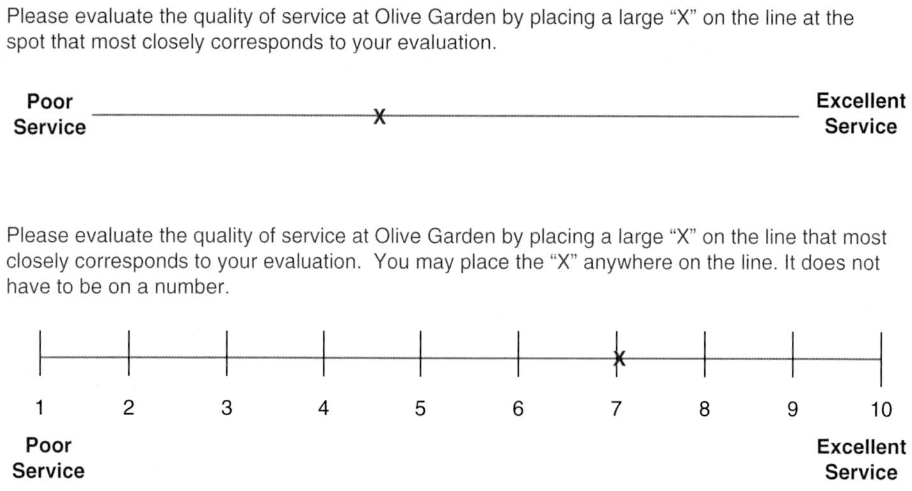

Please evaluate the quality of service at Olive Garden by placing a large "X" on the line at the spot that most closely corresponds to your evaluation.
Poor Service
X
Excellent Service
Please evaluate the quality of service at Olive Garden by placing a large "X" on the line that most closely corresponds to your evaluation. You may place the "X" anywhere on the line. It does not have to be on a number.
1
2
3
4
5
6
7
8
9
10
Poor Service
Excellent Service

FIGURE 10.14 Examples of Graphical Rating Scales

feel corresponds to their evaluation of service quality. The second scale has numbers, but respondents do not have to place their X on the line that corresponds to a number. They can place it between numbers if they want.

Graphical rating scales have the advantage of allowing respondents to provide a response along a continuum. In traditional research, the challenge is in converting the response to a number. If the line is 6 inches long researchers may equate each inch with a number, thus a scale of 1 to 6. Alternatively, they could divide the line into 12 parts and have a scale of 1 to 12. Because of the continuous nature of a graphical scale it will produce interval data. It cannot be ratio data since there is no absolute zero. Descriptive results would be reported in terms of a mean and standard deviation. Thus, for the graphical scales in Figure 10.14, the value indicated by the X for the top scale using a six-point scale may be 4.2 and for the bottom using a 10-point scale it may be 7.1.

Graphical rating scales have become much easier to implement in online surveys using interactive sliders. Respondents move an interactive slider back and forth along a bar to a place that represents their opinion. Key advantages of this technique include ease of measurement, as shown in **Figure 10.15**, and increased respondent engagement. Again, the measure produces interval-level data, making the mean and standard deviation appropriate descriptive measures. However, not all sliders show a number corresponding to the slide level to assist respondents in making a precise determination of their attitude, and questions using interactive sliders are more prone to being skipped by respondents when compared to itemized rating scales that use radio buttons. Research has also shown that the initial position of the slider influences the item completion rate. Placing sliders at the far left results in the least amount of missing data, as opposed to setting the initial slider position in the middle or at the far right. Finally, the use of sliders adds to the time

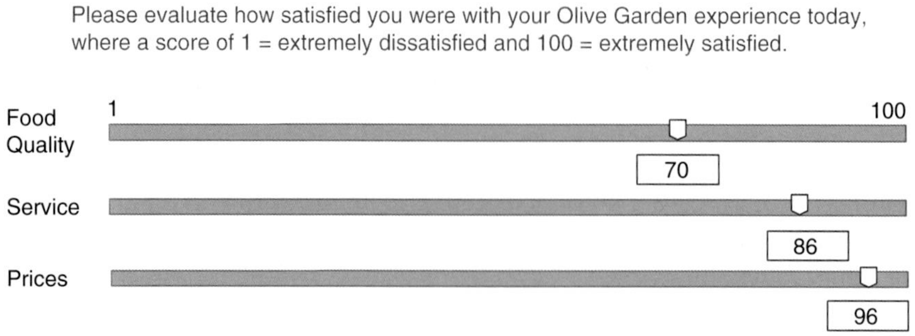

Please evaluate how satisfied you were with your Olive Garden experience today, where a score of 1 = extremely dissatisfied and 100 = extremely satisfied.

FIGURE 10.15 Example of an Interactive Slider Graphical Rating Scale

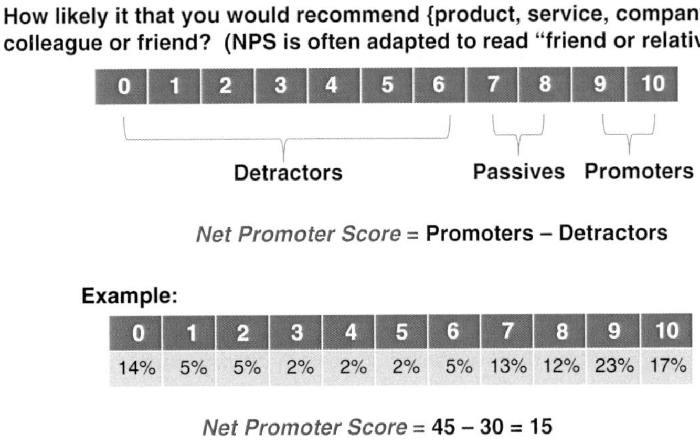

FIGURE 10.18 An Example of the Net Promoter Score Scale and How the NPS Scale Is Calculated

indicate whether consumers are actively telling others not to visit or do business with the firm.[5]

To achieve the "one number" that represents customer loyalty and will allegedly help firms to enhance profitability and growth, the percentage of detractors is subtracted from the percentage of promoters (see Figure 10.18). Passives are ignored in the calculation and many businesses pay this group—typically ranging between 20–35 percent of respondents— no further thought. TARP Worldwide argues that passives have often experienced some minor difficulty or problem, which if successfully addressed, could grow a passive into a promoter. Others argue that passives may be spreading negative word-of-mouth. Research has found that many passives are more price-sensitive, and that passives are at greater risk of switching brands. Furthermore, without a follow-up question, such as "Why do you say that?" a business doesn't know why consumers select the rating they do, which makes improving a business based on the NPS alone difficult. These are but a few of the potential problems associated with NPS measure.[6]

Businesses that adopt the NPS measure often engage in practices that misuse the scale's results, or detract from the quality of the data collected. For example, a survey by ORC International in 2017 found that over 60 percent of companies with customer experience programs tied executive compensation to achieving a target NPS. Predictably, a number of negative practices designed to raise NPS scores have detracted from the data quality, or cost firms millions of dollars. For example, coaching customers to provide high ratings or begging/pressuring customers to do the same detracts from the quality of data, yet is often used by employees who tell customers that any rating less than a "9" could be detrimental to their career. Reversing the scale, so that the customer sees the 10 first, followed by the 9, and so on, has been found to increase scores. Distributing the NPS survey following a major positive event, such as a stock split, can also artificially inflate scores. Some firms eliminate troublesome groups of consumers from the survey population, ensuring that their voice won't be heard. Others provide consumers with information on rating interpretation. By telling consumers that scores of 0–6 will categorize them as "Detractors," these details subtly influence some scores out of the detractor range and into the passive group, artificially inflating scores. Finally, it is argued that many firms trade "swag," or freebies, for positive ratings, which add up to millions of wasted dollars. In summary, many firms spend more time, money, and effort improving the NPS than they do the customer's experience.[7]

We now know that little empirical evidence exists to support the scale developer's contention that NPS is a superior measure when compared to existing loyalty scales. Studies have found that customer satisfaction, as measured by the American Customer Satisfaction Index, is just as good a predictor of revenue growth as NPS, while others have found that multi-item measures of overall satisfaction and likelihood to repurchase are not only more reliable due to lower measurement error, but also equally effective in predicting market share and cash flow. One study found that businesses randomly selected from the S&P 500 grew at a slightly higher rate than businesses who had adopted the NPS. Furthermore, the Net Promoter developers have been reluctant to fully disclose their methodology, which has caused many to question the rigor of the original research that led to the scale development. These issues beg the question, Why is NPS so popular? Well, the concept is easy for CEOs to understand and the idea of a single magic number is hard to resist. Loyalty is easy to measure using the NPS system. Many CEOS adopted NPS in part because of the implicit endorsement of *Harvard Business Review*, which published the original article. However, now that we have a greater understanding of NPS, businesses should think carefully about whether NPS has value for their firm, given its many misuses and problems. Multi-item measures of customer loyalty, satisfaction, or likelihood to recommend are often the superior choice.[8]

LEARNING OBJECTIVE 10.5
Identify and describe scales that can be either comparative or non-comparative.

10.4h Semantic Differential Scales

Semantic differential scale involves a finite number of choices anchored by dichotomous words or phrases.

A semantic differential scale can be either comparative or non-comparative depending on how a question is phrased. The **semantic differential scale** involves a finite number of choices anchored by dichotomous words or phrases. Most semantic differential scales have five or seven points, which allows for a neutral position. In some cases the neutral position is eliminated and a four- or six-point scale is used to force respondents to choose one side or the other of the scale. The key to good semantic differential scales is choosing the anchor phrases or words that will produce discriminate answers among respondents. Scale anchors should be bipolar, meaning that the anchors are perceived as opposites by respondents. Figure 10.19 provides an example of semantic differential scale items for Home Depot.

When properly constructed, a major advantage of the semantic differential scale is its ability to discriminate differences in the direction and intensity of attitudes.[9] The key is choosing anchor phrases or words that reflect opposite meanings. This isn't always an easy task. For example, most people would agree that "love" and "hate" are bipolar opposites. But what would be the appropriate opposite of "angry"? If you answered "happy," then what word would you choose as an opposite of "sad"? If the anchors are chosen well, the semantic differential is relatively easy for respondents to understand and therefore easy to answer. If the anchors are not chosen well, it will lead to respondent confusion and scores that tend to drift to the midpoint. Also, if anchors are too strong, the majority of responses will tend to be in the middle. However, if anchors are too weak, all of the answers will be at one extreme or the other.

Please evaluate the last purchase you made at Home Depot and the experience you had at the retail store.

Unfriendly staff	○	○	○	○	○	Friendly staff
Staff not very helpful	○	○	○	○	○	Staff very helpful
Poor selection	○	○	○	○	○	Excellent selection
Store unclean	○	○	○	○	○	Store clean
Poor value	○	○	○	○	○	Excellent value
Slow checkout	○	○	○	○	○	Fast checkout
Unsuccessful trip	○	○	○	○	○	Successful trip

FIGURE 10.19 Example of a Semantic Differential Scale

Semantic differential scales are excellent for assessing brand personality and brand image, and can be quickly answered by respondents. The results tend to be reliable. Semantic differential scales are also used frequently to assess attitudes toward an advertisement, a celebrity endorser, or a retail store.

A danger with using the semantic differential scale is the **halo effect**, which occurs when respondents have an overall feeling about the topic being surveyed, and that overall perception influences their response to individual items so that all of the answers are relatively close to the same. Little or no discrimination among individual items occurs. For instance, if Carla's overall experience at Home Depot was positive, she may just go through and mark the fourth circle on each item. While it is possible that those responses reflect her actual experience, it is also highly likely she did not think about each item sufficiently. It is unlikely that her experience would be a "4" for every single item. Past research using semantic differentials has shown that halo effects are more likely to occur when all favorable evaluations are placed on the left-hand side of the scale.[10]

Halo effect occurs when respondents have an overall feeling about the topic being surveyed, and that overall perception influences their response so that all of the answers are relatively close to the same.

The semantic differential scale shown in Figure 10.19 is a non-comparative scale because survey respondents are asked to evaluate their experience with Home Depot. No comparisons are made. If researchers want to compare Home Depot to Lowe's along the seven dimensions, then the scale can be modified to ask respondents to evaluate Home Depot in comparison to Lowe's. In addition, the anchors can be modified. For instance, the first item can have anchors "friendlier staff than Lowe's" and "unfriendlier staff than Lowe's."

Semantic differential scales produce interval data. Researchers assume there is equal distance between each of the points on the scale. Therefore, the appropriate descriptive measures would be a mean and standard deviation. **Figure 10.20** shows the results of the semantic differential scale about Home Depot. The two lowest ratings in this particular survey were for friendly staff and helpful staff.

Semantic differentials are often used to develop brand and image profiles. **Figure 10.21** shows an image profile for Williamson Hardware, a local retailer, compared to the national chain Home Depot. Instead of comparing a brand or business to a particular competitor, respondents can be asked to compare Williamson Hardware to other hardware stores in general. However, for this survey, individuals evaluated Williamson Hardware

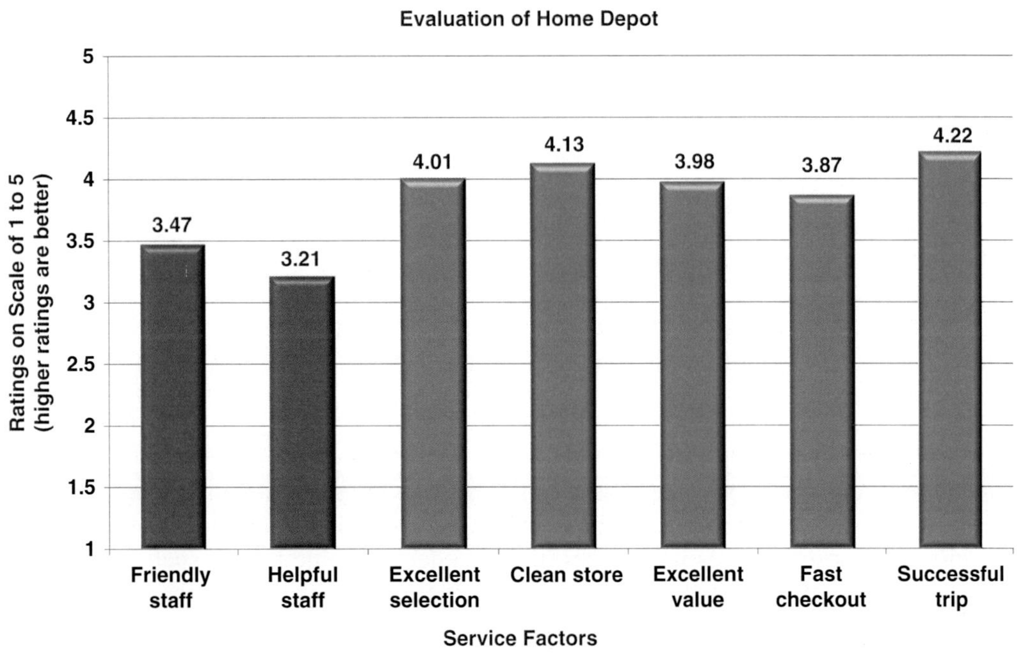

FIGURE 10.20 A Graph Showing the Results from Semantical Difference Scales

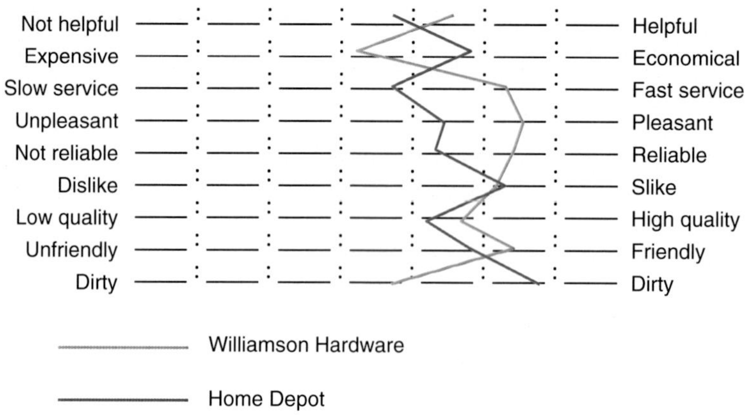

FIGURE 10.21 Image Profile of Williamson Hardware

along nine dimensions and also Home Depot along the same nine dimensions. The mean scores on each item for each brand are then plotted and connected to provide a visual representation of the resulting brand image profiles. A review of the results shows Williamson Hardware was evaluated higher on the dimensions of helpfulness, fast service, pleasantness, reliability, quality, and friendliness. On the negative side, Williamson Hardware was seen as being more expensive and not as clean. A paired sample t-test could be used to test whether the differences in the perceptions of cleanliness between Home Depot and Williamson Hardware are significant, meaning that they are not due to random sampling error. Should significant differences be found, the store manager can take steps to improve the cleanliness of the store, and thereby enhance the store's image.

When multi-item measures are used to assess an individual's attitude toward an advertisement or brand, the common practice is to create an overall average by summing the mean scores for each item. This summed score is then divided by the number of items in the scale to find the mean attitude score of the entire measure. This overall mean score for the scale or attitude dimension is then used in subsequent data analyses.

10.4i Likert Scales

Likert scale series of statements to which respondents indicate their level of agreement or disagreement with the statement.

Likert scales are among the most popular for marketing research. **Likert scales** list a series of statements, and respondents are asked to indicate their level of agreement or disagreement with each statement. Likert scales are used frequently because they are easy to construct. They avoid the difficulty of finding the right anchor words or phrases that are commonly encountered when creating a semantic differential. Likert scales are easy for respondents to read and understand. They are also easy to answer as subjects can respond to a whole series of statements that utilize the same scale. **Figure 10.22** contains some Likert statements about fashion.

Likert scales can be either comparative or non-comparative. The scale shown in Figure 10.22 is non-comparative. A comparative Likert scale might ask individuals to respond to a series of statements about a particular retail store, such as the Gap, as it compares to other clothing retail stores or a specific store such as Rue 21. An example of a comparative Likert statement would be "Rue 21 offers higher-quality clothing than the Gap."

Likert scales tend to be either a five or seven-point scale, with the five-point scale being the most common. Because Likert scales produce interval data, means and standard deviations are the appropriate descriptive measures. This allows the researcher to conduct various tests for differences in attitudes based on demographic factors such as age, gender, or race, as well as other classification variables. **Figure 10.23** graphs the results of the Likert scale about fashion.

Likert scales often include some items that have been reversed using negative phrasing. For instance, the last item in Figure 10.23 could be stated as, "Wearing the latest fashion is not important." Reversing a few items within a set of Likert statements tends to reduce

Please indicate your level of agreement or disagreement with each of the following statements.

	Strongly Disagree	Disagree	Neutral	Agree	Strongly Agree
1. Wearing the latest fashion is important to me.	○	○	○	○	○
2. The brand name is important to me.	○	○	○	○	○
3. I watch what celebrities wear. ...	○	○	○	○	○
4. I read magazines such as *Glamour* regularly.	○	○	○	○	○
5. In purchasing clothes, price is not a critical factor.	○	○	○	○	○
6. I am concerned about what others think of me.	○	○	○	○	○

FIGURE 10.22 Example of a Likert Scale

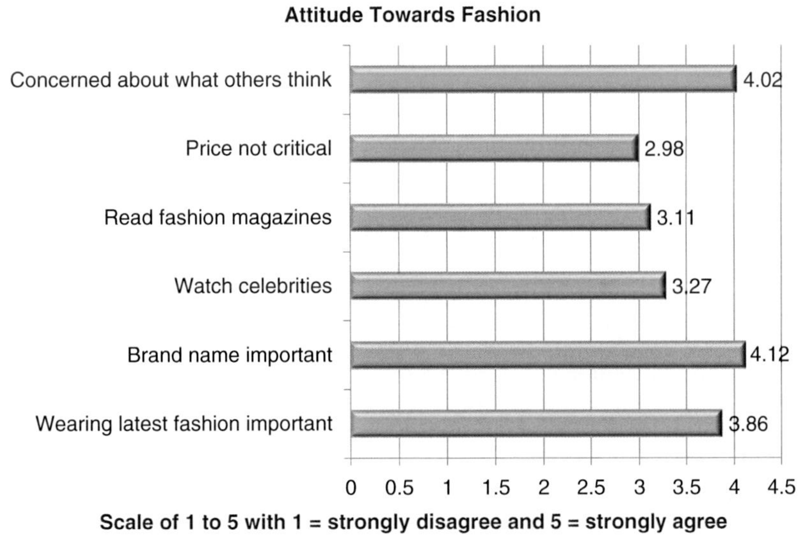

FIGURE 10.23 A Graph Showing the Results from a Series of Likert Statements

response bias from acquiescent respondents who are likely to be agreeable and rate everything positively.[11] Mixing positive and negative items is also important because some argue it helps to alert lazy or less attentive respondents that the question content varies.[12] Unfortunately, reversing scale items has been found to diminish the reliability of scales and can result in respondents selecting the exact opposite of their true attitude because they do not read the items carefully.[13]

10.5 Scale Category Considerations

LEARNING OBJECTIVE 10.6
Discuss the considerations involved in selecting marketing scales.

Choosing the best scale for a research project requires an understanding of the research objective, information needs, research subjects, mode of administration, and understanding of how the data will be analyzed. If the objective involves comparisons with other brands or products, one of the comparative scales should be used, or semantic differential or Likert scales should be used to assess multiple brands or products. The education level and reading ability of the respondents should also be considered. Some scales, such as the constant sum scale, require a higher level of education and math skills than do some of the other scales, though online surveys offering auto-calculation make these easier to complete now than in the past. To encourage respondents to complete a survey and to provide honest, beneficial answers, the scales need to be easy for the respondents to read, understand, and complete.

Researchers must also consider the information needs of the research study, especially in terms of the data that each scale will produce. This in turn requires thinking through how the data will be analyzed. Ordinal data might be sufficient for some research studies, while others might need interval or ratio data. Interval or ratio data is needed to calculate means so that t-tests or ANOVAs can be run during data analysis when comparing groups, be they brands or attitudes between men and women. Mode of administration has an impact on scale selection. Some scales are easier to use with telephone surveys. If the respondents can see the scale, as with a web or paper survey, then more complicated scales can be used. If they can only hear the scale as it is read to them, less complicated scales should be used. Mobile surveys may use graphical rating scales instead of words to save space, or alter the presentation of response options by using drop-down menus instead of radio buttons.

When it comes to actually creating a marketing scale, researchers must think about the number of categories, the use of balanced versus unbalanced scales, no opinion and don't know options, forced versus non-forced choices, and the extent of category description (see **Figure 10.24**). These decisions can have a significant impact on how respondents answer questions and the usefulness of the data that is produced.

10.5a Number of Categories

In developing scales, researchers must decide on the number of categories. A two or three-point scale lacks discrimination ability. Respondents tend to feel uncomfortable when using such a scale because it limits their freedom of expression. A Likert scale that has only three categories of disagree, neutral, and agree will not provide the researcher with a great deal of information. While it may technically be an interval scale, the mean will not be of much value. Frequency counts of how many agree and how many disagree may be more useful. By expanding the number of categories to 5, 7, or 10, greater detail is obtained and the scale increases in discriminatory power. While five- and seven-point scales produce comparable means, 10-point scales have been shown to result in slightly lower means.[14]

As the number of categories increases from three to nine, the reliability of the measure improves.[15] Thus, differences in responses are more likely to be found as the number of categories increases. But having a scale with 10 or more points may be too many for some respondents. It can be difficult for them to distinguish between values, such as 6 and 7 or 7 and 8. Thus, reliability may also suffer as scales with a large number of categories (10+) have been found to be less reliable than those with fewer categories.[16] As a result, most marketing researchers recommend scales with five to seven points as being optimal.[17] Often the decision on how many scale points comes down to researcher preference and the importance of the decision that needs to be made.

- Number of categories
- Balanced versus unbalanced scales
- No opinion and don't know options
- Forced versus non-forced choices
- Type of category description

FIGURE 10.24 Considerations in Creating Marketing Scales

Balanced scale How important is it to you to wear the latest fashions? ___very unimportant ____ somewhat unimportant ____ neutral ____ somewhat important____ very important **Unbalanced scale** How important is it to you to wear the latest fashions? ___very unimportant ____ somewhat unimportant ____ somewhat important ____ very important ___extremely important

FIGURE 10.25 Examples of Balanced and Unbalanced Scales

Another consideration in terms of number of categories is whether the scale should have an even or odd number of choices. When an odd number is used, such as five or seven, respondents can choose a neutral or middle position. With an even number of choices, respondents do not have that option. They must make a choice on one side or the other of the scale. It is a difficult decision. In some cases, individuals may not have an opinion and so having a neutral position is valid. Forcing them to choose one side or the other may distort the data. However, the downside of having an odd number of choices is that it provides an easy escape for individuals who do not want to state an opinion.

10.5b Balanced versus Unbalanced Scales

In addition to the number of categories, researchers must decide on whether to use a balanced or unbalanced scale. A **balanced scale** will have the same number of positive choices as negative choices, and the phrasing of each negative choice typically mirrors the phrasing of each positive choice. An **unbalanced scale** is weighted toward one of the anchors, either positive or negative. Figure 10.25 illustrates each of the scales in relation to an individual's attitude toward wearing the latest fashions.

Balanced scale has the same number of positive response choices as negative choices.

Unbalanced scale response categories are weighted toward one of the anchors, either positive or negative.

In the first example, the itemized rating scale has two negative response categories, a neutral position, and two positive response categories. It is balanced. In the second example, there are two negative responses categories, no neutral position, and three positive response categories. It is unbalanced. The researcher could still use a neutral position in the unbalanced category if he or she desires. In most cases, a balanced scale is preferred to an unbalanced scale. But, if past research shows that most people lean toward a negative or positive position, an unbalanced scale is a better choice because it will provide greater discrimination.

There are also situations where the target audience can dictate which scale is used. If a fashion question is asked of the general population, the balanced scale would be appropriate, and expanding the number of categories to a seven-point scale would produce even

Source: Rob Marmion/Shutterstock.

In some situations, the target audience may dictate which scale is used. An unbalanced scale would be better if teenage girls are studied, as most female teenagers are concerned about their personal appearance.

better results. If the population being studied is teenage girls, an unbalanced scale would be better since most female teenagers are concerned about personal appearance and fashion.

10.5c No Opinion and Don't Know/Not Sure Options

Another decision that must be made is whether to include a "no opinion," a "don't know" or a "not sure" option. As stated earlier, if an odd number of points is used in a scale, respondents tend to think of the center point as being neutral. They may also see it as a "don't know/not sure" or "no opinion" choice if none are provided. This is problematic, as researchers cannot be certain if the respondent is neutral about the issue, or if the respondent doesn't really have an opinion. To avoid this situation and reduce measurement error, a "no opinion" or "don't know" option can be placed to the right of the scale. By placing it on the right side, respondents are first encouraged to express an opinion. Usually just one of the options is included, but both options can be used if researchers feel that there is a significant difference between someone who doesn't want to express an opinion and someone who truly has no experience or knowledge with which to answer the question.

The downside of including a "no opinion" or "don't know" option is that its presence often encourages respondents to use it.[18] If a "no opinion" option is used on the Likert questions in Figure 10.22, a number of respondents might check it rather than indicate a level of agreement or disagreement with the statement. This is more likely to occur if an even-numbered scale is used in which a neutral position is not available. The same situation can occur with the semantic differential scales in Figure 10.19 if a "no opinion" option is available, though most semantic differentials do not include this category. While some professional researchers believe paid respondents should answer every question and thus advocate avoiding "don't know" or "no opinion" responses except when these answers could be legitimate responses to a question,[19] others advocate the use of "don't know" or "can't recall" options to improve data quality.[20]

In surveys where respondents might not have any experience with the brand or product being studied, a "not applicable" option is valuable. Suppose the respondent completing the questions about fashion (see Figure 10.22) was from France or another country and was not familiar with *Glamour* magazine. The respondent has to make a decision. She could skip the question and not answer it. She could answer it in terms of magazines in general, or guess what is meant by the question since she has no familiarity with *Glamour*. She might assume it is a magazine that features celebrities, tying it in with the previous item. By having a "don't know" option, the respondent can check it and the researcher is not left with biased data. A "not applicable" option is important when a question may not apply to the situation or individual answering the survey.

10.5d Forced versus Non-Forced Choices

With semantic differential and Likert scales that use an odd number of response categories, respondents can check the middle option and not have to take a stand on an issue. On the Likert scales about fashion shown in Figure 10.22, an individual can choose neutral. While the individual can certainly be neutral about the importance of fashion, brand names of clothes, pricing, and so forth, it is likely that they do have an opinion. They may just choose the easy route of checking neutral, or if the researcher has a "no opinion" category, he or she can check it.

To force individuals to take a stand on issues, such as fashion, researchers can use an even number of points such as the six-point scale in **Figure 10.26** that does not have a neutral point. If there are no other options such as "no opinion," the respondent must make a stand, either negative or positive. Thus, they have to either disagree or agree with the statement "I like wearing brand-name clothing." The only other option open to the respondent is to refuse to answer the question and leave it blank. Most individuals, however, when forced to make a stand on an issue or statement, will do so. Thus, by eliminating neutral, no opinion, and don't know options, researchers force respondents to either the positive or negative side of the statement or question.

For each of the following statements, indicate your level of agreement or disagreement by placing an X in the open box that most closely represents your feelings.

I like wearing brand-name clothing. .... Strongly Disagree__|__|__|__|__|__Strongly Agree
I prefer to purchase clothes that are on sale. .... Strongly Disagree__|__|__|__|__|__Strongly Agree
Wearing name-brand clothing makes me feel accepted by others. ... Strongly Disagree__|__|__|__|__|__Strongly Agree
Advertising influences my decision on what brand to purchase. ...... Strongly Disagree__|__|__|__|__|__Strongly Agree
I use coupons when I buy clothes. .... Strongly Disagree__|__|__|__|__|__Strongly Agree
I follow clothing trends so I can purchase the latest styles. .... Strongly Disagree__|__|__|__|__|__Strongly Agree
I normally buy clothes that are on a sales rack. .... Strongly Disagree__|__|__|__|__|__Strongly Agree
Price is important to me when selecting clothes. .... Strongly Disagree__|__|__|__|__|__Strongly Agree
The brand name is important in my selection of clothes. .... Strongly Disagree__|__|__|__|__|__Strongly Agree

FIGURE 10.26 Likert Scale Using Even Number of Points

10.5e Type of Category Description

Researchers must also decide whether each category in a scale should be labeled with a verbal description, a number, or whether only the scale anchors should be labeled. Figure 10.26 illustrates the latter situation. Alternatively, a Likert scale could be composed as was shown in Figure 10.21 in which each category is labeled. A final example which combines both verbal and numerical category descriptions is shown in **Figure 10.27**.

Using numbers to represent categories in a mail survey pre-codes the questionnaire and saves the person tabulating the results valuable time. The manual coding of each survey item is avoided. Interestingly, the numbers chosen for scales can significantly influence the resulting ratings. Multiple studies have compared scales containing all positive numbers, such 0 to 10, 1 to 9, or 1 to 5 with scales in which numbers were negatively and positively balanced (−5 to +5, 4 to +4, 2 to +2). In each instance, scales using negatively and positively balanced numeric response categories produced more positive evaluations.[21]

Limiting the use of verbal labels to anchors is desirable when the researcher wants to be certain that interval-level data is collected. However, describing each category can be helpful when the goal is to better explain the options available to respondents. One veteran researcher argues that "if you can't come up with verbal anchors that make sense for each scale point, it's a good indication you have too many scale points and that respondents won't be able to see the differences clearly either."[22] Obviously, the education level of respondents should be considered when making this decision. Respondents with lower levels of education are more likely to benefit from category descriptions that are applied to every option.

An additional consideration when choosing category descriptions relates to the strength of the anchors chosen when only anchors appear, and individual category descriptors are not provided. Suppose a question asked consumers to "Indicate your satisfaction level with your current cell phone service provider." How should the anchors be phrased? Satisfied vs. Dissatisfied? Very Satisfied vs. Very Dissatisfied? Extremely Satisfied vs. Extremely Dissatisfied? While the choice may be influenced somewhat by the number of categories used in the scale, it is also important to understand that the adjectives chosen

Please indicate your level of agreement or disagreement with each of the following statements by circling the number that best corresponds with your attitude.
1 = strongly disagree, 2 = disagree, 3 = neutral, 4 = agree, and 5 = strongly agree.

	SD	D	N	A	SA
1. Wearing the latest fashion is important to me.	1	2	3	4	5

FIGURE 10.27 Verbal and Numerical Descriptions in a Likert Scale

to accompany a category descriptor can influence respondents' choices. For instance, respondents would be less inclined to choose the first or last category when "extremely satisfied/dissatisfied" anchors exist than they would when the "very satisfied/dissatisfied" or "satisfied/dissatisfied" anchors are used. This also means that using strongly worded anchors, with a seven-point scale, may yield more insightful data.[23]

10.6 Validity and Reliability Measurement

LEARNING OBJECTIVE 10.7
Explain ways researchers can ensure the reliability and validity of scales.

In developing marketing scales, researchers have three basic options. First, they can use scales that have already been established by other researchers. The book *Marketing Scales Handbook* by Gordon C. Bruner, and co-authors on earlier volumes, is an excellent source of scales that have already been established. Additional scales can be found at https://marketingscales.com. A major advantage of using these scales is that many have already gone through rigorous validity and reliability tests. Thus, results from these scales are likely to have a high level of validity and reliability.

A second option is to use established scales, but modify them to fit the product or situation being studied. By starting with scales that have gone through validity and reliability tests, it is likely that the new, revised scales will also have a higher level of validity and reliability.

The final option is for researchers to develop their own scales. Scale development is a difficult and time-consuming process. A great deal of academic research has been devoted to the scale development process, and those wishing to develop their own scales are best served by following established procedures.[24] Whether existing scales are modified or new scales are developed from scratch, researchers need to check the validity and reliability of their scales. Chapter 9 presented various methods of measuring reliability and ensuring validity.

Multiple items (or indicators) are often used to measure consumer attitudes or other marketing-related variables (or constructs), such as brand image or attitude toward an ad. Using more than one item to measure a single construct provides a more accurate picture than using just one-item indicators. Consider the Likert statements shown in Figure 10.26 that were taken from a survey about purchasing clothes. Researchers that developed the survey believe the nine statements selected measure two constructs: branding and price. To check if this is true, researchers can use two statistical methods: correlation analysis and factor analysis.

10.6a Correlation Analysis

Correlation the degree with which one variable changes with another.

Correlation is the degree with which one variable changes with another. If the correlation involves only two variables, it is called bivariate correlation. A common statistical test to measure bivariate correlation is the Pearson product-moment correlation. The Pearson test examines the two variables to see the amount of change in one variable compared to the amount of change in the other variable. Pearson correlations can vary from a +1 to a −1. A +1 score would mean an identical change. If variable A increases by 2, then variable B would increase by 2. If variable A declines by 4, variable B would decline by 4. On the Likert scales shown in Figure 10.24, if two statements had a perfect +1 correlation, then the answers to both questions would always be the same.

A score of −1 would indicate an inverse relationship. If variable A increases by 2, then variable B would decline by 2 units. If variable A declines by 4, then variable B would increase by 4. A score of 0 would indicate no correlation at all. Changes in variable A had no relationship to the change in variable B. Scores of +1, −1, or 0 are extremely unlikely with a valid sample of respondents.

Referring back to the Likert statements about purchasing clothes, Pearson correlations that are positive indicate respondents tended to give the same answers to two different questions. The higher the value (i.e., the closer to 1 the correlation), the more often the same response was given to the two questions. A Pearson correlation that is negative

Likert Statements	Like Wearing Brands		Shop Clothes on Sale	
	Correlation	*P*-value	Correlation	*P*-value
Like wearing brand-name clothes	1		−0.310	0.000
Shop clothes on sale	−0.310	0.000	1	0.000
Wearing brands to feel accepted	0.712	0.000	−0.276	0.000
Advertising influences	0.359	0.000	−0.317	0.000
Use coupons	−0.222	0.002	0.497	0.000
Wearing latest fashions important	0.379	0.000	−0.342	0.000
Purchase from sales racks	−0.072	0.321	0.545	0.000
Price is important	−0.084	0.243	0.570	0.000
Brand name important	0.687	0.000	−0.468	0.000

FIGURE 10.28 Partial Bivariate Correlation Matrix

indicates that respondents tended to give opposite answers. Thus, if the respondent strongly agreed with statement A and it had a negative correlation with B, they would tend to disagree with statement B.

For simplification purposes, the Pearson correlation and significance level of the first two Likert statements are shown with all of the statements for a sample of 194 respondents in Figure 10.28. The values shown in the first "Correlation" column indicate how well the statement in each row is correlated with the statement "I like wearing brand-name clothing." The significance level of the correlation is reported next. The last two columns contain the Pearson correlation and significance level with the statement "I prefer to purchase clothes that are on sale."

Notice the Pearson correlation between, "I like wearing brand-name clothing" and "I prefer to purchase clothes that are on sale" is −0.310, which indicates an inverse correlation. The more the respondent liked wearing brand-name clothing, the less they preferred purchasing clothes off-of-the-sales rack. The *p*-value of .000 indicates that this is a significant inverse relationship that is unlikely to have been found by chance. Thus, we can be confident that the results indicate a true inverse relationship in the population since it was true for this sample. The correlation between the first and third statement is 0.712, indicating a strong, positive correlation between the statements "I like wearing brand-name clothing" and "wearing name-brand clothing makes me feel accepted by others." The 0.712 can be thought of as a percent of common answers. Thus, 71.2 percent of the respondents checked the same answer on the Likert scale for the two questions. In terms of the first and second statement correlations, it would indicate that 31 percent of the time respondents checked just the opposite answer. If they checked strongly agree for "I like wearing brand-name clothing," then 31 percent of the time they checked strongly disagree for "I prefer to purchase clothes that are on sale."

A review of the Pearson correlation matrix shows that the first item is highly correlated with the third statement and the last statement, "The brand name is important in my selection of clothes." It is positively related to the statements about advertising and importance of wearing the latest fashions, but the correlations are not as strong. It is inversely correlated to the statements about purchasing clothes on sale and using coupons. This would indicate that individuals who felt brand names were important tended to put less emphasis on sales and coupons. But notice that for the statements "I normally buy clothes that are on a sales rack" and "price is important to me when selecting clothes" the correlation is negative. As neither correlation is significant, it indicates very little correlation between these two statements and "I like wearing brand name clothing." So, from the correlation analysis, the researcher can say there is no correlation between individuals who like wearing brand names and their desire to shop from a sales rack and the importance of price to them.

A check of the final two columns shows just the opposite for the statement about shopping for clothes that are on sale. That statement is positively correlated with other statements about pricing and inversely correlated with statements about branding and fashions. All are significant.

10.6b Factor Analysis

Factor analysis reduces a larger number of items into a smaller subset of factors based on similarity.

A statistical procedure that is often used by researchers with multi-item attitude scales that are meant to represent multiple facets of an individual's attitude is factor analysis. A **factor analysis** involves analyzing a set of indicators (items) to determine underlying constructs (dimensions) by reducing a larger number of items into a smaller subset of factors. Through factor analysis, a researcher can determine which questions are measuring facets of the same component, or attitudinal dimension. For example, a researcher may start with 30 items that measure retail store image. Through factor analysis, these 30 items might be reduced to just five factors that measure different aspects of store image, such as atmospherics, layout, image, pricing and product selection. Each factor is typically measured by multiple questions that "load" highly on a particular factor. Questions which load on more than one factor are eliminated, as the goal is to develop question items that explicitly measure each individual factor, or dimension. The correlation matrix discussed in the previous section provides some information, but a factor analysis is a more comprehensive, statistical method that provides better information. A discussion of factor analysis can be found at the textbook's website (www.clowjames.net/students.html), along with instructions on how to conduct a factor analysis using the IBM SPSS software.

10.7 Global Concerns

In developing scales to be used in other countries, researchers must be cognizant of differences in culture. A literal translation from English (or whatever language the original questionnaire was developed) can yield scales that may actually have a different meaning, or at least not carry the same connotation. Engaging translators who understand the nuances of the language and culture can be extremely valuable. Double translation, in which one person translates the survey into the foreign language, and another translates this survey back into English, is often used to verify that the meaning between surveys is consistent.

Because translations are a costly and time-consuming process, researchers studying international populations that are bilingual (with one language being English) are often tempted to use surveys written in English rather than in the native language of the population being studied. While doing so eliminates translation costs and saves time, research has shown that the quality of data suffers due to an anchor contraction effect. The **anchor contraction effect (ACE)** is best defined as a systematic form of response bias in which international subjects "report more intense emotions" when answering questions in English, as opposed to when they answer the same questions in their native language. Thus, ACE introduces bias into the data.[25] Given the growing number of multilingual individuals worldwide, the increasingly global focus of the business environment, and the widespread influence of the Internet, this is of serious concern. ACE could artificially inflate product or business ratings in a significant fashion.

Anchor contraction effect (ACE) systematic form of response bias in which international subjects report more intense emotions when answering questions in English, as opposed to when they answer the same questions in their native language.

People do not always respond to scales in the same manner. Culture can impact the types of responses that are given. For instance, many individuals believe that the Likert scale is universal and easily understood by people of any language and culture. Such is not the case. Likert scales can yield different results, depending on the culture context where it is used. Respondents from some cultures show an acquiescence bias, or tendency to answer more favorably. Other cultures favor selection of the extreme points on the scale anchors while yet others tend towards moderation, in which responses are grouped around the middle of a scale.[26] Research has shown that using scales with numbers anchored only by "strongly agree" and "strongly disagree" can yield different results than using verbal words for each point on the scale.[27] The problem is that there is no conclusive evidence on which Likert scale is best because results were highly dependent on the topic being studied. With some topics, the numeric Likert scale performed better, but for other topics the verbal Likert scale was better. It is important for market researchers to carefully compare results across multiple countries since the scale used may affect results. It's possible that differences found are due to the scale rather than true differences in attitudes or opinions. To avoid this problem, researchers will often use numerical scales that have only anchors at each end. This approach appears to present the least problems in comparing results across cultures.[28]

As an alternative, researchers may benefit from using more semantic differential scales in international research. Semantic differential scales are less prone to response bias when compared with Likert scales. A study of U.S. and South Korea respondents found no statistically significant differences in extreme responses when the semantic differential was used, while both U.S. and South Korean respondents exhibited greater levels of extreme responses when Likert scales were employed.[29]

Another concern is with Hispanic cultures. In measuring attribute importance and brand performance, Hispanics have a tendency to rate both on the upper, positive side of the scale. With a five-point scale, nearly all responses are in the 3 to 5 range. With a 10-point scale, almost all responses are in the 6 to 10 range. These ratings tend to be higher than the general population. A study by Jeffry Savitz found that on the average Hispanics rate products about 6 percent higher than non-Hispanics. So comparing Hispanic populations to the general population or non-Hispanic cultures can be interpreted incorrectly. Researchers might see a significant difference, but that difference can be due to a cultural trend of Hispanics to rate more positively than due to an actual difference in evaluation.[30] One approach that can be used with Hispanics to obtain more useful information is to use an unbalanced scale that has more positive points than negative. This will allow for greater discrimination in answers. It does not, however, allow for more accurate comparisons to non-Hispanics.

10.8 Marketing Research Statistics

Since marketing research relies heavily on scales, researchers will often use a Cronbach's alpha test to determine if the multiple items within a scale are all measuring the same construct, or dimension. The Statistics Review and Dealing with Data sections examine Cronbach's alpha reliability and how it is typically used within marketing research analysis.

In reporting results of data analysis, there will be instances where a researcher wants to present results that have different scales. For example, a researcher might want to show the number of visits to a website and the sales revenue generated through those visits, but do so within the same graph. The Statistical Reporting section illustrates a technique for creating such a graph.

10.8a Statistics Review

Working with established scales improves the reliability and validity of the construct being measured. However, it is always a good idea to measure the reliability of the scale being used since the sample respondents and survey conditions vary. The best statistical tool to measure a scale's reliability is Cronbach's alpha. [31] Cronbach's alpha measures the internal consistency of the items, or the degree which items would produce the same results if a respondent were to retake a survey under the same conditions.

Reliability Statistics	
Cronbach's Alpha	N of Items
.837	5

Item-Total Statistics				
	Scale Mean If Item Deleted	Scale Variance If Item Deleted	Corrected Item-Total Correlation	Cronbach's Alpha If Item Deleted
Source Expertise 1: Experience	14.13	18.447	.753	.770
Source Expertise 2: Qualifications	13.79	19.799	.729	.779
Source Expertise 3: Expert	14.40	21.530	.626	.808
Source Expertise 4: Skills	13.93	24.525	.404	.862
Source Expertise 5: Knowledgeability	13.75	20.687	.697	.789

FIGURE 10.29 SPSS Initial Cronbach's Alpha Reliability Measures

A survey was developed to examine the source credibility of models used in print advertisements. One of the scales used measured the model's perceived expertise to endorse the product being advertised. A five-item scale was used. The results of the Cronbach's alpha statistical test are shown in Figure 10.29. The Cronbach's alpha score for the five-item scale is .837. Typically, Cronbach's alpha reliability scores above .700 are considered good scales.

The fourth column of the bottom table shows the correlation of each question with the overall correlation with the other items. Notice the correlation of the fourth question is only .404, which indicates only about 40 percent of the time do respondents give the same answer to this question. If the fourth question is deleted from the scale, the overall Cronbach's alpha score would improve to .862. This number is given in the last column of the table. If the Cronbach's alpha reliability test is run again in SPSS with question 4 deleted, the Cronbach's alpha score would be .862. This second SPSS analysis with question 4 deleted is shown in Figure 10.30.

The four items are a reliable measure of the expertise construct. An examination of the last column of the output shows the scale's reliability cannot be improved by dropping any additional questions. The Cronbach's alpha score of .862 shows that approximately 86 percent of the time, the responses to the four questions are the same, indicating the questions are measuring the same construct or dimension.

10.8b Statistics Reporting

Buzz score a measure of the relative amount of mentions and word-of-mouth communications a brand receives in social media.

Sometimes marketing researchers would like to report two different measures on the same graph, but the measures have two different scales. One method that can be used is a combination graph, shown in Figure 10.31. The left axis and the bars measure a company's buzz score. A **buzz score** is a measure of the relative amount of mentions and

Reliability Statistics	
Cronbach's Alpha	N of Items
.862	4

Item-Total Statistics				
	Scale Mean If Item Deleted	Scale Variance If Item Deleted	Corrected Item-Total Correlation	Cronbach's Alpha If Item Deleted
Source Expertise 1: Experience	10.55	13.036	.760	.803
Source Expertise 2: Qualifications	10.22	14.129	.743	.810
Source Expertise 3: Expert	10.83	15.682	.629	.808
Source Expertise 5: Knowledgeability	10.18	14.878	.712	.823

FIGURE 10.30 SPSS Cronbach's Alpha Score with Question 4 Deleted

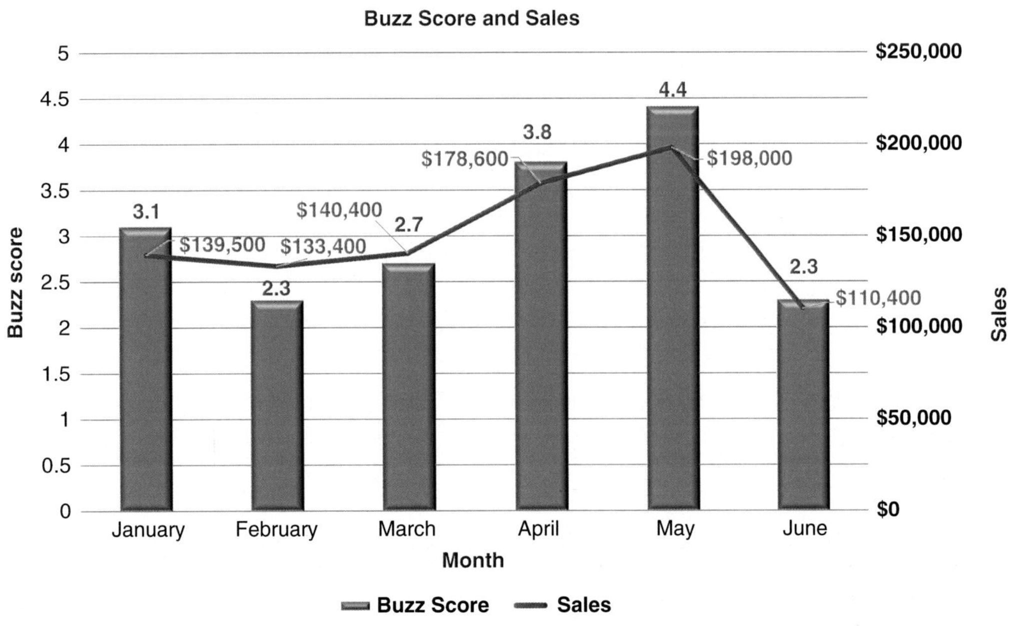

FIGURE 10.31 A Graph Utilizing Two Axes with Different Scales

word-of-mouth communications a brand receives in social media. The right axis measures sales for the company. The purpose of the graph is to show the correlation between buzz score and sales. While not perfect, sales do appear to fluctuate to a certain degree with the amount of buzz the brand receives. Sales were highest in May, when the buzz score also was the highest.

Month	Consumer Posts	Sales
January	161	$657,400
February	279	$684,900
March	294	$813,600
April	121	$609,600
May	236	$899,100
June	148	$868,000
July	139	$704,000
August	241	$605,200
September	236	$736,000

FIGURE 10.32 Data Showing the Total Number of Posts by Consumers on a Company's Social Media Pages and the Sales for Each of the Months

Statistical Reporting Exercise: Use the data in Figure 10.32 to create a combination graph. The second column shows the number of postings by consumers on a company's social media pages—Facebook, Twitter, Instagram, and the brand's blog. The third column is the sales for each month. Comment on the relationship between these two variables.

10.8c Dealing with Data

Source credibility of models in advertisements consists of five different dimensions. The Statistics Review examined one of the dimensions—expertise. The other dimensions are perceived trustworthiness of the model in the ad, attractiveness, similarity, and liking. *Trustworthiness* involves honesty and dependability. *Attractiveness* consists of the model's perceived physical beauty, elegance, and sex appeal. *Similarity* measures if the model is perceived to have similar values, tastes, and preferences as the respondent. *Liking* refers to the degree to which the model appears friendly, approachable, and likeable to the respondent.

Access the SPPS data file Chapter 10 Dealing with Data at www.clowjames.net/students.html. The variables for each of the remaining four source credibility dimensions are provided. Use SPSS to obtain a Cronbach's alpha score for each of the following dimensions: Final Source Trust, Final Source Attractiveness, Final Source Similarity, and Final Source Liking. When you are finished, answer the following questions:

1. What is the Cronbach's alpha score for the "trustworthiness" dimension? Can the scale be improved by deleting a question? If so, which question? Based on this initial printout, what would be the Cronbach's alpha if the item is deleted? Run a new Cronbach's alpha with the item deleted. What is the new Cronbach's alpha score?
2. What is the Cronbach's alpha score for the "attractiveness" dimension? Can the scale be improved by deleting a question? If so, which question? Based on this initial printout, what would be the Cronbach's alpha if the item were deleted? Run a new Cronbach's alpha with the item deleted. What is the new Cronbach's alpha score? Can the reliability measure be improved by dropping a second question? Why or why not?
3. What is the Cronbach's alpha score for the "similarity" dimension? Can the scale be improved by deleting a question? If so, which question? Based on this initial printout, what would be the Cronbach's alpha if the item is deleted?
4. What is the Cronbach's alpha score for the "liking" dimension? Can the scale be improved by deleting a question? If so, which question? Based on this initial printout, what would be the Cronbach's alpha if the item is deleted? Run a new Cronbach's alpha with the item deleted. What is the new Cronbach's alpha score?

Summary

Objective 1: Discuss the concept of attitude measurement.

Measuring consumer attitudes that influence purchase decisions is challenging because attitude is not visible and only exists in the minds of consumers. Attitude consists of three components: cognitive, affective, and behavioral. The cognitive component represents the belief and knowledge part of attitude. The affective component of attitude is the feelings and emotions. The behavioral component of attitude is the action or intentions aspect. Because attitude consists of multiple dimensions, is abstract, and in the minds of consumers, researchers typically develop multi-item scales to measure it.

Objective 2: Explain the concept of using scales for attitude measurement.

Scaling is the process of assigning numerical values or properties to subjective or abstract concepts. Scales can be unidimensional or multidimensional. Unidimensional scales measure only one attribute or concept, such as an overall attitude towards an advertisement. Multidimensional scales are designed to measure multiple dimensions or facets of a concept, idea, or attitude. Developing good scales is important if a concept is going to be measured with any degree of precision. Scales should be relatively easy for respondents to understand, making it advisable to use language that is used by respondents. Scale items should be developed that produce a wide range of responses yet limit response bias. Last, scales need to be valid and reliable. Researchers can use scales that have already been established by prior researchers and that have been validated through proper research methods. Scales can be divided into two primary categories: comparative scales and non-comparative scales.

Objective 3: Identify and describe the various comparative scales.

With comparative scales, respondents are asked to evaluate or rate a brand, product, object, concept, or person relative to other brands, products, objects, concepts, or individuals or to an ideal item. Typical comparative scales include rank-order, Q-sort, paired comparison, and constant sum. Rank-order scales involve respondents comparing two or more objects, concepts, or persons in some type of sequential order. They are relatively easy for respondents and tend to mimic reality, though researchers encounter many disadvantages with this type of scale. Q-sorting has respondents rank a set of objects into a prespecified number of categories. Q-sorting works well for a large number of items. With a paired comparison scale, respondents are asked to choose one of two items based on some criteria specified by the researcher. The number of comparisons grows quickly since all possible pairs must be evaluated. The constant sum scale has respondents allocating points (often 100) among various alternatives based on some prespecified criteria.

Objective 4: Identify and describe the various non-comparative scales.

Non-comparative scales involve respondents making judgments about a brand, product, object, concept, or person without reference to another or ideal item. Common non-comparative scales are graphical rating, itemized rating, and Net Promoter Score. Graphical rating scales allow respondents to place a response anywhere on a continuum. It may or may not have numbers. With itemized rating scales, respondents choose from a set of alternatives. The Net Promoter Score is widely used, though it is subject to misuse and has multiple disadvantages. Multi-item measures of customer loyalty are often a better choice.

Objective 5: Identify and describe scales that can be either comparative or non-comparative.

The semantic differential and Likert scales can be either comparative or non-comparative depending upon how the question is worded. Semantic differential scales involve a finite number of choices anchored by bipolar words or phrases. Semantic differential scales are easy for respondents to understand. The challenge, however, is choosing words or phrases that are opposites. Likert scales are commonly used in marketing and involve respondents indicating the degree to which they agree or disagree with statements. Likert scales are easy to understand and relatively easy to construct.

Objective 6: Discuss the considerations involved in selecting marketing scales.

Choosing the best scale for a marketing study requires an understanding of the research objective, target market, information needs, mode of administration, and data analysis process. When it comes to actually creating the marketing scale, researchers need to consider the number of category responses, balanced versus unbalanced scales, no opinion and don't know options, forced versus non-forced choices, and the type of category description. Scales can have as few as two choices and as many as 10, or even more. However, typically marketers use five-point to seven-point scales. A balanced scale will have the same number of positive choices as negative, while an unbalanced scale will be weighted in one direction. Researchers have to decide if they want to include a "no opinion" or "don't know" option. Allowing respondents to choose this option may encourage them to select it rather than state a view. Using an even number of categories forces individuals to either the negative or positive side since no neutral position exists. The last consideration is whether to use verbal descriptors for every category, verbal descriptors at the anchor points only, and/or numeric descriptors for categories. The choice made can influence respondents' answers.

Objective 7: Explain ways researchers can ensure the reliability and validity of scales.
In using scales, researchers have three options: use a scale that has already been developed, adapt a scale that has already been developed, or create a new scale. With the last two options, it is important to ensure reliability and validity of the scale. One method of doing this is through a correlation analysis. Items that have a high correlation are measuring the same construct and therefore fit together in a scale. Another option is a factor analysis. This procedure will examine data to determine underlying constructs by reducing a large number of items into smaller subsets of factors. Items that are related will be placed together within the same factor.

Key Terms

anchor contraction effect (ACE), p. 348
attitudes, p. 324
balanced scale, p. 343
buzz score, p. 350
comparative scale, p. 326
constant sum scale, p. 332
correlation, p. 346
factor analysis, p. 348
graphical rating scale, p. 333
halo effect, p. 339
itemized rating scale, p. 335
likert scale, p. 340
multidimensional scale, p. 325
Net Promoter Score, p. 336
non-comparative scale, p. 326
paired comparison scale, p. 330
Q-sort, p. 329
scaling, p. 325
semantic differential scale, p. 338
unbalanced scale, p. 343
unidimensional scale, p. 325

Critical Thinking Exercises

1. Suppose you work for a firm that sells products to other businesses over the Internet as well as through an external sales force. What types of attitudes might be important to assess if you surveyed your customers? Identify at least five separate attitudes that would be relevant to your firm.
2. Using the five attitude constructs you developed in response to Question 1, identify whether each attitude would likely be unidimensional or multidimensional. If multidimensional, what dimensions might be part of the overall attitude? Think carefully about the attitude in question as you do so, and justify your recommendations.
3. Critique the following scale in terms of the characteristics of a good scale that were discussed in the chapter. Make certain that you evaluate both the scale item and its response categories. Is a unidimensional scale appropriate to assess the beauty salon? Why or why not? Would a Net Promoter Score scale be a better choice? Why or why not?

> **Please rate Debbie's Beauty Salon using the following scale:**
> Outstanding Excellent Very Good Good Fair Poor The Worst

4. Compare and contrast rank-order scales with itemized rating scales. What are the advantages and disadvantages of each type of scale relative to one another?
5. Using examples other than those described in the text, identify two specific research scenarios in which a Q-sort could be used. Explain what objects would be sorted and what labels would be assigned to each category. How could the results of the research be used by marketers? Should respondents be allowed to select as many items for each category as they want? Why or why not?
6. You have been asked to develop a scale that assesses the relative importance of factors that influence the purchase of a smartphone. Begin by listing the product attributes or other factors that you believe could be influential. If the choice was between a ranking scale, paired comparison scale, or constant sum scale, which would you use and why? If the choice was between an itemized rating scale, Likert scale, or semantic differential scale, which would you use and why? Develop the scale type you ultimately would select given all possibilities, and defend your recommendation.
7. A sample of 200 individuals completed a series of paired comparison statements to assess preference for four national fast-food chain restaurants specializing in hamburgers. Interpret the results shown below and present them in a table, using percentages. Then create a graph with the percentages. The number of individuals selecting each restaurant for a paired comparison is shown in parentheses.

(160) Sonic	(40) McDonald's
(84) Wendy's	(116) McDonald's
(94) Sonic	(106) Burger King
(78) McDonald's	(122) Burger King

(134) Sonic	(66) Wendy's
(92) Burger King	(108) McDonald's

8. If a key research objective sought to develop brand image profiles for a local bank and a key competitor, what type of scale should be used? Why? Create a multi-item scale that measures a bank's brand image. Defend the scale category choices you make in terms of number of categories, balanced versus unbalanced, no opinion and don't know options, forced versus non-forced choices, and type of category description.
9. Create a Likert or itemized rating scale to determine student attitudes toward the university bookstore or cafeteria. Defend the scale category choices you made in terms of number of categories, balanced versus unbalanced, no opinion and don't know options, forced versus non-forced choices, and type of category description.
10. Given the relative advantages and disadvantages associated with providing a "don't know" response option, would you recommend its inclusion in a question which asks people who live within a given zip code to rate the effectiveness of the local school board? Why or why not?

Lakeside Grill

(Comprehensive Student Case)

Rather than develop their own questions to measure the quality of service at the Lakeside Grill, the student group decided to see if there was a scale that had already been established. The students were ecstatic when Brooke found a scale called SERVQUAL, which was developed by A. Parasuraman, Valarie A. Zeithaml, and Lenard L. Berry.[32] After examining the scale, the team chose 12 questions they thought would be good measures of service at the Lakeside Grill. The scales measured empathy, reliability, and tangibles. *Empathy* is the degree to which employees give attention to customers and understand their needs; *reliability* measures the degree to which the Lakeside Grill is responsible and can be depended on to perform as promised; and the *tangible* aspect relates to the degree to which the facilities and employees are visually appealing. The questions are listed in **Figure 10.33.**

The marketing team decided to use students at their university to test the three scales. After the pretest data were collected, the students used SPSS to run Cronbach's alpha tests. Complete results are located at www.clowjames.net/students.html in the PDF file Chapter 10 Lakeside Grill Output. The raw data is entitled Chapter 10 Lakeside Grill Data. The empathy scale had an initial Cronbach's alpha score of 0.743. Dropping the fourth question that dealt with convenient hours improved the Cronbach's alpha score to .806. The initial Cronbach's alpha score for the tangible scale was .868. The initial score for the reliability scale was .765. The score could not be improved by dropping any questions. So the group decided to keep all of the questions in that scale.

1. Employees of Lakeside Grill give you individual attention. (E1)
2. Lakeside Grill's facility is visually appealing. (T1)
3. Lakeside Grill gets your order right the first time. (R1)
4. Employees of Lakeside Grill understand your specific needs. (E2)
5. Lakeside Grill insists on error-free customer service. (R2)
6. Lakeside Grill's employees are well dressed and appear neat. (T2)
7. Lakeside Grill has employees who give you personal attention. (E3)
8. Tables and place settings are visually appealing at Lakeside Grill. (T3)
9. Lakeside Grill has convenient hours for all of its customers. (E4)
10. When Lakeside Grill promises to have food ready by a certain time, it does so. (R3)
11. The exterior appearance of Lakeside Grill is attractive and inviting. (T4)
12. When you have a problem, Lakeside Grill shows an interest in correcting it. (R4)

Scales ⟶ Empathy (E)
Reliability (R)
Tangibles (T)

FIGURE 10.33 Lakeside Grill Pretest Questions

Critique Questions:

1. Was the decision to use students to pretest the questions dealing with service quality a good decision? Why or why not?
2. How would you evaluate the Cronbach's alpha scores for each of the three scales? Would you agree with the final decision to drop the question about convenient hours? Why or why not?
3. What are the advantages and disadvantages of using these scales on the group's survey of Lakeside Grill versus creating their own questions?

Notes

1. Doug Berdie, "Advice from a Veteran Researcher—40 Years, 40 Lessons Learned," *Quirk's Media* (February 2017), https://www.quirks.com/articles/advice-from-a-veteran-researcher.
2. Trent Buskirk, "Are Sliders too Slick for Surveys?" *Quirk's Media* (June 2016), https://www.quirks.com/articles/are-sliders-too-slick-for-surveys.
3. Kristen Miles, "4 Tips for Incorporating Emojis and GIFs in Online Surveys," *Quirks Media* (December 4, 2017), https://www.quirks.com/articles/4-tips-for-incorporating-emojis-and-gifs-in-online-surveys.
4. F. F. Reichheld, "The One Number You Need to Grow," *Harvard Business Review* 81, no. 6 (2003): 46–54.
5. This section is based on Jerry Thomas, "Why NPS Is Not the Best Measure of Success," *Quirk's Media* (March 2015), https://www.quirks.com/articles/why-nps-is-not-the-best-measurement-of-success; Dennis Gonier and John Goodman, "Why You Should Be Careful with the Net Promoter Score," *Quirk's Media* (October 2011), https://www.quirks.com/articles/why-you-should-be-careful-with-the-net-promoter-score; Bob Hayes, "The Net Promoter Score Debate and the Meaning of Customer Loyalty," *Quirk's Media* (October 2008), https://www.quirks.com/articles/the-net-promoter-score-debate-and-the-meaning-of-customer-loyalty.
6. This section is based on Jerry Thomas, "Why NPS Is Not the Best Measure of Success," *Quirk's Media* (March 2015), https://www.quirks.com/articles/why-nps-is-not-the-best-measurement-of-success; Dennis Gonier and John Goodman, "Why You Should Be Careful with the Net Promoter Score," *Quirk's Media* (October 2011), https://www.quirks.com/articles/why-you-should-be-careful-with-the-net-promoter-score; Bob Hayes, "The Net Promoter Score Debate and the Meaning of Customer Loyalty," *Quirk's Media* (October 2008), https://www.quirks.com/articles/the-net-promoter-score-debate-and-the-meaning-of-customer-loyalty.
7. This section is based on Dave Fish, "Are You Misusing (or Misinterpreting) NPS Results?" *Quirk's Media* (December 11, 2017), https://www.quirks.com/articles/are-you-misusing-or-misinterpreting-nps-results; and Douglas Pruden and Terry Vavra, "7 NPS Boosters We Hope You Never Use," *Quirk's Media* (March 7, 2017), https://www.quirks.com/articles/7-nps-boosters-we-hope-you-never-use.
8. Bob Hayes, "The Net Promoter Score Debate and the Meaning of Customer Loyalty," *Quirk's Media* (October 2008), https://www.quirks.com/articles/the-net-promoter-score-debate-and-the-meaning-of-customer-loyalty.
9. William A. Mindak, "Fitting the Semantic Differential to the Marketing Problem," *Journal of Marketing* 25, no. 4 (1961): 28–33.
10. Hershey H. Friedman, Linda Weiser Friedman, and Beth Gluck, "The Effects of Scale-Checking Styles on Responses to a Semantic Differential Scale," *Journal of the Market Research Society* 30, no. 4 (1988): 477–481.
11. John J. Ray, "Reviving the Problem of Acquiescent Response Bias," *Journal of Social Psychology* 121, no. 3 (1983): 81–96.
12. Aimee L. Drolet and Donald G. Morrison, "Do We Really Need Multiple-Item Measurements in Service Research?" *Journal of Service Research* 3, no. 2 (2001): 196–204; Jum C. Numally, *Psychometric Theory* (New York: McGraw-Hill, 1978).
13. Scott D. Swain, Danny Weathers, and Ronald W. Niedrich, "Assessing Three Sources of Misresponse to Reversed Likert Items," *Journal of Marketing Research* 45, no. 1 (2008): 116–131.
14. J. Dawes, "Do Data Characteristics Change According to the Number of Points Used? An Experiment Using 5-Point, 7-Point, and 10-Point Scales," *International Journal of Market Research* 50, no. 1 (2008): 61–77.
15. A. W. Bendig, "The Reliability of Self-Ratings as a Function of the Amount of Verbal Anchoring and the Number of Categories on the Scale," *Journal of Applied Psychology* 37 (1953): 38–41.
16. Ibid.
17. Eli P. Cox, "The Optimal Number of Response Alternatives for a Scale: A Review," *Journal of Marketing Research* 17 (1980): 407–422.
18. Joe Hopper, "When 'Not Sure' Is a Survey Option," *Quirk's Media* (June 20, 2016), https://www.quirks.com/articles/when-not-sure-is-a-survey-option.
19. Ibid.
20. Annie Pettit, "Want to Write a Better Survey? Respect and Account for Human Bias," *Quirk's Media* (June 25, 2018), https://www.quirks.com/articles/want-to-write-a-better-survey-respect-and-account-for-human-bias.

21. T. Amoo and H. H. Friedman, "Do Numeric Values Influence Subjects' Responses to Rating Scales?" *Journal of International Marketing Research* 26 (1984): 41–46; C. Armitage and C. Deeprose, "Changing Student Evaluations by Means of the Numeric Values of Rating Scales," *Psychology of Learning and Teaching* 3, no. 9 (2004): 122–125; N. Schwartz, B. Knäuper, H.-J. Hippler, E. Noelle-Neumann, and L. Clark, "Rating Scales: Numeric Values May Change the Meanings of Scale Labels," *Public Opinion Quarterly* 55 (1991): 570–582.
22. Doug Berdie, "Advice from a Veteran Researcher—40 Years, 40 Lessons Learned," *Quirk's Media* (February 2017), https://www.quirks.com/articles/advice-from-a-veteran-researcher.
23. Ibid.
24. Gilbert A. Churchill, "A Paradigm for Developing Better Measures of Marketing Constructs," *Journal of Marketing Research* 16, no. 1 (1979): 64–73; Robert F. DeVellis, *Scale Development: Theory and Applications* (Newbury Park, CA: Sage Publications, 1991); David W. Gerbing and James C. Anderson, "An Updated Paradigm for Scale Development Incorporating Unidimensionality and Its Assessment," *Journal of Marketing Research* 25, no. 5 (1988): 186–192.
25. Bart De Langhe, Stefano Puntoni, Daniel Fernandes, and Stijn M. J. Van Osselaer, "The Anchor Contraction Effect in International Marketing Research," *Journal of Marketing Research* 48, no. 2 (2011): 366–380.
26. Peter B. Smith, et al. "Individual and Culture-Level Components of Survey Response Styles: A Multi-Level Analytical Using Cultural Models of Selfhood," *International Journal of Psychology* 31, no. 6 (2016): 453–463.
27. Kristin Cavallaro, "Data Use: Are Global Scales as Easy as 1-2-3 or A-B-C?" *Quirks Marketing Research Review* (January 2011): 18, 20–22.
28. Keith Chrzan and Joey Michaud, "Response Scales for Customer Satisfaction Research," *Quirk's Marketing Research Review* (October 2004): 50.
29. Joseph F. Rocereto, Marina Puzakova, Rolph E. Anderson, and Hyokjin Kwak, "The Role of Response Formats on Extreme Response Style: A Case of Likert-Type vs. Semantic Differential Scales," *Advances in International Marketing* 10, no. 22 (2011): 53–71.
30. Patrick Elms, "Using Decision Criteria Anchors to Measure Importance Among Hispanics," *Quirk's Marketing Research Review* (April 2001); Jeffrey N. Savitz, "Reconciling Hispanic Product Evaluation Ratings," *Quirk's Marketing Research Review* (December 2011): 26, 28–32.
31. Gilbert A. Churchill, "A Paradigm for Developing Better Measures of Marketing Constructs," *Journal of Marketing Research* 16, no. 1 (1979): 64–73.
32. A. Parasuraman, Valarie A. Zeithaml, and Lenard L. Berry, "SERVQUAL: A Multiple-Item Scale for Measuring Consumer Perceptions of Service Quality," *Journal of Retailing* 64, no. 1 (1988): 12–40.

Questionnaire Design

CHAPTER 11

Source: GaudiLab/Shutterstock.

Chapter Outline

Learning Objectives

After studying this chapter, you should be able to:

- Outline the questionnaire design process.
- Discuss the two primary question formats that can be used in questionnaire design.
- Elaborate on the three different types of closed-ended questions.
- Identify and describe the categories of questions used in questionnaires.
- Discuss the issues relating to the phrasing of questions.
- Identify and explain the contents of the survey invitation and each section of a questionnaire.
- Describe the negative consequences of long questionnaires.
- Discuss gamification and its use in online surveys.
- Discuss the steps in evaluating a questionnaire.

11.1 Chapter Overview

For many, designing a questionnaire is the fun part of marketing research. Creating a good questionnaire produces data that can be used for making smart business decisions. Consider the data obtained from a survey sent to customers and marketing managers shown in Figure 11.1. The data compares consumer's perceptions of ease of use for different customer service communication methods to the businesses' perceptions of ease of use for these same communication channels. The differences are astounding, with businesses overestimating their perceptions of how easy it is for consumers to use every channel of communication. For example, telephone's ease of use was overestimated by 27 percent when compared to how customers actually felt. Disturbingly, Figure 11.1 shows that none of these communications channels were rated as "easy" or "very easy" by more than 50 percent of the 1,000 consumer respondents. Even more interesting are comparisons to past surveys from 2015. Preferences for both web-self service and online chat increased over 20 percent, while the preference for telephone resolution of customer service problems dropped from 49 percent to 43 percent. Why? Sixty-nine percent of respondents indicated difficulty navigating automated systems, and the same percentage indicated long wait times to reach a human agent. Scripted responses were also problematic for 58 percent of respondents who indicated they did not receive a solution personalized to their situation. Still, consumers view the phone and online chat as offering the fastest speed of response, as problems were resolved within an hour in 69 percent and 66 percent of the time respectively. Email was the least speedy response, solving customer service issues in a day or more 81 percent of the time. How can marketers use these and other results from the Northridge Group's survey? Customers want shorter wait times as a top priority, closely followed by better trained customer service representatives. Nearly equally important were 24/7 customer service and easier to navigate phone menus. Redesigning phone menus to make them easier to navigate would also help lessen customer frustration. Businesses' top priority, personalized customer experience, was only important to 32 percent of the consumers surveyed, and ranked fifth in their priority list.[1] Surveys can be very helpful in understanding what consumers like and dislike, and helping management to overcome misperceptions that may be steering the company down the wrong path.

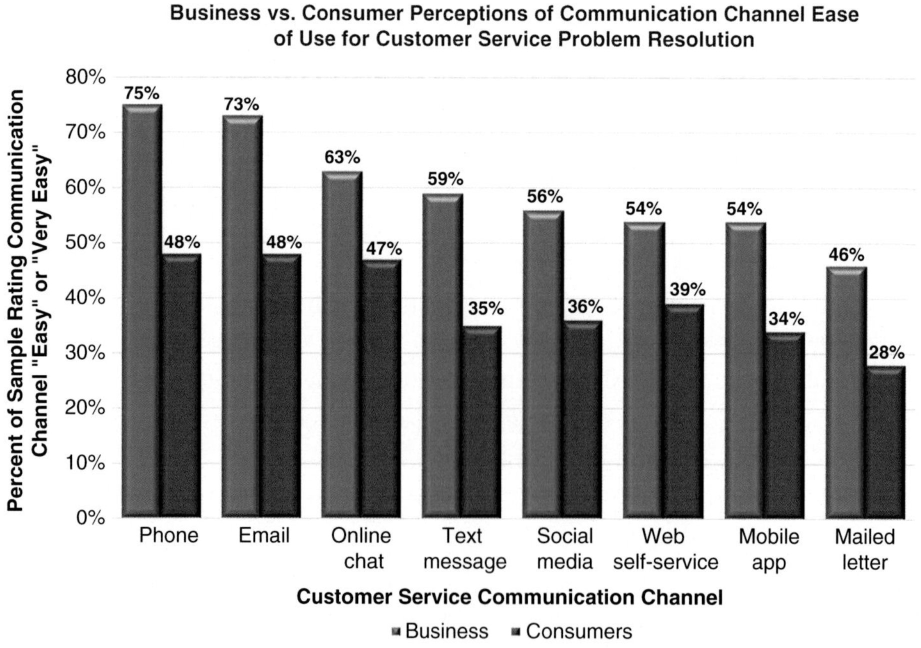

FIGURE 11.1 A Graph Comparing Business and Consumer Perceptions
Source: Adapted from "State of Customer Service Experience, 2018," *The Northridge Group*, 2019, p. 5.

Some would argue that questionnaire design is really an art form—some people are good at it, others are not. This chapter covers some basic principles that, if followed, will increase the probability that useful information will result from a questionnaire. The chapter begins with a discussion of the questionnaire design process. Next will be an examination of the primary question types that are used in survey questionnaires and the pros and cons of each type. Phrasing of questions is important, so a discussion of some common pitfalls is presented. The chapter concludes with material on how a questionnaire is composed, how it is evaluated, and a new format of questionnaire design-gamification.

11.2 The Questionnaire Design Process

LEARNING OBJECTIVE 10.1
Outline the questionnaire design process.

Survey research relies on some type of questionnaire to solicit information from a sample or census of respondents. A **questionnaire** is a set of questions used to generate data that meets specific research and survey objectives. The quality of the data obtained is directly related to the quality of the questionnaire designed. While there is not a perfect format for a questionnaire, there are principles that can enhance the quality of a questionnaire, thereby increasing the usefulness of the data generated. Questionnaires standardize the data collection process and ensure all respondents are asked the same questions in the same manner. This process is especially important for intercept surveys, telephone surveys and other situations where the interviewer is reading the question to the respondent.

Questionnaire a set of questions or items used to generate data that meets specific research and survey objectives.

Figure 11.2 outlines the steps in developing a questionnaire. The process begins with the research questions or objectives. Quite often the research objectives are provided by upper management or a client and given to the marketing department or marketing research firm. It is important to understand the research objectives before designing a questionnaire. It is also imperative to limit the research objectives to a manageable number to ensure that questionnaire length does not negatively affect the response rate. Finally, discussing the decisions that will result from the data obtained through the questionnaire will increase the chances the right data are collected.

The first step in the questionnaire design process is to determine the survey objectives. These **survey objectives** are derived from the research questions or objectives and clearly spell out the data that the questionnaire should generate. The survey objectives guide the process of selecting the types of questions asked and the way questions are worded.

Survey objectives objectives that are derived from the research questions or research objectives and clearly spell out the data that the questionnaire should generate.

Consider the case of a video game manufacturer that wants to prepare a new product launch for the personal computer (PC). The video game will be distributed in stores on DVD and through Amazon and other online retailers. However, there is concern within the company that limiting the new product to PC distribution only may be a mistake. Industry trends show a growing preference for online gaming via social network sites, smartphones, tablets, and consoles (such as Nintendo and Xbox). Secondary research confirms that there is cause for concern, as sales of the firm's most recently released product were lower than expected, and the PC gaming market in general is no longer growing. Some

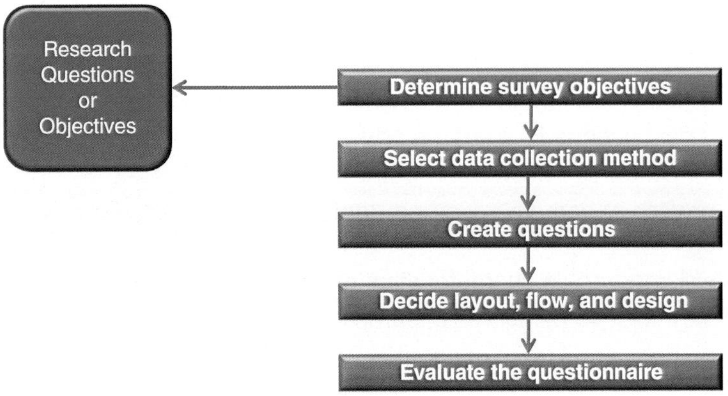

FIGURE 11.2 Questionnaire Design Process

individuals believe that this decline may be due to a pirating problem rather than a changing preference for gaming platforms. The decision management faces is whether the game should be released for the PC market only or whether it should be released in multiple platforms suitable for smartphones, tablets, consoles, and online.[2] With this background information, specific research objectives can be written. These research objectives, shown in **Figure 11.3**, highlight what the researcher wants to accomplish.

It is tempting to skip directly from the research objectives to writing survey questions. But doing so can result in incomplete information. Using research objectives as the basis for writing survey objectives ensures that the right questions are asked and that the purpose of the study is achieved. **Figure 11.4** identifies survey objectives for each of the research objectives. Notice that for the first research objective, three survey objectives have been written. In order to determine the preference of gamers for the various platforms, it is necessary to 1) solicit the preference for each of the various gaming platforms, 2) determine the usage level of each gaming platform, and 3) identify which gaming platforms gamers most prefer.

Once the survey objectives have been written, the second step in the questionnaire design process is to decide on the data collection methodology. How questionnaires are

- Determine the preference of gamers for the various gaming platforms (social networks, gaming consoles, PCs, smartphones, and tablets).
- Determine if gamers prefer online games to PC-based games and if there is a preference for games that can be played across multiple platforms.
- Investigate gamers' attitude toward in-game marketing efforts.
- Determine the characteristics of successful in-game promotions.
- Develop profiles of gamers based on demographic, lifestyle, and behavioral traits.

FIGURE 11.3 Sample Research Objectives

1. Determine the preference of gamers for the various gaming platforms (social networks, gaming consoles, PCs, smartphones, and tablets).
   - Solicit the preference for each of the various gaming platforms.
   - Determine the usage level of each gaming platform.
   - Identify which gaming platforms gamers most prefer.
2. Determine if gamers prefer online games to PC-based games and if there is a preference for games that can be played across multiple platforms.
   - Determine if gamers prefer online games to PC-based games.
   - Ascertain if gamers want games that can be played across multiple platforms.
   - If so, identify which platforms are the most desirable.
3. Determine gamers' attitude toward in-gaming marketing efforts.
   - Measure attitudes toward in-game advertisements.
   - Measure attitudes toward in-game promotions.
4. Determine the characteristics of successful in-game promotions.
   - Identify past actions for in-game advertising and promotions.
   - Solicit intention-to-action for in-game advertising promotions.
5. Develop profiles of gamers based on demographic, lifestyle, and behavioral traits of gamers.
   - Identify demographic characteristics of sample.
   - Solicit key lifestyle measures of sample.
   - Measure behavioral traits of sample.

FIGURE 11.4 Sample Survey Objectives

designed varies based on how data are collected. Questions for a telephone survey will be written differently from questions for an online survey, a mobile survey, or a questionnaire that is handed to a respondent to answer. At times researchers may decide on the data collection method and survey objectives simultaneously because the data collection methodology might affect the questionnaire design. For instance, if an online questionnaire is used, respondents can be shown a product, advertisement, or other material to evaluate. These visuals would not be possible with a telephone survey.

Once the data collection method is determined, researchers are ready to create the survey that will be used to measure the survey objectives. Key considerations include determining the question format, the types of scales to use, and the best way to phrase questions to minimize measurement error.

11.3 Question Format

LEARNING OBJECTIVE 11.2
Discuss the two primary question formats that can be used in questionnaire design.

The primary decision researchers make in terms of question format is whether to use open-ended questions, closed-ended questions, or a combination of both. Recall that Chapter 9 discussed the various levels of measurement: nominal, ordinal, interval, and ratio. The general rule of thumb in deciding question format is that the higher-order scales are better than the lower-order scales because they provide more valuable data and higher forms of data analysis. Thus, if an interval scale can be used, it is better than using an ordinal or nominal scale.

However, two cautions must be mentioned. First, while ratio-level data might meet the survey objective, a lower-order scale might capture the data in a way that is more useable by the decision maker and could even be more accurate. For example, respondents in a survey about Super Bowl ads were asked what they thought a 30-second television ad cost. A blank was provided for their response. The question yielded ratio data with answers ranging from $10,000 to $50 million. What to do with the data is problematic because of these extreme answers. Neither extreme is close to the cost of $5.1 million. It might have been better to use an ordinal scale that had mutually exclusive categories, and instruct the respondent to choose a category from the list.

Source: WAYHOME studio/Shutterstock.

Respondents aren't always able to accurately recall answers to some questions requesting ratio-level data. Or, they may not be willing to provide ratio-level information, especially in relationship to sensitive questions such as age and income.

A second caution deals with a respondent's ability and willingness to provide information, especially in relationship to sensitive questions. Requesting the specific dollar amount of a person's household income is very likely to result in a large number of non-responses. Using an ordinal scale increases the probability a respondent will respond. Also, there may be an inability to accurately recall information, such as when a person is asked how many soft drinks were purchased during the last 30 days. The respondent might not really know if it was 20 or 22 or 27 or 30. A category that says 20 to 30 could be just as accurate and result in more people answering the question. It is best to limit questions requesting ratio data—actual amounts—to instances in which knowing the specific number is of critical importance to accomplishing the survey objectives.

Chapter 10 provided information about the various scales, including rank-order, constant sum, Likert, and semantic differential. In examining the survey objective, a researcher must decide which type of scale would best capture the data needed. In almost all cases, more than one type of scale can be used. Consider the survey objective in Figure 11.4 that states "solicit the preference for the various gaming platforms." This objective could be measured using a semantic differential scale or a Likert scale. Although the data quality may not be as strong, graphical rating or itemized rating scales could also be used. In deciding the appropriate scale, the researcher will want to consider the target audience. Which scale would be the easiest for the respondent to use and yet obtain the most accurate responses? The researcher will also want to consider the data collection method. For instance, a graphical rating scale would not be possible with a telephone survey, while a semantic differential would be difficult and time consuming to administer over the phone. The Likert scale might be easier for respondents to answer in a phone survey and also easier for the interviewer to administer.

11.3a Open-Ended Questions

Open-ended questions questions that allow a respondent to answer in his or her own words.

Open-ended questions allow a respondent to answer a question in his or her own words. It can be simple questions, such as "What is your favorite brand of shampoo?" or "In a typical month how many times do you go out to a nightclub?" both of which would be followed by an answer blank. Open-ended questions of this type are also valuable in soliciting recall information when researchers do not want to bias an answer by listing alternative choices. Open-ended questions are used in survey pretests to help identify possible response category options when the researcher is unable to anticipate the possible range of responses.

However, open-ended questions can also be phrased in a more challenging and thought-provoking fashion, and as such, require detailed answers. Examples include, "Describe the decision-making process you used to purchase your vehicle" or "How do you feel about advertising to children?" Questions of this nature are far less suited to survey research than are those that simply require the respondent to input a number or to list one or more brand names.

Open-ended questions requiring detailed answers are best used for exploratory research when researchers want a better understanding of a problem or are seeking information to develop hypotheses. Focus groups or in-depth interviews are the natural choice for detailed questions. Regrettably, when incorporated into questionnaires, such questions are rarely successful in practice.[3] **Figure 11.5** identifies the major advantages and disadvantages of open-ended questions.

11.3b Advantages of Open-Ended Questions

A major advantage of open-ended questions is that the answers are in the respondents' own words. They use their own language and terms, which may be different from terminology used by the marketing researcher. Open-ended answers can provide researchers with information about the thought processes behind decisions and attitudes and often provide new or different insights. Sometimes researchers go into a research study with biased views, or feel they already know what people think and want based on past research studies. Open-ended questions might yield new information that taps into attitudinal

- Advantages
  - Answer is in respondent's own words
  - Can provide new or different insight
  - Can provide additional alternatives
  - Allows for probing
- Disadvantages
  - Can be difficult to interpret answer
  - Editing and coding can be challenging
  - Potential for interviewer bias
  - Answer may be shallow and insufficient
  - Lower response rates

FIGURE 11.5 Advantages and Disadvantages of Open-Ended Questions

changes among the target market, or provide a new way of looking at a situation that researchers never considered.

Open-ended questions can provide additional alternatives. For instance, in looking at factors consumers might consider in the purchase of resort vacation packages, an open-ended question could produce additional alternatives researchers had not identified. These can then be used later in a closed-ended question if desired. Finally, open-ended questions allow the researcher to probe and understand why people respond in a certain fashion. For example, a closed-ended question on a survey might ask respondents to identify their preferred retail store for purchasing formal wear. An open-ended question might then ask the individuals to explain why that store is their favorite. The responses could be helpful in identifying the store's competitive advantage, as perceived by customers.

11.3c Disadvantages of Open-Ended Questions

Open-ended questions have a number of disadvantages. Major problems involve the difficulty researchers have interpreting, editing, and coding answers. Suppose a survey placed in consumers' shopping bags asked, "How was your shopping experience at the {STORE} today?" Three responses may be:

"It was a hassle."

"It was slightly better than last week."

"It would have been great if my son hadn't gotten sick."

The first response is negative, but non-specific. There is no additional information to help understand what the respondent meant by "hassle." The second statement is also problematic to interpret and code. The researcher would need to understand the respondent's frame of reference. If last's week shopping experience was terrible, "slightly better" is by no means a positive endorsement. Last, the final statement also presents difficulties because the response is phrased in a conditional fashion. It would be incorrect to label this as a positive shopping experience as the "would have . . . if" implies that the shopping experience, in fact, was *not* great, though the circumstances which made for a negative experience were external to anything under the control of the store.

While some open-ended responses can be analyzed by text analytics software as discussed in Chapter 5, not all responses can be accurately processed by machines. The human interaction required during the process of reading, interpreting and coding responses manually normally involves a considerable amount of time, which makes the process expensive. The time, expense, and questionable value of the resulting data provide strong incentives to avoid open-ended questions of an exploratory nature in most survey research.[4]

Open-ended questions pose the risk of interviewer bias. Although interviewers are trained to reduce the chances of interview bias from occurring, the possibility increases when open-ended questions are used. If the interviewer is recording answers given verbally from a respondent, the way the answers are recorded is important. Ideally, answers should be recorded verbatim. However, often the respondent talks too fast and says too much for the researcher to record every word. Therefore, the general idea of what is said is recorded. But in so doing, the response may be biased by the perceptions of the interviewer and what he or she perceived the respondent said or meant by the response. One solution is to obtain written permission from the subject to audio record answers that can later be transcribed by software.

A second way interviewer bias occurs is with the use of probing questions. While probing questions are normally written in advance, there are situations where the researcher must ask respondents to clarify a response, or probe deeper to ensure the response is understood correctly. The manner and tone of voice used can influence the response given in a manner similar to that which occurs when the original questions are asked verbally by the researcher.

The next disadvantage occurs when an interviewer is not present. As demonstrated earlier by the retail shopping survey situation, the answer to open-ended questions in a self-administered survey may be shallow or insufficient. Without an interviewer, there is no opportunity to ask for clarification or additional information. The response may be a short one-sentence statement, when the researcher was looking for a paragraph explaining the respondent's thinking process. To minimize this problem, the researcher can provide clear instructions in the question. A phrase such as "please provide a detailed answer" can be used. Alternatively, instructions might ask that the response be "50 or more words."

Finally, many people refuse to answer open-ended questions altogether. If open-ended questions are asked at the beginning of the survey, they often negatively impact the response rate for the entire survey. Many respondents break-off from answering the survey once they see open-ended questions, so these types of questions can also negatively influence survey completion rates.

Before including open-ended questions in a survey, researchers should consider how the data will be analyzed and used. It is possible that one or more closed-ended questions can obtain the same information. However, if open-ended questions are used, interviewers must have the training, experience, and motivation to elicit high-quality data from the responses provided.[5]

11.3d Closed-Ended Questions

Closed-ended questions questions that give respondents a finite number of responses from which to choose.

The disadvantages of open-ended questions can largely be overcome by using closed-ended questions. With **closed-ended questions** respondents are given a finite number of responses from which to choose. The respondent can be asked to choose one response from the alternatives list or all of the alternatives in the list that apply. Figure 11.6 lists the advantages and disadvantages of using closed-ended questions.

11.3e Advantages of Closed-Ended Questions

Coding and entering the data into a spreadsheet is easier and more accurate for closed-ended questions because the respondent's answer is limited to response options listed by the researcher. Each question has a specific set of response choices. A question might have four response choices and so could be coded 1 through 4. If the survey is taken on a computer, tablet or mobile phone, the response is automatically entered into a spreadsheet, saving a great deal of time and preventing possible process errors.

For paper surveys, a data coder must first physically write the number associated with each survey item's answer on the survey itself, then transcribe the number into a spreadsheet. Errors can occur in one of three ways. First, the person coding the paper survey might write down the wrong number, perhaps writing "1" for a male respondent when in fact males should be coded as "2". Second, the respondent might mark his or her response in such a way that it is unclear which answer was checked. The line or X may be between answers or cover two different responses, and the coder might arbitrarily choose one or the other as the answer. Establishing rules that clearly tell the coder what to do in these cases is essential if measurement error is to be avoided. The adage, "When in doubt, throw it out" often applies. Finally, process error might occur when the individual inaccurately

- Advantages
  - Easy and accurate data coding and entry
  - Limited number of responses
  - Alternative list may help respondent recall
  - Limited interviewer bias
- Disadvantages
  - Researchers must generate alternatives
  - Respondents must select from given alternatives
  - No freedom for respondent in answering beyond choices given

FIGURE 11.6 Advantages and Disadvantages of Closed-Ended Questions

transcribes the data by entering a number different from the true answer. As mentioned in Chapter 6, frequency tables and random checks of data entry can help to identify these errors.

Another advantage is that responses to a closed-ended question can jog a respondent's memory and generate a more accurate response. For instance, with the gaming study mentioned earlier, a question might ask respondents to identify each of the platforms on which they have played games. A respondent might have forgotten she played a game at a social network site until she saw the response category in the question. Similarly, respondents might recognize brand names from a list that they would be unable to recall from memory.

Source: Andrey_Popov/Shutterstock.

Interviewer bias is greatly reduced with closed-ended questions since the respondent selects from a list of possible responses. Interview bias can occur when questions and responses are read verbally to respondents.

Interviewer bias is greatly reduced with closed-ended questions since the respondent selects from a list of possible responses. Interviewer bias can occur only when questions and responses are read verbally to respondents, and when interviewers or researchers code an "other" fill-in-the-blank response to a question. In the first situation, tone of voice and body language can influence which answer the respondent selects. In the second situation, coding of other responses should be left to the researcher, rather than assigned to the individual interviewers.

The researcher is best able to decide whether to add a new category based on the "other" response, pool all of the "other" responses into a single category called "other," or re-code the item into an existing category that matches closely. Interviewer bias can occur due to the subjective nature of interpretation. Pooling all "other" responses into a category called "other" eliminates interviewer bias in how the response is handled, and when performed consistently by a single person, recoding responses into new categories minimizes interviewer bias. Allowing interviewers to re-code the "other" response into an existing category will certainly produce a greater level of interviewer bias since it involves interpretation.

11.3f Disadvantages of Closed-Ended Questions

Closed-ended questions have three primary disadvantages. First, researchers must generate the list of alternative answers for the question. The ideal list of response categories should be mutually exclusive and categorically exhaustive. Recall, mutually exclusive means that each response category is uniquely different from the other response categories and that no overlap occurs between any of the categories. If responses are categorically (or collectively) exhaustive, the categories listed for a question contain all possible answers. Having mutually exclusive response categories is easier to achieve than is having a list that is categorically exhaustive.

Suppose a researcher has the question, "What brand of jeans did you last purchase?" followed by a series of brands. While the list of brand names would be mutually exclusive, it would be virtually impossible to list all of the various brands. If such a list could be created, it would be so long that respondents would be challenged to find the brand they last purchased, and seeing a large number of brands might even cloud their memory in terms of which brand was really bought. Researchers can overcome this problem by listing the major brands followed by an "other" category with a fill-in-the-blank for brands not shown on the list.

A second disadvantage is that respondents are restricted to the answers given, especially if an "other" category is not available. In such cases respondents have to either choose the item from the list that is most closely associated with their response or not answer the question at all. Either response produces inaccurate data, especially when online surveys force an answer before allowing respondents to proceed to the next question. This disadvantage can be particularly troublesome when researchers do not have a "don't know" option for questions related to topics that respondents legitimately might know nothing about. Forcing them to select an answer introduces substantial error into the data by mixing the opinions of those who truly are knowledgeable, with those who should not even be answering the question. As an example, consider an online survey that contains a typical brand image question that lists a series of brand in rows, and a series of attributes or perceptual factors in columns. Respondents are told to check all of the column factors they associate with each brand. But what if they don't associate any factors with a brand? Without a "don't know" option, an online survey that forces respondents to select a factor before allowing them to move on in the survey increases error in the data.

Alternately, suppose the question, "What is the most important factor in purchasing textbooks for your classes?" was asked as a closed-ended question. Perhaps the primary factor for a particular student is whether her friend is in the same class. If she is, they then purchase a book and share it. If that response is not available from the list provided, the student will either have to choose one of the other answers or just leave it blank. Thus it might also be appropriate to have a "None of the Above" or similar response in certain circumstances. The last drawback of closed-ended questions is that respondents have no freedom in how they answer the question. They must select from the list of alternatives. The only way to offer some variation is to provide an "Other" option with a fill-in-the-blank response where they can enter their answer.

11.4 Types of Closed-Ended Questions

LEARNING OBJECTIVE 11.3
Elaborate on the three different types of closed-ended questions.

Closed-ended questions can be dichotomous, multiple-choice, or scaled-response. The researcher should choose the type that best fits the survey objectives to yield the results needed and at the same time provide the highest quality data.

11.4a Dichotomous Questions

Dichotomous question closed-ended question with two options.

A **dichotomous question** is a closed-ended question with two response options. **Figure 11.7** shows four different dichotomous questions. Each has two response choices. Because each question has only two alternatives, they can be answered easily and quickly by respondents. Coding and entering the data into a spreadsheet for analysis is straightforward.

The first two questions are clear and easy to answer. The respondents are either female or male and they have either played a video game on a smartphone or they have not. But the last two questions illustrate some of the problems with dichotomous questions. The third question is clear and straightforward in terms of yes, they like playing games on their Smartphone or no, they do not. However, having respondents reply "yes" or "no" does not provide insight about intensity. The individual may be ambivalent about playing games on a smartphone. Or they may have never played a game on their smartphone, and thus have no knowledge of whether or not they like doing so. The dichotomous option does not allow for a neutral position. More importantly, some individuals might have strong positive feelings about it while others have rather weak positive feelings. The simple "yes" or "no"

1. What is your gender? ☐ Female ☐ Male

2. Have you played video games on your smartphone? ☐ Yes ☐ No

3. Do you like playing video games on your smartphone? ☐ Yes ☐ No

4. Which platform to you prefer for playing video games? ☐ Online ☐ Computer

FIGURE 11.7 Examples of Dichotomous Questions

response option does not allow respondents to indicate this intensity. The same criticism is true for the last question. Some may have only a slight preference for one of the options while someone else may feel more strongly. Scaled response questions would elicit more useful data for questions 3 and 4.

11.4b Multiple-Choice Questions

With **multiple-choice questions** individuals have multiple (three or more) answers from which to choose. **Figure 11.8** shows two possible multiple-choice questions. In the first question, individuals are to choose one of the platforms listed. The responses appear to be mutually exclusive and categorically exhaustive. A response would clearly indicate which platform the individual prefers. But it does not provide any measurement of the degree of intensity. Individuals who prefer games at online websites can differ greatly in how strongly they feel about that preference. Some might have only a slight preference over the other alternative platforms while others have a strong preference. Multiple-choice questions are often used for demographic or other classification variables, but may not be the best choice for preference.

Multiple-choice question questions with multiple (three or more) answers from which to choose.

The second question is actually a better multiple-choice question, and is often referred to as a **multiple-response question**, in which respondents are instructed to check all response options that apply. The response options are mutually exclusive and categorically exhaustive, and each response option is treated as a separate variable in the spreadsheet. Not only is the question easy for individuals to answer, the results can be quickly tabulated.

Multiple response question form of multiple choice question in which respondents are instructed to check all response options that apply.

An additional challenge faced by researchers when generating response categories is the length or number of items in the list. If the list is too long, a respondent may not take the time to look at all of the responses but just check the first one that applies. This phenomenon is known as **position bias**. Asking individuals to identify the best brand in a list of 30 brands is likely to produce position bias. So would a question that asks a respondent to check all of the reasons why they chose to do cosmetic surgery from among 15 different choices. One way to alleviate position bias is to randomize the list of responses by creating different versions of the questionnaire. This can be done easily with online surveys.

Position bias in a long list of response items individuals may not take time to look at all of the possible choices but simply check the first one that applies.

1. Of the following platforms for playing video games, which do you most prefer?

☐ Online website
☐ Social network sites
☐ Gaming console
☐ Computer
☐ Smartphone
☐ Tablet

2. Of the following gaming platforms, which ones have you used to play video games? (Check all that apply)

☐ Online website
☐ Social network sites
☐ Gaming console
☐ Computer
☐ Smartphone
☐ Tablet

FIGURE 11.8 Examples of Multiple-Choice Questions

For each of the following gaming platforms, please indicate how likely you would be to use each gaming platform, ranging from "highly unlikely" to "highly likely."

	Highly Unlikely	Unlikely	Somewhat Unlikely	Neutral	Somewhat Likely	Likely	Highly Likely
Online website	○	○	○	○	○	○	○
Social network site	○	○	○	○	○	○	○
Gaming console	○	○	○	○	○	○	○
Computer	○	○	○	○	○	○	○
Smartphone or tablet	○	○	○	○	○	○	○

FIGURE 11.9 Example of a Scaled-Response Question

It is more difficult with paper surveys since multiple copies would have to be printed. Mobile surveys present a special challenge, as questions and response options should be short enough to fit on a screen with minimal vertical scrolling. Horizontal scrolling should be avoided at all costs.[6]

11.4c Scaled-Response Questions

Scaled-response question questions that allow respondents to indicate a level or degree of intensity.

To capture the intensity of response, researchers will often use **scaled-response questions**. Figure 11.9 is an itemized rating scale assessing the likelihood of using different gaming platforms, with response categories ranging from "highly unlikely" to "highly likely." By using a seven-point scale, researchers can solicit the degree of intensity, or likelihood of usage, that each respondent has toward a particular gaming platform. In addition, the question should yield interval data that can be analyzed using more powerful statistical tests. Rather than just frequency counts, means and standard deviations can be obtained. The means can be compared across the different gaming platforms or based on other factors, such as respondents' demographics.

In terms of drawbacks, the scaled-response question takes more time for individuals to answer. It requires thought. They can't just check a box or boxes. With the question shown in Figure 11.9, individuals must think about each platform and the degree to which they are likely to use it. The answer may be clear for some of the platforms, but for others it may not be easy to decide.

The number of categories provided influences responses. If the scale in Figure 11.9 had been designed with only five categories instead of seven, respondents might have found it more difficult to decide among responses. The elimination of the "somewhat likely/somewhat unlikely" option would force respondents to choose "likely" or "unlikely" if they have even the slightest leaning in either direction. An individual might mark the "likely" category for online websites on a five point scale. The person might feel more inclined to use social network sites, but not to the degree that they are comfortable selecting the "highly likely" answer. From the researcher's perspective if both answers are marked a "likely", the researcher would assume there is equal preference for the two platforms. In reality, such may not be the case. Increasing the number of scale points from five to seven can help determine finer distinctions in attitudinal differences since it would allow the respondent in this example to choose "somewhat likely" for online websites, and "likely" for social networks.

11.4d Interaction of Device Type and Question Format

Researchers have long been concerned whether the type of device used to access a mobile or online survey impacts the quality of survey responses, or limits the usage of certain types of questions in surveys.

For example, conventional wisdom suggests that mobile surveys should not contain open-ended questions. Logically, it could be argued that it is more difficult for mobile users to type in responses on their phones considering the larger keypads available on tablets or PCs. Studies published in 2013 and 2014 found that mobile respondents provided shorter responses to open-ended questions compared to PC users. A separate study found mixed results when analyzing responses to sensitive questions.[7] Yet there is some evidence to suggest the smartphone users have become more comfortable typing on smartphones in recent years, perhaps due to auto-complete and voice-to-text typing. A study of more 1,390 Dutch research panel members found that smartphone users typed longer answers to open-ended questions than did those who answered the survey on a PC.[8] A 2018 study by Culturati Research and Consulting found similar results using a sample of 301 respondents, of whom 201 respondents were Hispanic and 100 respondents were Non-Hispanic. Another key finding was that Hispanic respondents typed more characters in response to open-ended questions than did non-Hispanics, averaging 51 characters for smartphones and 40 for PCs/tablets.[9] Although these recent studies contradict earlier findings, and seem to indicate that researchers needn't worry about the quality of responses to open-ended questions taken on mobile devices, there is another consideration. Sometimes individuals will start the survey, but quit because they feel it is too long. The percentage of individuals who start a survey but do not complete it is called the **break-off rate**. Research has consistently shown that mobile surveys are subject to higher break-off rates than other devices, and open-ended questions[10] are a known trigger for break-off behavior. If the reward is worth the risk, then a researcher may wish to include an open-ended question.

Break-off rate percentage of individuals who start a survey but do not complete it.

The majority of online survey software today automatically translates "grid" or "matrix" questions such as those shown in Figure 11.9 to multiple single screen questions when viewed on mobile devices.[11] Reformatting grid questions into consecutive single question items is necessary to avoid excessive horizontal and vertical scrolling that may cause the respondent frustration, and negatively influence completion rates. Yet this begs the question of whether or not the altered presentation format influences the response patterns differently for mobile devices, when compared to PCs and tablets. Historically, for surveys that have been optimized for mobile delivery, little to no differences have been found in survey responses by device type within demographically similar samples.[12]

Culturati's study found no differences in response patterns between smartphone and PC/tablets respondents for a series of question items with a single response scale, such as that shown in Figure 11.9. However, when respondents are told to "select all that apply" from among the response categories presented horizontally (such as brand attributes) for a list of items presented vertically (such as brands), there were differences in the response patterns based on device. These differences occurred as a result of the presentation format, as the PC/tablet respondents evaluating the brands in a large grid format selected fewer attributes per brand than did the smartphone respondents who evaluated each brand as a separate "select all that apply" question. Perhaps by presenting the brand to be evaluated as a single question, mobile respondents focused greater attention on the task at hand. To avoid potential measurement error stemming from differences in the device and corresponding presentation format, it is may be better to avoid using grids in online surveys when asking multiple response, brand evaluation questions.[13]

11.5 Questionnaire Development

In developing the questionnaire, it is helpful to think about the various categories of questions that can be used. **Figure 11.10** identifies the six most common categories used in marketing research.[14] It is not critical to have questions from each category, but the categories can serve as a guide to determining the best way to word questions. The categories can also be beneficial in ensuring questions are asked in such a way that they will provide the information management needs to make the decision.

LEARNING OBJECTIVE 11.4
Identify and describe the categories of questions used in questionnaires.

- Demographic or classification
- Knowledge
- Attitudes
- Preferences
- Intentions
- Behaviors

FIGURE 11.10 Categories of Questions Used in Questionnaire Development
Source: Based on David M. Ambrose and John R. Anstev, "Questionnaire Development: Demystifying the Process," *International Management Review*, Vol. 6, No. 1, 2010, pp. 83–90.

11.5a Demographic or Classification

Practically all questionnaires will ask for respondent demographic information, such as gender, age, income, race, and education. The respondent just checks the appropriate category. In addition, questionnaires will often contain classification-type questions that apply to a situation. It might be a question relating to the last brand of hiking boots purchased, store where they were purchased, or when they were purchased.

Demographic and classification questions are often used at the beginning of a questionnaire as screening questions. Any survey that uses automated sampling which requires respondents to enter qualifying characteristics should list the key qualifying demographic or ownership questions at the front of the survey. For instance, a question may ask if an individual has purchased an automobile within the last year. If the person has, the survey continues. If not, it is terminated since the survey deals with the car-buying process. Researchers may also want to fill certain demographic quotas, such as 300 males, 200 individuals ages 20 to 29, and so forth. When the quota of 300 males or the 200 individuals ages 20 to 29 have been reached, anyone falling into that category is terminated and not allowed to complete the questionnaire. When demographic questions do not function as screening questions, they are placed at the end of the survey.

Classification and demographic questions typically utilize nominal or ordinal scales. As such, the appropriate descriptive statistic would be a frequency count, and data might be presented in tables or charts that display percentages. Mode might also be of importance for nominal questions, and median might be used with questions that collect ordinal data. Researchers are limited in the data analyses they can do with demographic and classification questions. While such questions are needed in surveys, it is important to realize they produce lower-order data.

Source: ChristianChan/Shutterstock.

Knowledge measures can be used in advertising research to measure recall of ads and comprehension of their content.

11.5b Knowledge

At times it is beneficial to assess the knowledge consumers have of a topic. At the basic level would be a measure of awareness and recognition. Do consumers know the brand exists? Do they recognize the brand or logo? More in-depth knowledge can be measured to see what consumers know about a particular brand and if that knowledge is correct.

Knowledge measures can be used in advertising to measure recall of ads and comprehension of their content. It is not uncommon for individuals to recall seeing an ad for vehicles while watching television, but mistakenly say it was a Toyota ad when it was actually for Nissan. In addition to recall, advertisers want to see if the ad content was understood. Did they get the message or did they focus on a peripheral cue such as the ad model instead? Knowledge-based questions typically provide nominal or ordinal data, though questions assessing the degree to which a respondent is knowledgeable about a topic can use a scaled-response format providing interval data.

11.5c Attitudes

Questionnaires are often used to measure feelings and attitudes. In fact, a study could be focused entirely on measuring attitudes. It can be attitudes toward a product category, specific brands, attributes of a brand, or the purchase process. It might include the service component and the interaction with the company, whether in person or online. Attitudes are important because attitude formation typically precedes behavior. Before someone will purchase a particular brand, they will develop a positive attitude toward it, even if it is an impulse buy.

With attitude measures, level of intensity is important, so using some type of scaled-response question works best. It might be a series of Likert statements in which respondents can indicate their level of agreement or disagreement. It might be a semantic differential that uses bi-polar adjectives. It could even be a graphical scale. Whichever scale is used, it is important that the respondent be able to indicate a level of attitude beyond yes and no.

Most attitudinal measures will yield interval-type data. Since it is one of the higher order scales, it allows researchers to obtain means and standard deviations. It allows for comparisons across other variables through higher-order data analysis techniques. A researcher can see if a respondent's demographics have an impact on how they feel about a particular brand of snow skis or advertising of Nabisco products.

11.5d Preferences

Surveys often include preference questions. In terms of brands, it can be done by asking which brand is preferred from among a list of brands. Alternatively, individuals might be asked to rank various brands from most preferred to least preferred. The intensity of preference might be assessed via an itemized scale response question. The best method to measure preference is affected by the information needs of management, the target audience of the survey, and the type of preferences being requested.

If management wants to see where their brand falls among the primary competitors, a ranking-type of survey question might work best as long as the number of brands in the list is relatively small. When the list becomes long, then asking individuals to rank them becomes problematic. Ranking three to five brands is easy; ranking 12 to 15 brands is virtually impossible. In the latter case, it might be best to ask from the list of 12 to 15 brands which three or four brands individuals most prefer, or even just indicate their first and second choices. Itemized scaled response questions can be used in situations in which understanding the intensity of brand preference is of primary importance, or in instances when researchers want to know whether preferences differ significantly among demographic groupings or by some classification variable.

Source: Ivan Marc/Shutterstock.

If management wants to see where their brand falls among the primary competitors, a ranking type of survey question might work best as long as the number of brands is five or fewer.

11.5e Intentions

Researchers will often want to know consumer intentions. Will they purchase a particular brand in the future? It can be asked as a dichotomous question—yes or no. While helpful, it might be better to ask it using some type of scale that has four or five points ranging from "not at all likely" to "will definitely purchase." The scaled-response question provides higher-order data and indicates the degree of purchase intention.

Past research has indicated a significant difference between purchase intention and actual purchase behavior. The percentage of respondents who indicate intention to purchase a product at the end of a survey is always higher than the percent that actually make a purchase. While intention may be good, a number of extraneous variables can affect the final decision, such as promotions by other brands, advertising, product placement in the store, product availability in the store, and even consumer moods.

11.5f Behaviors

Behavioral questions are important in surveys since the ultimate goal of marketing is to sell products. While it is important to measure knowledge and even attitude toward ads and brands, did it result in a purchase? Asking people when, where, and how they purchased products seems to be fairly straightforward. Unfortunately, it is not because of the limited ability of humans to accurately recall past behaviors.

If consumers were asked what brand of dish detergent they last purchased, the brand loyal consumer who always purchases the same brand would be able to recall the information accurately. But the price-sensitive and the promotion-sensitive consumer who purchases different brands may not remember which brand was purchased last. If given a list of brands, individuals might choose a brand they know they have purchased in the past. It may not necessarily be the last one purchased, or even the one they purchase most often. But if researchers ask about the purchase of a high-ticket item such as an automobile, a computer, or furniture, purchase knowledge would tend to be more accurate. As the price and social visibility of a product increases, so does the ability to accurately recall purchase information. Also, the more infrequent the purchase or the shorter the time period involved, the greater the chance that the individual will recall the information accurately.

Source: OrangeVector/Shutterstock.

If consumers were asked what brand of dish detergent they last purchased, the brand loyal consumer who always purchases the same brand would be able to recall the information accurately.

In addition to purchase behavior, researchers often want to examine other behaviors such as media consumption, store patronage, social media postings, and word-of-mouth engagement. In determining how to spend advertising dollars, it is important to know what media individuals use and how much time they spend with each. Even information about the television shows watched and websites accessed is important. Store patronage is important to retail outlets, but it is also important to manufacturers. They will want to place their brands in stores that are patronized by shoppers that fit their target market. With the rise of the Internet, understanding how consumers communicate brand information has become more important. Where do they post information—good or bad? Do they read product reviews before making a purchase decision? If so, where do they read these? While surveys can provide insights to many of these questions, researchers should also strongly consider observational data collection alternatives, as the accuracy of results may be enhanced.

11.6 Question Phrasing

LEARNING OBJECTIVE 11.5
Discuss the issues relating to the phrasing of questions.

Writing the actual questions is one of the most challenging aspects of creating a survey. Good questions will yield useful data that can be analyzed and interpreted to provide beneficial information for management decisions. Poor questions will not only produce poor data, but can lead to poor decisions that cost a company thousands or millions of dollars.

- Questions should be clearly written free of jargon and ambiguity
- Questions should be applicable to respondents
- Questions should use the vocabulary of respondents
- Questions should be in a conversational style
- Questionnaire should have logical flow
- Scales should be easy to understand and use
- Questions should account for the limitations of human memory
- Either/or questions should be avoided
- Questions should not be double-barreled
- Questions should not be leading

FIGURE 11.11 Suggestions for Writing Good Questions

Good survey questions are those in which the respondent is both able and willing to answer truthfully. Properly phrased questions will be 1) clear, 2) concise, 3) understandable to the respondent and 4) written in such a way that the respondent's answer is not biased. A well-phrased questionnaire will maintain the interest and cooperation of respondents. Figure 11.11 provides some suggestions for writing good questions.

11.6a Ambiguity, Jargon, and Clarity

Ambiguity in survey questions is a frequent problem. The researcher knows what the question is asking, but sometimes it is not clear to the respondent. Consider the following question that appeared on a retail sales gun application form, "Are you a nonimmigrant alien?" Despite appearances, the question is not asking about the applicant's planetary status but rather refers to foreigners traveling in the U.S. or people studying in the U.S. who retain a residence in another country.

It is easy to slip jargon or language into a question that the researcher understands, but the respondent does not. Marketing terms such as cognitive dissonance, attribute evaluation, evoked set, and information search are understood by marketing experts, but may not be understood by the individual who is taking the survey.

Certain words may not be clear because they are interpreted differently by respondents. "Where did you eat dinner last night?" may seem fairly straightforward. Yet the word "dinner" is problematic because in the South, "dinner" often refers to the noon meal, while Northerners consider "dinner" to be the evening meal. It is also critical that researchers write questions in a way that ensures different respondents will answer by using the same frame of reference. The question "What is your annual income?" could be interpreted from multiple frames of reference. Does "your" mean you, personally, or your household? What type of money should be included in calculations of income? Is it salary only, or should money earned from investments, property management, gifts, grants, loans, child support, or welfare be included? To be able to make meaningful classifications on the basis of income, the question must be phrased in a manner such that respondents understand exactly what does and does not constitute income.

Words such as "often," "some," "occasionally," or "usually" are also ambiguous and likely to be interpreted differently among respondents. Failing to account for differing interpretations of words, or the potential for questions being answered from multiple frames of reference, will result in substantial measurement error and detract from the quality of data.

Because the person writing the question knows what information is being sought, ambiguity and the potential for interpretational differences may not be recognized. To ensure questions are clear and free of jargon and ambiguity, researchers can do three things. First, they can leave the questionnaire for a couple of days then come back to it. Ambiguity that was not present when the question was written may be evident at a later time. Second, the questionnaire can be given to individuals who do not have the marketing background to see how they interpret what is being asked and if the questions make sense. Third, the questionnaire can be administered to a few individuals that fit the profile of the survey's target audience. Pretesting of this nature also involves a debriefing session where the participants point out ambiguous wording or explain how they interpreted certain questions.

Substantial measurement error can also be avoided by making certain that the questions asked are applicable to the respondent. Qualifying questions such as, "Are you the primary individual responsible for grocery shopping?" can be used to skip respondents who are not the primary grocery shopper. Measurement error often occurs when respondents don't really know the answer to a question, but answer it anyway. Providing a "Don't Know" response category can minimize this form of error. Questions such as, "How frequently do you drink energy drinks?" assume that the respondent does in fact drink energy drinks. To accommodate this assumption, one of the response categories should be, "Do not drink energy drinks."

11.6b Vocabulary and Scales

It is important to use the vocabulary of the respondents, not the vocabulary of the individual writing the questions. Usually the individuals involved in questionnaire design have a college degree and many will have post-graduate degrees. The respondents for the survey may have only a high school education. In addition to using the vocabulary of the target audience, it is helpful to write the questions in a conversational style as people would talk. This makes it much easier for them to understand what is being asked. This is especially true for telephone or personal interview surveys where the questions are being read to the respondent by the interviewer. But even for self-administered questionnaires, conversational style wording is advised.

The questionnaire should have a logical flow that makes sense to the respondent and that provides the information that is needed without biasing responses. Asking individuals a recall question, such as what was the last brand of toothpaste purchased, should precede a recognition question that lists various brands of toothpaste. More information about questionnaire layout and flow is given in a following section.

If scales are used, they should be easy to understand. It is important to use descriptors that fit with the subject matter and are relevant to the target audience. For instance, if you want to ask individuals how they feel about ads shown during the Super Bowl, using "like and dislike" would be better descriptors than "good and bad" or "satisfied and dissatisfied." This approach is sensible because most people, if asked verbally how they felt, would reply with various degrees of "like or dislike," such as *"I really liked them."*

Consistency in using scales can aid in obtaining good data. This means using similar scales, similar formats, and similar arrangements. If a semantic differential scale is being used, switching to a paired comparison for the next question may be confusing. However, using a Likert scale along with the semantic differential scale is an easier transition. It is helpful if formats are similar. If a seven-point scale is used on the first semantic differential, it makes it easier if other scales use the same format. Switching from seven-point to five- or three-point may be confusing to some of the respondents. Also, if some scales have an even number of points and others have an odd number of points, it can make the questionnaire more difficult for respondents. Last, the arrangement of the scales should be consistent because individuals become quickly accustomed to a particular format. If one set of questions has "strongly disagree" on the left and "strongly agree" on the right, but the next set has the scale reversed, individuals may never notice the change and answer an entire sequence of questions incorrectly. The more consistency among the various scales, the easier it is for the respondent to answer the questions and the greater the probability that good data are obtained.

11.6c Limitations of Human Memory and Either/Or Questions

It is important to understand the limitations of human memory. While measures of human behavior are important, researchers must understand memory limitations and construct questions in a way that will yield useful data, not just a guess. As stated earlier, individuals' recall of information is not always accurate, especially with low-cost items or matters that are not very important to them. Asking a respondent to indicate how many tubes of toothpaste were purchased in the previous year is a useless question. The respondent won't be able to accurately recall the answer. While unusual events, such as purchasing carpet, are more memorable, a different memory error occurs because individuals typically remember events as happening more recently than they actually did. The best way to avoid memory errors is to keep the recall period short. For instance, a research panel used to track information related to restaurant dining first asks respondents to indicate what day of the week they are answering the survey, then frames all questions regarding their restaurant dining behavior in terms of the previous day.

Beware of using either/or questions. While they seem a good way to obtain comparative information, they are not. For instance, asking respondents if they prefer coffee black or with cream and sugar seems straightforward. But, suppose they don't like it either way. Maybe they like to put honey in their coffee or want cream but not sugar. An either/or question eliminates other possibilities and forces respondents to choose from the two alternatives when an optimal answer may be something else. The only place an either/or question is assured to work well is with the paired comparison scale where every possible combination of pairs is evaluated.

11.6d Double-Barreled and Leading Questions

In a **double-barreled question**, respondents are asked two questions in one. For instance, they might be asked to indicate their level of agreement or disagreement with the statement: "The prices at Walmart are reasonable and provide shoppers with a good value." The respondent might feel prices are reasonable, but not a good value, or vice versa. Although researchers and most people might associate the two concepts, they should never be placed together in the same question. It forces respondents to accept both or neither.

Double-barreled question question that involves asking respondents two questions in one.

Another problem that can occur is a **leading question**, where the survey question leads the respondent to the desired answer. A questionnaire might ask, "Because of the harmful impact of second-hand cigarette smoke, are you in favor of banning smoking on college campuses?" The wording of this question is leading to an affirmative answer by pointing out that second-hand cigarette smoke is harmful. Another example of a leading question appeared as a Likert statement on a green marketing survey. It stated, "Consumers are switching to brands that use bio-degradable packaging because of the large amount of plastics now filling our landfills." Respondents were asked to indicate their level of agreement or disagreement on a seven-point scale. While the statement does not specifically say the plastics are not bio-degradable, it is implied, and the statement further implies that our landfills are full of plastics that are not degradable.

Leading question survey question that leads the respondent to the desired answer.

11.7 Survey Invitation and Questionnaire Layout

11.7a Invitation or Cover Letter

LEARNING OBJECTIVE 11.6
Identify and explain the contents of the survey invitation and each section of a questionnaire.

While not an actual component of the questionnaire, the survey invitation is critically important. Cover letters are only used for mail surveys and in some cases personal interview surveys that involve giving respondents a questionnaire and asking them to complete it. With the overwhelming shift toward online survey research, email invitations are much more common today. Text invitations sent to sample member's mobile phones are also being used, and seem to be preferred by younger consumers.[15] Whether an email, text, or a cover letter, the purpose of a survey invitation is to obtain the person's cooperation and willingness to participate in the research study. Figure 11.12 highlights what should be contained in an invitation or cover letter.

The first challenge for online survey invitations is to develop a subject line that will motivate the respondent to open the email. If targeting current customers, non-profit organization members, or other populations that are not part of a research panel, it is often productive to send an email prior to the survey invitation, simply to let them know they

- Contact information, opt-out link for survey/text invitations
- Organization/company conducting the study
- Purpose of study
- Target audience of the study
- Survey URL
- Statement of anonymity or confidentiality
- Importance of participation and incentive (if appropriate)
- Time frame for completing and returning questionnaire
- Advance thank you for participating

FIGURE 11.12 Content of Invitation (Email, Text, Cover Letter)

will be receiving an invitation to participate in a survey. A similar strategy is used with mail surveys, as postcards often provide forewarning of surveys that will arrive in the mail. If the pre-notification email (or postcard) is sent from the owner, manager, or some other recognizable employee of the organization, it is more likely to garner attention.

Spam blockers often stop survey invites before they reach potential research subjects. The practices that trigger their filters aren't published, but survey invites have a better chance of reaching the intended target when researchers:

1. Avoid trigger words such as "free" and "win".
2. Avoid using words in all caps, and the use of excessive punctuation (e.g. !!!).
3. Comply with the CAN-SPAM Act, found at https://www.ftc.gov/tips-advice/business-center/guidance/can-spam-act-compliance-guide-business. In particular, this means including an opt-out line, a physical mailing address and an email address, which are generally placed at the bottom of the email.
4. Avoid spoofing emails. Using your firm's (or the research firm's) own mail servers helps emails pass authentication tests used to identify spam.

The FROM line for the email is typically the company name, or that of a known representative of the firm. The SUBJECT line can strongly influence whether or not your email is opened. Keep the subject to 50 words or less; the more clear and concise, the better. If possible, convey the topic of the email and highlight the benefit to the respondent without using the trigger words previously mentioned.

Emails delivered during the working day Tuesday through Thursday seem to be have a better chance of being opened, barring holidays or other special occasions. Personalizing the email with the name of the respondent is often possible by using merge fields, and helps the respondent to feel that are receiving personal attention.

Your phrasing of the survey invitation may differ depending upon whether you are targeting research panel members or other individuals. For example, the word "survey" has a negative connotation for many people who are not members of research panels, so avoid its use when targeting non-panel members, if possible. Instead, use a phrase such as, "take a few minutes to answer some questions" to convey the intent of the invitation. Identifying the organization can help motivate respondent's willingness to provide answers, and simply stating the study purpose—even in a brief and vague fashion—will persuade more respondents to complete the survey. Informing respondents about the targeted audience, and why you believe they fit into that group is also important. Promoting the idea that their opinions represent others like them enhances the importance of their participation.

One key component specific to online or mobile survey invitations is the survey URL. The link should be located in the upper half of the email or text, and it is normally offset by white space so that it stands out and is easily noticed even by those who don't read the entire invitation. If a password is required to enter the survey, that information should be located near the URL. The invitation should then close with a statement thanking the respondent in advance for participating.

People are increasingly concerned about sharing personal information, so be very clear about privacy. It is critically important to state if the responses will be anonymous or confidential. **Anonymity** means the responses given by a particular respondent can never be identified or tied to that particular person. **Confidentiality** means that although the researcher can identify who completed a particular survey, the researcher pledges to keep that information confidential and never reveal the identity of the respondent.

Anonymity responses given by a particular respondent can never be identified or tied to that particular person.

Confidentiality although a researcher can identify who completed a particular survey, the researcher pledges to keep that information confidential and never reveal who completed the survey.

The invitation or cover letter should reinforce the importance of completing the study, and describe any incentives for participation. If incentives are needed to motivate respondents to participate, realistic options are the best. A one-in-ten chance of winning a $25 cash or prize is a better motivator than a chance to win $10,000. If incentives are used, researchers need to be careful that the incentive does not encourage people to lie or provide bogus answers in order to receive the incentive. Two time frames should be given. The first is an *honest* estimate of the time needed to complete the actual survey. The second is the date by which the survey should be completed. In the first case, the invitation might say it will take approximately 20 minutes to complete the survey. In the second case, the individual is asked to complete the survey by a specific date.

One problem with incentives is that while they increase response rates, they also tend to influence respondents to provide more favorable feedback than they might otherwise have done without the promise of an incentive. To avoid this bias, multiple survey invitations can be created that do not mention incentives. One version might request feedback in a friendly, conversational manner. A second might suggest that if the respondent had a negative experience (or negative thoughts/responses to questions), their feedback needs to be heard as it is very important to the firm. The third might suggest that all respondents, even those with non-memorable experiences (or neutral thoughts) are important to the firm and that they shouldn't hesitate to express their true feelings. Randomly rotating the use of survey invitations throughout the sample should reduce non-response bias, especially when non-respondents receive additional invitations to participate in the study.[16]

Figure 11.13 identifies the primary sections of a questionnaire and the typical order in which the sections appear. Note that, for more complex surveys or questionnaires dealing with potentially sensitive information, the screening questions can precede the instructions. This allows the exclusion of individuals that do not meet the survey participant criteria before time is spent on providing instructions.

11.7b Introduction and Instructions

An effective introduction to the survey will increase your response rates, and the shorter the introduction, the better. Still, clear instructions are essential! Respondents need to know before starting a survey what they will be doing and what is expected of them. Explain the tasks in simple language that is easily understood. If the survey is long, and the software allows for respondents to stop, and then complete the questionnaire at a later time, mentioning this in the instructions can help reduce respondent fatigue and meaningless answers, though follow-up reminders to finish the survey are also recommended.

Some information listed in the survey invitation will likely need to be repeated. Are the results confidential? If you can promise true anonymity, do so. If respondents are not anonymous, tell them why it is important that you know who they are. How will the data be used? Will it be destroyed at some point? If the privacy and data usage terms

- Introduction and instructions
- Screening questions
- Survey questions
- Demographic information
- Closing

FIGURE 11.13 Questionnaire Layout

require more room than can be accommodated in an introduction screen or page, consider adding a separate page that details this information, and providing the URL link to the privacy page in your survey introduction. Reiterate the amount of time the survey will take to answer, who is collecting the data, the name of the client (if possible), and the study purpose.[17] While complete information might not be given (to prevent biasing the responses), sufficient information should be provided so the respondent feels comfortable in answering the questions. This becomes especially important if respondents are being asked personal or potentially sensitive questions. However, the less detail provided about the *topic* of the survey, the better, since it is important that respondents not reply based on interests. If only those interested in a topic complete the survey, biased results will be more likely. What often occurs in these situations is that those who really like a topic or brand respond, as do those who have strong negative feelings. So the data is bipolar, with the two extreme views, and as such may not adequately represent the population.

In self-administered surveys, the initial instructions should also indicate the date and method by which the survey should be returned. While researchers may have a preference that respondents answer online instead of using a smartphone, or that they use a certain browser or operating system, multiple research studies have shown that respondents will answer an online survey using the device and platform of their choosing, and ignore researcher's specific instructions to use a tablet, smartphone, or PC. So instead of providing instructions telling people to use a certain device or operating system, it is recommended that the survey be designed in a manner that allows it to be read and easily answered on all operating systems and devices.[18]

11.7c Screening Questions

Not everyone is a candidate for a particular questionnaire. Before administering the questionnaire, the target audience for the survey needs to be identified along with the purpose of the research. This information allows researchers to develop screening questions to determine if someone fits the profile needed. For instance, a company that manufactures lawn equipment wants to survey individuals who purchase and use lawn equipment. It is not always the same person and their insights can be quite different. Thus, the screening question might ask if the individual mows and trims his or her own lawn. Another question might ask if they have purchased lawn equipment in the past month. This second question is important if the company wants to investigate the purchase decision process. If someone uses lawn equipment, but never makes an actual purchase, that person would not be a good choice to participate in a survey about purchasing equipment. However, if the manufacturer wants to study features of lawn equipment to gather information on the development of new products, then a user can provide valuable information.

Good screening questions save researchers considerable time and money by eliminating individuals who cannot answer the questions or who should not be involved in the study. In the previous example, someone who only uses lawn equipment cannot provide useful information pertaining to the purchase process. In fact, their answers may lead to erroneous results and poor decisions by management. A similar situation is sometimes found in the healthcare industry. While the sick person might provide some useful information, the caregiver should probably be surveyed since he or she is making the decision on medical equipment and supplies.

When it comes to business surveys, good screening questions are very important. The title of a person in a company does not always indicate the individuals who should participate in a study. The higher a person is in a company, in terms of title and rank, the less likely they are to evaluate or offer insight into purchase and usage situations of products and services. However, these higher-ranking individuals could be good candidates for surveys dealing with larger, strategic issues.

Another reason for using screening questions is in an attempt to identify professional respondents or survey bots programmed to answer surveys on their behalf. Survey bots and "bad" professional respondents randomly select answers to questions, damaging the data quality. Inserting a reCAPTCHA widget into an online survey is one method of identifying survey bots. reCAPTCHA pops up a screen that says, "I am not a robot." Respondents check the box next to the message and are able to proceed through the survey; bots do not.[19] Bots and professional respondents can often be identified by a question that ascertains whether the respondent is paying attention. However, it may be best if this type of screening question is placed after the demographic screening questions (in case the bot programmer is answering the demographics manually in order to qualify for the survey). In one version, the question instructions may look very complex, and be somewhat long to read, while the question itself offers many different response options. Those who do read the instructions are told to select a particular answer while those who fail to select the proper answer are eliminated from the survey. Yet this type of question may eliminate some legitimate survey prospects, because many individuals do not read the question instructions, or at least, all of the instructions. So if using this method, it would be a wise to have the correct response option listed in the first or second sentence of the instructions. As an alternative, a general, easy to answer multiple choice question might be asked that has only a single obvious correct answer.[20] While some bots and professional respondents will randomly select the correct answers, following the tips for identifying professional respondents discussed in a previous chapter will also help to eliminate error in the data.

One final note regarding screening questions is worth mentioning. Programmatic sampling and the use of artificial intelligence in sample selection has the *potential* to make demographic screening questions obsolete in many situations. A well-developed automated sampling system could be programmed to review the demographic characteristics of a panel member's profile to see if an individual matches the criteria needed *before* a survey invitation is sent. The same logic applies to sample providers. The largest barrier to implementation is a lack of standardization between sample suppliers regarding how the data is stored. For example, some might use the term "gender" while others might use the term "sex" to store information on whether an individual is male or female. Age ranges might also differ between panels or sample providers, and some may use different classifications for race or ethnicities.[21]

11.7d Survey Questions

After the instructions and screening questions comes the body of the questionnaire. Generally, the survey should begin with broad questions and proceed to more focused ones. As necessary, questions may be prefaced by instructions to clarify how a question should be answered. Most important, the questionnaire should have a logical flow. If scales are used, placing similar scales together makes it easier for the respondent. Changing scale formats too often can be confusing and may even become frustrating. Scaled response questions are normally found in the middle of the survey, along with other questions that require thought or effort. This may include open-ended questions, if asked after any scaled-response questions. Asking open-ended questions at the beginning of the survey will likely lead to a higher refusal rate, while asking such questions after the respondent has invested time in answering the survey enhances the likelihood they will finish the survey. If open-ended questions are used, it is important that the researcher allow adequate room for answers. A one-line blank cues the respondent to provide a limited response; several lines worth of open space indicates that a lengthier response is desired. Still, subjects often fail to provide answers or they give limited responses to open-ended questions.

If a questionnaire has sensitive or potentially embarrassing questions, they should be near the end of the question sequence. Asking such questions too early may cause individuals to quit the survey. If asked properly and at the right time, respondents are more likely to answer such questions. The goal is to gain the confidence of the respondent by the time the sensitive questions are asked. Prefacing sensitive questions with the reason why the information is needed, or a reassurance as to how the data will be used or reported, can help increase response rates to these questions.

To prevent the questionnaire from becoming too long, only questions that pertain to the research and survey objectives should be asked. It is tempting to tack on additional questions that a researcher or someone with the client feels would be nice to ask, but may not relate to any survey objective.

Another approach is to use branching where additional questions are asked based on the respondent's responses to specific questions. Branching can be done easily with online and mobile surveys. For instance, suppose respondents are asked if they purchased an energy bar within the last week. If they say yes, they see additional questions about the energy bar. If they say no, the next question seen in the survey does not deal with energy bars. Online and mobile surveys also allow for piping, which means that an answer from a previous question can be inserted into the text of a later question. So, for those indicating they purchased a particular energy bar, the brand name will be incorporated into any additional questions asked about the energy bar. Piping keeps the survey taker focused on the particular brand they are evaluating, which can be very helpful if evaluating the most recent brand bought, when that brand is not their normal purchase.

11.7e Demographic Information

Demographic questions should be at the end of the questionnaire, unless they are used as screening questions. In that case, the appropriate demographics used for screening are asked at the beginning to determine if the person continues taking the survey or is terminated. For demographic questions at the end of the survey, a sentence explaining the importance of such questions, and a disclaimer stating that the answers will be used for purposes of classification only, will increase the likelihood that this section will be completed.

11.7f Closing

The closing provides an opportunity to thank the respondent. It can also be used to debrief the respondent with more information on how the data will be used and the purpose of the study, especially if the purpose was disguised or presented in a vague manner. Making the respondent feel he/she has contributed useful information that will be used for management decisions increases the likelihood the respondent will participate in future research studies. Typically, researchers include a phone number or email address that respondents can use if they have questions about the study.

It is advantageous to prepare respondents for additional research by adding a question in the closing that says, "Additional research may be required. Would you be interested in participating in future research?" If they respond yes, the researcher can then ask for their email address or another mode of contact.

11.7g Design Considerations

Providing adequate white space in the form of margins and empty space between questions can make the questionnaire easier to read and reduce refusal rates. Question instructions should be distinguished from the question itself. Choices include 1) bold text, 2) bold italic text, or 3) using a different font. Using all caps to display instructions or underlining instructions are not recommended. Both tactics reduce the readability of the information. Furthermore, in an online world, underlining is often associated with links, while all caps is considered poor etiquette and equated to "shouting."

With surveys that are taken over the Internet, additional design considerations come into play. Using a secure survey link for online and mobile surveys is highly recommended. Hyper Text Transfer Protocol Secure (HTTPS) encrypts the URL of the survey, which prevents unauthorized parties from reading the URL and accessing the data. Secure links are also essential for maintaining respondent anonymity as they don't store IP or location data that could be used to personally identify individuals. Secure survey links help to mitigate respondent's privacy concerns, while convincing them that what data

- Increase size of question text and response options
- Design questions with touch tap and swiping inputs
- Simplify content for ease of use with mobile
- Consider interview length
- Test and re-test prior to implementation

FIGURE 11.14 Designing Smartphone Friendly Surveys
Source: FocusVision Staff, "Five Steps to Getting the Most out of Mobile Surveys," *Quirk's Media*, (www.quirks.com), October 8, 2018.

they do provide will be handled securely. On occasion, researchers may wish to password protect surveys to ensure they are only answered by specifically invited sample members. Cookies—small pieces of data stored in the surveytaker's browser—can also be used to prevent respondents from taking a survey more than once. Finally, survey invitations and links may be personalized for each member of the sample to ensure easy tracking of who has responded versus who has not.[22]

Radio buttons are the common choice for multiple response, multiple choice, and scaled response questions in online surveys, and in some mobile surveys. Drop-down menus are reserved for questions that contain a multitude of response options, such as country-of-origin, or the state within which a respondent resides. While there is some evidence to suggest that drop-down boxes are more difficult to use, the choice of button vs. drop-down menu does not appear to impact survey completion rates or survey completion times.[23] Dragging and dropping response options are often used in online surveys, especially for ranking questions. Dragging is more engaging than simply assigning numbers to indicate ranks, and is one form of gamification discussed later in the chapter.

FocusVision is one of many research firms that specializes in mobile and online survey design. FocusVision's recommendations for smartphone friendly mobile survey designs are displayed in Figure 11.14.[24] First, make it easy for users to read and answer questions by increasing the font size of the questions, as well as the font size used for the response options. Many smartphones simply rescale a webpage to fit the width of mobile phone. The resulting text is often too small to be easily readable and does not optimize the screen space available. Designing a survey specifically for a mobile screen allows better control over question display and font sizes.

Second, consider the native input aspect of the device. Smartphone users are most comfortable touch tapping and swiping, as opposed to clicking and dragging which is common with PC users. Compare the two question formats in Figure 11.15. Questions that feature large, easy to touch answers like the format shown on the right are both easier to read and easier to select, and therefore less likely to encounter measurement error than are questions using dropdown menus, checkboxes, or radio buttons for input.

Simplifying content for mobile use means removing extraneous graphics, such as logos or banners from a heading, or any other extraneous graphic. If a graphic is necessary, offer users the ability to zoom in, if needed. Ideally, the survey elements should be large enough that the user can complete the survey without zooming. Rearranging content or altering the question format is necessary if horizontal scrolling is required to see the entire question or series of response options. For example, if a question has ten response categories that span beyond the edge of the screen, one way to simplify the content would be to reduce the number of categories in *both* the online and mobile surveys to seven categories. Changing both surveys ensures measurement equivalency between mobile and online survey takers.

The amount of time it takes to answer the survey is important as break-offs occur more frequently as time progresses. All things being equal, studies have consistently shown that mobile surveys take longer to complete then do PC surveys. One reason is because mobile survey takers often have to wait for graphics or videos to download. Reducing the clutter

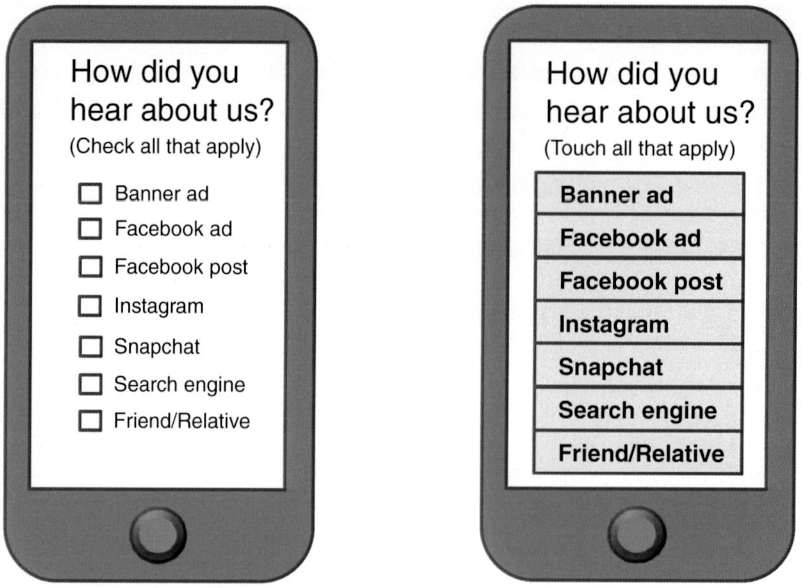

FIGURE 11.15 Customizing Mobile Response Options
Source: FocusVision Staff, "Five Steps to Getting the Most out of Mobile Surveys," *Quirk's Media*, (www.quirks.com), October 8, 2018.

- Lower cooperation rates
- Higher break-off rates
- Higher item non-responses
- Reduced data quality

FIGURE 11.16 Negative Consequences of Long Questionnaires

of unnecessary graphics helps reduce the interview time. Eliminating videos from mobile surveys will increase the completion rate, as many users won't wait for the download to complete. Mobile surveys also take longer when grid questions are split into individual items shown on consecutive screens. Plus, mobile survey takers are more prone to distractions while taking surveys. In general, shorter surveys are better, though estimates of what constitutes the proper number of questions or amount of time varies widely.

11.8 Consequences of Long Surveys

LEARNING OBJECTIVE 11.7 Describe the negative consequences of long questionnaires.

A major problem that often creeps into survey research is questionnaires that become too long. When this happens, it results in negative consequences that are not always easily anticipated by the researcher. The most common are declining cooperation rates, higher break-off rates, increasing item non-responses, reduced data quality, and panel attrition. Unfortunately, these negative consequences have become more pronounced, as reduced research budgets often result in lower participant incentives (see **Figure 11.16**).[25]

If respondents feel that a questionnaire is too long and thus will take too much time to complete, they may opt not to take the survey. This can affect the validity of a research study because the researcher does not know if the refusal to participate is due to the topic being investigated or the length of the questionnaire. Sometimes individuals will start the survey, but quit because they feel it is too long. Recall that the percentage of individuals who start a survey but do not complete it is called the break-off rate.

With mail surveys or surveys handed to a respondent, the individual can easily see how long the survey is and approximate how long it will take to complete. If it is viewed as being too long, the person is not likely to even start. But with online surveys, the respondent cannot really tell how long it will take, which is why the invitation to participate should accurately state the approximate length of the survey or the time involved in completing it. Some online surveys will also have an indicator on each page showing what percent of the survey has been completed. But this can be misleading because some components may take 30 seconds to complete while others may take several minutes. Online surveys typically take 20 minutes to complete, yet respondents begin getting bored half-way through, and they pay less attention to questions. Break-offs begin in earnest near the 15 minute mark. Even those who keep answering experience severe respondent fatigue around 20 minutes into the survey, and randomly select answers in order to finish the survey.[26] Millennials have even less patience, with approximately one in seven survey takers breaking off at the 13 minute mark, and 33 percent breaking off at 20 minutes.[27] So if respondents feel the survey is too long or taking too much time to complete, they may just quit answering questions and leave the survey. Fortunately, most online survey software packages allow for the respondents to leave a survey and pick up where they left off at a later time. This technology reduces the break-off rate.

Instead of quitting, respondents might just skip questions, especially those that look as if they will take too much time or too much thought to answer, leading to item non-response. Open-ended questions are the most likely to be skipped since they require more time and thought than closed-ended questions. Questions that have multiple or long response options that the respondent has to read through suffer a similar fate. Questions presented within a grid format, such as Likert or Semantic Differential scale questions, may also be at risk. Questions near the end of a survey are more likely to be skipped than are questions near the beginning.

Reduced data quality is the most serious problem stemming from long questionnaires, though specific instances can be difficult to detect. Respondents will answer the questions, but not spend time thinking about the best response. They may mark any response.

While the research industry recognizes the problem, they have been slow to abandon longer surveys. Still, some firms are attempting to change the research process in an attempt to address the issue. For example, many firms have attempted to make surveys more fun through gamification techniques, believing that more engaged respondents are less likely to break-off. Other firms are turning to observation research and using less survey-based attitudinal data. The surge in mobile surveys has forced firms to write more succinct questions while changing the style of survey questions, as discussed in the previous section on mobile survey research.[28] The most obvious solution to a long questionnaire is to shorten it and to give researchers credit, they have made strides toward reducing redundant questions. But if it is not possible to do so and still meet the research objectives, researchers can use a split questionnaire design. A **split-questionnaire design** involves splitting a questionnaire into one core component and multiple subcomponents. All respondents complete the core component. Each respondent is then randomly given one of the subcomponents.

Split questionnaire design involves splitting a questionnaire into one core component that all respondents answer and multiple subcomponents with respondents answering only one subcomponent.

Consider **Figure 11.17**. Respondent 1 answers the core component questions and the items in questionnaire component A. Respondent 2 answers the core questions and the

	Respondent 1	Respondent 2	Respondent 3	Respondent 4
Core Component	X	X	X	X
Component A	X			
Component B		X		
Component C			X	
Component D				X

FIGURE 11.17 Illustration of Split-Questionnaire Design

items in component B. Respondent 3 does the core and component C and respondent 4 does the core with component D. The sub-components should be randomly assigned among respondents. Approximately 25 percent of the total sample will respond to each of the subcomponents. To achieve a sufficient sample size it will be necessary to survey more individuals. So if a research study requires a sample of 300, 1,200 would have to be interviewed to ensure 300 people answer each of the components.

A study examining the validity and reliability of using the split-questionnaire design showed that the quality of data obtained was superior to data collected using a long, single questionnaire.[29] This is because respondents were able to answer the core questions and one component without the fatigue and negative consequences associated with a long questionnaire. The key to using a split-questionnaire design is the development of the core component and then each of the subcomponents.

Data mining and machine learning algorithms provide an additional alternative for shortened questionnaires. Similar to the split-questionnaire design, a long survey is parsed into separate components, so that each participant answers as few as a quarter of the total survey questions. Question sets are either randomly presented by the software, or the survey designer designates a set for all respondents, and then assigns other sets for random presentation. Following data collection, the data mining and machine learning algorithm is "seeded" with patterns of which the researcher is aware, or the software is instructed to review the data and find patterns on its own. One pattern may indicate that people of a certain age tend toward a certain response on a particular question, for example. Then it forecasts answers for each respondent's missing data. The natural assumption is to think that such a technique would introduce massive amounts of error into the data and reduce the overall data quality. Yet the results of a study by Lightspeed Research suggest otherwise. In their study, 4,464 individuals answered the complete twenty-nine question survey. A percentage and standard deviation were computed for each variable in the questionnaire. Then the survey was administered to four groups, each with over a thousand respondents, who answered only 25 percent of the questions in the full survey. The missing data for each individual's survey was predicted by the data mining and machine learning algorithm and added to the data set. In comparing the results of those who answered the full survey, to those who answered the partial survey and had 75 percent of their answers predicted by the software, the highest percentage difference among the twenty-nine questions was only 1 percent. Differences in the standard deviation of the survey variables were virtually meaningless. In light of this study, Lightspeed Research suggests that longer surveys can be eliminated by using data mining and machine learning algorithms, resulting in less respondent fatigue, lower costs, and better data quality while satisfying respondents preferences for mobile surveys.[30]

11.9 Gamification in Online Surveys

LEARNING OBJECTIVE 11.8
Discuss gamification and its use in online surveys.

Surveys are an integral source of marketing research data. Yet the quality of survey data has steadily declined due to increased refusal rates, increased panel member drop-outs, and growing participant dissatisfaction with the survey-taking experience. As a result, survey takers become less engaged and are less likely to read and think about questions carefully. They are also less likely to answer open-ended questions in a meaningful manner. Finally, due to their lack of attention, less engaged survey participants are not as likely to differentiate attributes or brands in a manner that is consistent with their actual thoughts or purchase behavior.[31]

Gamification process of applying gaming mechanics to survey tasks to encourage more active participation.

While definitions vary, one researcher defines **gamification** in marketing research as "the process of applying gaming mechanics to everyday tasks [such as surveys] to encourage more active participation."[32] What this essentially means is that survey-taking can become more fun and engaging, minimizing the negative consequences addressed in the previous paragraph.

Gamification has been studied in a variety of contexts. Using more than 5,000 participants, a year-long study of thirty different gamification research experiments concluded that certain types of gamification can reduce straight-lining of answers, improve data quality, improve respondent engagement and improve the quantity of data collected from individual respondents.[33] Some believe that gamification paints a more realistic portrait of consumer behavior, as consumer behavior is not always rationale due to behavioral biases.[34] A recent study found that consumers were more likely to accurately predict their grocery spending in a gamified survey vs. a standard survey, when forecasts were compared against shopping receipts for the month following the survey. This finding suggests improved data quality for purchase predictions. Gamified surveys also provided richer data, a greater quantity of data, and clearly engaged participants better than standard online surveys in the same study.[35] Similar results have been found in other studies. The research industry's interest in gamification is growing, as the results of the 2018 Quarter 3–4 *Greenbook Research Industry Trends Report* revealed that 26 percent of the research suppliers and buyers who answered the questionnaire are currently using gamification techniques compared to the 20 percent who were using gamification in 2015.[36]

11.9a Altering the Instructions and Question Style

The Global Market Institute (GMI) has been at the forefront of studying gamification and its impact on data quality and respondent engagement. GMI conducted over 100 experiments related to gamification. Their research indicates that a respondent's attitude and time spent on survey tasks can be positively influenced just by asking subjects to "play a survey game" in the invitation or instructions.[37]

Previously, this chapter discussed how question phrasing can affect respondents' ability and willingness to read and answer questions. Gamification techniques, such as those shown in **Figure 11.18**, can be applied to question phrasing to enhance positive outcomes. Through a series of experiments, GMI found that use of these techniques helps to engage respondents—they might spend up to 50 percent more time answering questions. Plus, more information was given in response to open-ended questions.[38]

Figure 11.19 illustrates how questions can be rephrased using each gamification technique. Despite the fact that respondents enjoy answering gamified questions more than those that are traditionally phrased, the researcher must be careful to ensure that rephrased questions are in keeping with the study's objective. For instance, it might be argued that the personalized question example in Figure 11.19 yields little in the way of usable data if the person answering has children or a spouse whose desires would affect the purchase decision in real life.

Triggering emotions or latent feelings by altering the question phrasing is a special type of personalization. The benefit of this technique is that respondents spend more time thinking about the question and offer increased levels of feedback. Similarly, using projection in online surveys engages participants, and under the right circumstances may double the attention and feedback from participants. Injecting creative imaginary situations and fantasy into questions also engages the respondent, and may lead to higher levels of satisfaction with the survey process. However, many researchers wonder if the phrasing itself invalidates the *quality* of the data gathered, as altering the context of the questions changes its meaning.[39]

- **Personalization**—personalizes questions
- **Triggering latent feelings**—adds emotional context
- **Projection**—projects respondent's thoughts onto another
- **Forced imagery situations**—participant responds in context of the situation
- **Fantasy**—presents questions in context highly unlikely to occur in real life

FIGURE 11.18 Gamification Techniques

- **Personalization**
  - *Traditional*: Which of the following is your favorite cereal?
  - *Gamification*: If you were buying cereal for yourself, which would you buy?
- **Triggering latent feelings**
  - *Traditional*: What would you wear to a three-star restaurant?
  - *Gamification*: What would you wear to a three-star restaurant if you were meeting your significant other's parents for the first time?
- **Projection**
  - *Traditional*: Evaluate the following product attributes on a scale of 1 (poor) to 5 (excellent).
  - *Gamification*: As marketing director, it is your job to evaluate the following product attributes on a scale ranging from 1 (poor) to 5 (excellent)
- **Forced imaginary situations**
  - *Traditional*: What brand of pants do you purchase for work?
  - *Gamification*: Imagine a waitress dumped spaghetti in your lap on a workday and you quickly had to go out and buy a new pair of pants to wear that afternoon. What brand would you buy?
- **Fantasy**
  - *Traditional*: What clothes would you wear to a special event?
  - *Gamification*: What would you wear if you were the sole winner of a million dollar lottery and Mark Zuckerberg invited you to a party?

FIGURE 11.19 Gamification and Question Phrasing

11.9b Survey Design

Designing the survey to include competitive elements heightens the engagement level of survey participants. A question phrased as, "Thinking about mobile phones, here is a little game. You have 60 seconds to write down all of the brands of mobile phones you can think of, to a maximum of 10. Your time starts now!" makes a game of what might otherwise be a tedious task and has a positive impact on the number of responses generated.[40]

Similarly, offering rewards and feedback mechanisms to participants piques their competitive nature and substantially increases their enjoyment and satisfaction with the survey process.[41] This technique has been successfully used when asking respondents to predict an outcome. A stock market survey might ask respondents, "What is your prediction for Nike's stock value during the next 30 days?" Response options would show a variety of positive and negative percentage changes. Rewards are offered in the form of points or badges accumulated for answers that match the predictions of market experts. Alternatively, the game and reward aspect can be enhanced by instructing participants to "bet" on their answer using money from a fictional account. Those who correctly match the experts' predictions "win" and double their bet. Unfortunately, the use of rewards can also detract from the data quality if respondents become *too* competitive and let their desire to "win" override their true thoughts, thereby decreasing the accuracy of the data.[42] Researchers continue to explore gamification, and one study recommended using gamified, modern question formats for research studies matching the parameters in **Figure 11.20**.[43]

11.9c Use of Visual and Interactive Elements

Questionnaire layouts have traditionally focused on text-based questions arranged in grid patterns with response categories arranged to the right of questions, or directly underneath. When multi-item scaled response questions are asked, several items are listed on the same page using vertically arranged response option columns to make answering easier for respondents.

- Surveys are shorter and more engaging (less than 10 minutes)
- Surveys are primarily taken on mobile devices
- Respondents are tech savvy or smartphone dependent
- When an immediate gut reaction to a brand or product is desired
- When feedback should mirror rating systems found in online and social media environments (e.g., star ratings)

FIGURE 11.20 Conditions for Using Gamified Question Formats
Source: Adapted from: Koski, Lilah, "Gamified Approaches: Testing Survey Design Techniques," *Quirk's Media*, (www.quirks.com), April 5, 2017.

Research by the Global Market Institute suggests that one way to make surveys more fun is to deviate from the traditional survey layout design. Each question could be presented on a separate page, incorporating visual representations of responses in addition to words.[44] **Figure 11.21** provides one example of how visualization can be incorporated into a gamified survey.

In creating gamified surveys, researchers should strive for visual intuity. **Visual intuity** involves transforming questions into micro-games that can be mastered by respondents with little or no explanation.[45] Typically this involves adding interactive elements to a survey that enhance respondent engagement and satisfaction in the survey process. For example, one survey instructed participants to press the stop button when a blurry image of a logo became recognizable. The amount of time it took respondents to recognize the image was recorded.[46] Another example would be asking respondents to drop and drag the advertising slogan next to the matching brand name. Interactivity can be incorporated in a variety of ways. The question listed in Figure 11.21 could instead have asked participants to rank order their choices by dropping and dragging photos into a single column, where the top photo would be the first choice, the one below that the second choice, and so on. Alternatively, a person might be asked to use their mouse to rate an item by holding the mouse button and sliding it along a visual graphic scale (a slider) that tracks and follows the mouse movement. Participants then release the mouse button to assign their rating. Dropping and dragging icons of images into categories ranging from unappealing to very appealing, instead of marking radio buttons in a grid format, or moving meter gauges or thermometers, offers additional methods of using interactivity in surveys. The use of visual elements and interactivity improves data quality substantially by reducing both straight-lining behavior and survey dropout rates.[47]

Visual intuity transforming questions into micro-games that can be mastered by respondents with little or no explanation.

Which of the following countries would you most like to visit?

FIGURE 11.21 Example of Visualization in a Gamified Survey
Sources: (*Top row, left to right*) Shutterstock—zhu difeng, Abdoabdalla, Taras Vyshnya, canadastock. (*Bottom row, left to right*) Shutterstock—IR Stone, Chr. Offenberg, Catarina Belova.

More advanced micro-games borrow from projective techniques and involve theme collage-building, where respondents choose photos to represent their responses, then explain what the photos mean. Virtual environments are common in pricing, packaging, and shelf-placement research where respondents are challenged to examine the virtual environment for something that doesn't fit, something that items have in common, or are briefly shown a scene and asked to recall brands. Researchers believe that by allowing respondents to experience the virtual environment, it triggers more natural emotional reactions as well as higher satisfaction with the survey process.[48]

Context gamification occurs when participants are totally immersed in game elements and the questionnaire itself takes the form of a video game.

A final form of gamification is called context gamification (or hard gamification). **Context gamification** occurs when participants are totally immersed in game elements and the questionnaire itself takes the form of a video game.[49] For example, GMI tested a downhill skiing game in which participants would manipulate the skier underneath one of several gates listing potential question answers. A different contextual game survey encouraged respondents to "shoot" the appropriate answer using their starship. Preliminary results suggest that contextual games have the potential to confuse participants and negatively impact the data quality.[50] Additional experiments revolved around the Second Life virtual reality platform and asked respondents to create avatars for use in virtual conversations and surveys. MRII found the time, cost, and effort to create the survey research gaming environment simply overwhelming given the value of the research results received.[51] The vast majority of firms have abandoned context gamification in favor of micro-games, interactivity and textual forms of gamification. While gamification is no longer in its infancy, the increasing reliance on Internet and mobile surveys suggest that the use of gamification techniques will still continue to grow in the future.

11.10 Evaluating the Questionnaire

LEARNING OBJECTIVE 11.9
Discuss the steps in evaluating a questionnaire.

Before administering the questionnaire it is important for it to be evaluated. Figure 11.22 identifies typical steps used in the evaluation process. The evaluation should begin by comparing the questions in the survey to the survey objectives. Was each survey objective addressed adequately? Are there questions in the survey that do not meet one of the survey objectives? If so, the questions should be deleted.

A very beneficial second step is to have colleagues evaluate the questionnaire. These may be individuals that work in the same office but who are working on other projects. They may be individuals who work outside the organization but understand marketing research and don't mind contributing some time in evaluating a questionnaire. Sometimes these individuals can catch wording that is not quite clear, jargon, or problematic phrasing.

Once the researcher is comfortable with the questionnaire, it should be shown to the client. The purpose of showing it to the client is to ensure the data that are being collected meets the information needs. It is not to inspect the wording of each question. Most clients are not marketing researchers and they might want to re-write questions. When this happens, the re-written questions often only confuse respondents or do not produce the level of data needed. The client's role is to make sure the questionnaire meets the objectives of the research study and that the results produced from the questionnaire will provide useful information.

Once these reviews are finished, it is time for a pretest. Typically, 20–40 individuals are chosen who mirror the sample that will be used for the research study. They are given

- Check questions against survey objectives
- Colleagues review
- Client review
- Pre-test
- Revise questionnaire
- Pre-test again if necessary

FIGURE 11.22 Steps in Evaluating a Questionnaire

the questionnaire and asked to take the survey. Their input can be obtained in two different ways. The first is to have them complete the entire questionnaire just as the sample respondent would. Once it is complete, the researcher will ask the pretest participant to discuss any questions that were not clear or were difficult to answer. The researchers can also ask about the length of the questionnaire, the sequencing of questions, terminology, jargon, and any signs of boredom or fatigue that they may have noticed in the respondent. The second approach is for the person doing the pretest to talk out loud as he takes the survey rather than wait until the end. The idea behind this approach is that it will help the researcher to see the thought processes used in answering the questions. It could reveal information that waiting until the end would not.

In most cases the pretest will indicate revisions that should be made to the questionnaire. If these are minor, they can be made and the questionnaire is ready to launch. If major changes are made, then another pretest should be conducted. It may also be worthwhile to go through the entire process again. Time spent on questionnaire evaluation is time well spent. It will result in better data and will aid in the reduction of errors.

11.11 Global Concerns

In the last several years online research has become prevalent internationally. The more advanced countries have a higher Internet penetration rate that makes it possible to complete online surveys. However, companies sometimes try to conduct research in countries where a significant number of people do not have Internet access. This becomes an issue if the input from those who are not online is important to fulfilling the survey objectives.

Another challenge globally is the thought that to save money the survey should be offered in English only, or only in the native language where the study is being conducted. With business surveys, offering surveys only in English might be permissible. But in doing so a researcher might be missing valuable input. For example, suppose a survey is conducted in France and the survey is in French only. Not everyone who works in businesses in France is fluent in French. Asians, Hispanics, and even Americans may be able to converse in French but not feel comfortable answering a survey in French. If the survey were offered in both French and English, more respondents could respond and better data would be obtained.

Furthermore, recognize that each language has its own vernacular and dialects. For example, creating survey items that offer measurement equivalency can be particularly challenging when surveying Hispanic cultures from multiple countries of origin. To avoid other common problems when creating international surveys, use translations that are more formal, 0–10 rating scales that are much more familiar internationally than Likert scales, and plan more time for multiple pretests.[52]

11.12 Marketing Research Statistics

Scales are used frequently in marketing research. In the Statistics Review section the concept of recoding is reviewed since scales with multiple items will usually contain some positively worded statements as well as negatively worded statements. The Dealing with Data section has an exercise requiring recoding of statements as well as summing and averaging scale values that can be used for analytical purposes. The Statistics Reporting section contrasts reporting of data using a pie chart, bar chart, and a radar chart. Sometimes using an unusual type of graph will grab an audience's attention.

11.12a Statistics Review

Scales are an important part of marketing research. To ensure individuals read a series of statements within a scale, researchers often reverse questions. Some will be positively stated, others will be negatively worded. Consider the scale shown in Figure 11.23 that measures an individual's loyalty to local retail stores.

1. I will pay slightly more for products if I can buy them locally.	Never Occasionally Frequently Always
2. I shop outside my local retail area before looking to see what is offered locally.	Never Occasionally Frequently Always
3. I shop at local stores because it is important to help my community.	Never Occasionally Frequently Always
4. I shop locally because the convenience outweighs the other advantages of shopping outside the community.	Never Occasionally Frequently Always
5. I shop locally to support the local merchants and business district.	Never Occasionally Frequently Always
6. Shopping at local stores is an enjoyable experience.	Never Occasionally Frequently Always
7. Local stores have inferior products/services so I prefer shopping out of town.	Never Occasionally Frequently Always
8. Because I am more familiar with the local stores, I prefer shopping locally than out of town.	Never Occasionally Frequently Always
9. I shop locally even when the selection/variety of goods is poor.	Never Occasionally Frequently Always
10. I am not loyal to my local shopping area.	Never Occasionally Frequently Always

FIGURE 11.23 Scale to Measure Loyalty to Local Retail Stores

Notice items 2, 7, and 10 are worded so that an "always" response measures a more favorable attitude toward shopping outside the local area. Responses for individuals who are loyal to the local retail stores would be a low value. To make the scale consistent and to measure loyalty to local retail stores, these three items need to be recoded after the data has been collected, reversing these scale items. In SPSS this can be done with the recode command. The coding of the original scale shows "never" was coded a 1, "occasionally" a 2, "frequently" a 3, and "always" a 4. To recode items 2, 7, 10, the 1 is changed to a 4, the 2 is changed to a 3, the 3 is changed to a 2 and the 4 is changed to a 1. Recoding these three items makes the responses consistent with the other seven items that together constitute the scale. Following recoding, the higher the value, the greater is the loyalty the respondent displays to local retail stores.

It is always a good idea to recode data into a new variable. If recoding is done with the original variable, it is easy to forget whether or not it has been recoded, especially a month or a year later. It is further recommended that new variables be created for every item in the scale even though some will be identical to the original scale, since this allows the researcher to keep the original data, in case it is ever needed, and makes it easier to select the variables to be used in a particular analysis. For example, the new set of store loyalty items might be named FinalSL1 through FinalSL10, though only items 2, 7, and 10 would differ from the original data.

In examining local retail store loyalty using this scale, researchers have two options. They can either sum the responses to obtain a total score for the ten items or they can average the responses for the measure as a whole. Which method is used depends on how the results will be used and what will be the easiest for reporting to management. If the scale items are summed, the mean value for the ten items is 25.32 with a standard deviation of 4.55. If an average score is used for ten items, it is 2.53 with a standard deviation of 0.45.

Summing or averaging the items in the scale allows researchers to make comparisons with other variables. For instance, the level of loyalty to local retail stores can be compared

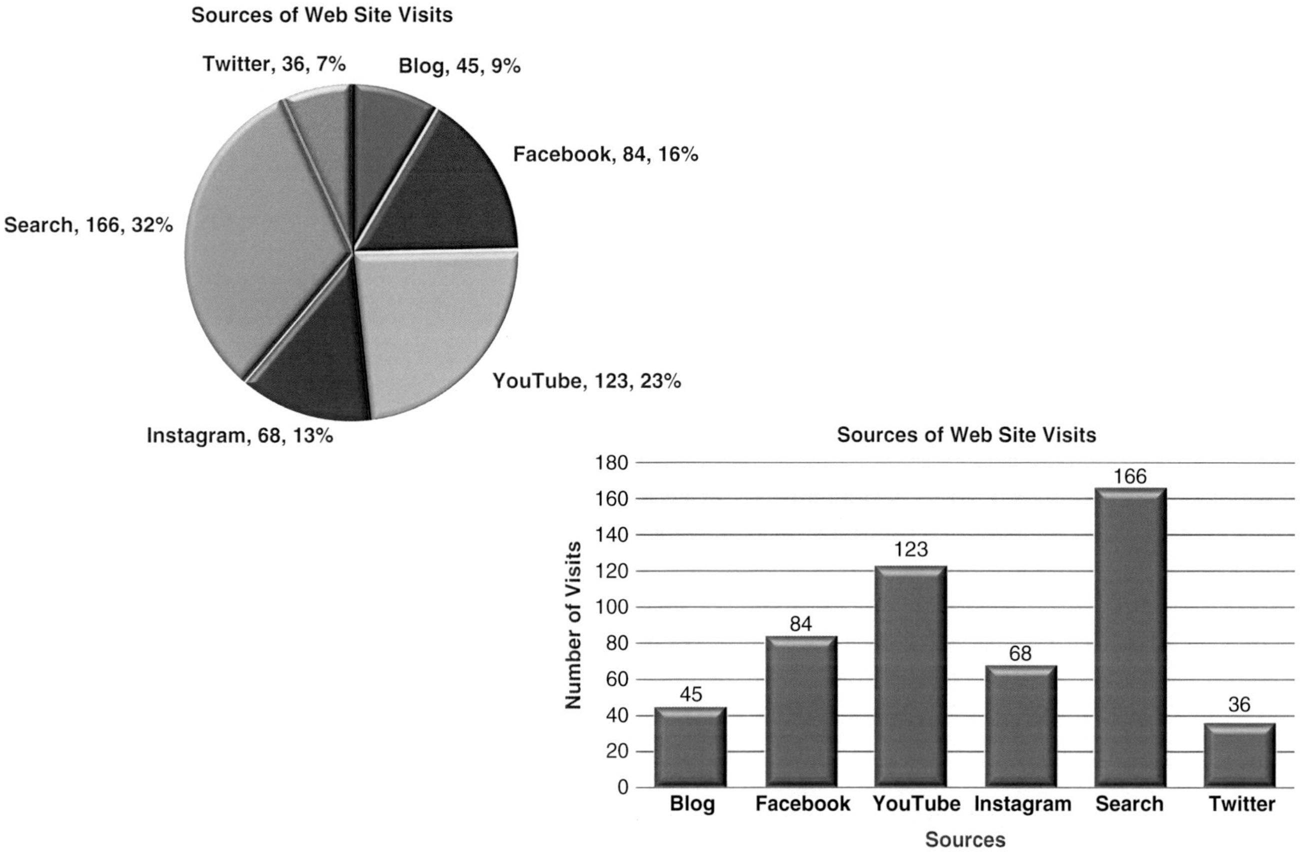

FIGURE 11.24 An Example of Data Graphed Using a Pie Chart and Bar Chart

based on a respondent's gender, age, income, how long they lived in the community, and other variables the researcher deems may be important in local store loyalty.

11.12b Statistics Reporting

Researchers often have multiple ways of reporting data. Two common graphs are the pie chart and bar chart. Figure 11.24 illustrates data that is graphed using each of these methods. The data are the sources of a company's website visits over a 90-day period. The pie chart allows the researcher to show the number of visits that originated from each source and the percentage each source is of the total. The bar chart shows the number of visits from each source. The researcher could have graphed the percentages instead, but not both as was done with the pie chart.

Because pie charts and bar charts are used so frequently, sometimes a researcher wants to use a different type of chart to grab the attention of individuals looking at a report or listening to a presentation. A seldom-used graph that could be used with this data is the radar chart, shown in Figure 11.25. The points of the hexagon are the sources of the websites visits. The red line in the center charts the number of visits from each of the sources. The graph shows the highest number of visits originating from search and YouTube.

To create a radar chart like the one showing in Figure 11.25, you will need to create a table similar to Figure 11.26. The second, third, fourth and fifth columns are bogus data used to create the rings in the radar chart. The last column is the actual data and is the dark red line in the figure. For instructions on how to create a radar chart, such as Figure 11.25, go the author's website at www.clowjames.net/students.html.

Statistical Reporting Exercise: Use the data provided in Figure 11.27 to create a radar chart. Also, graph the data using a pie chart and a bar chart. Comment on the pros and cons of each graph.

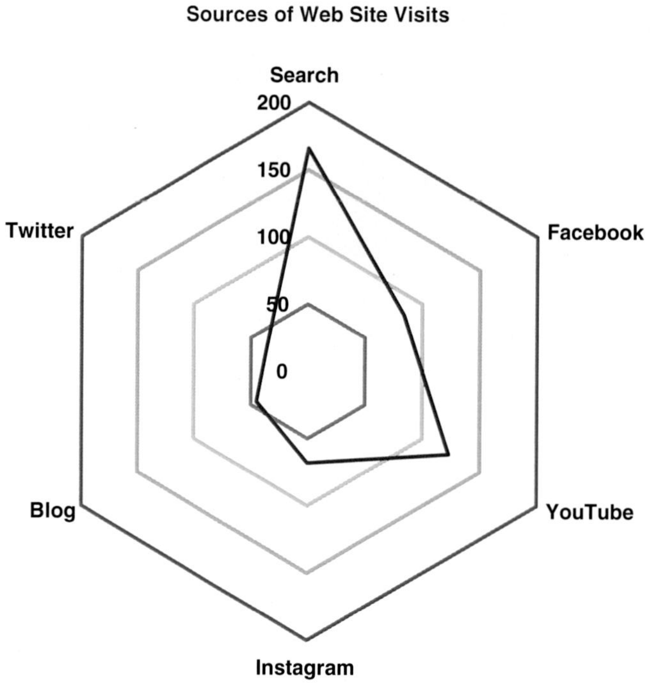

FIGURE 11.25 An Example of a Radar Chart

Source	Rings				Data
Blog	50	100	150	200	45
Facebook	50	100	150	200	84
YouTube	50	100	150	200	123
Instagram	50	100	150	200	68
Search	50	100	150	200	166
Twitter	50	100	150	200	36

FIGURE 11.26 Data Used to Create Radar Chart

Source	Purchases
Banner ad	375
Direct mail	188
Email blast	271
Facebook ad	113
Mobile ad	244
Search ad	205
TV Direct response ad	133

FIGURE 11.27 Data for Statistical Reporting Exercise

11.12c Dealing with Data

The loyalty to local retail stores that was shown in the previous section was part of a larger study that also examined skepticism toward advertising, buying impulsiveness, and materialistic attitude. The questionnaire for this study is entitled Chapter 11 Dealing with Data Survey, and the SPSS data is entitled Chapter 11 Dealing with Data. Both files are located at www.clowjames.net/students.html.

Access the data and questionnaire. Start by reading through the items and noting which items are reversed and need to be recoded. For the local shopping loyalty scale, the previous Statistics Review section already identified items 2, 7, and 10 as those to be reverse coded. Once you have identified the items in need of recoding for the "skepticism to advertising," "buying impulsiveness," and "materialistic attitude" scales, answer the following questions.

1. For each of the scales, which items need to be reverse coded?
2. What is the mean of these scale items (before recoding)?
3. Recode these items. What is the mean of each of these items after being recoded?

Using SPSS, sum the responses for each of the scales by creating a new variable for each scale. Repeat the same process, but average the scores for each of the scales. You will create a total of eight new variables. When finished, answer the questions below.

1. What is the sum for each of the four scales?
2. What is the average for each of the four scales?
3. If a researcher wanted to compare the overall responses from the four scales, which would be easier to understand—comparing the summated scale scores or the average scale scores? Why?

Summary

Objective 1: Outline the questionnaire design process.
Questionnaire design begins with the research questions or objectives, from which survey objectives are developed. The next step is to select the data collection method since it influences how questions are written. Questions are carefully written for each survey objective. Then the layout and design of the questionnaire are determined. Once the questionnaire is complete, it is evaluated. The last step is to develop an invitation or cover letter.

Objective 2: Discuss the two primary question formats that can be used in questionnaire design.
The two primary question formats are open-ended questions and closed-ended questions. Open-ended questions allow respondents to answer in their own words, and can provide new or different insights for researchers, as well as additional alternatives for closed-ended questions. Open-ended questions in surveys administered by interviewers allow for additional probing for understanding. The problems with open-ended questions include difficulty in interpreting the answer, challenges in editing and coding the responses, potential for interviewer bias, and insufficient and shallow answers. In contrast, closed-ended questions are easy to code and the possibility of interviewer bias is limited. Also, the response categories can jog respondents' memories, enhancing recall. However, generating the list of alternative answers to closed-ended questions is challenging for researchers, and individuals must select from the list provided, so respondents have no freedom in how they answer a question.

Objective 3: Elaborate on the three different types of closed-ended questions.
The three types of closed-ended questions include dichotomous questions, multiple-choice questions, and scaled-response questions. Dichotomous questions have only two options. Multiple-choice questions offer multiple (three or more) options. Neither dichotomous nor multiple-choice questions allow respondents to indicate a degree of intensity. To capture intensity, researchers often use scaled-response questions, such as Likert or semantic differential scales.

Objective 4: Identify and describe the categories of questions used in questionnaires.
Survey questions can be classified into one of six categories. Demographic or classification questions ask respondents for demographic information or to identify one or more responses that apply to a situation. Knowledge questions are designed to assess the level of knowledge respondents have about a topic. Attitude questions involve

measuring feelings toward a brand, object, or concept. Attitude measurement is important because attitude often precedes actions. Preference questions involve asking consumers to rate or rank objects or ideas. While intentions do not always equate to actions, measuring intentions can provide valuable information. Behavior questions involve past actions, such as purchases or media consumption.

Objective 5: Discuss the issues relating to the phrasing of questions.
Questions should be clearly written, free of jargon and ambiguity, and should be interpreted as meaning the same thing by different respondents. They should use respondents' vocabulary in a conversational style. The questionnaire should have a logical flow. If scales are used, they should be easy for respondents to understand and use. In wording questions, it is important to keep recall periods short, avoid either/or questions and double-barreled questions. Leading questions do not provide honest responses since respondents may feel uncomfortable providing an answer other than what is suggested, and thus should be avoided. Care should be taken to ensure that the questions asked are applicable to the respondents.

Objective 6: Identify and explain the contents of the survey invitation and each section of a questionnaire.
Though not part of the questionnaire, the survey invitation is a critical factor influencing respondent participation. The questionnaire should begin with and introduction and instructions that not only explain how to complete the questionnaire but why it is important. A screening question or questions should then be used to see if the person meets the target audience criteria. In some cases, the screening question might be asked before instructions are given. The body of the questionnaire, containing the survey questions, then follows. Questions should follow a logical order and funnel from more general questions to more specific ones. Scaled response questions should be toward the middle. If sensitive questions are asked, they should be near the end of the survey. After all of the questions have been asked, respondents then should be asked demographic information. The questionnaire should end with a closing that thanks the respondent for participating and, if possible, provides more information about the purpose of the research.

Objective 7: Describe the negative consequences of long questionnaires.
Negative consequences of long questionnaires include lower cooperation rates from respondents, more individuals breaking off from answering questions after they started but before finishing, higher item non-response rates where questions are left blank, reduced data quality from respondents either just randomly answering or not taking time to provide good answers, and, for panels, a higher attrition rate. The split-questionnaire avoids the problems of long questionnaires because each respondent answers a core component of the survey and only one subcomponent.

Objective 8: Discuss gamification and its use in online surveys.
Gamification is the process of applying gaming mechanics to survey tasks to encourage more active participation. Individuals will become more engaged in the survey process by injecting fun elements into the survey. The primary text-based gamification techniques are personalization, triggering latent feelings, projection, forced imagery situations, and fantasy. Adding interactive aspects and micro-games to the survey, as well as incentive and visual elements can further enhance the participant's experience, producing higher levels of satisfaction and survey completion.

Objective 9: Discuss the steps in evaluating a questionnaire.
Questionnaire evaluation has six steps. First is checking questions against the survey objectives to be sure all survey objectives have been adequately met and that no superfluous questions have been asked. Second, colleagues should be asked to review the questions to make sure they are clear and concise. Third, clients should be asked to evaluate the questions, not for wording, but to make sure the data provided will provide the information needed to make management decisions. Fourth is a pretest with 20 to 30 individuals that mirror the target audience for the study. The fifth step is to revise the questionnaire based on the pretest information. The last step, if major changes were made to the questionnaire, is to pretest again.

Key Terms

anonymity, p. 379
break-off rate, p. 371
closed-ended questions, p. 366
confidentiality, p. 379
context gamification, p. 390
dichotomous question, p. 368
double-barreled question, p. 377
gamification, p. 386
leading question, p. 377
multiple-choice question, p. 369
multiple response question, p. 369
open-ended questions, p. 364
position bias, p. 369
questionnaire, p. 361
scaled-response question, p. 370
split questionnaire design, p. 385
survey objectives, p. 361
visual intuity, p. 389

Critical Thinking Exercises

1. Suppose that a key research objective is "To understand how different consumer segments use and share social media content." Create a minimum of three survey objectives for this research objective.
2. Your client believes that attitudes toward the firm's brand should be assessed using a semantic differential or an itemized rating scale. How will the scale chosen affect the choice of data collection method? Which scale and data collection technique would you recommend and why? If the research objectives did not require comparing attitudes between subgroups, would you still use this scale and data collection method you chose? Why or why not?
3. The use of open-ended questions in quantitative research studies is appropriate only in certain circumstances. Explain.
4. For each of the following, identify the type of closed-ended question being asked and the question category each represents.
   a. In the last week, have you visited a hair salon or barber?____Yes____No
   b. How did you hear about our salon (check all that apply)?
      _______ Radio Ad ____ TV Ad ___ News paper ad
      _____Online search

      _______ Website ____ Friend ____ Other: (please specify)______
   c. Please indicate your level of agreement or disagreement with the following statements, where 1 = strongly disagree to 7 = strongly agree:
      In general, the higher the price of a product, the higher the quality. 1 2 3 4 5 6 7
      The old saying, "you get what you pay for" is generally true. 1 2 3 4 5 6 7
      You always have to pay a bit more for the best. 1 2 3 4 5 6 7
5. Select one of the survey objectives developed in response to question 1. Write at least three complete questions for an online survey that will help to obtain the necessary information.
6. Itemized rating questions, paired comparisons, and rank order questions are the most common methods of determining preference. Create survey questions of each type in the context of fast food restaurants. Under what circumstances would you recommend using each and why?
7. Suppose you were tasked with developing separate questionnaires targeting 1) individuals who have immigrated to the U.S. from Mexico in the past 90 days; 2) welfare recipients; 3) physicians. Explain how the respondent characteristics could influence the questionnaire development and question phrasing process.
8. Critique the following questions and response options:
   How much do you normally pay for milk?
   __________ $3.00– $3.50_________ $3.50– $3.99
   __________ $4.00– $4.50 More than $4.50
   Please indicate your level of satisfaction with the quality tools made by Craftsman.
   _____ Very satisfied ___ Satisfied _____ Somewhat satisfied ___ Dissatisfied. How old are you and how much do you make in a year?__________
   Do you have soda with your mixed drinks?__________
   Yes__________No
   Please rate the Recreation Center's natatorium using the following scale:
   Clean:____:____:____:____:____:____:____: Dirty
   1 2 3 4 5 6 7
   Too warm:____:____:____:____:____:____:____: Too cold
   1 2 3 4 5 6 7
   Crowded:____:____:____:____:____:____:____: Just right
   1 2 3 4 5 6 7
9. A 50-item survey regarding attitudes toward used cars, salespersons, and dealerships will be conducted online. Compose 1) a survey invitation, and 2) instructions that will appear at the beginning of the survey. You may make any reasonable assumptions that you would like when creating instructions or phrasing your invitation.
10. Describe a specific research study in which a split questionnaire design might be appropriate. What types of questions would constitute the core component of the survey? How many subcomponents would you recommend, and what would be the primary focus of each?
11. Develop a standard survey question for an online survey using the topic of your choice. Now create two gamified versions of survey questions designed to collect the same data. One survey question should include a micro-game or interactive feature, and the other should feature and a gamified question phrasing as discussed in Figure 11.19. Do you think the items you created will be successful in engaging respondents? Why or why not? Do you believe the data they collect will be of similar or superior quality? Why or why not?

Lakeside Grill

(Comprehensive Student Case)

Alexa, Brooke, Destiny, Juan, and Zach went back to their notes and found the research questions the team had developed previously. Based on these research questions, the team created the following survey objectives.

1. What is the current level of customer satisfaction and patronage with the various aspects of Lakeside Grill?
   a. Identify level of satisfaction with customer service, food, aesthetics, and atmosphere.
   b. Request frequency of patronage of Lakeside Grill.
   c. Solicit likes and dislikes with Lakeside Grill.
2. Why have individuals not patronized Lakeside Grill?
   a. Determine reasons for not patronizing Lakeside Grill.
3. How has the addition of a new competitor down the street affected Lakeside Grill's customer base?
   a. Determine attitudes toward new competitor in relation to Lakeside Grill.
   b. Determine if frequency of patronage of Lakeside Grill declined.
4. Would changing the Lakeside Grill's menu, advertising, and/or promotional practices increase sales?
   a. Solicit attitudes toward new menu items.
   b. Determine impact of advertising on patronage decision.
   c. Identify promotions that may influence patronage decisions.

Using these survey objectives, the team next developed the questionnaire entitled Chapter 11 Lakeside Grill Survey (www.clowjames.net/students.html). Almost every question resulted in some level of discussion among the team members. But the questions that raised the most controversy were Questions 2, 4 and 5. Brooke argued that they should not use open-ended questions at all because they would get too many different answers. The other team members felt the open-ended questions were important because respondents could provide their thoughts in their own words. Juan commented that "asking for the one thing they like and dislike about Lakeside Grill would provide valuable insight into what individuals are thinking."

While Alexa thought that the SERVQUAL instrument should have been used in place of the items in Question 6, others disagreed, arguing that not all of the items were relevant, and that doing so would make the survey too long. When it came to Question 10, Destiny felt the way it was worded was like an "either or" question because changes in eating at Lakeside Grill may not have been caused by Fisherman's Paradise. But Zach argued that it was clearly stated that the respondent was to answer how Fisherman's Paradise affected eating at Lakeside Grill.

Critique Questions:

1. Review the research questions. Do they appear to be adequate for this study?
2. Evaluate the survey objectives. Are each of the research objectives covered adequately by survey objectives? Are there any survey objectives that are not clear? Are there any survey objectives that would solicit unnecessary information?
3. Match each survey question with its appropriate survey objective. What is your evaluation of the questionnaire in terms of meeting the survey objectives?
4. Using Figure 11.10, classify each question. Do you think the team used the best question type, or could a different category of questions be used that would provide better data?
5. What do you think about Questions 2, 4, and 5? Would you agree with the team or with Brooke?
6. Do you agree with Alexa that the SERVQUAL instrument should have been used in place of Question 6? Why or why not?
7. What do you think of Questions 7 through 10 about Fisherman's Paradise and its impact on Lakeside Grill? Are these good questions? Why or why not?
8. Evaluate the total questionnaire. What changes would you make in the questionnaire? Why?

Notes

1. *State of Customer Service Experience, 2018* (Rosemont, IL: The Northridge Group, 2019), 5–6, 8, 10–11, 13.
2. Based on reports available at http://www.emarketer.com/reports/all/emarketer_2000815.aspx.
3. Jonathan E. Brill, "The Exploratory Open-Ended Survey Question," *Quirk's Marketing Research Review* (March 1995), https://www.quirks.com/articles/the-exploratory-open-ended-survey-question.
4. Ibid.
5. Ibid.
6. FocusVision Staff, "Five Steps to Getting the Most Out of Mobile Surveys," *Quirk's Media* (October 8, 2018), https://www.quirks.com/articles/five-steps-to-getting-the-most-out-of-mobile-surveys.
7. Antoun Mavletovta, "Data Quality in PC and Mobile Web Surveys," *Survey Research Methods* 7, no. 3 (2013): 191–205; T. Wells, J. T. Bailey, and M. W. Link, "Comparison of Smartphone and Online Survey Administration," *Social Science Computer Review* 32,

no. 2 (2014): 238–255; Antoun Maveltova and Mick P. Couper, "Sensitive Topics in PC Web and Mobile Web Surveys," *Survey Research Methods* 7, no. 3 (2013): 191–205.

8. Antoun, Christopher, Mick. P. Couper and Frederick G. Congrad, "Effects of Mobile versus PC Web on Survey Response Quality. A Crossover Experiment in a Probability Web Panel," *Public Opinion Quarterly* 81, Special Issue (2017): 280–306.
9. Patrick Elms, "Optimizing Questionnaire Design for Mobile Surveys," *Quirk's Media* (December 2018), https://www.quirks.com/articles/optimizing-questionnaire-design-for-mobile-surveys.
10. Tom Wells, "What Market Researchers Should Know about Mobile Surveys," *International Journal of Marketing Research* 57, no. 4 (2015): 521–532.
11. Patrick Elms, "Optimizing Questionnaire Design for Mobile Surveys," *Quirk's Media* (December 2018), https://www.quirks.com/articles/optimizing-questionnaire-design-for-mobile-surveys.
12. Tom Wells, "What Market Researchers Should Know about Mobile Surveys," *International Journal of Marketing Research* 57, no. 4 (2015): 521–532.
13. Patrick Elms, "Optimizing Questionnaire Design for Mobile Surveys," *Quirk's Media* (December 2018), https://www.quirks.com/articles/optimizing-questionnaire-design-for-mobile-surveys.
14. David M. Ambrose and John R. Anstey, "Questionnaire Development: Demystifying the Process," *International Management Review* 6, no. 1 (2010): 83–90.
15. Andrew Grenville, "Text Message vs. E-Mail Survey Invites," *Quirk's Media* (August 15, 2017), https://www.quirks.com/articles/text-message-vs-e-mail-survey-invites.
16. This section is based on Charles Coby and Robert Devall, "How to Maximize Survey Response Rates," *Quirk's Media* (January 2016), https://www.quirks.com/articles/how-to-maximize-survey-response-rates; Sofie Nelen, "Tips for Crafting the Perfect Survey Intro," *Quirk's Media* (October 9, 2017), https://www.quirks.com/articles/tips-for-crafting-the-perfect-survey-intro; Rill Hodari, "Survey Participation: Balancing the Influence of Invitation Language and Incentives," *Quirk's Media* (March 2016), https://www.quirks.com/articles/survey-participation-balancing-the-influence-of-invitation-language-and-incentives; and interview with Debbie Peternana, ReRez, December 1, 2011.
17. This section is based on Sofie Nelen, "Tips for Crafting the Perfect Survey Intro," *Quirk's Media* (October 9, 2017), https://www.quirks.com/articles/tips-for-crafting-the-perfect-survey-intro.
18. Tom Wells, "What Market Researchers Should Know about Mobile Surveys," *International Journal of Marketing Research* 57, no. 4 (2015): 521–532; A. Jue, "FocusVision Mobile Trend Report," 2016, http://www.focusvision.com.
19. Bill McDowell, "Minimizing the Impact of Survey Bots," *Quirk's Media* (February 21, 2019), https://www.quirks.com/articles/minimizing-the-impact-of-survey-bots.
20. Sarah Faulkner, "How to Follow Consumer Research's Golden Rule," *Quirk's Media* (May 4, 2017), https://www.quirks.com/articles/how-to-follow-consumer-research-s-golden-rule.
21. J. D. Deitch, "Programmatic Sampling: The Basics" (December 12, 2017), https://greenbookblog.org/2017/12/18/programmatic-sampling-the-basics/; J. D. Deitch, "10 Ways Sample Companies Should Be Using Automation," June 14, 2018, https://greenbookblog.org/2018/06/14/10-ways-sample-companies-should-be-using-automation/.
22. Mario X. Carrasco, "The Importance of Using Secure Survey Links," *Quirk's Media* (February 4, 2019), https://www.quirks.com/articles/the-importance-of-using-secure-survey-links.
23. Alexander Cernat and Mingnan Liu, "Radio Buttons in Web Surveys: Searching for Alternatives," *International Journal of Marketing Research* 61, no. 3 (2019): 266–286.
24. This section is adapted from FocusVision Staff, "Five Steps to Getting the Most Out of Mobile Surveys," *Quirk's Media* (October 8, 2018), https://www.quirks.com/articles/five-steps-to-getting-the-most-out-of-mobile-surveys.
25. Marco Vriens, Michael Wedel, and Zsolt Aandor, "Split-Questionnaire Design: A New Tool in Survey Design Panel Management, *Market Research* (Summer 2001): 14–19.
26. Frank Kelly and Phil Doriot, "Using Data Mining and Machine Learning to Shorten and Improve Surveys," *Quirk's Media* (May 22, 2017), https://www.quirks.com/articles/using-data-mining-and-machine-learning-to-shorten-and-improve-surveys.
27. Dan Coates, MaryLeigh Bliss, and Xavier Vivar, "The Impact of Survey Duration on Completion Rates among Millennial Respondents," *Quirk's Media* (February 2016), https://www.quirks.com/articles/the-impact-of-survey-duration-on-completion-rates-among-millennial-respondents.
28. Frank Kelly and Phil Doriot, "Using Data Mining and Machine Learning to Shorten and Improve Surveys," *Quirk's Media* (May 22, 2017), https://www.quirks.com/articles/using-data-mining-and-machine-learning-to-shorten-and-improve-surveys.
29. Feray Adiguzel and Michel Wedel, "Split Questionnaire Design for Massive Surveys," *Journal of Marketing Research* 45, no. 5 (October 2008): 608–617.
30. Frank Kelly and Phil Doriot, "Using Data Mining and Machine Learning to Shorten and Improve Surveys,"

Quirk's Media (May 22, 2017), https://www.quirks.com/articles/using-data-mining-and-machine-learning-to-shorten-and-improve-surveys.
31. Trish Doran and Shellie Yule, "How Game-Enhanced Design Can Improve Respondent Satisfaction and Data Quality," *Quirks Marketing Research Review* (January 2015), https://www.quirks.com/articles/how-game-enhanced-design-can-improve-respondent-satisfaction-and-data-quality.
32. Jon Puleston, "Gamification 101—From Theory to Practice—Part 1," *Quirk's Media* (January 2012), https://www.quirks.com/articles/gamification-101-from-theory-to-practice-part-i.
33. J. Puleston and D. Sleep, "The Game Experiments: How Gaming Techniques Can Be Used to Improve the Quality of Feedback from Online Research," ESOMAR Congress, Amsterdam, September 2011, pp. 18–21.
34. Tom Ewing, "Where Gamification Came From and Why It Could Be Here to Stay," *Quirk's Marketing Research Review* (March 2012): 30–32, 34.
35. Pippa Bailey, Gareth Pritchard, and Hollie Kernohan, "Gamification in Market Research. Increasing Enjoyment, Participant Engagement and Richness of Data, but What of Data Validity?" *International Journal of Market Research* 57, no. 1 (2015): 17–28.
36. "Adoption of Emerging Methods," in *GRIT Report: GreenBook Research Industry Trends Report, Quarters 3–4, 2018* (New York: GreenBook, 2018), 22.
37. Jon Puleston, "Gamification 101—From Theory to Practice—Part 1," *Quirk's Media*, (January 2012), https://www.quirks.com/articles/gamification-101-from-theory-to-practice-part-i.
38. Ibid.
39. Tom Ewing, "Where Gamification Came From and Why It Could Be Here to Stay," *Quirk's Marketing Research Review* (March 2012): 30–32, 34; Jon Puleston, "Gamification 101—From Theory to Practice—Part 1," *Quirk's Media* (January 2012), https://www.quirks.com/articles/gamification-101-from-theory-to-practice-part-i.
40. Pete Cape, "The Impact of Gamifying to Increase Spontaneous Awareness," *Quirk's Media* (November 2015), https://www.quirks.com/articles/the-impact-of-gamifying-to-increase-spontaneous-awareness; and Jon Puleston, "Gamification 101—From Theory to Practice—Part 1," *Quirk's Media* (January 2012), https://www.quirks.com/articles/gamification-101-from-theory-to-practice-part-i.
41. Jon Puleston, "Gamification 101—From Theory to Practice—Part II," *Quirk's Media* (February 2012), https://www.quirks.com/articles/gamification-101-from-theory-to-practice-part-i.
42. Ibid.
43. Lilah Koski, "Gamified Approaches: Testing Survey Design Techniques," *Quirk's Media* (April 5, 2017), https://www.quirks.com/articles/the-impact-of-gamifying-to-increase-spontaneous-awareness.
44. Trish Doran and Shellie Yule, "How Game-Enhanced Design Can Improve Respondent Satisfaction and Data Quality," *Quirks Marketing Research Review* (January 2015), https://www.quirks.com/articles/how-game-enhanced-design-can-improve-respondent-satisfaction-and-data-quality.
45. Bill MacElroy, "Engagement Gamification: How to Play the Game," Market Research Institute International, July 12, 2017, https://blog.mrii.org/engagement-gamification-how-to-play-the-game/.
46. Bill MacElroy, "What Is Gamification?" Market Research Institute International, June 1, 2017, https://blog.mrii.org/what-is-gamification/.
47. Jon Puleston, "Gamification 101—From Theory to Practice—Part II," *Quirk's Media* (February 2012), https://www.quirks.com/articles/gamification-101-from-theory-to-practice-part-i.
48. Bill MacElroy, "Engagement Gamification: How to Play the Game," Market Research Institute International, July 12, 2017, https://blog.mrii.org/engagement-gamification-how-to-play-the-game/.
49. Trish Doran and Shellie Yule, "How Game-Enhanced Design Can Improve Respondent Satisfaction and Data Quality," *Quirks Marketing Research Review* (January 2015), https://www.quirks.com/articles/how-game-enhanced-design-can-improve-respondent-satisfaction-and-data-quality.
50. Jon Puleston, "Gamification 101—From Theory to Practice—Part II," *Quirk's Media* (February 2012), https://www.quirks.com/articles/gamification-101-from-theory-to-practice-part-ii.
51. Bill MacElroy, "What Is Gamification?" Market Research Institute International, June 1, 2017, https://blog.mrii.org/what-is-gamification/.
52. Loren Chase, "Overcoming the Challenges of Cross-Cultural Research," *Quirk's Media* (November 2017), https://www.quirks.com/articles/overcoming-the-challenges-of-cross-cultural-research.

PART IV

Analyzing and Reporting Marketing Research

Source: everything possible/Shutterstock.

Fundamental Data Analysis

CHAPTER 12

Source: Voronin76/Shutterstock.

Chapter Outline

Learning Objectives

After studying this chapter, you should be able to:

- Identify the steps in the data preparation process.
- Discuss the processes of validating and coding data.
- Describe the processes of data entry and data cleaning.
- Discuss the advantages of pre-coding questionnaires.
- Describe the various ways of tabulating data.
- Explain the descriptive statistics that should be used with each type of scale.

12.1 Chapter Overview

Preparing data for analysis is important. It requires validating the data collected, coding responses to questions, entering the data into a data file, and cleaning the data. Each of these steps is necessary to minimize errors before the data are ever analyzed. Once the data has been properly prepared, it is time to tabulate the results of each question in the survey and the demographic information that was requested. This information can be presented in tables or graphs. If graphs are used, it is important to prepare graphs that contain complete information, are easy to read, and are properly labeled, such as the one in **Figure 12.1**. This graph shows the differences between B2B and B2C marketers in how the various social media platforms are used. It is easy to see that B2C marketers use Facebook considerably more than any other type of social media. B2B marketers use Facebook, but also use both LinkedIn and Twitter more than B2C marketers.[1]

Parameter characteristic of a population, such as the mean or mode.

Statistic characteristic of a sample used as an estimator for the population parameter.

In discussing fundamental data analysis, it is important to understand the difference between the terms "parameter" and "statistic." A **parameter** refers to a characteristic of an entire population, such as the mean or mode for the age of the population. A **statistic** describes a characteristic of the sample, such as the mean or mode of the age of the sample respondents, and is used as an estimator for the population parameter. If collected properly, the sample should be representative of the population, and thus a statistic obtained from the sample should be a good estimation of the population parameter. In the graph shown in Figure 12.1, the statistics obtained from the sample of B2C and B2B marketers are used to estimate which social media platforms are used by each type of marketer. If the sample was selected properly, it is not necessary to interview every B2C and B2B marketer. In fact, it would be impossible to do so. Therefore, it is important for companies using the data from this study to have confidence in the way the data were collected and analyzed.

12.2 Preparing Data for Analysis

LEARNING OBJECTIVE 12.1
Identify the steps in the data preparation process.

The purpose of collecting data is to gather information to make marketing decisions. The quality of those decisions is dependent on the quality of data obtained. To ensure high

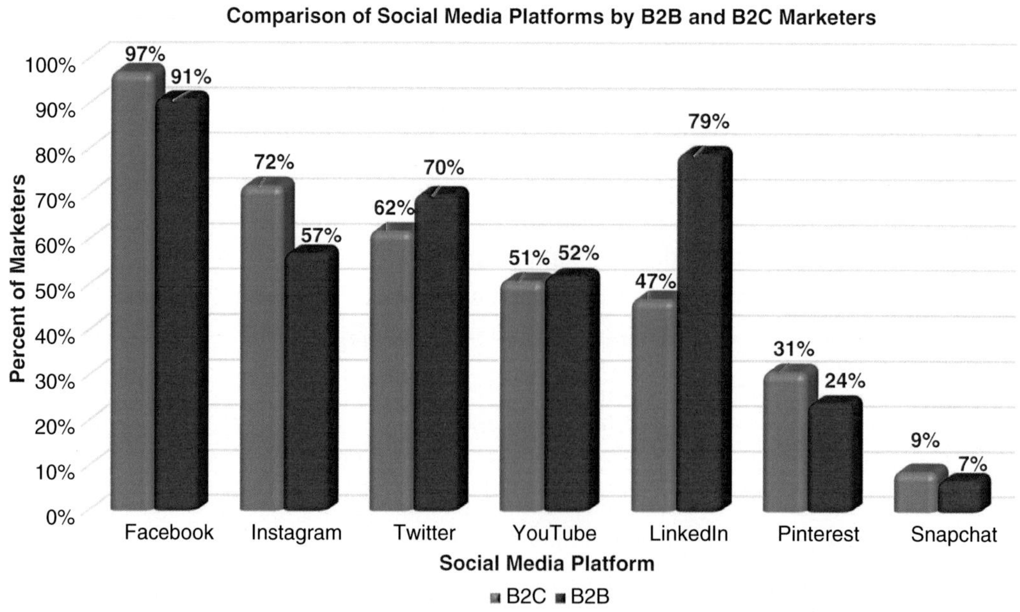

FIGURE 12.1 A Clustered Bar Chart Showing the Differences between B2B and B2C Marketers and How They Use the Various Social Media Platforms
Source: Adapted from Michael A. Stelzner, "2018 Social Media Marketing Industry Report," *Social Media Examiner*, 2018

- Validation
- Coding
- Data entry
- Data cleaning

FIGURE 12.2 Data Preparation Process

quality data, it is important to follow a methodical process that will help in detecting and reducing errors. These steps are highlighted in Figure 12.2.

12.3 Data Validation

LEARNING OBJECTIVE 12.2
Discuss the processes of validating and coding data.

Data validation process to ensure data were collected properly and are as free of error and bias as possible.

The purpose of **data validation** is to ensure the data were collected properly and are as free of error and bias as possible. As discussed in Chapter 6, error will always occur in the process of collecting data. Random error cannot be eliminated, but can be reduced by increasing the sample size. Despite a researcher's best efforts, systematic error will occur, so the purpose of data validation is to check for any recognizable systematic error. Figure 12.3 highlights the areas that are checked in the data validation step. The first three checks occur in the field where the data are collected, and the last two are the responsibility of the research firm or research department where the data are being tabulated and analyzed.

12.3a Data Collection Process

Data validation begins by thoroughly examining the data collection process. If interviewers are involved, this validation often occurs while the interviews are taking place. It is important for interviewers and individuals collecting the data to follow the process that has been outlined. If not, the results can be affected. For example, if an intercept study is being conducted at a theme park and interviewers are requested to stop every fifteenth person and read the questions to the respondent, then it is important every interviewer follow that procedure. Sample selection error can occur if some interviewers stop every fifteenth person while others stop individuals around the fifteenth person who they think will take time to complete the survey. It might be the thirteenth person, the eighteenth person, or some other number.

Interviewer error is also of concern. If some of the interviewers read the questions while others hand the questionnaire to the respondent, it is very possible that the answers will vary. Interviewer error can occur when interviewers don't give respondents proper instructions or when they fail to follow skip patterns. Insufficient probing of open-ended questions also can result in interviewer error. For instance, a respondent might be asked why he or she purchased a certain brand of dog food. Taking an answer such as, "Because of the price" at face value and failing to probe further can lead to

- Field Validation
  –Data collection process
  –Proper screening
  –Fraud
- Primary Research Firm
  –Data completeness
  –Data usability

FIGURE 12.3 Areas Check During Data Validation

erroneous conclusions. While it would be natural to assume that the answer reflects the respondent's preference for low price, further probing might reveal that the respondent purchased a higher-priced brand because he or she felt price signaled a higher quality food with superior nutrition.[2]

Confederates people who pose as potential interviewees and who evaluate the interviewers' data collection procedure as part of the field validation process.

Field supervisors should be on the alert for these problems and might observe interviewers' behavior either directly or remotely via camera. **Confederates** who pose as potential interviewees can also be used to evaluate the interviewers' data collection procedure, similar to a mystery shopper. Should it be determined that a particular interviewer systematically conducts the data collection process in a manner different from all other interviewers, the data collected by the problem interviewer should be discarded, and the interviewer should be dismissed or sent for retraining. Field supervisors should also check to make certain that written responses to open-ended questions are legible and that they have been sufficiently probed. Answers to closed-ended questions on paper and pen surveys should be clearly marked in a single category and checked to make certain that no marks exist on lines between categories or spanning categories, which would make the correct answer difficult to determine. Surveys that lack answers to key questions, or that are only partially complete, should be eliminated from the data pool, though sometimes field service firms that specialize in data collection will forward incomplete surveys back to the research firm that employed their services. Data collection or custom research firms should also perform quality control checks such as those outlined in Chapter 6.

12.3b Proper Screening

Almost all survey research has some type of screening question or questions to ensure the respondent fits the criteria stipulated by the study design. It is important that all interviewers and individuals involved in collecting the data ask the screening questions and use only respondents who pass all of the screeners. In the quest to obtain a quota, data collectors can be tempted to allow individuals who do not meet all of the criteria to complete the survey. This is especially true in situations where the incidence rate is very low, meaning that only a low percentage of the population is qualified to be part of the study. It is also more common when interviewers are paid on the basis of the number of surveys completed. Field supervisors can randomly talk with interviewees after they have finished the questionnaire to determine whether or not they really qualified. It is very common to randomly contact about 10 percent of individuals who completed a survey to validate that they passed the screening criteria and to investigate whether or not the interviewer was in any way guilty of fraud, which is discussed in more detail in the next section.

Detecting those who fail screening questions can be easier in online research, especially in studies that use panel members. Each panel members fills out a complete demographic and psychographic profile before joining a panel. If a screening question is based on gender or participation in some type of lifestyle activity, such as fishing, the respondent's answer to the screening question can be easily compared against the respondent's profile to determine whether or not they qualify. Typically, panel members will be prescreened so that only those who meet the criteria are invited to complete the survey, resulting in a superior sample.

Source: Christos Georghiou/Shutterstock.

Almost all survey research has some type of screening question or questions to ensure the respondent fits the criteria stipulated by the study design.

12.3c Fraud

The third area to be checked in the field may be the most difficult to detect, and that is fraud. With fraud, the interviewer or data collector falsifies the data by completing the questionnaire themselves, or they may fill in questions the respondent left blank in order to complete the questionnaire. The latter fraudulent situation can occur when individuals are paid for completed surveys. It is easier and faster to fill in a few missing questions than discard the questionnaire and find a new respondent. The former situation can occur when individuals responsible for data collection are under time and cost constraints. To ensure deadlines are met at the quoted price, it may be tempting to falsify the data rather than go back to the client and admit they either did not collect the number of surveys promised, or to ask for additional time.

Source: SuperStock 2018/Shutterstock.

Detecting fraud in the field is difficult. Fraud occurs when the interviewer or data collector falsifies the data by completing the questionnaire themselves, or when they fill in questions the respondent left blank.

One method of detecting fraud is to contact some of the respondents. The respondents should be told that the purpose of contacting them is to validate the data collection process. Respondents can be asked questions to help verify whether or not 1) they indeed did answer the survey, 2) they answered all the questions in the study, and 3) their answers to key questions were accurately recorded. With telephone research, requiring interviews to be conducted from a central location, under the supervision of a field supervisor or recorded, will result in less fraud than if individuals are allowed to conduct telephone surveys from their home with no supervision. Artificial intelligence and a heuristic or algorithmic decision-making process is used to analyze online survey data for potential fraudulent activity. The use of artificial intelligence requires a large amount of historical data in order for the AI to learn patterns and better determine which surveys are fraudulent. However, it is essential that AI users know how to define fraudulent behavior and which data to use to check for potential problems.[3]

12.3d Data Completeness

Data collection duties are often outsourced to firms that specialize in this process. Once the data are returned to the central office, an additional editing phase is typically undertaken. During this phase the completeness and usefulness of the data are examined.

Surveys can contain incomplete information. Sometimes individuals unknowingly skip a question, while other times people refuse to answer one or more questions. Surveys missing answers to entire sections or pages are likely to be of little value to the firm, and are typically eliminated at this stage on the basis of incompleteness. For example, if one of the survey objectives sought to determine whether significant differences in attitudes existed on the basis of gender, age, and education, then a survey lacking answers to these demographic questions is of no value. However, it also must be remembered that skip patterns often direct individuals away from answering questions that are not relevant. In this case, what appears to be at first glance an incomplete survey may in fact contain all the relevant information for that subject.

It is best if one individual undertakes the decision of which incomplete surveys can be retained, and which should be thrown out, because this ensures consistency in how the data are treated. Only someone with an intimate knowledge of the survey objectives and the design of the questionnaire should be given this task. Deciding which questions or how many questions must be answered in order for a survey to be included in a data set can be highly subjective. Online survey software can help ensure data completeness by requiring answers to key questions.

12.3e Data Usability

The usability of the data must also be considered. Illegibly written answers, bizarre abbreviations, or responses that are understandable only to the original interviewer can hinder the coding process of open-ended responses. If the original interviewer cannot be reached for clarification, the responses to these questions may be eliminated from the data; or, if the questions are central to the research purpose, the entire survey might be eliminated.

Obvious patterns that indicate response bias are also identified at this stage. For example, the heart of the survey might consist of different Likert or semantic differential "grid" questions. Two types of patterns may indicate problematic responses that could lead to elimination of surveys from the data pool: 1) straight-lining answers, and 2) zig-zagging or entering responses that create a visual pattern on that page of the questionnaire.[4]

Straight-lining occurs when a respondent selects the same response category for all or the majority of responses to "grid"-based questions.

Straight-lining occurs when a respondent selects the same response category for all or the majority of responses to grid-based questions such Likert or semantic differential. If an individual selects all neutral responses for multiple scale items, it is likely that the subject either didn't read the question or doesn't have the knowledge or experience necessary to answer the question. Straight-lining of neutral responses is particularly likely to occur in cases in which a "don't know" option is not available, or when a skip pattern was not used to determine relevance of the topic to the individual before asking the scaled response questions. It is also common when respondents are simply not engaged in the survey process. College students who are required to participate in research studies may not read questions and straight-line neutral responses in order to finish their task as quickly as possible. It is in the best interest of the researcher to eliminate these questionnaires from the data pool when the attitude questions are central to the study purpose.

Individuals who select "strongly agree" or "strongly disagree" to every question or who otherwise straight-line their answers may be demonstrating one of three things. First, they may have a very strong opinion which they wish to express quite forcibly. Responses could be legitimate if no reversed items were included in the set of scaled questions. Second, if the scale being answered is a semantic differential, responses could be a manifestation of the halo effect discussed in Chapter 10. Third, this response pattern could be indicative of a respondent who is not reading and considering the questions carefully, but rather speeding through the questionnaire in order to finish quickly.

One advantage of collecting data online is that "speeders" can be easily identified since the amount of time taken to complete a question, section of questions, or the survey itself can be timed. This information can be forwarded to the client, along with the data, so that it can be used to determine which respondents should be eliminated. The data collecting entity can also use this information as part of its internal quality control, and eliminate certain respondents from the data pool before forwarding the data to the research client.[5]

In rare circumstances, the responses to a series of questions with scaled response categories might be marked in a fashion that creates a visual design.[6] This type of response bias can be caught using pattern recognition algorithms with online surveys. Respondents who demonstrate such behavior are not allowed to complete the survey and are usually removed from the online panel.[7] However, this behavior is also easy to identify in mail or other self-administered paper-based surveys by simply examining the responses. Some patterns experienced by the authors of this text include perfect zig-zag lines, in which a respondent starts by selecting 1 for the first question, then 2, 3, 4, 5, 4, 3, 2, 1, 2, 3, 4, 5, etc. for additional questions. Alternatively, some respondents will "X" multiple categories for each semantic differential item in order to create pictures of circles, or alphabet letters such as "N" or "Y". Any surveys exhibiting these characteristics should be immediately discarded.

The individual tasked with determining the usability of the data should look carefully at the questions asked, to see whether answers seem to be consistent. Two scale items might read, "The ad held my attention," and "The ad was boring." An individual who marks "strongly agree" to both questions is probably not paying attention to the question content. Often researchers will eliminate a survey on the basis of such inconsistencies.[8]

Other researchers might require multiple problems to be present before eliminating the survey from the data pool.

Bruzzone Research tested eight factors thought to negatively affect the quality of data. Using a study of Super Bowl ads, Bruzzone and their research partners sought to identify whether these factors actually influenced the answers to ad-tracking questions. Straight-lining answers, speeding through the survey, and failing trap questions involving specific instructions were found to have a noticeable effect on data quality, while inconsistent answers to conflicting questions such as those outlined in the previous paragraph did not. Specifically, three percent of the survey respondents finished the survey in less than half the normal time, three percent straight-lined answers to 60 percent or more of the grid-based questions, and 10 percent failed to follow the instruction to select the slightly disagree category for the trap question. Overall though, only two percent of the respondents engaged in two or more of these behaviors. Bruzzone chose to eliminate only this two percent, rationalizing that a respondent could inadvertently engage in any of the questionable behaviors without "evil intent."[9] It is up to the researcher to decide how fast is "too fast" (especially when skip patterns are present), the percentage of straight-lining that is permissible, and whether or not data from those who fail trap questions or who provide inconsistent answers is usable.

12.4 Data Coding

After the data are validated, it is time to begin the coding process. **Coding** involves assigning numerical values to each response on the questionnaire. For written questionnaires the coding process typically occurs after the surveys are completed. However, the codes can be built into the questions at the time the questionnaire is developed. Thus, a Likert scale that uses the anchors "strongly disagree" to "strongly agree" may also have numbers under each of the possible answers ranging from 1 to 5. This makes it easy for the person recording the data from the survey response sheet.

Coding assigning numerical values to each response on the questionnaire.

With most quantitative research now shifting to online, mobile or electronic mechanisms, the majority of coding will be done before the data are collected. This is necessary since the data from the online, mobile or electronic mechanism is automatically placed into some type of spreadsheet. While the spreadsheet can collect the actual words used by respondents, it makes the process simpler and reduces errors if the numerical code is placed into the spreadsheet when the questionnaire is completed. However, open-ended questions and open-ended responses associated with the "other" category can only be coded once the data have been collected. In these cases, the words typed by the respondent will be listed in the spreadsheet verbatim.

The coding process begins by assigning a unique identifying number to each questionnaire. This facilitates the process of checking the accuracy of data coding and data entry errors. In coding surveys, every question and every response needs to be coded. For closed-ended questions and scales, this process is rather simple. Each response can be given a numerical code. To aid in understanding the results, higher values are typically coded with higher numbers and lower values with lower numbers. In addition, positive responses tend to be coded with higher numbers than negative responses. Thus "very satisfied" would be assigned a value of "7" on a seven-point scale ranging from 1 to 7 while "very dissatisfied" would be assigned a value of "1". Figures 12.4 through 12.10 illustrate various ways questions can be coded.

12.4a Coding Closed-Ended Questions

The coding of dichotomous questions is shown in **Figure 12.4**. Most are coded either with a 1 or 2 or a 0 and 1. The numbers chosen really does not matter as long as each response is coded in the same manner. In Figure 12.4 gender was coded 1 for females and 2 for males. When questions ask for a yes or no response, the most common coding is to use a 1 for yes and a 0 for no. The numbers chosen for question 4 can be anything, but it is easier

1. What is your gender? ☐ Female (1) ☐ Male (2)

2. Have you played video games on your smartphone? ☐ Yes (1) ☐ No (0)

3. Do you like playing video games on your smartphone? ☐ Yes (1) ☐ No (0)

4. Which platform to you prefer for playing video games? ☐ Online (1) ☐ Computer (2)

FIGURE 12.4 Coding Dichotomous Questions

1. Your household income from all sources (salary, investments, gifts, etc.) is:
   - ☐ Less than $24,999 (1)
   - ☐ $25,000 to $49,999 (2)
   - ☐ $50,000 to $74,999 (3)
   - ☐ $75,000 to $99,999 (4)
   - ☐ $100,000 or more (5)
2. Of the following gaming platforms, which ones have you used to play video games? *(Check all that apply)*
   - ☐ Online website (0 or 1)
   - ☐ Social network sites (0 or 1)
   - ☐ Gaming console (0 or 1)
   - ☐ Computer (0 or 1)
   - ☐ Smartphone or tablet (0 or 1)

FIGURE 12.5 Coding Multiple-Choice and Multiple-Response Questions

and usually creates fewer errors if the first response is given a code of 1 and the second response a code of 2 (or 0 and 1 could also be used).

Figure 12.5 illustrates how multiple-choice questions and multiple-response questions can be coded. In the first question about income, codes of 1 to 5 are used to represent ordinal data. The responses are coded such that the higher a person's income, the higher the code number. Thus, someone with an income of $80,000 would be coded a 4 while someone with an income of $33,000 would be coded a 2.

The second question presents a unique coding situation because respondents can choose all the answers that apply. That means that the individual may check one answer, three different answers, or even all five answers. So coding the responses as a single variable ranging from 1 to 5 will not work. With questions of this type, separate variables must be created for each response option, and a process called dummy coding is used. With **dummy coding** responses are coded with a 0 or a 1. If the respondent checks an item, such as online website or gaming console, then each of these responses would be coded as a 1. The items not checked would be coded as a 0. Thus, the question is listed in the spreadsheet as five different variables, one for each response item. In contrast, question 1 about income is only one variable with codes ranging from 1 to 5.

Dummy coding responses are coded a "1" if a response option is selected and a "0" if it is not selected.

Most scaled-response questions are relatively straightforward to code, with the caveat that higher numbers should represent more positive responses while lower numbers are used for negative responses or less desirable responses for surveys administered in the United States. For the question in **Figure 12.6**, a code of 1 to 5 is used with the

For each of the following gaming platforms, please indicate your level of preference ranging from "very unlikely to use" to "very likely to use."

	Very unlikely to use 1	2	3	4	Very likely to use 5
Online website	○	○	○	○	○
Social network site	○	○	○	○	○
Gaming console	○	○	○	○	○
Computer	○	○	○	○	○
Smartphone or tablet	○	○	○	○	○

FIGURE 12.6 Coding a Scaled-Response Question

For each of the following pairs of criteria in purchasing a laptop computer, indicate which item in each pair is most important to you by placing a checkmark on the appropriate line.

0 or 1 Price or Size of computer 0 or 1

0 or 1 Physical appearance or Technical specifications 0 or 1

0 or 1 Price or Physical appearance 0 or 1

0 or 1 Physical appearance or Size of computer 0 or 1

0 or 1 Technical specifications or Price 0 or 1

0 or 1 Size of computer or Technical specifications 0 or 1

FIGURE 12.7 Coding a Paired Comparison Scale

1 representing "very unlikely to use" and the 5 representing "very likely to use". With this coding the lower numbers indicate a gaming platform that the respondent is less likely to use while higher numbers represent platforms the respondent is more likely to use.

With a paired comparison scale, respondents can choose between two items. An example is shown in **Figure 12.7**. Since either can be checked, it is necessary to list each response as a separate variable and code them using the dummy coding procedure. With the first pair of items, if the individual indicated that price was more important than the size of the computer, then price would be coded as a 1 and size of computer as a 0. However, if the individual indicated that the size of computer was more important, it would be coded as a 1 and price would be coded as a 0. The same procedure would be used for the entire set of paired comparisons.

Graphical rating scales present a unique challenge because responses are not specific. Two different graphical rating scales are shown in **Figure 12.8**. Recall from Chapter 10 that respondents can indicate a response anywhere on either line. With the first scale no numbers are placed on the line at all. In this situation, the most common method of coding is to use a ruler or some other type of measuring device. Suppose a 6-inch line is used and the blue X falls on the 2 inch point, thus resulting in a code of 2. But suppose the red Y is at 4 and 3/4 inches. In this case the researcher can code it as 4.7, 4.8 or, if the two decimal

Please evaluate the quality of service at Olive Garden by placing a large "X" on the line that most closely corresponds to your evaluation.

Poor
Service

Excellent
Service

Please evaluate the quality of service at Olive Garden by placing a large "X" on the line that most closely corresponds to your evaluation. You may place the "X" anywhere on the line. It does not have to be on a number.

| 1 | 2 | 3 | 4 | 5 | 6 | 7 | 8 | 9 | 10 |

Poor Service Excellent Service

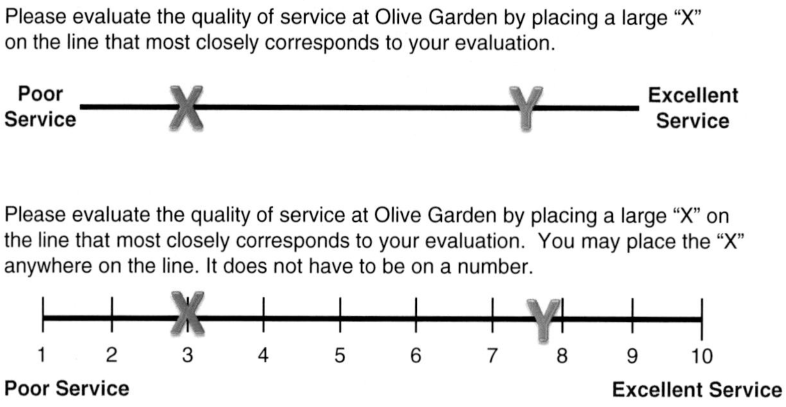

FIGURE 12.8 Coding Graphical Rating Scales

points are used, as 4.75. With the bottom scale, the blue X is clearly on the 3. But, the red Y is between 7 and 8. The researcher will have to choose the value he/she thinks best represents the response, which in this case may be a 7.8. Rules should be developed prior to coding to ensure consistency. A metric ruler is often used in international research or in studies that have international applications, since the metric system is prevalent everywhere except in the United States.

Semantic differential scales are usually straightforward to code. As shown in **Figure 12.9**, the code of 1 to 5 is being used with the 1 representing the first circle, a 2 the second circle, and on to a 5 for the last or fifth circle. For most of the questions, the higher number would represent a more desirable experience at Home Depot. For instance a 5 would indicate friendly staff while a 1 would indicate unfriendly staff. However, to make sure the respondent is reading the questions, the second, fourth, and fifth items have been reversed. The most desirable experience is on the left of the scale and the least desirable experience on the right. In recording the data, these questions would typically be coded just as they appear on the question. Then after all of the data is recorded, the researcher can reverse the code by using the process discussed in the Statistics Review section of Chapter 11. By reversing the codes on those three items, the higher responses will then represent the more desirable characteristics. If the questions were part of an online survey, the correct codes would be used since they would not be visible to the respondent. Reverse coding would not then be necessary.

Please evaluate the last purchase you made at Home Depot and the experience you had at the retail store.

Unfriendly staff	○	○	○	○	○	Friendly staff
Staff very helpful	○	○	○	○	○	Staff not very helpful
Poor selection	○	○	○	○	○	Excellent selection
Store clean	○	○	○	○	○	Store unclean
Excellent value	○	○	○	○	○	Poor value
Slow checkout	○	○	○	○	○	Fast checkout
Unsuccessful trip	○	○	○	○	○	Successful trip
Code →	1	2	3	4	5	

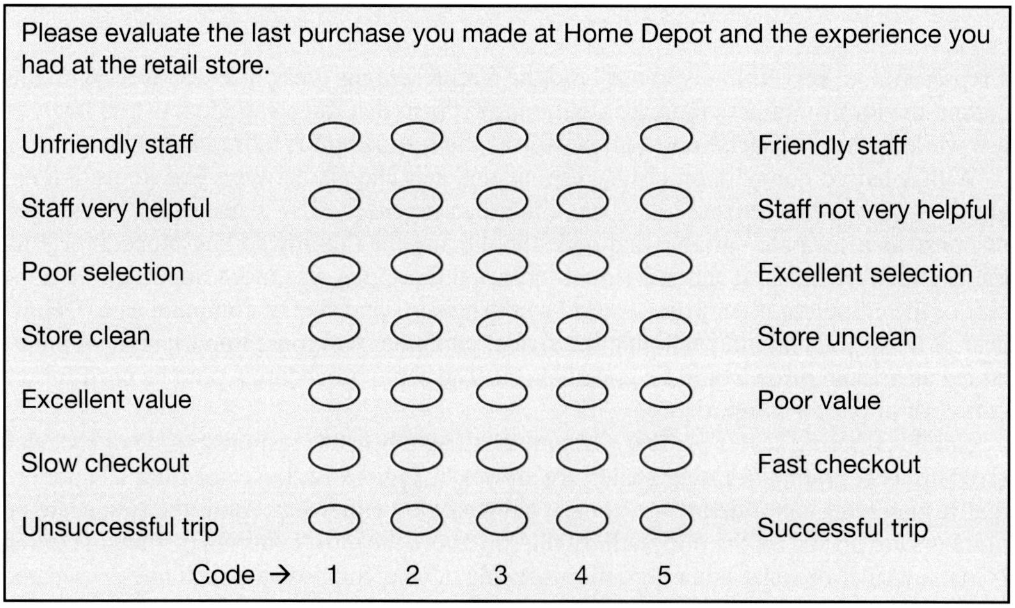

FIGURE 12.9 Coding a Semantic Differential Scale

Please indicate your level of agreement or disagreement with each of the following statements.

	Strongly Disagree	Disagree	Neutral	Agree	Strongly Agree
1. Wearing the latest fashion is important to me.	◯	◯	◯	◯	◯
2. The brand name is not important to me.	◯	◯	◯	◯	◯
3. I do not watch what celebrities wear.	◯	◯	◯	◯	◯
Code →	1	2	3	4	5

	Strongly Agree	Agree	Neutral	Disagree	Strongly Disagree
1. I read magazines such as Glamour regularly.	◯	◯	◯	◯	◯
2. In purchasing clothes, price is not a critical factor.	◯	◯	◯	◯	◯
Code →	1	2	3	4	5
Values after Recoding or Alternate Coding →	5	4	3	2	1

FIGURE 12.10 Coding a Likert Scale

A Likert scale is shown in **Figure 12.10**. In the top example the codes of 1 to 5 are used such that the 1 represents the negative or strongly disagree while the 5 represents the positive, or strongly agree. The problem comes when questions are reversed, such as in questions 2 and 3 ("The brand name is not important to me" and "I do not watch what celebrities wear"). This problem can be resolved after all the data is recorded as shown by reversing the code in a recoding process. Again, if it is an online survey, the correct coding can be used when the questionnaire is developed.

In the second Likert scale, the strongly agree is on the *left* side of the scale and the strongly disagree is on the *right* side of the scale. The typical code that would be used would list the 1 on the left and the 5 on the right. However, coding in this manner makes strongly agree a lower value and strongly disagree a higher value, just the opposite of what is desired. This can be corrected by either reversing the code at the end of the process or reversing the code sheet so it goes from 5 to 1.

If surveys are answered on paper and recorded by humans, coding low numbers to the left and higher numbers to the right produces the fewest errors. If the list is vertical, it should be coded from lowest at the top to highest at the bottom. But if the survey is completed on a computer or other electronic device, coding can be done in any fashion the researcher desires since the respondent will see only the response options and not the codes. Reverse codes can also be done automatically in programs such as SPSS, eliminating the need to do this manually after the data have all been recorded.

A final issue involves the coding of "don't know", "no opinion", or "not applicable" responses. For purposes of the following discussion, reference will be made to the "don't know" option, though the same logic discussed can apply to the "no opinion" or "not applicable" choices. Initially, these responses are often coded with a number that breaks from the sequence used by scaled response categories. Thus, if possible responses ranged from 1 "strongly dissatisfied" to 5 "strongly satisfied", then the "don't know" option may be coded as 9. Coding in this fashion allows the researcher to run frequency reports and to create pie charts that show the percent who responded to each scaled response category, the percent who responded with "don't know", and even the percent who failed to respond to the question and are designated as "missing" data. Using "9" to designate the "don't know" response option helps to remind the researcher that these responses should not be included in the calculation of means and standard deviations that are often necessary in analyzing the attitudes of individuals. After all, if they don't know, don't have an opinion, or the question is not applicable to them, their response is not a legitimate expression of the attitude being sought and thus should not be grouped with the responses of those who do know, who do have an opinion, or to whom the question is appropriate. So prior to calculating means, standard deviations, or performing advanced statistical analyses, the researcher will either filter the data so that "don't know" responses are no longer included, or the researcher will recode the "9" values to system missing data, which automatically eliminates them from further analysis.

12.4b Coding Open-Ended Questions

Coding open-ended questions presents unique challenges that were discussed in Chapter 11. Figure 12.11 outlines a five-step process that can be used to code open-ended questions. The first step occurs prior to data collection and involves generating a list of possible answers. These responses can be obtained through past research, input from interviews with experts in the field, or even focus groups. Typically, researchers will want to code answers into a manageable set of responses that includes an "other" category. If the number of categories is too small, the richness obtained from open-ended responses can be lost, and the percentage of responses falling into the "other" category increases. If the number of categories is too large, tabulating and summarizing the results might not produce meaningful information that can be used by managers. For instance, possible answers to an open-ended question related to key factors that influence the purchase of a particular brand of sofa may initially generate the following list: price, promotional incentives/financing, quality, brand name, style, appearance and "style-related".

Once the initial list has been developed, a coding guide is sometimes created that defines each category and provides examples of words or phrases that are indicative of each group. While a coding guide is not always developed, at a minimum the researcher will list some basic rules for coding open-ended questions. For instance, categories are generally assumed to be mutually exclusive so that the same comment does not appear in two different categories.[10] In the example cited earlier, care would have to be taken to clearly differentiate "style-related" comments from those that would be classified as "appearance." Furthermore, respondents often make multiple comments that can be separated into different categories since each represents a unique thought. Making it clear to coders whether one or more responses are acceptable for a given open-ended question is critical.

To illustrate, when asked to indicate the key factors considered when purchasing a sofa, a subject may say, "I bought an Ethan Allen sofa because they make a quality product. Plus, the color contrasted nicely against our new carpeting." In coding this response, the coder would have to decide whether the first portion of the comment should be coded in the brand name category, the quality category or both. Without a coding guide or rules in place to guide the decision, one coder could classify the first sentence of the response as "brand name" related, while another could classify it as "quality" based, and yet a third could double-count the same comment by classifying it in both categories. The second portion of the comment regarding color might fall into the "appearance" category, or be treated as a new response, depending upon the coding rules that are in place.

Once the initial list has been generated, the next step is to go through the completed surveys. Each new response that is seen should be added to the list. No attempt to force it into a current response category should be made unless it is clear that it fits well with a given response category.

1. Generate list of possible responses
2. Create coding rules and guides
3. Add new responses to the list
4. Consolidate related responses
5. Assign numerical code to each response

FIGURE 12.11 Process for Coding Open-Ended Questions

When all the surveys have been examined, related responses should be consolidated. This is a difficult task because it relies on the researcher's judgment. Decisions have to be made if two responses are really the same and should be consolidated into one category or should instead remain as two separate answers.

The greatest challenge in this process is interpreting an answer. While many responses will fit the codes that have been developed, some responses will not. The researcher then must decide between creating a new category or choosing a category that already exists and appears to be close to what the respondent is saying. Creating a new category for only one or two responses is not productive because that data is not very useful. Forcing it into a category requires researcher judgment, and may not truly reflect the respondent's thoughts. Consider the following response that was provided to the question, "What is the most important factor in purchasing textbooks for your classes?"

"Price is really the most important, but also convenience is too. So I always go for the lowest price, but it depends too. If I didn't have time to buy the book online before class starts, then I will go to the campus bookstore and just get it there even though it costs more."

In terms of coding this response, three possible categories that could be used are price, convenience, and time. Into which category should it be coded? While this respondent is saying price is the most important factor, the respondent is also saying convenience is important and she is willing to pay more if she doesn't have time to get it online before classes begin. A case could also be made that time is most important because when a book is purchased influences the decision more than price. The response could fit into all three categories, or it could be discarded since the coder is not sure what to do. While predetermined rules can help guide the coder, whatever decision is made represents the judgment of the coder and may not truly reflect the opinion of the respondent since the respondent's view is not clear.

The last step is to assign a numerical code to each response, using a process similar to that discussed when coding close-ended questions. If the question asks for the single most important factor, then a single variable is created and responses are coded from 1 to X, where X is equal to the number of response categories. If a respondent is allowed multiple answers, each response category would represent a separate variable in the data set and dummy coding would be used.

Within the marketing research industry, a common practice is to code only 20 to 30 percent of the responses to open-ended questions. Research companies have found that this practice will actually yield the same results as if 100 percent of the open-ended responses had been coded. It can be the first 20 to 30 percent of the items or it can be a random selection of items. Either process will tend to yield the same results as long as the methodology in collecting the data was the same throughout the entire data set. However, it is critical that at least 50 open-ended responses are coded.[11]

12.5 Data Entry

LEARNING OBJECTIVE 12.3
Describe the processes of data entry and data cleaning.

Data entry is the process of entering data into a computer spreadsheet such as SPSS or Excel that can be used for data tabulation and analysis. With the increased use of online surveys, the need for manual data entry has been reduced substantially. With electronic surveys, responses from individuals taking the survey are automatically placed into a spreadsheet based on the coding that was programmed into the survey software.

Data entry process of entering data into a computer spreadsheet such as SPSS or Excel that can be used for data tabulation and analysis.

When questionnaires are completed on paper, researchers have two options. The first is to have someone manually enter the data into a computer spreadsheet or SPSS. The data being entered may have been manually coded on each paper survey, or transferred to a coding sheet in which the correct numerical response for each variable is listed on a subject-by-subject basis. The second is to use a scanning device that can read the answers. If a scanning device is used, usually responses are recorded on answer sheets or within a designated area on the survey that will allow for electronic scanning.

Online survey data are entered by the respondents when taking the survey. Online survey software programs allow for easy validation of certain data. For example, responses can be required for key questions so that missing data is minimized. A number input—such as the year born—can be checked to see if it is within a range of years, such as 1928–2000. Data inputs related to the number of children, or dollar values can also be checked against an acceptable input range defined by the researcher. A person who tries to enter 299 children is obviously providing invalid data. The data field can be set to accept only a single digit, or a range of digits between 0 and 12.

12.6 Data Cleaning

Data cleaning process of checking the data for inconsistency.

Data cleaning occurs once all of the data are entered into a spreadsheet and before results are tabulated and analyzed. **Data cleaning** is the process of checking the data for any inconsistency and involves four steps:

- Examine the data in each column
- Examine data for values out of the coded range
- Examine data for values that are extreme
- Compare responses that show inconsistency

The first step is to examine the data in each column. Does it fit the data label, or is income in the age column, and age in the income column? Does the data meet the field parameters? For example, if an email address is expected, does the field contain an "@" character between a user name and a domain name?[12]

The second step in data cleaning is to look for values outside of the accepted range. This can easily be done by running a frequency count for each question using SPSS or Excel. In Figure 12.12, responses for Question 1 must be either a 1 or 2. For Question 2 values should be either a 1 or 0. If a 3, or any other number is found, then there has been an error in data entry. If the data were manually entered or scanned, the question response can be located through the questionnaire number and then checked to see what number should have been recorded. For question 3, values should be from 1 to 5. Any other response is out of this range and is an error. As another example, perhaps a question asked individuals to enter the amount of time they've spent on a task. An answer that is negative would indicate bad data. Finding values outside of the accepted range is relatively easy to detect and correct with SPSS. With online and electronic questionnaires, any value out of the accepted range is almost always due to a coding error in the computer program since the individual taking the survey can only select the options that appear on the screen.

1. What is your gender? ☐ Female (1) ☐ Male (2)

2. Have you played video games on your smartphone? ☐ Yes (1) ☐ No (0)

3. Your household income from all sources is:

☐ Less than $24,999 (1)

☐ $25,000 to $49,999 (2)

☐ $50,000 to $74,999 (3)

☐ $75,000 to $99,999 (4)

☐ $100,000 or more (5)

FIGURE 12.12 Examining Data for Coding Values

The third step in data cleaning is checking for extreme values that can occur with open-ended questions. For instance, respondents might be asked how many energy drinks they have purchased in the last week. Suppose someone has written 110. That is over 15 energy drinks a day, which is extremely unlikely. But did the person intend to write 11 or was it 10, or could it even have been just a 1? If the respondent can be contacted again, then the correct answer can be obtained. But the cost of doing so is probably not worth the effort since one survey among 200 or 300 is not going to change the results. Therefore, either the response is deleted or the entire survey is discarded, depending on the quality of the remaining answers on the questionnaire. Extreme values can be easily detected through obtaining a frequency count in SPSS. Also, consider running cross-tabulations that help you make sense of the data in context by filtering the data so only the suspect questionnaire is analyzed. A clerical worker with a multi-million dollar income is suspicious, especially if additional analysis indicates this person is single.

Checking for answer inconsistencies can be the very difficult as one cannot search for an outlier like in the previous two situations. Researchers will often put a couple of questions in a survey to make sure the respondent is reading the questions and answering thoughtfully. Suppose a respondent has said they do not like playing video games on a smartphone (checking the no response). Suppose this same person later in the survey checked "very likely to use" in response to a question about their level of preference for playing games on a smartphone. So in one question the respondent says he or she does not like playing video games on a smartphone, but then later in the survey says he or she is very likely to use a smartphone for playing video games. Because of this inconsistency, the questionnaire might be discarded. Either the person did not read the questions or intentionally provided random responses or answers that did not show thought and sincerity.

12.7 Pre-Coding Questionnaires

LEARNING OBJECTIVE 12.4
Discuss the advantages of pre-coding questionnaires.

Pre-coding questionnaires requires that the code numbers be placed on the survey instrument prior to individuals filling it out. Questions in Figures 12.4 and 12.6 have been pre-coded. It is very easy for the individual recording the data to see what code number should be placed in the computer spreadsheet. Pre-coding in this fashion reduces transcription errors (also called data processing errors). One disadvantage to pre-coding is that some researchers feel it can influence or affect respondents' answers to questions if they see how a question will be coded. Studies have compared scales containing all positive pre-coded numbered scales (e.g., 1 to 5) with those in which precoded numbers for scales were negatively and positively balanced (e.g., –2 to +2). Scales using negatively and positively balanced numeric response categories produced more positive evaluations.[13] Others argue that no bias or influence would occur if the codes are seen by the respondents. A second potential disadvantage is that pre-coding can take up more space on a survey, reducing its readability and potentially negatively influencing perceptions of survey length.

Of course, only closed-ended questions can be pre-coded. Pre-coding open-ended questions where a respondent would see possible answers would certainly bias the person's response. But if the question is administered by telephone or in person and read to the respondent, having pre-coded answers allows the interviewer to check the person's response. If it is not in the list of possible answers, it can be added. Suppose a question asks individuals what their favorite platform is for playing video games. The list of possible answers can be on the interviewer's list and the response given by the individual can then be checked.

With online or mobile surveys and other electronic-type surveys, questions can be coded in advance. This allows the computer to enter a respondent's answer into a spreadsheet, saving labor costs and time spent in the data validation, data entry, and data checking stages. These time savings ultimately translate into cost savings for the firm and allow for research projects to be completed more quickly. This works well for closed-ended and scale-type questions. For open-ended questions, whatever the person types into the survey will be transcribed into the spreadsheet. Researchers can then code those responses once the survey collection is complete.

12.8 Tabulation

LEARNING OBJECTIVE 12.5
Describe the various ways of tabulating data.

Tabulation counting the number of responses in each answer category of a question.

One-way tabulation counting the number of responses for each answer category within one question.

Cross-tabulations counting the number of responses in two or more categories simultaneously.

Tabulations involve counting the number of responses in each answer category of a question. While the raw number of counts can be used, more often researchers are concerned about percentages. The two types of tabulations used are one-way tabulations and cross-tabulations. **One-way tabulations** involve counting the number of responses for each answer category within one question. **Cross-tabulations** involve counting the number of responses in two or more categories simultaneously.

12.8a One-Way Tabulation

One-way tabulation involves obtaining the frequency and percentage of responses to a question. Figure 12.13 contains the SPSS output for the question "Have you played video games on your smartphone?" Responses were yes and no. Yes responses were coded a 1 while no responses were coded a 0. The total number of completed surveys was 688.

The first column of the output identifies the possible responses to the question. The second column shows the frequency. For this question 417 respondents said "no" to the question, 263 said "yes," and 8 individuals did not answer the question. The third column provides the percent of responses for each category. Out of the sample of 688 respondents 60.6 percent indicated "no," 38.2 percent indicated "yes," and 1.2 percent did not answer the question. The fourth column entitled "valid percent" shows the percent of responses for each category of those who answered the question. In this case, of those who answered this question 61.3 percent said "no" and 38.7 percent said "yes."

The last column produced by SPSS is the cumulative percent. Figure 12.14 shows how likely respondents are to use video games on social network sites. In looking at the last column (cumulative percent), 26.3 percent of the respondents said they are "very unlikely" to play games on a social network website. The next row shows a total of 53.8 percent. This percent value combines the responses from the first two rows. Thus, a researcher can say 58.3 percent of the respondents are "very unlikely to use" or "somewhat unlikely to use" social network sites for video games. Taken one step further, a researcher could say 76.1 percent are not likely or neutral about playing games at a social network site. Subtracting 76.1 percent from 100 percent, the researcher could also state that only 23.9 percent of those who answered the question indicated any type of positive likelihood of playing games on social networking sites.

In many questions, the value of the missing data is not relevant. It just tells the researchers how many respondents did not answer the question. Usually it is a very small percentage. But, occasionally the missing value number (or percentage) is important to a researcher. Notice the results in Figure 12.15, which asks respondents where they purchased their last video game. In looking at the third column, 27.3 percent purchased their

Have You Played Video Games on Your Smartphone?					
		Frequency	Percent	Valid Percent	Cumulative Percent
Valid	No	417	60.6	61.3	61.3
	Yes	263	38.2	38.7	100.0
	Total	680	98.8	100.0	
Missing	System	8	1.2		
Total		688	100.0		

FIGURE 12.13 Example of SPSS Output for Dichotomous Question

Usage Likelihood for Social Network Site					
		Frequency	Percent	Valid Percent	Cumulative Percent
Valid	Very unlikely to use	172	25.0	26.3	26.3
	Somewhat unlikely to use	179	26.0	27.4	53.8
	Neither likely nor unlikely to use	146	21.2	22.4	76.1
	Somewhat likely to use	98	14.2	15.0	91.1
	Very likely to use	58	8.4	8.9	100.0
	Total	653	94.9	100.0	
Missing	System	35	5.1		
Total		688	100.0		

FIGURE 12.14 Example of SPSS Output for Usage Likelihood Question

Where Did You Purchase Your Last Video Game?					
		Frequency	Percent	Valid Percent	Cumulative Percent
Valid	Retail store	188	27.3	36.9	36.9
	Online	302	43.9	59.2	96.1
	Rented—did not purchase	20	2.9	3.9	100.0
	Total	510	74.1	100.0	
Missing	System	178	25.9		
Total		688	100.0		

FIGURE 12.15 Example of SPSS Output with a Relevant Missing Value

last game from a retail store, 43.9 percent purchased it online, 2.9 percent rented the game, and 25.9 percent did not answer the question. Sometimes a large number of non-responses are due to the sensitive nature of the question and a respondent's desire to protect his or her privacy. In this case, the large percent of missing data is likely due to the fact that the response options are not categorically exhaustive. This brings up the interesting question that if the game was not purchased online or from a retail store, and was not rented, then where/how was it obtained? At this point, the researcher can only speculate. Identifying other sources for video game purchases would require additional investigation, which could be accomplished via personal interviews, a focus group, by asking an open-ended question, or by offering an "other" with a fill-in-the blank option to the existing question.

12.8b Cross-Tabulation

Cross-tabulations analyze relationships and involve comparing data across two different variables, at least one of which is measured at the nominal or ordinal level. Figure 12.16 displays the SPSS output for the question "Have you played video games on social network sites?" by the respondent's gender. It shows the frequency count for the "yes" and "no" responses as well as the column percentages. For females, 85.4 percent said "no" to the question and 14.6 percent responded "yes," that they had played games on social networking sites. For the males in the sample, 93.7 percent said "no" and only 6.3 percent indicated "yes."

Three-way crosstabs are occasionally used when researchers believe two different variables might be affecting a response. For example, with video games a researcher might think that both gender and income drive attitude toward the various gaming platforms. Using SPSS, a three-way crosstab table can be produced, as shown in Figure 12.17. Thus, two- and three-way cross tabulations divide the sample into subgroups in order to better understand how the dependent variable is related to and varies by the different subgroups.

Of concern to researchers is the percentage for each gender in each income group. For the first two income groups (Less than $24,999 and $25,000–49,999) the percentage of females and males that indicated they had played video games (yes responses) on social networking sites is relatively equal. But, beginning with the $50,000–79,999 income bracket, differences appear. 15.1 percent of females said "yes" compared to only 6 percent of males who said "yes." Differences are also present in the $75,000-99,999 income group. The most dramatic differences are in the $100,000+ income bracket, where 24.4 percent of females have played video games on social networking sites compared to only 2.9 percent of males.

12.8c Basic Descriptive Statistics

LEARNING OBJECTIVE 12.6
Explain the descriptive statistics that should be used with each type of scale.

Reporting the results of every question in a survey, including the demographic profile of the sample, is basic descriptive statistics. It provides researchers with an overview of the data that was obtained through the questionnaire. The type of descriptive statistics obtained is dictated by the type of scale within each question. Figure 12.18 provides an overview of the type of data and appropriate descriptive statistic. For nominal and ordinal data, the appropriate descriptive statistic measure would be a frequency count. For interval and ratio data the key appropriate descriptive statistics are the mean, a measure of central tendency, and standard deviation, a measure of dispersion.

Played Games on Social Network Sites * Gender Crosstabulation

			Gender		Cumulative Percent
			Female	Male	Total
Played games on social network sites	No	Count	223	385	608
		% within gender	85.4%	93.7%	90.5%
	Yes	Count	38	26	64
		% within gender	14.6%	6.3%	9.5%
Total		Count	261	411	672
		% within gender	100.0%	100.0%	100.0%

FIGURE 12.16 Example of Cross-Tabulation SPSS Output

Played Games on Social Network Sites * Gender * Income Crosstabulation						
				Gender		
				Female	Male	Total
Less than $24,999	Played games on social network sites	**No**	Count	37	63	100
			% within gender	88.1%	90.0%	89.3%
		Yes	Count	5	7	12
			% within gender	11.9%	10.0%	10.7%
$25,000–49,999	Played games on social network sites	**No**	Count	53	84	137
			% within gender	93.0%	93.3%	93.2%
		Yes	Count	4	6	10
			% within gender	7.0%	6.7%	6.8%
$50,000–74,999	Played games on social network sites	**No**	Count	45	79	124
			% within gender	84.9%	94.0%	90.5%
		Yes	Count	8	5	13
			% within gender	15.1%	6.0%	9.5%
$75,000–99,999	Played games on social network sites	**No**	Count	43	68	111
			% within gender	82.7%	91.9%	88.1%
		Yes	Count	9	6	15
			% within gender	17.3%	8.1%	11.9%
$100,000+	Played games on social network sites	**No**	Count	34	68	102
			% within gender	75.6%	97.1%	88.7%
		Yes	Count	11	2	13
			% within gender	24.4%	2.9%	11.3%

FIGURE 12.17 Example of a Three-Way SPSS Crosstab Output

Type of Scale	Descriptive Measure
Nominal	Frequency
Ordinal	Frequency
Interval	Mean Standard Deviation
Ratio	Mean Standard Deviation

FIGURE 12.18 Type of Scale and Descriptive Statistics

Figure 12.19 provides the SPSS output for one of the questions about how likely the respondent would be to use each of gaming platforms. Means and standard deviations are appropriate because this variable represents interval-level data, based on the assumption that the distances between categories will be perceived by respondents as being equal. With regard to the mean, the platform with the lowest likelihood of usage is social network sites (2.53) and the platforms with the highest likelihood of usage are smartphones (3.52) and the computer (3.44).

Standard deviation a measure of dispersion that provides an indication of the degree of variation in the responses.

The **standard deviation** provides an indication of the degree of variation in the responses. Of the five variables listed in Figure 12.19, the likelihood of playing games on online websites has the highest standard deviation, while preference for games on social networking sites has the lowest. This would indicate that responses in reference to online websites are spread out or dispersed more than are the responses for social networking sites, and suggests that tests for differences should be performed on the basis of gender, income, age, or other factors that might help to account for the differences, or dispersion in responses.

Respondents in the gaming platform study were asked to enter how many games they purchased in the last year, which generates ratio data. The SPSS analysis provided a mean of 3.73 with a standard deviation of 2.98. Although the mean and standard deviation are appropriate descriptive statistics for ratio data, it sometimes is helpful to obtain the mode and median as well. The frequency count for the various responses is shown in Figure 12.20.

Mode a measure of central tendency indicating the most frequent response within a frequency count.

Median a measure of central tendency indicating the mid-point of the data in a frequency count, below which 50 percent of the observations fall.

The **mode** is the most frequent response, which, according to the SPSS output, is two video games (114, or 16.7 percent of the valid percent column). It would also be important to note that "1" is also high with 100 responses, or 14.6 percent. The **median** is the mid-point of the data, below which 50 percent of the observations fall. In examining the cumulative percentage, the 50 percent point is within the response "3." This is useful information because the researcher can say that 53.9 percent of the respondents purchase three or fewer games a year.

With the array of numbers shown in Figure 12.20, researchers might want to collapse the data into categories so it can be presented either in a table or graphically. In doing so the researcher will look at the data array in three ways. First, are there any natural breaks in the data? Second, approximately how many categories are desirable? Third, what would be logical groupings of the data?

Descriptive Statistics					
	N	Minimum	Maximum	Mean	Std. Deviation
Usage likelihood for online website	662	1	5	3.03	1.528
Usage likelihood for social network site	653	1	5	2.53	1.269
Usage likelihood for gaming console	653	1	5	2.89	1.351
Usage likelihood for computer	666	1	5	3.44	1.313
Usage likelihood for smartphone	648	1	5	3.52	1.279
Valid N (listwise)	616				

FIGURE 12.19 Descriptive Statistics for Interval Data

Number of Games Purchased in Last Year					
		Frequency	Percent	Valid Percent	Cumulative Percent
Valid	0	87	12.6	12.7	12.7
	1	100	14.5	14.6	27.4
	2	114	16.6	16.7	44.1
	3	67	9.7	9.8	53.9
	4	68	9.9	10.0	63.8
	5	59	8.6	8.6	72.5
	6	55	8.0	8.1	80.5
	7	47	6.8	6.9	87.4
	8	33	4.8	4.8	92.2
	9	28	4.1	4.1	96.3
	10	12	1.7	1.8	98.1
	11	6	.9	.9	99.0
	12	3	.4	.4	99.4
	14	2	.3	.3	99.7
	15	2	.3	.3	100.0
	Total	683	99.3	100.0	
Missing	System	5	.7		
Total		688	100.0		

FIGURE 12.20 Frequency Count of Ratio Data

Figure 12.21 illustrates one possible grouping of the data. It makes sense to have a category for zero since this indicates the number of individuals who did not make any purchases in the last year. Such individuals should be separated from those who did make purchases. A logical grouping may be zero, one to three video games, four to six video games, seven to nine video games, and 10 or more games.

12.9 Global Concerns

Many U.S. client firms and research providers are outsourcing global survey design, data collection and validation tasks to international firms specializing in these areas. Outsourcing of international research is predicted to increase. Cost savings help research firms to remain profitable in today's demanding economic climate, which continually expects research firms to cut costs while producing results more quickly. By outsourcing tasks, research firms are also able to engage in more projects, increasing their capacity to do business. Finally, disaggregation is becoming more and more prevalent in the marketing research industry as a whole; the international research community is no exception.[14]

To ensure that the validation process is relatively trouble free, U.S. client firms or their U.S. research partners must take care when selecting their primary international outsourcing firm. Only those firms with strong references that can provide evidence of

Number of Games Purchased (Categories)					
		Frequency	Percent	Valid Percent	Cumulative Percent
Valid	0 games	87	12.6	12.7	12.7
	1–3 games	281	40.8	41.1	53.9
	4–6 games	182	26.5	26.6	80.5
	7–9 games	108	15.7	15.8	96.3
	10+ games	25	3.6	3.7	100.0
	Total	683	99.3	100.0	
Missing	System	5	.7		
Total		688	100.0		

FIGURE 12.21 Ratio Data Reported in Groups

Source: mindscanner/Shutterstock.

The benefits of costs and quicker results have led many U.S. firms to outsource global survey design, data collection and validation tasks to international firms specializing in these areas.

having completed similar projects in the countries in question should be considered.[15]

Once the primary outsourcing firm has been selected, careful thought must be put into creating playbooks. According to Kumar Mehta, "Playbooks establish clear standards, protocols, and processes to be followed by all parties to ensure error-free deliverables and success. They are meant to ensure every process and quality step is followed. The playbook should identify clear detailed roles and responsibilities, timeliness, process flows and quality-control procedures."[16]

Playbooks are particularly important because many international partners in turn subcontract work at the country, region, and even local levels. This means that client firms or U.S. research partners could be working with data that has passed through as many as four levels of subcontractors. Consistency in performance and adherence to the playbook standards are of critical importance. Data accuracy and completeness should be stressed, not only within the playbook, but during the negotiation process. Costs related to ensuring that complete and accurate data is delivered should be built into the price of the primary outsourcing firm's services. The playbook should require the primary outsourcing firm to fully disclose its hiring and training procedures for interviewers, to describe upfront how interviewers will be compensated, and that all adhere to a standard training process and use standardized training materials. The primary outsourcing firm should also be required to provide a list of all subcontractors, and agree upon and fully disclose the quality control process used to validate data at the field level.

Furthermore, the primary outsourcing firm should be required to deliver evidence of validation activities as part of their deliverables. The contract should specify that subcontractors clarify ambiguous data in the field and that they provide both the original information as well as the validated information as part of their deliverables. This is important because cost, local custom, and language barriers make validating information by the primary outsourcing agency virtually impossible. If the primary outsourcing firm or a subcontractor is responsible for cleaning the data, the original and cleaned data files should also be required as part of the deliverables. While many factors affecting the validation process vary by country, adhering to this process can help to maximize the accuracy and completeness of data collected in an international setting.[17]

12.10 Marketing Research Statistics

Checking data for inconsistencies and errors is the topic of the Statistics Review. In addition, the concept of filtering data is presented. This procedure can be used when the researcher wants to examine a particular subset of the data. The Statistical Reporting section examines various ways of reporting ratio data. The key is to report the data in a way that accurately reflects the data and provides useful information to management. The Dealing with Data section involves examining data for inconsistencies and errors, then filtering it for a specific subset of respondents.

12.10a Statistics Review

As discussed in the chapter, data cleaning is the process of checking the data for inconsistencies. **Figure 12.22** shows the SPSS output for a scaled-response question with inconsistencies. The question asked respondents to indicate their level of preference for video games on smartphones. It is a five-point scale from "would not use" to "highly prefer." Notice in the output there is a "0" response and two "6" responses. Neither can be correct.

To locate the questionnaires with these three incorrect responses, the data can be sorted by this question. If using Excel, make certain that all fields are selected as part of the sort, or only data in the selected column will be sorted and will not match up with the original questionnaires. For SPSS, the variable related to this question is selected for the sorting. Depending on whether the data are sorted in ascending or descending order, the "0" response and "6" responses will be at the top and bottom of the data file. Once these are located on the spreadsheet, the questionnaire number can be identified. The questionnaire

Preference for Smartphone					
		Frequency	Percent	Valid Percent	Cumulative Percent
Valid	0	1	.1	.2	.2
	Very unlikely to use	54	7.8	8.3	8.5
	Somewhat unlikely to use	95	13.8	14.7	23.1
	Neither unlikely nor likely to use	152	22.1	23.5	46.6
	Somewhat likely to use	155	22.5	23.9	70.5
	Very likely to use	189	27.5	29.2	99.7
	6	2	.3	.3	100.0
	Total	648	94.2	100.0	
Missing	System	40	5.8		
Total		688	100.0		

FIGURE 12.22 Data Cleaning of a Scaled-Response Question

can then be checked to see if there was an entry error or some other mistake that resulted in the incorrect responses. In most cases, the incorrect value can be replaced with the correct value.

Open-ended questions that produce ratio data are more challenging. **Figure 12.23** shows the SPSS printout for the number of games individuals purchased last year. Notice the last two items, the "77" response and the "115" response. Both seem highly unlikely since the nearest response is 15. If the researcher has the paper survey, then it is possible that the correct answer can be found.

But what if this survey was completed online and there is no paper questionnaire to examine? Is it possible the person meant "7" and just accidentally typed in "77", or perhaps this person was not being serious and just typed it in to throw off the results? There is no way of knowing. In the latter situation, the researcher could check all of the person's other answers to see if they make sense and if they appear to be consistent. If not, then the questionnaire can be discarded. The same process can be used for the "115." Here it is more difficult because there is no way of knowing if the person meant "11" or "15" since

Number of Games Purchased in Last Year					
		Frequency	Percent	Valid Percent	Cumulative Percent
Valid	.00	87	12.6	12.7	12.7
	1.00	100	14.5	14.6	27.4
	2.00	114	16.6	16.7	44.1
	3.00	66	9.6	9.7	53.7
	4.00	68	9.9	10.0	63.7
	5.00	59	8.6	8.6	72.3
	6.00	55	8.0	8.1	80.4
	7.00	47	6.8	6.9	87.3
	8.00	32	4.7	4.7	91.9
	9.00	28	4.1	4.1	96.0
	10.00	12	1.7	1.8	97.8
	11.00	6	.9	.9	98.7
	12.00	3	.4	.4	99.1
	14.00	2	.3	.3	99.4
	15.00	2	.3	.3	99.7
	77.00	1	.1	.1	99.9
	115.00	1	.1	.1	100.0
	Total	683	99.3	100.0	
Missing	System	5	.7		
Total		688	100.0		

FIGURE 12.23 Data Cleaning of an Open-Ended Ratio Scale

both would be legitimate answers. Regardless, the researcher must decide whether to keep extreme data points that cannot be validated, or whether they should be deleted. Most researchers would opt to remove the data points since their inclusion would significantly influence the mean number of games purchased and the answers do not appear legitimate.

In data cleaning, another situation that must be considered is constant sum questions. In the questionnaire dealing with gaming platforms, a constant sum question asked respondents what percent of the games they played across four platforms: game consoles, online, computer, and smartphone. The total of the four should add to 100 percent. While this can be automatically checked in online surveys, self-administered surveys rely on the user to correctly complete the question. Sometimes respondents make mistakes and their answers do not add to the necessary 100 percent. Since the researcher cannot really know what the respondent meant to answer, the constant sum scale should be deleted from the analysis and values changed to missing data. Failure to add properly does not necessarily mean that the rest of the questionnaire data is bad, so unless multiple validation problems exist within the survey, the rest of the data can be retained.

To check if the four responses did indeed add to 100 percent a new variable can be created that sums the answers to the four categories (each represented by a separate variable). Results of the gaming platform study for the constant sum question are shown in Figure 12.24. Notice out of the 617 individuals who answered this question, 603 or 97.7 percent did so correctly. That means 14 responses did not sum to 100. Totals ranged from 80 to 200. Some were close, such as the 95 and the 105, but the researcher cannot know what happened and cannot arbitrarily subtract or add five percentage points from one of the four platform responses. Neither can the response of the individual whose total came to 200 be halved for each category. The same is true for the other cases where the constant sum did not equal 100.

Summed Score of Constant Sum Scale

		Frequency	Percent	Valid Percent	Cumulative Percent
Valid	80.00	1	.1	.2	.2
	90.00	2	.3	.3	.5
	95.00	1	.1	.2	.6
	100.00	603	87.6	97.7	98.4
	105.00	3	.4	.5	98.9
	115.00	1	.1	.2	99.0
	125.00	1	.1	.2	99.2
	130.00	1	.1	.2	99.4
	132.00	1	.1	.2	99.5
	160.00	1	.1	.2	99.7
	200.00	2	.3	.3	100.0
	Total	617	89.7	100.0	
Missing	System	71	10.3		
Total		688	100.0		

FIGURE 12.24 Totals for a Constant Sum Question

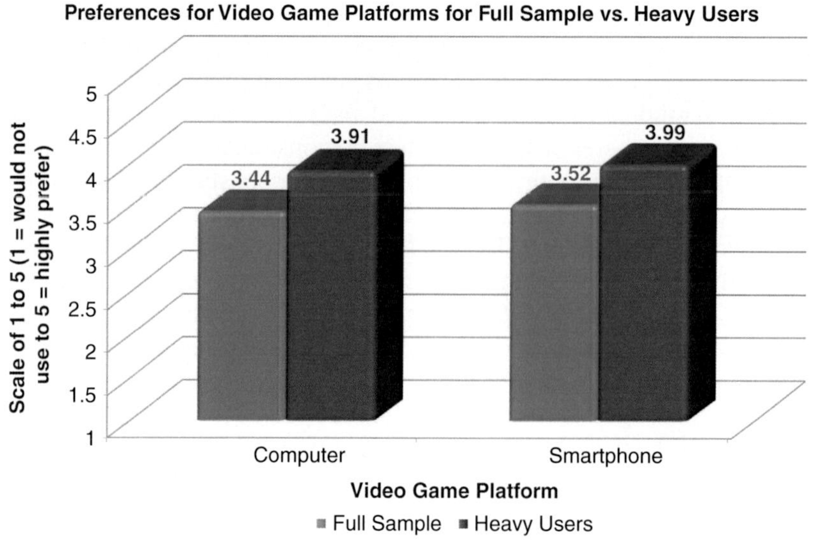

FIGURE 12.25 An Example of Results Using Filtering to Isolate only Heavy Game Users

In examining data, sometimes researchers want to know how a specific segment of the sample, rather than the entire group, responded to questions. For instance, in developing video games it would be important to know what heavy purchasers think. Instead of looking at all individuals, it might be a good idea to look only at those who purchased five or more video games during the last year. This would be approximately one-third of the sample. Researchers can do this by filtering or selecting only those who purchased five or more games. Out of the original sample of 688 respondents, 247 indicated they had purchased five or more video games during the last year.

The view of these individuals can be important in terms of developing an application for smartphones. When asked if they like playing video games on smartphones, the percentage of "yes" responses for the entire sample was 38.7, but for those who had purchased five or more video games in the last year it was 53.1. Clearly, those who are heavy purchasers of video games like playing video games on smartphones more than the sample as a whole.

Figure 12.25 shows the difference in preference for video games played on the computer and smartphones for the entire sample compared to heavy users. By using filtering, researchers can advise the video game producer that providing games on both platforms is important in reaching the heavy purchasers.

12.10b Statistics Reporting

Results of marketing research can be reported in a variety of ways. Consider the data shown in Figures 12.20 and 12.21, the number of video games purchased in the last year. The original data were ratio, as shown in Figure 12.20, but could be put into groups, as shown in Figure 12.21. In making a presentation of the descriptive statistics from this study a researcher can show these data in three different ways. First, an area graph of the ratio data could be created, illustrated in **Figure 12.26**. The graph is an excellent visual image of the number of games purchased by respondents of the study and clearly shows that the highest frequencies are for 0, 1, and 2. The frequency then makes a sharp decline for three games and then slowly declines all the way to the maximum value of 15.

As discussed previously, the data could be grouped into categories and graphed using a bar chart, shown in **Figure 12.27**. Someone looking at the graph can quickly see the majority of respondents purchased one to three games. Recall from the previous discussion, the grouping was arbitrary. A researcher could use unequal categories of 0, 1, 2, 3–4, 5–7,

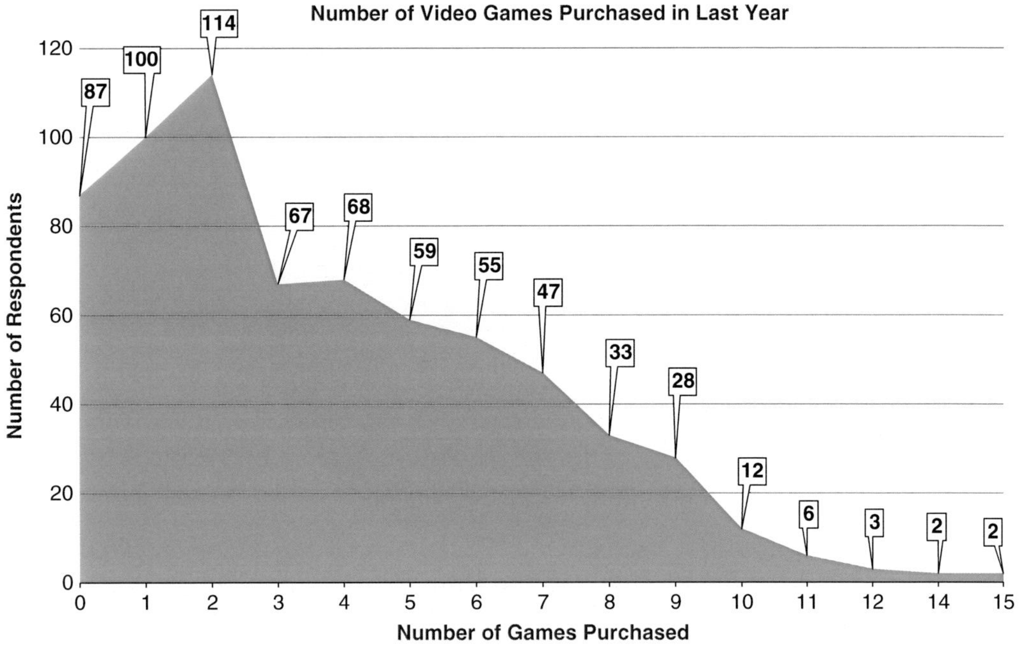

FIGURE 12.26 An Area Chart Showing the Number of Video Games Purchased during the Last Year

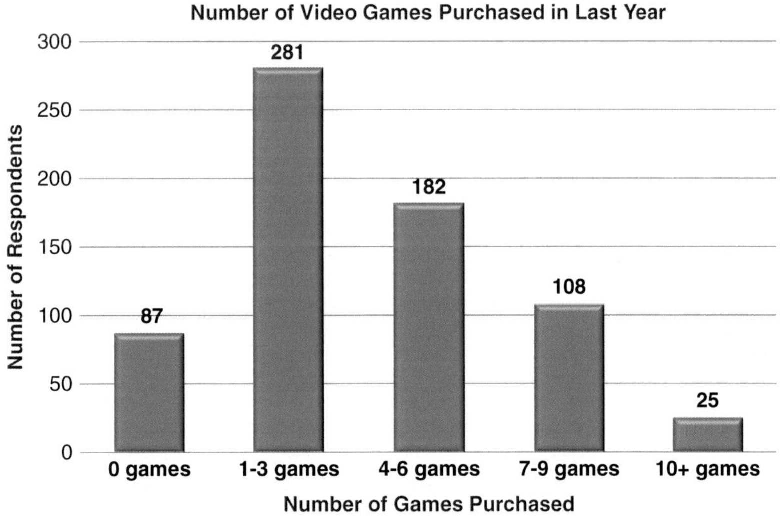

FIGURE 12.27 A Column Chart Showing the Number of Video Games Purchased during the Last Year

and so on. The way the data are grouped is at the discretion of the researcher. The objective should be to report the data in a way that accurately reflects the results of the study and is the most usable for management decisions.

A third way these data could be reported is a pie chart, shown in Figure 12.28. With the pie chart, the researcher can show both the frequency count and the percentage of the total. The same groupings were used that are in Figure 12.27. Again, the researcher does not have to use these particular groups. He can choose different categories if doing so fits better with the research report and the emphasis that is being presented.

Statistical Reporting Exercise: Respondents to a survey were asked, "What is the acceptable load time for apps for a cell phone?" A total of 297 individuals responded to the question. Results are shown in Figure 12.29. The acceptable load time, in seconds, is

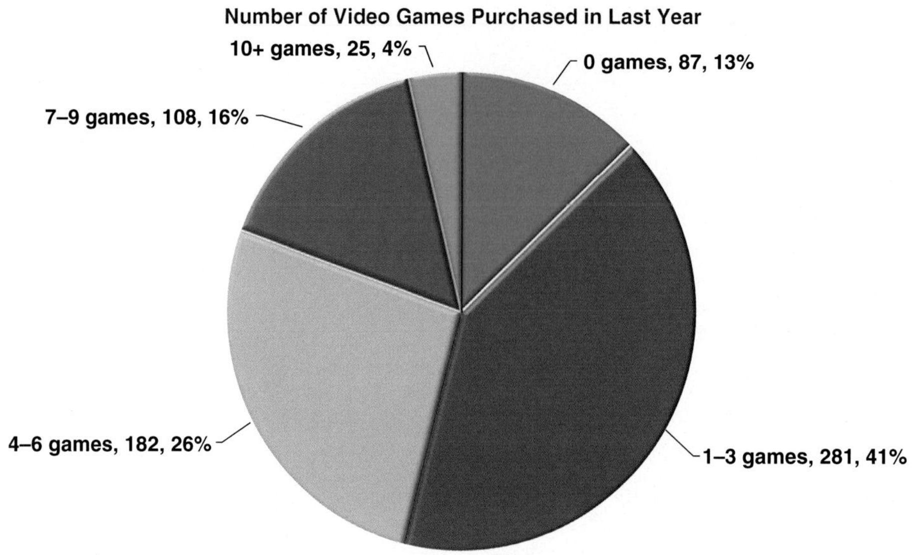

FIGURE 12.28 A Pie Chart Showing the Number of Video Games Purchased during the Last Year

Load Time (seconds)	Frequency
1	14
2	36
3	62
4	44
5	31
6	22
7	20
8	17
9	15
10	10
11	9
12	8
13	5
14	3
15	1

FIGURE 12.29 Acceptable Load Time for Cell Phone Apps

shown in the first column, and the frequency is shown in the second column. Create an area chart, a bar chart, and a pie chart of the data. Create groups for the bar and pie charts that you believe best represent the data. Explain your rationale for the groupings. Identify the primary advantages of each method of graphing the data.

12.10c Dealing with Data

A study was conducted with 180 respondents concerning criteria in selecting a retail clothing store. The questionnaire is entitled Chapter 12 Dealing with Data Survey and the data is entitled Chapter 12 Dealing with Data. Both files are located on the textbook website: www.clowjames.net/students.html

Exercise One: Data Cleaning: Respondents were asked to indicate how important nine different criteria were in selecting a retail clothing store. A five-point scale was used with responses ranging from very unimportant to very important. Another question asked respondents to indicate what percentage of clothing they purchased in discount stores, department stores, specialty stores, and online.

The first step in cleaning the data is to run a frequency count of every question to make sure no responses are outside the accepted range from very unimportant to very important. For those that fall outside the range, it is important to identify the specific questionnaire or "case" number of the invalid data so it can be fixed. This can be done by sorting the data on that variable.

The second step in the data cleaning is to create a new variable that is the sum of the constant sum categories. The total should add to 100 percent. Again, the specific case number where problems occur must be identified. After completing these steps, answer the following questions.

1. Of the nine criteria individuals use to select retail clothing stores, which ones have answers outside the five-point scale? Identify the question and the response that was incorrect, as well as the specific case number that corresponds with each error. (This can also be done by running a crosstab with Case ID as the row variable and the criteria question as the column variable.)
2. Looking at the summed total for the constant sum question, how many individuals were identified as "missing system"?
3. Looking at the summed total for the constant sum question, what percent of the answers add to the correct 100 percent? What other totals are seen in the output? Link the case number to each incorrect constant sum total. (Again, this can be done by using the crosstab function, or sorting the data by the sum variable.)
4. Do any of the questionnaires indicate multiple validation problems? If so, which specific cases (questionnaires) would you recommend eliminating entirely from data pool and why?

Exercise Two: Data Filtering: Filter the data by selecting all of the cases where the percentage of clothing purchases at specialty stores (Question 2) is 40 percent or greater. Obtain the mean for the items in Question 1 by using the descriptive option in SPSS for those respondents who purchase 40 percent or more of their clothes from specialty stores. Clear the filter. Filter the data by selecting all of the cases where the percentage of clothes purchased at department stores is 50 percent or greater. Obtain the means of question 1 using the descriptive option in SPSS. Compare the means between those who purchase more of their clothes at specialty stores versus department stores. Create a bar graph comparing these means for the two filtered samples.

Summary

Objective 1: Identify the steps in the data preparation process.

The data preparation process involves four steps: validation, coding, data entry, and data cleaning. Data validation is a process used by researchers to ensure data were collected properly and are free of error and bias. The next step is data entry, which is actually entering data into a computer spreadsheet such as SPSS or Excel that can be used for data tabulation and analysis. The last step is data cleaning, which is the process of checking the data for inconsistencies.

Objective 2: Discuss the processes of validating and coding data.
Validation starts by checking the data collection process to make sure procedures were followed and data were collected properly. If multiple interviewers were used, data must have been collected the same way. The data are then checked to make sure only qualified respondents passed the screening questions and unqualified respondents were not interviewed or did not complete questionnaires. The next validation step is checking the data for fraud. While extremely difficult to detect, the researcher can check for signs that fraud might have occurred. Finally, the completeness and usability of the data must be checked by someone with excellent knowledge of the study purpose and survey objectives. The second step in the validation process is coding, which is assigning numerical values to each response on the questionnaire. Coding closed-ended questions and scaled questions tends to be rather easy. Open-ended questions, however, require some level of interpretation and classification of responses, a time-consuming and expensive process.

Objective 3: Describe the processes of data entry and data cleaning.
Data entry involves entering the data into a computer spreadsheet. With online surveys the data are automatically entered into a spreadsheet through the programming of the online survey. If entered manually, the person doing the data entry must be given a code sheet that specifies the code to be used for each response. Data cleaning involves checking the data for inconsistencies and involves four steps. First, the data are examined to be certain the data is recorded in the correct column. Second, the data are reviewed for values out of the range for a particular response. Third, the data are checked for extreme values that appear to be incorrect and not feasible. Fourth, the data are checked for responses that show inconsistency and lack of reading the question or inattention on the part of the respondent.

Objective 4: Discuss the advantages of pre-coding questionnaires.
Pre-coding involves putting the code numbers on the questionnaire prior to administering the survey. For online and computerized surveys, pre-coding automatically occurs in writing the program because the computer needs to know what numerical value to give to each response. Paper surveys can also be pre-coded. This makes it easier for the person entering the data into a computer. Most researchers feel this does not bias responses.

Objective 5: Describe the various ways of tabulating data.
Tabulation is counting the number of responses in each answer category of a question. One-way tabulation involves counting the number of responses for each answer category within one question. Cross-tabulation is counting the number of responses in two or more categories simultaneously. In tabulating responses, researchers must be cognizant of the number of missing items (individuals who left the question blank). In most cases it is small and insignificant to understanding the data. In other instances, non-responses are important and need to be considered in the tabulation.

Objective 6: Explain the descriptive statistics that should be used with each type of scale.
Descriptive statistics is the reporting of every question in a survey, including sample demographics. If the type of scale is nominal or ordinal, the appropriate descriptive statistic is a frequency count. If the type of scale is interval or ratio, then the appropriate descriptive statistic is the mean and standard deviation.

Key Terms

coding, p. 409
confederates, p. 406
cross-tabulations, p. 418
data cleaning, p. 416
data entry, p. 415
data validation, p. 405
dummy coding, p. 410
median, p. 422
mode, p. 422
one-way tabulation, p. 418
parameter, p. 404
standard deviation, p. 422
statistic, p. 404
straight-lining, p. 408
tabulation, p. 418

Critical Thinking Exercises

1. In validating an intercept survey, a field supervisor asked a recent interviewee what she answered when asked, "What is the one thing you dislike most about your SeaWorld experience today?" The respondent answered, "I was surprised that the trainers did not interact with Orcas during the show like they have in the past. We didn't get to see the Dolphin show because there were only two shows scheduled. It seems like all of the animals are doing fewer tricks compared to when we came a few years ago." The response

written by the interviewer read, "Animal shows." Is the interviewer's recorded response an accurate representation of the interviewee's opinion? Why or why not?

2. An open-ended question asked, "What is your favorite thing about football? Critique the phrasing of the question, create a list of possible response categories, and code the following responses into categories. Justify your decisions.
   a. "High scoring games are exciting."
   b. "Men in tight pants."
   c. "There's nothing better than being with friends in the stands, watching your college team beat up on a rival, especially if you sneak a flask into the game. I love close games."
   d. "I hate football."
   e. "Watching an NFL game on TV is the perfect way to spend a rainy Sunday afternoon."
   f. "It's fun."
   g. "I love playing football on nice fall days, but I really don't like playing when it rains."
   h. "The guys on the team are so cute, strong, and muscular, I just love them! I wish they would play better though."
   i. "I like watching well-matched defenses play against one another. But the rules favor the offense now."
   j. "Tailgating is great! I love visiting with friends, eating lots of food, and getting drunk. The game is ok, I guess."
   k. "Rugby is much more exciting than Football."

3. Identify whether the data below are nominal, ordinal, interval, or ratio data. What type of chart or graph would you recommend to present the results of this table?

Rank Walmart

		Frequency	Percent	Valid Percent	Cumulative Percent
Valid	Least desirable	139	69.5	69.5	69.5
	4th most desirable	26	13.0	13.0	82.5
	3rd most desirable	20	10.0	10.0	92.5
	2nd most desirable	10	5.0	5.0	97.5
	Most desirable	5	2.5	2.5	100.0
	Total	200	100.0	100.0	

Should data from other brands be included as well? Why or why not? What additional information would be needed in order to create a chart that is clear and easily understood?

4. Suppose you developed a Likert scale to assess the degree to which attracting new customers was given priority in the marketing plan. Which of the following items need to be reversed so that more positive responses are expressed by higher numbers? Assume that respondents will use a scale ranging from 1=strongly disagree to 5=strongly agree.
   1. Formal strategies are in place to attract new clients.
   2. We do not give enough attention to attracting new clients.
   3. Our employees are not motivated to sell our services to potential customers.

The following questions require you to access the textbook's website at: www.clowjames.net/students.html

The SPSS data file is named Chapter 12 Critical Thinking Data and the Word file Chapter 12 Critical Thinking Survey has the survey questions.

5. Review the survey questions that accompany the data file and think about whether they represent nominal, ordinal, interval, or ratio level data. Open the SPSS data file, and look at the column entitled MEASURE. For each variable, change the measure from SCALE to either ORDINAL or NOMINAL if appropriate. Remember, interval and ratio-level measures are designated by SCALE in SPSS. String characters (such as responses to open-ended questions) by default are classified as NOMINAL data.

6. Except for the first variable IDNO (the survey number corresponding to each respondent), run frequencies for each of the variables contained in the data file. Create a table based on this output that lists the variable name, incorrect value, and IDNO for each problem found.

7. Variables 4aCSRunning through 4aCSSwimming represent the results of a constant sum scale. Validate the data by creating a new variable that sums the constant sum variables. Run a frequency for the new variable, then create a table listing this variable's name, the incorrect percentages, and the IDNO for each problem case.
8. Question 6 of the survey asks individuals why they joined a health club. Code the open-ended responses into categories. Justify why you chose the categories that you did. For each category, create a table that lists the category name and the verbatim responses that fall into that category. Should any of the open-ended remarks be thrown out? Why or why not? Next, create a new variable in SPSS containing these classifications and code each case. Save your data file.
9. Examine the items in question 3. Which need to be recoded so that the more positive attitudes are represented by higher numbers? Recode these into new variables. Be sure to keep the old variables. When you are finished, run descriptive statistics (frequencies, means, range and standard deviations) for each of the question 3 variables. If you were to present this information visually, what type of graph or chart would you recommend? Why? What portion of the data would you graph, the frequency count, percentage, mean, or standard deviation? Justify your answer.
10. Create a chart or graph that accurately displays a cross-tabulation of Q6WhyJoin by Q7Gender. Comment on the results. What other variables might make good candidates for cross tabulations? List your recommendations.
11. Which of the variables in the dataset would be good candidates for pie charts? Why? Which would be better represented by some type of bar/column chart? Why? Are any variables in this data set suitable for area chart or line graphs? Why or why not?

Lakeside Grill

(Comprehensive Student Case)

The student team collected data using four different methods. First, they passed the questionnaire out to patrons at the Lakeside Grill and asked them to fill it out while waiting for their food. Second, they sent emails to businesses that were members of the Chamber of Commerce and asked that the email be circulated among the business's employees. The email directed respondents to an online version of the survey. Third, they used an intercept approach asking individuals to fill out the questionnaire during a local food festival. The fourth approach was email sent by students in three different marketing classes to family and friends that lived in the area, directing them to an online survey. These approaches produced 247 completed surveys.

Located on the textbook website (www.clowjames.net/students.html) is the final questionnaire used for the study, Chapter 12 Lakeside Grill Survey. The data that were collected is in a SPSS file called Chapter 12 Lakeside Grill Data. The data were validated, coded, and entered into the SPSS spreadsheet. During the data cleaning process several errors were detected. The original questionnaires were obtained to determine the cause of the error. Several items were corrected and eight questionnaires were discarded because of inconsistencies in answers.

Upon completion of the data preparation process, descriptive statistics for each question were run. This output file is entitled Chapter 12 Lakeside Descriptive Output. From the data, the team developed graphs for each question and placed them in a PowerPoint file. The title of this file is Chapter 12 Lakeside Descriptive Graphs. All of these files can be found at the website (www.clowjames.net/students.html).

Access all of these files and then answer the questions below.

Critique Questions:

1. Critique the four methods the team used to collect the data. Should they have identified the source (data collection method) from where each response came? Why or why not?
2. Critique the final questionnaire.
3. Look carefully at the responses to questions 2, 4, and 5 in the SPSS data file. Evaluate how these open-ended questions were coded.
4. Open the output file entitled Chapter 12 Lakeside Grill Descriptive Output. Compare the output file to the questionnaire. Did the team run the correct descriptive statistics? If not, what descriptive statistics should have been run? Are there any other statistics that should be obtained using SPSS?
5. Open the Chapter 12 Lakeside Grill Descriptive Graphs file. Examine each graph. Are they clear, understandable, and properly labeled? What are some of the problems that can occur when graphing in SPSS? Compare each graph with the SPSS output file. Discuss each graph in terms of being appropriate for its descriptive statistic.

Notes

1. Michael A. Stelzner, "2018 Social Media Marketing Industry Report," *Social Media Examiner* (2018).
2. Jonathan E. Brill, "The Exploratory Open-Ended Survey Question," *Quirk's Marketing Research Review* (March 1995): Article ID 19950301.
3. Mathijs de Jong, "Using New Technologies to Mitigate Fraud in Online Research," RW Connect, April 12, 2018, https://rwconnect.esomar.org.
4. Bill MacElroy, "How to Catch a Cheat," *Quirk's Marketing Research Review* (July 2004): Article ID 20040704, p. 46.
5. Shawna Fisher, "How to Spot a Fake," *Quirk's Marketing Research Review* (January 2007): 44.
6. Bill MacElroy, "How to Catch a Cheat," *Quirk's Marketing Research Review* (July 2004): Article ID 20040704, p. 46.
7. Ibid.
8. Ibid.
9. Don Bruzzone, "Sampling the Impact. How Do Respondent Behaviors and Online Sample Quality Affect Measures of Ad Performance?" *Quirk's Marketing Research Review* (April 2009) Article ID 20090404, pp. 32, 34–37.
10. Stephen J. Hellebusch, "By the Numbers: To Double-Code or Single-Code?" *Quirk's Marketing Research* (December 2003): Article 20031210.
11. Interview with Debbie Peternana, ReRez, December 1, 2011.
12. Brenden Bailey, "Data Cleaning 101," Towards Data Science, June 14, 2017, https://towardsdatascience.com/data-cleaning-101-948d22a92e4.
13. T. Amoo and H. H. Friedman, "Do Numeric Values Influence Subjects' Responses to Rating Scales?" *Journal of International Marketing Research* 26 (2012): 41–46; C. Armitage and C. Deeprose, "Changing Student Evaluations by Means of the Numeric Values of Rating Scales," *Psychology of Learning and Teaching* 3 (2004): 122–125; N. Schwartz et al., "Rating Scales: Numeric Values May Change the Meanings of Scale Labels," *Public Opinion Quarterly*, Vol. 55, pp. 570–582.
14. Kumar Mehta, "Best Practices in Managing Offshore Research Processes," *Quirk's Marketing Research E-Newsletter* (July 25, 2011): Article ID 20110726-2.
15. Karl Field, "Do You Know Where Your Data Came From?" *Quirk's Marketing Research Review* (November 2007): Article 20071101, p. 24.
16. Kumar Mehta, "Best Practices in Managing Offshore Research Processes," *Quirk's Marketing Research E-Newsletter* (July 25, 2011): Article ID 20110726-2.
17. Karl Field, "Do You Know Where Your Data Came From?" *Quirk's Marketing Research Review* (November 2007): Article 20071101, p. 24..

Analysis of Differences and Regression Analysis

CHAPTER 13

Source: paulista/Shutterstock.

Chapter Outline

Learning Objectives

After studying this chapter, you should be able to:

- Identify and explain the steps in hypothesis testing.
- Understand statistical significance and practical importance.
- Explain the difference between Type I and Type II errors.
- Explain how the chi-square test is used.
- Identify and describe the various tests for differences in means.
- Demonstrate an understanding of regression analysis.

13.1 Chapter Overview

Companies collect data in order to make better decisions. Once data are collected and have been validated, it is time for more intensive analysis that will reveal significant differences that can be used by management. According to Newzoo's recent report, the multibillion-dollar video gaming industry is comprised of three primary segments: Mobile, Console, and PC. The report shows several years of past revenues divided by segment, as well as projected future revenues.[1] Some of the results are shown in Figure 13.1.

A couple of conclusions can be drawn from the graph. The video gaming industry as a whole is still growing, as the 2015 revenues of $93.1 billion are projected to nearly double by 2021 to $180.1 billion. Mobile game revenues grew between 2015 and 2018, and forecasts suggest that revenues from this segment will triple between 2015 and 2021. While the overall revenue level associated with PC games and Console games has remained fairly stable and is projected to grow a little by 2021, the percentage of the overall revenue generated by each segment is in decline. In 2015, the Mobile and PC segments each accounted for 34 percent of the revenue pie while the Console segment contributed 32 percent of revenues. Fast forward to 2021 when the Mobile segment is expected to account for 59 percent of all global games revenues, and PC and Console game segments are forecast to decline to 19 percent and 22 percent of gaming revenue, respectively. Are these trends significant? Most people would think so, but researchers rely on statistical tests to determine if differences are truly meaningful.

This chapter first reviews hypothesis testing and how data analysis can be used to support and reject the null hypothesis. The second part of the chapter examines various tests that are often used in marketing research. These include goodness-of-fit tests and various tests for measuring differences in means between populations or components of a sample.

LEARNING OBJECTIVE 13.1
Identify and explain the steps in hypothesis testing.

13.2 Hypothesis Testing

In Chapter 2, the concept of a research hypothesis was briefly introduced in the text and reviewed in the Statistics Review section of the chapter. Understanding the research

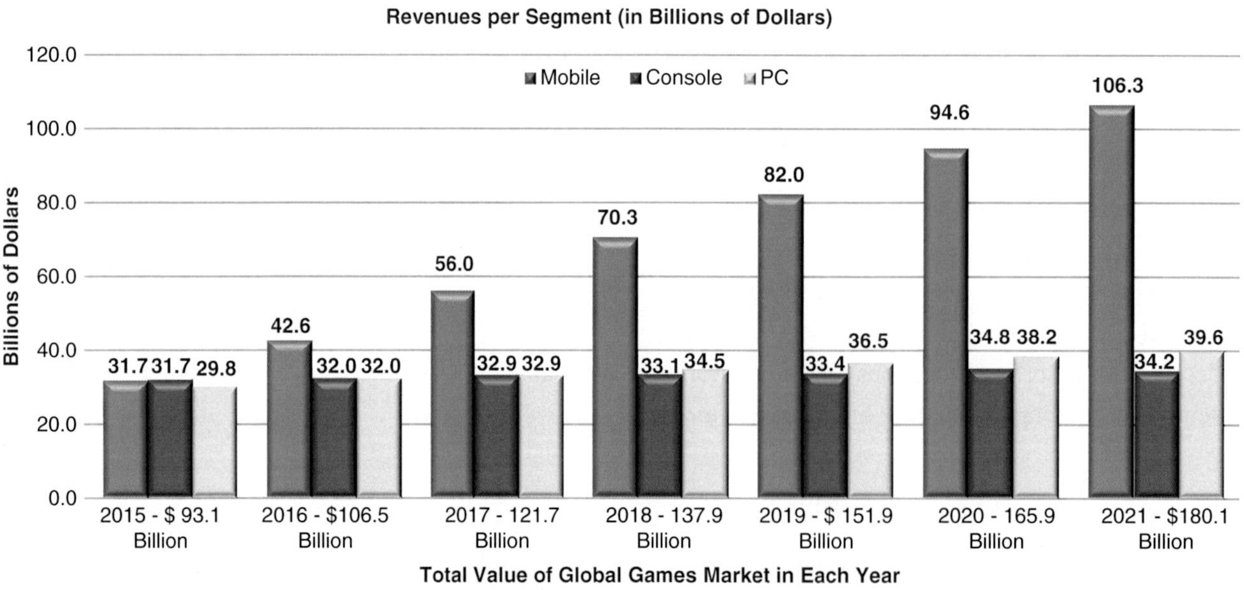

FIGURE 13.1 Global Video Games Market

Note: Segment totals may not match market total due to rounding errors.

Source: Adapted from Tom Wigman, "Mobile Revenues Account for More Than 50% of the Global Games Market as It Reaches $137.9 Billion in 2018," Newzoo, April 2018, www.newzoo.com.

1. State the hypothesis
2. Select statistical test
3. Decide decision rule
4. Calculate test statistic
5. State conclusion

FIGURE 13.2 Steps in Hypothesis Testing

hypothesis is important because marketers want to know if conditions or situations constitute a change in the marketing strategy being used. While differences may exist, researchers want to know if the differences are significantly different, meaning that they are likely true for the population as a whole and not due to random sampling error. Furthermore, does that significant difference warrant a change in a firm's marketing strategy or the development of a separate marketing campaign? Figure 13.2 identifies five steps involved in testing a hypothesis.

13.2a Step One: State the Hypothesis

Hypothesis testing involves writing a null hypothesis (H_O) and an alternative hypothesis (H_A). The null hypothesis is a statement or claim that can be statistically tested. It is derived from the research questions or research objectives of the study, or the research hypothesis. It can be based on past research, the current situation, or a supposition on what might be the situation. The purpose of the null hypothesis is to state the claim in such a way that it can be measured and tested.

If the subject of a hypothesis is a single variable, the null hypothesis is usually stated in terms of equality. For instance, a manufacturer of computers has a null hypothesis that "Individuals purchase a new laptop computer on average every three years." A firm that is testing a newly designed coupon might have a null hypothesis that states, "The coupon redemption rate is equal to 0.85 percent." The 0.85 percent is based on an average of previous coupon issuances and the percent of coupons redeemed.

The alternative hypothesis (H_A) states what must be true if the null hypothesis is false. For the null hypothesis about computer purchases, the alternative hypothesis would be "Individuals do not purchase a new laptop computer on average every three years." For the coupon redemption, the alternative hypothesis would be "The coupon redemption rate is not equal to 0.85 percent."

In situations when comparisons are made between groups or variables, the null hypothesis is usually stated as the status quo situation or in terms of no differences between the groups being tested. For instance, in examining the loyalty toward local stores, a null hypothesis might state, "Loyalty toward local retail stores does not vary by a person's gender." The alternative hypothesis would then state the opposite—"Loyalty toward local retail stores does vary by a person's gender." Often the alternative hypothesis rephrases the proposed research hypothesis, but in more general terms.

Source: PlusONE/Shutterstock.

For example, perhaps researchers expect that women will be more loyal to fashion retail stores than will men. In this case, it is important that two alternative hypotheses be proposed, one stating that men are more loyal, and the other stating that women are more loyal. Rejecting the null hypothesis only tells us that loyalty does vary by gender, but not how. Either men or women could be more loyal, so both alternatives must be listed because only one alternative hypothesis can be true.

The null hypothesis and alternative hypothesis do not have to be limited to two groups in the comparison. Local store loyalty could be examined based on a person's age or ethnicity, but each hypothesis should specify only one test variable. Thus, age and ethnicity should not be listed together in a single hypothesis. A possible null and alternative hypothesis for age could be:

H_O: Loyalty toward local retail stores does not vary based on a person's age.

H_A: Loyalty toward local retail stores does vary based on a person's age.

13.2b Step Two: Select Statistical Test

Parametric procedures statistical tests that can be used only with interval or ratio-level data.

Non-parametric procedures statistical tests that are appropriate for nominal and ordinal data.

Once the null and alternative hypotheses have been stated, the researcher can choose the appropriate statistical test. As **Figure 13.3** illustrates, the correct statistical test depends upon the nature of data, the number of variables, and the nature and size of the sample. You may recall from your statistics course that **parametric procedures** are statistically more robust, but can only be used with interval or ratio level data (metric data). **Non-parametric procedures** are appropriate for tests in which at least one variable is nominal or ordinal in nature (nonmetric data). For nominal and ordinal data, the primary statistical test is a chi-square goodness-of-fit test. With the chi-square test, actual frequency counts are compared to what would be expected based on the researcher's null hypothesis. For interval and ratio data, the most common statistical tests are t-tests and ANOVA. Z-tests

Statistical Test	Number of Variables	Nature of Data	Nature of Sample
Chi-square	1	Nonmetric	1 sample, Independent
	2+	At least one nonmetric	2 or more samples, Independent
T/Z-tests *			
One sample	1	Metric: means or proportions	1 sample, Independent
Independent	2	DV = metric, IV = nonmetric**	2 samples, Independent; *(e.g., DV limited to 2 categories)*
Paired comparison	2	Metric	2 samples, Dependent
One-way ANOVA	2	DV = metric, IV = nonmetric	3 or more samples, Independent; *(e.g., DV has 3 or more categories)*

FIGURE 13.3 Types of Statistical Tests

* T-tests are used when $n < 30$; z-tests are used when $n > 30$.

** DV= dependent variable (test variable); IV = independent variable (grouping or factor variable)

or T-tests are used when comparing two groups, and ANOVA tests are used when comparing three or more groups.

13.2c Step Three: Decide Decision Rule

It is important to state the decision rule prior to conducting the data analysis to prevent the results from affecting whether the null hypothesis should be accepted or rejected. The decision rule is a measure of certainty in the conclusion that is drawn. Most marketers use a significance level or alpha of .05, which means the researcher is willing to accept a five percent chance he or she is wrong, but a 95 percent chance that the conclusion is correct. For decisions involving millions of dollars, marketing managers may want a lower significance level of .02 or even .01, which would mean the probability of being wrong is two and one percent, respectively. For minor decisions, a 10 percent probability of error may be adequate.

13.2d Step Four: Calculate the Test Statistic

Using the sample data that have been collected, the researcher can calculate the test statistic using the appropriate statistical test. The test statistic is then compared to the decision rule. If a significance level of .05 is chosen, then the null hypothesis is rejected if the test statistic has a significance level of .05 or lower. It is not rejected if the significance level of the test statistic is above .05.

Figure 13.4 shows a null hypothesis, alternative hypothesis, decision rule, and output from SPSS with the test results. The null hypothesis stated that the importance of service in selecting a clothing store does not vary based on the respondent's gender. Service importance was measured on a scale of 1 to 5, where 1 was very unimportant to 5 was

H_O: The importance of service in selecting a clothing store does not vary based on a person's gender.

H_A: The importance of service in selecting a clothing store does vary based on a person's gender.

Decision rule: significance level of .05

Group Statistics						
	Q8. What is your gender?		N	Mean	Std. Deviation	Std. Error Mean
Q5d. Service		Male	73	3.78	1.003	.117
		Female	145	3.99	1.086	.090

	T-Test for Equality of Means						
					95% Confidence Interval of the Difference		
	t	df	Sig. (2-tailed)	Mean Difference	Std. Error Difference	Lower	Upper
Q5d. Service	−1.351	216	.178	−.205	.152	−.505	.094

FIGURE 13.4 Example of Hypothesis Test for Importance of Service
Scale: 1 = Very unimportant; 2 = Unimportant; 3 = Neither important nor unimportant; 4 = Important; 5 = Very important

H_O: In selecting a clothing store, the importance of offering amenities (such as gift wrapping and alterations) does not vary based on a person's gender.

H_A: In selecting a clothing store, the importance of offering amenities (such as gift wrapping and alterations) does vary based on a person's gender

Decision rule: significance level of .05

Group Statistics					
	Q8. What is your gender?	N	Mean	Std. Deviation	Std. Error Mean
Q5i. Amenities (such as gift wrapping, alterations)	Male	73	2.30	1.009	.118
	Female	145	2.65	1.128	.094

	T-Test for Equality of Means						
						95% Confidence Interval of the Difference	
	t	df	Sig. (2-tailed)	Mean Difference	Std. Error Difference	Lower	Upper
Q5i. Amenities (such as gift wrapping, alterations)	−2.219	216	.028	−.347	.156	−.655	−.039

FIGURE 13.5 Example of Hypothesis Test Showing Significant Difference
Scale: 1 = Very unimportant; 2 = Unimportant; 3 = Neither important nor unimportant; 4 = Important; 5 = Very important

very important. The alternative hypothesis would then state there is a difference based on gender. The decision rule chosen by the researcher is a significance (or alpha) level of .05.

The SPSS procedure used to test this hypothesis was an independent t-test, which will be explained in more detail later in the chapter. The mean for males was 3.78 and the mean for females was 3.99. The sample had a total of 218 individuals respond to this question, 73 of whom were male. Is the difference between the mean for males and females significant at the decision rule of α (alpha) $= .05$? The last table shows the SPSS output from the t-test. The t-value is –1.351 with a significance level, or p-value, of 0.178.

Figure 13.5 shows a null hypothesis, the alternative hypothesis, the decision rule, and the SPSS results for the importance of offering amenities such as gift wrapping and alterations when selecting a retail clothing store. The null hypothesis states there is no difference in the importance of amenities on the basis of gender while the alternative states there is a difference. The decision rule of $\alpha = .05$ is again used. The mean for males is 2.30 and for females it is 2.65. The results of the t-test show a t-value of –2.219 and a significance level of .028.

13.2e Step Five: State Conclusion

The conclusion is based on the statistical test in comparison to the decision rule. Researchers will often maintain a list of research hypotheses for their own internal use, which they update to indicate whether the null hypothesis was rejected, or whether they failed to reject the null hypothesis. One may wonder why the researcher simply doesn't "accept" the null hypothesis as having been proven true. "Failing to reject the null hypothesis" is more accurate because it reflects the fact that the researcher is drawing conclusions (or making an inference) about a population based on sample data. While the results may *seem* to indicate that there are no differences in the population, one can never be 100 percent certain. There is always at least that 1-alpha (the decision rule) chance that the researcher is wrong in stating his or her conclusion about the null hypothesis. Keep in mind that errors in the measurement, sampling, or data collection process may also negatively impact the validity of the sample data.

When dealing with clients, the conclusion should be stated in the context of the research question or objective it addresses, and provide the manager with information that is needed to make a decision. Suppose the manager of a boutique retail clothing store wanted information on whether she should increase the number of retail employees working in the women's departments of her stores compared to the men's departments. The results of the first hypothesis test shown in Figure 13.4 indicate that there is insufficient evidence to reject the null hypothesis, as the two-tailed significance level of .178 exceeds the decision rule, or cut-off value, of .05. So the researcher can conclude with 95 percent confidence that there is no difference between males and females concerning the importance of service in selecting a retail clothing store. In practice, researchers typically do not mention confidence levels or the term "significant differences" when discussing the results with clients unless the client is well versed in statistics. Instead, the researcher might state the conclusion as, "The study found no meaningful differences between men and women in terms of their perceptions of the importance of service when selecting a retail clothing store."

In the second situation shown in Figure 13.5, one would conclude that the null hypothesis should be rejected since the significance value of .028 is less than the .05 decision rule. The researcher would conclude on the basis of this evidence that offering amenities such as gift wrapping and alterations is slightly more important to females than to males. As we will see in the next section, and in more detail in Chapter 14, conclusions must be interpreted beyond examining results for significance, and should ultimately influence recommendations made to the client.

13.3 Statistical Significance versus Practical Importance

LEARNING OBJECTIVE 13.2
Understand statistical significance and practical importance.

Professionals associated with commercial market research firms have long argued that the concept of statistical significance has been misused in industry by some individuals and relied upon too much by others. For those in management positions who must make decisions based on marketing research, statistical significance is not always the same as practical importance.

13.3a Misuses of Statistical Significance

Some researchers have been guilty of interpreting highly significant results (such as statistical test significance levels, or p-values that are $<= .01$, or $<= .001$) as providing insight into the magnitude of differences found.[2] Actually, the significance level has nothing to do with how much the mean of group A differs from the mean of group B. The significance level simply states the probability of finding these results in the sample, when the differences noted are not true in the population. Thus, it is important to understand that the significance level indicates the probability that random (sampling) error has occurred and does not indicate magnitude of the difference.

Another misperception is that statistical significance can be used to gauge the validity of the data. This is false. The significance level assesses only the probability that random error is present in the sample data (due to the fact that the entire population has not been studied). The significance level implies nothing about the presence or absence of systematic error due to other problems. Measurement error stemming from the phrasing of or interpretation of questions is a major factor in determining data validity. Issues such as non-response bias, response bias, interviewer error, sample selection error, and process error will all influence the validity of the data collected.[3] Significance levels do not reflect the extent to which any of these factors are present or absent from the data.

13.3b Relevancy and Statistical Significance

Statistical significance can also be misused when researchers turn a blind eye to any results that are not significant, or when they form recommendations on the basis of statistically significant results that have little practical value to managers.[4] Consider the previous discussion of Figures 13.4 and 13.5. The results displayed in Figure 13.4 are not significant at the .05 level. In forming recommendations for the client, researchers who seek only "significant results" would ignore the data regarding the importance of service in selecting a clothing store because the results suggest that importance does not vary by gender. However, this overreliance on significance tests can cause researchers to develop recommendations that miss key insights of importance to the client.[5] As another example, consider a taste test that finds no significant differences in preference between a current drink and a potential new product. This is an important finding, as it would be inappropriate to recommend that the manufacturer continue developing the new product *unless* it was tapping into an entirely different market segment. New products often cost millions of dollars to develop, and wasting that money on a product that would only cannibalize existing offerings does not make sense. Good researchers rarely rely on tests of statistical significance alone.

To illustrate, when interpreting the data for an independent t-test it also important to compare the mean scores for each gender against the scale used. Comparing the mean scores in Figure 13.4 to the five-point scale used indicates that both men and women rated service as important even though their attitudes did not differ significantly from one another. The mean scores are greater than the neutral point of 3, and actually fall much closer to 4. Thus, service is important to both genders, and the researcher should recommend that the manager offer the same, fairly high level of service in both the men's and women's departments.

Figure 13.5 illustrates an example in which the null hypothesis is rejected. This means that the sample data suggests women place a higher level of importance on amenities than do men. Yet are these differences important enough to generate actionable recommendations? The researcher again needs to consider the overall mean values before determining whether gift wrapping and alteration services should really be recommended to the client. Although gift wrapping and alterations were found to be significantly more important to females, the mean scores for both genders fall between "unimportant" and "neutral," which leads one to wonder whether offering the amenities is truly worth the cost they would entail.

A second instance in which the meaningfulness of statistically significant results must be considered relates to sample size. The larger the sample size, the easier it is to find statistically significant differences in the data. The theory behind this idea is that larger sample sizes better represent the population and thus reduce random error. According to Doug Berdie, senior business manager at Maritz Research, "Large enough samples almost always lead to statistically significant results and very small samples rarely do."[6]

Commercial researchers argue that that the real question to be asked is not whether results are significant, but whether or not significant differences found have practical importance to managers. Suppose a national survey of 20,000 soft drink consumers found that Brand A was preferred to its direct competitor Brand B, on the basis of sweetness of taste. It would be foolish to immediately assume that Brand B needs to change their formula, or introduce a sweeter tasting brand spin-off, without first examining the effect size, or magnitude of the difference, between the mean scores for each brand.

With such a large sample, it is very likely that the difference between mean scores could be as little as one-tenth of a point (.1). Thus, if the mean for Brand A was 5.8 while the mean for Brand B was 5.7 on a seven-point scale, rational individuals would reason that investing millions of dollars in research and development to introduce a new brand, or improve the "sweetness" of Brand B would not be a wise investment. Though significant, the results in this scenario would have little practical value to managers.

Furthermore, in the grander scheme of things, this difference—though real in the population—may have little practical value in terms of marketing application. Understanding the market and environment must come into play. Do factors other than sweetness of taste influence which brand is purchased? If so, the differential in taste preference may be moot when compared to preferences based on brand image, availability, promotions, price, or some other marketing factor.

In summary, more practical considerations must be brought to bear when considering whether or not a given result has practical relevance for management. Clearly the absolute value of the difference (effect size) must be considered. On a seven-point scale, a difference in mean scores of two points warrants more attention that does a 0.1 difference. The cost-to-benefit ratio of taking a prescribed course of action must be evaluated[7] as well as existing marketing objectives and strategies.[8]

13.4 Types of Errors

LEARNING OBJECTIVE 13.3 Explain the difference between Type I and Type II errors.

Figure 13.6 illustrates the correct and incorrect decisions that can be made in regard to hypothesis testing. It is important to keep in mind that in most situations researchers are using a sample to make inferences to a population. If the state of the population was actually known, there would be no need to conduct research. But, since it is not known, researchers will use a sample to draw conclusions about the entire population being studied. If the researcher does not reject the null hypothesis on the basis of the study, and indeed the null hypothesis is correct in the population, then a correct decision has been made. Conversely, if the researcher rejects the null hypothesis when the null hypothesis is in fact false among the population, then the correct decision has also been made.

In either failing to reject, or rejecting the null hypothesis, researchers can make two types of errors. **Type I error** occurs when the null hypothesis is rejected, when the null hypothesis is actually true. In statistical terms, Type I error is referred to as *alpha* with the Greek symbol α. Type I error, or α, as mentioned earlier, is used to determine the decision rule that guides statistical tests. If the decision rule is set at .05, it means that $\alpha = .05$ and the researcher is comfortable with a 5 percent chance of a Type I error occurring. For the null hypotheses shown previously, the researcher feels comfortable with making a conclusion about the results of the study when there is a 5 percent chance that an incorrect decision has been made. Of course this also means that recommendations implemented on the basis of this data may fail, if the premise on which they are based is incorrect.

Type II error occurs if a null hypothesis is not rejected on the basis of the sample data, even though it is actually false in the population. Type II errors are important because of the potential opportunity costs they represent. For example, a study might have consumers evaluate the attributes and benefits of a new product concept versus those of a competitor's brand. A Type II error can lead to a recommendation that a marketer drop the product concept from the new product development process, or send it back for revision. This represents an opportunity cost because the product concept is actually preferred to the competitor's product by the population.

Type I error occurs when the null hypothesis is rejected when it is actually true.

Type II error occurs when the null hypothesis is accepted when it is actually false.

Decision	In population, the null hypothesis is true.	In population, the null hypothesis is false.
Accept Null Hypothesis	Correct Decision	Type II Error
Reject Null Hypothesis	Type I Error	Correct Decision

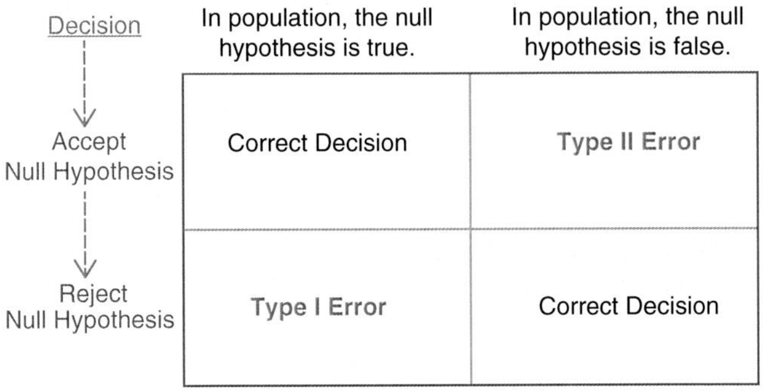

FIGURE 13.6 Types of Errors with Hypothesis Testing

The nomenclature for Type II error is *beta* or the Greek symbol β. While the level of α is set by the researcher in deciding the decision rule, the level of β can be calculated but is rather complicated and beyond the scope of this textbook. The level of β cannot be set in advance. It can be calculated only after data are collected and the analysis performed because it is influenced by the final sample size used in a particular statistical test.[9]

However, the value of β is inversely related to the value of α. As α decreases, β increases and the reverse is also true: as α increases β decreases. So to decrease the chances of retaining a false null hypothesis (and not finding differences when they exist in the population), the value of β needs to be reduced. This is accomplished by increasing the value of *alpha* which, in effect, makes significant differences easier to find. If the value of α was increased from .05 to .10, the researcher increases the chances of a Type I error, but decreases the value of β and thus reduces the chances of a Type II error. Therefore, in setting the significance level (α), the researcher needs to decide which error is more serious, Type I or Type II, in light of the decision that is to be made from the data.

Academic researchers strive to minimize Type I errors, especially when testing theoretical models. Rarely will academic researchers use an α greater than .05. Medical researchers studying the impact of new drugs often use double-blind studies based on very small samples. Due to the large potential for random error in small samples, medical research tends toward very stringent decision rules using small alphas, such as .01 or even lower. In the medical industry, the negative consequences of making a Type I error are substantial and include the millions of dollars spent developing and marketing a drug that may ultimately prove to be ineffective. Throw in the potential lawsuits that might be initiated by patients or their survivors, and it is no wonder that medical researchers stress Type I error over Type II error. Lives could be at stake. It also explains why new drugs require such a long approval process by the FDA. Multiple studies must be conducted to help demonstrate that the results are real, and that Type I error is not responsible for the drug's alleged efficacy.

In some situations, commercial practitioners of market research may be more comfortable with alphas of .10 so as to reduce the possibility that a Type II error occurs. If the cost of a proposed course of action is minimal while the potential returns are large, then such actions are warranted. As mentioned previously, commercial firms also evaluate factors other than significance levels when drawing conclusions. Their focus is to find results that have practical relevance to managers. Even though a decision rule may use .05, results showing a significance of .061 may be deemed "close enough" by commercial researchers to be actionable, depending upon the magnitude of the finding (effect size) and other factors.

13.5 Chi-Square Test

LEARNING OBJECTIVE 13.4
Explain how the chi-square test is used.

Marketing researchers often want to examine if there are significant differences in the frequency counts of nominal and ordinal data. It may involve a one-way frequency count or a cross-tabulation. With one-way frequencies researchers may be looking to see if the frequencies are equal across the various categories or if they follow a specific pattern determined by the researcher prior to collecting the data. With cross-tabulations researchers are interested in knowing if the frequency counts differ across multiple categories. The chi-square test compares the actual frequency counts from a data sample to what would be expected if the null hypothesis were true.

Researchers often call the single variable chi-square test a "goodness-of-fit" test because the procedure evaluates how well the actual frequencies "fit" the expected frequencies. When the differences between the actual and expected frequencies are large, there is not a good fit. If the null hypothesis states that there is no significant difference between the expected and the actual values observed, the null hypothesis is rejected. When differences are small, the chi-square value is small, and therefore there is a good fit between the expected and the actual frequency counts.

Certain assumptions and conditions must be met for the chi-square test to yield useful results. In using the chi-square test, it is important that each cell has a minimum expected count of five. Also, if more than 20 percent of the cells have actual counts less than five, results will not be reliable. Finally, if any cell has an expected value of zero, the results will not be reliable. For this reason, a researcher may "collapse" two categories that border on one another by recoding the variable to contain fewer categories, thereby increasing the number of observations falling into each cell before running a chi-square analysis.

13.5a One-Way Frequency

A common use of the chi-square test is to see if a sample represents a particular target audience that is being studied. A small clothing boutique store chain collected data from a sample of 221 respondents. Before analyzing the data, the researcher in charge of data collection wanted to see if the sample represented the firm's current target base. Using the retailer's database, the researcher was able to identify that 70 percent of its customers were female and 30 percent were male. In terms of age, 50 percent of the customers were 18 to 29, 30 percent were 30 to 49, and 20 percent were 50 or older. **Figure 13.7** shows the chi-square tests for both gender and age.

The left side of Figure 13.7 shows the chi-square test results for gender. The sample consisted of 74 males and 146 females. If 30 percent of the customers are male, then a sample of 220 individuals should have 66 males (220 * 30%). The sample should have 154 females (220 * 70%). The sample size of 220 is used because one person in the overall sample did not indicate his or her gender. Comparing the actual frequency count to the expected count, the chi-square value is 1.385, with a significance level of .239. At the 95 percent confidence level, there is no significant difference between the actual gender count and the expected values, which means the sample is representative of the customer base in terms of gender for this retail chain.

For age, the sample had 3.5 too many individuals in the 18 to 29 age category and 22.8 too many in the 50-plus category. But, in the 30 to 49 age group the sample was short 26.3 individuals. If the decision rule is at the 95 percent level, then the conclusion is that there

Q8. What Is Your Gender?			
	Observed N	Expected N	Residual
Male	74	66.0	8.0
Female	146	154.0	–8.0
Total	220		

Q8. What Is Your Age?			
	Observed N	Expected N	Residual
18–29	114	110.5	3.5
30–49	40	66.3	–26.3
50+	67	44.2	22.8
Total	221		

Test Statistics	
	Q8. What is your gender?
Chi-Square	1.385[a]
df	1
Asymp. Sig.	.239

[a] 0 cells (.0%) have expected frequencies less than 5. The minimum expected cell frequency is 66.0.

Test Statistics	
	Q8. What is your gender?
Chi-Square	22.305[a]
df	2
Asymp. Sig.	.000

[a] 0 cells (.0%) have expected frequencies less than 5. The minimum expected cell frequency is 44.2.

FIGURE 13.7 Chi-Square Test of a Single Frequency Count

is a significant difference between the sample's age breakdown and the ages of the firm's customers. Thus, the sample is not representative of the customer base in terms of age. Note that the significance value of .000 means that the p-value is a decimal *less* than .000.

13.5b Cross-Tabulations

A second common use of the chi-square test is with cross-tabulation tables to see if differences are present in responses across multiple categories. Suppose the clothing boutique store wanted to see if there was a difference in the age composition of its customers among three of its stores. Respondents were asked which of the three stores they patronized the most. The null hypothesis would be that there is no difference in the ages of its customers in the three stores. The alternative hypothesis would be there is a difference in the age composition of the customer base of the three stores. The hypothesis was tested at the 95 percent confidence level, which means a significance level of .05 or lower was needed to reject the null hypothesis. Results of the SPSS chi-square test are shown in **Figure 13.8**.

Q17. Which Store Do You Patronize the Most? * Q7. What Is Your Age? Cross-Tabulation

			Q7. What Is Your Age?			Total
			18–29	30–49	50+	
Q17. Which store do you patronize the most?	Walnut Street Store	Count	23	18	28	69
		Expected Count	35.8	12.5	20.7	69.0
		% within Q7. What is your age?	20.2%	45.0%	42.4%	31.4%
	Highland Boutique Store	Count	70	11	6	87
		Expected Count	45.1	15.8	26.1	87.0
		% within Q7. What is your age?	61.4%	27.5%	9.1%	39.5%
	Riverwalk Mall Store	Count	21	11	32	64
		Expected Count	33.2	11.6	19.2	64.0
		% within Q7. What is your age?	18.4%	27.5%	48.5%	29.1%
Total		Count	114	40	66	220
		Expected Count	114.0	40.0	66.0	220.0
		% within Q7. What is your age?	100.0%	100.0%	100.0%	100.0%

Chi-Square Tests

	Value	df	Asymp. Sig. (2-sided)
Pearson Chi-Square	53.245[a]	4	.000
Likelihood Ratio	57.851	4	.000
Linear-by-Linear Association	.234	1	.628
N of Valid Cases	220		

[a] 0 cells (.0%) have expected count less than 5. The minimum expected count is 11.64.

FIGURE 13.8 Chi-Square Test with Cross-Tabulation

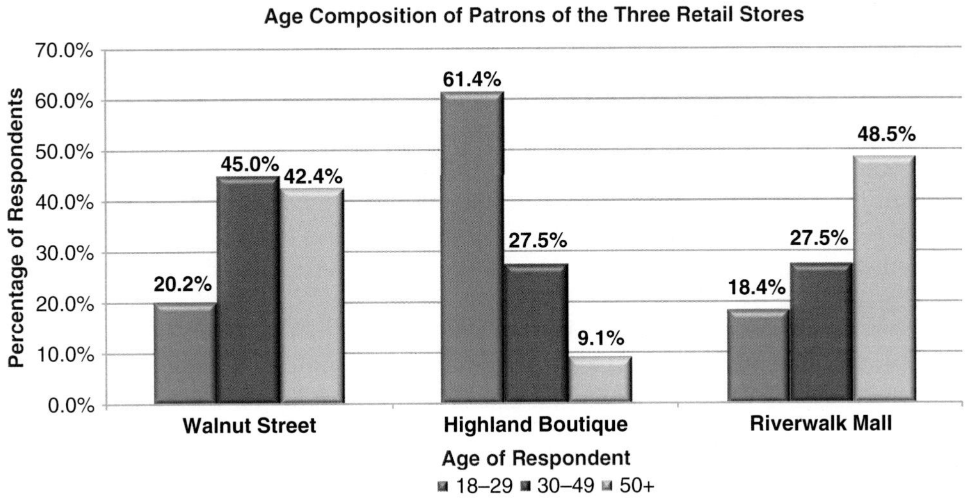

FIGURE 13.9 Graphical Results of a Crosstab Chi-Square

To understand the top table in Figure 13.8, start with the last column. Out of the sample of 220 respondents, 69 (31.4%) indicated they shopped at the Walnut Street store the most, 87 (39.5%) indicated they shopped at the Highland Boutique store the most, and 64 (29.1%) said they shopped at the Riverwalk Mall store the most. These percentages are then used to calculate the expected values shown in the table. The assumption with the chi-square test is that the percentages of each age group within a row should be the same. Thus, the chi-square will test for the Walnut Street store if the percentage of individuals 18 to 29, 30 to 49, and 50+ are the same. Based on the last column, there should be 31.4 percent for each column. For the Highland Boutique store, the chi-square will compare the actual counts to the 39.5 percent expected. For the Riverwalk store, the expected percentage is 29.1 percent.

Comparing the actual count for each store and age group against the expected values yields a Pearson chi-square value of 53.245 with a significance level of less than .000. Since the test was at the 95 percent confidence level and the significance level is below .05, the conclusion is that there is a significant difference in the age composition of the patrons of each store. This information is helpful to the managers of the stores because they can merchandise the store with fashions appropriate for the ages of their primary shoppers. These differences can be seen more clearly in the graph in **Figure 13.9**. With 61 percent of the 18 to 29 year olds shopping in the Highland Boutique store, it should have a large collection of clothes that cater to younger shoppers. Similar merchandise decisions can be made for the other store locations.

13.6 Testing for Differences in Means

Researchers often want to compare two or more means. The means can be from the same sample or from different samples. For instance, in the first case (same sample) researchers may want to compare the average or mean number of meals eaten at quick service restaurants, dine-in restaurants, and pickup or carryout for male respondents. If the researcher wanted to compare the means for those three variables between males and females, it would be a comparison of two different samples.

LEARNING OBJECTIVE 13.5
Identify and describe the various tests for differences in means.

The two primary statistical tests used by researchers are t-tests (or z-tests) and ANOVA (analysis of variance). T-tests (or z-tests) are used when comparing two means. The **one-way ANOVA test** is used when comparing three or more means. With both tests, the data being analyzed must be either interval or ratio (metric data).

One-way analysis of variance (ANOVA) test used when comparing three or more means.

13.7 T-Tests and Z-Tests

T-tests used with samples containing fewer than 30 subjects per cell.

Z-tests used for larger samples of 30 or more per cell.

As stated, t-tests and z-tests are used to compare the means of two groups. **T-tests** are used with samples containing fewer than 30 subjects per cell. **Z-tests** are used for larger samples of 30 or more per cell. SPSS and most statistics programs automatically compute the correct test, though both are uniformly referred to as t-tests by the software. The groups compared by t-tests can be from the same sample or different samples. The formula for the t-test is not provided in this text. It can be obtained from most statistics books as well as a number of websites. The goal of this discussion is to 1) explain how to use t-tests and 2) how to interpret the results.

The t-test is used with interval and ratio data. It is especially useful with small samples ($n < 30$), but is commonly used by researchers with samples of any size. It is a good test for situations where the population standard deviation is not known, which occurs in almost all research conducted by companies and marketing research firms. In order to use the t-test, researchers assume the sample is drawn from populations with normal distributions and the variances of the populations are equal. Three types of t-tests will be discussed: one sample t-tests, independent sample t-tests, and paired sample t-tests.

13.7a One Sample T-Test

One sample t-test tests if the mean of a sample distribution is different from a specified (test value) mean.

A **one sample t-test** is used to test if the mean of a sample distribution is different from a specified (test value) mean. For the clothing boutique stores, the manager would like to see if the email campaign conducted this year yielded significantly better results than the direct mail campaign that was used last year. Both campaigns were conducted using the firm's database of customers that was obtained from individuals filling out loyalty cards. The results of the one sample t-test are shown in **Figure 13.10**.

The top table shows the sample size was 221 respondents and the mean number of purchases made in the 90 days following the email marketing campaign was 5.10 with a standard deviation of 3.14, after rounding. The mean for a direct mail campaign last year was 4.23, as indicated in the "Test Value" section of the second table. Using SPSS, the number of purchases this year in the last 90 days was compared to the test value of 4.23. The one sample t-test produced a t-value of 4.120 with 220 degrees of freedom and a significance level of less than .000. The difference between the current sample mean (5.0995) and the test mean (4.23) is 0.86955. Based on the Confidence Interval of the

One Sample Statistics

	N	Mean	Std. Deviation	Std. Error Mean
Q14. Number of purchases in last 90 days	221	5.0995	3.13761	.21106

One Sample Test

	Test Value = 4.23					
	t	df	Sig. (2-tailed)	Mean Difference	95% Confidence Interval of the Difference: Lower	95% Confidence Interval of the Difference: Upper
Q14. Number of purchases in last 90 days	4.120	220	.000	.86955	.4536	1.2855

FIGURE 13.10 Results of One Sample T-Test

Difference data, the manager conducting this research can be 95 percent confident that the mean difference in purchases between the two campaigns is somewhere between 0.45 and 1.28. The t-test shows there was a significant increase in the number of purchases using the email campaign versus the direct mail campaign.

While the one sample t-test showed this year's email campaign yielded significantly higher purchases than last year's direct mail campaign, the manager must be aware that other factors could have created the differences. Since the two campaigns were a year apart, economic conditions may have changed. The fashions being sold in the stores would certainly be different. The customer base may have even shifted. So from a managerial perspective, it is important to examine the entire situation before concluding that the email marketing campaign was significantly superior to the direct mail campaign.

13.7b Independent Sample T-Test

Quite often managers want to know if there is a significant difference between two groups. The appropriate SPSS test to use is the **independent sample t-test**. This test requires that the dependent variable be an interval or ratio-level variable that is being tested for differences. The grouping, or factor variable, must contain mutually exclusive categories that are usually nominal or ordinal in nature. Mean values are computed and compared for the dependent variable between groups. In the clothing store study, the manager of the retail stores wanted to see if there was a significant difference in the purchases made by male and female customers exposed to the email marketing campaign. Gender serves as the grouping variable, while purchases made is the dependent variable being tested. The results of the study can aid in advertising efforts and influence how future email messages are designed. The researcher found that the mean for females was 5.13 while the mean for males was 4.97, a mean difference, or "effect," of 0.16. But is this effect significant at the 95 percent confidence level? The results of the independent sample t-test are shown in **Figure 13.11**.

Independent sample t-test tests for a significant difference between two groups.

The top table in Figure 13.11 shows the sample size, mean, and standard deviation for the two genders. The standard error is calculated from the standard deviation and sample size. It identifies the precision of the mean for each of the two samples. The smaller the standard error the more likely the sample mean equals the true population mean. So for this sample, the standard error for the female portion of the sample is lower than that of the males, 0.253 compared to 0.381. The primary reason for the lower standard error for females is the larger sample size. Since the denominator used in calculating the standard error is the square root of the sample size, the standard error can be reduced by increasing the sample size.

SPSS will calculate two t-values, one assuming the variance of the two populations is equal and the other assuming the variances of the two populations is not equal. In most cases, the same significant or not significant results will be obtained with both methods of calculating the t-value. But to ensure the correct values are used, SPSS will produce a Levene's test for equality of variances. For the independent sample t-test that was run, the F-value for the Levene test was .578 with a p-value of .448. If the same 95 percent confidence level is used, the researcher can assume the variances of the male and female samples are the same, as .448 is greater than the decision rule of .05. To assume the variances are different, the significance level would have to be .05 or below.

Using the top row (equal variances assumed), the t-test for equality of means is -0.366 with a significance level of .715. The negative value of the t-test is not important. It can be either negative or positive depending on how the mean difference between the two samples is calculated. In this case it was calculated by subtracting 5.13 from 4.97, thus producing a negative number –0.16401. Because the significance level is .715, the conclusion of the t-test is that there is no significant difference in the mean purchases of males and females. The last two columns show the confidence level of the differences. The researcher can be 95 percent confident that the mean difference between males and females in terms of purchases is between –1.04 and 0.71.

	Q8. What is your gender?		N	Mean	Std. Deviation	Std. Error Mean
Group Statistics						
Q14. Number of purchases in last 90 days		Male	74	4.9730	3.28122	.38143
		Female	146	5.1370	3.06623	.25376

		T-Test for Equality of Means						
						95% Confidence Interval of the Difference		
		t	df	Sig. (2-tailed)	Mean Difference	Std. Error Difference	Lower	Upper
Q14. Number of purchases in last 90 days	Equal variances assumed	–.366	218	.715	–.16401	.44805	–1.04708	.71906
	Equal variances not assumed	–.358	138.283	.721	–.16401	.45813	–1.06987	.74184

Levene's Test for Equality of Variances
F-Value = .578
Sig. = .448

FIGURE 13.11 Results of an Independent Sample T-Test

13.7c Paired Sample T-Test

Paired sample t-tests compares two different responses from an individual respondent

Paired sample t-tests are used when a researcher wants to compare two different responses from an individual respondent. With the clothing store study, the manager wanted to know if the email campaign produced immediate results. Through the company's database it was able to identify the number of purchases individuals made in the 90 days prior to the email campaign and the number of purchases that were made in the 90 days following the campaign. To see if there is a significant difference between pre- and post-campaign sales, a paired t-test is used. With the paired sample approach, the computer will compare for each individual the number of purchases made during the 90 days prior to the campaign to the number of purchases made in the 90 days after the campaign. Results of this paired sample t-test are shown in **Figure 13.12**.

From the top table, the manager can see the mean number of purchases made after the email campaign was 6.25 and the number before was 4.93. The second table measures the correlation between each person's first response and the person's second response. If a person made a high number of purchases before the campaign, it would be expected that the individual will make a high number of purchases after the campaign. Similarly, individuals who made a low number of purchases before the campaign are likely to make few purchases after the campaign. A high correlation value shows this pattern exists. A low correlation value shows the relationship between the two values is random. With this study, the correlation of 0.677 is relatively high, indicating there is a high level of correlation between the purchases before and after the campaign. The sig. value of less than .000 offers support that the correlation is significant.

The bottom table provides the t-test statistical value. The mean difference between pre- and post measures is 1.32, which indicates that on the average, customers made 1.32 more

Paired Samples Statistics					
		Mean	N	Std. Deviation	Std. Error Mean
Pair 1	Q16. Number of purchases in 90 days after campaign	6.2534	221	3.70860	.24947
	Q15. Number of purchases in 90 days prior to campaign	4.9321	221	3.16370	.21281

Paired Samples Correlations				
		N	Correlation	Sig.
Pair 1	Q16. Number of purchases in 90 days after campaign Q15. Number of purchases in 90 days prior to campaign	221	.677	.000

Paired Samples Test									
		Paired Differences					t	df	Sig. (2-tailed)
		Mean	Std. Deviation	Std. Error Mean	95% Confidence Interval of the Difference				
					Lower	Upper			
Pair 1	Q16. Number of purchases in 90 days after campaign Q15. Number of purchases in 90 days prior to campaign	1.32127	2.80761	.18886	.94906	1.69347	6.996	220	.000

FIGURE 13.12 Results of a Paired Sample T-Test

purchases in the 90 days after the campaign than in the 90 days prior to the campaign. The t-value for this mean difference is 8.996 with a significance level of less than .000. The researcher can conclude the campaign was successful since on the average purchases increased by 1.32. The researcher can also be 95 percent confident that the mean increase was somewhere between 0.94 purchases and 1.69 purchases.

13.8 Analysis of Variance (ANOVA)

For situations involving the comparison of three or more means, researchers use analysis of variances (ANOVA) tests. As with the t-test, the formula for calculating ANOVA is not provided, but students are referred to statistics textbooks. The ANOVA procedure tests if the means of the groups are equal. An ANOVA test comparing the number of purchases by the respondent's age is shown in Figure 13.13.

The mean number of purchases for individuals 18 to 29 years of age is 5.07, for individuals 30 to 49 it is 3.82, and for individuals 50 and older it is 2.04. In addition to the mean, SPSS provides calculations for the standard deviation, the standard error, the confidence interval for the mean at 95 percent confidence level, and the minimum and maximum values.

Descriptives								
Q14. Number of purchases in last 90 days								
					95% Confidence Interval for Mean			
	N	Mean	Std. Deviation	Std. Error	Lower Bound	Upper Bound	Minimum	Maximum
18–29	114	5.0702	3.29580	.30868	4.4586	5.6817	.00	10.00
30–49	40	3.8250	1.93334	.30569	3.2067	4.4433	.00	8.00
50+	67	2.0448	1.22391	.14952	1.7462	2.3433	.00	5.00
Total	221	3.9276	2.90676	.19553	3.5422	4.3130	.00	10.00

ANOVA					
Q14. Number of purchases in last 90 days					
	Sum of Squares	df	Mean Square	F	Sig.
Between Groups	386.762	2	193.381	28.638	.000
Within Groups	1472.079	218	6.753		
Total	1858.842	220			

FIGURE 13.13 Results of an ANOVA Test

The second table provides the statistical information from the ANOVA test. The test statistic is an F-value. For an understanding of the F-statistic and how it is calculated, a basic statistics book or the Internet can be accessed. For this situation, the resulting F-value is 28.638 with a significance level of less than .000. The ANOVA test shows there is a significant difference in the number of purchases made by the three age groups. The results are graphically displayed in **Figure 13.14**.

The results of the basic ANOVA test indicate that significant differences exist somewhere in the data, meaning that the differences in the means for at least two categories of the factor variable (age) differ significantly from one another. Determining which age categories differ requires that multiple "pairwise comparisons" be performed. Pairwise comparisons test the mean of each subgroup against the mean of each other subgroup to determine whether the numerical difference between the two mean scores is significant. Thus, a comparison for the basic ANOVA test shown in Figure 13.13 would first compare

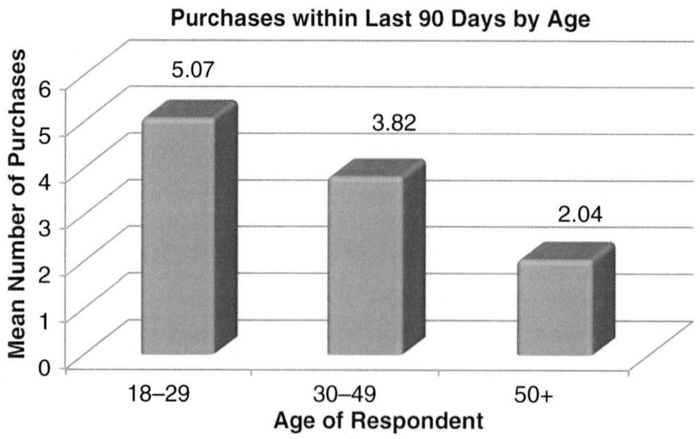

FIGURE 13.14 Graph of ANOVA Test Results

the mean of the 18 to 29 year-old group (5.07) against the mean of the 30 to 49 year-old group (3.82) to determine if the difference between the two means is significant. Pairwise comparisons would also be performed for the 18 to 29 year-old and 50+ groups, and for the 30 to 49 year-old group and 50+ year-old groups.

Various methods can be used to calculate post-hoc comparisons such as these since it occurs after the initial analysis. The correct choice depends first upon whether equal variances can be assumed for the means within each category. The Duncan, Tukey, Tukey's-b, and Scheffe tests are common forms of post-hoc comparison tests when equal variances are assumed. Of these, many researchers prefer to use the Scheffe test because it is the most conservative, meaning that significant results for the Scheffe test require larger differences between subgroup mean scores than do most other methods.[10] The implication, then, is that the Scheffe test minimizes Type I error when making pairwise comparisons. The results of the Scheffe post-hoc comparison tests are illustrated in Figure 13.15.

Post Hoc Tests

Multiple Comparisons						
Dependent Variable: Q14. Number of purchases in last 90 days Scheffe						
(I) Q7. What is your age?	(J) Q7. What is your age?	Mean Difference (I-J)	Std. Error	Sig.	95% Confidence Interval Lower Bound	95% Confidence Interval Upper Bound
18–29	30–49	1.24518*	.47755	.035	.0682	2.4222
	50+	3.02540*	.40002	.000	2.0395	4.0113
30–49	18–29	−1.24518*	.47755	.035	−2.4222	−.0682
	50+	1.78022*	.51923	.003	.5005	3.0600
50+	18–29	−3.02540*	.40002	.000	−4.0113	−2.0395
	30–49	−1.78022*	.51923	.003	−3.0600	−.5005

* The mean difference is significant at the .05 level.

Homogeneous Subsets

Q14. Number of purchases in last 90 days				
Scheffe[a,b]				
		Subset for alpha = .05		
Q7. What is your age?	N	1	2	3
50+	67	2.0448		
30–49	40		3.8250	
18–29	114			5.0702
Sig.		1.000	1.000	1.000

Means for groups in homogeneous subsets are displayed.

a Uses Harmonic Mean Sample Size = 61.605.

b The group sizes are unequal. The harmonic mean of the groupsizes is used. Type I error levels are not guaranteed.

FIGURE 13.15 Scheffe Ad-Hoc ANOVA Test Results

The top table shows the individual t-tests for each age group when contrasted with the other two groups. The results are interpreted as previously explained when discussing independent t-tests. In this case each age group differs significantly from the others. The bottom table lists the means and sample size for each age subgroup. The fact that every mean is shown in its own unique column visually demonstrates that the results differ significantly from one another. If the means of two groups were numerically different, but appeared in the same column, it would indicate that the means are not significantly different at the alpha level chosen for the decision rule.

A note of caution is appropriate at this juncture. The Scheffe test should only be performed after the basic one-way ANOVA has been found to be significant. Some researchers may select an ad-hoc test when specifying the initial run of an ANOVA. While this saves some time and is more convenient for the researcher, it is inappropriate to make use of ad-hoc test results if the overall ANOVA test result is not significant.

13.9 Regression Analysis

LEARNING OBJECTIVE 13.6
Demonstrate an understanding of regression analysis.

Simple regression examination of the relationship of one independent or predictor variable and one dependent or outcome variable.

Multiple regression examination of the relationship of multiple independent or predictor variables and one dependent or outcome variable.

Regression analysis provides a test for measuring the relationship or correlation among two or more variables. If the number of variables being examined is two, it is simple regression. If more than two variables are being examined, it is called multiple regression. With both simple and multiple regression, the researcher has one dependent (or outcome) variable that is being examined. With **simple regression** the researcher is examining the relationship of one independent or predictor variable to the outcome variable. With **multiple regression**, multiple independent or predictor variables are being examined to determine which ones are good predictors of the outcome variable.

It is extremely important to understand that mathematical relationships do not prove cause and effect. Just because one variable is highly correlated with another does not mean that a researcher can say that one causes the other to occur. As discussed previously, a researcher may see a high level of correlation between temperature and the sales of snow shovels and other snow removal equipment. But it is not the cold weather that causes the sales to increase. It is the snow that comes with the cold weather. Thus, in building regression equations researchers should select variables that logically can influence the dependent or outcome variable.

13.9a Simple Regression

The manager of the clothing boutique stores noticed that age appeared to be related to the number of purchases made at the three stores. Before deciding if she should enlarge her young women's fashions, she thought it would be good to run a simple regression. The dependent variable would be the number of purchases made in the last 90 days. The independent or predictor variable would be the respondent's age. The SPSS outcome of this analysis is shown in **Figure 13.16**.

The top table in Figure 13.16 provides model summary information on how well the model fits the data, and how well the predictor variable, the person's age, is able to predict the number of purchase made in the last 90 days. The first value shown is R, which is a measure of how well the predictor variable predicts the outcome. However, to obtain a more accurate measure it is necessary to square the R value, which is the third column. **R-Square** is also known as the coefficient of determination as it shows the percentage of variation explained by the predictor variable(s). R-Square values range between 0 and 1. A zero score indicates no predictive ability at all and that the two numbers are just random. A "1" score would indicate a perfect predictor. The .207 shown in this table says that 20.7 percent of the variance in the number of purchases in the last 90 days is based on the person's age. That is a fairly low level of predictability. While 20 percent is explained by age, the other 80 percent is caused by other factors not present in the regression equation.

R-Square also known as the coefficient of determination as it shows the percentage of variation explained by the predictor variable(s).

The second table measures if the regression is significant or not. Since the F-value is 57.104 with a significance level of less than .000, it is a significant predictor of purchases in the last 90 days. Although the regression model is significant, keep in mind that the R-Square is only .207, indicating it has a low level of predictability.

Model Summary				
Model	R	R-Square	Adjusted R-Square	Std. Error of the Estimate
1	.455[a]	.207	.203	2.59469

[a] Predictors: (Constant), Q7. What is your age?

ANOVA[b]						
Model		Sum of Squares	df	Mean Square	F	Sig.
1	Regression	384.448	1	384.448	57.104	.000[a]
	Residual	1474.394	219	6.732		
	Total	1858.842	220			

[a] Predictors: (Constant), Q7. What is your age?

[b] Dependent Variable: Q14. Number of purchases in last 90 days

Coefficients[a]						
		Unstandardized Coefficients		Standardized Coefficients		
Model		B	Std. Error	Beta	t	Sig.
1	(Constant)	6.608	.395		16.717	.000
	Q7. What is your age?	–1.499	.198	–.455	–7.557	.000

[a] Dependent Variable: Q14. Number of purchases in last 90 days

FIGURE 13.16 Results of a Simple Regression Analysis

The bottom table in Figure 13.16 provides the coefficients. The constant is where the regression line crosses the Y-axis. The unstandardized coefficient (B) for the age variable is –1.499, which indicates an inverse relationship. This means that as the customer's age increases, the number of purchases made decreases, which confirms what the manager suspected. The unstandardized coefficient shows the amount of change in the outcome variable based on an increase or decrease of one unit in the predictor variable. Recall that the age variable consists of three categories: 18 to 29, 30 to 49, and 50+. So if the age category is increased by one unit to the next category, the number of purchases declines by 1.499. Based on the unstandardized coefficient, the regression equation can be written in the following manner:

$$Y = 6.608 + (-1.499 * X)$$

$$\text{Purchases in last 90 days} = 6.608 + (-1.499 * \text{age category})$$

Using this equation, the number of purchases can be predicted for each of the three age categories. The results are shown in Figure 13.17. If a customer is between 18 and 29, the age category would be 1 and the predicted number of purchases would be 5.11. If the individual is 30 to 49, it would be 3.61, and if 50 and over it would be 2.11. When the means of these three groups are obtained from SPSS, it is very close to the purchases made for each category, which are listed in the last column in the table.

Purchases in last 90 days = 6.608 + (–1.499 * age category)					
Age Category	Code	Regression Equation: Constant	Regression Equation: Age Beta	Predicted # of Purchases	Sample Mean
18–29	1	6.608	–1.499	5.11	5.07
30–49	2	6.608	–1.499	3.61	3.82
50+	3	6.608	–1.499	2.11	2.04

FIGURE 13.17 Outcome of Simple Regression Equation

The standardized coefficient will be discussed in the next section on multiple regression since it really only has meaning when multiple independent variables are in the equation. The t-value and corresponding significance level show if the variable being considered is significant. With this simple regression, both the constant and age variable are significant and therefore should be part of the regression equation.

13.9b Multiple Regression

With the simple regression explaining only 20.7 percent of the variance in the number of purchases, the manager of the boutique stores decided to run a multiple regression analysis with additional variables in the model. Each respondent was asked to evaluate the clothing store along eight dimensions. In addition to these eight and the age variable, the person's household income was added to the model. The model summary and fit statistics are shown in **Figure 13.18**.

Model Summary

Model	R	R-Square	Adjusted R-Square	Std. Error of the Estimate
1	.754[a]	.568	.547	1.93932

[a] Predictors: (Constant), Q12. What is your family income?, Q5a. Product selection, Q5i. Amenities (such as gift wrapping, alterations), Q7. What is your age?, Q5b. Price, Q5d. Service, Q5h. Parking, Q5g. Store image, Q5f. Location, Q5c. Convenience

ANOVA[b]

Model		Sum of Squares	df	Mean Square	F	Sig.
1	Regression	1000.905	10	100.090	26.613	.000[a]
	Residual	759.715	202	3.761		
	Total	1760.620	212			

[a] Predictors: (Constant), Q12. What is your family income?, Q5b. Price, Q7. What is your age?, Q5a. Product selection, Q5h. Parking, Q5d. Service, Q5g. Store image, Q5f. Location, Q5e. Store atmosphere, Q5c. Convenience

[b] Dependent Variable: Q14. Number of purchases in last 90 days

FIGURE 13.18 Model Summary for Multiple Regression

According to the ANOVA table, the multiple regression equation is a significant fit with the data. The R-Square has improved,; .568 compared to .207 with the simple regression. Approximately 56.8 percent of the outcome variable is explained by the multiple regression equation. The beta coefficients for the multiple regression analysis are shown in Figure 13.19.

It is helpful to look first at the t-value and significance level for each of the independent variables. At the 95 percent confidence level, any variable that has a significance level of .05 or lower would be considered a significant predictor of the outcome variable, or the number of purchases made in the last 90 days. According to the SPSS analysis, significant predictors of the number of purchases made by customers are product selection, level of service, store atmosphere, store image, the person's age, and household income. These are the variables the researcher and store manager will want to address in marketing efforts as they drive purchase behavior.

The standardized beta coefficient can help the researcher and store manager understand which significant variables are the most important and the relative magnitude of importance. The standardized coefficients convert all of the variables to a 0 to 1 scale so they can be compared. With this process the beta weights gain ratio properties. For example, in reviewing the standardized betas in Figure 13.19, household income and service have the highest values at .336 and .320, respectively. While the manager has no control over the household income of her customers, she can control the level of service customers receive. When the .320 beta weight for service is compared to the .132 for product selection, .172 for store image, and .134 for store atmosphere, the manager can make the assumption that the level of service is approximately twice as important as the other three variables (.32/.132 = 2.42; .32/.172=1.86; .32/.134 =2.39).

Coefficients[a]

		Unstandardized Coefficients		Standardized Coefficients		
Model		B	Std. Error	Beta	t	Sig.
1	(Constant)	.804	.969		–.829	.408
	Q5a. Product selection	.380	.153	.132	2.492	.014
	Q5b. Price	–.009	.176	–.003	–.052	.958
	Q5c. Convenience	–.139	.200	–.048	–.699	.485
	Q5d. Service	.799	.140	.320	5.704	.000
	Q5e. Store atmosphere	.364	.176	.134	2.064	.040
	Q5f. Location	–.056	.193	–.019	–.289	.772
	Q5g. Store image	.428	.140	.172	3.047	.003
	Q5h. Parking	–.116	.129	–.047	–.902	.368
	Q7. What is your age?	–.689	.169	–.210	–4.064	.000
	Q12. What is your household income?	.928	.140	.336	6.644	.000

[a] Dependent Variable: Q14. Number of purchases in last 90 days

FIGURE 13.19 Multiple Regression Coefficients

As age is inversely related to the number of purchases, it would make good management senses to focus on fashions for younger consumers.

To spend money on training and motivating employees to provide high-quality service appears to be a wise decision, at least according to the regression analysis. Notice that price, convenience, location, and parking do not have a significant impact on purchases. To say they have none is incorrect. But, their impact is minimal. Resource allocations should focus on service, product selection, store image, and store atmosphere.

As was found with the simple regression, age is inversely related to the number of purchases. It would make good management sense to focus on fashions for the younger consumers.

To understand the predictive ability of a regression model, consider **Figure 13.20**. On the left is a good customer. Assume this customer evaluates each of the store attributes as a four on the five-point scale, is in the youngest age category, and the highest income bracket. The regression model predicts this customer would purchase 8.82 items over a 90-day period. Now consider the poor customer who may rate each of the store's attributes as a two out of five, is in the oldest age category, and the lowest income bracket. This customer would generate only 1.36 purchases in the same time period.

Just like the simple regression, the unstandardized beta weights provide useful information. It shows the change in the outcome variable, the number of purchases, with a one-unit increase in that particular variable. Suppose the poor customer shown in the right table in Figure 13.20 marked a 3 on service instead of a 2. Just that one change would increase the outcome variable by 0.799 (the beta weight), from 1.36 to 2.16. If the customer rated service a 4 instead of a 2, it would jump to 2.96. This change in the number of purchases reinforces the idea that service is extremely important.

13.10 Global Concerns

Mathematics, statistics, and the process of analyzing quantitative data using traditional statistical tests and software packages are well-accepted throughout the world. The primary concern for the global researcher is making certain that all parties have access to the same version of the software since this facilitates collaboration during data analysis, as well as the sharing of findings.

Specialized software packages also exist to assist in the analysis of qualitative data. While a variety of software packages are available, collectively, they are referred to as computer assisted qualitative data analysis software, or simply by the acronym, CAQDAS. The growth of qualitative research in an international context has recently spurred renewed interest in CAQDAS.[11]

CAQDAS programs such as NVivo (http://www.qsrinternational.com) allow users to organize, synthesize, and integrate qualitative data from interview transcripts, secondary data from articles, videos, photos, survey data, and more. Characteristics of those interviewed or the internal data pertinent to the firms they work for can also be stored. NVivo works in just about any language, and the software allows for qualitative data to be retained in multiple languages concurrently. The software saves the user time by helping to identify themes or categories in the data, and users can write notes on insights found at any point in the process. As NVivo is multi-user compatible; different researchers can analyze the same data from their unique perspective concurrently, or they can choose to work collaboratively. Finally, the software assists in creating visual displays of information, including models, charts, and more.[12]

Good Customer:

1. Evaluate items as 4 out of 5
2. Youngest age group
3. Highest income bracket

Good Customer	Value	Beta	Value*Beta
Constant		–0.804	–0.804
Product selection	4	0.380	1.520
Price	4	–0.009	–0.036
Convenience	4	–0.139	–0.556
Service	4	0.799	3.196
Store atmosphere	4	0.364	1.456
Location	4	–0.056	–0.224
Store image	4	0.428	1.712
Parking	4	–0.116	–0.464
Age	1	–0.689	–0.689
Income	4	0.928	3.712
Summed Total (Number of Purchases)			**8.82**

Poor Customer:

1. Evaluate items as 2 out of 5
2. Oldest age group
3. Lowest income bracket

Poor Customer	Value	Beta	Value*Beta
Constant		–0.804	–0.804
Product selection	2	0.380	0.760
Price	2	–0.009	–0.018
Convenience	2	–0.139	–0.278
Service	2	0.799	1.598
Store atmosphere	2	0.364	0.728
Location	2	–0.056	–0.112
Store image	2	0.428	0.856
Parking	2	–0.116	–0.232
Age	3	–0.689	–2.067
Income	1	0.928	0.928
Summed Total (Number of Purchases)			**1.36**

FIGURE 13.20 Comparison of Good/Poor Customers

Despite the apparent sophistication and usefulness of CAQDAS programs, a recent study demonstrated that CAQDAS are not frequently used in Britain. In fact, only nine percent of the research industry professionals surveyed used the software to assist with qualitative data analysis.[13] As the marketing research industry in the United Kingdom is second in size only to the United States, this finding is somewhat surprising. The use of CAQDAS among researcher practitioners in Spain was also found to be low, and typically reserved for projects requiring large volumes of data to be analyzed, or a team-based analysis approach. Barriers to usage in Spain appear to be related to a lack of knowledge on how to use the software, as well as attitudinal perceptions that suggest researchers are skeptical of the software's benefits.[14] Only time will tell if advances in technology and the benefits of CAQDAS software eventually result in increased usage in the context of global marketing research.

13.11 Marketing Research Statistics

A primary objective of marketing research is to identify significant differences within a sample. The Statistical Reporting section illustrates one way to graph the results of a regression analysis. Various graphs throughout the chapter showed ways to graphically illustrate results from chi-square, t-test, and ANOVA tests.

The Dealing with Data section requires analysis of a data set. In the analyses, chi-square, t-tests, and ANOVA tests are used.

13.11a Statistical Reporting

Results of chi-square, t-tests, and ANOVA analyses are normally reported using bar charts. Typically, only significant differences are reported. But a researcher may want to show all of the groups or results of an analysis to allow for comparisons. It is also important to remember that practical significance may require reporting results that might not be statistically significant. The reverse can also be true. Something that is statistically significant may have no or very little impact on a management decision and therefore is not reported in the main body of a report. It may be put in an appendix instead.

In graphing the results of a regression analysis, the most common practice is to graphically show the standardized beta values, as shown in Figure 13.21. The standardized beta scores allow for comparisons between variables that are significant. Thus, a researcher can easily compare the magnitude of service to the other store variables of product selection, store image, and store atmosphere. The graph shows only the variables that were significant at the 95 percent confidence level. A researcher presenting the results might want to put all of the variables on the graph to show relative impact of those that are significant to those that are not.

Notice the value for age is negative, which indicates an inverse relationship. As age increases, the number of purchases at a clothing boutique decreases. The sign on standardized beta scores are important because they show the type of relationship between the independent and dependent variables.

13.11b Dealing with Data

A marketing research firm that specializes in social media marketing conducted a study about social media usage by consumers. Data were collected from 502 respondents. The data set is entitled Chapter 13 Dealing with Data. After accessing the data at www.clow-james.net/students.html, perform the following analyses. In a word document, highlight all of the significant and/or managerially relevant findings from the analysis. The questionnaire is found in the document called Chapter 13 Dealing with Data Survey.

1. Run a descriptive analysis of the data, obtaining frequency counts of nominal and ordinal data and means for interval and ratio data.
2. Run a chi-square test of the following variables by the demographics of gender, age, and race using the crosstab function.
   a. Visited a social media site within last 30 days.
   b. Have a Facebook profile page.
   c. Type of site visited after leaving the social media page.
   d. Uploaded photos or video within the last 30 days.

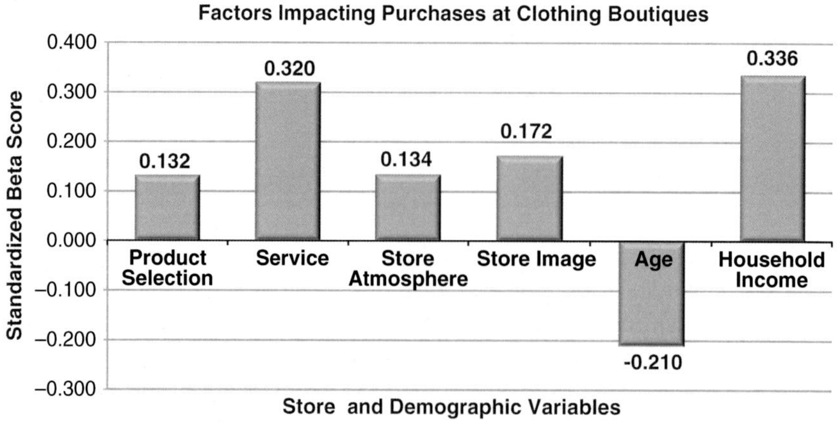

FIGURE 13.21 Graph Showing Regression Analysis Results

3. Run a one sample t-test for the following variables against the test variable indicated in parenthesis.
   a. Number of Facebook visits within the last 30 days (mean for the same month last year was 14.83).
   b. Percentage of purchases made online (mean in prior 60 days was 6.88).
4. Run an independent sample t-test of the following variables based on gender.
   a. Number of Facebook visits within the last 30 days.
   b. Average time of each visit on Facebook.
   c. Number of online purchases in last 60 days.
   d. Percentage of purchases made online.
   e. Percent of online communications with friends, siblings, children/parents, significant other, and colleagues.
   f. Likert statements about branding.
5. Run an ANOVA test of the following variables based on age and race.
   a. Number of Facebook visits within the last 30 days.
   b. Average time of each visit on Facebook.
   c. Number of online purchases in last 60 days.
   d. Percentage of purchases made online in last 60 days.
   e. Percent of online communications with friends, siblings, children/parents, significant other, and colleagues.
   f. Likert statements about branding.

Summary

Objective 1: Identify and explain the steps in hypothesis testing.

Hypothesis testing involves five steps: 1) state the hypothesis, 2) select the statistical test, 3) decide the decision rule, 4) calculate the test statistic, and 5) state the conclusion. The hypothesis should have both a null and an alternative hypothesis, with the null hypothesis typically assuming equality or no effect. The statistical test appropriate for nominal and ordinal data is the chi-square test. For interval and ratio data the appropriate tests are the t-test (z-tests) and ANOVA. The decision rule is the level of confidence the researcher desires. The test statistic is calculated from the sample using SPSS or another appropriate statistical software. Based on the test statistic and decision rule, either the null hypothesis is accepted or rejected.

Objective 2: Understand statistical significance and practical importance.

Statistical significance is not a proxy for effect size. It is incorrect to assume that more highly significant results indicate a greater magnitude of difference. P-values do not measure the probability that a null hypothesis is true or that sample data was produced by random chance. Statistical significance also cannot be used to assess the validity of the data, as significance only assesses random error. When evaluating tests of differences, the means score must be considered, in addition to whether or not results are significant, in order to determine if results have practical value for managers. Larger sample sizes increase the likelihood that significant differences will be found for small effect sizes; before recommending action, cost-to-benefit ratio, marketing objectives, and strategy must be considered.

Objective 3: Explain the difference between Type I and Type II errors.

Type I error occurs when the researcher rejects the null hypothesis when it is actually true. Type I error is set by the researcher in selecting the decision rule. For instance, if a 95 percent confidence level is chosen, then there is a 5 percent chance of Type I error occurring. Type II error is when the null hypothesis is accepted when it is actually false. While the level of a Type II error can be calculated, it is beyond the scope of this text. It is important to know there is an inverse relationship between Type I and Type II errors. When a researcher decreases the chances of a Type I error occurring by increasing the level of desired confidence, the probability of a Type II error occurring will increase. To decrease the probability of a Type II error occurring requires an increase in the probability of a Type I error.

Objective 4: Explain how the chi-square test is used.

Chi-square is used to test for significant differences in the frequency counts of nominal and ordinal data. The test compares the actual frequency count of the sample with the expected count. The chi-square test can be used for a single variable or it can be used with crosstabs. With a single variable the frequency count of the sample is tested against an expected frequency count supplied by the researcher. With crosstabs, chi-square tests for equality across specified categories based on the sample characteristics for the test variable.

Objective 5: Identify and describe the various tests for differences in means.

To test for differences in means with interval and ratio data, researchers utilize either t-tests (z-tests) or an ANOVA test. The t-test is used when comparing two categories, and ANOVA is used when comparing three or more categories. Common t-tests include one sample t-test, independent sample t-test, and paired sample t-test. The one sample t-test is used when comparing the mean of a sample variable to a test mean. The independent sample t-test involves comparing the mean of two different groups, such as males and females. The paired sample t-test looks at before and after (or related) scores for each individual case, or compares responses to two questions for each respondent.

Objective 6: Demonstrate an understanding of regression analysis.

Regression analysis provides a test for measuring the relationship or correlation among two or more variables. If the number of variables being measured is two, it is simple regression. If more than two variables are involved, it is multiple regression. With both types of regression, there is one outcome or dependent variable that the researcher wants to predict. Simple regression involves one predictor or independent variable while multiple regression involves two or more independent or predictor variables. How well the regression model predicts the outcome variable is measured by R-Square. The t-value and corresponding significance level of each predictor variable determines if it is a significant predictor of the outcome variable.

Key Terms

independent sample t-test, p. 451
multiple regression, p. 456
non-parametric procedures, p. 440
one sample t-test, p. 450
one-way analysis of variance (ANOVA) test, p. 449
paired sample t-tests, p. 452
parametric procedures, p. 440
R-Square, p. 456
simple regression, p. 456
t-tests, p. 450
Type I error, p. 445
Type II error, p. 445
z-tests, p. 450

Critical Thinking Exercises

1. Critique the following null and alternative hypotheses. If not appropriate, re-write them using acceptable language.
   H_O: No differences will be found on the basis of income.
   H_A: Higher incomes will be as likely to purchase as will low incomes.
2. A retailer is interested in investigating whether doubling the value of manufacturer coupons will a) increase the number of shoppers, and b) increase store profits. "Doubling" means that the store would give consumers a discount equal to twice the coupon face value, with the retailer absorbing the cost of the extra discount. The retailer would also like to know whether the redemption percentage of doubled coupons varies by gender, income, or age. Write the null and alternative hypotheses associated with each of the three statistical tests. For each null hypothesis, indicate the type of data that should be collected to best test the null hypothesis, and the type of statistical test that would need to be performed.
3. In speaking with your friend Lauren, you learn that she is performing community service by analyzing the attitude data collected on behalf of a not-for-profit organization. Lauren tells you, "I'm just going to run the analyses and find the most statistically significant results and base my recommendations off of that. After all, the more statistically significant the result, the bigger the difference in attitudes." What do you think of Lauren's data analysis strategy? Should she ignore all nonstatistically significant results? Why or why not? Is her assumption regarding the degree of statistical significance and the size of the attitude difference correct? What factors influence the ease with which statistical differences are found in a sample?
4. A study was conducted to assess undergraduate college students' attitudes toward the student bookstore. Since many students attend a local junior college before transferring to a university, the classification of those responding to the study is a key demographic. Is the sample representative of the population according to the chi-square test shown in Figure 13.22, given that the student body is composed of 7 percent freshman, 6 percent sophomores, 42 percent juniors, and 35 percent seniors? Why or why not? If the sample is not representative, what action(s) would you suggest that the researcher take?
5. Suppose Nike commissioned a study to better understand factors that influence men and women when purchasing sneakers, as the firm believes different

Frequencies

Classification				
Model	Category	Observed N	Expected N	Residual
1	freshman	18	14.2	3.8
2	sophomore	21	12.1	8.9
3	junior	76	84.9	–8.9
4	senior	67	70.8	–3.8
Total		182		

Test Statistics

Model	Classification
Chi-Square[a]	8.665
df	3
Asymp. Sig.	.034

[a] 0 cells (.0%) have expected frequencies less than 5. The minimum expected cell frequency is 12.1.

FIGURE 13.22 Chi-Square Results for Critical Thinking Question 4

factors are important to each gender. The results of key independent samples t-tests based on gender are shown in Figure 13.23. What conclusions can you draw regarding key differences between male and female attitudes? Now interpret this information. What findings are meaningful for Nike, and how they can make use of the information?

6. A local credit union is interested in creating a credit card product that would appeal to graduating college seniors. A marketing research class conducted a study of 72 graduating seniors in which their attitudes were assessed toward various credit card features. For each of the paired comparison t-tests shown in Figure 13.24, state the null hypothesis and your conclusion based on the findings. Do you have any reservations about the study? Explain. What would you recommend the credit union do? Justify your decisions.
7. Exit surveys from the previous year indicated that visitors to a theme park spent, on average, $217 on food, mementos, and merchandise per family during their stay. The theme park's general manager is wondering if the economic downturn has negatively affected sales for these items in the current year. The results of a one sample t-test comparing last year's average sales to the current year's average sales, as determined by the most recent exit survey, are shown in Figure 13.25. State the null hypothesis being tested and your conclusion. Now interpret these findings. Is the general manager correct in his assumption?
8. Women who live in the South participate more frequently in hunting and fishing activities than do women in other parts of the country, and thus represent a market of interest to sporting goods stores. A national sporting goods chain conducted a study of Texans who hunt and fish regularly. The study, among other questions, asked participants to rank their store preferences for purchasing hunting and fishing equipment. The CEO of the sporting goods chain was curious to see if men and women differed in their store preferences. Five national store brands were ranked, and a cross-tabulation and chi-square analysis was performed by gender for each store. The results for Brand A are shown in Figure 13.26. Do men and women's preferences differ for the store? If so, how do they differ? What recommendations would you make to the CEO?

The following questions require that you access the textbook's website at www.clowjames.net/students.html. Open the SPSS data file entitled Chapter 13 Critical Thinking Data, and the questionnaire that accompanies the data file, entitled Chapter 13 Critical Thinking Survey.

9. Is gender associated with playing intramural basketball (question 5)? Is gender associated with playing

basketball in high school (question 4)? Run the appropriate analyses, state your conclusion, and interpret the findings.

10. Do males and females hold similar attitudes toward the statements assessed in question 3 of the survey? State the null hypothesis, perform the appropriate statistical test, explain your conclusions, and interpret the findings.
11. Do people spend as much money on other expenses associated with attending an NBA game (parking, food, merchandise, etc.) as they do on the price of the ticket itself (questions 8 and 10)? State the null hypothesis, perform the appropriate statistical test, explain your conclusions, and interpret the findings.
12. Does the number of professional basketball games attended vary by income (question 2)? State the null hypothesis, run the appropriate test, explain your conclusion, and interpret the finding.
13. Your friend believes that the average price paid for a single NBA ticket is $95.00 a game (question 8). Run the appropriate statistical test, explain your conclusion, and interpret the finding. What is the confidence interval for the average price paid for a single NBA game ticket?

Group Statistics					
Model	**Gender**	**N**	**Mean**	**Std. Deviation**	**Std. Error Mean**
The brand name of a sneaker influences my purchase decision.	Female	104	3.8462	1.27538	.12506
	Male	96	3.8750	.93189	.09511
I prefer to buy sneakers when they are on sale.	Female	104	3.5865	1.56174	.15314
	Male	96	4.2083	1.05548	.10772
Advertising Influences which sneaker brand I purchase.	Female	104	3.3942	1.21014	.11866
	Male	96	2.7292	1.37251	.14008
Price is important to me when selecting sneakers.	Female	104	4.0288	1.24211	.12180
	Male	96	4.1563	.87453	.08926
I choose style over comfort when buying sneakers.	Female	104	2.1442	1.32503	.12993
	Male	96	2.8021	1.64553	.16795
I prefer to shop online.	Female	104	2.6250	1.43593	.14080
	Male	96	3.2292	1.44717	.14770
Athlete endorsements affect my sneaker purchase decision.	Female	104	2.0096	1.22669	.12029
	Male	96	2.5729	1.49909	.15300

Scale: Ranging from 1 = Strongly disagree to 5 = Strongly agree

FIGURE 13.23a Independent Samples T-Test Results for Critical Thinking Question 5

The Fantastic Five Lakeside Grill (Project Class Discussion)

The Fantastic Five team had looked forward to this part of their project. The questionnaire had been created, data were collected, and now it was time to focus on the analysis. After validating and cleaning the data, the team divided the analyses among the team members.

However, the first task was to code the open-ended questions and create a few new variables. This task was given to Alexa. She added the number of noon meals eaten at Lakeside to the number of evening meals eaten to create a new ratio variable that represented the total meals eaten at Lakeside. She then used this information to create a variable containing three categories called light users, moderate users, and heavy users. Light users were defined as those who ate six or fewer meals; moderate users

Independent Samples Test

		Levene's Test for Equality of Variance		T–Test for Equality of Means						
									95% Confidence Interval of the Difference	
		F	Sig.	t	df	Sig. (2-tailed)	Mean Difference	Std. Error Difference	Lower	Upper
The brand name of a sneaker influences my purchase decision.	Equal variances assumed	14.700	.000	–.181	198	.856	–.02885	.15905	–.34250	.28480
	Equal variance not assumed			–.184	188.305	.855	–.02885	.15712	–.33879	.28109
I prefer to buy sneakers when they are on sale.	Equal variances assumed	41.910	.000	–3.372	198	.001	–.62179	.19006	–.99660	–2.4699
	Equal variance not assumed			–3.321	181.871	.001	–.62179	.18723	–.99123	–.25236
Advertising Influences which sneaker brand I purchase.	Equal variances assumed	7.978	.005	3.641	198	.000	.66506	.18266	.30485	1.02528
	Equal variance not assumed			3.623	190.015	.000	.66506	.18359	.30294	1.02719
Price is important to me when selecting sneakers.	Equal variances assumed	4.116	.044	–.832	198	.406	–.12740	.15306	–.42925	.17444
	Equal variance not assumed			–.844	185.369	.400	–.12740	.15100	–.42531	.17050
I choose style over comfort when buying sneakers.	Equal variances assumed	31.971	.000	–3.125	198	.002	–.65785	.21053	–1.073	–.24269
	Equal variance not assumed			–3.098	182.463	.002	–.65785	.21234	–1.007	–.23890
I prefer to shop online.	Equal variances assumed	.376	.541	–2.962	198	.003	–.60417	.20400	–1.006	–.20188
	Equal variance not assumed			–2.961	196.470	.003	–.60417	.20406	–1.007	–.20173
Athlete endorsements affect my sneaker purchase decision.	Equal variances assumed	14.111	.000	–2.917	198	.004	–.56330	.19308	–.94406	–.18254
	Equal variance not assumed			–2.894	183.923	.004	–.56330	.19462	–.94728	–.17932

Scale: Ranging from 1 = Strongly disagree to 5 = Strongly agree

FIGURE 13.23b Independent Samples T-Test Results for Critical Thinking Question 5

Paired Samples Statistic

		Mean	N	Std. Deviation	Std. Error Mean
Pair 1	Prefer 0% interest promotion for 12 months	1.67	72	.475	.056
	Prefer $0 balance transfer fee	4.68	72	.470	.055
Pair 2	Prefer cash back reward program	4.40	72	.522	.061
	Prefer points rewards program for Amazon.com	4.54	72	.502	.059
Pair 3	Prefer higher credit limit with higher standard interest rate	4.51	72	.503	.059
	Prefer lower credit limit with lower standard interest rate	3.64	72	1.079	.127

Paired Samples Correlations

		N	Correlation	Sig.
Pair 1	Prefer 0% interest promotion for 12 months Prefer $0 balance transfer fee	72	.337	.004
Pair 2	Prefer cash back reward program Prefer points rewards program for Amazon.com	72	.123	.302
Pair 3	Prefer higher credit limit with higher standard interest rate Prefer lower credit limit with lower standard interest rate	72	.113	.344

Paired Samples Test

		Paired Differences					t	df	Sig. (2-tailed)
					95% Confidence Interval of the Difference				
		Mean	Std. Deviation	Std. Error Mean	Lower	Upper			
Pair 1	Prefer 0% interest promotion for 12 months Prefer $0 balance transfer fee	−3.014	.544	.064	−3.142	−2.886	−47.039	71	.000
Pair 2	Prefer cash back reward program Prefer points rewards program for Amazon.com	−.139	.678	.080	−.298	.020	−1.739	71	.086
Pair 3	Prefer higher credit limit with higher standard interest rate Prefer lower credit limit with lower standard interest rate	.875	1.138	.134	.608	1.142	6.527	71	.000

Scale: 1 = Not strongly prefer to 5 = Strongly prefer

FIGURE 13.24 Paired Sample T-Test Results for Critical Thinking Question 6

One Sample Statistics

	N	Mean	Std. Deviation	Std. Error Mean
How much did your spend on other expenses (food, merchandise, etc.)?	88	187.8409	132.31101	14.10440

One Sample Test

	Test Value = 217					
					95% Confidence Interval of the Difference	
	t	df	Sig. (2-tailed)	Mean Difference	Lower	Upper
How much did your spend on other expenses (food, merchandise, etc.)?	−2.067	87	.042	−29.15909	−57.1931	−1.1251

FIGURE 13.25 One Sample T-Test Results for Critical Thinking Question 7

Crosstab

			Rank Brand A				
			4th Most Desirable	3rd Most Desirable	2nd Most Desirable	Most Desirable	Total
Gender	Female	Count	21	10	20	53	104
		% within Gender	20.2%	9.6%	19.2%	51.0%	100.0%
		% of Total	10.5%	5.0%	10.0%	26.5%	52.0%
	Male	Count	16	15	45	20	96
		% within Gender	16.7%	15.6%	46.9%	20.8%	100.0%
		% of Total	8.0%	7.5%	22.5%	10.0%	48.0%
Total		Count	37	25	65	73	200
		% within Gender	18.5%	12.5%	32.5%	36.5%	100.0%
		% of Total	18.5%	12.5%	32.5%	36.5%	100.0%

Chi-Square Tests

	Value	df	Asymp. Sig. (2-sided)
Pearson Chi–Square	14.659[a]	4	.005
Likelihood Ratio	18.538	4	.001
Linear-by-Linear Association	1.419	1	.234
N of Valid Cases	200		

[a] 4 cells (40.0%) have expected count less than 5. The minimum expected count is 2.40.

FIGURE 13.26 Chi-Square Results for Critical Thinking Question 8

consumed seven to ten meals, and heavy users at eleven or more meals per month at the Lakeside Grill. Another new variable used categories to classify if the respondent ate at the Lakeside Grill primarily for lunch, primarily for dinner, or a combination of both. To determine the correct classification, Alexa subtracted the number of evening meals from the number of lunch meals. If the result was –2 or below, the person was labeled as an evening diner, if from -1 to +1 the label was both meals, and if the result was 2 or greater the person was labeled as a lunch diner. The last two variables created related to the distance that respondents A) lived from Lakeside Grill and B) worked from Lakeside Grill. For each of these variables, the two categories with the largest distances were collapsed into a single category using the recoding process.

After this work was done, Destiny ran the descriptive analysis of every question. The SPSS data file used in this and subsequent analysis is entitled Chapter 13 Lakeside Grill Data Coded. The questionnaire is entitled Chapter 13 Lakeside Grill Survey. With each part of the analysis, the team decided to write down significant or interesting findings. This document is entitled Chapter 13 Analyses Findings. All of the files for this exercise are located at the textbook website: www.clowjames.net/students.html.

Using independent t-tests, Brooke compared answers to questions 6, 11, and 12 based on the respondent's gender and whether the person ate primarily at noon or in the evening. Using ANOVA tests, Brooke analyzed responses to question 6, Juan to question 11, and Alexa to question 12. To see if the new restaurant, Fisherman's Paradise, had an impact on Lakeside Grill, Destiny analyzed the evaluation of the food at Fisherman's Paradise compared to the Lakeside Grill (question 9) and the resulting change on dining at Lakeside (question 10). The last part of the analysis included chi-square tests. Brooke examined the ranking of the Lakeside Grill and Zach examined the change in dining at Lakeside Grill since the Fisherman's Paradise opened. For this last test, Zach collapsed the first two categories, quit eating and eating less, into a single category.

Critique Questions:

1. Evaluate the work Alexa did on the original data set in terms of coding the three opened-ended questions and the creation of the new variables.
2. Access the "Significant and Interesting Findings" for the Lakeside Grill analyses. For each of the following sections, evaluate the work of the team. The output file's name is given in the parenthesis following the analysis technique. Open each and compare the output results to the findings indicated by the team.
    a. Descriptive analysis (Chapter 13 Lakeside Grill Descriptives)
    b. Independent Sample T-Tests (Chapter 13 Lakeside Grill Independent T-Tests)
    c. ANOVA Tests for Question 6 (Chapter 13 Lakeside Grill ANOVA Question 6)
    d. ANOVA Test for Question 10 (Chapter 13 Lakeside Grill ANOVA Question10)
    e. ANOVA Tests for Question 11 (Chapter 13 Lakeside Grill ANOVA Question 11)
    f. ANOVA Tests for Question 12 (Chapter 13 Lakeside Grill ANOVA Question 12)
    g. Chi-Square of Ranking of Lakeside Grill (Chapter 13 Lakeside Grill Chi-Square Ranking)
    h. Chi-Square of Changes in Eating at Lakeside Grill Because of New Competitor (Chapter 13 Lakeside Grill Chi-Square Competitor)
3. Based on the findings from the SPSS analysis, what recommendations would you make to the owner of the Lakeside Grill?

Notes

1. Tom Wigman, "Mobile Revenues Account for More than 50% of the Global Games Market as It Reaches $137.9 Billion in 2018," Newzoo, April 2018, http://www.newzoo.com.
2. Patrick Baldasara and Vikas Mittel, "The Use, Misuse, and Abuse of Significance," *Quirk's Marketing Research Review* (November 1994): Article ID 19941101.
3. Terry Grapentine, "Data Use; Statistical Significance Revisited," *Quirk's Marketing Research Review* (April 2011): Article ID 20010401, pp. 18, 20–23.
4. Patrick Baldasara and Vikas Mittel, "The Use, Misuse, and Abuse of Significance," *Quirk's Marketing Research Review* (November 1994): Article ID 19941101.
5. Grapentine, "Data Use; Statistical Significance Revisited"; Doug Berdie, "Significant Differences," *Quirk's Marketing Research Review* (January 2012): 30, 32–35.
6. Doug Berdie, "Significant Differences," *Quirk's Marketing Research Review* (January, 2012), pp. 30, 32–35.
7. Doug Berdie, "Significant Differences," *Quirk's Marketing Research Review* (January, 2012), p. 33.
8. Patrick Baldasara and Vikas Mittel, "The Use, Misuse, and Abuse of Significance," *Quirk's Marketing Research Review* (November 1994): Article ID: 19941101.
9. Gary M. Mullet, "The Statistics of Missed Opportunities (or) You Better Beware of Beta," *Quirk's Marketing Research* (December 1991): Article ID 19911208.
10. Marija Norusis, *SPSS Base System User's Guide* (Chicago, IL: SPSS Inc., 1990).
11. Rudolph R. Sinkovics and Elfriede Penz, "Multilingual Elite-Interviews and Software-Based Analysis. Problems and Solutions Based on CAQDAS," *International Journal of Market Research* 53, no. 5 (2011): 705–724.

12. Jesús Cambra-Fierro and Alan Wilson, "Qualitative Data Analysis Software: Will It Ever Become Mainstream?" *International Journal of Market Research* 53, no. 1 (2011): 17–24.
13. R., Rettie, H. Robinson, A. Radske and X. Ye, "CAQ-DAS: A Supplementary Tool for Qualitative Market Research," *Qualitative Market Research: An International Journal*. Vol. 11, No. 1, (2008), pp. 76–88.
14. Jesús Cambra-Fierro and Alan Wilson, "Qualitative Data Analysis Software: Will It Ever Become Mainstream?" *International Journal of Market Research* 53, no. 1 (2011): 17–24.

Research Reports and Presentations

CHAPTER 14

Chapter Outline

Learning Objectives

After studying this chapter, you should be able to:

- Identify the goals of preparing marketing research reports and presentations.
- Describe the various components of a marketing research report.
- Explain the four principles of an executive-ready report.
- Discuss the use of oral presentations in marketing research reporting.
- Explain how to use graphs and charts effectively.

14.1 Chapter Overview

While the descriptive information obtained from a study's data is interesting and the significant results obtained through t-tests, ANOVA tests, and chi-square tests are important, companies want to know what it all means. What are the study conclusions? What insights can be drawn from the data? What are the marketing implications? How can the findings be used to make management and marketing decisions?

A study by $Reach_3$ Insights investigated what motivates consumers to subscribe to products or services that are delivered digitally or to their home. While many people associate these services with online video subscriptions or meal kits, subscription services sales are growing in a variety of industries, and even major brands such as Nike are attempting to jump on the bandwagon and offer their own subscription sales. The key insight uncovered by the study was that emotions, not logic, motivate consumers to sign-up for subscription sales. The top three reasons for signing up for subscription service are listed in **Figure 14.1** along with key barriers to adoption. The ultimate goal of marketing research is to turn data into information that can be used by individuals and companies making decisions. While the study investigated logical reasons for subscription services, such as making shopping easier, saving time, saving money, and avoiding hassle, the most factors that motivated subscribers were emotional in nature. The information identified by $Reach_3$ Insights can guide marketing managers in developing marketing plans, as communications should focus more on the excitement, fun, and surprise aspect of the subscription delivery, while reassuring potential subscribers that items can easily be returned if they don't like what they receive. The study also asked the sample of 1,000 consumers how they originally learned about subscriptions. Word-of-mouth recommendations from friends or family were the most common method at 42 percent, followed by social media. Only 7 percent of the consumers in this study mentioned influencer marketing leading one to conclude that influencer marketing is not very effective in the context of subscription service marketing.[1] As many marketers are investing heavily in influencer marketing today, this finding would be helpful in developing a marketing budget and deciding how much is going to be allocated for the various digital components of marketing.

This chapter takes the data analysis discussed in the previous chapters and outlines how those conclusions and the key insights are to be presented. While most reports are written, some are oral. In the past, all reporting was done in person by the marketing research agency or marketing research personnel within a company. Today, other alternatives exist. Formal reports may not even be written. It may just be a presentation that is given via Skype, attached to an email, or delivered through a website. Infographics and other forms of data visualization are also becoming a common way of communicating research results.

Key motivational insight: Emotions drive subscriptions.
Top reasons for signing up for subscription services:

- Getting unique products I wouldn't normally find or get for myself
- Excitement of getting a fun surprise in the mail
- It's a special treat for myself

Barriers to subscription service/product adoption:

- Fear of being trapped into a long-term commitment
- High-cost
- Possibility that delivered items won't be liked

FIGURE 14.1 Motivations and Barriers in E-Commerce Subscription Market
Source: Adapted from, Mackenzie Hollister "Motivations and barriers: Unboxing the e-commerce subscription market" *Quirk's Media*, https://www.quirks.com/articles/motivations-and-barriers-unboxing-the-e-commerce-subscription-market, November 13, 2019.

14.2 Goals of Reports and Presentations

LEARNING OBJECTIVE 14.1
Identify the goals of preparing marketing research reports and presentations.

The quality of a marketing research report is directly related to the effort put into it by the research staff. It is tempting to spend all of the time doing the research, then throw the report together at the last minute. Such an approach can leave a lasting negative impression and waste the valuable research that was performed. To ensure quality, it is important to consider the goals of preparing reports and making presentations shown in Figure 14.2.

14.2a Effectively Communicate Findings

The first and ultimate goal is to effectively communicate the findings. If the results cannot be communicated in an effective manner, then it doesn't matter how well the research was conducted or what was learned. The recipients of the research will not be able to make informed management decisions if they don't understand the results.

Writing effective research reports begin with understanding the different groups of individuals who will be reading the report or listening to the presentation. There will be individuals who are only interested in the executive summary, and who only want to hear the conclusions and recommendations. They don't want to bother with anything else or get bogged down in a discussion of the research methodology. Another type of individual will want to read or hear the findings from the marketing research, in addition to learning the conclusions and listening to recommendations. These people are interested in how the findings tie into the conclusions and how the recommendations are then derived. The third group is composed of those people who have some expertise in marketing research, or at least believe they do. This group wants to gain a detailed understanding of how data were collected, how it was analyzed and how the findings were drawn. That said, most individuals involved in reading or listening to a marketing research report or presentation fall into the first two categories.

In addition to understanding the type or types of individuals who will be involved, it is important to understand that most individuals have an extremely limited knowledge of research. They do not know what a t-test, ANOVA, or chi-square analysis is, and their knowledge of the meaning of "statistical significance" is very low. Even those who have heard of various statistical tests typically have no idea of how the test was performed and how the results are read, much less what they mean. As a result, the report and presentation need to be free of marketing research jargon and terminology. Definitions, detailed explanations, and statistical test printouts can be placed in the appendices where the individual who is interested can go for in-depth information. In most cases, though, even the appendices often contain few actual statistical analyses or tables. But competent providers of research should be willing and able to make this information available to the client upon request in a timely manner.

14.2b Provide Interpretations of the Findings

It is important to focus on the fact that the marketing research was conducted because of the research objectives stated at the beginning of the project. The findings and corresponding interpretations of the research must relate to these research objectives. More important, the interpretations of the findings need to be written or presented in a non-technical manner that can be easily understood by someone without any marketing

1. Effectively communicate findings
2. Provide interpretations of findings
3. Draw conclusions
4. Provide insight
5. Make recommendations
6. Discuss limitations

FIGURE 14.2 Goals of Reports and Presentations

research knowledge. This can be a challenge for individuals trained in marketing research because research terminology has become such a critical part of their vocabulary. More difficult is discussing results of the research without using research terminology such as t-values, level of significance, and confidence interval.

Findings results of the data analysis.

Interpretations presentation of findings in a context that the listener or reader can more easily understand.

At this juncture it is important to distinguish between findings and interpretation. **Findings** are the results of the data analysis. Findings include the data analysis output, frequency tables, descriptive statistics, cross tabulations, chi-square analyses, factor analysis, scale reliability, tests for differences in means, and regression analysis. **Interpretations** put these findings into a context that the listener or reader can more easily understand. For example, findings related to descriptive statistics may be placed into summary tables that show the key attitude questions that were asked, the number of subjects (n) who expressed an opinion, and the means and standard deviations for each question. Normally, a small note would appear under this table explaining the scale. The notation might say, "Subjects answered each question by selecting a response ranging from 1 = strongly disagree, to 5 = strongly agree."

Discussion in the report might interpret this finding by pointing out that a mean of 4.5 on an item assessing satisfaction with customer service is very strong. Data from the frequency chart can be cited to expand on this finding to report the percent of total respondents who answered either agree or strongly agree in response to the question.

Alternatively, the report discussion for a different question assessing satisfaction with the company's pricing might point out that while a mean score of 3.5 is positive (as 3 indicates a neutral position), the large standard deviation of 1.57 indicates that pricing satisfaction varies widely from individual to individual. This interpretation can then provide a lead-in for additional analyses that may test for differences in satisfaction, perhaps on the basis of gender, age, education, income, buyer loyalty, or some other key variable being investigated.

Data visualization provides a visual representation of information and data.

Data visualization provides a visual representation of information and data. Charts, graphs, and infographics help to visually interpret and display information. Information presented visually is easier to understand and recall. Software products such as Tableau are increasingly being used to create dashboards that allow users to find and visualize data relationships, especially in huge data sets.[2] For example, Douglas White, Director of the LSUS Center for Business and Economic Research, used Tableau to create data visualization dashboards for several census variables of interest to the Louisiana Business community. Figure 14.3 shows the data visualization for residents of Louisiana who have any type of Broadband access. The dropdown list in the upper left-hand corner shows other variables related to Internet access and cellular plans that can be visualized. Dashboard users can narrow the data to specific parishes (which are similar to counties) and census tracts within a given parish. Colors help to define the differences in access percentages. Dark green corresponds with low access percentages, while dark blue indicates high access percentages. Such information could be useful to local marketers in a particular parish who are trying to decide whether investing in YouTube marketing is appropriate. If the census tract where there customer base is located is associated with low levels of "Broadband Access" or high levels of "No Internet Access" then YouTube marketing would not make sense even if similar stores in different states have had success with using YouTube marketing to reach their target market.

Source: Pressmaster/Shutterstock

Data visualization provides a visual representation of information and data. Charts, graphs videos, and infographics help to visually interpret and display information.

Sometimes researchers will discover findings that to them are interesting, but do not relate to the research objectives in any way. In such situations, they must avoid the temptation to put them in the main body of the report. Findings that don't relate to the research objectives can be placed in the appendices if the researcher feels they are important or will be of interest to the client. Furthermore, not all findings have to be reported. If a variety of crosstabulation analyses revealed that no relationships

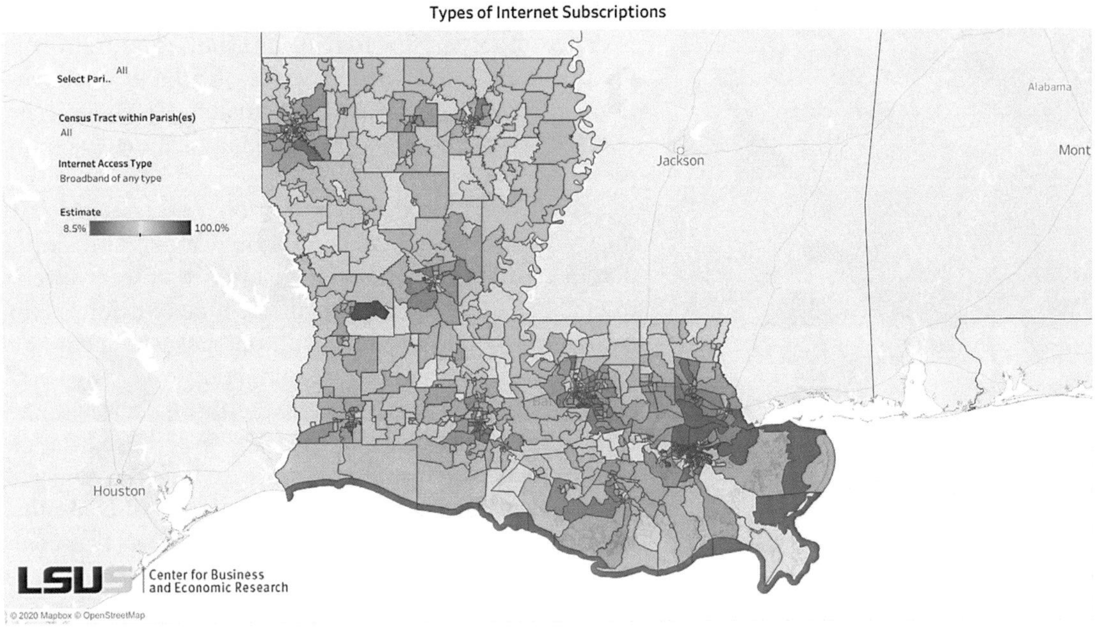

FIGURE 14.3 Data Visualization Dashboard
Source: LSUS Center for Business and Economic Research, "Types of Internet Subscriptions," https://public.tableau.com/profile/douglas.white#!/vizhome/LouisianaCensusTract-TypesofInternetSubscriptions/Dashboard1, retrieved January 9, 2017.

were present between the variables being tested, the researcher will likely choose to limit discussion of these tests to a single sentence stating that no relationships were found. Cross tabulation analyses will be included in the appendices but not discussed them in the report. Alternately, any reference to these findings may be eliminated altogether. Which approach is taken depends upon the degree to which the findings relate to specific research objectives.

14.2c Drawing Conclusions

The third goal of reports and presentations is to draw conclusions based on the findings and interpretations. **Conclusions** expand upon the interpretations and attempt to explain to the reader or listener what the results of the study actually mean. It is critical that the conclusions tie into the research objectives. Specifically, conclusions should be explicitly stated for each research objective. After all, that is the why the research agency was contracted to conduct the study. In drawing these conclusions the researcher needs to have an understanding of the client's business, its customers, and its marketing strategy.

Conclusions expanding of the interpretation to explain what the results of a research study actually mean.

For instance, if the firm under study had recently implemented a customer service training program for its personnel, the high satisfaction scores pertaining to customer service provide strong evidence to conclude that the training program was most likely a success. The conclusion could be further bolstered if current satisfaction scores could be compared against satisfaction scores achieved by the firm prior to implementing its training program. In phrasing the conclusion, the researcher would need to be careful in the claims made. "The training program appears to have been successful. The differences in customer satisfaction scores from before and after the training program were implemented indicate a large improvement. Slightly more than 93 percent of the respondents to our recent survey indicated that they agreed or strongly agreed with the question, compared to only 72 percent who expressed these same levels of agreement before the training program was implemented."

As the example above illustrates, it is important that every conclusion drawn is based on solid interpretations of the research. If the study does not provide sufficient information or evidence to state a conclusion for a particular research objective, this fact must be

Source: IQoncept/Shutterstock

Marketing research clients want more than conclusions and recommendations; they want insights that will lead to a competitive advantage for their company or brand.

made clear. Drawing evidence-based conclusions is especially important if a conclusion is different from what the client expected. In such cases, the client may question the credibility of the conclusion. The researcher needs to be prepared to present analytical evidence that provides justification.

Conclusions regarding causation can be especially misleading. Researchers should be wary of concluding that one variable definitively "caused" another variable to change. In most circumstances, a conclusion of this nature will be inconsistent with the research methodology used in the market research study. You may recall from an earlier chapter that experiments under highly controlled conditions are used for proving causation. Marketing research studies performed outside of an academic setting are rarely experimental in nature and thus lack the necessary control over other variables that could have an influence on the dependent variable. Finally, remember that correlation analysis alone is grossly insufficient to prove causation. High correlations between two variables do not provide sufficient evidence to indicate that one variable caused the other variable to change, and may simply be coincidental.

14.2d Provide Insight

In the past, marketing research companies went from the third goal of drawing conclusions directly to the fifth goal of making recommendations (as listed on Figure 14.2). With increased global competition and tighter marketing research budgets, companies now want more than conclusions and recommendations. They want to know how the conclusions derived from the research apply to their business and how they can use them to make more intelligent marketing decisions. They want **insights** that will lead to a competitive advantage for their company or brand.

Insights conclusions derived from research that help firms to make more intelligent marketing decisions that result in competitive advantage for their company or brand.

Generating insights is a complex, challenging, and labor-intensive process. It requires thinking beyond numbers. It involves using analytical and creative skills and an in-depth knowledge of the firm's operation and especially its customers. It involves spending time with the client to gain a better understanding of the situation the firm is facing. In our example, the researcher would need to gain a detailed understanding of how the customer service training program was implemented and exactly what customer service standards were set. Additional changes to business policies, processes, and procedures that could affect customer service should also be learned through discussions with the client. Finally, pending client approval, the researcher may conduct additional focus group interviews to better understand why customers feel satisfied with customer service and what factors influenced their ratings.

A key insight gained from this process might be that multiple customer service and information access options should exist to satisfy every type of patron. Thus, older adults can "speak to a human" in person or over the phone, a person who graciously helps them in a warm, friendly, and positive fashion. On the other hand, those who desire self-serve are satisfied because they are able to find needed information on the company's website using the FAQ section, technical support manuals, or company blog. Those who fall in between the two extremes may be satisfied because they can mostly find what they need online, but can email a technical support person directly and receive a response within 24 hours. These insights can provide a competitive advantage when generalized to other aspects of the business, such as designing, ordering, and returning products.

The challenge faced by marketing researchers is that they feel compelled to share data and provide information that is garnered from data. However, business executives want less data and more insights that lead to solutions. To make this change, researchers need to shift from tables, charts, and graphs to strategic storytelling. Stories are engaging, and video clips, anecdotes, descriptive adjectives, metaphors and analogies all help stories to come alive in the mind of client. Stories simplify data. They inspire. They take numbers and facts and translate them into living, relatable experiences. Strong stories create mental imagery and stimulate the imagination, and are more successful at persuading the client to action than are data alone. Key insights that are tied to stories are more memorable when condensed and highlighted in the context of a story, especially when the clients can draw personal or emotional parallels to the information provided. Graphs and charts can be used to support the stories, but the prime emphasis is stories that recapitulate customer experiences or that solve a business problem. These types of insights require marketing researchers to think more like entrepreneurs. It requires taking risks, using data to suggest why something is occurring and not just that it is occurring. Usually, the executives know it is occurring. What they don't know, and the reason the research is conducted, is why it is occurring and, most important, what changes the company needs to make to create the desired outcomes.[3]

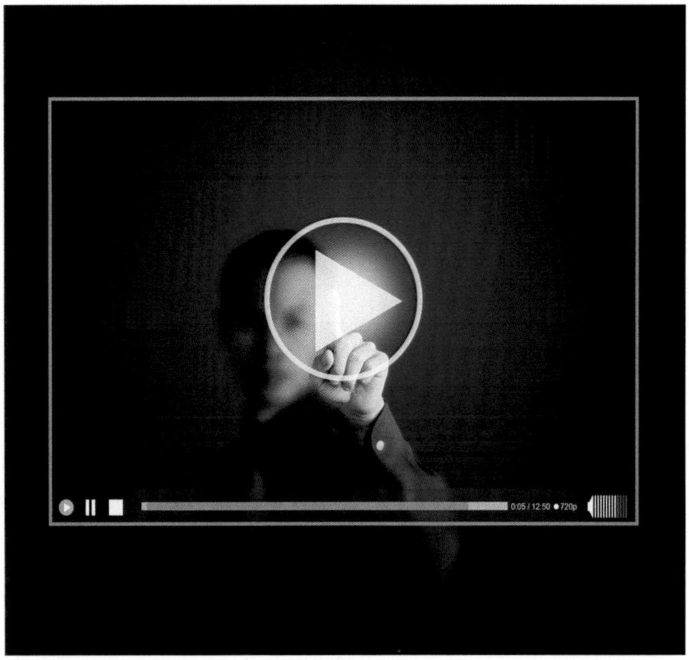

Research reports and presentations often use storytelling to help present insights. Stories are engaging, and video clips, anecdotes, descriptive adjectives, metaphors and analogies all help stories to come alive in the mind of client.

14.2e Make Recommendations

The fifth goal of research reports and presentations is to make recommendations that result in action. **Recommendations** are courses of actions that should be taken by the firm based on the results of the study. The recommendations need to be based on the insights that were gained from the data analysis and the conclusions that were drawn. They also need to be tied into the objectives of the research. Making recommendations is typically the most difficult part of the report since many marketing researchers are not marketing strategists. They often are venturing into areas where they have limited knowledge. So consultations with the client may occur prior to writing the recommendations to ensure the recommendations are appropriate. However, researchers must be careful doing this. It is easy to offer recommendations the client wants, and not recommendations based on the research findings and conclusions.

Recommendations courses of actions that should be taken by the firm based on the results of the study.

Recommendations must be actionable. "Investing in additional research" would be a poor recommendation if unaccompanied by specific details outlining the research objectives, proposed methodology, cost, timeline, and expected value of the study. A well-presented recommendation section will provide support for the proposed actions and justify why these actions should be implemented. Recommendations should also be prioritized to help managers make the best-informed decisions. Using stories and metaphors can help persuade the client to action. One senior researcher recounted an instance where he compared the client's product to regular milk purchased from a supermarket. He used this metaphor to help the CMO understand that consumers thought the firm's brand was pretty similar to other brands competing in the same category, and added weight to his recommendation that advertising dollars be invested to build perceptions of differentiation between the brand and its competitors.[4]

In the example cited previously, it would be particularly important to offer recommendations for action, given the disparate results related to satisfaction with the company's customer service. Depending upon the conclusions and insights generated, the recommendations could fall into the area of customer relationship management. Strategically, the recommendation might be to "fire" a particularly unprofitable or hard-to-please segment. Specific actions to be taken may include recommending the removal of specific customers from the firm's direct marketing database to prevent future marketing communications from reaching those individuals. Alternatively, depending upon the conclusions or insights that are relevant, recommendations might suggest that promotional incentives be targeted toward specific consumer segments. More specific suggestions regarding the type of promotional incentive, the timing, and how the promotion should be communicated to the target audience would constitute an actionable plan, as long as the suggestions are based on insights into consumers and the interpretations and conclusions.

14.2f Discuss Limitations

Limitations any potential problems that may have arisen during the data collection process or because of assumptions that were made during the research study.

The last goal of reports and presentations is to discuss any limitations of the study. **Limitations** include any potential problems that may have arisen during the data collection process or assumptions that were made during the research study. The most frequently cited limitation is the sample used for the study. Non-probability samples, such as convenience samples, yield results that cannot be generalized to the larger population. Even when probability sampling is attempted and every effort is made to ensure the sample is representative of the target market, it may not be an identical match in terms of important demographic, geographic, or psychographic characteristics. The size of the sample may also be of concern.

Other limitations can involve the manner in which the data were collected or the analytical tools used to interpret the data. The use of self-reported data in marketing research is often criticized due to memory errors or perceptual differences that might not be relevant to the questions being asked, but that introduce response error into the results. Both overall non-response and item non-response levels should be discussed. Thus, if only five percent of the sample answered an open-ended question that was critical to fulfilling a key research objective, the client must be informed since this low response rate calls into question the validity of the interpretation, conclusion, insights, and recommendations related to the research objective.

14.3 Preparing Research Reports

The typical format of the marketing research report is shown in Figure 14.4. The terminology and section headings may differ depending on the industry, the client, and the marketing research firm. But most reports will cover the basic elements shown. This section will cover the long version of the marketing research report. In the next section, a newer, shorter version will be presented.

Title page front cover of the research report.

LEARNING OBJECTIVE 14.2
Describe the various components of a marketing research report.

14.3a Title Page

The **title page** or front cover of the report should have four basic pieces of information. The first is the title of the report or study. Titles do not have to be complete sentences, but should convey the essence of the topic contained in the report. Next should be the name of the person to whom the report is directed and/or the name of the organization

1. Title page
2. Table of contents
3. Executive summary
4. Introduction
5. Research methodology
6. Data analysis findings
7. Conclusions and recommendations
8. Appendices

FIGURE 14.4 Format of the Marketing Research Report

for which the report is prepared. The third piece of necessary information is the date of the report. The last informational segment should relate to the individual and company that prepared the report. This typically includes the name of the firm, the primary contact person's name within the firm, and contact information such as phone number, address, email, and corporate URL.

14.3b Table of Contents

The **table of contents** lists the different sections of the report in sequential order. Usually the first page of each section of the report is identified along with the corresponding page number. Some reports will have a separate listing of the figures and tables. This is handy for those who are looking for a specific piece of information, or for those who want to see a table that was used as the basis for a chart or graph presented on a slide during the oral presentation. In addition to the regular sections, the table of contents will also contain a listing of the appendices, if relevant.

Table of contents lists the different sections of the report in sequential order.

14.3c Executive Summary

The executive summary is a key component of the report. The **executive summary** presents a summary of the entire research report including the purpose of the research, key findings, insights, conclusions, and recommendations. Although the summary is placed at the beginning of the research report, it is the very last portion of the report to be written because it summarizes what is in the report.

Executive summary presents a summary of the entire research report including the purpose of the research, key findings, conclusion, and recommendations.

It is important to remember that this will be the only section some individuals will read. It must be written concisely. These individuals are not interested in research methodologies used, type of analyses that were performed, and the individual significant results. They want to know why the research was conducted, the method of sampling, and the sample size. It should contain the key findings—not all of the findings—just those that are the most critical and that support the conclusions, insights, and recommendations. It is these latter topics, conclusions, insights, and particularly recommendations, that are the most important to an executive. They need to be identified clearly, but concisely. If the executive wants further information, he or she can refer to other sections of the report.

14.3d Introduction

The introduction contains background information for the study. Background information may contain secondary information, or summaries of other studies that were conducted on the topic that relate to the current study. Events or factors that led to the study will be explained. For instance, declining market share over the last year may have triggered a need to look for alternative methods of reaching consumers. Or, a revision of the current marketing plan may be pending. As a result, the current study may have been commissioned.

The introduction will contain the specific research objectives or questions that the study addresses. If hypotheses were developed, they will be stated. Usually the hypotheses are not stated in formal null and alternative fashion. Instead, the research hypotheses will be summarized in layman's terms. In fact, the word hypothesis is seldom used. A hypothesis written in layman's words might read "We expected no differences between the rate of responses for males and females."

14.3e Research Methodology

This section is often difficult for a marketing researcher to write. The reader just wants to know what was done and how it was done. The researcher, on the other hand, often wants to provide specific step-by-step details of the entire project from sample selection to questionnaire design to data analysis. When writing this section, it is important to remember that readers do not care about details. Information that should be contained in this section is listed in **Figure 14.5**.

1. Research design
2. Secondary data used
3. Procedure for collecting primary data
4. Sampling plan
5. Sampling procedure
6. Data collection process
7. Analytical techniques

FIGURE 14.5 Information in the Research Methodology Section

The research design is the plan that was used for conducting the research. At a minimum, the research design specifies whether qualitative, quantitative, or both types of research were implemented. The use of descriptive, observational, or causal research techniques should also be specified. In discussing the research design, reference should be made back to the research objectives or questions by showing how the research that was conducted was appropriate for answering these questions or objectives.

If secondary data was incorporated into the study beyond that which was already identified in the introduction, details should be provided. It is especially important to identify the source of the secondary data and how it was utilized in the study.

Most research reports involve primary data collection. The procedure for collecting this data should be outlined in the report. The sampling plan must be thoroughly explained since sampling is a critical component of any research study. The client needs to be shown that the sample is representative of the population being studied, and as such, provides accurate information for the problem being addressed. The procedure that was used to obtain the sample needs to be discussed to assure the reader that it was a quality sample. Special attention may be given to the quality control measures used to prevent or identify professional or unengaged respondents.

The researcher next should explain the data collection process. Some processes such as online surveys need little explanatory information. Other methods such as observation research, experimentation, mixed method research, or a focus group will need more details.

The last component in the methodology section is a brief explanation of the analytical techniques used. This information is there if someone wants to know, but it is seldom reviewed. However, in case it is reviewed, it is important to describe the analytical methods accurately, yet without overusing confusing statistical terms. For example, instead of saying a t-test was used to test for differences based on gender, the researcher can say the analysis examined purchase behavior to see if there was a difference between males and females.

14.3f Data Analysis Findings

This will be the largest section of the report. It contains the findings from the data analysis as well as a description of the sample respondents. How to organize the section can be a challenge. A common method of organization is to begin by describing the characteristics of the sample and then arrange the findings by research objectives or questions. The analysis and findings for each research objective would be shown under a heading listing that specific research objective. Care must be taken when presenting findings so that undue emphasis is not placed on findings that lack statistical or practical significance. A major advantage of this type of organization is that it discourages researchers from adding findings that do not pertain to a particular objective.

A second approach is to organize the report in the order of the questionnaire. This approach allows an individual reading the report or listening to the presentation to follow along with the questionnaire and understand how each question or item has been analyzed and the corresponding findings. If this organizational method is used, some distinction must be made to explain that while some comparisons between groups may appear to indicate that differences exist, they likely would not represent a real difference in the population. The issue of statistical significance again is at the heart of this challenge; explaining why two results that are numerically different in the sample aren't really different at all, without getting into statistical language can be quite challenging. Another disadvantage is that because most questionnaires leave demographics until the end of the survey, the discussion of the nature of the sample would take place last, and will seem out of place. Modifying the presentation of information so that the sample characteristics are presented before the rest of the questionnaire can help to reduce confusion and frustration on the part of the reader.

Throughout this process, the key challenge for the marketing researcher is to present the findings in a way that is understood by the audience. Using statistical terminology tends to confuse rather than clarify, and thus should be avoided unless the audience is well versed in statistical terms. The researcher should instead rely on graphs, charts, infographics, and tables to present the results. Graphs and charts especially are easier to understand and allow the findings to be grasped rather quickly. In addition to graphs, charts, infographics, and tables, the researcher needs to write about the results. This is important in case the reader wants additional information. It also can provide details that may not be easily recognizable in a graph or figure. Furthermore, not all information warrants an infographic, chart, graph, or table.

14.3g Conclusions and Recommendations

The conclusions and recommendations are obtained from the data analysis and corresponding findings. The conclusions should be specific, clear, and concise. Each conclusion should be tied with a specific research objective. The number of conclusions will vary depending on the type of research conducted and the findings that were discovered from the analysis. Some objectives may have only one conclusion while others may have multiple conclusions. It is also possible that no conclusions can be drawn for a specific research objective.

The recommendations are clear statements of action. They are derived from the conclusion. They are the result of critical thinking and application of the conclusions to the research problem that was the catalyst for the research study.

When citing conclusions and making recommendations, it is also a good idea to identify any limitations associated with the research. Although researchers strive to conduct errorless research, it is impossible to eliminate all error. As was discussed in previous chapters, the goal is to reduce or eliminate systematic error and reduce the level of random error. But even the best-designed studies are likely to have some error, and therefore limitations that affect the conclusions and recommendations should be addressed. The most common limitations cited include a sampling bias and measurement error. The researcher may also want to cite time limitations or budget constraints if either affected the quality of the data.

14.3h Appendices

The content of the appendices and the number of appendices will vary greatly. Almost all studies will put a copy of the questionnaire or survey instrument in an appendix for referral. Tables and information that is technical may be put in an appendix and referred to in the text of the report. Some reports will put copies of pertinent or specific data analysis output in an appendix. It would be extremely rare to include all of the analysis because the analysis alone may be 100 to 200 pages long. More likely is the enclosure of data analyses that deal with a specific issue that the researcher feels the client may want to see. This is often the case if a finding is contrary to what the client expected. Having the analysis available in an appendix can be valuable to assure the client the correct interpretation was made.

14.4 Executive-Ready Report

LEARNING OBJECTIVE 14.3
Explain the four principles of an executive-ready report.

In the past, marketing research executives as well as executives of client firms considered a long, detailed marketing research report to be the norm. Clients and marketing managers wanted all of the details. They wanted every possible piece of information and analysis that was conducted. Marketing research agencies believed that by providing length and details they were producing quality research. But times have changed. Email, smartphones, and instant messaging have changed the way people communicate and even the way executives communicate. Today's executives want a shorter, more readable version that can be read on a smartphone or tablet and dissected on the plane, in an airport, or in a taxi on the way to a business meeting. As a result, a newer, trimmer version of the marketing research report is being used by many companies. This **executive-ready report** is based on four principles: conciseness, adaptability, readability, and balance.[5]

Executive-ready report shorter marketing research report based on principles of conciseness, adaptability, readability, and balance.

A concise report eliminates all of the unnecessary words, figures, tables, and charts. While there is written content, bullet points, headlines, and subheads are used frequently to provide emphasis and conciseness. The idea is if it can be said in five words, why use fifteen? The goal is to allow the reader the opportunity to quickly grasp the point or idea without reading an entire paragraph. Additional information can be provided in appendices or a supporting document.

In making the executive-ready report concise, it is important to realize this does not simply refer to the elimination of word content. It also does not dictate that all information be presented in bullet points. While bullet points are used, some may need further explanations or justifications. Thus, some written content is needed. Conciseness does not imply that only major points or conclusions should be addressed, while minor ones should be left out. Conciseness does require full reporting, but looks for ways of doing it more efficiently and succinctly.

Adaptability refers to the ability of the report to be adapted to different individuals within an organization. Some members of the executive team may read only headlines and subheads and by means of this process are able to grasp the research findings, conclusions, and recommendations. By reading the executive summary, the executive will know the stated research objectives, how the study met those objectives, and the future strategic or management decisions that need to be made. The marketing director and other mid-level managers will likely read the bullet points and examine the figures, graphs, tables, and charts. But, this can be done rather quickly. The executive-ready report is not 200 pages long. Further, the report should be provided in a format such as PDF, so that reviewing can be done on a smartphone or tablet, wherever the executive may be.

While the executive-ready report is condensed, it is important for it to be readable. The report should tell a story. One point should lead to the next. To make it readable, the report needs to be visually appealing. This involves spatial placement of headlines, subheads, bullet points, and content. But it also involves the use of visuals. Tables, charts, infographics, and graphs are helpful. However, a report that is full of tables, graphs, and figures quickly becomes boring and tedious to read. Other visuals can be used, such as photographs, line drawings, and even cartoons. Links to video clips such as snippets of focus groups, in-depth interviews, usability studies, or ethnographic research that emphasize important findings might also be included. The idea is to create a report that is visually appealing and draws the reader in.

Balance is the last principle of an executive-ready report. Balance is important from two perspectives. First, it involves a balance between visual interest and professional presentation. While visuals add interest to the report, if overdone, they can make the report look cartoonish and unprofessional. However, a lack of visuals makes the report boring and tedious to read. Second, balance is required between brevity and wordiness. Using headlines, subheads, and bullet points makes the report smaller and easier to scan, but if overdone can leave out critical information. The reader should never be left wondering what was meant by a bullet point, subhead, or head. Because of the abbreviated nature of the executive-ready report, every word is important and should be carefully considered.

14.5 Oral Presentations

LEARNING OBJECTIVE 14.4
Discuss the use of oral presentations in marketing research reporting.

In addition to a formal written report, clients may want an oral presentation. An oral presentation allows for a personal meeting between the client and researcher firm or the research specialist within a company research department. It allows for two-way communication. Clients are able to ask questions and seek clarification. The research firm not only has the opportunity to respond, but they can also check to make sure the points they are making are clearly understood.

With current technology, oral presentations can be presented virtually. It may be a live video conference over the web or a recorded presentation that is viewed at the convenience of the client. The use of virtual presentations is becoming more popular primarily due to the high cost of travel, although saving high-level corporate executives time is often another factor.

If an oral presentation is requested, it is extremely important that the presentation be done well. It is very likely that top management will attend to hear the results. These are individuals who are not likely to read the written report, so the oral presentation will be their only exposure to the study. If they do access the written report, it will be either just to read the executive summary or to check for more details about some aspect of the oral presentation.

Source: IQoncept/Shutterstock

Oral presentations of research insights and recommendations allow clients to ask questions and seek clarification. Virtual presentations are becoming more popular as they often save busy executives time, and reduce travel costs of presenters.

14.5a Creating Effective Presentations

A conversation with the president of a Fortune 500 company and communications consultant Gary A. Schmidt resulted in what he termed "The Five Things Top Management Wants to Tell Research—But Just Can't."[6] These five things were based on attending hundreds of meetings and listening to multiple marketing research presentations. They are:

1. You're boring us to tears.
2. Enough with all the numbers already—what do we do?
3. I don't have all day to listen to you—how about 10 pages next time instead of 50?
4. I don't care about fancy methodology—what's the bottom line?
5. Take a position. I don't care about "confidence levels" or "statistical significance."

These statements reinforce the need for firms to embrace the executive-ready marketing research reporting style. They also highlight the fact that listeners want the same type of approach during the oral presentation. Long, boring presentations loaded with facts are out; short to-the-point, concise presentations are desired.

Data, analysis, and significant findings are the core of marketing research. But when it comes to making the presentation, these should be left in the marketing research lab. Attendees at the presentation want to know what it all means for their business or their brand. The purpose of the presentation is not to showcase marketing research and the methodologies that were used, but to provide insight that can help managers make good decisions. To accomplish this purpose, Gary Schmidt suggests presenters adhere to the "Fab Five Principles" shown in **Figure 14.6**.

The first principle "Keep it right" refers to the idea of keeping the findings of the research brief, on point, and most important, focused on insights. To relay that there is a significant difference based on age is presenting the findings. Management wants to know what this means for their business. How does this difference affect marketing strategy and marketing decisions? The answer to that question provides valuable insight.

- Keep it right
- Keep it simple
- Focus on the audience needs (not yours)
- Be engaged and engaging
- Take a risk

FIGURE 14.6 "Fab Five Principles" in Effective Research Presentations
Source: Adapted from Gary A. Schmidt, "Take a Risk, Keep it Simple," *Quirk's Marketing Research Review*, April 2007, Article ID 20070404.

Marketing research is very complex and to most managers is filled with statistical jargon they don't really understand (although they often pretend that they do). The second principle "Keep it simple" means taking the complex marketing research analysis and making it simple so that managers can comprehend it and do not have to pretend they understand when in fact they may not. The key is to tell the audience what is important, no more or no less, in terminology they understand.

Keeping it right and keeping it simple helps with the next principle – focusing on the audience's needs. The research presentation is not about showing how skilled a researcher is or how knowledgeable he or she is about marketing research techniques. It is about the audience and the business or brand they represent. The audience does not care how difficult it was to get the data or how many hours were spent interviewing respondents; they want to know what was learned and how will it help them to make better marketing decisions.

Focusing on the audience needs will necessitate that presenters "be engaged and engaging," which is principle four. No one wants to attend a boring meeting, and if that meeting is also long, it becomes unbearable. The t-test, the significance level, or the sampling design may be exciting to the researcher, but they are not exciting to the audience. What gets them engaged are results, conclusions, recommendations, and insights into what has happened and what needs to be done. To engage the audience requires the right message be delivered in an exciting tone and with enthusiasm. Excitement and enthusiasm are contagious. If the presenter is excited about the finding and the corresponding insights, it will infect the audience.

The last principle cited by Gary Schmidt is to "take a risk." Marketing researchers tend to want to play it safe. They want significant results. They want to stay within the confidence interval. They want to hide behind potential systematic and random error. However, to make a presentation that is effective requires taking a risk. It means suggesting a strategy, a course of action and then supporting it with research. It is very unlikely that research can eliminate all risk. But, it can provide insight to the "better" decision. Managers make decisions every day without perfect information, so they understand that insights and recommendations from research contain risk. Their goal is to reduce that risk and choose the path that has the highest probability of success. The marketing research presentation should not only direct the client or management to that path, but provide support for why it is a better decision.

14.5b Creating Effective Visuals

In terms of format, the oral presentation is usually similar to the written report, except it begins with the introduction and then proceeds through the other steps of the research methodology, description of sample respondents, data analysis findings, conclusions, and recommendations. To engage the audience, oral presentations need to be accompanied by visuals. The most commonly used visual is PowerPoint®, although handouts, infographics and flip charts can be used. But PowerPoint® allows for much greater creativity in making the presentation. Changes can be made at the last minute. Graphs, figures, and tables can be easily embedded into a slide. Multiple people can be involved in preparing the PowerPoint® as long as someone coordinates the final version so it is uniform and fits together.

The keys to effective visuals are: visibility, simplicity, and legibility (see Figure 14.7).[7] Whatever visuals are used, they must be easily seen by everyone in the audience. They should be colorful, simple, and most important, illustrate or convey only one point. They should be legible and easy to understand. If the audience is staring at a visual trying to figure out what it says or what it means, they are not listening to the speaker. The visual should assist the speaker, not be a distraction from what is being said. Thus, animated visuals are usually not recommended. Experts on presentations suggest that no more than one visual for every 30–60 seconds should be used. Changing visuals too frequently can be distracting.

14.5c Making PowerPoint® Presentations Come Alive

Microsoft's PowerPoint® has almost become the standard for presentations of all kinds, including marketing research presentations. Unfortunately, PowerPoint® is often used improperly and ineffectively. Figure 14.8 provides a list of some common mistakes

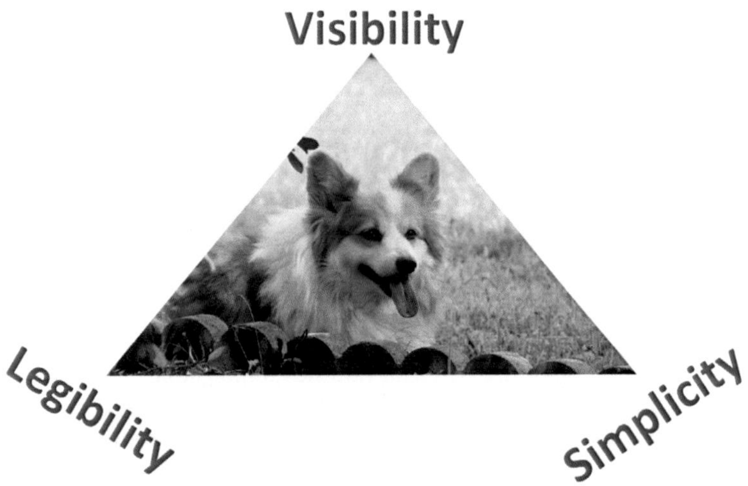

FIGURE 14.7 Keys to Effective Visuals
Source: Adapted from N. Carroll Mohn, "How to Effectively Present Marketing Research Results," *Quirk's Marketing Research Review*, January 1989, Article ID 19890104.

- Too many slides
- Slides with all text—no graphics or white space
- Cluttered slides with clip art, visuals, animation
- No visuals
- Too much variance in colors, fonts, font sizes, and slide formats
- Excessive bullet points
- Long sentences
- Too much information on one slide

FIGURE 14.8 Poor and Ineffective PowerPoint® Presentations
Source: Adapted from Melissa Murray, "Making the Results Come Alive," *Quirk's Marketing Research Review*, October 2006, Article ID 20061005.

that have been made with PowerPoint® slides.[8] It ranges from using too many slides to placing too much information on each slide, to ineffective use of visuals or no visuals at all. Too much variance with colors, fonts, font sizes and slide formats and cluttered slides are also problematic. Bullet points may become excessive in length and phrased as long sentences.

In contrast to the list in Figure 14.8 of poor and ineffective PowerPoint® slides, **Figure 14.9** highlights five ways to make PowerPoint® presentations come alive.[9] The first step is to start strong. Think about the audience and the purpose of the PowerPoint® presentation. Choose fonts and colors that are appropriate considering who will be viewing the slides and what the presenter wants to accomplish. Select a slide background, body text style, heading placement, fonts, and accent colors that fit, and apply these in the master slide for consistency. This will ensure every slide in the presentation utilizes the same stylistic elements.

The amount of text on each slide should be minimal. The purpose of the text or bullet points is to highlight the main ideas or thoughts. It serves as an aid to keep the presenter on track and gives the audience an idea of what will be covered. Slides with too much text can easily become a distraction because the audience reads the slide instead of listening to the presenter.

Consistency is important and makes a PowerPoint® presentation look professional. The best way to ensure consistency is to utilize pre-made templates. The ones provided by Microsoft within PowerPoint® are used frequently by many types of businesses, so it is a good idea to either create a new template or access one of the thousands of templates that are now online. While some variance among the slides is good, too much variance can be distracting and make the presentation look amateurish.

In terms of fonts, it is a good idea to use no more than two font families. If the presentation will make use of the client's computer, care should be taken to select font families that are commonly installed on all PCs, such as Arial, Calibri, Times New Roman or Tahoma. There's nothing more embarrassing then opening a presentation, only to find that the font substituted for the one you had chosen has altered the displayed information, perhaps by forcing words off the slide, or creating a "look" that is inconsistent with the image promoted by the rest of the template. Fonts can be varied by using bold and italics, even shadowing. But by using only two font families, consistency is maintained. It is also a good idea to add the company's name or the client's name or logo on each side, along with a copyright symbol. This can be done through the master slide and will make the presentation look more credible as well as professional. Last, slide transitions can improve the presentation. However, if used, the same transition should be used throughout the entire presentation.

As has already been discussed, visuals are critical to engaging an audience. Photographs, clip art, line drawings, tables, figures, and charts can be easily embedded into a slide. Typically, only one visual should be used per slide. However, there are instances where a photograph may be included with a table, graph or chart to reinforce the data being shown or to illustrate the impact of the result. Photographs are more professional and persuasive then line art or clip art. Clip art tends to be negatively viewed by many and

- Start strong
- Minimize text
- Be consistent
- Be visually engaging
- Use technology to add life

FIGURE 14.9 Making PowerPoint® Presentations Come Alive
Source: Adapted from Melissa Murray, "Making the Results Come Alive," *Quirk's Marketing Research Review*, October 2006, Article ID 20061005.

often detracts from the professionalism of the presentation. While visuals can help engage the audience, too many can be distracting. It is a matter of creating a balance between text and visuals.

Expanding the PowerPoint® to include videos and audio recordings can further enhance a presentation and make it come alive. It provides variety to the presentation, but also can provide support for research findings. A short video of actual customers talking about a product or making points that reinforce a conclusion, insight, or recommendation can be powerful. The goal of using video and audio recordings is not just to break up a presentation and simply add variety, it is to present information in a unique way that communicates effectively. A story told in a short video can make an impression on a client or marketing executive that is difficult to do in a PowerPoint® slide or from the lips of the presenter.

14.6 Creating Charts and Graphs

LEARNING OBJECTIVE 14.5
Explain how to use graphs and charts effectively.

Charts and graphs are an essential component of conveying the results of marketing research. They provide a visual picture of data, which is easier for someone to grasp than numbers in a paragraph or even in a table. Basic concepts have been presented through the Statistical Reporting sections in previous chapters. This section will explore additional options that should be considered.

Prior to graphing results, the researcher must decide what "base" will be used when presenting data. The research can choose to use 1) the entire sample; 2) only respondents who were asked the question; 3) or only those respondents who answered the question. The choice is important, because the percentages calculated and reflected in the graph will be influenced by the selected base. Most of the time researchers select option two or three, though there are exceptions. Selecting the appropriate base to use for charting data is particularly important when skip patterns are present since some respondents might not have been eligible to answer a particular question. In these cases, only the responses of those who were asked the question should be graphed.

Similarly, when graphing responses to questions such as product ownership, preference, level of agreement or disagreement with a statement, or likelihood of usage, the graphed data is often restricted to those who were asked the question. However, some researchers may choose to display the results from only those who answered the question, particularly when the scaled response question being graphed is part of a multi-item measure. In such cases, subjects who do not answer one question within a multi-item measure are dropped from subsequent analyses. Also, when questions are meant to express an attitude, those who did not answer or who answered but checked the "don't know" or "not applicable" response categories are typically not included in data on which the graph is based.

14.6a Pie Charts

Pie charts are used frequently in presentations and are excellent for conveying nominal and ordinal data. With pie charts, the data is limited to a single variable typically containing a minimum of three and generally no more than ten mutually exclusive categories. The pie chart itself consists of a 360 degree circle, sliced into segments, where each segment represents a category within the variable. Ideally, each category should be large enough in size so that each pie slice is easily identified in the chart.

Because pie charts are visual representation of data, the way the pie is created is important. Consider the pie chart at the upper left corner in Figure 14.10. Most people will look first in the upper right hand corner of a pie chart then move clockwise around the pie. Thus, the first slice that is seen is Chuck E Cheese. The eyes then move to Domino's, Godfather's, and on around to Johnny's. Very little attention will be paid to the last two

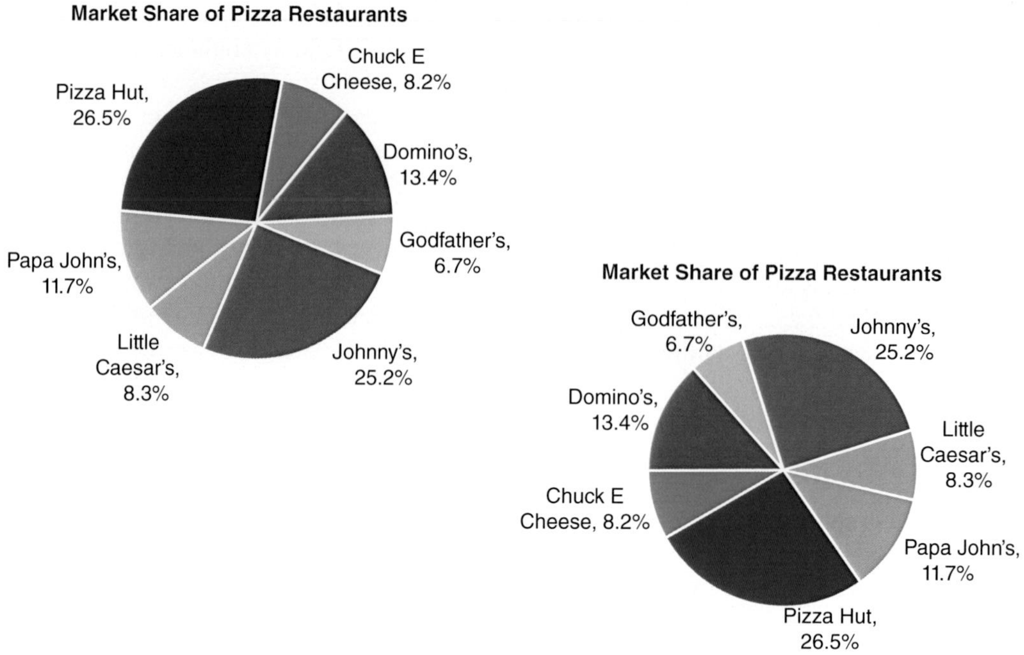

FIGURE 14.10 Rotating a Pie Chart to Change Perception

brands. Simply by the way it is designed, the pie appears to emphasize Chuck E Cheese. At least that is the perception.

Suppose the marketing research study was done for a local pizza chain called Johnny's Pizza. The perception of the pie chart can be changed by simply rotating it to the right, in this case by 250 degrees. Now Johnny's is on the upper right and would be the first part of the pie that is noticed. This fits with the perception the research agency wants to create since the study was conducted for Johnny's.

To create an even stronger perception, the slice for Johnny's can be cut and pulled from the rest of the pie (see Figure 14.11). Now, it clearly becomes the immediate focus of the pie chart. Another more subtle change was positioning two smaller pieces of the pie on each side of Johnny's. This gives it the impression that Johnny's share is even larger. Also, the names of the two pieces, Godfather's and Little Caesar's were moved slightly away from Johnny's. Again, these actions create the perception that the central focus of the pie chart is Johnny's Pizza.

14.6b Line and Area Charts

Recall from Statistical Reporting that line and area charts are used to graph ratio data. These charts cannot be used to graph nominal, ordinal, or interval data because line charts imply a continuous variable. Line charts are often used to express patterns in variables over time, such as sales, gross margins or market share percentages. Figure 14.12 shows a line chart of the number of complaints at a tanning salon over the last year. It is easy to see that the number of complaints spiked in March and were considerably higher, for some reason, than during the rest of the year. It is also evident that the number of complaints increased in the spring and summer months presumably because a tanning salon's business increases during those months.

Multiple lines can be shown on one graph, or a stacked area graph can be used. While stacked area charts look good, their usage sometimes makes it difficult for the viewer to decipher the information being represented. The key to understanding stacked charts is to realize that each additional level represents incremental values. Consider the sales figures at the tanning salon from four different types of tanning products. Because there are four different shaded areas for each tanning bed's sales

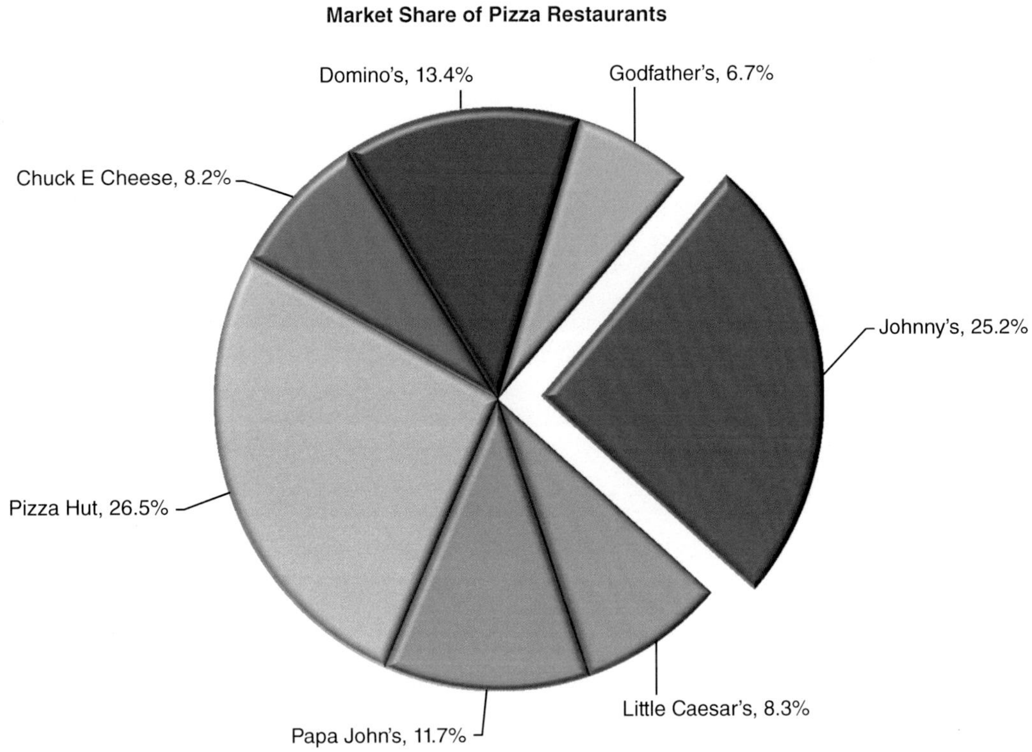

FIGURE 14.11 Cutting a Slice to Provide Emphasis

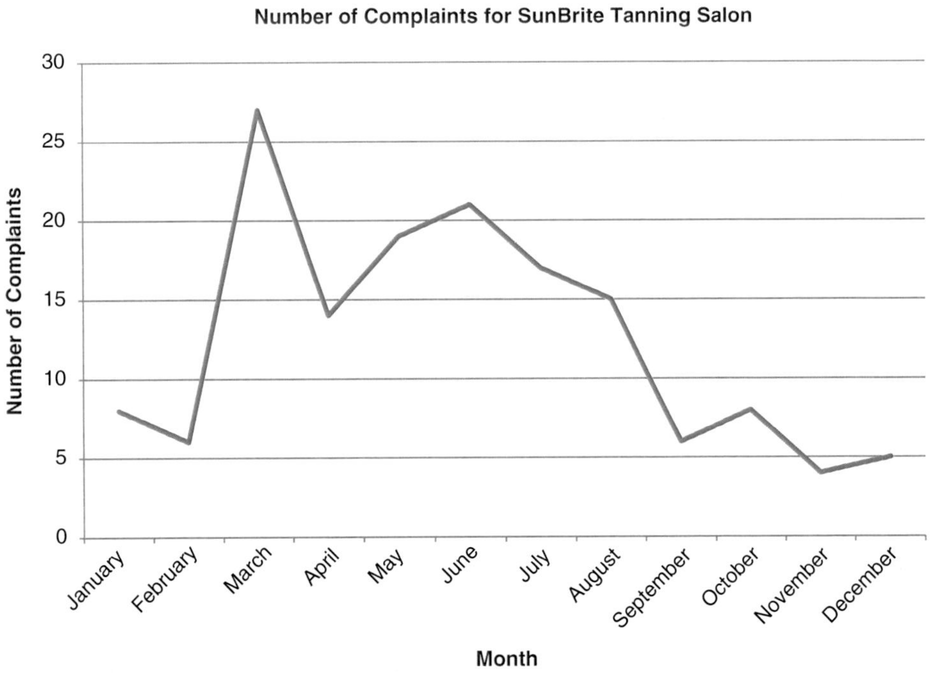

FIGURE 14.12 Line Chart Showing the Number of Complaints

data, it is necessary to have a legend. **Legends** provide a key for understanding the data, and in this case differentiate the types of tanning products on the basis of their relative sales. The stacked area chart in **Figure 14.13** provides an excellent visualization of the changes in sales between the four different brands of tanning products. Sales from using the UltraSun tanning beds tend to stay rather stable all year, as do

Legend explains what each different color-coded portion of the graph or chart represents.

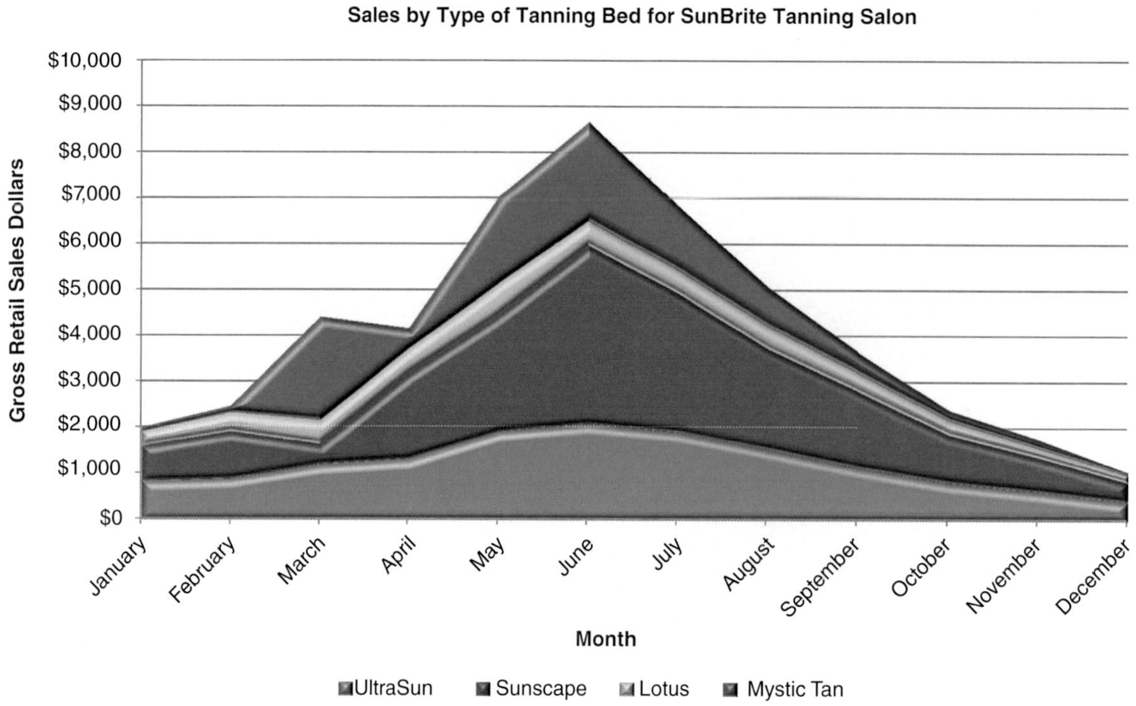

FIGURE 14.13 Stacked Area Chart Showing Sales

sales for Lotus. However, use of the Sunscape tanning beds increases sharply from April through September and represents a high percentage of total sales. Mystic Tan is a spray-on that can give the skin the appearance of a tan. It is quick, easy, and provides an even tan. Notice sales of Mystic Tan shoot up in March around spring break, then again in May and June for the summer months.

14.6c Bar/Column Charts

Bar charts allow the highest level of flexibility when presenting data and will fit almost all types of data. Simple bar charts can be used to display responses to nominal, ordinal, or interval-based questions. Clustered bar charts are excellent for visually presenting the results of cross-tabulations. Stacked bar charts serve as an alternative to pie charts and show the cumulative percent of respondents who selected each response option for a particular variable, with the final percentage equaling 100.

Bar charts are also excellent ways to show the results of paired t-tests and ANOVA tests since multiple columns of data can be shown. Figure 14.14 is a graph showing the percentage of online purchases compared to a person's total purchases in six different categories for males versus females. It is easy to see that females purchase a higher percentage of apparel, books, videos, and shoes online, while males purchase a higher percentage of electronics, home/garden items, and sporting goods.

While bar charts provide excellent visual representations of data, they can be created to deceive or at least give a false impression. Examine the graph in Figure 14.15 of the level of satisfaction at Tony's Diner across six categories. Food is rated the highest at 4.89. The menu and appearance of the facility also appear to be rated relatively high. The only real concern for Tony's is level of service, which shows a mean value of 3.12. But it appears not to be dangerously low, maybe midway on the scale.

However, when you examine the graph more diligently you notice the y-axis labeling is incomplete, as all it says is "level of satisfaction." The viewer of the graph has no idea what scale was used. Was it a five-point scale, a six-point scale, or even a higher level of scale? Most will assume that it is a five-point scale, based on the

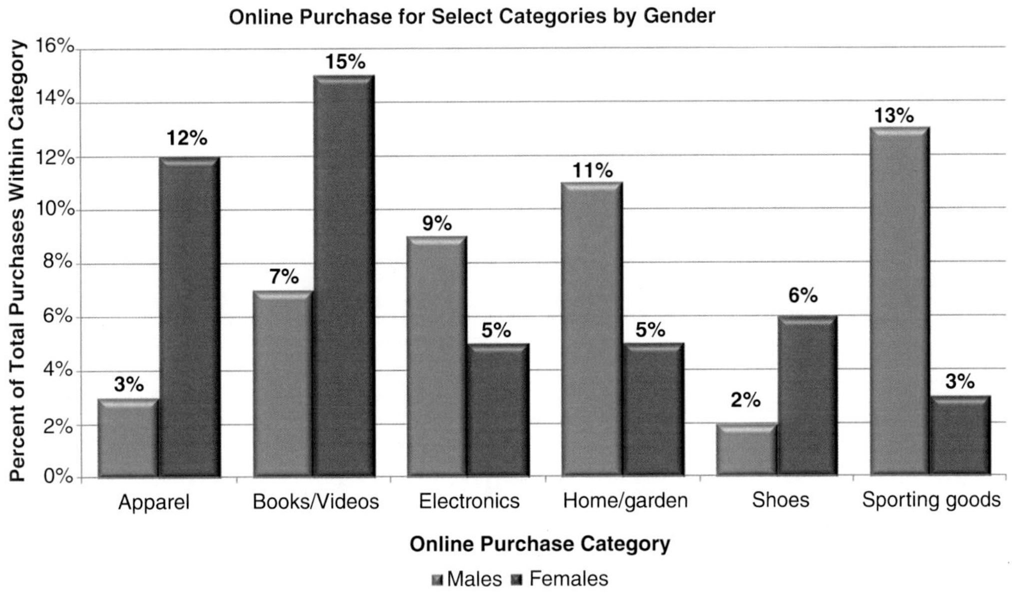

FIGURE 14.14 A Graph Showing Results of a T-test

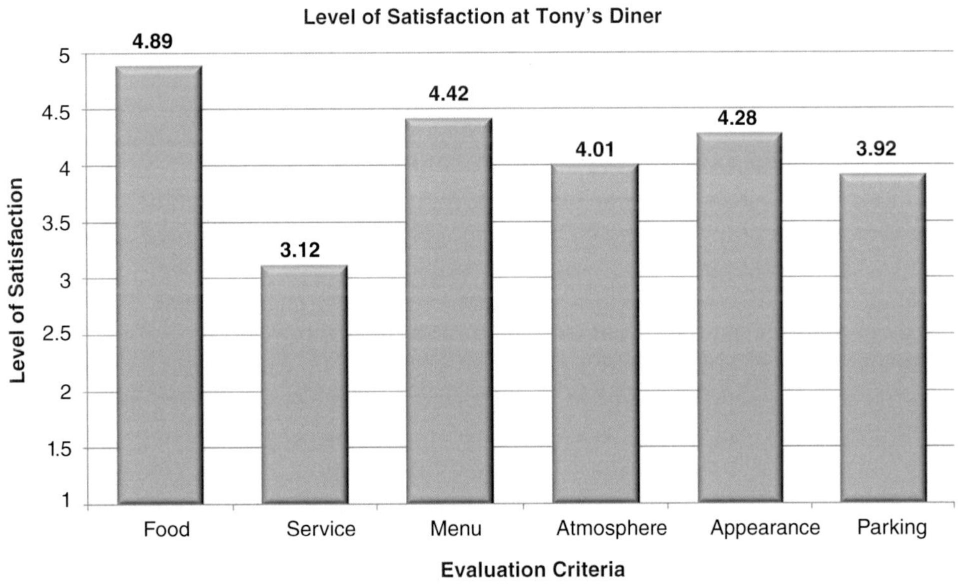

FIGURE 14.15 A Potentially Misleading Graph or One that Gives a False Impression

manner in which the data was presented. However, this is misleading since it was actually a seven-point scale. Figure 14.16 shows the results from Tony's Diner with the true vertical scale indicated, which was a seven-point scale ranging from 1 = very unsatisfied to 7 = very satisfied. When the data is viewed from this perspective, the picture of satisfaction with Tony's changes dramatically. Now the food rating, which looked good before, is just barely above the mid-point on the scale and the service score is now even lower. The other categories that were evaluated also appear to be less positive, ranging from slightly below the neutral point of 4 to slightly above. By just adjusting the scale that is used for the vertical column, the perception of satisfaction with Tony's Diner is altered.

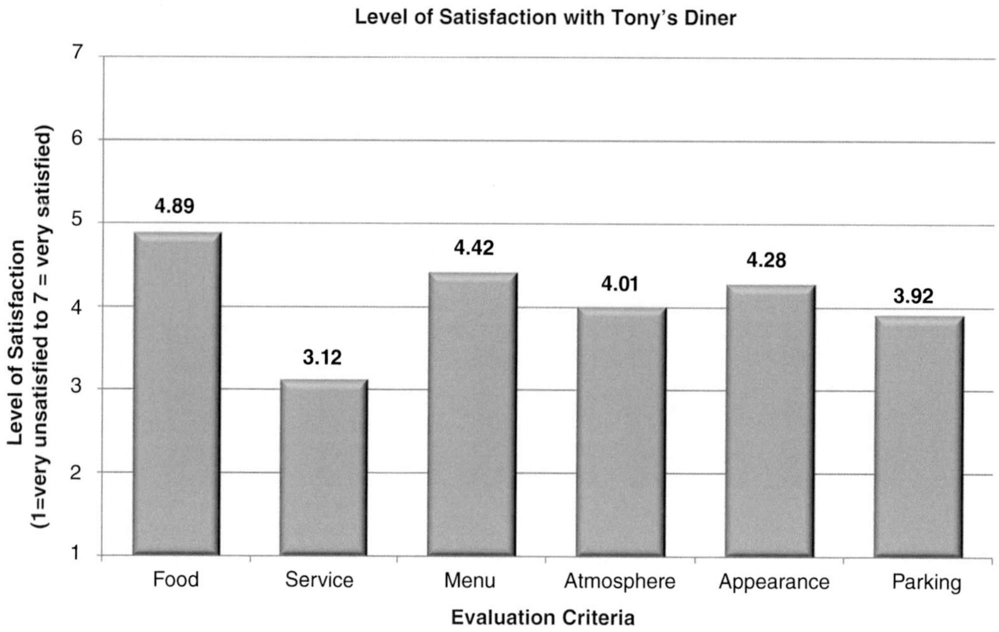

FIGURE 14.16 Level of Satisfaction at Tony's with the Y-axis Properly Labeled

To present an even more accurate picture of Tony's Diner, it is beneficial to compare it to other restaurants in the area. **Figure 14.17** does this. The first thing a person will notice when looking at the graph is that Tony's was evaluated lower across all six dimensions. However, in terms of food, it is not that far below the competitors' average. Neither is parking. However, service is extremely low and it is obvious that is where Tony's Diner needs to invest resources and improve if they want to stay in business. The visual picture and resulting perception of Tony's Diner changed considerably from the first graph in Figure 14.15 to the last one shown in Figure 14.17.

Another bar chart option is the stacked bar or column chart. **Figure 14.18** shows a stacked bar chart of the four types of suntan beds or methods for a local tanning salon. The stacked chart provides a relative picture of total sales for each method. Total sales are highest for the Sunscape tanning bed while lowest for the Lotus bed. The individual bars can be examined to see, in this case, which age group is using which bed or method. The Mystic Tan appeals the most to the 20–29 year old age group and the least to individuals 40 and older. Sales of the UltraSun and Sunscape are highest for the two middle-age categories. While the Lotus bed has the lowest sales, it appeals to older customers more than younger customers.

14.6d Infographic Charts

Infographic representation of information, data, or knowledge in both text and visual form that present bite-sized information quickly and clearly.

Infographics are a recent phenomenon being used increasingly by market research firms to enhance the visualization of data in an eye-catching and engaging manner. **Infographics** are a representation of information, data, or knowledge, in both text and visual form that present bite-sized information quickly and clearly. At first, researchers scoffed at the idea of infographics because they looked cartoonish and, it was felt, detracted from the message being conveyed. However, as the popularity of infographics rose, so did the sophistication and ability to create stunning infographics that looked professional. Proponents argue that infographics are beneficial to client firms; they provide bite-sized information that is easy to understand and convey to others. Infographics can also be helpful in attracting attention from the media, should a firm wish to share information from a study.

Well-executed infographics are typically kept to a standard letter or legal-sized page, use non-linear paths to encourage reader engagement, and don't leave readers to draw

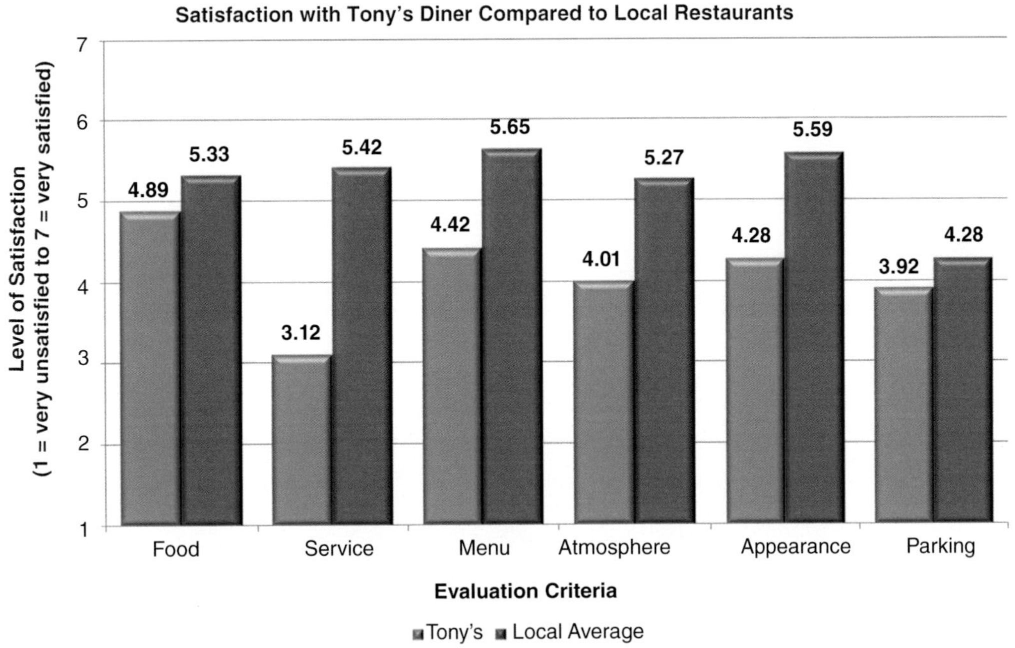

FIGURE 14.17 Graph Comparing the Level of Satisfaction with Tony's Diner to the Average Rating of Local Restaurants

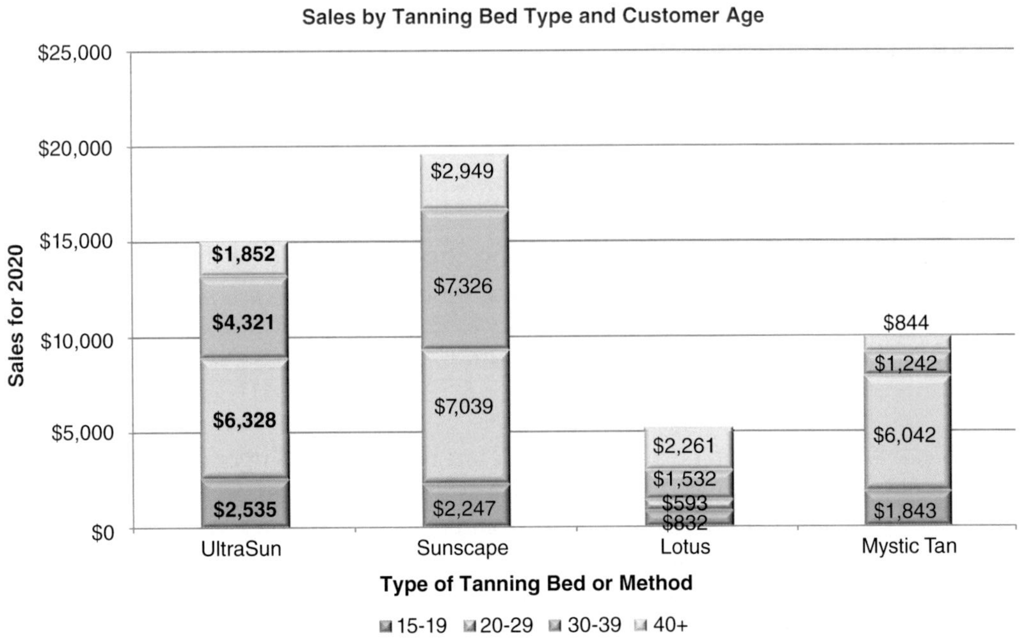

FIGURE 14.18 Example of Stacked Bar Chart

their own conclusions but instead tell a story. Infographics typically focus on a theme or data and insights related to a key research question. Simplifying data representations, using subheads or text as graphics, and organizing blocks of information in a fashion that encourages exploration of the data can help to engage the reader. Creation of the infographic begins with an understanding of the audience and what information they most want to learn from the infographic. Next, consideration should be given to the output format. Will this be a static infographic suitable for an online article, or should it be prepared as a poster sized graphic?[10] Increasingly, data visualization software such

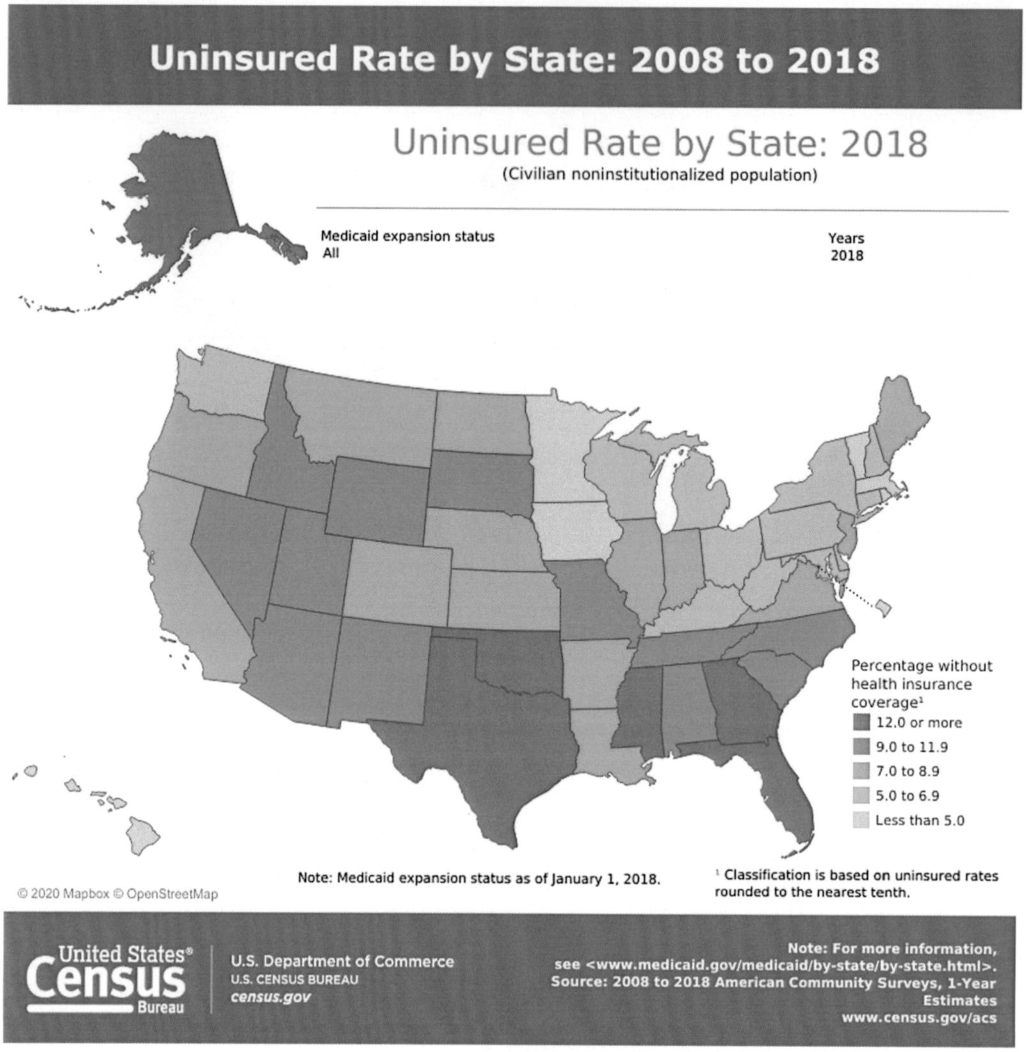

FIGURE 14.19 An Infographic Presenting the Percentage of the U.S. Civilian Population without Healthcare Insurance by State for 2018
Source: U.S. Department of Commerce, U.S. Census Bureau, https://www.census.gov/library/visualizations/interactive/uninsured-rate-2008-2018.html

as Tableau is being used to create infographics of portions of a larger dataset to provide on-demand infographics. For example, Figure 14.19 shows census data in an infographic that reports the percentage of the U.S. civilian population without health insurance by state for the year 2018. The infographic allows for pictures, visuals, and charts within a single presentation, and the chart can be downloaded from the Census website. Because the Tableau software is accessing the Census data to create the infographic, users have the flexibility of creating additional infographics by changing the year, or focusing on particular states.

The concepts that have been presented in this section about graphs and in the *Statistical Reporting* sections of each chapter apply to infographics as well. Each chart needs to be clearly labeled. The infographic needs a title and copy that will convey a complete message. Someone looking at an infographic should be able to understand everything within the infographic. It is important in designing infographics not to get carried away with visuals, charts, and text that make it look cluttered and difficult to read. Simplicity, conciseness, and clarity are good rules for infographic design. The bonus is that information can be conveyed in a way that attracts the attention of the viewer and adds variety to a presentation.

14.7 Global Concerns

Reporting the results of a global research study can be particularly challenging. Effectively communicating results can be difficult when the audience is composed of people from different countries. While English is typically used for oral presentations because it tends to be the language that audience members are most likely to have in common, comprehension may suffer among those for whom English is their second language. Misinterpretation can even occur among those who speak English in the U.K. versus America. For example, a report given by a researcher from England might state, "It is recommended that the planned expansion into Eastern Europe be tabled." To an American, this recommendation would seem to indicate that expansion plans be abandoned or shelved. Yet in England the word "tabled" means to put forth for approval, which is the exact opposite of the meaning as understood by Americans.[11]

Interpreting data collected in another country and then drawing conclusions from that data can be difficult and fraught with risk. Reineke Reitsma, Research Director at Forrester Research has over twenty years of experience with conducting international research projects. "It's really hard to understand the real drivers of behavior in different regions. Just looking at the results and comparing them with those of other countries might result in the wrong conclusions.[12]

Reitsma believes it is essential that research firms collaborate with local teams in the country under study. She strongly recommends that local teams serve as a resource for gaining additional insights into the data and brainstorming potential recommendations. Local teams help to provide perspectives that may be lacking on the part of a researcher who is not as familiar with cultural nuances. "One of the challenges is that our brain translates new information into concepts with which it is familiar . . . But is it true?"[13]

In the past, marketers have ignored cultural norms to their detriment. "These norms are very influential forces, and can represent the difference between successful products introduction and failure. Unfortunately, cultural norms are usually very subtle rather than blatant or obvious, which makes them hard to discern and detect."[14] Thus, understanding cultural norms is a key area in which local teams can be particularly helpful, especially when developing insights and brainstorming potential recommendations.

Summary

Objective 1: Identify the goals of preparing marketing research reports and presentations.

The goals of marketing research reports and presentations are to effectively communicate research findings, provide interpretations of the findings, draw conclusions, provide insight, make recommendations, and highlight limitations of the research. Effective research reports begin with understanding the different types of individuals who will read the report or listen to the presentation. These individuals are looking for insights and information to make a business decision.

Objective 2: Describe the various components of a marketing research report.

The components of a research report include title page, table of contents, executive summary, introduction, research methodology, data analysis findings, conclusions and recommendations, and appendices. The title page indicates who the report is for and who prepared it. The executive summary is written last and should provide an overall summary of the report's content. The introduction lays the foundation for the report by providing background information and the original research objectives. The research methodology discusses the research design, secondary data used, procedure for collecting primary data, sampling plan, sampling procedure, data collection process, and analytical techniques. The largest section of the paper is the findings from the data analyses. Each finding should be tied to a specific research objective. The conclusions and recommendations should be derived from the findings of the data analysis and insights gained from the research. The appendices will contain any supporting documents.

Objective 3: Explain the four principles of an executive-ready report.

A newer, trimmer version of the research report is the executive-ready report. It is based on the four principles of conciseness, adaptability, readability, and balance. Conciseness refers to eliminating all unnecessary words, figures, tables, and charts. Adaptability refers to a report that can be adapted by different people within an organization, from high-level executives to marketing personnel. Readability means the report tells a story, is visually appealing, and engages the reader. Balance involves obtaining a balance between visual interest and professional content. It also refers to a balance between being too wordy and too brief.

Objective 4: Discuss the use of oral presentations in marketing research reporting.
Oral reports are often part of research report. Creating effective oral presentations involves five principles: keep it right, keep it simple, focus on the audience needs, engage the audience, and take a risk. Keeping it right involves providing insights, not just reporting findings. Keeping it simple means not using research terminology. Focusing on the audience needs refers to presenting information the audience wants, which primarily means insights into how to solve the problem at hand. Such an approach will engage the audience. Last, the presenter needs to take some risk and take a stand on what should be done.

Objective 5: Explain how to use graphs and charts effectively.
Charts and graphs are an essential component of reports and provide visual appeal. It is important to make sure they are well prepared, properly labeled, and provide the correct perception. With pie charts, individuals look at the upper right corner first, so the pie needs to be rotated so the correct piece is displayed. Pie charts are excellent for nominal and ordinal data. For ratio data, line or area charts can be used. In creating line or area graphs, it is important to label both axes. Column and bar charts can be used for graphing nominal, ordinal, or interval data. They are excellent for tests that involve differences of means or percentages, such as chi-square, t-test, and ANOVA. A new format is infographics, which can be used to embellish presentations through creative combinations of graphs, text, and visuals.

Key Terms

conclusions, p. 477
data visualization, p. 476
executive summary, p. 481
executive-ready report, p. 484
findings, p. 476
infographic, p. 494
insights, p. 478
interpretations, p. 476
legend, p. 491
limitations, p. 480
recommendations, p. 479
table of contents, p. 481
title page, 480

Critical Thinking Exercises

1. Critique the bar chart shown in Figure 14.20. What problems need to be addressed? Is any information missing that would aid in interpretation? Explain.

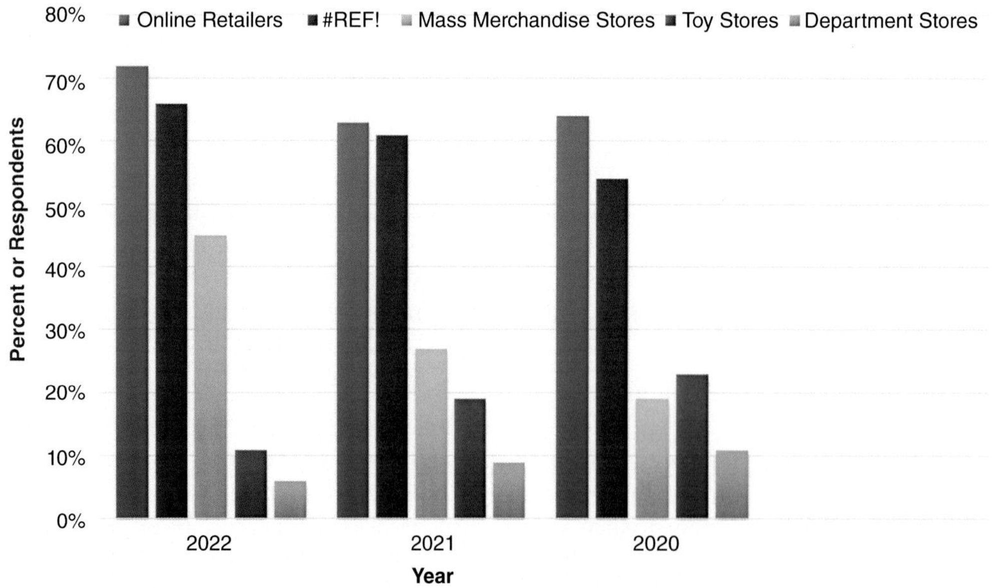

FIGURE 14.20 A Bar Chart of Data for Critical Thinking Question 1

2. Critique the pie chart shown in Figure 14.21. What problems need to be addressed? Is any information missing that would aid in interpretation? Explain.

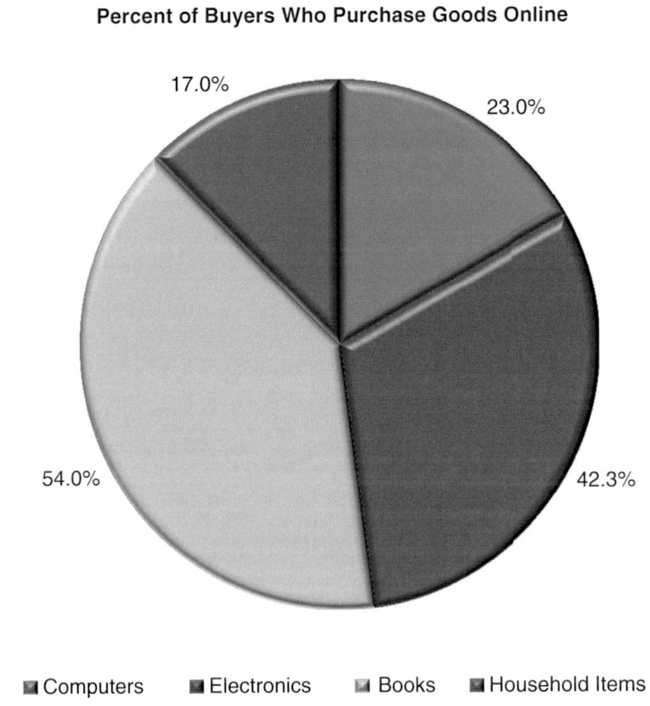

FIGURE 14.21 A Pie Chart of Data for Critical Thinking Question 2

3. Critique the stacked area chart shown in Figure 14.22. What problems need to be addressed? Is any information missing that would aid in interpretation? Explain.
4. Critique the line chart shown in Figure 14.23. What problems need to be addressed? Is any information missing that would aid in interpretation? Explain.
5. In reporting the nature of the sample, should the percent of individuals who failed to pass the screening criteria be mentioned in the report? Why or why not?
6. Compare and contrast the nature of findings, conclusions, insights, and recommendations in your own words. In what ways are they related? How do they differ? Use an example to illustrate your discussion.
7. A Nielsen research study found that 60 percent of social media users generate product or service ratings/reviews online. Only five percent and seven percent of those who engaged in online reviewing rated baby care, or toys, respectively. However, an additional 16 percent, and 22 percent of social media users read reviews related to baby care, and toys, respectively. These findings contributed to Nielsen's insight that "creation of content about toys, jewelry, and baby care is concentrated—far more people consume this content vs. creating."[15] How could you use this insight to help create actionable recommendations for the marketing of either toys or baby care items?

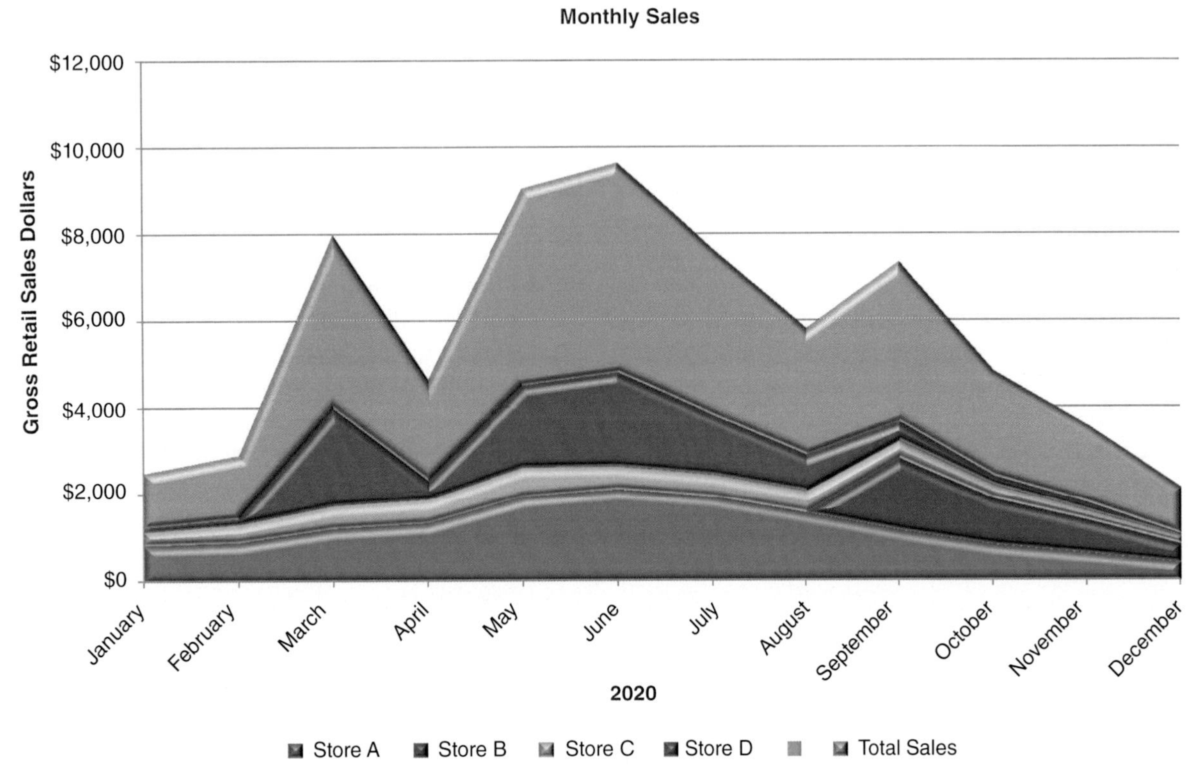

FIGURE 14.22 An Area Chart of Sales Data for Critical Thinking Question 3

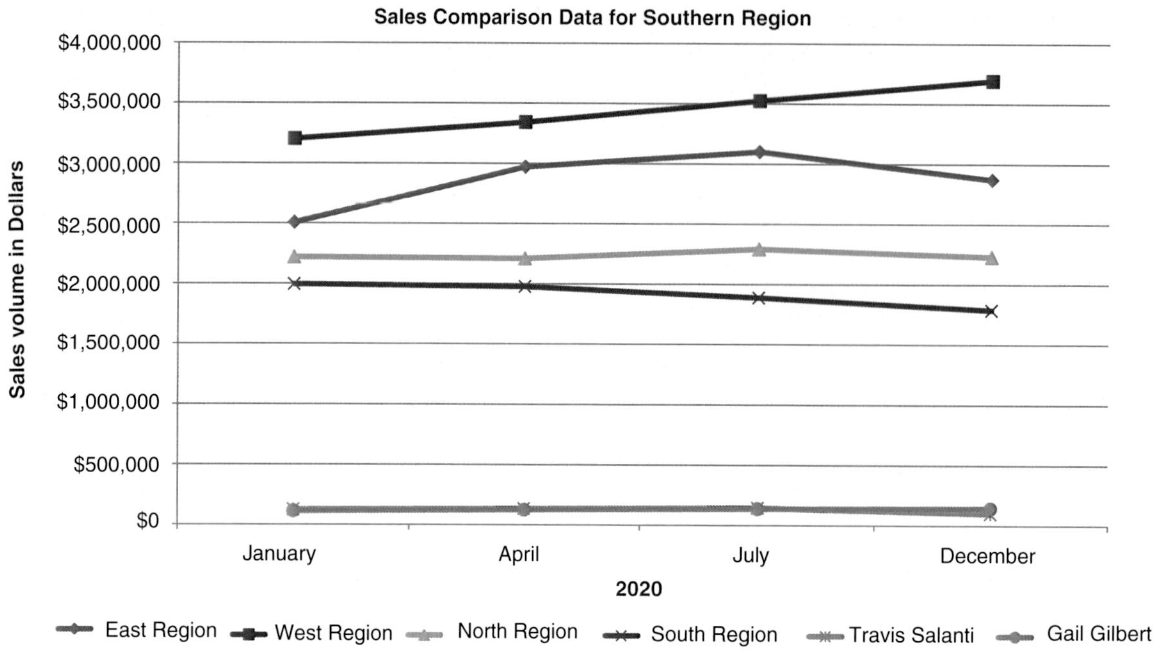

FIGURE 14.23 A Line Chart of Sales Data for Critical Thinking Question 4

8. Go the Internet and do a search for infographic images. Locate two that you think are good. Explain why they are good. Locate two that you think are difficult to understand or done poorly. Discuss why you think they are poor examples and then provide ideas how to improve them.
9. Use the Internet to locate an online company that offers a free trial version of an infographic software. Create an account or login into the software and create your own infographic. Use the data from one or more of the graphs shown in Figures 14.9 through 14.17.

The following questions require that you access the SPSS data file entitled Chapter14 Critical Thinking Data, as well as the files entitled, Chapter14 Critical Thinking Analysis and Chapter 14 Critical Thinking Survey located at: www.clowjames.net/students.html

10. Assume you have been tasked with creating the visuals for a PowerPoint® presentation related to this study. As part of the planning process, your manager has requested that you create a table listing the following information: chart title, name(s) of variable(s) to be charted, level of data corresponding to each variable (nominal, ordinal, interval, and ratio), type of chart recommended, base to be used, and special instructions. Be specific in making recommendations. Specify whether a bar chart should be a simple bar chart, clustered bar chart, or stacked bar chart. For pie charts, note if an exploding slice is desired. Area charts can be plain or stacked. Indicate whether the base to be used should be all members of the sample, only those who were asked the question, or just those who answered. Special instructions may include directions to eliminate those who chose "don't know/no opinion/or not applicable" response categories.
11. Create a pie chart, a bar chart, and a stacked bar chart for question 1 and for question 3 of the questionnaire. Which chart would you recommend using to display the answers to each question, and why?
12. Review the independent t-test results for question 2 of the survey. Create one or more charts or graphs to display the results of these tests. Should your charts be limited to displaying only those variables for which significant differences were found? Why or why not?
13. Devise a table, chart, or graph to display the results to question 4 of the questionnaire. Justify your choice for presenting the data in this fashion.
14. Create a clustered bar chart to display the cross-tabulations between question 3 and 5, question 3 and 6, and question 3 and 7. Would you recommend including all of these charts in the final report? Why or why not?

Lakeside Grill

(Comprehensive Student Case)

With the analysis finished, the team of Alexa, Juan, Destiny, Brooke, and Zach jumped into discussing insights they gained from the research. Using their analysis as well as discussions with their marketing professors and the owner of the Lakeside Grill, the team drew some conclusions. Based on these conclusions, they generated some recommendations.

The team debated about the best approach for the report and presentation. After talking it over with their marketing advisor and the owner of the Lakeside Grill, the team decided to create a PowerPoint® presentation since there would be an oral presentation. They developed two versions of the presentation. The first was a PowerPoint® with all of the findings, conclusions, insights, and recommendations. They would give this to the owner in case he wanted additional information or wanted to see everything they learned. The second PowerPoint® had only the findings that were relevant to the conclusions, insights, and recommendations.

In the process of preparing the report, the team realized that "wait time" for food and service was an issue. So they went back and pulled the data from the restaurant relating to sales and costs, especially labor costs. This information was then added to the primary research that was conducted through the survey.

Access the report and PowerPoint® presentation at the textbook website:

www.clowjames.net/students.html

The first PowerPoint® is entitled Chapter 14 Lakeside Grill Full Report and the second is entitled Chapter 14 Lakeside Grill Presentation.

Critique Questions:

1. Review the full PowerPoint® presentation in terms of factors that are commonly associated with poor and ineffective PowerPoint® presentations (see Figure 14.7). How well did the students avoid these pitfalls?
2. Now review the full PowerPoint® presentation in terms of the factors presented in Figure 14.8, how to make a presentation come alive. How well did the team do?
3. Examine the conclusions, insights, and recommendations. Do these fit the findings? Do you see any additions, deletions, or modifications that should be made? Justify your thoughts.
4. Evaluate the Chapter 14 Lakeside Grill Presentation PowerPoint® that was used for the formal presentation to the owner of Lakeside Grill. What is your evaluation of the conclusions, insights, and recommendations? Evaluate the merits of each recommendation.
5. Now compare the presentation (second PowerPoint®) to the full PowerPoint®. Do you agree or disagree with the slides that were not included? Why? Are there slides in the final presentation that should not have been included? If so, which ones? Why?
6. Overall, how well did the team do with their presentation?

Notes

1. Adapted from Mackenzie Hollister, "Motivations and Barriers: Unboxing the e-Commerce Subscription Market," *Quirk's Media* (November 13, 2019), https://www.quirks.com/articles/motivations-and-barriers-unboxing-the-e-commerce-subscription-market.
2. Hugh J. Watson, "Data Visualization, Data Interpreters, and Storytelling," *Business Intelligence Journal* 22, no. 1 (2017): 5–9.
3. This section is based on Scott Fiaschetti, "More Insights, Less Data—Why Your Research Should Tell a Story," *Quirk's Marketing Research Review* (August 2012): Article 20120926-1; Nik Werk, "The Power of Storytelling in Research," *Quirks Media* (December 2017), https://www.quirks.com/articles/the-power-of-storytelling-in-research; Denise Christie, "Seven Steps for Taking Action on Insights," *Quirk's Media* (September 22, 2016), https://www.quirks.com/articles/7-steps-for-taking-action-on-insights; Jim Kraus, "How to Write High-Impact Marketing Research Reports," *Quirk's Media* (July 15, 2013), https://www.quirks.com/articles/how-to-write-high-impact-marketing-research-reports.
4. David Santee, "Evolving the Role of Research Professionals," *Quirk's Media* (May 2016), https://www.quirks.com/articles/the-evolving-role-of-marketing-research.
5. Carla Penel and Will Leskin, "Mixing Art with Science: A Guide to Executive-Ready Reporting," *Quirk's Marketing Research Review* (May 2006): Article 20060504, pp. 48, 50–51.
6. Gary A. Schmidt, "Take a Risk, Keep It Simple," *Quirk's Marketing Research Review* (April 2007): Article 20070404, pp. 52, 54–55.
7. N. Carroll Mohn, "How to Effectively Present Marketing Research Results," *Quirk's Marketing Research Review* (January 1989): Article 19890104.
8. Melissa Murray, "Making the Results Come Alive," *Quirk's Marketing Research Review* (October 2006): Article 20061005, pp. 58, 60–62, 64, 66.
9. Ibid.
10. Joe Hopper, "Bite-Sized Information: How to Make Great Infographics," *Quirks Marketing Research Review* (October 2014): Article ID 20141025-1; Jack Weber and Kevin Sturmer, "Visual Storytelling: The Art of Developing an Infographic" [sponsored content], *Quirk's Media* (January 2019), https://www.quirks.com/articles/visual-storytelling-the-art-of-developing-an-infographic.
11. Robert B. Young and Rajshekhar G. Javalgi, "International Marketing Research: A Global Project Management Approach," *Business Horizons* 50 (2007): 113–122.

12. ESOMAR, "Running Global Research Projects," *RW Connect* (December 2, 2011), http://rwconnect.esomar.org/2011/12/02/the-challenges-of-running-global-research-projects/.
13. Ibid.
14. Robert B. Young and Rajshekhar G. Javalgi, "International Marketing Research: A Global Project Management Approach," *Business Horizons* 50 (2007): 113–122.
15. Radha Subramanyam, "Television Gets Social," in *NM Incite—The State of Social Media Survey 2011* (Chicago, IL: Nielsen, 2011).

Glossary

absolute zero point Measurement designation of "0" indicates a total absence of the property being measured.
accounting database Database containing a record of customer transactions which follows the rules of accounting and is used for accounting purposes.
advertising effectiveness research Research that examines the effectiveness of advertising and marketing communications.
advocacy research Research which is purposively designed to advocate or support a particular position.
anchor contraction effect (ACE) Systematic form of response bias in which international subjects report more intense emotions when answering questions in English, as opposed to when they answer the same questions in their native language.
anonymity Responses given by a particular respondent can never be identified or tied to that particular person.
applied marketing research Research designed to solve a specific marketing problem, to investigate a particular marketing phenomenon, or to understand the results of previous decisions.
artificial intelligence (AI) Relates to computers that are programmed to learn in a way that mimics how humans think and act.
asynchronous online focus groups Take place over several days, allowing participants to login and off at their convenience.
attitudes Relatively enduring predispositions to respond to an object in a consistent fashion.
attrition The loss of subjects during the time the experiment is being conducted (also called mortality).

balanced scale Has the same number of positive response choices as negative choices.
basic marketing research Research conducted to advance marketing knowledge in general or to verify a proposed marketing theory or concept.
behavioral targeting Uses consumers' online behavioral data and some offline secondary data to display relevant advertising and marketing messages, and personalized content such as product recommendations.
benefit and lifestyle studies Research that examines the similarities and differences consumers seek in products and how these benefits fit into particular lifestyles.
bibliographic databases Digital databases that provide references to magazine and journal articles.
big data Extremely large data sets holding structured and unstructured data that are analyzed to reveal patterns, trends, and associations, especially those related to human behavior and interactions.
blogs Regularly updated webpages containing online discussions or musings.
bots Computer programs that attempt to mimic human behavior automatically.
branching A process by which the answer to a multiple-choice question indicates the next survey question to be asked.
break-off rate Percentage of individuals who start a survey but do not complete it.
buzz score A measure of the relative amount of mentions and word-of-mouth communications a brand receives in social media.

cartoon tests Projective technique in which respondents are asked to fill in a dialogue bubble of a cartoon illustration in which one or more characters are present.
categorically exhaustive All possible responses are included in the answer categories.
causal research Research used to determine cause-and-effect relationships between variables.
census Survey of the entire population.
closed-ended questions Questions that give respondents a finite number of responses from which to choose.
cluster sample Probability sample method that involves dividing the population into mutually exclusive and categorically exhaustive groups or subsets where each group or subset is assumed to be representative of the population, then randomly selecting elements from within each group or subset.
clusters Sample groups that are assumed to be representative of the population as a whole rather than homogenous groups based on some criterion.
coding Assigning numerical values to each response on the questionnaire.
cognitive neuroscience Research process involving brain-image measurements through the tracking of brain activity.
comparative scale Respondents are asked to evaluate or rate a brand, product, object, concept, or person relative to other brands, products, objects, concepts, or individuals or to an ideal item.
competitive analysis studies Research that examines competitors within a market industry.
computer-assisted personal interviewing (CAPI) Allows the interviewer or respondent to record the answers to questions on an electronic device, such as a phone, tablet, or laptop, during a face-to-face interview.
computer-assisted telephone interviewing (CATI) Interviewers read questions and response options from a computer

screen over the telephone and select the answer indicated by the respondent.
conclusions Expanding of the interpretation to explain what the results of a research study actually mean.
concomitant variation Condition for causality in which two variables are either positively or inversely correlated and vary together in a predictable manner.
confederates People who pose as potential interviewees and who evaluate the interviewers' data collection procedure as part of the field validation process.
confidentiality Although a researcher can identify who completed a particular survey, the researcher pledges to keep that information confidential and never reveal who completed the survey.
confounds (results) Occurs when extraneous effects that represent competing explanations for the dependent variable call into question the results of the study.
constant sum scale Asks respondents to allocate points among various alternatives so the total sums to a specified amount designated by the researcher.
construct validity Method of evaluating validity by assessing how well the measurement captures the construct or concept under consideration and how well it logically connects to underlying theories.
contact rates The percent of sample phone numbers reached by an interviewer.
content validity Systematic process to evaluate validity by assessing the adequacy of the items used to measure a concept or construct.
context gamification Occurs when participants are totally immersed in game elements and the questionnaire itself takes the form of a video game.
continuous data Can take on any value within a specified range including decimals.
contrived setting Individuals are studied in a controlled or laboratory setting where they know they are being observed.
control group Group of experimental subjects who are not exposed to the treatment or manipulation of the independent variable.
convenience sample Nonprobability sample method where individuals or objects are chosen based on convenience.
convergent validity Refers to the degree of correlation among constructs, and tests whether constructs which should be related actually are related.
correlation The degree with which one variable changes with another.
cronbach alpha Internal consistency reliability method that produces a reliability coefficient for all possible combinations of a set of items within a scale.
cross-sectional studies Research conducted at a single point in time that provides a snapshot of the subject or topic being studied at that particular time.
cross-tabulations Counting the number of responses in two or more categories simultaneously.
crowdsourcing Distributes tasks to a large number of people via a flexible, open call.
customer experience studies Provide information on how customers interact with a firm and the type of experiences they have with the company.
customer satisfaction studies Track satisfaction levels of current customers with a firm's product's services, facilities, or experiences of current customers on an ongoing basis.

data cleaning Process of checking the data for inconsistency.
data entry Process of entering data into a computer spreadsheet such as SPSS or Excel that can be used for data tabulation and analysis.
data minimalism A philosophy that examines data collection from the user perspective and strives to assure that the data collected and stored is in the consumer's best interest and is helpful in driving business outcomes.
data mining The process of scanning and analyzing data to uncover patterns or trends.
data validation Process to ensure data were collected properly and are as free of error and bias as possible.
data visualization Provides a visual representation of information and data.
deliberate falsification An individual provides false answers on purpose.
dependent variable Outcome variable of the experiment that the independent variable seeks to influence, the *effect* component of a cause-and-effect relationship.
descriptive function Gathering and presentation of information about a marketing phenomenon or situation.
descriptive research Answers the questions who, what, when, where, and how in describing the characteristics of consumers, brands, and other marketing phenomena.
descriptive text analytics Looks for word associations, the frequency of word counts, words that are in proximity to one another, or other patterns.
diagnostic function Data analysis techniques used to investigate relationships and phenomena within data that have been gathered through marketing research.
dichotomous question Closed-ended question with two options.
digital fingerprinting Occurs when a panel provider creates and tracks a unique ID for a panel member's computer, tablet, or smartphone.
direct observation Researchers watch participants as the behavior takes place.
discrete data Have specific integer values with no decimals.
discriminant validity Items designed to measure one construct have a low correlation with items that measure a different construct.
discussion guide Series of questions that will be asked of participants by the moderator during the focus group interview.
disguised observation Participants do not know they are being observed.
double-barreled question Question that involves asking respondents two questions in one.
dummy coding Responses are coded a "1" if a response option is selected and a "0" if it is not selected.

electroencephalogram (EEG) Records signals on the scalp from neurons firing inside of the brain.
emotion language analysis (ELA) A form of targeted event extraction text analytics that identifies both surface feelings

and the deeper emotions that consumers feel toward brands or other topics.

equivalent form reliability Method to evaluate reliability in which a second measurement instrument is developed that is equivalent to the first and then administered to the same subjects.

ethnographic research Observing individuals in their natural settings using a combination of direct observation and video and/or audio recordings.

executive-ready report Shorter marketing research report based on principles of conciseness, adaptability, readability, and balance.

executive summary Presents a summary of the entire research report including the purpose of the research, key findings, conclusion, and recommendations.

exhaustive fact extraction Computer-based linguistic problem-solving techniques to identify, pattern, and refine key facts and concepts within the source data.

experiment A research study where all variables are held constant except the one under study consideration.

exploratory function Occurs when researchers have a limited understanding or no knowledge at all about a marketing situation or a particular outcome.

exploratory research Preliminary examination of a problem or situation to identify parameters to be studied further or to define the research problem itself.

external validity The extent to which the findings of an experiment (or research study) can be generalized to the population as whole, or to the particular population being studied.

eye tracking analysis Infrared technology that shows where the pupil is tracking by reflecting off of the eye's retina.

face validity Opinion of the researcher or experts that an instrument measures what it is intended to measure.

factor analysis Reduces a larger number of items into a smaller subset of factors based on similarity.

field experiments Conducting an experiment in a real-world setting.

field studies Pre-experimental and quasi-experimental designs that take place outside of a laboratory setting and study behavior rather intentions or attitudes.

findings Results of the data analysis.

fixed sample Sample size is determined prior to conducting the research.

focus groups Qualitative research method in which a group of 6 to 10 individuals unknown to each other are brought together to discuss a particular topic.

frame error Use of an incorrect sample frame.

functional magnetic resonance imaging (fMRI) A brain-image measurement process that tracks the flow and movement of electrical currents in the brain associated with increased neural activity.

galvanometer Measures changes in the electric resistance in the skin that results from a subject's exposure to stimuli.

gamification Process of applying gaming mechanics to survey tasks to encourage more active participation.

geo-aware ads Mobile ads triggered by a consumer's location around a retail outlet.

geocoding A secondary data compilation process which involves combining geographic information with demographic and psychographic information.

graphical rating scale Non-comparative scale that allows respondents to place a response anywhere on a continuous line.

group think Phenomenon that occurs when individuals within the group come to a consensus on a thought or idea through the informal leadership of one or two individuals.

halo effect Occurs when respondents have an overall feeling about the topic being surveyed, and that overall perception influences their response so that all of the answers are relatively close to the same.

history effects Occur when some external event takes place between the beginning and end of an experiment that changes the outcome of the event.

homonyms Words that have multiple meanings.

immersion An ethnographic study that last hours, not days, and involves prompting by the researcher.

incidence Percentage of individuals, households, or businesses in the population that would be qualified as potential respondents in a particular study.

independent sample t-test Tests for a significant difference between two groups.

independent variables Variables that are manipulated, or changed, in order to observe the effect on the dependent variable, the *cause* element in the cause-and-effect relationship.

in-depth interviews (IDIs) Qualitative research method involving one-on-one interviews for the purpose of probing deeply into an individual's thoughts and ideas to better understand a person's mental activities and behaviors.

indirect observation Observing the results of consumer actions rather than the action itself.

infographic Representation of information, data, or knowledge in both text and visual form that present bite-sized information quickly and clearly.

insights Conclusions derived from research that help firms to make more intelligent marketing decisions that result in competitive advantage for their company or brand.

instrumentation effects Occur when a change in the measurement instrument or other procedures used to measure the dependent variable cause an unwarranted change in the dependent variable.

internal consistency reliability Method to evaluate reliability that involves using one measuring instrument and assessing its reliability through using different samples or different items within each scale.

internal validity The extent to which a particular treatment in an experiment produced the sole effect observed in the dependent variable.

internet of things (IoT) Growing network of home appliances, vehicles, security systems, heart monitors, and items other than computers and smartphones that connect to the Internet.

interpretations Presentation of findings in a context that the listener or reader can more easily understand.

interval scales Scale in which numbers are assigned for the purpose of identification, the numbers indicate order, and

the distances between the numbers assigned are considered to be equal.
interviewer error or bias When an interviewer influences a respondent to give erroneous answers, either intentionally or unintentionally.
itemized rating scale Respondents choose a response from a select number of items or categories.

journey mapping studies Identify different stages in the shopping process, as well as the customer's relationship with a brand over time, and across different distribution channels or communication touchpoints.
judgment sample Nonprobability sample method where researchers use personal judgment to select the sample.

keyword analysis Form of text analytics that looks for predefined sequences in text through analyzing unstructured text and identifying key phrases and relationships.

leading question Survey question that leads the respondent to the desired answer.
legend Explains what each different color-coded portion of the graph or chart represents.
Likert scale Series of statements to which respondents indicate their level of agreement or disagreement with the statement.
limitations Any potential problems that may have arisen during the data collection process or because of assumptions that were made during the research study.
longitudinal study Research study over time in which the same questions are asked at different points in time.
low-ball pricing Submitting an extremely low-priced bid in response to a RFP simply for the purpose of getting the contract, with no intention of doing the work at the quoted price.

machine learning A form of artificial intelligence that uses statistical processes to help computers "learn" from data, without being explicitly programmed.
market analysis study Research that examines the current marketing situation faced by a company or brand and then identifies potential markets.
market basket analysis Modeling and analysis of items purchased by households on shopping trips to retail stores or e-commerce websites.
marketing database Database containing records of customers that involve communication interactions, demographic profiles, and any other information that company has collected or purchased from an independent marketing data research firm.
marketing mix Specific combination of product, pricing, promotional, and distribution decisions made for the purpose of targeting a particular group of consumers.
marketing research Systematic gathering and analysis of marketing-related data to produce information that can be used in decision-making.
market research online community (MROC) Online group of either brand advocates or highly involved individuals who agree to participate in research related to an activity or brand that is of interest to the researcher.
maturation Changes in the subject over time that can affect the results of an experiment.
measurement Process of assigning numbers or labels to phenomena or characteristics.
measurement error Difference between the responses that are obtained and the true responses that were sought.
measurement instrument error or bias Errors caused by the questionnaire or instrument being used for measurement.
median A measure of central tendency indicating the midpoint of the data in a frequency count, below which 50 percent of the observations fall.
media studies Research that identifies the most appropriate media to reach a specific target market.
metric A standard of measurement such as counts, percentages, or averages.
micro surveys Mobile surveys that contain no more than 5 questions which can be answered in a short amount of time, often a minute or less.
mode A measure of central tendency indicating the most frequent response within a frequency count.
moderator Trained interviewer who guides the focus group discussion, encourages respondent participation, and prepares the client report.
multidimensional scale Measures multiple dimensions or facets of a concept, idea, or attitude.
multiple-choice question Questions with multiple (three or more) answers from which to choose.
multiple regression Examination of the relationship of multiple independent or predictor variables and one dependent or outcome variable.
multiple response question Form of multiple choice question in which respondents are instructed to check all response options that apply.
mutually exclusive Each response category is uniquely different from others and respondents either fit into one category or another, but cannot belong to multiple categories.

named entity recognition Identifies and extracts classes of entities (e.g., people, brands, firms, products, locations) and related information.
natural language processing (NLP) Technologies that require training a software program to understand language and the way it is used by people.
natural setting observation Individuals are observed in their natural environment where they may or may not know they are being observed.
net promoter score Calculates the likelihood that customers will recommend a given product, service, or business to their friends, relatives, or colleagues.
network behavioral targeting Collects and shares non-personally identifiable data across multiple Internet sites, and categorizes the consumers based on interests, purchase intent, and other factors.
neuromarketing The measurement of consumers' physiological and neural signals to gain insight into their motivations, preferences, and decisions.
nominal scales Scale in which numbers are assigned to objects or sets of objects for the purpose of identification.
non-comparative scale Respondents make judgments about a brand, product, object, concept, or person without reference to another or ideal item.

non-parametric procedures Statistical tests that are appropriate for nominal and ordinal data.
nonprobability sample The chance or probability of someone being selected within a target population is not known and cannot be determined.
non-response bias Difference between the responses of those who participate in a study and those who do not participate in the study.

observation Measurement of a variable or group of participants during an experiment.
observation research Systematic process of recording the behaviors or the results of behaviors of people, objects, and occurrences.
one-group pretest-posttest design Pre-experimental design in which measurements of the dependent variable are taken prior to the experiment and again after the experiment.
one sample t-test Tests if the mean of a sample distribution is different from a specified (test value) mean.
one-shot pre-experimental design Pre-experimental design that exposes test subjects to a treatment variable that is then followed by a measurement of the dependent variable.
one-shot static group design Pre-experimental design that uses a control group for comparison purposes and takes measurements after the experimental treatment.
one-stage cluster sample Probability cluster sample method that involves randomly selecting clusters, then surveying all of the elements within the clusters that are selected.
one-way analysis of variance (ANOVA) test Used when comparing three or more means.
one-way tabulation Counting the number of responses for each answer category within one question.
onsite behavioral targeting Occurs within a particular website as part of the website's personalization strategy.
open-ended questions Questions that allow a respondent to answer in his or her own words.
open (or undisguised) observation Individuals know they are being observed.
order bias Occurs when respondents are influenced to select a certain response or set of responses based on the order in which they appear in the survey.
ordinal scales Scale in which numbers are assigned for the purpose of identification, but also have the property of being arranged in some type of array or order.

paired comparison scale Asks respondents to choose one of two items in a set based on some specific criterion or attribute.
paired sample t-tests Compares two different responses from an individual respondent
parameter Characteristic of a population, such as the mean or mode.
parametric procedures Statistical tests that can be used only with interval or ratio-level data.
people meters Devices that log who is watching television and what content is being viewed.
picture sort Projective technique requiring participants to sort through a stack of cards containing images or photos and select those that are representative of the topic of interest.
pilot study An abbreviated study with a limited number of respondents designed to provide information to the researcher useful in developing a larger, more definitive study.
piping Occurs in online surveys when the answer to one question is incorporated into the text of sequential questions.
points Number of intervals in a scale.
population Group from which a sample is drawn and which is the target of the research study.
population specification error Population is incorrectly identified.
position bias In a long list of response items individuals may not take time to look at all of the possible choices but simply check the first one that applies.
posttest only control group design Experimental design in which subjects are randomly assigned to experimental and control groups, followed by exposure to the treatment in the experimental group, after which both groups take a posttest, with no pretest.
predictive function Marketing research used to predict or forecast the results of a marketing decision or consumer action.
predictive text analytics Use text to predict the outcome of a target variable.
predictive validity Measure of validity that assesses how well a measurement can predict future actions or behavior.
pre-experimental designs Offer little or no control over extraneous variables and no randomization of subjects.
pretest-posttest control group design True experimental design in which subjects who have been randomly assigned to experimental and control groups take a pretest, followed by exposure to the treatment in the experimental group, then both groups take a posttest.
pricing studies Research that evaluates the elasticity of a brand's price and the impact pricing changes will have on demand.
primary research Research studies specifically developed to help fulfill the research purpose currently being investigated.
private labels Products manufactured by a third party and sold under a retailer's brand name.
probability sample Each member of the target population has a known and nonzero chance of being selected.
probing questions "Why, what, how, please explain," or "tell me more" types of questions that will lead to deeper thinking.
process error When data from a survey instrument are incorrectly entered into the computer program that is being used to tally the data and to analyze it.
product testing studies Research that identifies how a product fits the needs of consumers and what changes need to be made to the product to make it more attractive.
professional respondents Individuals who belong to multiple research panels for the purpose of participating in many research studies, often deceitfully, in order to obtain financial rewards or gifts.
programmatic advertising Automated software-based advertising auction system.
programmatic sampling Automates the buying and selling of a sample and automatically directs respondents into survey projects.
projective techniques Indirect methods of qualitative research using ambiguous stimuli that allow respondents to

project their emotions, feelings, thoughts, attitudes, and beliefs onto third-party or inanimate objects.
pupilometer Measures the degree of pupil dilation which occurs in response to stimuli.

q-sort A comparative technique whereby respondents rank a set of objects into a prespecified number of categories along a particular attribute or criterion.
qualitative research Involves unstructured data collection methods that provide results that are subjectively interpreted.
quantitative research Structured data collection methods that provide results that can be converted to numbers and analyzed through statistical procedures.
quasi-experimental designs Type of research design in which researchers are unable to randomly assign subjects to group or lack control of when the treatment occurs.
questionnaire A set of questions or items used to generate data that meets specific research and survey objectives.
quota sample Nonprobability sample method of selecting a sample based on the target population's characteristics or criteria specified by the researcher.

random digit dialing (RDD) A probability sampling technique in which area codes and phone prefix numbers are entered in an auto-dialer, which then randomly generates the remaining phone number digits and then dials the phone number.
random error Results from chance variation between the sample surveyed, and the population that they represent.
randomization Process by which subjects are randomly assigned to treatment and control groups.
ratings A form of audience measurement that represent the percentage of a base population that is watching a television program or listening to a particular radio station at a given time.
ratio scale Scale in which numbers are assigned for the purpose of identification, the numbers indicate order, the distances between the numbers are equal, and the scale has an absolute zero.
recommendations Courses of actions that should be taken by the firm based on the results of the study.
reliability The degree to which a measurement is free from error and provides consistent results over time.
request for proposal (RFP) Written document containing an official request for a research proposal (also referred to as an "invitation to bid").
research databases Group of individuals who are part of a firm's database and are asked to participate in research studies sporadically.
research design Plan to address the research problem, question, and/or hypothesis.
research hypothesis Expected research outcome which seems reasonable in light of existing information.
research proposal Written document prepared in response to a RFP that provides basic information about the research process that will be used.
research purpose Statement that broadly specifies the situation, phenomenon, opportunity, or problem to be investigated, and guides the creation of research questions and hypotheses.
research panels Group of individuals who have agreed to provide input on research studies and are asked to participate in research studies on a regular basis.
research question Specifies the type of information needed to fulfill the research purpose and to make managerial decisions.
response rate The percentage of individuals who complete a study from among those who are contacted and asked to participate.
r-square Also known as the coefficient of determination as it shows the percentage of variation explained by the predictor variable(s).

sales forecasts Research that estimates future sales for a company or brand.
sales potential studies Research that estimates potential sales for a product industry.
sample Group of individuals chosen to survey.
sample aggregator Firm that collects data through utilizing multiple sample companies.
sample frame The listing of people or objects from which the sample will be drawn.
sample size The number of usable responses needed by the client.
sampling error Refers to the amount of error that the researcher is willing to accept as a result of the sampling process.
sampling Process of choosing the group of individuals to survey.
scaled-response question Questions that allow respondents to indicate a level or degree of intensity.
scale item (or item) A question or statement that needs to be evaluated.
scaling The process of assigning numerical values or properties to subjective or abstract concepts.
search costs Costs associated with locating individuals that meet the sample criteria for a study.
search engine optimization (SEO) The process of increasing the probability of a particular company's website emerging from an Internet search.
secondary data Data collected previously for purposes other than for the current study at hand.
selection effects Occurs when the sample selected for a study is not representative of the population or the samples selected for different groups within the study are not statistically the same.
selection error Sampling procedures are not followed or are not clearly defined.
semantic differential scale Involves a finite number of choices anchored by dichotomous words or phrases.
sentence completion Projective technique in which respondents are given a partial sentence and asked to complete it with the first thoughts that come to mind.
sentiment analysis A form of named entity recognition which identifies a brand or business, then extracts and classifies words as positive, negative, or neutral.
sequential sample Sample is selected in stages or sequences, stopping when sample size is sufficient for research purpose.

simple random sample Probability sample method where each element of the population has a known and equal chance of being selected.
simple regression Examination of the relationship of one independent or predictor variable and one dependent or outcome variable.
simulated test markets Attempt to imitate real-life consumer behavior in a simulated purchase or usage environment, such as a laboratory setting or in-home use test.
site selection Research study to help retailers determine the best locations for retail outlets.
skip interval The total population is divided by the number of elements desired in the sample to yield the "Nth" number of elements skipped when implementing systematic sampling.
snowball sample Nonprobability sample method of selecting a few respondents to participate in a study, then asking each respondent for names of additional individuals to participate.
split-half technique Method to evaluate reliability through randomly splitting items designed to measure a construct into two groups and then measuring the correlation between the two groups.
split questionnaire design Involves splitting a questionnaire into one core component that all respondents answer and multiple subcomponents with respondents answering only one subcomponent.
spurious association Apparent cause-and-effect relationship between two variables that is actually caused by other factors.
spurious correlation A coincidental correlation between variables that does not indicate causality.
standard deviation A measure of dispersion that provides an indication of the degree of variation in the responses.
standard test markets Typically used when companies introduce a new product and wish to test every element of the marketing mix in a small number of representative test cities.
statistic Characteristic of a sample used as an estimator for the population parameter.
storytelling Qualitative projective approach that involves showing respondents a picture, cartoon, or series of pictures and asking them to tell a story about what they see.
straight-lining Occurs when a respondent selects the same response category for all or the majority of responses to "grid"-based questions.
stratified sample Probability sampling method that requires dividing the population into mutually exclusive and categorically exhaustive groups related to the behavior or variables of interest, then randomly selecting elements independently from within each group.
structured observation research Researchers know beforehand what behaviors to expect and even the various categories or options within each behavior that should be recorded.
subjects Participants in an experimental research study.
survey objectives Objectives that are derived from the research questions or research objectives and clearly spell out the data that the questionnaire should generate.
survey research Research in which individuals are asked a series of questions about the topic under study.
synchronous focus group interviews Online chat, audio, or video focus groups conducted in real time.
syndicated research service A marketing research firm that supplies standardized information to a number of clients for a fee.
systematic error Mistake or problem in the research design or the research process.
systematic random sample Probability sample method that involves randomly selecting the first respondent, then selecting each Nth element of the population.

table of contents Lists the different sections of the research report in sequential order.
tabulation Counting the number of responses in each answer category of a question.
targeted event extraction Occurs when complex rules for finding and grouping data are initiated based on specific trigger words.
targeted social ads Use behavioral data, demographic data, geo-targeting, and other profile data gathered by social platforms to target only those consumers whose profiles interest marketers.
target market analysis Research that provides basic demographic, psychographic, and behavioral information about specific target markets.
temporal sequence Condition for causality in which the cause precedes the effect.
testing effects Occur when exposure to a pretest sensitizes subjects to the test or experiment in a manner that affects the results of the experiment.
test marketing Uses pre-experimental or quasi-experimental designs to test new product introductions and various aspects of the marketing mix.
test markets Research that provides information on how well a new product or product modification will do in a limited market before a national or international launch.
test-retest reliability Method to evaluate reliability by repeating the measurement process with the same instrument with the same set of subjects.
third-person technique Qualitative projective technique that involves asking individuals how someone else (a third person) would react to the situation, or what his/her attitude, beliefs, and actions might be.
time series control group design Time series design that includes a control group that includes both a pretest and posttest at the same intervals as the treatment group.
time series design Quasi-experimental design in which several pretests are conducted over time prior to exposure to the treatment, followed by several posttests over time.
title page Front cover of the research report.
traditional controlled test markets Panels of stores who have agreed to participate, for a fee, in test markets maintained by professional research firms carry new products and provide sales or other data to the research firm.
treatment Change or manipulation in the independent variable.
true experimental designs Experiments in which subjects are randomly assigned to treatment conditions from a pool of subjects.

t-tests Used with samples containing fewer than 30 subjects per cell.
two-stage cluster sample Probability cluster sample method that involves randomly selecting clusters, then randomly selecting elements within the clusters that were selected.
type 1 error Occurs when the null hypothesis is rejected when it is actually true.
type II error Occurs when the null hypothesis is accepted when it is actually false.

unbalanced scale Response categories are weighted toward one of the anchors, either positive or negative.
unidimensional scale Measures only one attribute or concept.
unstructured data Text-dominant data that is not organized in a predefined manner when input by the source, nor does it have a pre-defined data model.
unstructured observation research Researchers watch participants and record behaviors they feel are relevant to the study being conducted.
user experience studies Seek to understand how consumers use a product to achieve their goals.

validity Refers to the degree to which an experiment (or research study) measures what it is supposed to measure.
virtual voice interviewing Respondents dial into a telephone line and leave voice mail responses to a set of automated questions.
visual gamification Occurs when "fun" game elements are mixed into a survey.
visual intuity Transforming questions into micro-games that can be mastered by respondents with little or no explanation.
voice-pitch analysis Focuses on subtle, involuntary physiological changes and anomalies in respondent's voice to reflect various emotions, stress, truth, or deception.

web analytics Information resulting from the logical analysis of various data, or metrics, collected from a website.
word association Qualitative projective research technique where respondents are given a series of words and asked to respond with the first word that comes to mind.

ZMET Qualitative projective technique that uses an in-depth interview to uncover emotional and subconscious beliefs and attitudes over a two- or three-week period of time.
z-tests Used for larger samples of 30 or more per cell.

Index

Note: Page numbers in *italics* indicate figures.

E

F

G

H

I

J

K

L

M

N

O

P

Q

R

S

T

U

V

W

Y

Z